Enterprise Information Systems V

Enterprise Information Systems V

edited by

Olivier Camp
ESEO,
Angers, France

Joaquim B.L. Filipe
Escola Superior Tecnologia de Setúbal,
Portugal

Slimane Hammoudi
ESEO,
Angers, France

and

Mario Piattini
Universidad de Castilla-La Mancha,
Ciudad Real, Spain

KLUWER ACADEMIC PUBLISHERS
DORDRECHT / BOSTON / LONDON

Library of Congress Cataloging-in-Publication Data

ISBN   978-90-481-6473-8 (PB)
ISBN   978-1-4020-2673-7 (e-book)

Published by Kluwer Academic Publishers,
P.O. Box 17, 3300 AA Dordrecht, The Netherlands.

Sold and distributed in North, Central and South America
by Kluwer Academic Publishers,
101 Philip Drive, Norwell, MA 02061, U.S.A.

In all other countries, sold and distributed
by Kluwer Academic Publishers,
P.O. Box 322, 3300 AH Dordrecht, The Netherlands.

Printed on acid-free paper

TABLE OF CONTENTS

PREFACE

This book comprises a set of papers selected from those presented at the fifth « International Conference on Enterprise Information Systems », (ICEIS'2003) held in Angers, France, from 23 to 26 April 2003. The conference was organised by École Supérieure d'Électronique de l'Ouest (ESEO) of Angers, France and the Escola Superior de Tecnologia de Setúbal, Portugal.

Since its first edition in 1999, ICEIS focuses on real world applications and aims at bringing together researchers, engineers and practitioners interested in the advances and business applications of information systems. As in previous years, ICEIS'2003 held four simultaneous tracks covering different aspects of enterprise computing: *Databases and Information Systems Integration, Artificial Intelligence and Decision Support Systems, Information Systems Analysis and Specification* and *Software Agents and Internet Computing*. Although ICEIS'2003 received 546 paper submissions from over 50 countries, only 80 were accepted as full papers and presented in 30-minutes oral presentations. With an acceptance rate of 15%, these numbers demonstrate the intention of preserving a high quality forum for future editions of this conference. From the articles accepted as long papers for the conference, only 32 were selected for inclusion in this book

Additional keynote lectures, tutorials and industrial sessions were also held during ICEIS'2003, and, for the first time this year, the 1st Doctoral Consortium on Enterprise Information Systems gave PhD students an opportunity to present their work to an international audience of experts in the field of information systems. On behalf of the conference organising committee, we would like to thank all invited speakers and panel members for their important contribution to ICEIS'2003: Albert Cheng (University of Houston, USA), Jean-Paul Haton (University of Nancy 1, France), Stefan Jablonski (University of Erlangen-Nürnberg, Germany), Michel Léonard (University of Geneva, Switzerland), Kecheng Liu (Staffordshire University, UK), Leszek A. Maciaszek (Macquarie University, Australia), Colette Rolland (University of Paris 1, France), Pierre Sablonière (IBM, France) and Marc Shapiro (Microsoft Research, UK). We would also like to thank all the members of the programme committee for their work in reviewing and selecting the papers for the conference; the detailed classifications they provided us with were used to select the articles in this book. The complete list of all reviewers is provided below.

The success of such a conference relies on the dedicated effort of many individuals. We wish to thank all members of the organising committee, listed below, for their help and commitment. Special thanks go to Caroline Harrault and Vitor Pedrosa for their hard work and patience in replying to the numerous mails we received and keeping a nice and clean website. Last but not least, our thanks also go to all the people who helped in the final organisation of ICEIS'2003; their help was invaluable and undoubtedly participated to the success of the conference.

Considering the growing success of ICEIS since its first edition in 1999 we can reasonably believe that ICEIS is now a well established conference and will still continue to grow over the next few years. People from various countries have expressed their interest in organising future editions of ICEIS and it was finally agreed that the sixth edition of ICEIS, to be held in 2004, would return to Portugal and would be hosted by Universidade Portucalense in the famous city of Porto.

Olivier Camp
Joaquim Filipe
Slimane Hammoudi
Mario Piattini

CONFERENCE COMMITTEE

Honorary President:
Victor Hamon, École Supérieure d' Electronique de l' Ouest, France

Conference Co-Chairs:
Joaquim Filipe, Escola Superior de Tecnologia de Setúbal, Portugal
Slimane Hammoudi, École Supérieure d' Electronique de l' Ouest, France

Programme Co-Chairs:
Olivier Camp, École Supérieure d' Electronique de l' Ouest, France
Mario Piattini, E.S. Informática - Univ. de Castilla-La Mancha, Spain

Organising Committee:
Jacky Charruault, Jean-Marc Percher, Slimane Hammoudi, Patrick Plainchault, Olivier Camp, Patrick Albers, Olivier Beaudoux, Jérôme Delatour, Daniel Schang, Denivaldo Lopes, École Supérieure d' Electronique de l' Ouest, France.

Senior Programme Committee:

Amaral, L. (PORTUGAL)
Baeza-Yates, R. (CHILE)
Bézivin, J. (FRANCE)
Bonsón, E. (SPAIN)
Carvalho, J. (PORTUGAL)
Cheng, A. (USA)
Coelho, H. (PORTUGAL)
Delgado, M. (SPAIN)
Dietz, J. (THE NETHERLANDS)
Dignum, F. (THE NETHERLANDS)
Figueiredo, A. (PORTUGAL)
Fox, M. (CANADA)
Greene, T. (USA)
Guimarães, N. (PORTUGAL)
Gupta, J. (USA)
Haton, J. (FRANCE)
Laender, A. (BRAZIL)
Lenzerini, M. (ITALY)
Leonard, M. (SWITZERLAND)
Liu, K. (UK)

Luker, P. (UK)
Lyytinen, K. (FINLAND)
Manolopoulos, Y. (GREECE)
Martins, J. (PORTUGAL)
Matsumoto, M. (JAPAN)
Odell, J. (USA)
Pirotte, A. (BELGIUM)
Pohl, K. (GERMANY)
Rolland, C. (FRANCE)
Sharp, B. (UK)
Smirnov, A. (RUSSIA)
Stamper, R. (THE NETHERLANDS)
Tari, Z. (AUSTRALIA)
Toro, M. (SPAIN)
Tribolet, J. (PORTUGAL)
Vernadat, F. (LUXEMBOURG)
Warkentin, M. (USA)
Weigand, H. (THE NETHERLANDS)
Wieringa, R. (THE NETHERLANDS)

Programme Committee:

Aguilar-Ruiz, J. (SPAIN)
Ahonen-Myka, H. (FINLAND)

Albers, P. (FRANCE)
Alderson, A. (UK)

Al-Jadir, L. (LEBANON)
Antunes, P. (PORTUGAL)
Aparício, J. (PORTUGAL)
Baranauskas, C. (BRAZIL)
Barn, B. (UK)
Barro, S. (SPAIN)
Belguith, L. (TUNISIE)
Bellalem, N. (FRANCE)
Bernus, P. (AUSTRALIA)
Bertok, P. (AUSTRALIA)
Biddle, R. (NEW ZEALAND)
Bittel, O. (GERMANY)
Boavida, F. (PORTUGAL)
Bratko, I. (SLOVENIA)
Brisaboa, N. (SPAIN)
Boulanger, D. (FRANCE)
Calero, C. (SPAIN)
Carvalho, F. (BRAZIL)
Castro-Schez, J. (SPAIN)
Cernuzzi, L. (PARAGUAY)
Chapelier, L. (FRANCE)
Christofol, H. (FRANCE)
Chu, W. (TAIWAN)
Clarke, R. (UK)
Claude, C. (FRANCE)
Corchuelo, R. (SPAIN)
Costa, E. (PORTUGAL)
Coulette, B. (FRANCE)
Cox, S. (UK)
Cesare, S. (UK)
Dolado, J. (SPAIN)
Dubois, G. (FRANCE)
Dubois, J. (FRANCE)
Duval, B. (FRANCE)
Eardley, A. (UK)
Emery, D. (UK)
Estay, J. (FRANCE)
Fadier, E. (FRANCE)
Favela, J. (USA)
Fernández-Medina, E. (SPAIN)
Ferneda, E. (BRAZIL)
Ferreira, P. (PORTUGAL)
Flory, A. (FRANCE)
Frank, U. (GERMANY)
Fred, A. (PORTUGAL)

Garbajosa, J. (SPAIN)
Genero, M. (SPAIN)
González, P. (SPAIN)
Gordillo, S. (ARGENTINA)
Gouveia, F. (PORTUGAL)
Gouveia, L. (PORTUGAL)
Govaere, V. (FRANCE)
Grönlund, Å. (SWEDEN)
Grusenmeyer, C. (FRANCE)
Gustavsson, R. (SWEDEN)
Hanseth, O. (NORWAY)
Heng, M. (AUSTRALIA)
Herrera, F. (SPAIN)
Higgins, P. (AUSTRALIA)
Hu, J. (AUSTRALIA)
Huang, K. (NETHERLANDS)
Jahankhani, H. (UK)
Jaime, A. (SPAIN)
Linares, L. (SPAIN)
Joyanes, L. (SPAIN)
Karacapilidis, N. (GREECE)
Karagiannis, D. (AUSTRIA)
Kolp, M. (BELGIUM)
Krogstie, J. (NORWAY)
Labidi, S. (BRAZIL)
Lallement, Y. (CANADA)
Langlois, D. (FRANCE)
Lehner, F. (GERMANY)
Mora, C. (SPAIN)
Leung, H. (HONG KONG)
Libourel, T. (FRANCE)
Lim, J. (SINGAPORE)
Linna, M. (FINLAND)
Ljungberg, J. (SWEDEN)
Loiseau, S. (FRANCE)
Lopes, J. (PORTUGAL)
Lucia, A. (ITALY)
Lueg, C. (AUSTRALIA)
Madeira, E. (BRAZIL)
Magnin, L. (CANADA)
Malekovic, M. (CROATIA)
Mamede, N. (PORTUGAL)
Marcos, E. (SPAIN)
Maria-Amparo, V. (SPAIN)
Marir, F. (UK)

Martins, M. (PORTUGAL)
Meier, A. (SWITZERLAND)
Mendes, E. (NEW ZEALAND)
Michelis, G. (ITALY)
Moghadampour, G. (FINLAND)
Mokhtar, H. (USA)
Molli, P. (FRANCE)
Muñoz-Avila, H. (USA)
Nguifo, E. (FRANCE)
Olivas, J. (SPAIN)
Santos, L. (ARGENTINA)
Papadopoulos, G. (CYPRUS)
Parets-Llorca, J. (SPAIN)
Pastor, O. (SPAIN)
Gramaje, M. (SPAIN)
Penzel, T. (GERMANY)
Lopes, G. (PORTUGAL)
Péridy, L. (FRANCE)
Peters, S. (NETHERLANDS)
Pimentel, E. (SPAIN)
Pires, F. (PORTUGAL)
Pires, J. (PORTUGAL)
Plodzien, J. (POLAND)
Poels, G. (BELGIUM)
Polo, M. (SPAIN)
Prasad, B. (USA)
Quang, N. (VIET NAM)
Ramos, P. (PORTUGAL)
Reimer, U. (GERMANY)
Revenu, M. (FRANCE)
Ribeiro, N. (PORTUGAL)
Richir, S. (FRANCE)
Riquelme, J. (SPAIN)
Rivreau, D. (FRANCE)
Roddick, J. (AUSTRALIA)
Rodriguez, P. (SPAIN)
Rosa, A. (PORTUGAL)
Rossi, G. (ARGENTINA)

Roztocki, N. (USA)
Ruiz, F. (SPAIN)
Rumpe, B. (GERMANY)
Sahraoui, H. (CANADA)
Salem, A. (EGYPT)
Samier, H. (FRANCE)
Schang, D. (FRANCE)
Scharl, A. (AUSTRIA)
Schoop, M. (GERMANY)
Shao, J. (UK)
Shi, Z. (CHINA)
Silva, A. (PORTUGAL)
Silva, A. (PORTUGAL)
Silva, M. (PORTUGAL)
Siris, V. (GREECE)
Skaf-Molli, H. (FRANCE)
Sobral, J. (BRAZIL)
Soule-Dupuy, C. (FRANCE)
Sun, L. (UK)
Taniar, D. (AUSTRALIA)
Torkzadeh, R. (USA)
Toval, A. (SPAIN)
Ultsch, A. (GERMANY)
Vallecillo, A. (SPAIN)
Vasconcelos, J. (PORTUGAL)
Vasiu, L. (UK)
Verdier, C. (FRANCE)
Vinh, H. (VIET NAM)
Weghorn, H. (GERMANY)
Weiss, G. (GERMANY)
Wilson, D. (UK)
Winstanley, G. (UK)
Wojtkowski, W. (USA)
Wrembel, R. (POLAND)
Yang, H. (UK)
Yano, Y. (JAPAN)
ZongKai, L. (CHINA)

Invited Speakers:
Thomas Greene, MIT Laboratory for Computer Science, USA
Jean-Paul Haton, LORIA/INRIA, France
Colette Rolland, Université de Paris 1, France
Albert Cheng, University of Houston, USA
Michel Léonard, University of Geneva, Switzerland
Dov Dori, Israel Institute of Technology, Israel
Stefan Jablonski, University of Erlangen-Nuernberg, Germany
Ilia Petrov, University of Erlangen-Nuernberg, Germany
Leszek A. Maciaszek, Macquarie University, Australia
Qusay H. Mahmoud, University of Guelph, Canada
Christophe Roche, University of Savoie, France

EVOLUTION OF ENTERPRISE INFORMATION SYSTEMS IN THE INTERNET ERA:
Contribution and Limits of new technologies and architectures

Abstract: In the era of the Internet, small and large Enterprise Information Systems around the world are looking for Internet related solutions to evolve and maintain their new Internet Information Systems. In recent years, new technologies and architectures have emerged as solutions for the new requirements and challenge of future enterprise information systems such as: inter-enterprise cooperation, interoperability and integration, migration and heterogeneity management...etc. Among these technologies and architectures, Web services and Components technology, Workflow technology, Model Driven Architecture (MDA : MOF, UML, CWM,XMI,...), and the Grid Computing seem promising to face this challenge. This panel will focus on how these new technologies and architectures can contribute to shape human activities especially in organizations, in the support they may give for designing future information systems and on the trend of development, evolution and maintenance of such future Internet Enterprise Information Systems.

1 TOWARDS SUPPORTABLE TECHNOLOGIES AND ARCHITECTURES

Leszek A. Maciaszek

The modern IT landscape of the Internet era is characterized by an increased use of distributed service-oriented architectures and the rapid adoption of object-oriented technology. This translates to various Business-to-Business (B2B), Business-to-Customers (B2C) and Business-to-Employee (B2E) web-based systems. The buzzwords are plenty among the reality of robust technologies and standards such as UML, MDA, CWM, XMI, MOF, DCOM, CORBA, .NET, EJB, J2EE, XML, UDDI, WSDL, RDF, SOAP.... Lost in the cyberspace of acronyms? Let us try to separate the wheat from the chaff. Frankly, many of these acronyms are just new names for established technologies and standards. Almost all of them are about multi-tier client/server reincarnations. They are about the middleware in a new disguise. They are about "applications and technologies come and go, data stays for ever" (Bob Epstein, Sybase, quoted from memory). They are much about hype, technology reconciliations, power struggles, inertia; about politics and business; about two steps forward and one step back. Remember how relational databases came about at the time when navigational object databases were just behind the door? Remember what happened to object databases? Why do we still program applications (as opposed to system software) in the assembly language of the new millenium – C (well, how many programmers actually program in C++, C#)?

So, I am learning from Internet era technologies and architectures and then... I design in UML, forward-engineer to Java and relational databases (but cannot quite reverse-engineer from either), generate business components for Java and XML (but cannot quite plug into it my existing Java/Oracle applications), give clear architectural designs to programmers (but get a mess of intercommunicating objects that do not resemble my design), I write regression tests that only work once in initial tests, I establish traceability links from use cases to programs that are invalidated by the beginning of the second project iteration, etc.

New technologies and architectures are important, but they do not ship products. People and processes ship products. Technologies and architectures are just facilitators. They can contribute to product shipment only as much as the tools, based on these technologies and architectures, are available and used.

The bottom line is that we need more organizational maturity, improved management, better quality control. We need to invest more in the "soft component" of people and processes than in the hard technology. We need to build supportable systems – systems that are understandable, maintainable, and scalable; systems that are not becoming "legacy" at the moment they are deployed to users.

We seem to know how to build such systems. We seem to understand the required technology and

1

architectures for supportable systems. Yet, we are not delivering them. Somewhere between the phases of the development lifecycle we fail in "soft components". The failures are typically in "interfaces" between requirements analysis and system design and between the design and implementation.

Too often designers do not understand system stakeholders. Too often programmers do not understand the intentions of designers and construct buildings that have little to do with their architectural designs. Too often project managers are unable to enforce the architectural designs because they do not understand these designs, never mind the coding of these designs.

Perhaps rather than equipping designers and programmers with ever more sophisticated tools and technologies, we should use technological advances to equip managers with means of understanding the projects under development. To start with, we should teach them how to harness complex problems, how to simplify solutions with good architectural designs (Fowler, 2003; Maciaszek et al., 2004), and how to monitor and enforce the chosen architecture (Maciaszek and Liong, 2003; Smallwords, 2002).

One does not have to be a rocket scientist to understand that there are only a couple of prerequisites for building supportable systems. The first one is a hierarchical layering of software modules that reduces complexity and enhances understandability of module dependencies by disallowing direct object intercommunication between non-neighboring layers (well, client/server and middleware revisited again). The second is the enforcement of programming standards that make module dependencies visible in compile-time program structures and that forbid muddy programming solutions utilizing just run-time program structures.

Without these two simple prerequisites we will never win the "application backlog" war and we will always be talking about "legacy systems". Why "legacy" in the first place? Systems rarely retire because they are not useful any more. They retire because they are not supportable. It is not funny that today's legacy is yesterday's great technology. Consider CORBA and DCOM, for example.

"For every complex problem, there is a simple solution - that won't work" (H.L. Mencken). New technologies, architectures and standards have always been and will be in a catch-up business, trying to respond to the growing needs of new and ever more complex applications. The gap between application needs and available and affordable architectures and technologies is increasing rather than shrinking. This gap further exaggerates the most fundamental problem that we fail in "soft components".

REFERENCES

FOWLER, R.C. (2002): *Patterns of Enterprise Application Architecture*, Addison-Wesley, 533p.

MACIASZEK, L.A. LIONG, B.L. and BILLS, S. (2004): *Practical Software Engineering. A Case-Study Approach*, Addison-Wesley, ~600p (to appear)

MACIASZEK, L.A. and LIONG B.L. (2003): Scalable System Design with the BCEMD Framework, in: *Information Systems Development: Advances in Methodologies, Components and Management*, Kluwer Academic Press, pp.279-292

SMALLWORLDS (2002): *SmallWorlds 2.0*, http://www.thesmallworlds.com/ (accessed October 2002)

2 EVOLUTION OF ENTERPRISE INFORMATION SYSTEMS IN THE INTERNET ERA: CONTRIBUTIONS OF REAL-TIME SYSTEMS TECHNOLOGY

Albert M. K. Cheng

On-time response/delivery (and not just fast), consistent quality-of-service, and adaptive behavior characterize today's and future successful enterprise information systems in the Internet era. The same features are exhibited in real-time systems, though at a more stringent scale.

In this abstract, I propose looking beyond Internet technologies to advance enterprise information systems connected to the Internet. I describe how real-time scheduling, quality-of-service guarantees, and rule-based systems can help improving EISs.

The speed of business information processing has increased dramatically in the Internet era. This also means that more and more decisions must be made at a much faster pace than ever before. Such decisions are often based on a massive amount of data about suppliers, consumers, products, and/or market conditions. With conventional scheduling strategies such as first-come-first-served (FCFS) or shortest-job-first (SJF), deadlines for information retrieval or order delivery may be missed even though on average, the performance is fast. To reduce or eliminate deadline misses, it is necessary to use real-time scheduling techniques [1,6]. For examples, an earliest-deadline-first (EDF) scheduler gives highest priority to the job with the earliest deadline whereas a least-laxity-first (LLF) scheduler assigns highest priority to the job with the least laxity, which is defined as the job's deadline minus its remaining computation time.

Quality-of-service (QoS) is another desirable property of EISs as seen by customers and suppliers. QoS is often a metric associated with network performance. For instance, we expect that trading items in a remote database can accessed within a certain time interval across the Internet, or we expect that a certain number of frames per second can be achieved in a video conference. Again, real-time network technology can be used to achieve a desirable QoS according to the cost and network conditions [2,5,8,9].

The ability to used feedback and adapt to a changing environment is needed to today's and future EISs so that the cost of re-programming is reduced and versatility is enhanced. Research in real-time caching [7] can help reduce access time and work on intelligent rule-based systems [3,4] can make EISs more flexible and self-evolving.

REFERENCES:

[1] A. M. K. Cheng,
Textbook ``Real-Time Systems: Scheduling,
Analysis, and Verification,"
ISBN# 0471-184063,
John Wiley & Sons,
August 2002.

[2] A. M. K. Cheng and S. Rao,
``Real-Time Traffic Scheduling and Routing in Packet-Switched
Networks using a Least-Laxity-First Strategy,"
Special Issue on Multimedia Communications,
Journal of VLSI Signal Processing - Systems for Signal,
Image and Video Technology,
Kluwer Academic Publishers,
Vol. 34 Nos. 1-2, pp. 139-148,
May/June 2003.

[3] P.-Y. Lee and A. M. K. Cheng,
``HAL: A Faster Match Algorithm,"
IEEE Transactions on Knowledge and Data
Engineering,
Vol. 14, No. 5, pp. 1047-1058,

September/October 2002.

[4] A. M. K. Cheng and J.-R. Chen,
``Response Time Analysis
of OPS5 Production Systems,"
IEEE Transactions on Knowledge and Data
Engineering,
Vol. 12, No. 3, pp. 391-409, May/June 2000.

[5] A. M. K. Cheng and K. Rajan,
``A Digital Map/GPS-Based Routing and Addressing Scheme for
Wireless Ad Hoc Networks,"
Proc. IEEE Intelligent Vehicles Symposium,
Columbus, OH, USA, June 9-11, 2003.

[6] Ming Zu and Albert M. K. Cheng,
``Real-Time Scheduling of Hierarchical Reward-Based Tasks,"
Proc. IEEE-CS Real-Time Technology and Applications Symp.,
Toronto, Canada, May 27-30, 2003.

[7] A. M. K. Cheng and Z. Zhang,
``Adaptive Proxy Caching for Web
Servers in Soft Real-Time Applications,"
Proc. WIP Session, 23rd IEEE Real-Time Systems Symposium,
Austin, TX,
December 3-5, 2002.

[8] L. Miller and A. M. K. Cheng,
``Admission of High Priority Real-Time Calls
in an ATM Network via Bandwidth Reallocation
and Dynamic Rerouting of Active Channels,"
Proc. 21st IEEE-CS Real-Time Systems Symposium,
Orlando, FL, pages 249-258,
Nov. 2000.

[9] R. Agarwal and A. M. K. Cheng,
``Reducing Variation in Bit-Rate Produced by Encoder
in MPEG Video,"
Proc. IEEE-CS Intl. Conf. on Multimedia Computing
and Systems,
Florence, Italy, pages 6-10, June 1999.

3 EVOLUTION OF ENTERPRISE INFORMATION SYSTEMS IN THE INTERNET ERA: CONTRIBUTIONS OF THE GRID COMPUTING

Pierre Sablonière

Life used to be simple for the IT people back in the god old days of the main frame. One machine, one operating system, one development model, total control by IT operations. the drawback was a constrained level of service for the users. With the maturity of the internet, the simplicity is on the user side and the complexity stays now on the shoulders of the IT operations. Multiple operating systems, multiple application development model, in house legacy, vendor applications, glue code for integration. The result is now built of fractured layers delivering independent service level to the end users. The overall complexity becomes unbearable to the IT operations.

There is a role that must be played by the leading IT research community to restore simplicity within the IT shops. This is underway. Technology is now on the edge to producing meta-operating system managing a Grid infrastructure in such a was that applications will used the distributed and heterogeneous machines as a single meta-computer. Technology is underway to produce more robust services below the OGSI layer. Autonomic computing functions are being implemented to harden the technology under the cover. Technology is being used to simplify the usage of technology by self configuration, self healing, self management, self discovery, self protection. Those functions are in labs and research centre reaching early adopters.. They will reach next the large companies but they will cascade very quickly down to the SMB market and to the individuals. The vision is that computer resources will be used as simply as any other utility such as water or electricity.

The role of this IT community is to unveil new ways of IT techniques, to identify new areas where those IT techniques can be used for real application (e.g. research, medical, mechanics simulation, etc). The next step is for those new ways have to follow the standard body process to open up their usage to the broadest part of the IT industry. This is the fuel of the new generation of the IT industry components. The heat is on and we see already very significant momentum.

MANAGING CHANGE – EVOLVING THE EIS VISION

Thomas J. Greene, Ph. D.
MIT Laboratory for Computer Science
Email: tjg@mit.edu

Keywords: EIS, web services, GRIDs, dotcom, semantic web, converging technologies,

Abstract: The visions and models of the future of the enterprise information system and the other models that effect it are important because such tools are used to commit the resources in our world of very rapidly change. The details of specific models at a MICRO (microtime or microspace) level may not be determinable , while those of the MACRO set (system boundry conditions?) may be very clear. The position argued here is that this is true for the EIS space. It is possible to say what will happen, but it is very diificult to asy when. Reasons for this conclusion are presented beginning with the drivers of change for Information Technology, and the drivers of change for human industry.

O. Camp et al. (eds.), Enterprise Information Systems V, 5.

AUTOMATIC SPEECH RECOGNITION: A REVIEW

Jean-Paul Haton

LORIA/INRIA BP 239 54506 Vandoeuvre, France
Email, jph@loria.fr

Keywords: Speech recogntion, signal processing, stochastic models, robustness, man-machine interaction

Abstract: Automatic speech recognition (ASR) has been extensively studied during the past few decades. Most of
present systems are based on statistical modeling, both at the acoustic and linguistic levels, not only for
recognition, but also for understanding. Speech recognition in adverse conditions has recently received
increased attention since noise resistance has become one of the major bottlenecks for practical use of
speech recognizers. After briefly recalling the basic principles of statistical approaches to ASR (especially
in a Bayesian framework), we present the types of solutions that have been proposed so far in order to
obtain good performance in real life conditions.

1   INTRODUCTION

The use of speech as a man-machine communication medium has been extensively studied during the past few decades. This paper deals with one aspect of this problem, i.e., automatic speech recognition (ASR) that consists of accessing to a machine by voice. Commercial products have existed for more than 20 years, at first for isolated word recognition, and then for connected words and continuous speech. Most of these systems are based on statistical modeling, both at the acoustic and linguistic levels.

However, if automatic speech recognition systems perform remarkably well, even for large vocabulary or multi-speaker tasks, their performance degrades dramatically in adverse situations, especially in the presence of noise or distortion. In particular, problems are created by differences that may occur between training and testing conditions (noise level as measured by the signal-to-noise ratio (SNR), distance to the microphone and orientation, type of speakers, etc.). If training and testing can be carried out in the same conditions, performance turns out to be significantly better than that obtained when training takes place in a noise-free environment.

Speech recognition in adverse conditions has recently received increased attention since noise resistance has become one of the major bottlenecks for practical use of speech recognizers in real life. After briefly recalling the basic principles of statistical approaches to ASR (especially in a Bayesian framework), we present the types of solutions that have been proposed so far to increase the robustness of ASR systems in order to obtain good performance in real life conditions.

2   EFFECT OF NOISE ON SPEECH

The various kinds of noise cause substantial alterations to the speech signal. The main sources of speech variation can be classified into three main categories:

• a d d i t i o n   o f   a m b i e n t   n o i s e : it is generally accepted that a recorded speech signal is the sum of the speech produced by a speaker and the ambient noise. This noise is usually a colored noise, and its structure can vary significantly according to the source: office machinery (typewriters, workstations, etc.), human conversations (babble noise), car (originating from engine, wind, tires, road, etc.), plane cockpit, industrial plant, etc. Non-acoustic noise (electronic, quantization, etc.) is also always present but its level is very low and does not affect the recognition process, except in some situations of telephonic applications;

• d i s t o r t i o n   o f   t h e   s i g n a l : the speech signal undergoes various distortions that may affect its frequency structure and phase in a usually non-linear way. Such distortions result from the convolution of the speech signal in a particular system. They can for instance be produced by room reverberation. Microphone transduction can also distort the speech spectrum in a way specific to each

O. Camp et al. (eds.), Enterprise Information Systems V, 6-11.
© 2004 *Kluwer Academic Publishers. Printed in the Netherlands.*

type of microphone and mounting position. Therefore, the use of different microphones for training and testing can lead to significant spectrum mismatch and causes important discrepancies in recognition. Finally, in telephonic applications, the transmission channel can also cause speech distortions, mainly through a frequency-dependent attenuation. The resulting distortions in the speech spectrum, or spectral tilt, are a major cause of performance degradation in automatic speech recognition. Some of the methods proposed so far are able to carry out simultaneously a compensation of noise and spectral tilt. Such a joint compensation has been shown to be more effective than a combination of independent compensators;
• variations in articulation: a speaker can be affected in his speaking manner by different factors like stress, emotion, physiological state, etc. But the most important factor is perhaps the influence of a noisy environment. When speakers speak under heavy noise and/or stress conditions, they dramatically change their utterance in terms of formant frequencies, pitch, sound duration, etc. This Lombard effect has a strong influence on the performances of a speech recognizer, even if speakers can be trained to some extent to avoid to some extent Lombard speech in noisy environments.

3 A STATISTICAL FRAMEWORK FOR SPEECH RECOGNITION

Most current speech recognition systems rely on a statistical framework. The basic idea is to compute the conditional probability P(W/O) of recognizing a sequence of words W for an acoustic input signal O, thanks to Bayes' formula.

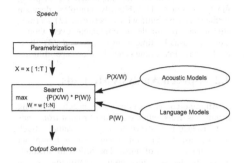

Figure 1: Principle of statistical speech recognition

As illustrated in figure 1, this computation involves two kinds of models:
- a c o u s t i c m o d e l s , usually under the form of Hidden Markov Models, HMM, which are stochastic automata whose parameters are learned during a preliminary training phase from large corpora of acoustic data.
- l a n g u a g e m o d e l s that are used to compute the probability of a word sequence P(W).
The sequence $w_{i-1}, w_{i-2}, \ldots w_1$ of preceding words is called the history of w_i. If this sequence is too long, it is likely that no exemplar of the sequence followed by word w_i would exist in the training corpus. It is then necessary to introduce approximations of histories, usually under the form of a single word w_{i-1} (bigrams) or of two words (trigrams).
A large number of methods have been proposed to increase the robustness of ASR, even though none is totally satisfactory. These methods are used at some steps in the basic sequence of speech recognition processing:
- speech signal acquisition,
- acoustic analysis and parameterization,
- segmentation and speech-non speech detection,
- reference patterns modeling,
- recognition algorithms and distance measures.
These different methods are not exclusive and can be combined in order to obtain satisfactory performances. The following sections present the main different categories of methods.

4 ACOUSTICAL PROCESSING AND PARAMETERIZATION

4.1 Speech Enhancement

As a first step in the recognition process, speech enhancement techniques tend to suppress the noise which corrupts the speech signal. Besides these methods using several microphones, many different types of speech enhancement systems using a single microphone have been proposed and tested. All these systems are based on techniques designed to recover the clean speech signal by enhancing the signal-to-noise ratio. The performance depends upon the type of noise that corrupts speech and the information required about noise. It should be noted at this point that the increase of SNR will improve the quality of the speech signal without always improving its intelligibility. Therefore, as far as automatic speech recognition is concerned, a trade-

7

off has to be found between SNR improvement and recognition accuracy. Moreover, speech enhancement techniques have initially mainly dealt with the improvement of speech quality and intelligibility for human listeners. Even though the problem is not totally similar, these techniques will also improve automatic recognition.

Several types of methods are used for speech enhancement:

• *noise subtraction:* this a very common method based on the assumption that noise and speech are uncorrelated and additive. In the spectral subtraction approach, the power spectrum of cleaned speech is obtained by subtracting the noise power spectrum from the spectrum of noisy speech. The noise spectrum is estimated during pause intervals by averaging short-term power spectra over successive frames. The method assumes that the noise varies slowly so that the noise estimation obtained during a pause can be used for suppression. Obtaining a good estimate of the noise spectrum is obviously the most difficult part of the method.

This process is quasi-linear: the only non-linearity is introduced by the specific solutions to the avoidance of negative spectral magnitudes in the subtraction operation (e.g. thresholding). There are several biases in the process: thresholding, approximation on signal phase (the phase of noisy signal is used for reconstructing the spectrum of the cleaned signal), non-stationarity of real noise, etc.). These biases result in the introduction of a "musical" noise in the cleaned signal due to the presence of spurious peaks in the spectrum. A solution to this problem is to design a non-linear spectral subtraction which basically consists in overestimating the noise spectrum, either in a uniform way, or else based on the perceptual evidence that the ear is more sensitive to the peaks of a power spectrum than to the valleys and that noise in the frequency regions of the valleys contributes the most to perceptual distortions. This latter solution has significantly improved the recognition performances compared to normal subtraction;

• *filtering:* traditional adaptive filtering techniques like Wiener or Kalman filtering have been used for speech enhancement, but more for speech transmission than for recognition purposes. As for the noise subtraction techniques, the most difficult aspect is the proper estimation of noise characteristics from observations. The Wiener filter provides an optimal solution to the adaptive filtering problem in the sense of least mean square error. It necessitates the estimation of some parameters of the noise. Unless the noise is stationary and perfectly known this must usually be done iteratively. A recursive optimal estimation can be obtained with a Kalman filter. In this method an AR speech model is

estimated by an autocorrelation method at each speech frame s_n. This speech model together with the noise model are used by a Kalman filter in order to extract from s_n a better estimate of the enhanced signal. This method results in a substantial improvement in the SNR but, at the same time, it introduces several distortions to the speech signal which deteriorate the recognition rate and lead to performances lower than those obtained with non-linear spectral subtraction;

• *space mapping:* speech enhancement can be viewed as the process of transforming noisy speech into clean speech by some kind of mapping. For instance, spectral mapping has been implemented by a set of rules obtained by vector quantization techniques. A statistical mapping of spectra has also been done. This technique is based on the extraction of noise-resistant features from speech, and can thus be considered as noise-independent to some extent. Another method based on the use of multiple linear regression techniques applied to MFCC vectors has been reported to give better results than linear spectral subtraction for word recognition in a car. The idea can be generalized to arbitrarily complex space transformations thanks to connectionist neural networks. Even simple models such as multi-layer perceptrons have been trained on learning samples to produce a mapping of noisy signals to noise-free speech that has been tested successfully in an auditory preference test with human listeners. They have also been used for learning to differentiate between similar patterns such as plosive consonants in the recognition of letters spelled out in noise, and for normalizing speech data in order to adapt a recognizer to variations in telephone line conditions. Some improvements have been brought to the method based on the fact that the separation between speech and noise is easier to carry out at the output of a hidden layer of the network rather than in the initial physical space. More generally, connectionist models are attractive for implementing mapping functions since (1) arbitrarily complex decision surfaces can be built with a network, (2) learning algorithms are simple to implement even though they are usually time consuming, and (3) these models have interesting generalization capabilities.

4.2 Speech Analysis Methods

An important category of noisy speech processing techniques deals with the design of robust front-ends that produce noise-resistant acoustic features. Such methods usually do not make any assumptions about the characteristics of noise. The following methods have produced substantial improvements in recognition accuracy:

• non-parametric representations: Mel Frequency Cepstrum Coefficients (MFCC) are to some extent resistant to noise, and certainly more so than conventional LPC analysis. Their efficiency can be significantly improved by adding dynamic features, i.e. the temporal slopes obtained by regression on the MFCC coefficients. More generally, the use of dynamic and acceleration (second derivative) MFCC and energy features makes it possible to enhance the recognition performance for noisy and/or Lombard speech. It is worth noticing that time derivatives are high-pass functions. These techniques are therefore related to the subband or cepstral domain filtering methods such as RASTA (cf. below), subband high-pass filtering, or spectral normalization.

Data analysis techniques have been used in the IMELDA system in order to obtain a robust representation of noisy speech (but also of clean speech, as further experiments have demonstrated). IMELDA carries out a linear transformation based on discriminant analysis with minimization of within-class differences and maximization of between-class differences. The result is a low dimensionality representation space in which recognition algorithms perform well. An advantage of the method is that recognition is also computationally inexpensive. IMELDA coefficients are computed from an initial parameter space which varies according to the version of the system: outputs of a large filter bank, static and dynamic outputs of the filter bank, outputs of a simulated auditory model based on Seneff's model. This latter representation has given good results for both clean and noisy speech recognition. The combination of IMELDA with a non linear spectral subtraction method has also been shown as giving improved performance in the recognition of speech in a car;

• parametric representations: several improvements of LPC analysis in the presence of noise have been tested with some success. Some of these methods are based upon an alternative solution to the speech deconvolution problem. The classical solution consists in identifying the impulse response of the vocal tract by AR or ARMA modeling. The other solution is to map the time signal space into a linear structure by using a homomorphic transformation that corresponds to a filtering in the cepstral domain. The logarithm homomorphic deconvolution can be further generalized to a spectral root deconvolution. This root scheme differs from the original homomorphic deconvolution scheme by changing the logarithmic and exponential functions respectively by $(.)^\beta$ and $(.)^{1/\beta}$ with $-1 < \beta < +1$, $\beta \neq 0$. This scheme has been proven as

significantly less affected by noise than the log scheme.

PLP (Perceptual Linear Prediction) differs from LPC by the use of three concepts derived from the study of human hearing, i.e. critical band spectral resolution, pre-emphasis with an equal-loudness curve, and spectral compression according to an intensity-loudness power law. A comparative study has shown the superiority of PLP over LPC for noisy speech recognition, especially in conjunction with a liftered cepstral distance (cf. section 5).

The RASTA (Relative Spectral) approach can be considered as another improvement of basic LPC. The method consists in operating in the log power spectral domain. That makes it possible to remove, or at least efficiently reduce, by filtering techniques, slow-varying communication noise, which is additive in the log domain. On the other hand, noise which is additive in the time domain will not be removed and could possibly be exaggerated by the log operation. A proposed solution consists in designing a filter function that is linear for low values in the auditory spectrum and approximately logarithmic for large values with a threshold related to the SNR value.

4.3 Noise Masking

In the presence of noise, certain low energy regions of the speech frequency spectrum will be more heavily corrupted by noise than others. This can cause distortions in the computation of a distance between spectra during the recognition phase. This problem was mentioned by D. Klatt in the use of a filter-bank analyzer. He proposed a solution based on a speech masking method in which only those frequency regions of the spectrum with energy level higher than the masking level are used in the distance computation.

Klatt's initial method was further improved in order to overcome its limitations, especially for the comparison of two speech patterns with very different noise levels. Noise masking has been demonstrated as giving particularly robust recognition performances down to a very low 3 dB SNR. The masking operation is also possible in a transformed representation space obtained from the initial frequency spectrum. Experiments reported in have demonstrated the interest of masking in the cepstral domain, even for very low SNRs. Performances compare favorably with the HMM decomposition method for less computation power.

5 RECOGNITION TECHNIQUES

5.1 Position of the Problem

The robustness against adverse conditions can also be obtained at the level of recognition itself. Rather than trying to only remove noise from speech, the idea is to develop robust recognition models and techniques capable of coping with noise.

A first problem that occurs is related to the segmentation of an utterance (the so-called speech/non-speech problem). Although very good solutions exist for clean speech, the problem is very difficult to solve in case of noisy speech.

Since the best performance for a system is obtained when the training and testing conditions are similar, a first idea that has been investigated consists in training a recognizer with a multi-style training procedure. The training data are made up of speech signals produced in different talking styles and noise conditions, thus resulting in a multi-reference recognition system. Although this solution was demonstrated as feasible, it is not easy to implement in practice, and it does not really satisfy the requirement of robustness in noisy speech recognition.

Two other types of techniques have been proposed. The first one deals with robust distance measure in recognition algorithms. The second one consists in introducing noise in the reference models used in the matching process of a pattern recognizer, or in adapting those models.

5.2 Robust Distance Measures

The definition of an appropriate speech representation is not sufficient for characterizing the classification space. It must be complemented by an adapted distance measure so that the recognition algorithm can take full advantage of the robustness of the representation. Of course, the definition of an appropriate distance measure is intimately related to the type of acoustic features used. Amongst the various distance measures used in pattern recognition, the following ones have been specifically adapted to the problem of noisy speech recognition:

• Weighted spectral measures have long been considered as efficient. Many weighted distortion measures are based on the log power spectral difference:

$$V = \log | X |^2 - \log | Y |^2$$

where X and Y are respectively the speech and noise spectra.

This distance and some variances have been shown to be robust against white noise by weighting spectral peak regions that are less affected by noise;

• Cepstral distances have yielded good results in speech recognition. However, their performances degrade in case of varying environments or speakers. A solution to this problem consists in defining weighted (liftered) cepstral distances.

The Mahalanobis distance can be considered as a special case of weighted cepstral distance with $w(n) = 1 / \sqrt{V(n)}$, where $V(n)$ is the variance. This distance is well known in pattern recognition; it has proved more efficient than the cepstral distance for speech recognition;

• Cepstral projection has also be proven to be effective in coping with mismatched noise conditions. The principle is based on the observation that additive white noise causes a shrinkage of the cepstral vector norm as a function of the noise level, and that the vector orientation is less affected. This shrinkage obviously affects a traditional distance calculation. It has been suggested to use a projection operation to formulate a new family of distortion measures.

5.3 Adaptation Methods

Since a major cause of performance degradation is the discrepancy between training and testing conditions, it seems interesting to transform the parameters of recognition models in order to adapt them to new conditions. Such adaptation techniques have received considerable interest during the past few years.

One of the first of this category is the Parallel Model Combination (PMC) scheme. This method applies to stochastic models like HMMs or trajectory models. It consists of choosing a representation space that makes it possible to obtain an adapted noisy model by simple combination of a clean speech model and of a noise model (the noise being supposed stationary), as illustrated in Figure 2.

Regression methods can also be used to adapt the parameters of a model. Among the most popular is the linear regression by maximum likelihood (*Maximum Likelihood Linear Regression, MLLR*). In this method, the means of the statistical model, and possibly the variances, are estimated as linear combinations of the original means and of a bias.

Another method consists of a *maximum a posteriori* Bayesian estimation. In that case, the probability distribution function of the model parameters is chosen *a priori*. Parameters are then estimated by a *Maximum a Posteriori* (MAP) technique, instead of a classical maximum likelihood. This incremental method is interesting, but it necessitates more adaptation data than the MLLR method.

5.4 Noise Contamination of Reference Patterns

A technique for avoiding the mismatch between training and testing conditions consists in adding estimated noise to the reference patterns instead of trying to clean up the observed speech signal. This technique is quite easy to implement and has sometimes given better results than those obtained with more sophisticated speech enhancement techniques. For instance, good results have been obtained for word recognition in a car by adding noise in the time and frequency domains.

6 CONCLUSION

A large variety of methods have been proposed so far in order to increase the robustness of statistical automatic speech recognition in adverse conditions. This problem is very difficult and diverse; it constitutes a major bottleneck for the practical use of speech recognizers in real conditions. This paper has reviewed some methods that try to reduce the mismatch between training and testing conditions, ranging from signal acquisition and preprocessing to adapted recognition algorithms. All these methods can be classified into two main categories. Firstly, signal processing and parameterization techniques can be used as a preprocessing step in order to enhance the SNR of the corrupted speech signal. Secondly, the different steps of the statistical pattern matching process can be modified in order to account for the effects of noise. The two approaches are not mutually exclusive; they can be combined for obtaining better performance.

Despite significant results, several questions are still open. As a matter of fact, it can be said that the problem of robust, environment-independent or environment-adaptive speech recognition is still in a state of infancy. A major issue is that the present methods depend on the noise level as well as on its type. Another important point is the need for methods which are capable of dealing with non-stationary noise conditions, such as door slams, telephone rings or other transitory sounds.

It can be expected that substantial improvements in the robustness of speech recognition systems will be obtained through clever combinations of methods and models related to different levels of the speech communication process, depending on noise types and levels.

REFERENCES

FURUI, Sadaoki (2001): Digital Speech Processing, Synthesis, and Recognition, Marcel Dekker.
HUANG, Xuedong, ACERO, Alex, and HON, Hsiao-Wuen (2001): Spoken Language Processing, Prentice-Hall.
JELINEK, Frederick (1997): Statistical Methods for Speech Recognition, MIT Press.
JUNQUA, Jean-Claude and HATON, Jean-Paul (1996): Robustness in Automatic Speech Recognition: Fundamentals and Applications, Kluwer.
MARIANI, Joseph (réd.) (2002): Reconnaissance automatique de la parole, Hermès.
RABINER, Lawrence and JUANG, Biing-Hwang (1993): Fundamentals of Speech Recognition, Prentice-Hall.

REASONING WITH GOALS TO ENGINEER REQUIREMENTS

Colette Rolland

Colette Rolland , Université de Paris 1, Panthéon Sorbonne 75013 Paris Cedex 13,
Email: rolland@univ-paris1.fr

Keywords: Systems goals, goal-driven requirements, goal-oriented requirements, requirements engineering, requirements elicitation Internet services, Dial-up networking

Abstract: The concept of a goal has been used in multiple domains such as management sciences and strategic planning, artificial intelligence and human computer interaction. Recently goal driven approaches have been developed and tried out to support requirements engineering activities such as requirements elicitation, specification, validation, modification, structuring and negotiation. The paper reviews various research efforts undertaken in this line of research. It uses L'Ecritoire, an approach which supports requirements elicitation, structuring and documenting as a basis to introduce issues in using goals to engineer requirements and to present the state-of-the art.

1   INTRODUCTION

Motivation for goal-driven requirements engineering (RE) : In (Lamsweerde, 2000), Axel van Lamsweerde defines RE (RE) as "concerned with the identification of goals to be achieved by the envisioned system, the operationalisation of such goals into services and constraints, and the assignment of responsibilities of resulting requirements to agents as humans, devices, and software". In this view, goals drive the RE process which focuses on goal centric activities such as goal elicitation, goal modelling, goal operationalisation and goal mapping onto software objects, events and operations.

Many authors will certainly agree to this position or to a similar one because goal driven approaches are seen today as a means to overcome the major drawback of traditional RE (RE) approaches that is, to lead to systems technically good but unable to respond to the needs of their users in an appropriate manner. Indeed, several field studies show that requirements misunderstanding is a major cause of system failure. For example, in the survey over 800 projects undertaken by 350 US companies which revealed that one third of the projects were never completed and one half succeeded only partially, poor requirements was identified as the major source of problems (Standish, 1995). Similarly, a

recent survey over 3800 organisations in 17 European countries demonstrate that most of the perceived problems are related to requirements specification (>50%), and requirements management (50%) (ESI, 1996).

If we want better quality systems to be produced i.e. systems that meet the requirements of their users, RE needs to explore the objectives of different stakeholders and the activities carried out by them to meet these objectives in order to derive *purposeful system requirements*. Goal driven approaches aim at meeting this objective.

As shown in Figure 1, these approaches are motivated by establishing an *intentional relationship* between the *usage world* and the *system world* (Jarke and Pohl, 1993). The *usage world* describes the tasks, procedures, interactions etc. performed by agents and how systems are used to do work. It can be looked upon as containing the objectives that are to be met in the organisation and which are achieved by the activities carried out by agents. The *subject world*, contains knowledge of the real world domain about which the proposed system has to provide information. Requirements arise from both of these worlds. However, the subject world imposes domain- requirements which are facts of nature and reflect domain laws whereas the usage world generates user-defined requirements which arise from people in the organisation and reflect their goals, intentions and wishes. The *system world* is the world of system specifications in which the requirements arising from the other two worlds must be addressed.

O. Camp et al. (eds.), Enterprise Information Systems V, 12-20.
© 2004 *Kluwer Academic Publishers. Printed in the Netherlands.*

These three worlds are interrelated as shown in Figure 1. User-defined requirements are captured by the *intentional relationship*. Domain-imposed requirements are captured by the *representation relationship*.

Understanding the *intentional relationship* is essential to comprehend the reason why a system should be constructed. The usage world provides the rationale for building a system. The purpose of developing a system is to be found outside the system itself, in the *enterprise,* or in other words, in the context in which the system will function. The relationship between the usage and system world addresses the issue of the system purpose and relates the system to the goals and objectives of the organisation. This relationship explains *why* the system is developed. Modelling this establishes the conceptual link between the envisaged system and its changing environment. *Goal-driven approaches* have been developed to address the semiotic, social link between the usage and the system world with the hope to construct systems that meet the needs of their organisation stakeholders.

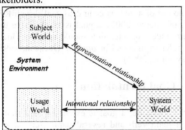

Figure 1: The relationships between the usage, subject and system worlds.

Roles of goal in RE: Goal modelling proved to be an effective way to *elicit requirements* (Potts, 1994; Rolland et al, 1998; Dardenne et al., 1993; Anton, 1994; Dubois et al., 1998; Kaindl, 2000; Lamsweerde, 2000). The argument of goal driven requirements elicitation being that the rationale for developing a system is to be found outside the system itself, in the enterprise (Loucopoulos, 1994) in which the system shall function.

RE assumes that the To-Be developed system might function and interact with its environment in many alternative ways. Alternative goal refinement proved helpful in the systematic *exploration of system choices* (Rolland et al, 1999; Lamsweerde, 2000; Yu, 1994).

Requirements completeness is a major RE issue. Yue (Yue, 1987) was probably the first to

argue that goals provide a criterion for requirements completeness : the requirements specification is complete if the requirements are sufficient to achieve the goal they refine.

Goals provide a means to ensure *requirements pre-traceability* (Gotel et al., 1994; Pohl, 1996; Ramesh, 1995). They establish a conceptual link between the system and its environment, thus facilitating the propagation of organisational changes into the system functionality. This link provides the rationale for requirements (Bubenko et al., 1994; Sommerville and Sawyer, 1997; Ross, 1977; Mostov, 1985; Yu, 1993) and facilitates the explanation and justification of requirements to the stakeholders.

Stakeholders provide useful and realistic viewpoints about the To-Be developed system but requirements engineers know that these viewpoints might be conflicting (Nuseibeh, 1994). Goals have been recognised to help in the *detection of conflicts* and their resolution (Lamsweerde, 2000; Robinson, 1989).

Difficulties with goal driven approaches : However, several authors (Lamsweerde et al., 1995; Anton, 1998; Rolland et al, 1998; Haumer et al, 1998) also acknowledge the fact that dealing with goal is not an easy task. We have applied the goal driven approach as embodied in the EKD method (Bubenko et al., 1994; Kardasis, 1998; Loucopoulos, 1997; Rolland et al., 1997b) to several domains, air traffic control, electricity supply, human resource management, tool set development. Our experience is that it is difficult for domain experts to deal with the fuzzy concept of a goal. Yet, domain experts need to discover the goals of real systems.

It is often assumed that systems are constructed with some goals in mind (Davis, 1993). However, practical experiences (Anton, 1996; ELEKTRA, 1997) show that goals are not given and therefore the question as to where they originate from (Anton, 1996) acquires importance. In addition, enterprise goals which initiate the goal discovery process do not reflect the actual situation but an idealised environmental one. Therefore, proceeding from this may lead to ineffective requirements (Potts, 1997). Thus, goal discovery is rarely an easy task.

Additionally, it has been shown (Anton, 1996) that the application of goal reduction methods (Dardenne et al., 1993) to discover the components goals of a goal, is not as straight-forward as literature suggests. Our own experience in the F3 (Bubenko et al., 1994) and ELEKTRA (Rolland et

13

al., 1997a) projects is also similar. It is thus evident that help has to be provided so that goal modelling can be meaningfully performed.

Paper outline : The objective of this paper is (a) to highlight some of the issues of goal driven approaches in RE, (b) to provide an overview of the state-of-the art on these issues and (c) to illustrate how L'Ecritoire approach deals with them. In section 2 we briefly introduce L'Ecritoire, a goal driven approach developed in our group (Rolland et al, 1998; Tawbi, 2001; Ben Achour, 1999; Rolland et al, 1997b; Rolland et al, 1999) to support requirements elicitation, specification and documentation. The presentation of this approach in section 3 will be used as the means to raise issues in goal driven RE, and to provide a state-of-the art on these issues.

2 L'ECRITOIRE: AN OVERVIEW

L'Ecritoire is a tool for requirements elicitation, structuring, and documentation. Figure 2 shows that the approach underlying L'Ecritoire uses *goal-scenario coupling* to discover requirements from a computer-supported analysis of textual scenarios. L'Ecritoire produces a requirements document which relates system requirements (the functional & physical levels in Figure 2) to organisational goals (behavioural level in Figure 2).

Central to the approach is the notion of a *requirement chunk* (RC) which is a pair <goal, scenario>. A goal is 'something that some stakeholder hopes to achieve'(Plihon, 1998) whereas a scenario is a possible behaviour limited to a set of purposeful interactions taking place among agents'(CREWS, 1998). Since a goal is intentional and a scenario operational in nature, a RC is a possible way of achieving the goal.

L'Ecritoire aims at eliciting the collection of RCs through a *bi-directional coupling* of goals and scenarios allowing movement from goals to scenarios and vice-versa. As each goal is discovered, a scenario is authored for it. In this sense the goal-scenario coupling is exploited in the forward direction from goals to scenarios. Once a scenario has been authored, it is analysed to yield goals. This leads to goal discovery by moving along the goal-scenario relationship in the reverse direction. By exploiting the goal scenario relationship in the reverse direction, i.e. from scenario to goals, the approach proactively guides the requirements elicitation process.

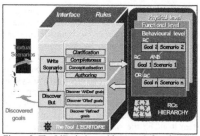

Figure 2: The L'Ecritoire architecture & functionality

The next section introduces the approach in more details with the aim to raise general issues reasoning with goals to engineer requirements and present the related state-of-the art. General issues are introduced with the ❖ symbol whereas the L'Ecritoire concepts are presented under the • symbol.

3 ISSUES IN GOAL REASONING

The notion of a goal is central to goal driven RE. In (Lamsweerde, 2001), a goal is an objective the system under consideration should achieve. Goals thus, refer to intended or *optative* (Jackson, 1995; Lamsweerde, 2001).

3.1 Goal formulation

• In L'Ecritoire, a goal is expressed as a clause with a main verb and several parameters, where each parameter plays a different role with respect to the verb. For example in the goal statement :

$\textit{'Withdraw }_{verb}\textit{ (cash)}_{target}\textit{ (from ATM)}_{means}\textit{'}$

• *'Withdraw'* is the main verb, *'cash'* is the parameter target of the goal, and *'from ATM'* is a parameter describing the means by which the goal is achieved. We adopted the linguistic approach of Fillmore's Case grammar (Fillmore, 1968), and its extensions (Dik, 1989; Schank, 1973) to define goal parameters (Prat, 1997). Each type of parameter corresponds to a case and plays a different role with respect to the verb, e.g. target entities affected by the goal, means and manner to achieve the goal, beneficiary agent of the goal achievement, destination of a communication goal, source entities needed for goal achievement etc.

❖ Goal statements are often texts in natural language (Anton, 1996; Cockburn, 1995) and may be supplemented as suggested by (Zave, 1997) with an informal specification to make precise what the goal name designates.

The motivation for semi-formal or formal goal expressions is to be the support of some form of automatic analysis. We will see later in the paper how the L'Ecritoire goal template helps reasoning about goals. Typical semi-formal formulations use some goal taxonomy and associate the goal name to a predefined type (Anton, 1998; ELEKTRA, 1997; Dardenne et al., 1993).This helps clarifying the meaning of the goal. For instance, in (Mylopoulos, 1992) a non functional goal is specified by the specific sub-type it is instance of. Similarly, in Elektra (Elektra, 1997), goals for change are pre-fixed by one of the seven types of change: *Maintain, Cease, Improve, Add, Introduce, Extend, Adopt* and *replace*. Graphical notations (Chung et al., 2000; Mylopoulos, 1992; Lamsweerde, 2001) can be used in addition to a textual formulation.

Formal specifications of goals like in Kaos (Dardenne et al, 1993) require a higher effort but yield more powerful reasoning.

3.2 Coupling Goal and Scenario

- In L'Ecritoire, a *goal* is coupled with a *scenario*. In this direction, from goal to scenario, the relationship aims to concretise a goal through a scenario. Thus, the scenario represents a possible behaviour of the system to achieve the goal. In L'Ecritoire, a scenario is defined as composed of one or more *actions* which describe a unique path leading from an *initial* to a *final state* of agents. Below is an example of scenario associated to the goal *'Withdraw cash from the ATM'*.

> The user inserts a card in the ATM.
> The ATM checks the card validity.
> If the card is valid a prompt for code is given by the ATM to the user, the user inputs the code in the ATM.
> The ATM checks the code validity.
> If the code is valid, the ATM displays a prompt for amount to the user.
> The user enters an amount in the ATM.
> The ATM checks the amount validity.
> If the amount is valid, the ATM ejects the card to the user and then the ATM proposes a receipt to the user.
> The user enters the user's choice in the ATM.
> If a receipt was asked the receipt is printed by the ATM to the user but before the ATM delivers the cash to the user.

❖ Many authors suggest to combine goals and scenarios (Potts, 1995; Cockburn, 1995; Leite et al, 1997; Kaindl, 2000; Sutcliffe, 1998; Haumer et al., 1998; Anton, 1998; Lamsweerde et Willemet, 1998). (Potts, 1995) for example, says that it is « unwise to apply goal based requirements methods in isolation » and suggests to complement them with scenarios. This combination has been used mainly, to make goals concrete, i.e. to operationalise goals. This is because scenarios can be interpreted as containing information on how goals can be achieved. In (Dano et al., 1997; Jacobson, 1995; Leite, 1997; Pohl and Haumer, 1997), a goal is considered as a contextual property of a use case (Jacobson, 1995) i.e. a property that relates the scenario to its organisational context. Therefore, goals play a documenting role only. (Cockburn, 1995) goes beyond this view and suggests to use goals to structure use cases by connecting every action in a scenario to a goal assigned to an actor. In this sense a scenario is discovered each time a goal is. Clearly, all these views suggest a unidirectional relationship between goals and scenarios similarly to what we introduced in L'Ecritoire so far. We will see later on, how L'Ecritoire exploits the goal/scenario coupling in the reverse direction.

3.3 Relationships among Goals

- In L'Ecritoire, RCs can be assembled together through *composition, alternative and refinement* relationships. The first two lead to AND and OR structure of RCs whereas the last leads to the organisation of the collection of RCs as a hierarchy of chunks of different granularity.

AND relationships among RCs link complementary chunks in the sense that every one requires the others to define a completely functioning system. RCs linked through *OR relationships* represent alternative ways of fulfilling the same goal. RCs linked through a *refinement relationship* are at different levels of abstraction. The goal *'Fill in the ATM with cash'* is an example of *ANDed* goal *to 'Withdraw cash from the ATM'* whereas *'Withdraw cash from the ATM with two invalid code capture '*is *ORed* to it. Finally *'Check the card validity'* is linked to the goal *'Withdraw cash from the ATM'* by a *refinement* relationship.

❖ Many different types of *relationships* among goals have been introduced in the literature. They can be classified in two categories to relate goals: (1) to each other and (2) with other elements of requirements models. We consider them in turn. AND/OR relationships (Bubenko et al, 1994; Dardenne et al, 1993; Rolland et al, 1998; Loucopoulos et al, 1997; Mylopoulos 1999) inspired from AND/OR graphs in Artificial Intelligence are used to capture goal decomposition into more operational goals and alternative goals, respectively. In the former, all the decomposed goals must be satisfied for the parent goal to be achieved whereas in the latter, if one of the alternative goals is achieved, then the parent goal is satisfied.

In (Mylopoulos, 1992; Chung et al., 2000), the inter-goal relationship is extended to support the capture of negative/positive influence between goals. A sub-goal is said to *contribute* partially to its parent goal. This leads to the notion of goal *satisfycing* instead of goal *satisfaction*. The 'motivates' and 'hinders' relationships among goals in (Bubenko et al, 1994) are similar in the sense that they capture positive/negative influence among goals.

Conflict relationships are introduced (Bubenko et al, 1994; Dardenne et al 1993; Nuseibeh, 1994; Easterbrook, 1994) to capture the fact that one goal might prevent the other to be satisfied.

In addition to inter-goal relationships, goals are also related to other elements of requirements models. As a logical termination of the AND/OR decomposition, goals link to operations which ensure them (Anton, 1994; Anton and Potts, 1998; Kaindl, 2000; Lamsweerde et Willemet, 1998). Relationships between goals and system objects have been studied in (Lee, 1997) and are inherently part of the KAOS model (Lamsweerde et al., 1991; Dardenne et al., 1993)).

Relationships with agents have been emphasized in (Yu 1993; Yu 1997) where a goal is the object of the dependency between two agents. Such type of link is introduced in other models as well (Dardenne et al, 1993; Lamweerde et al., 1991; Letier, 2001) to capture who is responsible of a goal. As discussed earlier, goals have been often coupled to scenarios (Potts, 1995; Cockburn, 1995; Leite, 1997; Kaindl, 2000; Sutcliffe, 1998; Haumer et al., 1998; Anton, 1998; . et al., 1998). In (Bubenko et al, 1994) goals are related to a number of concepts such as *problem*, *opportunity* and *thread* with the aim to understand better the context of a goal. Finally the interesting idea of *obstacle* introduced by (Potts, 1995) leads to obstructions and resolution relationships among goals and obstacles (Lamweerde, 2000a; Sutcliffe, 1998).

3.4 Levels of Abstraction

• The L'Ecritoire approach identifies three levels of requirements abstraction, namely the *behavioural*, *functional* and *physical* levels. The aim of the *behavioural level* is to couple the services that a system should provide so a business goal. At the *functional level* the focus is on the

interactions between the system and its users to achieve the services assigned to the system at the behavioural level. The *physical level* focuses on what the system needs to perform the interactions selected at the system interaction level.

❖ As in L'Ecritoire goals many approaches suggest to formulate goals at different *levels of abstraction*. By essence goal centric approaches aim to help in the move from strategic concerns and high level goals to technical concerns and low abstraction level goals. Therefore, it is natural for approaches to identify different levels of goal abstraction where high level goals represent business objectives and are refined in system goals (Anton et al., 2001; Anton and Potts, 1998) or system constraints (Lamsweerde and Letier, 2000a). Inspired by cognitive engineering, some goal driven RE approaches deal with means-end hierarchy abstractions, where each hierarchical level represents a different model of the same system. The information at any level acts as a goal (the end) with respect to the model at the next lower level (the means) (Leveson 2000; Rasmussen, 1990; Vicente and Rasmussen, 1992).

3.5 Eliciting Goals

• The L'Ecritoire requirements elicitation process is organised around two main activities : *goal discovery* and *scenario authoring*.

In this process, *goal discovery* and *scenario authoring* are complementary activities, the former following the latter. As shown in Figure 3, these activities are repeated to incrementally populate the RCs hierarchy.

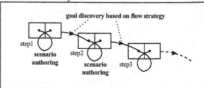

Figure 3: Goal reasoning in l'Ecritoire.

Each of the two main activities is supported by enactable rules, (1) *authoring rules* and (2) *discovery rules*. Authoring rules allow L'Ecritoire scenarios which are textual to be authored. Discovery rules are for discovering goals through the analysis of authored scenarios. We focus here on exemplifying the discovery rules. Details about the authoring rules and the linguistic approach underlying them can be found in (Rolland and Ben Achour, 1997; Ben Achour, 1999).

Discovery rules guide the L'Ecritoire user in discovering new goals and therefore, eliciting new RCs. The discovery is based on the analysis of scenarios through one of the three proposed discovery strategies, namely the *refinement, composition* and *alternative* strategies. These strategies correspond to the three types of relationships among RCs introduced above. Given a pair <G,Sc>:

- the *composition strategy* looks for goals Gi ANDed to G,
- the *alternative strategy* searches for goals Gj ORed to G,
- the *refinement strategy* aims at the discovery of goals Gk at a lower level of abstraction than G.

Once a complete scenario has been authored, any of these three strategies can be followed.

L'Ecritoire uses six discovery rules, two for each strategy. Rules can be applied at any of the three levels of abstraction, contextual, functional and physical. A detailed description of rules can be found in (Rolland et al., 1998; Tawbi, 2001, Rolland, 2002). As an example of a rule, we present the refinement rule R1 and exemplify it with the example of the ATM system engineering.

Refinement guiding rule (R1) :
Goal : Discover *(from RC* <G,Sc>$)_{So}$ *(goals refined from G)$_{Res}$ (using every atomic action of Sc as a goal)$_{Man}$*
Body :
1. *Associate a goal Gi to every atomic action Ai in Sc. Gi refines G*
2. *Complement Gi by the manner 'in a normal way'*
3. *User evaluates the proposed panel of goals Gi and selects the goals of interest*
4. *RCs corresponding to these selected goals are ANDed to one another*

The guiding rule R1 aims at refining a given RC *(from RC*<G,Sc>$)_{So}$ by suggesting new goals at a lower level of abstraction than G *(goals refined from G)$_{Res}$.* The refinement mechanism underlying the rule looks to every interaction between two agents in the scenario Sc as a goal for the lower level of abstraction (step1). Let us take as an example the scenario SC associated to the goal *Improve services to our customers by providing cash from the ATM.*
Scenario SC :
1. *If the bank customer gets a card from the bank,*
2. *Then, the bank customer withdraws cash from the ATM*
3. *and the ATM reports cash transactions to the bank.*

This scenario includes three interactions namely 'Get card', 'Withdraw cash' and 'Report cash transactions' corresponding to the three

services involving the ATM. These services are proposed as the three a finer grained goals :
- *'Get card from the bank in a normal way'*
- *'Withdraw cash from ATM in a normal way'*
- *'Report cash transactions to the bank in a normal way'*

Assuming that the user accepts the three suggested goals (step3), the corresponding RCs are ANDed to one another (step4).

❖ As illustrated above, L'Ecritoire develops a requirements/goal inductive elicitation technique based on the analysis of conceptualised scenarios. The conceptualisation of a scenario results of powerful analysis and transformation of textual scenarios using a linguistic approach based on a Case Grammar inspired by Fillmore's Case Theory (Fillmore, 1968) and its extensions (Dik, 1989; Schank, 1973). The pay-off of the scenario conceptualisation process is the ability to perform powerful induction on conceptualised scenarios. In (Lamweerde, 1998), a similar approach is developed that takes scenarios as examples and counter examples of the intended system behaviour and generates goals that cover positive scenarios and exclude the negative ones.

An obvious informal technique for finding goals is to systematically ask WHY and WHAT-IF questions (Potts et al, 1994), (Sutcliffe et al, 1998). In L'Ecritoire the refinement strategy helps discovering goals at a lower level of abstraction. This is a way to support goal decomposition. Another obvious technique to perform decomposition is to ask the HOW question (Lamsweerde et al., 1995). A heuristic based decomposition technique has been developed in (Loucopoulos et al., 1997) and (Letier, 2001).

An attempt to retrieved cases from a repository of process cases was developed in (Le, 1999). The software tool captures traces of RE processes using the NATURE contextual model (Nature, 1999) and develops a case based technique to retrieve process cases similar to the situation at hand.

4 CONCLUSION

Goal-driven RE was introduced mainly to provide the rationale of the To-Be system. Beyond this objective, we have seen that there are some other advantages :
- goals bridge the gap between organisational strategies and system requirements thus providing a conceptual link between the system and its organisational context;

- goal decomposition graphs provide the pre-traceability between high level strategic concerns and low level technical constraints; therefore facilitating the propagation of business changes onto system features;
- ORed goals introduce explicitly design choices that can be discussed, negotiated and decided upon;
- AND links among goals support the refinement of high level goals onto lower level goals till operationalisable goals are found and associated to system requirements;
- Powerful goal elicitation techniques facilitate the discovery of goal/requirements;
- Relationships between goals and concepts such as objects, events, operations etc. traditionally used in conceptual design facilitates the mapping of goal graphs onto design specification.

There are other advantages which flow from issues which were not verified with in the paper and that we sketch here :

- Goal-based negotiation is one of them (Boehm and In H, 1996).
- Conflict resolution is another one. (Nuseibeh, 1994) explains how conflicts arise from multiple view points and concerns and in (Lamsweerde et al., 1998a) various forms of conflict have been studied.
- Goal validation is a third one. (Sutcliffe et al, 1998) use a scenario generation technique to validate goal/requirement and in (Heymans and Dubois et al., 1998) the validation is based on scenario animation.
- Qualitative reasoning about goals is provided by the NFR framework (Mylopoulos, 1992; Chung et al, 2000).

REFERENCES

Anton, A. I., 1996,Goal based requirements analysis. Proceedings of the 2nd International Conference on Requirements Engineering ICRE'96, pp. 136-144.

Anton, A. I, and Potts C., 1998,The use of goals to surface requirements for evolving systems, International Conference on Software Engineering (ICSE '98) , Kyoto, Japan, pp. 157-166, 19-25 April 1998.

Anton, A. I., Earp J.B., Potts C., and Alspaugh T.A., 2001,The role of policy and stakeholder privacy values in requirements engineering, IEEE 5th International Symposium on Requirements Engineering (RE'01), Toronto, Canada, pp. 138-145, 27-31 August 2001.

Ben Achour, C., 1999,Requirements extraction from textual scenarios. PhD Thesis, University Paris6 Jussieu, January 1999.

Boehm, B., 1976,Software engineering. IEEE Transactions on Computers, 25(12): 1226-1241.

Boehm, B., 1996,Identify Quality-requirements conflicts, 1996, Proceedings ICRE, Second International Conference on Requirements Engineering, April 15-18, 1996, Colorado spring, Colorado, 218.

Bowen, T. P., Wigle, G. B., Tsai, J. T., 1985,Specification of software quality attributes. Report of Rome Air Development Center.

Bubenko, J., Rolland, C., Loucopoulos, P., de Antonellis V., 1994,Facilitating 'fuzzy to formal' requirements modelling. IEEE 1st Conference on Requirements Enginering, ICRE'94 pp. 154-158.

Cockburn, A., 1995,Structuring use cases with goals. Technical report. Human and Technology, 7691 Dell Rd, Salt Lake City, UT 84121, HaT.TR.95.1, http://members.aol.com/acocburn/papers/usecases.ht m .CREWS Team, 1998,The crews glossary, CREWS report 98-1, http://SUNSITE.informatik.rwth-aachen.de/CREWS/reports.htm

Chung, K. L., Nixon B. A., and Yu E., Mylopoulos J., 2000,Non- Functional Requirements in Software Engineering. Kluwer Academic Publishers.. 440 p.

Dano, B., Briand, H., and Barbier, F., 1997, A use case driven requirements engineering process. Third IEEE International Symposium On Requirements Engineering RE'97, Antapolis, Maryland, IEEE Computer Society Press.

Dardenne, A., Lamsweerde, A. v., and Fickas, S., 1993,Goal-directed Requirements Acquisition, Science of Computer Programming, 20, Elsevier, pp.3-50.

Davis, A. .M., 1993, Software requirements :objects, functions and states. Prentice Hall.

Dik, S. C., 1989, The theory of functional grammar, part i : the structure of the clause. Functional Grammar Series, Fories Publications.

Dubois, E., Yu, E., and Pettot, M., 1998, "From early to late formal requirements: a process-control case study". Proc. IWSSD'98 – 9th International Workshop on software Specification and design. Isobe.IEEE CS Press. April 1998, 34-42.

ELEKTRA consortium, 1997,Electrical enterprise knowledge for transforming applications. ELEKTRA Project Reports.

ESI96, European Software Institute, 1996,"European User survey analysis", Report USV_EUR 2.1, ESPITI Project, January 1996.

Fillmore, C., 1968,The case for case. In ''Universals in linguistic theory'', Holt, Rinehart and Winston (eds.),Bach & Harms Publishing Company, pp. 1-90.

Gote, O., and Finkelstein A., 1994,Modelling the contribution structure underlying requirements, in Proc. First Int. Workshop on Requirements

Engineering : Foundation of Software Quality, Utrech, Netherlands.

Haumer, P., Pohl K., and Weidenhaupt K., 1998,Requirements elicitation and validation with real world scenes. IEEE Transactions on Software Engineering, Special Issue on Scenario Management, M. Jarke, R. Kurki-Suonio (eds.), Vol.24, N°12, pp.11036-1054.

Heymans, P., and Dubois, E.,.1998, Scenario-based techniques for supporting the elaboration and the validation of formal requirements. RE Journal, P. Loucopoulos, C. Potts (eds.), Springer, CREWS Deliverable N°98-30, http://SUNSITE.informatik.rwth-aachen.de/CREWS/

Jacobson, I., 1995,The Use case construct in object-oriented software engineering. In Scenario-Based Design: Envisioning Work and Technology in System Development, J.M. Carroll (ed.), pp.309-336.

Jarke, M., and Pohl, K., 1993,Establishing visions in context: towards a model of requirements processes. Proc. 12th Intl. Conf. Information Systems, Orlando.

Kaindl, H., 2000, "A design process based on a model combining scenarios with goals and functions", IEEE Trans. on Systems, Man and Cybernetic, Vol. 30 No. 5, September 2000, 537-551.

Kardasis P., and Loucopoulos P., 1998,Aligning legacy information system to business processes. Submitted to CAiSE'98.

Lamsweerde, A. v., Dardenne, B., Delcourt, and F. Dubisy, 1991,"The KAOS project: knowledge acquisition in automated specification of software", Proc. AAAI Spring Symp. Series, Track: "Design of Composite Systems", Stanford University, March 1991, 59-62.

Lamsweerde, A. v., Dairmont, R., and Massonet, P., 1995,Goal directed elaboration of requirements for a meeting scheduler : *Problems and Lessons Learnt*, in Proc. Of RE'95 – 2nd Int. Symp. On Requirements Engineering, York, pp 194 –204.

Lamsweerde A. v., and Willemet, L., 1998, "Inferring declarative requirements specifications from operational scenarios". In: IEEE Transactions on Software Engineering, Special Issue on Scenario Management. Vol. 24, No. 12, Dec. 1998, 1089-1114.

Lamsweerde, A. v., Darimont, R., and Letier, E., 1998a, "Managing conflicts in goal-driven requirements engineering", IEEE Trans. on Software. Engineering, Special Issue on Inconsistency Management in Software Development, Vol. 24 No. 11, November 1998, 908-926.

Lamsweerde, A. v., 2000,Requirements engineering in the year 00: *A research perspective*. In Proceedings 22nd International Conference on Software Engineering, Invited Paper, ACM Press, June 2000.

Lamsweerde, A. v., and Letier, E., 2000a,"Handling obstacles in goal-oriented requirements engineering", IEEE Transactions on Software

Engineering, Special Issue on Exception Handling, Vol. 26 No. 10, October 2000, pp. 978-1005.

Lamsweerde, A.v., 2001, "Goal-oriented requirements engineering: a guided tour". Invited minitutorial, Proc. RE'01 International Joint Conference on Requirements Engineering, Toronto, IEEE, August 2001, pp.249-263.

Le, T. .L., 1999,Guidage des processus d'ingénierie des besoins par un approche de réutilisation de cas, Master Thesis, CRI, Université Paris-1, Panthéon Sorbonne.

Lee, S. P., 1997, Issues in requirements engineering of object-oriented information system: a review, Malaysian Journal of computer Science, vol. 10, N° 2, December 1997.

Leite, J. C. .S., Rossi, G., Balaguer, F., Maiorana, A., Kaplan, G., Hadad, G., and Oliveros, A., 1997, Enhancing a requirements baseline with scenarios. In Third IEEE International Symposium On Requirements Engineering RE'97, Antapolis, Maryland, IEEE Computer Society Press, pp. 44-53.

Letier, E., 2001,Reasoning about agents in goal-oriented requirements engineering. Ph. D. Thesis, University of Louvain, May 2001; http://www.info.ucl.ac.be/people/eletier/thesis.html

Leveson, N. G., 2000,"Intent specifications: an approach to building human-centred specifications", IEEE Trans. Soft. Eng., vol. 26, pp. 15-35.

Loucopoulos, P, 1994, The f² (from fuzzy to formal) view on requirements engineering. Ingénierie des systèmes d'information, Vol. 2 N° 6, pp. 639-655.

Loucopoulos, P., Kavakli, V., and Prakas, N., 1997,Using the EKD approach, the modelling component. ELEKTRA project internal report.

Mylopoulos, J.,. Chung K.L., and Nixon, B.A., 1992,Representing and using non- functional requirements: a process-oriented approach . IEEE Transactions on Software Engineering, Special Issue on Knowledge Representation and Reasoning in Software Development, Vol. 18, N° 6, June 1992, pp. 483-497.

Mylopoulos, J.,. Chung, K..L., and Yu, E., 1999,"From object-oriented to goal6oriented requirements analysis". Communications of the ACM. Vol 42 N° 1, January 1999, 31-37.

Mostow, J., 1985, "Towards better models of the design process". AI Magazine, Vol. 6, pp. 44-57.

Nature, 1999, The nature of requirements engineering . Shaker Verlag Gmbh. (Eds.) Jarke M., Rolland C., Sutcliffe A. and Dömges R., Jily 1999.

Nuseibeh, B., Kramer, J., and Finkelstein, A., 1994,A framework for expressing the relationships between multiple views in requirements specification. In IEEE Transactions on Software Engineering, volume 20, pages 760-- 773. IEEE CS Press, October 1994.

Plihon, V., Ralyté, J., Benjamen, A., Maiden, N. A. M., Sutcliffe, A., Dubois, E., and Heymans, P., 1998, A reuse-oriented approach for the construction of scenario based methods. Proceedings of the International Software Process Associations 5th

International Conference on Software Process (ICSP'98), Chicago.

Pohl K., 1996, Process centred requirements engineering, J. Wiley and Sons Ltd.

Pohl K., and Haumer, P., 1997, Modelling contextual information about scenarios. Proceedings of the Third International Workshop on Requirements Engineering: Foundations of Software Quality REFSQ'97, Barcelona, pp.187-204, June 1997.

Potts, C., Takahashi, K., and Anton, A. I., 1994,Inquiry-based requirements analysis. In IEEE Software 11(2), pp. 21-32.

Potts, C., 1995, "Using schematic scenarios to understand user needs", Proc. DIS'95 - ACM Symposium on Designing interactive Systems: Processes, Practices and Techniques, University of Michigan, August 1995.

Potts, C., 1997,Fitness for use : the system quality that matters most. Proceedings of the Third International Workshop on Requirements Engineering: Foundations of Software Quality REFSQ'97 , Barcelona, pp. 15-28, June 1997.

Prat, N., 1997,Goal formalisation and classification for requirements engineering. Proceedings of the Third International Workshop on Requirements Engineering: Foundations of Software Quality REFSQ'97, Barcelona, pp. 145-156, June 1997.

Ramesh, B., Powers, T., Stubbs, C., and Edwards, M., 1995, Implementing requirements traceability : a case study, in Proceedings of the 2nd Symposium on Requirements Engineering (RE'95), pp89-95, UK.

Rasmussen, J., 1990, Mental models and the control of action in complex environments. Mental Models and Human--Computer Interaction, D. Ackermann and M.J. Tauber , eds., North-Holland : Elsevier, pp. 41-69.

Rolland, C, and Ben Achour, C., 1997,Guiding the construction of textual use case specifications. Data & Knowledge Engineering Journal Vol. 25 N° 1, pp. 125-160, (ed. P. Chen, R.P. van de Riet) North Holland, Elsevier Science Publishers. March 1997..

Rolland, C., Grosz, G., and Nurcan, S., 1997a,Guiding the EKD process. ELEKTRA project report,

Rolland, C., Nurcan, S., and Grosz, G., 1997b,Guiding the participative design process. Association for Information Systems Americas Conference, Indianapolis, Indiana, pp. 922-924, August, 1997

Rolland, C., Souveyet, C., and Ben Achour, C., 1998,Guiding goal modelling using scenarios. IEEE Transactions on Software Engineering, Special Issue on Scenario Management, Vol. 24, No. 12, Dec. 1998.

Rolland, C., 2002,L'e-lyee: l'ecritoire and lyeeall, Information and software Technology 44 (2002) 185-194

Rolland, C., Grosz, G., and Kla, R., 1999,Experience with goal-scenario coupling. in requirements engineering, Proceedings of the Fourth IEEE International Symposium on Requirements Engineering, Limerik, Ireland,

Ross, D. T., and Schoman, K. .E., 1977,Structured analysis for requirements definition. IEEE Transactions on Software Engineering , vol. 3, N° 1, , 6-15.

Robinson, W. N., 1989, "integrating multiple specifications using domain goals", Proc. IWSSD-5 - 5th Intl. Workshop on Software Specification and Design, IEEE, 1989, 219-225.

Schank, R. C., 1973,Identification of conceptualisations underlying natural language. In ''Computer models of thought and language'', R.C. Shank, K.M. Colby (Eds.), Freeman, San Francisco, pp. 187-247.

Sommerville I.,1996, Software Engineering. Addison Wesley.

Sommerville, I., and Sawyer, P., 1997, Requirements engineering. Worldwide Series in Computer Science, Wiley.

Standish Group, 1995,Chaos. Standish Group Internal Report, http://www.standishgroup.com/chaos.html

Sutcliffe, A.G., Maiden, N. .A., Minocha, S., and Manuel D.., 1998,"Supporting scenario-based requirements engineering", IEEE Trans. Software Eng. vol. 24, no. 12, Dec.1998, 1072-1088.

Tawbi, M., 2001,Crews-L'Ecritoire : un guidage outillé du processus d'Ingénierie des Besoins. Ph.D. Thesis University of Paris 1, October 2001.

Thayer, R., Dorfman, M. (eds.), System and software requirements. IEEE Computer Society Press.1990.

Vicente, K. J., and Rasmussen, J., 1992, Ecological interface design: Theoretical foundations. IEEE Trans. on Systems, Man, and Cybernetics, vol. 22, No. 4, July/August 1992.

Yu, E., 1994,Modelling strategic relationships for process reengineering. Ph.D. Thesis, Dept. Computer Science, University of Toronto, Dec. 1994.

Yue, K., 1987,What does it mean to say that a specification is complete?, Proc. IWSSD-4. Four International Workshop on Software Specification and Design, Monterrey, 1987.

Zave P., and Jackson M., 1997, "Four dark corners of requirements engineering", ACM Transactions on Software Engineering and Methodology, 1-30. 1997.

REAL-TIME KNOWLEDGE-BASED SYSTEMS FOR ENTERPRISE DECISION SUPPORT AND SYSTEMS ANALYSIS*

Albert M. K. Cheng

Real-Time Systems Laboratory
Department of Computer Science
University of Houston
Houston, Texas 77204, USA
Email: cheng@cs.uh.edu

Abstract: This keynote paper explores the use of real-time knowledge-based systems (RTKBSs) for enterprise decision support as well as for systems specification and analysis. Knowledge-based systems for monitoring and decision-making in a real-time environment must meet stringent response time and logical correctness requirements. Modern enterprise information systems are requiring shorter response time and greater reliability for businesses to stay competitive. The critical nature of such decision-making systems requires that they undergo rigorous and formal analysis prior to their deployment. This paper describes how knowledge-based systems for decision support are formally analyzed. It also shows how the requirements and operations of enterprise systems can actually be modeled as a rulebase which can then be formally analyzed.

1 INTRODUCTION

Enterprise information systems must perform faster and more reliably than ever before in order for businesses to stay competitive. The increasing amount of information in these systems also necessitates automated decision support to meet often time-critical requirements. This keynote paper explores the use of real-time knowledge-based systems (KBSs) for enterprise decision support as well as for systems specification and analysis.

There is a rapid increase in the use of embedded computers in time-critical systems ranging from the anti-lock braking controller in automobiles to the onboard safety mechanism in the Space Shuttle. The ability of these real-time monitoring and control computers to deliver results *on time* becomes as important as the ability of such computers to deliver *correct* results whenever needed. Since these embedded computers are used to perform increasingly complex monitoring, diagnosis, and control functions, real-time knowledge-based expert systems (KBSs) are becoming increasingly popular in the implementation of these embedded computer systems (Payton, et al. 1991). Other emerging motivations for employing KBSs include the increasing complexity of operations

*This material is based upon work supported in part by the National Science Foundation under Award No. CCR-9111563 and by the Texas Advanced Research Program under Grant No. 3652270.

performed by the system being monitored and controlled, the repetitive nature of the monitoring and control functions which also impose very short time for computer response, the unavailability of efficient deterministic algorithms for solving the real-time decision problems which are more amenable to rule-based reasoning, and a rapidly changing environment requiring learning and adaptive capabilities.

Real-time KBSs are embedded artificial intelligence (AI) systems which must respond to the environment being monitored and controlled within stringent timing constraints. They are programs which encode application-specific knowledge expressed in the form of *if-then* rules. Based on input sensor values, the embedded KBS must make decisions within bounded time to respond to the external environment; the result of missing a deadline may be catastrophic. Thus a real-time KBS makes critical decisions that are used to guarantee the safety and progress of the environment in which they are embedded. However, these decisions are only useful if they are produced within the timing constraints imposed by the environment. Therefore, it is required not only to verify the logical correctness of a real-time expert system but also to determine whether the computation time required to compute a logically correct decision is within the imposed timing constraint. This added constraint of timing requirements makes the design and maintenance of these systems particularly difficult.

Although a KBS may perform well on the average

O. Camp et al. (eds.), Enterprise Information Systems V, 21-34.

in terms of computation time, it may fail to deliver results while meeting deadlines in some critical cases. In fact, the performance of a KBS is highly unpredictable in a real-time environment owing to the fact that the control flow of the rules in these systems is embedded in the data and cannot be easily deduced (Wang, et al. 1990). This is not acceptable in a *hard* real-time system (as in the case of the anti-lock braking controller or the Space Shuttle safety mechanism) where the failure to meet a single deadline may be catastrophic. There have been few attempts to formalize the question of whether rule-based systems can deliver adequate performance in *bounded time*. Thus the technology for building the next generation of real-time KBSs must be developed before we can rely on these smart systems to perform complex monitoring and control functions in a real-time environment as we currently do on software programs implemented in procedural languages such as C and C++.

We examine some fundamental issues in the design and development of real-time KBSs in this paper, including response time analysis and parallel rule-base execution. Past research focused only on performance analysis and optimization of KBSs for *soft* real-time applications, where the failure to meet some timing constraints can be tolerated(Gupta 1991). Although several researchers have begun addressing real-time issues in the design of KBSs in recent years (Benda 1987; Laffey, et al. 1988; Marsh 1988; O'Reilly, et al.), there is a lack of work in the formal verification and validation of KBSs in the real-time environment, especially in time-critical enterprise systems.

We begin this paper by describing some basic features of real-time KBSs. The concept of a real-time decision system model is also formulated. For motivation, several small examples of rule-bases written in OPS5 and EQL are given. Then we show how to represent and visualize the execution of a KBS using a state space graph. We also show how to meet stringent response time constraints without modifying the rule base by reducing the execution time via parallel rule-base execution. Practical solutions for these fundamental problems are outlined and examples are given to demonstrate their capabilities. To show that our tools are practical enough to verify realistic real-time decision systems, we show some results from the analysis of the Integrated Status Assessment Expert System (Marsh 1988). We describe how the requirements and operations of operators in an assembly line can be captured and modeled as a rulebase which can then be formally analyzed. Finally, the conclusion ends this paper with some relevant remarks.

2 REAL-TIME RULE-BASED PROGRAMS

We begin by describing the basic features of the popular OPS5 rule-based programming language [5]. Then we show a simpler rule-based language called EQL which we use to study the response time analysis problem. An OPS5 rule-based program consists of a finite set of rules each of which is of the form:

```
(p rule-name
    (condition-element-1)
         :
    (condition-element-m)
-->
    (action-1)
         :
    (action-n)
```

and a database of assertions each of which is of the form

```
(class-name ^attribute-1 value-1
            ^attribute-2 value-2
                 :          :
            ^attribute-p value-p).
```

The set of rules is called the *production (or rule) memory* (PM) and the database of assertions is called the *working memory* (WM). Each assertion is called a *working memory element* (WME). A rule has three parts:

(1) The name identifying the rule: rule-name,

(2) LHS: the left-hand-side, i.e., a conjunction of condition elements each of which can be either a *positive condition element* or a *negative condition element*, and

(3) RHS: the right-hand-side, i.e., the action(s) each of which may create, modify, or delete a WME, perform I/O, or halt.

The following is an OPS5 rule for processing sensor information from a wind-speed detection system:

```
(p wind-scan    ; an OPS5 rule
     (region-scan1 ^sensor high-wind-speed)
       ; positive condition element
     (region-scan2 ^sensor high-wind-speed)
       ; positive condition element
     (status-check ^status normal)
       ; positive condition element
   - (interrupt ^status on)
       ; negative condition element
   { <Uninitialized-configuration>
       ; positive condition element
     (configuration ^high-wind 0) }
 -->
     (modify <Uninitialized-configuration>
             ^high-wind 1))
       ; action
```

If both wind sensors (region-scan1 and *region-scan2*) detect high-speed wind, the status of the sensor system is normal (attribute `status` of element class `status-check` is *normal*), there is no interrupt (attribute `status` of element class `interrupt` is not *on*), and the attribute `high-wind` in the element class `configuration` is 0, then assign 1 to `high-wind`. `<Uninitialized-configuration>` is used to refer to the WME matched in the LHS. Comments are given following the semicolon ';'. When the working memory contains the WMEs (updated periodically by reading from sensor input values and system status):

```
(region-scan1 ^sensor high-wind-speed)
(region-scan2 ^sensor high-wind-speed)
(status-check ^status normal)
(configuration ^high-wind 0)
```

but does not contain the WME

```
(interrupt ^status on)
```

then the above rule is said to have a successful matching. More precisely, a rule is enabled if each of its positive condition elements is matched with a WME in the working memory and each of its negative condition elements is *not* matched by any WME in the working memory. A rule firing is the execution of the RHS action(s) in the order they appear in the rule. The above rule fires by modifying the attribute `high-wind` in the element class `configuration` to have the value 1.

The OPS5 rule interpreter executes an OPS5 program by repeatedly performing the match-select-act cycle until a `halt` action is executed or until none of the rules in the PM are matched:

(1) Match: for each rule, determine all sets of WMEs which match the condition elements of the rule. Note that a rule may have more than one matching. The result of a successful match is called an *instantiation*.

(2) Select: select one instantiation according to a specified *conflict-resolution* strategy. Two common strategies are LEX (lexicographic ordering) and MEA (means-end analysis).

(3) Act: perform the RHS actions in the order they appear in the selected rule instantiation.

To provide motivation for studying the response time analysis problem, let's consider the following OPS5 rule-based program for processing sensor data from an intruder detection system in an organization such as a bank vault.

Example 1. A simple OPS5 intruder-detection program.

```
(P sensor-a-detect-t          ; rule 1
  (sensor-a ^value 1 ^status good)
  -->
  (modify configuration ^intruder-detected true) )

(P sensor-b-detect-t          ; rule 2
```

```
  (sensor-b ^value 1 ^status good)
  -->
  (modify configuration ^intruder-detected true) )

(P sensor-a-detect-f          ; rule 3
  (sensor-a ^value 0 ^status good)
  -->
  (modify configuration ^intruder-detected false) )

(P sensor-b-detect-f          ; rule 4
  (sensor-b ^value 0 ^status good)
  -->
  (modify configuration ^intruder-detected false) )
```

If the working memory contains the WMEs

```
(sensor-a ^value 1 ^status good)
(sensor-b ^value 0 ^status good)
```

indicating that `sensor-a` and *sensor-b* read in values '1' and '0' respectively, then the above program will never terminate since the attribute `intruder-detected` of the element class `configuration` will be set to *true* and `false` alternatively by rules 1 and 4. Rule 1 and rule 4 are said to be not compatible. Similarly, if the working memory contains the WMEs

```
(sensor-a ^value 0 ^status good)
(sensor-b ^value 1 ^status good)
```

indicating that `sensor-a` and *sensor-b* read in values '0' and '1' respectively, then the above program will never terminate since the attribute `intruder-detected` of the element class `configuration` will be set to *true* and `false` alternatively by rules 2 and 3. Rule 2 and rule 3 also are not compatible. This cyclic rule firing is one of the many timing violations which must be detected and corrected in a real-time KBS. The general goal is to guarantee that the KBS converge to a fixed point within a bounded time period as imposed by the environment being controlled. In our example, the KBS must decide whether an intruder is detected before the next sensor readings erase the current working memory values. One subproblem is to determine whether or not the rule-based program will reach a fixed point in a bounded number of rule firings. Another subproblem is to determine the computation time required for each match.

For a program of this size, the answer is obvious. However, the problem is not trivial for larger programs. In general, the analysis problem to determine whether a rule-based program will reach a fixed point is undecidable if the program variables can have infinite domains, i.e., there is no general procedure for answering all instances of the decision problem (Cheng, et al. 1993) To get a better handle on this complex problem, we shall use a simpler rule-based language to study the analysis problem so that we can concentrate on the problem itself and not on the complexity of the language. This simpler language is called EQL (Equational Logic rule-based language), which is more predictable in terms of response time and thus easier to analyze.

Consider a real-time system model (Figure 1) where the decision module D is implemented as a rule-based EQL program and the environment A is the enterprise system.

Figure 1: A real-time decision system.

This EQL program has a set of rules for updating variables which denote the state of the physical system under control. The firing of a rule computes a new value for one or more state variables to reflect changes in the external environment as detected by sensors. Sensor readings are sampled periodically. Every time sensor readings are taken, the state variables are re-computed iteratively by a number of rule firings until no further change in the variables can result from the firing of a rule. The equational rule-based program is then said to have reached a *fixed point*. Intuitively, rules in an EQL program are used to express the constraints on a system and also the goals of the controller. If a fixed point is reached, then the state variables have settled down to a set of values that are consistent with the constraints and goals as expressed by the rules.

EQL differs from OPS5 and other popular expert system languages such as CLIPS in some important ways. These differences reflect the goal of our research, which is not to invent yet another expert system shell but to investigate whether and how performance objectives can be met when rule-based programs are used to perform safety-critical functions in real time. Whereas the interpretation of a language like OPS5 is defined by the recognize-act cycle (Forgy 1981), the basic interpretation cycle of EQL is defined by fixed point convergence. It is our hypothesis that the time it takes to converge to a fixed point is a more pertinent measure of the response time of a rule-based program than the length of the recognize-act cycle. More importantly, we do not require the firing of rules that lead to a fixed point to be implemented sequentially. As we will see later, rules can be fired in parallel if they do not interfere with one another (Cheng 1993). The definition of response time

in terms of fixed point convergence is architecture independent and is therefore more robust.

The RULES section of an EQL program is composed of a finite set of rules of the form:
$$a_1 := b_1 ! a_2 := b_2 !...! a_m := b_m \text{ IF EC}$$
A rule has three parts:

(1) VAR: the left-hand-side variables of the multiple assignment statement, i.e., the a_i's,

(2) VAL: the right-hand-side expressions of the multiple assignment statement, i.e., the b_i's, and

(3) EC: the enabling condition.

An enabling condition is a predicate on the variables in the program. A rule is enabled if its enabling condition becomes true. A rule firing is the execution of the multiple assignment statement. A rule is *firable* only when it is enabled and if by firing it will change the value of some variable in VAR. A multiple assignment statement assigns values to one or more variables in parallel. The VAL expressions must be side-effect free. The execution of a multiple assignment statement consists of the evaluation of all the VAL expressions, followed by updating the VAR variables with the values of the corresponding expressions. An invocation of an EQL program is a sequence of rule firings. When two or more rules are enabled, the selection of which rule to fire is nondeterministic or up to the run-time scheduler.

An EQL program is said to have reached a *fixed point* when none of its rules is firable. An EQL program is said to always reach a fixed point in *bounded time* if and only if the number of rule firings needed to take the program from an initial state to a fixed point is always bounded by a fixed upper bound imposed by environmental constraints. It is possible that a program can reach different fixed points starting from the same initial state, depending on which and how rules are fired. This may suggest that the correctness of the program is violated, whereas for some applications this is acceptable. Our concern in this paper is, however, on designing KBSs that meet the specified timing requirements.

EQL is an equational rule-based language which we have implemented to run under BSD UNIX. The current system includes a translator eqtc which translates an EQL program into an equivalent C program for compilation and execution in a UNIX-based machine. Rewriting the OPS5 intruder-detection program in EQL, we obtain the program below.

Example 2. EQL RULES section of a simple intruder-detection program.

```
(*1*)    intruder_detected:=true
            IF sensor_a=1 AND sensor_a_status=good
(*2*)[]intruder_detected:=true
            IF sensor_b=1 AND sensor_b_status=good
(*3*)[]intruder_detected:=false
            IF sensor_a=0 AND sensor_a_status=good
(*4*)[]intruder_detected:=false
```

```
IF sensor_b=0 AND sensor_b_status=good
```

As in the equivalent OPS5 program, if `sensor_a` and *sensor_b* read in values '1' and '0' respectively, then this EQL program will never reach a fixed point since the variable `intruder_detected` will be set to *true* and `false` alternatively by rules 1 and 4. Recall that a rule is enabled if its enabling condition is true, and that a rule can fire when it is enabled and if by firing it will change the value of at least one VAR variable. Thus a rule can fire more than once as long as it remains firable. Rule 1 and rule 4 are not compatible. Similarly, if `sensor_a` and *sensor_b* read in values '0' and '1' respectively, then this EQL program will never reach a fixed point since the variable `intruder_detected` will be set to *true* and `false` alternatively by rules 2 and 3. Rule 2 and rule 3 also are not compatible.

3 STATE SPACE REPRESENTATION

The execution of an EQL program can be modeled by a labeled directed graph called a state space graph $G = (V, E)$. Each vertex is labeled by a distinct tuple: $(x_1, ..., x_n, s_1, ..., s_p)$ where x_i is a value in the domain of the $i - th$ input sensor variable and s_j is a value in the domain of the $j - th$ internal variable. A rule is *enabled* at vertex i if and only if its enabling condition is satisfied by the tuple of variable values at vertex i. Each edge denotes the firing of a rule such that an edge (i, j) connects vertex i to vertex j if and only if there is a rule r which is enabled at vertex i, and firing r will modify the program variables to have the same values as the tuple at vertex j. Obviously, if the domains of all the variables in a program are finite, then the corresponding state space graph must be finite. Note that the state space graph of a program need not be connected.

A path in the state space graph corresponds to the sequence of states generated by a sequence of rule firings of the corresponding program. A vertex in a state space graph is said to be a *fixed point* if it does not have any out-edges or if all of its out-edges are self-loops (i.e., cycles of length 1). Obviously, if the execution of a program has reached a fixed point, then every rule is either not enabled or its firing will not modify any of the variables.

An invocation of an EQL program can be thought of as tracing a path in the state space graph. A *monitor-decide* cycle starts with the update of input sensor variables and this puts the program in a new state. A number of rule firings will modify the program variables until the program reaches a fixed point. Depending on the starting state, a monitor-decide cy-

cle may take an arbitrarily long time to converge to a fixed point if at all.

Figure 2: State space graph of a real-time decision program.

Figure 2 illustrates these concepts. If the current state of the program is A, then the program can reach the fixed point FP2 in 4 rule firings by taking the path (A,D,F,H,FP2). If the path (A,D,E,...,FP1) is taken, then the fixed point FP1 will be reached after a finite number of rule firings. The dotted arrow from E to G in the graph represents a sequence of an unspecified number of uniquely labeled states. State A is stable because all paths from A will lead to a fixed point. If the current state of the program is B, then the program will iterate forever without reaching a fixed point. All the states B,I,J,K in the cycle (B,I,J,K,B) are unstable. Note that there is no out-edge from any of the states in this cycle. Once the program enters one of these states, it will iterate forever. If the current state of the program is C, then the program may enter and stay in a cycle if the path (C,L,J,...) is followed. If the path (C,L,M,...) is taken, then the cycle (M,P,N,M) may be encountered. The program may eventually reach the fixed point FP3 if at some time the scheduler fires the rule corresponding to the edge from P to FP3 when the program is in state P. To ensure this, however, the scheduler must observe a *strong fairness* criterion: if a rule is enabled infinitely often, then it must be fired eventually. In this case, paths from state C to FP3 are finite but their lengths are unbounded. C is a potentially unstable state.

In designing real-time KBSs, we should never allow the KBS to be invoked from an unstable state. Potentially unstable states can be allowed only if an appropriate scheduler is used to always select a sufficiently short path to a fixed point whenever the program is invoked from such a state. A fixed point is an *end-point* of a state s if that fixed point is reachable from s. Note that not every tuple which is some combination of sensor input and program variable values can be a state from which a program may be invoked. After a program reaches a fixed point, it will remain there until the sensor input variables are updated, and the program will then be invoked again in this new state. The states in which a program is invoked are called *launch states*.

In this paper, the timing constraint of interest is a deadline which must be met by every monitor-decide cycle of an EQL program. In terms of the state space representation, the timing constraint imposes an upper bound on the length of paths from a launch state to a fixed point. Integrity constraints are assertions that must hold at the end-points of launch states. Note also that the state space graph as defined only considers the length of a path in terms of the number of rule firings. However, the match time and the rule selection time at each state must also be included in determining the total response time of a KBS from a launch state to a fixed point (Wang, et al. 1990; Zupan, et al. 1993).

4 RESPONSE TIME ANALYSIS

In a real-time KBS-controlled system, the goal is to ensure that the KBS converges to a fixed point within a bounded time period at each invocation. Therefore, the analysis problem is to determine whether or not the program will reach a fixed point within a bounded time period. The problem is not trivial even for some small programs. In general, the analysis problem to determine whether a rule-based program will reach a fixed point is *undecidable* if the program variables can have infinite domains. The computational complexity of the analysis problem restricted to finite-domain programs is PSPACE-complete (Cheng, et al. 1993).

Existing software engineering techniques and tools for analyzing and validating procedural programs cannot be applied to KBSs due to two main differences between expert system programming and procedural programming. First, unlike programs written in a procedural language, the control flow of KBSs is embedded in the data and cannot be easily derived. It can also be implementation dependent. Second, the contents of the working memory of a KBS change continually with each rule firing. In the real-time control environment, there is the added complexity of timing constraints which makes the development of correct real-time programs more difficult even if such programs are written in procedural languages.

There exist computer-aided design (CAD) tools such as CHECK and EVA (Gupta 1991) for verifying and validating KBSs but we are not aware of any tools which are capable of determining response time prior to KBS execution so that specified timing constraints can be satisfied at every monitor-decide cycle. There has been very little work in the formal verification and validation of KBSs in the real-time environment (see the Introduction for references). To tackle this problem for a large class of EQL KBSs, a powerful analysis methodology to determine whether a program in this class has bounded response time was developed (Cheng, et al. 1993). Since the verification is based on a static analysis of the EQL rules and does not require checking the state space graph corresponding to these rules, this methodology makes the analysis of programs with a large number of rules practical for the first time. The flexibility of the analysis tools is further extended by the introduction of the special form specification language Estella (Cheng, et al. 1993). A suite of computer-aided software engineering (CASE) tools based on this analysis approach have been implemented and used successfully to analyze several real-time expert systems developed by MITRE and NASA for the Space Shuttle and the planned Space Station (Marsh 1988).

5 FINITE STATE SPACE ANALYSIS

Even though the analysis problem is undecidable in general, it is trivially true that the analysis problem is decidable if all the variables of an equational rule-based program range over finite domains. In this case, the state space graph of the program must be finite and can thus be analyzed by an algorithm which performs an exhaustive check on the finite graph. The default approach there is to generate the reachability graph from the initial state and use a model checker to determine whether a fixed point is always reachable on any path from the initial state. Fixed points are expressed by an atomic predicate on a state which is true if and only if out-edges from the state are self-loops. This approach is viable if the state space graph is reasonably small, but in the worst case may require exponential computation time as a function of the number of variables in the program.

Analysis example

The EQL program in example 2 given a set of initial input values can be translated into a finite state space graph by using the ptf translator:

```
ptf   example.eql
```

which also labels each state

```
(sensor_a,sensor_a_status,sensor_b,
 sensor_b_status,intruder_detected);
G = good, B = bad, T = true, F = false.
```

ptf also generates a temporal logic formula for checking whether this program will reach a fixed point in finite time from the launch state corresponding to the initial input and program variable values. This formula is stored in the file *mc.in* which is generated as input to the model checker and the timing analyzer. *mc.in* contains the representation of the labeled state space graph. The temporal logic model checker mcf can then be used to determine whether a fixed point is always reachable in a finite number of iterations by analyzing this finite state space graph with the given launch state:

```
mcf   mc.in.
```

To verify that the program will reach a fixed point from any launch state, the (finite) state space reachability graph of every launch state need to be analyzed by the model checker. The graph with launch state $(1, good, 1, good, false)$, corresponding to the combination of input values and initial internal values is one of $2^5 = 32$ possible subgraphs that must be checked by the model checker.

In general, for a finite-domain EQL program with n input variables and m internal variables, the total number of reachability graphs that have to be checked in the worst case (i.e., all combinations of the values of the input and internal variables are possible) is $(\Pi|X_i| \cdot \Pi|S_j|)$ where $|X_i|, |S_j|$ are respectively the size of the domains of the i-th input and j-th program variable. If all variables are binary, then this number is 2^{n+m}. In practice, the number of reachability graphs that must be checked is substantially less because many combinations of input and program variable values do not constitute launch states. In the above example, only $2^4 = 16$ subgraphs need to be checked by the model checker since the internal variable `intruder_detected` does not affect any enabling conditions. Other techniques like the one discussed in the next section are also available that do not require examination of the entire state space graph.

Finally, the timing analyzer fptime can be invoked to determine the longest sequence of rule firings leading to a fixed point, if at least one exists, by the command:

```
fptime   mc.in.
```

The following is the partial output of the fptime module corresponding to the reachability graph with launch state $(1, good, 0, good, false)$:

```
> initial state:   0
> fixed-point(s):  none
> maximal number of rule firings: infinity
```

The module ptaf performs the above translation and analysis on the entire state space graph of the example EQL program automatically.

```
> The program may not reach a fixed point in finite
> time.
```

5.1 Special Forms of Rules with Bounded Execution Time

In practice, it is often not necessary to check the complete state space in order to solve the analysis problem. Under appropriate conditions, efficient procedures exist which can be applied to reduce the size of the state space by a simple static analysis of the program. In particular, rules of certain forms are always guaranteed to reach a fixed point in a bounded number of rule firings. A suite of these special forms which are especially useful have been discovered. We shall show later that it is unnecessary for all the rules of a program to be in a special form in order to be able to reduce the state space. Techniques exist that can be applied recursively to fragments of a program and the result used to transform the whole program into a simpler one. For ease of discussion, we define three sets of variables for an EQL program:

$L = \{ v|v$ is a variable appearing in VAR$\}$
$R = \{ v|v$ is a variable appearing in VAL$\}$
$T = \{ v|v$ is a variable appearing in EC$\}$

Let L_x denote the set of variables appearing in LHS of rule x. Two rules a and b are said to be *compatible* if and only if at least one of the following conditions holds:

(CR1) Enabling conditions a and b are mutually exclusive (cannot be true simultaneously).

(CR2) $L_a \cap L_b = \emptyset$.

(CR3) Suppose $L_a \cap L_b \neq \emptyset$. Then for every variable v in $L_a \cap L_b$, the same expression must be assigned to v in both rule a and b.

Let T_x denote the set of variables appearing in the test (enabling condition) of rule x. We are now ready to present one special form of rules with bounded execution time for which the analysis problem can be solved efficiently.

5.2 Special form A

A set of rules are said to be in special form A if all of the following three conditions hold.

(A1) Constant terms are assigned to all the variables in L, i.e., $R = \emptyset$.

(A2) All of the rules are compatible pairwise.

(A3) $L \cap T = \emptyset$.

An EQL rule-based program whose rules are in special form A will always reach a fixed point in at most n iterations, where n is the number of rules in the program (Cheng, et al. 1992).

5.3 Complexity of the recognition procedure for special form A

It is easy to see that the complexities of the recognition algorithms for checking a set of rules for the satisfiability of the conditions A1, A2:CR2 and A2:CR3, and A3 are respectively $O(n)$, $O(n^2)$, and $O(k^2)$, where n is the number of rules in the set, and k is the number of variables appearing in set L. Note that in the worst case, the checking of condition A2:CR1 (mutual exclusion) may require exponential time. However, programmers do not write unstructured tests in practice and many pairs of rules are compatible by conditions CR2 or CR3 (which are checked first by the recognition procedure), the checking of condition CR1 is usually not a problem.

5.4 Application of special form A

To illustrate the application of the special form A, consider the programs in example 3 below. Each program read in the values for b and c prior to execution.

Example 3a. These rules satisfy condition CR1.

```
(*1*)  a1 := true   IF b = true AND c = false
(*2*)[]a2 := false IF b = true AND c = true
```

Example 3b. These rules satisfy condition CR2.

```
(*1*)   a1 := true   IF b = true
(*2*)[]a2 := false IF c = true
```

Example 3c. These rules satisfy condition CR3.

```
(*1*)   a1 := true   IF b = true
(*2*)[]a1 := true   IF c = true
```

The utility of the special form above might seem quite limited since the three conditions of the special form must be satisfied by the *complete* set of rules in a program. However, the main use of the special form in our analysis tools is not to identify special-case programs. The leverage of the special form comes about when we can apply it to a subset of rules and conclude that at least some of the variables must attain stable values in finite time. The exploitation of the special form in a general strategy is explained next.

The General Analysis Strategy

Our general strategy for tackling the analysis problem is best understood by an example.

Example 4.

```
          input: read(b,c)
(*1*)      a1 := true
              IF b = true AND c = true
(*2*)  [] a1 := true
              IF b = true AND c = false
(*3*)  [] a2 := false
              IF c = true
(*4*)  [] a3 := true
              IF a1 = true AND a2 = false
(*5*)  [] a4 := true
              IF a1 = false AND a2 = false
(*6*)  [] a4 := false
              IF a1 = false AND a2 = true
```

For this program, $L \cap T \neq \emptyset$ and thus the rules are not of the special form described above. However, observe that rules 1, 2 and 3 by themselves are of the special form and that all the variables in these rules do not appear in LHS of the rest of the rules of the program and thus will not be modified by them. We can readily conclude that the variables $a1$ and $a2$ must

attain stable values in finite time, and these two variables can be considered as *constants* for rules 4, 5 and 6 of the program. We can take advantage of this observation and *rewrite* the program into a simpler one, as shown below.

```
(*4*) [] a3 := true
          IF a1 = true AND a2 = false
(*5*) [] a4 := true
          IF a1 = false AND a2 = false
(*6*) [] a4 := false
          IF a1 = false AND a2 = true
```

Note that $a1$ and $a2$ are now treated as input variables. This reduced program is of the special form since all assignments are to constants, L and T are disjoint, and all tests are mutually exclusive. Hence this program is always guaranteed to reach a fixed point in bounded time. This also guarantees that the original program must reach a fixed point in finite time.

There are in fact more special forms that can be exploited in the above fashion. The outline of the general strategy for tackling the analysis problem is as follows. Detailed discussions of the specific algorithms used can be found in another paper (Cheng, et al. 1993). Let S and Q be two disjoint sets of rules. S is *independent* from Q if the following conditions hold:

I1. $L_S \cap L_Q = \emptyset$. I2. the rules in Q do not potentially enable rules in S. I3. $R_S \cap L_Q = \emptyset$.

Algorithm Build_HLD. High-level dependency (HLD) graph construction.

Input: An EQL program.

Output: A high-level dependency graph corresponding to the EQL program.

a. For each rule i in the EQL program, create a vertex labeled i.

b. For every pair of rules j and k, let S contain rule j and let Q contain rule k. If one of the conditions I1, I2 or I3 is not satisfied, create a directed edge from vertex k to vertex j.

c. Find every strongly connected component in the dependency graph $G(V, E)$ constructed by step a and step b.

d. Let $C_1, C_2, ..., C_m$ be the strongly connected components of this graph $G(V, E)$. Define $\bar{G}(\bar{V}, \bar{E})$ as follows:

$$\bar{V} = C_1, C_2, ..., C_m$$

$\bar{G}$ is the HLD graph of the EQL program. Each of the vertices C_i in this high-level dependency graph is called a *forward-independent ruleset*.

Algorithm.   General Analysis Algorithm.

Input: A complete EQL program or a set of EQL rules; a list of special forms and exceptions, if any, specified in Estella.

Output: If the program will always reach a fixed point in bounded time, output 'yes'. If the program may not always reach a fixed point in bounded time according to the analysis, output 'no' and the rules involved in the possible timing violations.

(1) Construct the high-level data dependency graph corresponding to the EQL program. This graph shows dependence relations of one set of rules from another set.

(2) WHILE there are more rules for analysis DO:

Identify forward-independent sets of rules which are in special forms. If at least one rule set in special form is found and there are more rules to be analyzed, then mark those forward-independent sets identified as checked (which effectively removes those rules from further analysis), rewrite the remaining rules to take advantage of the fact that some variables can be treated as constants because of the special form, and repeat this step. If there are no more rules for analysis, output 'yes' (the EQL rules have bounded response time) and exit WHILE loop. If no independent set of rules is in a special form catalogue but the variables in some rule set have finite domains, check whether this rule set can always reach a fixed point in bounded time by using a state-based model checking algorithm. If the rule set is determined to be able to always reach a fixed point in bounded time, repeat this step. If the rule set is determined to be unable to always reach a fixed point in bounded time, report the rules involved in the timing violations. Prompt the user for new special forms or exceptions. If no new special forms or exceptions are entered, output 'no' (the EQL rules do not have bounded response time) and exit WHILE loop.

End While.

To compute precise bounds after the general analyzer has determined that a program has a bounded response time, the analysis tool invokes specialized algorithms (Cheng, et al. 1992) to compute a tight response time bound for the program. As an example, we analyze the Integrated Status Assessment Expert System next.

Analysis of the Integrated Status Assessment Expert System

The purpose of the Integrated Status Assessment Expert System (ISA) (Marsh 1988) is to determine the faulty components in a network. A component can be either an *entity* (node) or a *relationship* (link). A relationship is a directed edge connecting two entities. Components are in one of three states: nominal,

suspect, or failed. A failed entity can be replaced by an available backup entity. This expert system makes use of simple strategies to trace failed components in a network. Consider the first rule in the ISA program.

```
(P FIND-BAD-RELATIONSHIPS
  (ENTITY ^NAME <NAME> ^STATE << SUSPECT FAILED >>)
  (RELATIONSHIP ^FROM <NAME> ^STATE { <> SUSPECT }
    ^TYPE DIRECT ^MODE ON)
  -->
  (MODIFY 2 ^STATE SUSPECT))
```

This rule says that if entity A is in the suspect or failed state and the relationship L connects A to some other entity, then change the state of L to suspect.

The original ISA program is written in the OPS5 rule-based language. It contains 15 production rules and some Lisp function definitions. The EQL version of the ISA Expert System consists of: 35 rules, 46 variables (29 of which are input variables), and 12 constants. All the attributes of class *entities* and *relationships* of OPS5 are now represented by variables in EQL. For example, the working memory class

```
(ENTITY ^NAME ^STATE ^MODE)
```

is decomposed into variables $state1$ to $state4$ and $mode1$ to $mode4$ with the attribute NAME being '1' to '4'. Actually, there are no variables corresponding to NAME explicitly. By using $state2$, for example, we actually refer to the state of the entity of the name '2'. Again, we use the first rule from the original ISA program as an example to illustrate how it is translated into EQL rules.

```
rel1_state := suspect
  IF (state1 = suspect OR state1 = failed) AND
    rel1_state <> suspect AND
    rel1_mode = on AND rel1_type = direct

[]rel2_state := suspect
  IF (state2 = suspect OR state2 = failed) AND
    rel2_state <> suspect AND
    rel2_mode = on AND rel2_type = direct

[]rel3_state := suspect
  IF (state3 = suspect OR state3 = failed) AND
    rel3_state <> suspect AND
    rel3_mode = on AND rel3_type = direct
```

Note that it is translated into three EQL rules. Each rule checks the status of one *relationship*. This can be done only when the topology of the network is fixed.

5.5   Partial Analysis

The analysis makes use of special form A and special form B (Cheng, et al. 1993). One of the timing violations detected is the following two bad cycles: $(10- > 18- > 34- > 10)$ and $(10- > 18- > 35- > 10)$. This indicates that the program may not reach a fixed point given a particular initial state. The rules involved in these two cycles are reproduced below.

```
(*10*)[] state3 := failed
          IF find_bad_things = true AND
             state3 = suspect AND
          NOT (rel1_state = suspect AND rel1_mode = on
          AND rel1_type = direct) AND
          NOT (rel2_state = suspect AND rel2_mode = on AND
             rel2_type = direct)

(*18*)[] state3 := nominal ! reconfig3 := true
          IF state3 = failed AND mode3 <> off
                          AND config3 = bad

(*34*)[] sensor3 := bad ! state3 := suspect
          IF state1 = suspect AND
             rel1_mode = on AND rel1_type = direct AND
             state3 = nominal AND rel3_mode = on AND
             rel3_type = direct AND state4 = suspect AND
             find_bad_things = true

(*35*)[] sensor3 := bad ! state3 := suspect
          IF state2 = suspect AND
             rel2_mode = on AND rel2_type = direct AND
             state3 = nominal AND rel3_mode = on AND
             rel3_type = direct AND state4 = suspect AND
             find_bad_things = true
```

6 SPECIFYING ENTERPRISE SYSTEMS AS RULEBASES FOR ANALYSIS

Using an example, we show how systems requirements and operations can be modeled as KBSs, which can then be formally analyzed for logical and timing correctness using the above methodology. Two algorithms (centralized algorithm A and distributed algorithm B) have been proposed for solving a timing-based mutual exclusion problem in (Attiya, et al. 1989). In addition to computer processes, this algorithm can be applied to machine operators in a manufacturing assembly line. To illustrate the feasibility of our analysis approach, we shall utilize GAA to determine whether algorithm A has bounded response time. First, we manually encode the Attiya-Lynch algorithm in EQL such that the original algorithm has bounded response time iff the corresponding EQL version has bounded response time. Our first research objective is to develop an automatic encoding technique for converting any embedded system specification into an equivalent rule-based system. More specifically, the EQL program has the property such that the time between the request of any operator and the corresponding grant is bounded iff the EQL program has bounded response time. Then, we analyze the EQL program with GAA. The RULES part of the EQL version of Attiya-Lynch algorithm A follows. The declarations of variables and other housekeeping instructions are omitted.

```
PROGRAM mutual_exclusion_algorithm_a;
INIT
     request := empty,
     ticked := true,
```

```
     queue_head := empty,
     queue_tail := 0,
     queue_0 := empty,
          :
     queue_n_1 := empty,
     timer := 0

RULES
(* rules to encode add-request-to-queue operations *)

[] queue_0 := request ! queue_head := 0
                      ! queue_tail := 1
               IF  request <> empty
                   AND queue_head = empty
                   AND queue_tail = 0
          :
          :
[] queue_n_1 := request ! queue_tail := 0
                  IF  request <> empty
                  AND queue_tail = n-1

(* rule to simulate clock tick *)

[] timer := timer - 1 ! ticked := true
          IF  tick = true AND timer > 0

(* rules to encode grant operation to first request
   in queue *)

[] queue_head := 1 ! timer := (m+1) DIV c1 + 1
                   ! ticked := false
          IF queue_head = 0 AND queue_0 = 0
          AND timer <= 0 AND ticked = true
          :
[] queue_head := 0 ! timer := (m+1) DIV c1 + 1
                   ! ticked := false
          IF queue_head = n-1 AND queue_n_1 = 0
          AND timer <= 0 AND ticked = true
          :
          :
[] queue_head := 1 ! timer := (m+1) DIV c1 + 1
                   ! ticked := false
          IF queue_head = 0 AND queue_0 = n-1
          AND timer <= 0 AND ticked = true
          :
[] queue_head := 0 ! timer := (m+1) DIV c1 + 1
                   ! ticked := false
          IF queue_head = n-1 AND queue_n_1 = n-1
          AND timer <= 0 AND ticked = true

[] ticked := false
          IF queue_head = empty OR timer > 0
          OR ticked = false
          OR queue_head = queue_tail
END.
```

We now apply the analysis tool consisting of GAA and a facility called Estella (Cheng, et al. 1993;

Chen, et al. 1995; Cheng, et al. 2000) for specifying application-specific constraint assertions to perform the analysis on the EQL program. Only the pertinent analysis part is presented. First, we present the definitions of special form B and special form D. The enable-rule graph and the variable-modification graph encode information about the structure of and relationships among the rules. Note that the size of these graphs is proportional to the size of the program being analyzed, and is much smaller than the program's state space.

Rule a is said to *potentially enable* rule b if there exist at least one reachable state where (1) rule b is disabled, and (2) firing rule a enables rule b. The *enable − rule* (ER) graph of a set of rules is a labeled directed graph $G = (V, E)$. V is a set of vertices such that there is one vertex for each rule. E is a set of edges such that an edge connects vertex a to vertex b iff rule a potentially enables rule b.

Definition of Special Form B.

A set of rules are said to be in special form B if all of the following four conditions hold.

(B1) Constant terms are assigned to all the variables in L, i.e., $R = \emptyset$.

(B2) All of the rules are compatible pairwise.

(B3) $L \cap T \neq \emptyset$.

(B4) For each cycle in the enable-rule graph corresponding to this set of rules, no two rules in the cycle assign different expressions to the same variable. (A cycle is said to be bad if at least two rules in it assign different expressions to the same variable.)

(B5) Rules in disjoint simple cycles (with at least two vertices) in the enable-rule graph do not assign different expressions to a common variable appearing in their LHS.

The *variable − modification* (VM) graph of a set of rules is a labeled directed graph $G = (V, E)$. V is a set of vertices each of which is labeled by a tuple (i, j) corresponding to a distinct single-assignment subrule, where i is the rule number and j is the single-assignment subrule number within rule i (counting from left to right). E is a set of edges each of which denotes the interaction between a pair of single-assignment subrules such that an edge (m, n) connects vertex m to vertex n iff $L_m \cap R_n \neq \emptyset$, i.e., the variable appearing in LHS of single-assignment subrule m also appears in RHS of single-assignment subrule n.

To define special form D, we extend this graph to include a new type of edges: the *disable* edge. To distinguish the original type of edge from the new *disable* edge, we call the original edge an LR (set L → set R) edge to reflect the fact that an LR edge (m, n) connects vertex m to vertex n iff $L_m \cap R_n \neq \emptyset$, i.e., the variable appearing in the set

L of single-assignment subrule m also appears in the set R of single-assignment subrule n. A *disable* edge (r, s) connects vertex r to vertex s iff the firing of rule r always disables the enabling condition of rule s.

Definition of special form D.

A set of rules are said to be in special form D if all of the following five conditions hold.

(D1) Expressions with variables are assigned to the variables in L, i.e., $R \neq \emptyset$.

(D2) All of the rules are compatible pairwise.

(D3) $L \cap T \neq \emptyset$.

(D4) For each distinct cycle consisting of LR edges only in the variable-modification graph corresponding to this set of rules, there is at least a pair of rules (subrules) in the cycle that are compatible by condition CR1 (mutual exclusivity), or there is at least one *disable* edge in the cycle. (If a disable edge connects one rule vertex a to another rule vertex b, then there is one *disable* edge connecting every subrule vertex of rule a to every subrule vertex of rule b.)

(D5) For each cycle in the enable-rule graph corresponding to this set of rules, no two rules in the cycle assign different expressions to the same variable.

(D6) Rules in disjoint simple cycles (with at least two vertices) in the enable-rule graph do not assign different expressions to a common variable appearing in their LHS.

The analysis results for a system with four operators are as follows.

```
                    ⋮
                    ⋮
Commands:rp(read program)        sf(new special form)
         ls(load special form)   ps(print special forms)
         ds(delete special form) vm(verbose mode?)
         cp(compatible set)      bc(break condition)
         an(analyze)             ex(exit)

command > an

Select the rules to be analyzed:
   1. the whole program
   2. a continuous segment of program
   3. separated rules
Enter your choice: 1


Step 1:
   2 strongly connected components in dependency graph.
   20 rules in special form d.

1 rules remaining to be analyzed: 21

Step 2:
   1 strongly connected components in dependency graph.
     1 rules in special form b.

0 rules remaining to be analyzed:
```

Textual analysis is completed.
The program always reaches a fixed point in bounded time.

In step 1, 20 rules have been found to be in special form d and thus these rules are always guaranteed to reach a fixed point in bounded time. There are two independent components in the dependency graph representing data dependencies amongst rules. In step 2, the remaining rule is found to be in special form B. Without checking the state space graph of the program, the GAA tool concludes that the program always reaches a fixed point in bounded time. This analysis result is the same as the proof result obtained in (Attiya, et al. 1989). Using model checking or other state-space-based techniques to verify the correctness of algorithm A leads to a combinatorial state space explosion (Clarke, et al. 1986; Burch, et al. 1990; Cheng 2002) as the number of operators increases. We plan to characterize the class of embedded/real-time systems that can be analyzed with the proposed analysis approach.

A numeric bound on the number of rule firings for a program to reach a fixed point can be derived as follows. Note that the analysis algorithms breaks the EQL program into smaller rule sets, and the rules in the rule sets selected in iteration i are independent from those in the rule sets selected in iteration j, for $i < j$. This suggests an optimal schedule for firing the rules in the program. Rules in the rule sets selected during the first iteration should be fired first until a fixed point is reached, followed by the firing of those rules in the rule sets selected during the second iteration and later iterations. With this scheduling policy and a uniprocessor system, the bound on the number of rule firings is the sum of all the bounds (associated with the special forms identified or computed by the state space analyzer for non-special-form rule sets) on the number of rule firings of each rule set. A different upper bound can also be easily derived if a different scheduling policy and an alternative run-time architecture are assumed. To compute a response time bound for the system encoded in an EQL program, we need to assign appropriate weight to each rule in the program to reflect actual computation requirements of the system encoded.

7 RULE BASE PARALLELISM

An approach to meet stringent response time constraints without modifying the rule base is to reduce the execution time by introducing parallelism in both the pattern matching phase and/or the rule firing phase of the recognize-act cycle. Here, we consider briefly a parallel rule-firing approach for automated extraction of parallelism in KBSs via the response time analysis technique introduced earlier. An extension to the general analyzer can be used to automatically extract rule-firing parallelism in production systems without any programmer's assistance. The approach is discussed in detail and a list of recent work in parallel implementation of KBSs can be found in another paper (Cheng 1993).

7.1 Automated extraction of parallelism and optimal scheduling

We can extract parallelism in an EQL production system program using the General Analysis Algorithm introduced earlier. The following condition must be observed when rules are fired in parallel. A set of rules can be fired in parallel if the resulting values following the rule firings do not differ from the resulting values following any possible sequences of sequential firings of the same set of rules. To satisfy this condition, note that GAA builds the HLD graph corresponding to the program in step 2 by checking the data dependencies among all pairs of rules. This effectively decomposes the original program into an acyclic graph of inter-dependent rule sets some of which may be executed in parallel at a given time. Before describing our approach to parallel rule firing, let's first consider the scheduling of the rules in a program in a uniprocessor system.

7.2 Optimal rule set scheduling

In a uniprocessor system, the scheduler can be optimized to select the rules to fire such that a fixed point is always reached within the response time constraint, assuming that there is at least one sufficiently short path from a launch state to every one of its fixed points. This can be done by sorting the rule sets in topological order and then executing the rules in the list of inter-dependent rule sets in the sorted order.

Suppose A and B are two adjacent rule sets in the HLD graph $\bar{G}$ corresponding to a program and A precedes B. Let t_A and t_B be respectively the maximal number of rule firings required for rules in A and B to converge to a fixed point. Let $t_{A \cup B}$ be the time it takes for the rules contained in both rule sets to reach a fixed point. Since rule set A is forward-independent relative to rule set B, once the rules contained in A have reached a fixed point, firing any rules contained in B will not affect the fixed point convergence of A. Rules contained in B may not reach a fixed point before rules contained in A have reached a fixed point. Thus firing rules contained in B before those rules contained in A have converged to a fixed point will not decrease $t_{A \cup B}$, but may increase $t_{A \cup B}$. Consequently, firing the rules contained in A until a fixed point is reached in A and then firing those rules contained in B until a fixed point is reached in B will minimize the total number of rule firings in these two rule sets. Thus the optimal worst-case time needed for the rules contained in both rule sets to reach a fixed point using this schedule is $t_A + t_B$. With the rules decomposed as in step 2 of algorithm Build_HLD, this computation time is the best one can guarantee without further knowledge about the interaction of the rules within each rule set. This result can be extended to optimally schedule all rule sets selected firing the rules in each rule sets (until a fixed point is reached) in topological order.

7.3   Inter-ruleset parallelism

Note that in the HLD graph corresponding to a program, rules in rule sets without any in-edge can be fired in parallel because their fixed-point convergences are independent of each other. This observation forms the basis of an algorithm for maximizing rule-firing parallelism.

7.4   Intra-ruleset parallelism

We can also fire rules in parallel within each interdependent rule set detected by algorithm Build_HLD, thus further reducing the execution time of production systems. Since rules in each rule set may be mutually dependent, they must be analyzed for interference as a result of parallel rule firings. For each inter-dependent rule set, the analysis tool constructs a *disable graph*.

A *disable edge* connects vertex r to vertex s if and only if the firing of rule r always inhibits the enabling condition of rule s. The *disable graph* of a set of rules is a labeled directed graph $G = (V, E)$. V is a set of vertices such that there is a vertex for each rule in the program. E is a set of disable edges. The algorithm for detecting intra-ruleset parallel rule-firing interference first identifies all strongly connected components in G. Then, it labels rules in each strongly connected component C_i as interfering. Note that rules in C_i and in C_j, $i \neq j$, are not interfering.

We do not have to consider the case where there exists a variable v, v *member* $L_a \cap L_b$ and v is assigned conflicting values in rule a and rule b since such a pair of rules are not compatible if they can be simultaneously enabled and thus the timing violation is reported by the General Analysis Algorithm. The database constructed by this technique is used at run-time to determine whether the rules enabled in a recognize-act cycle interfere with one another. If no interference exists amongst the enabled rules, then all enabled rules in this cycle can be fired in parallel.

7.5   Automated Extraction of Parallelism in the ISA Expert System

We now apply this technique to extract parallelism in the ISA program analyzed earlier, which exhibits varying degrees of potential inter-ruleset and intra-ruleset parallelism. The General Analysis Algorithm has detected nine inter-dependent rule sets (strongly connected components) in the ISA expert system. After the rules in C_1 have reached a fixed point, rule 12 (C_2), rule 13 (C_3), rule 14 (C_4) and rule 15 (C_5) can be fired in parallel without interference. Finally, the rules in C_6, C_7, C_8 and C_9 can be fired in parallel without interference.

Furthermore, intra-ruleset parallelism is also detected in C_1, C_6, C_7, C_8 and C_9. More specifically, all rules in C_6, as well as those in C_7, C_8 and C_9, if enabled, can be fired in parallel without interference. However, rules in four subsets of rules in C_1 have been found to cause interference if they are fired in parallel: $\{8,16,32\}$, $\{9,17,33\}$, $\{10,18,32,34,35\}$, and $\{10,18,33,34,35\}$. Enabled rules in a set which is not equal to or which is not a superset of any of these subsets may fire in parallel in C_1.

To summarize, this algorithm extracts parallelism by breaking a large production system into smaller, more manageable rule clusters, each of which can be further analyzed for potential parallel rule firings. Ongoing work considers the implementation of an efficient computational environment for parallel execution of production systems, and investigates further improvement of our proposed technique for the automated extraction of parallelism. In particular, we are developing techniques for solving the following problems: (1) How to reduce the number and the size of the interfering rule sets by rewriting the given production system so that parallelism can be further increased? (2) Given a fixed number of processors, determine an optimal way to allocate the parallel modules into these processors such that the time needed to compute the respective fixed points of all parallel modules is minimized. (3) How to incorporate match parallelism in this model so that the detection of enabled rules can be expedited? Solutions to these and other related problems are needed to exploit maximal parallelism in production systems with today's parallel computers.

8   CONCLUSION

The main focus of this paper is to describe the use of real-time knowledge-based systems for enterprise decision support as well as for systems specification and analysis. It addresses two fundamental issues in the development of real-time KBSs: (1) Response time analysis: is the KBS sufficiently fast to meet stringent response time requirements? (2) Parallel rule-base execution: how to exploit today's parallel processors to speed up the rule-base execution?

For problem 1, we have developed a general strategy which combines partial state space search and the recognition of special forms of subsets of rules by static analysis. For problem 2, we have shown how to automatically extract rule-firing parallelism by reusing and extending the analysis strategy. Although we have explored techniques to tackle these problems based on the EQL rule-based language for simplicity and clarity, most of the techniques described can be applied or ported to real-time KBSs implemented in more expressive languages. These techniques form a basis for the technology for building the next generation of real-time KBSs which we can rely on to perform complex monitoring and control functions in a real-time environment.

To show the usefulness of KBS for systems specification and analysis, the paper describes how the requirements and operations of operators in an assembly line can be captured and modeled as a rulebase which can then be formally analyzed. Modern enterprise information systems are requiring shorter response time and greater reliability for businesses to stay competitive. The critical nature of such decision-making systems requires that they undergo rigorous and formal analysis prior to their deployment. Using real-time KBSs for decision support and for capturing enterprise systems' requirements and operations will improve the performance of today's and future enterprise information systems.

REFERENCES

H. Attiya and N. A. Lynch, "Time Bounds for Real-Time Process Control in the Presence of Timing Uncertainty", *Proc. 10th Real-Time Systems Symposium*, Santa Monica, CA, pages 268–284, Dec. 1989.

M. Benda, "Real-Time Applications of AI in the Aerospace Industry," Presentation at the Fall School on Artificial Intelligence, The Research Institute of Ecole Normal Superieure, France, Sept. 4, 1987.

J. R. Burch, E. M. Clarke, K. L. McMillan, D. L. Dill, and L. H. Hwang, "Symbolic Model Checking: 10^{20} states and Beyo nd, " *Proc. 5th IEEE Intl. Symp. on Logic in Computer Sc ience*, pages 428–439,1990.

J.-R. Chen and A. M. K. Cheng, "Response Time Analysis of EQL Real-Time Rule-Based Systems," *IEEE Transactions on Knowledge and Data Engineering Vol. 7, No 1*, pp. 26-43, Feb. 1995.

A. M. K. Cheng, "Real-Time Systems, Scheduling, Analysis, and Verification," ISBN # 0471-184063, John Wiley and Sons, 2002.

A. M. K. Cheng, "Parallel Execution of Real-Time Rule-Based Systems," *7th Intl. Parallel Processing Symp.*, Newport Beach, California, Apr. 1993.

A. M. K. Cheng and J.-R. Chen, "Response Time Analysis of OPS5 Production Systems," in *IEEE Transactions on Knowledge and Data Engineering*, Vol. 12, No. 3, pages 391-409, May/June 2000.

A. M. K. Cheng, J. C. Browne, A. K. Mok, and R.-H. Wang "Analysis of Real-Time Rule-Based Systems with Behavioral Con straint Assertions Specified in Estella," *IEEE Transactions on Software Engineering Vol. 19, No. 9*, Sept. 1993.

A. M. K. Cheng and C.-H. Chen, "Efficient Response Time Bound Analysis of Real-Time Rule-Based Systems," *Proc. 7th Annual IEEE Conf. on Computer Assurance*, Gaithersburg, Maryland, June 1992.

E. M. Clarke, E. A. Emerson, and A. P. Sistla, "Automatic Verification of Finite State Concurrent Programs Using Temporal Logic: A Practical Approach," *ACM Transactions on Programming Languages and S ystems*, Vol. 8, No. 2, April 1986, pages 244–263.

C. L. Forgy, "OPS5 User's Manual," Department of Computer Science, Carnegie-Mellon University, Tech. Rep. CMU-CS-81-135, July 1981.

U. G. Gupta, editor, "Validating and Verifying Knowledge-Based Systems," IEEE Computer Society Press, Los Alamitos, CA, May 1991.

T. J. Laffey, P. A. Cox, J. L. Schmidt, S. M. Kao, and J. Y. Read, "Real-Time Knowledge-Based Systems," *AI Magazine*, Vol. 9, No. 1, Spring 1988, pp. 27-45.

C. A. Marsh, "The ISA Expert System: A Prototype System for Failure Diagnosis on the Space Station," MITRE Report, The MITRE Corporation, Houston, Texas, 1988.

C. A. O'Reilly and A. S. Cromarty, ""Fast" is not "Real-time": Designing Effective Real-time AI Systems," *Applications of Artificial Intelligence*, John F. Gilmore, editor, Proc. SPIE, 485.

D. W. Payton and T. E. Bihari, "Intelligent Real-Time Control of Robotic Vehicles," *Communications of the ACM*, Vol. 34, No. 8, Aug. 1991.

C.-K. Wang, A. K. Mok, and A. M. K. Cheng, "MRL: A Real-Time Rule-Based Production System," *11th Real-Time Systems Symp.*, Orlando, Florida, pp. 267-276, Dec. 1990.

B. Zupan and A. M. K. Cheng, "Optimization of Real-Time Rule-Based Systems Based on State Space Diagrams," manuscript submitted to *IEEE Conf. on AI for Applications (CAIA)*, 1993.

IS ENGINEERING GETTING OUT OF CLASSICAL SYSTEM ENGINEERING

Michel Léonard

Centre Universitaire d'Informatique, University of Geneva, 24, rue du Général Dufour, CH-1211 Genève 4.
Email : Michel.Léonard@cui.unige.ch
Tel: ++41-22 705 77 77   Fax: ++41-22 705 77 80

Keywords: Method, hyperclass, information overlap, dynamic space, integrity rule, and specialisation.

Abstract: An Enterprise Information System must be pertinent for the human and enterprise activities. It plays a central role because most of the activities are now supported by an information system (IS) and also because the Enterprise development process, itself, is depending on the IS development in most cases. Enterprise and IS developments are completely interwoven. It appears necessary to have concepts and rules, which are pertinent to explain difficulties and potentialities of IS thanks to information technologies. IS domain establishes a rendezvous between various competencies and responsibilities. The classical software engineering domain, which has not the same objectives, does not provide adequate concepts and rules to the IS engineering domain. With the point of view of this paper, IS engineering appears as a generalization of the software engineering domain.

1   INTRODUCTION

It is now a common fact that the information system (IS) of an enterprise or an organization is a fundamental factor of its success, survival or failure. During decades, databases (DBs) have been the central element and often the unique component of an IS. Nowadays, and even if DBs still play an important role for the storage and sharing of data and information in an IS, DBs need to be put interaction with the other elements of the IS, to face the complexity and the growing variety of tasks to be assumed. However, beyond the problems of performance, security, liability and data volume, it is especially a question of: (a) ensuring how information circulates, (b) coordinating activities, (c) supporting interactivity collaboration, (d) allowing a dynamic communication on Internet, a-s-o.

IS development process is then a collective, progressive, learning process, where evolution takes a central role. Indeed, an IS is only the reflection of a particular perception of how human activities might be efficiently supported by means of computerized systems for information storage, search and processes. This perception may evolve to take into account new needs, to adapt to organizational changes, to correct errors of design or to improve specifications ([ALJA97]). Practically,

an evolutionary IS must guarantee information coherence, consistency and relevance, and this, throughout the whole information life cycle. On another hand, due to the unceasingly increasing IS complexity, it becomes necessary to offer to the persons in charge of IS (e.g. Chief Information Officer) adapted services and functionalities, to manage it. This requires an environment offering a more significant level of abstraction and a concept of modularity of high level, enabling these persons to consider IS through components.

Thus, this paper introduces concepts, which are not traditional and even unknown in the classic system engineering (SE) domain, but are particularly relevant to the IS engineering (ISE) domain. Then, the concept of IS component is defined over the previous concepts with major differences with the traditional system component concept in the system engineering domain.

In conclusion, the IS engineering domain will appear as a very fruitful domain with its own concepts, rules and many differences with the classical systems engineering domain.

The concepts introduced in this paper are implemented in our CAISE environment M7. M7 is based on a repository composed of seven conceptual spaces (classes, hyperclasses, rules, life cycles, periods, events, transactions), which is implemented on a commercial DBMS.

O. Camp et al. (eds.), Enterprise Information Systems V, 35-45.

2   SPECIALIZATION

Specialization is an abstract concept, used in many scientific disciplines other than computer science, for example botany [STAC89]. It appears in the database field thanks to [SMSM77]. One of its first implementation inside a DBMS, may-be the first one, was in the DBMS ECRINS [JLT81, JFL86], which implemented it by the means of a mechanism of dynamic specialization.

Later, the object-oriented approach, in particular the object-oriented DBMS, introduced the inheritance mechanism to implement it. With the inheritance mechanism, an object is placed at a given level of inheritance hierarchy and will stay at this level definitively. So the inheritance mechanism implements in fact the static specialization.

In the opposite way, an object in a dynamic specialization can move inside a specialization hierarchy: a person can become a student. Furthermore a person can be both an employee and a student: the specialization hierarchy does not need a particular class assistant, except if assistant has special attributes, associations, and methods.

Considering that static specialization can be described in terms of dynamic specialization and not the contrary, the dynamic specialization concept is richer then the static one. It is much more powerful to define IS more rigorously. If inheritance in object-oriented DBMS is "a powerful modelling tool, because it gives a concise and precise description of the world and it helps in factoring out shared specifications and implementations in applications" ([ABWD89], then dynamic specialization is really a very powerful modelling tool.

They are **several possible mechanisms** to implement dynamic specialization. [ALLE99] described precisely the hologram mechanism to implement dynamic specialization: it seems to be the most interesting. This mechanism supports evolution of the specialization hierarchy, generally in a more large sense than the inheritance mechanism does: for instance, deletion of a class inside a specialization hierarchy is implemented without any useless loss of information and any recopy of objects with dynamic specialization contrary to static specialization.

The hologram approach [ALLE99] allows objects to be multi-instantiated and play many roles at once. Return to previous example, where a person may be both a student and an employee without being an assistant: this fact is stored with an object in Person, another in Student and another in Employee, both linked to the first one.

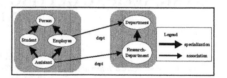

Figure 1: Dynamic specialization

The hologram approach allows objects to be dynamic and able to be migrated between classes of a specialization hierarchy: for instance it is possible that a person becomes an employee or that another person is no more a student. Of course, properties of student include properties of person, but it is possible to design following facts:

– an assistant, who is both an employee and a student, is assigned to a department as an employee; but, this department must be a research-department;

– an assistant cannot receive any regular grants, but other students can do.

In conclusion, the specialization concept appears as a fruitful concept for the IS domain. For IS modelling, dynamic specialization is a much more pertinent concept than static specialization: the modelling results can be written in a more rigorous way. Furthermore, as described in the next chapter, it appears to be a cornerstone to reconcile static and dynamic IS aspects. For IS implementation, the use of static specialization in database systems is the origin of severe difficulties to implement dynamic specialization: it produces severe bootless and artificial problems with only approximate, heavy and intricate solutions. Besides, an IS would become rigid and the modifications of its environment would be difficult to be taken into account. On the contrary, DBMS with dynamic specialization will be much more convenient; [ALJA97] tested performances of such a system, the system F2, with the classical object-oriented DBMS benchmark and showed F2 performances were comparable with any classic object-oriented DBMS.

3   IS DYNAMIC ASPECTS

The **difference** between static spaces and dynamic spaces is well known in many parts of computer science. Nevertheless, in the context of IS, these conceptual spaces have a lot of common properties and they are very interwoven. However, most of the methods separate them and their interrelations are difficult to establish and then to validate their consistency. In fact, at the level of IS conceptual schema, the difference between IS static and dynamic aspects, is not so important as in other computer domain. A concept as a reservation may be represented by means of a class or a transaction or both. Often, the decision would be taken only at the implementation level. But if a wrong decision was taken, it should be very costly to change specification. So it is important to consider seriously the nature of the difference between static and dynamic spaces, in the IS context. This is an attempt to understand it.

The main question concerns the interpretation of **transition**. Most of the classic dynamic models are convenient to take into account dynamic movements in the living world, for instance: a train moving from Angers to Geneva. So a transition between the state: the train is at Angers and the other state the train is at Geneva, corresponds to the train movement. Eventually, this transition corresponds to the processing, which simulates minute by minute the movement of the train and gives continuously its position. But there is another interpretation of usefulness of transition: transition between states only corresponds to human tasks or decisions. In this case, there is no movement. Transition is only in correspondence with programs, which fulfil automated task or decision support or both. In the example of Person and Student, a transition may be built between:

- in the first hand, the states of a request of curriculum inscription made by a person and prepaid taxes,
- and, in the second hand, the states of accepted request, refused request or supplementary courses. If the request is accepted, then the person becomes a student.

With this perspective, **several traditional points** of view must be re-examined. *Firstly*, even if the request is accepted and so the person becomes a student, nevertheless the person is always a person! It is not the case for the train: when it is at Geneva, it is no more at Angers! So, for IS modelling, an object, which participates in a transition, can keep its previous states and obtain new states. This is different from the traditional point of view.

Secondly, transition uses traditionally logical input and output conditions. Generally speaking, input conditions of transition are expressed with the AND logical connector, output connections with the XOR logical connector. Such a tradition is often pertinent in the case of movement. However in the context of IS, which must support human activities the most efficiently as possible, these conditions are not always so important. In fact, input/output conditions can be a mix of logical connectors.

Besides, these conditions often cannot be conceived without introducing too many rigid situations. In the previous example, the input states: a request of curriculum inscription made by a person and prepaid taxes indicate that the persons in charge of the transition must access to the objects in these states to assume responsibilities behind the transition. But, possibly, they can analyse a request without any information about prepaid taxes. The output states: accepted request or refused request or supplementary courses only indicate that their activities behind this transition can create some information in these states. Of course, they cannot accept and refuse a same request and so there is an output logical condition. But, possibly, they can accept/refuse a request with proposing supplementary courses, or propose supplementary courses without taking any other decision.

So input/output conditions, which are essential to traditional approaches, are not so important in IS modelling. Even, if they are used, they can be too rigid and become traps, where future persons in charge of activities would be caught.

Thirdly, graph is less powerful than bipartite graph to represent semantics. So, for the point of view of expressiveness, any dynamic model using graph as support is potentially less pertinent than another one using bipartite graph. Statecharts ([HARE87]) use graphs; Petri nets ([PETR80]) use bipartite graphs.

The Gavroche model uses bipartite graph with other semantics than Petri nets do. The nodes of Gavroche model correspond to states, its stars to transactions (like commercial transactions, financial transactions…). The entry nodes of a transaction correspond to its basic states: the tasks or decisions to be assumed by persons in charge of this transaction require the information in these states. The output nodes of a transaction correspond to its produced states: the previous tasks or decisions can produce information in these states.

Here is the representation of the previous example with this model:

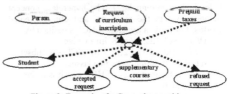

Figure 2: Example of a Gavroche transition

The **Gavroche model** contains other properties ([LEPH99]), which are out of the scope of this paper. However, with such an interpretation of IS dynamic space, then it is possible to combine static and dynamic space with using intensively dynamic specialization: states are subclasses of some class C, and represent some important steps of the life cycle of C-objects. Here is a schema, which mixes static and dynamic aspects. With such a model static spaces and dynamic spaces are interrelated together with more precision.

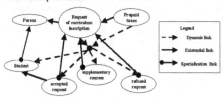

Figure 3: Static and dynamic schemas

4 HYPERCLASSES

The **classes** are commonly used as a pivot to model IS. They coordinate the various facets of specification (static, dynamic and functional). However IS modeling and implementation generally imply a lot of classes, and often the level of class is too restricted to take into account larger concepts of the domain. To be able to manage an IS schema with a higher level of abstraction we propose the concept of hyperclass. A hyperclass is formed on one subset of conceptual classes of the global IS schema, forming a unit with a precise semantic. Generally, it is associated with a managerial function around the IS and it delimits the informational domain necessary for the achievement of this function. So it is a representation of a particular field of competence around the IS.

A **hyperclass** is built in a similar way to a universal relation ([MUV84]); the links between two objects have the same semantics at the HCl level, and HCl attributes have unique names, except those belonging to foreign keys. The hyperclass concept belongs to both the relational and object-oriented worlds. Formally, a hyperclass HCl is defined by:

HCl=<SCl, RC, NGr, SHm> where
- SCl={RC, C1, C2,... Cn}. SCl is a subset of the set of the IS global schema classes;
- RC is the root class of HCl, which is a class of SCl (RC∈SCl);
- NGr is the navigation graph associated to HCl: NGr is connected, oriented and without circuit. This graph is composed of nodes corresponding one to one to the classes of SCl, and edges corresponding to

associations between these classes. It indicates how the objects of each class of SCl will be reached from the RC object;
- SHm is the set of hypermethods defined upon HCl.

The set of the attributes (HCl^+) of HCl is the union of the sets of the attributes of the HCl classes.

The instances of a hyperclass HCl are called **hyperobjects.** A hyperobject ho is a set of linked objects, built starting from an object oRC of the root class RC (its root object) and of the HCl closure of this root object. The HCl closure (ho*) of oRC is the set of objects composed of:
- the object oRC itself;
- the objects of HCl classes linked to oRC, and
- the objects of HCl classes, which are linked to an object belonging to the closure.

The values taken by a hyperobject ho for an attribute att of a class Cl belonging to HCl are the union of the set of values taken for att by the Cl objects belonging to ho. The update of the value v taken by the HCl hyperobject ho for the attribute att of the HCl class Cl into the value v', consists of updating the value v into v' taken for att by all the Cl objects of ho.

In the same way that methods are defined upon classes, it is possible to define **hypermethods** upon hyperclass. An hypermethod uses class methods of the HCl classes. Hypermethods are an advantage for the method designers, because they do not have to choose a class for the method. In fact the hypermethod designers do not have to know the detailed schema of the hyperclass, but only the attributes of the hyperclass: the mechanism of hyperclass undertakes to resolve access paths for each HCl involved attribute.

Example: we consider the generic example of a hyperclass HCl defined on the set of schema classes {A, B, C, D,E}. A is the root class of HCl.

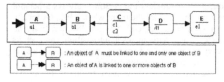

Figure 4: Example of HCl

The HCl attributes are: HCl^+ = {a1, b1, c1, c2, d1, d2, e1}.

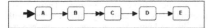

Figure 5: Example of navigation graph

The figure 5 represents the navigation graph of HCl. It indicates how the objects of the different classes of HCl are accessed from the object of the root class A.

Upon HCl, it is possible to define hypermethods. A hypermethod Hm is defined over several classes of HCl. It can use different HCl hyperattributes and invocate class methods of the HCl classes.

For example, here is an expression of Hm: hoi.Hm() = sum(b1j * e1k) where Hm manipulates the values taken for the attributes b1 and e1 by the objects of the classes B and E belonging to the hyperobject hoi.

If the **class D** is no more useful in HCl, it can be **excluded from HCl**. It will not be deleted from the global schema, but only hidden from HCl. Even if the exclusion maintains the class D at the level of global schema, it can cause a lost of important information at the level of HCl: connection with the class E is lost and information stored in this class cannot longer be reached in HCl. For that reason, HCl is consolidated, thanks to a new association linking the class C to E.

Thanks to the consolidation of HCl, the hypermethod HCl.Hm() will be still available and operational (method conservation) and will continue to return the same results (method results conservation), without any modification of its source code or any recompilation. These two results are obtained because the class D is not directly involved in the hypermethod HCl.Hm(). Hyperobjects has fitted the new structure of HCl and information in its different classes continues to be reachable.

The **hyperclass concept is useful** to facilitate the steps of IS analysis, design, implementation and maintenance. It introduces a kind of modularity in the definition and the management of an IS schema. As demonstrated in [TULE02a], thanks to hyperclasses, there is a powerful kind of independence between the data schema level and the hypermethod level. A HCl hypermethod Hm can be performed even after some HCl schema transformations, except of course, if they remove necessary information for Hm from HCl.

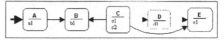

Figure 6: Example of class exclusion

The effects of every hyperclass modification method are divided into two levels: the local level of the hyperclass, in which the modification is fired, and the global level where the modifications are negotiated among the involved hyperclasses and the whole DB. A particularity of hyperclasses is that the hyperobjects fit automatically the new structure of their modified hyperclass, without need to delete or copy objects.

5   INTEGRITY RULES

Integrity rules (IRs) of an IS represent most often the business rules of an organization. An IR is a logical condition defined over classes, which can be described formally and verified by transactions or methods. At the first time of databases, IRs were often considered only as domains of attributes: the objective was to avoid data inconsistency (for instance the domain of Day is an integer between 1 and 31 with eventually a null value). Then, in a more general definition, an IR was defined over only one class C and can be verified at the level of one C-object without considering the other C-objects: for instance, the date-of-inscription is posterior to the date-of-birth, except in the case of unknown values. These two kinds of IRs are taken into account by DBMS.

But, now, IRs can play other important roles. They not only, ensure objects to be coherent, but also help IS architecture to be precisely established (for instance, normal forms in the relational model), and IS transactions to be well coordinated. Since, in the most cases, they correspond to business rules, they play a crucial role in the IS evolution. Indeed, modifications of the IS environment often lead to the modifications of business rules. These changes most often influence IRs, which must be modified, deleted or added.

Therefore, an **integrity management system** (IRMS) ([LELU03]) seems to be necessary: it will support the IRs management during their life cycle: analysis, design, implementation and evolution. Then, activities of IS analysts, designers and administrators relative to IRs would be much safer and much more coordinated.

But, several major challenges have to be overcome, such as the followings:
- an IR must be validated in various cases of data manipulations (for instance create, delete, modify or query an object);
- for a given case of data manipulation, generally there are different IRs to be validated;
- in the most cases, validation of the set S of IRs is not equivalent to the set of validations of any IR belonging to S, due to performance reasons;
- when an IR is infringed, the response may be different following the situation, when this event happens.
So, IR validation is implemented in numerous pieces of codes: modifying an IR requires to find all these pieces of codes and then to modify them. An IRMS supports efficiently these activities.

6 OVERLAP

An **overlap situation** occurs when there is at least one class common to several semantic universes. Then, the semantic universes cannot be considered independently, and therefore it is necessary to specify coordination rules, which regulate their interactions. A semantic universe corresponds, in the first hand, to a responsibility area like department, section… and, in the second hand, to a hyperclass.

The overlap area of several semantic universes is the subset of the classes, which belong to these semantic universes. There are two analysis levels of an overlap situation: the level of common classes with information sharing protocols, and the level of transactions with the interwoven activities protocols.

Here is an **example of a travel agency**: the figure 7 gives the static schema of two semantic universes named travel preparation and travel selling.

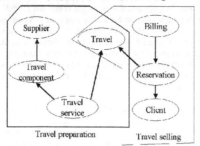

Travel preparation   Travel selling

Figure 7: Example of a travel agency

The first one corresponds to the responsibility area, where persons have charge of setting up of new

travels or new travel components. These travel components are offered by the agency with eventually the help of a supplier. For instance the travel "France for IS specialists" includes the component "visit of Descartes' native place".

The second one concerns the responsibility area in charge of buying some travels and also of managing clients and travel sales.

At the class level, a cross-analysis table (table 1) indicates what are the classes of the semantic universes, and shows all the overlap situations. So the Travel class must be analyzed to determine which responsibility areas are in charge of creating, deleting, updating or questioning Travel objects, and how their activities, which are involved by these operations, are coordinated.

Class/ Semantic Universe	Travel Preparation	Travel Selling
Supplier	*	
Travel Component	*	
Travel Service	*	
Travel	*	*
Billing		*
Reservation		*
Client		*

Table 1: Example of class cross-analysis table

At the transaction level, the object life cycle of any common class indicates how the activities of the involved responsibility areas would be interwoven. In the case of the Travel example, and for this presentation, we start from the collaborative object life cycle of the Travel class (fig. 8), which is described in the Gavroche model.

The initial state of a Travel object is "Initialized". Then two alternatives are possible:
at the right-hand side, the agency decides to buy it [Buy-Travel] and customize [Describe-Travel] travel products; at the left-hand side, the agency decides to collect internal custom-made travel components [Collect-Travel-Components] in order to build a Journey, then makes a travel service allocation to this new Journey [Allocate-Travel-Services].
After this alternative processing, "Saleable" travel can be sold to customers [Sell-Travel].

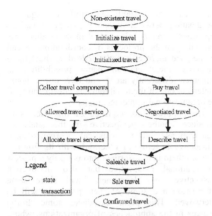

Figure 8: Life cycle example for the "Travel" class using the Gavroche model

The different parts of an object life cycle of a common class are generally in charge of different responsibility areas. As often happens, various responsibility situations occur during the object evolution. They depend on sharing of responsibilities for the methods and states defined in the object life cycle. This sharing of responsibilities can also be represented by means of a table, which analyses transactions and states in relation to the semantic universes (see table 2).

Transaction-State / Semantic Universe	Preparation	Selling
Non-existent travel		
Initialize travel	*	*
Initialized travel		
Collect travel component	*	
Allowed travel service	*	
Allocate travel service	*	
Saleable travel	*	*
Buy travel		*
Negotiated travel		*
Describe travel service		*
Sell travel		*
Confirmed travel		*

Table 2: Cross-analysis table for the Travel object life cycle

A classic question is how to obtain a **local view** from a **collaborative view**? It means in our example, what information is given to every responsibility area to explain how to have locally a coherent behavior with the activities of the other involved responsibility areas?

A *first approach* is to apply the *simple projection* of an object life cycle onto the corresponding semantic universe with considering only states and transactions related with it. The

following figure 9 shows this projection for the responsibility area "Travel preparation".

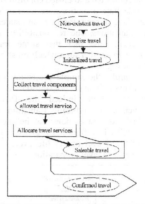

Figure 9: Example of a simple projection

But then any person working inside the semantic universe "Travel preparation" do not have any information related to the choice between the transactions Collect-Travel-Component and Buy-Travel and can imagine that an initialized travel must always be built by collecting components. Furthermore this person can not understand how a saleable travel becomes a confirmed travel. The simple projection seems not to be convenient at a cognitive level. Nevertheless it seems normal to reject the following approach at the opposite way: each responsibility area knows the semantic universe of all other involved areas. Indeed this approach would overload the understanding of activities without any efficiency in counterpart.

A *second approach* is to apply the *shade projection* of an object life cycle: it tries to give to any responsibility area the minimum but necessary information about transactions and states in the other responsibility areas, which can influence its activities.

An object life cycle is **connected** for a semantic universe SU if its simple projection onto SU is connected. An object life cycle is *closed* for a semantic universe SU if its simple projection P onto SU contains:
- all the incoming and outgoing states of every transaction of P,
- all incoming (respectively outgoing) transactions of every place of P, if the semantic universe contains at least one of them.

A *shade projection* of an object life cycle Ocl onto a semantic universe SU is another object life cycle built from the simple Ocl projection onto SU by introducing shade state transitions, if necessary, to satisfy the connected and closed conditions.

These shade state transitions are used to 'outline' the contour of the missing methods and states. With these shade transitions, one responsibility area can take into account the fact that some important activities occur in another area which must be taken into account locally.

In our **example**, the simple projection onto the semantic universe "Travel preparation" is neither connected nor closed: indeed the Buy-Travel method, which is an outgoing transition for the "Travel Initialized" place, does not belong to the projection result. The figure 10 gives the shade projection of the Travel object life cycle onto the semantic universe "Travel preparation".

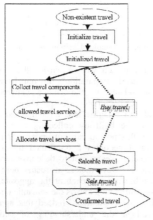

Figure 10: Example of a shade projection

Here, the configuration of the shade projection on the Selling semantic universe shows that a set of transactions and states represented by the shade transition "shade-Buy-Travel" is an alternative choice with the local connected Gavroche sub-network [Collect travel components, allowed travel service, Allocate travel services].

From the standpoint of the responsibility area, the **role of a shade transition** is to inform it that something of significance for the coordination can occur in another responsibility area.

In conclusion, the information overlap concept seems to be a cornerstone between the living world and the artificial world. From it, it is possible to settle up the implications between organization and IS. So overlaps must clearly be explicitly described in any IS modeling because from them organization plans can be established and consequently coordination between human activities of various departments can be also established. Furthermore, depending on the protocols of coordination, IS can be specified more efficiently: indeed, without these protocols, there are so many possibilities to implement differently an IS and developers should implement one of them without any consideration of the organizational implementations.

An important consequence of this fact is to introduce another perspective in the study of organizations. The classical organizational perspective in terms of functions with its frontiers between them is transformed into not only a process organizational perspective but also an overlap perspective: two departments will share same information and some of their processes will be interwoven. This point introduces some drastic changes in the approaches of organizations, whose activities are supported by IS.

This concept has another interest in the IS development management. Indeed, since one of the very difficult IS situations is the integration of several IS parts [LELE02], such situations must be avoided. Since it is impossible to conceive the global schema of an enterprise IS, the IS work must be divided into several parts, which were developed by different teams. One main charge of the IS development coordination is to determine the most soon as possible the overlaps between the domain of investigation of these different teams and so to avoid the so tricky situations of integration.

7 IS COMPONENTS

Due to the huge activities of an Enterprise, which are supported by an IS, it is more and more **impossible to obtain a pertinent IS global view** of its different parts and the overlaps between these parts. Besides, development of Enterprise and development of its IS are interrelated together with a gordian knot. So, it is necessary to discover some concepts and some methods to settle strategic IS plans without using soap sentences and smooth points of view, or technical arguments with fabulous perspectives. Furthermore, to face the unceasingly increasing IS complexity, it becomes necessary to offer to the persons in charge of IS (e.g. Chief Information Officer) adapted services and functionalities, to manage it. This requires an environment offering a more significant level of abstraction and a concept of modularity of high level, enabling these persons to consider IS through components.

In the last few years, there is a significant trend towards a **component-based development**, that handles components at the earlier phases of IS development life cycle, as well as supports wide distribution and coordination of components. These new CBD approaches may possibly be classified according to the IS development life cycle, which they address such as:
- Analysis component [ROLL93] [CNM96] [FOWL97] handles the problem appears during the requirement analysis phase of IS development life cycle. The analysis components help designers in the construction of conceptual models, that are best suited to representing IS requirements.
- Design component [GHJV95] captures the experience and knowledge used for the design phase by identifying objects, their collaborations and the distribution of their responsibilities.

In **our approach**, the concept of IS components (ISC) is linked to both the level of organization and the level of implementation. It requires precise specifications of ISC and of overlaps between ISCs of IS designers. IS component ([LELE02] [TULE02b]) is defined over:
- an hyperclass Hcl, with its classes and hypermethods,
- a dynamic schema with the Gavroche model including the object life cycles of the Hcl classes,
- a set of integrity rules.
Furthermore, there is a set of ISC consistency rules: by example, an ISC integrity rule must be defined over classes of the ISC hyperclass.
An ISC appears as an IS itself, which is reduced to only one hyperclass. It can be generic when it is devoid as much as possible of organizational information: in this case it has ontological properties.

One major operation is **to implement an ISC** into an operational information system IS_0. New activities not supported by IS_0, will be supported by the new IS: IS_1 thanks to ISC: $IS_1 = IS_0 * ISC$.
In the last example of a travel agency, IS_0 supports the activities of travel selling since ISC is designed to support the activities of travel preparation. IS_1 should support the activities of both travel selling and travel preparation.
But, what are the *consequences* of the ISC insertion into an IS?
A first one is at the conceptual level.
- ISC and IS_0 might contain common classes; in this case, it is impossible to implement two different classes in IS_1 without considering interactions between their objects. In fact the starting point is the contrary point of view: any class belonging both to ISC and IS_0, would be implemented by only one

class in IS_1 as a starting point. Then, only due to technical reasons, it is possible to implement it following another architecture schema than a simple class, by example two classes with strong interrelations between their objects.
- In any situation, where new elements are introduced into IS_0, the IS_0 integrity rules must be re-analyzed. In particular there are the following remarkable situations:
- an ISC (respectively IS_0) integrity rule is defined over classes, which belong both to IS_0 and ISC, and is not implemented in IS_0 (resp. ISC). In this case its validation must be added in IS_0 (resp. ISC).
- an ISC (respectively IS_0) integrity rule must be validated by transactions of IS_0 (resp. ISC).
- due to the extension of the IS_0 (resp. ISC) schema, it might happen that new integrities rules appear. In that case IS_0 (resp. ISC) transactions and methods must be re-analyzed and re-implemented to take into account these new integrity rules.
- In any situation, where new elements are introduced into IS_0, the IS_0 static and dynamic schemata must be re-analyzed. Some associations or transactions in IS_0 (resp. ISC) must be introduced or deleted due to the presence of associations or transactions in ISC (resp. IS_0).
- Finally ISC must be adapted to the activities supported by in IS_0: ISC may be built with an ontological point of view, since in IS_0 is relevant to a particular enterprise. By example, ISC can be a generic component for travel preparation. For its introduction into the IS of a travel agency, which is specialized in travels of IS specialists, it must contain a travel component relative to visiting IS centers.

A second one is the organizational level.
The consequences of the ISC insertion into IS_0 at the organizational level is to adapt, in the first hand, ISC to the organization and reciprocally, and, in the second hand, the processes P implemented in IS_0 to ISC, because activities supported by P may be enriched if P is extended thanks to ISC.
Consequently, other important situation arise:
- previous IS_0 overlaps must be involved by some ISC parts : they must be re-analyzed;
- new overlaps can crop up: they must be analysed. By example, the introduction of the component travel preparation into the IS of the travel agency will induce the overlap situation, which was studied in the overlap paragraph.

Then it is clear, that the concept of software component (SC), of most classical software methods, is quite **inappropriate** to support the activities of persons in charge of enterprise and IS developments, at any level. An ISC can not be only a black or wide or transparent box. It can not be process-functionality oriented with public and private functionalities; it must be submitted to the rules of sharing objects, validating objects, overlapping objects, transitions, object life cycles, organizations... An ISC is not a simple box with input/output information. Introducing ISC into an IS is fundamentally not a simple question of assembling or of plug-in.

This proposition is concept/rule oriented, in opposition with a traditional process-functionality oriented proposition. Thus an IS component overlaps other IS parts for every IS level: for instance, static, dynamic, integrity rule, organizational level. Then, no ISC part should be kept hidden from IS designers. IS component may be a very fruitful concept for the enterprise and IS developments because of its use at so various levels: strategic level, conceptual level, specification level, implementation level.

8 CONCLUSIONS

The Information System engineering domain has its own concepts and rules, which have to be discovered to be able to place IS persons in charge of IS developments in situation of dialogues with other persons for the Enterprise developments. An Enterprise IS is never finished, it is not simply a project. It must support efficiently human activities, tasks, responsibilities. These activities are interwoven with the IS to be efficient. So, the persons, who assume these activities, are not simple IS users: their responsibilities, their way of thinking their activities, their own efficiency are dependent on the IS. So they must be able to propose IS developments, not in order to improve usability and efficacy of the system, but in order to improve their own effectiveness, to defend their own position: this is completely different from the situation of users in classic SE. For instance, it is no more a simple question of *user satisfaction*, it is a question of enterprise development, personal professional positions. Furthermore human activities become much more interesting with the help of IS than without.

Considering an IS as a solution to a problem is quite irrelevant. Such a position hides the IS worth and especially the difficulties to obtain pertinent IS. IS difficulties come from IS *unity* and IS *identity*. In the case of SE, the objective of the project is clearly comprehensible for all the persons in charge of its development (unity). An IS has no global objective and a permanent difficulty is to keep its unity, which

is never stable. Besides, in the case of SE, the objective is also clearly comprehensible inside the enterprise (identiy), since the identity of an IS inside an enterprise is so difficult to maintain: never the IS identiy is definitely accepted, it must be always defended. Of course, some IS parts can have the same behavior as a classic system, but fundamentally ISE domain must consider IS unity and IS identiy as basic aspects for IS development.

Furthermore, the concepts of dynamic specialization, hyperclass, Gavroche model, IS component are generalizations of the concepts of, respectively, static specialization and inheritance, class, statecharts and Petri nets, classic system component; IS overlap is unknown in system engineering domain.

For all these reasons, the Information System engineering domain appears to get out of the classical System engineering domain.

ACKNOWLEDGMENTS

We would like to thank Abdelaziz Khadraoui, Thang Le Dinh, Hong Luu, Thoa Pham, Jolita Ralyté, Slim Turki and Mehdi Snene, members of the MatisGe research group.

REFERENCES

[ABWD89] Atkinson M., Bancilhon F., De Witt D., Dittrich K., Maier D., Zdonik S., The Object-Oriented Database System Manifesto, Proc. Int. Conf. on Deductive and Object-Oriented Databases, DOOD, Kyoto 1989.

[ALJA97] Al-Jadir, L., Evolution-oriented database systems, PhD thesis, University of Geneva, 1997.

[ALLE99a] Al-Jadir L., Léonard M., Transposed Storage of an Object Database to Reduce the Cost of Schema Changes, Proc. of ER'99 Int. Workshop on Evolution and Change in Data Management (ECDM'99), Paris (France), 1999.

[ALLE99] Al-Jadir L., Léonard M., If we refuse the Inheritance... Proc. Int. Conf. on DEXA, Firenze, 1999.

[CACM96] Software Patterns, Communications of the ACM, Vol. 39, No. 10, 1996.

[CACM00] Component-based enterprise frameworks. Communications of the ACM, Vol. 43, No. 10. October 2000.

[COAD92] Coad P, Object-oriented patterns, Communications of the ACM, Vol.35, 1992.

[CNM96] Coad P., North D., Mayfield M., "Object Models – Strategies, Patterns and Applications", Yourdon Press Computing Series, 1996

[FGJL88] Falquet G., Guyot J., Junet M., Léonard M., et al.., Concept Integration as an Approach to Information Systems Design, in Computerized Assistance during the Information Systems Life Cycle, T.W. Olle, A.A Verrijn-Stuart (Eds.), IFIP, North-Holland, 1988.

[FOWL97] Fowler M., Analysis Patterns – Reusable Object Models, Addison-Wesley, 1997.

[GHJV95] Gamma E., Helm R., Johnson R., Vlissides J., "Design patterns, Elements of Reusable Object-Oriented Software", Addison-Wesley Publishing Company, 1995.

[HARE87] Harel D., Statecharts: a visual formalism for complex systems, Science of computer programming, 8:231-274, 1987.

[JFL86] Junet M., Falquet G., Léonard M., ECRINS/86: An Extended Entity-Relationship Data Base Management System and its Semantic Query Language, Proc. Int. Conf. on Very Large Data Bases, VLDB, Kyoto 1986.

[JLT81] Junet M., Léonard M., Tschopp R., ECRINS/81, Workshop, IFIP 8.1, Sitgès, 1981

[LELE02] Le Dinh T., Léonard M., Defining Information System Components, Proceeding of Confederated International Conferences CoopIS, DOA, ODBASE, Springer, California, October 2002.

[LELU03] Léonard M., Luu H., Towards An Integrity Rules Management System, Matis report, CUI, University of Geneva, January 2003.

[LEPH00] Léonard M., Pham Thi, T.T., Conceptual model: an integration of static aspects and dynamic aspects of information system, Conference on IT 2000, Ho Chi Minh City, Vietnam.

[LGLS01] Léonard, M., Grasset A., Le Dinh, T., Santos, C., Information Kernel: an Evolutionary Approach to Integrate Enterprise Information Assets, Proceedings of the International Workshop on Open Enterprise Solutions: Systems, Experiences, and Organizations. OES-SEO2001. Rome, 14-15 September 2001.

[MUV84] Maier D., Ullman J.D., Vardi M. Y., On the foundations of the Universal Relation Model, ACM Transactions on Database Systems, Vol. 9, No. 2, June 1984, Pages 283-308.

[PETR80] Petri C.A., Introduction to general net theory, in Net theory and application, Springer Verlag, 1980.

[RALY02] Ralyté J., Requirements Definition for Situational Methods Engineering, Conf. EISIC 2002, IFIP WG 8.1, Kanazawa, Japan.

[ROLL93] Rolland C, Adapter les Méthodes à l'Objet: Challenges et Embûches, Journées Méthodes d'Analyse et de Conception Orientées Objet des Systèmes d'Information, ACFET, Paris, 1993.

[SMSM77] Smith J.M., Smith D.C.P., Database Abstractions: Aggregation and Generalization, ACM Transactions on Database Systems, vol. 2, no 2, June 1977.

[SNLE03] Snene M., Léonard M., Collaborative CASE Tools editors based on web-service: J2EE experiment. SETIT, Tunisia, 2003.

[STAC89] Stace C., Plant taxonomy and biosystematics, 2nd edition, Edward Arnold, 1989.

[TULE02a] Turki, S., Léonard, M., Hyperclasses: towards a new kind of independence of the methods from the schema. In the proceedings of the 4th International Conference on Enterprise Information Systems, ICEIS'2002, Vol.2, P. 788-794, ISBN: 972-98050-6-7. Ciudad-Real, Spain, April 3-6, 2002.

[TULE02b] Turki, S., Léonard, M., IS Components with Hyperclasses, Conference of the OOIS 2002 Workshops, Advances in Object-Oriented Information Systems, Montpellier, France, September 2, 2002, LNCS 2426, Springer, 2002.

45

PART 1

Databases and
Information Systems Integration

ON OPERATIONS TO CONFORM OBJECT-ORIENTED SCHEMAS

Alberto Abelló, Elena Rodríguez, Fèlix Saltor
Universitat Politècnica de Catalunya
Email: {aabello, malena, saltor}@lsi.upc.es

Marta Oliva
Universitat de Lleida
Email: oliva@eup.udl.es

Cecilia Delgado, Eladio Garví, José Samos
Universidad de Granada
Email: {cdelgado, egarvi, jsamos}@ugr.es

Keywords: Information Integration, Cooperative Information Systems, Federated Database Systems, Object-Oriented Schemas.

Abstract: To build a Cooperative Information System from several pre-existing heterogeneous systems, the schemas of these systems must be integrated. Operations used for this purpose include conforming operations, which change the form of a schema. In this paper, a set of primitive conforming operations for Object-Oriented schemas are presented. These operations are organized in matrixes according to the Object-Oriented dimensions -*Generalization/Specialization, Aggregation/Decomposition*- on which they operate.

1 INTRODUCTION

A "Cooperative Information System" (CIS) is built upon a number of pre-existing heterogeneous information systems. We assume that each one of them will have a schema in some data model (relational, object-oriented, ...). Because of the autonomy of design of these systems, their models will, in general, be different: "syntactic heterogeneity". One of the methods to overcome this heterogeneity is by adopting a data model as the "Canonical Data Model" (CDM) of the CIS, and translating schemas from their native models to the CDM, as explained in Sheth and Larson (1990). "Object-Oriented"(O-O) data models were found in Saltor et al. (1991) well suited as CDM of a CIS, and we will be assuming in this paper an O-O CDM.

The architecture of a CIS may follow different frameworks, but most likely it will be a "multilevel-schema architecture", with schemas at different levels, and schema *mappings* between consecutive levels. The now classical example is Sheth & Larson's 5-level schema architecture for "Federated Database Systems" (Sheth and Larson, 1990); it continues to be a useful reference framework (Conrad et al., 1999).

A system with a multilevel-schema architecture can be built by starting from one or more schemas, and applying operations to yield another schema at the next level (and their corresponding mappings), and so on. At each step, if all schemas follow the CDM, then the operations applied are precisely the schema operations of that model; this is the reason why it is important to use a CDM with adequate schema operations.

This paper discusses schema operations needed to *conform* "Object-Oriented" (O-O) schemas, i.e. to change the *form* of a given schema into a desired form. Our emphasis here is in the process to build a CIS using an O-O model as its CDM, particularly when constructing *Federated Schemas* from *Export Schemas* in the sense of Sheth and Larson (1990). This schema integration process has two steps: first, each *Export Schema* is transformed into a common form (conformation) and then all these conformed schemas are integrated by some "Generalization" operation, as in García-Solaco et al. (1996).

Here, a set of *primitive* operations to conform O-O schemas are presented. In these operations the

O. Camp et al. (eds.), Enterprise Information Systems V, 49-56.
© 2004 *Kluwer Academic Publishers. Printed in the Netherlands.*

schema *form* is taken explicitly into account; thus, from a starting schema, according to its patterns, operations can be applied to obtain a conformed schema to be integrated lately. We assume that these conforming operations do not add new information (they do not augment the information capacity of the schema in the sense of Miller *et al.* (1993)) to the obtained schema (all elements added must be derived from the source schema). All "semantic enrichment" takes place when producing *Component Schemas*, as was presented in Castellanos *et al.* (1994). This is so because of the "separation of concerns" of the architectures. For the same reason conforming operations do not change the data model; translating operations do that.

We use UML terminology (OMG, 2002). We add to this terminology some general integrity constraints to restrict the semantics of some operations. However our results are applicable to any O-O data model.

Conforming operations are defined on the *Generalization/Specialization* (G/S from now on) and on the *Aggregation/Decomposition* (A/D) dimensions. Each operation produces a mapping between the input and output schemas, and all these mappings will be stored in a repository; but this topic is out of the scope of this work.

This paper is organized as follows: the UML model elements are introduced in section 2; section 3 the schema patterns and *primitive* conforming operations are presented; related work, conclusions and references close it. We use **bold face** for UML terms, *italic* for new terms, and "quotes" for terms introduced by other authors.

2 MODEL ELEMENTS

Figure 1 shows the UML metaclasses meaningful for our purpose. We only consider three elements: **Class, Generalization**, and **Association**.

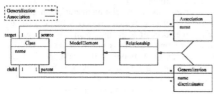

Figure 1: Subset of UML metaclasses.

- **Classes** describe sets of objects sharing structure and semantics, which can be given either extensionally, or intensionally.

- **Generalizations** are **Relationships** between two **Classes** along the G/S dimension.
- **Associations** are **Relationships** between two **Classes** along the A/D dimension.

2.1 Generalization Metaclass

A **Generalization** is a taxonomic relationship between a more general element (**parent**) and a more specific one (**child**). It uses a **discriminator** to show the criterion used in the specialization.

A set of **Generalizations** sharing the same **parent** and **discriminator** form a **Partition**. In our context, a **discriminator** is a function used to restrict the presence of instances of the superclass in each subclass. The **discriminator** of a **Generalization** is the set of functions added to the predicate of the **child** w.r.t. that of the **parent**.

Notice that **Generalizations** are absolutely independent of the information represented along the A/D dimension (which includes attributes, as explained below). We only know that an instance belongs to a subclass because it fulfils the intension predicate. Attributes corresponding to the **discriminator** do not necessarily exist, so that if the subclass is deleted, the information may be lost.

We assume that the generalization digraph is a semi-lattice, having **Class** *All_objects* as root. It is not a tree, because more than one generalization path is allowed between two **Classes**. Nevertheless, we impose a really strong Integrity Constraint (IC) on this allowance: both paths must involve the same set of functions, however, it is not possible that given any two **Classes** (one in each path) both sets of functions used in the **Generalizations** till them coincide. Figure 2 shows a correct and an incorrect example. In (b), **Classes** Girl and YoungWoman should be the same, since functions used to specialize them (i.e. {sex(x), agePerson(x)}) coincide. In addition, they are superclasses of the same **Class** (GirlScout) by the same **discriminator** (hobby(x)), thus they should be the same **Class**.

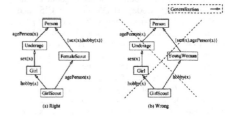

Figure 2: **Generalization** integrity constraint.

2.2 Association Metaclass

An **Association** defines a semantic relationship between **Classes**. An instance of an **Association** is a **Link**, which is a tuple of instances obtained from the related **Classes**. In general, UML allows n-ary **Associations**. However, we only consider binary unidirectional **Associations**. Having only binary **Associations** does not reduce the expressivity of an O-O schema, since n-ary **Associations** can always be represented by a **Class** and n binary **Associations**. UML refers to the **Association** ends as **source** and **target**; here, the **target** end is graphically expressed by the head of the arrow.

Moreover, as we did for **Classes**, we also consider that the instances of an **Association** can be given extensionally, or intensionally. The intension of an **Association** is given by a predicate showing which pairs of instances (from **source** and **target**) are related (i.e. which **Links** exist).

Although different kinds of **Associations** exist, we only emphasize the difference between **Aggregations** (i.e. a part-whole relationship) and those that are not **Aggregations** (i.e. those showing a class being either associated or used as attribute in another one). We consider that if **DataType** values would have identity, and could be freely associated to **Classes**, **Attributes** would just be a special case of **Association**. Thus, for the sake of simplicity, from here on, we will assume this.

There exist two ICs in the usage of **Associations**, both only concerning **Aggregations**. As depicted in Figure 3.b, **Aggregations** forming a cycle are not allowed (i.e. **Class** A being part of B, means **Class** B cannot be part of A). Moreover, between a **parent Class** and any of its **child Class** cannot exist an **Aggregation Relationship**.

Figure 3: **Aggregation** integrity constraint.

3 OPERATIONS ON OBJECT-ORIENTED SCHEMAS

The main difference among operations defined in this work and those defined by other authors is that we only consider operations modifying the form of the schema. For example, since operations that change names do not change any form, they are not

needed to conform schemas. Operations locate a particular pattern in the *source schema*, and change it to a different form in the *target schema*, leaving unaltered the rest.

We define a *pattern of interest* as that which represents the minimal information needed to apply a given conforming operation. As candidate patterns, we took digraphs, where nodes represent **Classes**, and arcs represent **Relationships** (either **Association** or **Generalization**) between **Classes**.

Many occurrences of patterns appear in each schema. Conformation operations are applied successively on each pattern until a conformed schema is obtained. The conformation is the *composition of operations*, which is associative, but not commutative. We call *primitives* the atomic operations needed to *conform* schemas; the *derived* operations are those that can be obtained by composition of *primitives*. We have established a set of fifteen *primitive* operations, in the sense that none of them can be left out without affecting the set of derived operations.

Patterns of interest and *primitives* can be represented in a digraph $G = (P,O)$, where P is the set of patterns, and O is the set of operations (Figure 4). An arc o_{ij} from p_i to p_j represents the operation that converts pattern p_i into pattern p_j. We distinguish three subgraphs corresponding to operations on G/S, A/D and inter dimensions. The reflexive arc on pattern p_6 reflects the existence of three operations acting on the same pattern, which give rise to three different forms (a, b, c), that can be seen as special cases of it.

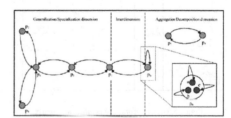

Figure 4: Patterns transition graph.

G is a symmetric graph, in the sense that for every arc o_{ij}, there is an arc o_{ji} representing the *opposite* operation, which may or may not be its mathematical *inverse*. When o_{ij} reduces the capacity of information, o_{ji} is not able to recover it, giving rise to a *target schema* different to the *source schema*; however, the patterns have the same *form*.

The matrixes depicted in Figures 5 and 10 show the *primitive* operations that work over the *patterns of interest* that we have identified for G/S and A/D respectively, while Figure 14 shows the matrix containing *primitive* operations that combine both dimensions. The cr_i are the criteria of the **discriminators** and the n_i the names of the **Associations**. Empty cells of the matrixes represent *derived* operations.

3.1 Operations along Generalization/Specialization

There are eight *primitive* conforming operations that work exclusively along the G/S dimension (Figure 5).

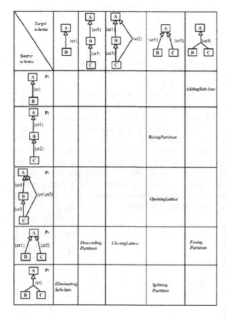

Figure 5: *Generalization/Specialization* matrix

AddingSubclass (cell c_{15}) adds a new subclass to a **Partition** by union, intersection, difference, etc. of instances of existing **Classes**, without changing the **discriminator** of the **Partition**. *EliminatingSubclass* (cell c_{51}) removes a subclass from a specialization, it can produce some loss of information capacity.

Figure 6 shows how, by difference, we add a new subclass Others, and it also shows how *EliminatingSubclass* removes the same subclass without producing any loss of information capacity. There are some cases where it is impossible to recover an eliminated subclass without augmenting

the information capacity (for example, we cannot recover Marine, if we only have Terrestrial and Animals).

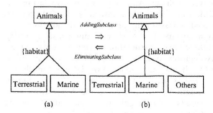

Figure 6: *Adding/EliminatingSubclass* example

RisingPartition (cell c_{24}) derives a new **Partition** of a superclass by applying the transitivity property. This operation converts an indirect subclass of a superclass in a direct one. *DescendingPartition* (cell c_{42}) does the *opposite* transformation.

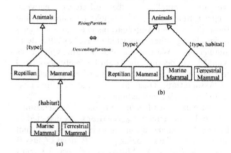

Figure 7: *Rising/DescendingPartition* example

Figure 7 shows an example of *RisingPartition*, where we obtain the subclasses Marine Mammal and Terrestrial Mammal as direct subclass of superclass Animals. To descend a **Partition**, its **discriminator** has to include the **discriminator** of the **Partition** of the subclass where we want to place it. So, whereas sometimes it is possible to directly apply *DescendingPartition*, in other cases it is necessary to previously use other operations to obtain an adequate **discriminator**.

OpeningLattice (cell c_{34}) changes a semi-lattice pattern into a tree pattern by removing part of one path between two **Classes**, eliminating multiple inheritance. This does not imply any loss of information capacity because, when there are two specialization paths between two **Classes**, both involve the same set of functions. The *inverse* transformation is carried out by *ClosingLattice* (cell c_{43}). Figure 8 shows an example where the **Partition** with habitat **discriminator** disappears and appears.

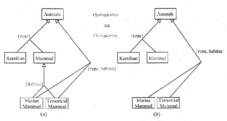

Figure 8: *Opening/ClosingLattice* example

FusingPartition (cell c_{45}) fuses all **Generalizations** in two different **Partitions** of a superclass into a unique **Partition** of it. The generated **Partition** has as **discriminator** the union of **discriminators** of the source **Partitions**. Its inverse, *SplittingPartition* (cell c_{54}), splits subclasses of a **Partition** into two **Partitions**. Figure 9 shows an example.

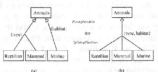

Figure 9: *Fussing/SplittingPartition* example

3.2 Operations along Aggregation/Decomposition

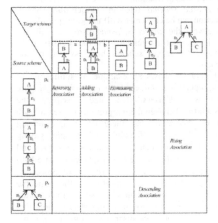

Figure 10: *Aggregation/Decomposition* matrix

The matrix associated to this dimension (Figure 10) contains three patterns (p_6, p_7, p_8). It shows conformation generic operations whose application depends on the kind of **Association**. Three operations can be applied over pattern p_6; for each one of them the form of its *target schema* is shown. The *forms* produced by *AddingAssociation* and *EliminatingAssociation* are not patterns but special cases of pattern p_6.

ReversingAssociation (cell c_{11}^a) changes the direction of an **Association**. Notice that it is not applicable to **Aggregations**, because it would change the meaning, not only the *form* of the schema. If it is applicable, the information capacity in the *source schema* is preserved, and itself is its inverse. For example, if there is an **Association** between Cars and People **Classes** showing the owner of each car (Figure 11a), the effect of this operation is to substitute this **Association** by its reversing one in the *target schema*, which shows the cars owned by each person (Figure 11b).

Figure 11: *ReversingAssociation* example

AddingAssociation (cell c_{11}^b) adds a new **Association** to the *target schema*. A new **Association** between two **Classes** can be derived by union, difference, complementarity, etc. of **Associations** between them. This operation preserves the information capacity in the *source schema*. *EliminatingAssociation* (cell c_{11}^c) carries out the *opposite* transformation, it eliminates an **Association** from the *source schema*; in this case, the information capacity of the *target schema* may be reduced.

In Figure 12, given a source schema with People and Universities **Classes**, and the **Associations** between them represented by means of their attributes students, teaching_staff and adm_staff, *AddingAssociation* derives a new **Association** in the *target schema* (Figure 12b) by union of pre-existing ones showing all people that belong to each university. The name of this new **Association** is community. The *target schema* in Figure 12a is obtained after applying *EliminatingAssociation* over the *source schema* in Figure 12b.

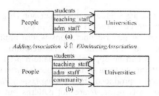

Figure 12: *Adding/EliminatingAssociation* example

RisingAssociation (cell c_{23}) derives a new **Association** between two **Classes** by applying the transitivity property. Whether the information capacity in the *source schema* is preserved in the *target schema* or not, depends on properties of **Association**s involved in the operation. The information capacity of the *target schema* may be reduced. *DescendingAssociation* (cell c_{32}) is its *opposite*; although it could seem that this operation is *derived* from successive application of *ReversingAssociation*, *RisingAssociation* and *ReversingAssociation*, this is not true, because the *ReversingAssociation* is not applicable when there is an **Aggregation**. The *target schema* obtained by *DescendingAssociation* does not always preserve the information capacity of the *source schema*.

Figure 13 depicts an example of these operations. The *source schema* (Figure 13a) includes **Classes** Languages, People, and Clubs; and the **Associations** among these **Classes** which show that people speak languages, and that clubs are conceived as compound objects from all their members. After performing *RisingAssociation*, a new *target schema* is obtained (Figure 13b). This schema incorporates a new **Association** connecting **Classes** Languages and Clubs. Therefore, in the *target schema*, we can obtain for a given club all its members and all the languages spoken in the club, but data about which languages were spoken for each person has been lost. The *target schema* in Figure 13a is obtained after applying *DescendingAssociation* over the *source schema* in Figure 13b; the new **Association** represents, for each person, the languages that are spoken in the clubs to which the person belongs instead of the languages spoken by the person.

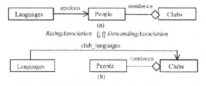

Figura 13: *Rising/DescendingAssociation* example

3.3 Interdimension Operations

Figure 14 shows the *primitive* conforming operations that work simultaneously along the G/S dimension as well as the A/D dimension.

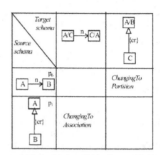

Figure 14: Interdimension matrix

ChangingToPartition (cell c_{12}) transforms an **Association** into a **Partition**, so one or more subclasses are added to the *target schema*. The contents and number of these subclasses depend, respectively, on the set of objects of the **Class** that is being specialized and the **Association** that is being transformed in a **Partition**. The **Class** to be specialized could be any of the two **Classes** related by the **Association**. Given that no new information can be added, the subclasses only incorporate those **Associations** that are inherited from their superclasses; the *target schema* preserves the information capacity of the source schema. *ChangingToAssociation* (cell c_{21}) carries out the *opposite* transformation, it converts a **Partition** of the *source schema* into an **Association** (whose direction can be chosen at will) in the *target schema*. Moreover, the *target schema* disregards all the subclasses that participated in the **Partition**. In general, the *target schema* has less information capacity.

Figure 15 shows an example of application of these operations. Given a *source schema* (Figure 15a) with **Classes** Sex and People, the **Association** between them represents the sex of each person. Assuming that there are people having associated object 'female' and people having associated object 'male', the subclasses Women and Men will be added to the *target schema* (Figure 15b) using *ChangingToPartition* . The set of objects of these subclasses are, respectively, those people whose sex is 'female' and whose sex is 'male' in the *source schema*. Finally, it is important to note that **Class** Sex does not disappear from the schema because it could be **Associated** to other **Classes**. Figure 15a is obtained after applying *ChangingToAssociation* over the *source schema* in Figure 15b.

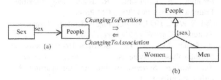

(b)

Figure 15: *ChanginToPartition/Association* example

4 RELATED WORK

Schema conformation is related to other topics such as Schema Evolution and View Definition (definition of External Schemas and Derived Classes). The main difference between them is in their aims. The Schema Evolution objective is to modify a schema to adapt it to changes in the modelled Universe of Discourse; hence, these changes can augment the information capacity. In the case of View Definition, its general objective is to transform and to present information stored in DB, all or part of it, according to end-user requirements.

4.1 Operations on Object-Oriented Data Models

Directly related to the Schema Conformation problem is the proposal found in Motro (1987), where a set of operations to build and modify the generalization hierarchy is presented. In Mannino *et al.* (1988) generalization hierarchies can be merged using a set of operations.

Several view mechanisms have been proposed for O-O models, as can be seen in Motsching-Pitrik (1996). In Rundensteiner (1992) proposal, Derived Classes are defined using Object Algebra, and then integrated in an O-O schema (the Global Schema) to define External Schemas as subschemas of it. In Bertino (1992), Derived Classes that include non-derived attributes can be defined using a specific language. In Santos *et al.* (1994) an External Schema definition methodology is proposed; in it, Derived Classes can contain existing or new objects. In Rundensteiner *et al.* (1998) a Schema Evolution mechanism based on a View Definition system is proposed, and it has no limitation on the accepted changes. In proposals where External Schemas are

built from the Conceptual or other External Schemas without augmenting their information capacity, the conformation operations presented in this paper can be directly used. As mentioned in Miller *et al.* (1993), one of the operational objectives of defining External Schemas is to restructure information to be integrated in others schemas, which is also the target of our work.

In Banerjee *et al.* (1987), a taxonomy of primitive operations for Schema Evolution in the Orion system is defined; each operation has a semantic based on a set of rules that preserve Schema Invariants. For the GemStone system (Penney and Stein, 1987), a set of primitive operations, based on Schema Invariants as well, is defined; in this case, the object model is simpler than the Orion one (since multiple inheritance is not allowed), and this fact is reflected on operations. The corresponding proposal for the O_2 system can be found in Zicari (1992). In Claypool *et al.* (1998) a framework is proposed based on the Object Data Management Group (ODMG) data model; in it, complex schema evolution operations can be defined as a sequence of primitive ones. In these models, subclass relationships are defined based exclusively on subtype relationships, without taking into account any specialization criteria; for this reason, the primitive operations defined along the G/S dimension perform only the addition or removal of subclass relationships. Related to the A/D dimension, the only association in these models corresponds to the definition of a class as an attribute domain; therefore, the only operation along this dimension is devoted to change attribute domains. In relation to the G/S and A/D dimensions, in this paper we have defined a set of operations wider than the above mentioned, the reason is that we consider specialization criteria and associations.

4.2 Operations on other Data Models

Operations to transform or restructure schemas have also been proposed in others data models. The complex object model put forward in Abiteboul and Hull (1988) allows the definition of typed hierarchical objects; in this environment, a set of operations over this kind of objects, based on rewriting rules, is defined. These operations work along the A/D dimension, since they restructure the type of a complex object by associating its components; most of them preserve the information capacity, only two augment it.

In Kwan and Fong (1999), a schema integration methodology is put forward, it is based on the

Extended Entity-Relationship model, but it could also be applied to the Relational model. This methodology offers a set of rules to solve semantics conflicts and to merge entities and relationships taken from different schemas in another schema. These rules operate along the G/S or A/D dimensions; the generated schema always preserves the information capacity.

5 CONCLUSIONS

Conforming operations change a pattern in a *source schema* into a different pattern in a *target schema*, thus changing the *form* of the schema, without augmenting the information capacity. We have presented a set of *primitive* conforming operations on Object-Oriented database schemas; these operations may be represented by arcs of a graph and by cells of a "pattern×pattern" matrix. Other conforming operations can be *derived* from these *primitives*.

The use of different O-O dimensions allows us to classify the operations into three groups, each one with its matrix: operations along the *Generalization/Specialization* dimension, operations along the *Aggregation/Decomposition* dimension, and operations changing from one dimension to the other. Each operation produces a *mapping* between its *source* and its *target schema*. These *mappings* lie along the *Derivability* dimension, and is subject of our research in progress, that will give rise to the implementation of a case tool for schema integration.

ACKNOWLEDGMENTS

This work has been partially supported by the Spanish Research PRONTIC under projects TIC2000-1723-C02-(01 and 02), as well as grant 1998FI-00228 from the Generalitat de Catalunya.

REFERENCES

Abiteboul, S., Hull, R., 1988. Restructuring Hierarchical Database Objects. *Theoretical Computer Science 62*. North-Holland.

Banerjee, J. et al., 1987. Semantics and Implementation of Schema Evolution in Object-Oriented Databases. In *ACM SIGMOD'87*.

Bertino, E., 1992. A View Mechanism for Object-Oriented Databases. In *EDBT'92, LNCS 580*. Springer.

Castellanos, M. et al., 1994. Semantically Enriching Relational Databases into an Object Oriented Semantic Model. In *DEXA'94, LNCS 856*. Springer.

Claypool, K. et al., 1998. SERF: Schema Evolution through an Extensible, Re-usable and Flexible Framework. In *CIKM'98*. ACM Press.

Conrad, S. et al., 1999. Engineering Federated Information Systems. *ACM SIGMOD Record, 28*.

García-Solaco, M. et al., 1996. Semantic Heterogeneity in Multidatabase Systems. In *Object Oriented Multidatabase Systems*. Bukhres, O., Elmagarmid, A. (eds.), Prentice-Hall.

Kwan, I., Fong, J., 1999. Schema Integration Methodology and its Verification by Use of Information Capacity. *Information Systems, 24*. North-Holland.

Mannino, M. et al., 1988. A Rule-Based Approach for Merging Generalization Hierarchies. *Information Systems, 13*. North-Holland.

Miller, R. et al., 1993. The Use of Information Capacity in Schema Integration and Translation. In *VLDB'93*. Morgan Kaufmann.

Motro, A., 1987. Superviews: Virtual Integration of Multiple Databases. *IEEE TSE 13*. IEEE Press.

Motsching-Pitrik, R., 1996. Requirements and Comparison of View Mechanisms for Object-Oriented Databases. *Information Systems 21*. North-Holland.

OMG, 2002. *Unified Modelling Language Specification*. Version 2.0. http://www.omg.org/uml/

Penney, D., Stein, J., 1987. Class Modification in the GemStone Object-Oriented DBMS. *ACM SIGPLAN Notices 22*. ACM Press.

Rundensteiner, E., 1992. MultiView: A Methodology for Supporting Multiple Views in Object-Oriented Databases. In *VLDB'92*. Morgan Kaufmann.

Rundensteiner, E. et al., 1998. Capacity-Augmenting Schema Changes on Object-Oriented Databases. In *OOIS'98*. Springer.

Saltor, F. et al., 1991. Suitability of Data Models as Canonical Models for Federated DBs. *ACM SIGMOD Record 20*.

Santos, C. et al., 1994. Virtual Schemas and Bases. In *EDBT'94, LNCS 779*. Springer.

Sheth, A., Larson, J., 1990. Federated Database Systems for Managing Distributed, Heterogeneous, and Autonomous Databases. *ACM Computing Surveys 22*.

Zicari, R., 1992. A Framework for Schema Updates in an Object-Oriented Database System. In *Building an Object-Oriented Database System*. Bancilhon, F., Delobel, C., Kanellakis, P. (eds.), Morgan Kaufmann.

ERP IMPLEMENTATION, CROSS-FUNCTIONALITY AND CRITICAL CHANGE FACTORS

Redouane El Amrani, Bénédicte Geffroy-Maronnat
CRGNA-LAGON, Université de Nantes / Ecole des Mines de Nantes, Nantes, France
E-mail : {Redouane.elamrani, benedicte.geffroy}@emn.fr

Frantz Rowe, Rolande Marciniak
CRGNA-LAGON, Université de Nantes, Nantes, France
E-mail : {rowe, marcinia}@sc-eco.univ-nantes.fr

Marc Bidan
CRGNA-LAGON, Université de Nantes, Nantes, France,

Email : *bidan@iut-nantes.univ-nantes.fr*

Keywords: ERP, cross-functional, change, functional coverage, lifecycle, critical success factors.

Abstract: ERP (Enterprise Resource Planning) systems are characterised by particular features such as functional coverage, interdependent relationships, single database and standard management and processing rules; all of which are capable of bringing about various degrees of change within the company and, potentially, encourage a more cross-functional overview of it. However, few quantitative studies have been conducted to measure these effects.

This is the background to this paper, which studied 100 French companies to arrive at the following assessment of ERP adoption. It then goes on to test the relationships between the factors influencing the ERP lifecycle ((preparation (organizational vision, process re-engineering), engineering (specific developments), implementation strategy (functional coverage and speed)), the perception of a more cross-functional overview of the company and, more globally, the scope of the change this technology brings about within the company.

All these factors play significant roles, with functional coverage appearing to be a particularly important consideration, which should be addressed in future research.

INTRODUCTION

Despite the considerable risks involved, the vogue for Enterprise Resource Planning (ERP) systems has had a considerable effect on changing the way company information systems are designed. This task now rests largely with software publishers and is independent of software learning cycles (Lesuisse, 2002). ERP systems have also been the subject of a large number of French[1] publications, as well as being covered extensively in English (Esteves & Pastor, 2001). However, most

---

[1] Special edition of *Systèmes d'Information et Management (SIM)*: ERP/PGI and change, vol.4, no. 4: (Rowe; Besson; Hanseth & Braa; Forest; Bouillot; Coat & Favier). 5th AIM symposium (2000), Montpellier, France (Adam, O'Doherty; Ravarini, Tagliavini, Pigni, Sciuto). 6th AIM symposium (2001), Nantes, France (Bidan; Besson & Rowe; Saint-Léger & Savall). 7th AIM symposium (2002), Hammemet, Tunisia (Geffroy, Saint-Léger)

57

of these publications fail to address one of the most important questions posed to companies by these systems: can they offer those involved a more cross-functional overview of the company's problems and enable profound change to be brought about by "breaking down" functional silos?

It is important to address this question, because the few quantitative studies available to us which have attempted to answer the ultimate question of how ERP systems contribute to business performance have reached negative conclusions. Poston and Grabski (2001) showed that the use of these systems in the USA made no significant contribution to company performance when compared with comparable companies who had not invested in ERP systems during the same period. However, their research does not address the functional coverage of ERP systems. All other things being equal, they restrict themselves to examining the link between the fact of having adopted an ERP system and the financial effects observed. Our observations of the French[2] context demonstrate that most companies who say that they have adopted an ERP system have actually adopted only a few modules. It is therefore perfectly possible that the business effects are dependent on the functional coverage delivered by the system and that these business effects come about from a modification of the organizational vision.

This paper has three aims:

1- To describe the way in which ERP systems have been adopted in French companies;

2- To examine if the implementation (functional coverage and speed) of these systems explains the emergence of a more cross-functional overview and, more generally, of more marked change throughout the company;

3- To evaluate the impact of such implementation in respect of the critical

change factors that emerge throughout the lifecycle of these projects.

As we have already emphasised, we cannot conduct a scientific study of such a complex and relatively new phenomenon without first describing it (Bachelard, 1938). No quantitative study has yet addressed these issues in the French context and we know that the French context is sufficiently specific (Besson, Rowe, 2001) to begin by describing the ERP phenomenon in France from a base that exceeds the sum of the case studies listed.

Literature on the impact made by information technologies has widely demonstrated that the process of change is an important consideration in explaining the paradoxes or surprises that emerge from the effects observed (Robey, Boudreau, 2000). In the case of ERP systems, the scale of investment and the level of risk involved make the process of change especially crucial. IT literature also underlines the fact that organisational dynamics differ depending on the technology concerned. In this respect, ERP leads us to address the central problem of cross-functionality; a problem to which it is potentially central.

In the first part of our paper, we examine the theoretical bases of change and cross-functionality, as well as the ERP literature on which we have formulated our hypotheses. We then proceed to present our methodology. This leads us on to the third part of our paper, in which we describe the adoption and implementation of ERP systems in France. Lastly, the fourth part of the paper presents the test results for our hypotheses.

I – Change theory, cross-functionality and hypotheses

I.1. Change theory

Within organisational theory, theories of change tend to involve four or so standard ideas concerning the development and change in organization (Van de Ven, Scott Poole, 1992), a process being defined here as a progression of events over time. These standard ideas differ in terms of their logic and their motors of change. Seen in terms of a lifecycle, the term "change" describes a sequence of events which unfolds in a logical and pre-designed fashion. Conversely,

---

[2] Observations made as part of a contractual research programme conducted for the French Ministry of Employment's DARES (Direction de l'Animation de la Recherche, des études et des statistiques) addressing the relative contribution of ERP systems of varying levels of (operational and strategic) flexibility and the effects of introducing ERP systems on the organisation of work and company functions in SMEs and major companies.

change can also be seen as the result of forces external to the organisation bringing about a kind of natural selection. Moving closer to the social sciences, change may even be seen as a teleological process of enaction, made possible by the involving participants in presenting the action to be taken and redefining the objectives sought or as a conflict-based dialectic process. In the French context, the difficulties encountered with ERP projects – and therefore the problems of change linked to them – have been addressed theoretically on the basis of ideas derived from enaction and conflict typology (Besson and Rowe, 2001). In the American context, the work of Robey et al. (2001) is based on a dialectic reading that takes account of the learning processes related to ERP configuration and the assimilation of new processes. Taking a complementary approach, we intend to return in this paper to a closer reading of traditional management literature by identifying the factors that contribute effectively to change. By presenting these factors in a logical fashion and testing them on the basis of a quantitative survey conducted amongst single participants, this reading is similar to viewing change as a lifecycle and may seem simplistic. However, given the current level of knowledge, it seems to us that there is a relatively good understanding of ERP in terms of case studies and that what we lack are truly comparative tests that enable us to explain change.

Many of the threads running through the existing literature on change can be adopted and applied to ERP projects (Boudreau, 1999). We have therefore retained several major contributions.

The work done on innovation in organisations by Leonard-Barton (1988) shows that innovation implementation characteristics are based on implementation strategies which, in turn, determine whether the innovation concerned is accepted or rejected. This outline is probably simplistic, but it effectively highlights the essential characteristics of innovation which are both constraints and choices for managing change in the organization. There are three subsets of such characteristics.

1. Whether or not innovation is transferable depends on the preparation made for it and the effectiveness with which it can be communicated. Preparation takes place either in laboratories or other fields of experimentation. It aims to achieve a suitable level of development at which there is sufficient proof of feasibility that the innovation becomes transferable. Communicability takes the form of initiatives to train users in new ways of working and the documentation of different rules and operating methods.

2. The complexity of implementation in relation to the participants involved. This complexity is linked not only to the number of people identified as users of the technology, but also – and particularly so from our point of view – to their organisational differentiation; the more functions an innovation addresses, the more difficult it is to ensure its acceptance since it must address a number of distinct cultures.

3. The divisibility of the innovation which rightly enables the difficulties involved in cross-organisation project implementation to be worked around. Divisibility is linked to the modularity of the innovation and the opportunities for personalising it, and therefore to the ability to adapt the product details to suit the vision population.

The modular and configurable nature of ERP systems makes them inherently divisible innovations and therefore capable of responding to complex implementation strategies.

What we mean by implementation strategy is the ability to set limits on those parts of the organisation to be affected by the innovation and the way in which those can be covered. If the level of functional coverage is high, the company will have the option of implementing a divisible technology in progressive stages.

A second major contribution to our research (Gallivan et al., 1994) clearly addressed the debate on the speed of implementation of radical innovations. They stress that in many cases, two quite different questions are confused: the extent of the change envisaged and the speed of the implementation. The vocabulary does not help us here, because according to Quinn (1980) and Hammer and Champy (1993), it is normal to distinguish radical change from incremental change. These two types of implementation strategies both link scope with speed. Radical change would be far-reaching and rapid, whilst incremental change would be a sequence of small steps made at a pace to suit the participants involved and adjusted by mutual agreement. Gallivan, Hofman and Orlikowski (op.cit.) demonstrate clearly that widespread innovation can be implemented gradually and more widely than one might think and even justify (depending on the context) cases that combine scope and speed of change in widely differing ways.

But would that really be an interesting debate? Wouldn't widespread innovation be simply a sum total of small-scale innovations obtained and added according to the principle of divisibility? Some strategies do not meet these criteria for a number of reasons. In practice, some innovations can only produce a beneficial effect when introduced at a certain scale. Just because it is possible to divide it in order to deploy it, it is not necessarily desirable to remain at a preliminary stage of distribution. On the other hand, implementation, even within a closely defined perimeter, has a fixed cost and requires a certain level of effort from the designers and users involved. This effort may, despite the potential benefits of the innovation, result in resistance to change. Crozier and Friedberg (1977) highlight the propensity of participants to resist innovation where it threatens their zone of uncertainty and leaves them no room for manoeuvre, that resistance taking the form of working around the innovation or even diverting it from its originally intended uses. Typically, ERP systems are affected by this tension between the search for widespread functional coverage in order to gain the expected benefits and the risk of provoking even stronger resistance. In practice, these systems would contribute to establishing the common language or single frame of reference that companies have always dreamed of, as long as the functional coverage is sufficiently extensive (Rowe, 1999). So, the argument over divisibility and, more especially, modularity of innovation as a way of ensuring its success through enabling potentially gradual implementation, seems to lose its persuasiveness where ERP systems are concerned. Or suggest that success would, in this case, be limited to the implementation stage only without progressing to make the anticipated potential gains.

Finally, the existing literature on innovation continually stresses the importance of champions (Beath, 1991) and the support of senior management in the success of IT projects (Jarvenppa, Ives, 1991). In the case of ERP projects, it is inconceivable that senior management would not be instrumental in the decision to introduce ERP, given the level of investment and challenge involved.

I.2. The application of these theories to ERP

According to the concept of change as a logical progression of stages in which key activities follow one another in sequence, it falls to us to identify as precisely as possible the questions raised by the existing literature on change in the context of ERP system implementation ((transferability, complexity (functional coverage), speed (implementation strategy) and management support)). Schematically, this can be represented by four stages (Markus and Tanis, 2000), as illustrated in figure 1:

- **Chartering**: during this phase, the opportunity to acquire an ERP system is examined from the viewpoint of the company's needs and the possibility of improving its performance. The impacts of such an acquisition on the company's organisation and strategy are defined and estimated.

- **Project**: this phase includes all the activities required to make ERP operational in all the departments concerned. ERP system configuration is particularly crucial here. This is also the stage at which processes are redefined and specific developments undertaken.

- **Shakedown**: this final project phase involves installing the ERP system, switching over from the old IS and user training. Implementation may be gradual (first by module, then by site, for example) or much more rapid (big-bang: all modules and all sites at once). A period during which the system is controlled by the project team will enable problems to be corrected and the system to be optimised. It is during this phase that ERP functionalities are practically matched to the company's organisational processes. Implementation ends with the completion of the ERP project.

- **Onward and Upward**: the ERP system now enters its operational phase and improvements are continually sought through its various maintenance cycles. The company may begin work on new projects incorporating new applications (CRM, SCM, e-business, etc.).

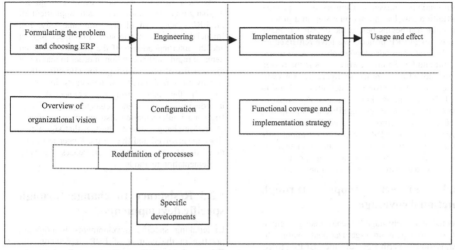

Figure 1: Stages in the process of change brought about by an ERP project

I.2.1 Definition of an organizational vision by managers

The company's managers play an essential role in an ERP project. The scope of such projects demands not only their approval of the decision to proceed, but also their involvement in resolving leadership conflicts and choosing suppliers; they should therefore remain at the heart of the decision making process. However, one key aspect of their role is not always clearly understood or taken fully into account: directors often arrive at their organizational vision having used a rather rudimentary map of the company's processes (Besson and Rowe, *op. cit.*). In this very complex type of project, the support and involvement of senior executives from the earliest phases are seen as key factors for success (Nelson and Somers, 2001). In practical terms, they must design the organisational model before delegating the task of putting that model into action and handing it over to the technical designers (the project team & external consultants). In some cases, this will involve the participation of key users from each function concerned. This visioning strategy affects every subsequent stage of the project's progress and finds its practical application in the parameterization and configuration of the ERP system. This technical modelling exercise is an interpretation of the organisational choices made during the previous stage. One question in particular seems important to us at this point: How important is this particular role of the company directors for the rest of the project and, ultimately, the scope of the changes actually brought about?

I.2.2 Redefinition of organizational process

The printed structure is transferred to the parameterized software package during the engineering phase and paves the way for implementation. More often than not, this transfer is accompanied by a redefinition of processes (Grover, 1995). This complex and painstaking task presupposes that the way the company wishes to work can be reconciled with the way the system will allow it to. Several studies (Davenport, 1998, Robey et al., 2002; Parr, 2000; Hong and Kim, 2002) have demonstrated that it is vital for the company's processes to be accurately aligned with those of the ERP system if the full benefits are to be realised. The literature often recommends starting the process before parameterization (Bancroft, 1996). However, we observe from the case studies (those conducted by ourselves, as well as those read by ourselves for the purposes of research) that this action runs in parallel with configuration phase. Conversely, process redefinition may be an important step in a process of change that begins before the decision is made to move to an ERP project. We have remarked on this observation in our monographs on Air France, Renault and Les Salins du Midi. This is the reason for the dotted area shown in figure 1. However, regardless of how process redefinition relates to the ERP decision-making process in terms of timing, it seems to us significant that in the absence of process redefinition, the implementation of ERP systems brings about little in the way of profound organisational change. In other words, process re-engineering promotes a more profound change within the company.

I.2.3 Project scope through functional coverage

Selected at an early stage by senior management as part of arriving at an organizational vision, the organisational perimeter of the ERP project provides a fair idea of the scope of the changes to be made. Where functional coverage is wide and takes in almost all the company's functions and departments, the ERP project assumes a strategic importance and leads to profound change (Parr, 2000). At this stage, change becomes inevitable and process re-engineering is often embarked upon in order to maximise the benefits of integration. The multiplicity of people involved and the increasing interdependence between selected modules makes the project extremely risky, both technically and organisationally (Urwin, 2001). On the other hand, where ERP is chosen to cover a number of support functions connected with standard processes, the strategic considerations become secondary and the scope of future change is narrower.

I.2.4 Speed through implementation strategy

There are two implementation strategies that may be adopted: the Big Bang or the progressive option. Progressive implementation proceeds module-by-module and/or site-by-site. In this approach, the ability of the ERP project to integrate is often limited. Change is not profound because the organisational processes concerned affect only a part of the organisation. The other units continue to function using their existing

practices as they await their turn to enter the integration perimeter.

Conversely, when a company decides to go for big-bang implementation, it elects to implement all the ERP modules on all sites simultaneously. The financial risks inherent in such a complex project and the interdependence of the modules involved demand rapid implementation in order to maximise the benefits of process integration (Beretta, 2001) and avoid a multiplicity of temporary interfaces and all the other problems connected with introducing organisational change progressively. Big-bang implementation also has more profound effects on change; despite the fact that significant risks are involved and that in the longer term one may doubt the ultimate differences between implementation methods.

I.2.5 Resistance to change through specific developments

Undertaking specific developments is common practice in the context of ERP implementation. They probably deliver operational flexibility by responding to special local needs; nevertheless, they constitute a major long-term restraint on ERP flexibility. According to the conclusions set out in the CIGREF report (1999), specific developments generate significant extra cost and delay, whilst destroying the ability to upgrade to new versions released by the publisher and reducing the relevance of the system.

Over and above providing a response to special local requirements poorly addressed or completely overlooked by the ERP system, the development of special software and interfaces between the installed modules and the other applications maintained by the company reflects the will of the organisation and its members to avoid modifying the existing overall structure and its operation. Seen from this point of view, the need for organisational adaptation is low (Bingi et al., 1999; Brehm et al., 2001) and the process of managing change becomes easier to handle since resistance to change is less pronounced. This practice also allows users to retain a certain amount of room for manoeuvre, whilst enabling IT specialists to protect their territory and continue to exercise power within the organisation (Markus, 1983). This may explain the high number of specific application development requests that emerge during ERP projects. So, the greater the number of specific developments, the less profound the resulting change will be.

ERP implementation poses the problem of change from two different angles: that of the theory of lifecycles and that of changes in the company's method of operation – the transition from a hierarchico-functional approach to a cross-functional one.

I.3 The cross-functional approach

The topics of horizontal process and project management, inter-functional collaboration and integration methods lie at the heart of the changes introduced by companies with the objective of providing greater control over their corporate performance. The literature on cross-functionality puts the emphasis on the precedence of processes over functions and ushers in a new vision of an organisation built around a partition-free horizontal structure and multifunctional/multidisciplinary working teams. It also shows a growing emphasis on the role played by technology in horizontal co-ordination.

I.3.1 Cross-functionality: a new vision of the organisation

The challenge of cross-functionality first appeared in the areas of quality and flow management before being broadened to include innovation (Tarondeau, 1998).

Total Quality approach revealed the limitations of over-compartmentalized organisations, in which lack of quality is generally the result of poor co-ordination between functions. These problems occur at the interfaces between functions and demand the rethinking of communication, co-ordination and co-operation methods as part of overall trans-functional integration. In Total Quality approach, the functional approach is replaced by multifunctional and process-based approaches to organisation and the resulting need for horizontal co-ordination.

This new view of the organisation is opposed to the hierarchico-functional company model. The unit of organisation therefore changes from being the function to become the process which "crosses over" between the formal vertical structures to produce a product or a service (Davenport and

Short, 1990). The horizontal process comprises "a suite of activities which uses one or more inputs to produce an output that offers value to the customer" (Hammer and Champy, *op.cit.*). This approach refocuses the company on its principal need for horizontal co-ordination in order to overcome the difficulties posed by the division of work and the fragmentation of the organisation into specialist activities. Control over processes comes from managing the interactions and relationships between the company's various functions.

Cross-functionality by means of processes also offers a way of describing the company in terms of its operating methods. As Lorino (1995) explains, the process describes the methods of action alongside the structures of power and responsibility conveyed by the formal vertical structure. It is also analysed in terms of the flows of goods or information passing through it. It puts particular emphasis on the information flows required to supply goods or services to the customer. Lastly, it no longer structures activities according to the task- or skill-based logic on which functions or job functions are based, but follows a logic of customer-orientated final objectives. It is instructive to emphasise the fact that, by their very nature, ERP systems match this approach point-for-point. As an organisational approach, ERP therefore comes very close to delivering the cross-functional co-ordination so sought after by companies. However, this pre-supposes that the decision-makers involved have defined an organizational vision prior to implementing the ERP solution.

I.3.2 Cross-functionality: one result of process re-engineering

At operational process level, what is required is the improvement of inter-functional co-ordination and the need to focus on the "management of interdependence" (Rockart and Short, 1995), since there are gains in competitiveness to be made at the interface between functions. Lawrence and Lorsch (1967) and Galbraith (1977) were already stressing the role played by integration facilitators and the horizontal co-ordination of inter-functional teams. The BPR approach (Al-Mashari and Zairi, 2000), whose aim is to improve customer service via process rationalisation, therefore suggests the removal of as many intermediaries as possible at as many different levels of the company as possible in order to shorten the time taken to access and exchange information. Nevertheless, taken overall, BPR is based on vertical integration via a process of vertical decompartmentalization. In the cross-functional organisation, information flows between services and functions without passing through hierarchical channels. Process re-engineering is based on rationalising the horizontal flows within the company to promote a process of horizontal decompartmentalization.

Over and above the relationship between the choice of a particular technology and the business and organisational objectives targeted, it is therefore essential to carry out preliminary work on the organisation to ensure that it will be capable of "absorbing" the new technical systems (Orlikowski, 1992). Added to this is the question that if companies want their ERP system to support a more cross-functional vision of the company, should they not then conduct a process re-engineering project beforehand?

I.3.3   Cross-functionality   and implementation strategy

Three key points emerge from the literature on IT integration as a vector of cross-functionality (Alsène, 1994; Fulk & DeSanctis, 1995; Hanseth & Braa, 1999):

- A process-based approach to flow management based on the sequential interdependence of units contributing to the provision of goods or services: the outputs (whether goods or information) of the upstream units that deliver the inputs for downstream units.

- A cross-functional approach based on pooled interdependence in which the functions concerned share a common database. This sharing of information is a necessary precondition, but is not sufficient in itself to improve customer service.

- Finally, a new company approach is implemented: global management. This means that everyone gains a more global overview of the company in which people learn to work together, rather than separately and sequentially. This requires that they also take account of reciprocal relationships based on

interdependence in the way they work (Lozzi et al., 2000).

Through the various forms of interdependence that it introduces, ERP encourages a cross-functional approach to organisation which takes the user out of his functional silo in direct proportion to the extent of ERP coverage. The wider the integration perimeter chosen, the greater the perception of cross-functionality becomes.

Moreover, it will be easier to make users aware of the organisational effects of ERP in terms of greater cross-functionality if the implementation strategy is introduced rapidly (Adam & O'Doherty, 2000). They will be obliged to take a cross-functional overview quickly and at an earlier stage in order to use ERP without causing major problems.

I.3.4 Cross-functionality and specific developments

Over and above the organisational methods put forward by Lawrence and Lorsch (op.cit.) and Galbraith (op.cit), the emergence of the cross-functional organisation has its origins in the development of IT integration, where the stated objective is to integrate the various functions of the company. The challenge posed by this form of cross-functional integration is to accomplish what the traditional mechanisms of co-ordination failed to deliver. However, it should be stressed that the type of integration selected by the company (interface rather than shared database) has its influence on two aspects of organisation: decompartmentalization and greater autonomy for certain functions; the increase in autonomy of these functions then runs contrary to the inter-functional collaboration sought through IT integration (Alsène, op cit). Is it not true then that, as with integration by means of interfacing applications, specific developments enable interconnections without necessarily providing a cross-functional overview?

I.4. Research model and hypotheses

We have assembled a set of hypotheses for testing, based on our review of existing literature on change, cross-functionality and ERP:

- **H1a**. Process re-engineering promotes a more profound change

- **H1b.** Process re-engineering promotes a more cross-functional overview of the company

- **H2a.** Defining an organizational vision promotes a more profound change

- **H2b.** Defining an organizational vision promotes a more cross-functional overview of the company

- **H3a.** Greater functional coverage promotes a more profound change

- **H3b.** Greater functional coverage promotes a more cross-functional overview of the company

- **H4a.** Faster implementation promotes a more profound change

- **H4b.** Faster implementation promotes a more cross-functional overview of the company

- **H5a.** Specific developments slow down the process of change

- **H5b.** Specific developments do not promote a more cross-functional overview of the company.

The general research framework is summarised in the model shown in figure 2.

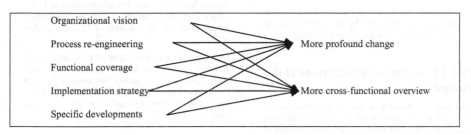

Figure 2: Research model

II – Methodology and results

Our lifecycle approach is based on a fundamentally quantitative method, although it was preceded in 2001 by a qualitative phase which produced eight monographs outlining ERP implementation in the French context (El Amrani et al., 2002). The use of a quantitative method must always be subject to caution when it relies on opinions (Bourdieu, 1994) and makes it difficult to do justice to the accuracy of other conflict- or enaction-based approaches to change. Having opted here for this quantitative approach, we did not want to include these other approaches when drawing up our questionnaire because of the difficulties involved in obtaining objective answers from single interviewees, overloading the questionnaire and reducing the response rate. Data on conflict within IT projects takes the form either of longitudinal work based on multiple measurements of a large base of respondents

(Marciniak, 1996) or case studies (Robey et al., *op.cit*).

The questionnaire[3] listed 62 items and was distributed to a population of 223 SMEs and 116 major companies, all of whom were members of CIGREF[4]. We received 177 responses. 100

---

[3] The questionnaire on which this quantitative survey is based, was divided into four parts. The first part took the form of a general introduction describing the characteristics of respondents and their companies, the type of ERP package installed and the deployment methods used. The second part contained a series of questions on the organisational perimeter addressed by the ERP system, the methods used for the reorganisation and formalisation of processes and the organisational changes observed in the functions concerned subsequent to the introduction of an ERP module. The third part aimed to evaluate the relative contribution made by ERP systems to the flexibility of the company, as well as the flexibility shown by the software package itself. The fourth and final part set out to analyse the effects of ERP introduction on the way work was organised, i.e. changes to task content, the distribution of tasks within and between departments and changes in user opinions. The questions contained in the 1st, 2nd and 4th parts were designed to test our hypotheses. The resulting data was analysed using SPSS statistics processing software.

[4] Club Informatique des Grandes Entreprises Françaises (the IT Club for Major French Companies).

questionnaires, 73 of them from SMEs and 27 from major companies, were useable for the purpose of this survey. The responses were gathered from ERP project managers, information system managers (ISM) and functional managers at a time when the individuals involved were best informed about the process and consequences of their companies' ERP projects.

II. 1 The construction of the variables to be explained

To test our hypotheses, we used items in the questionnaire to construct a change indicator. Two dimensions of change were constructed:

1. The scope of organisational change brought about within the functions of the company as a result of ERP implementation,

2. Changes in user opinion: a more global overview accompanied by an awareness of the cross-functional nature of the company.

II.1.1 Changes in the functions of the company

The scope of change was calculated on the basis of item 17 of the questionnaire: *"How would you score the scope of organisational change achieved in each function?"* This item offered 7 function options[5], each being measured on a scale from "0" (scope of change *zero*) to "4" (scope of change *extensive*). The change indicator relating to company functions could therefore range from the minimum value of *"0"* (no change in any function) up to the maximum value of *"28"* (extensive scope of change in all functions).

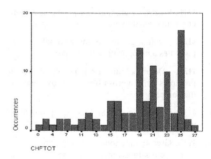

Diagram 1: Frequency diagram for the CHFTOT indicator

The mean obtained for the indicator relating to the scope of change in functions (CHFTOT) amongst the one hundred companies in our sample is 18.93, with a standard deviation of 5.90. We also note a modal value for the indicator of 25 and a median of 20.

One company response reported no change in any function, whilst the highest score of *"27"* also came from a single response. We observe that over two thirds of those companies who had installed at least one module reported a scope of change indicator of over 17.

II.1.2 Cross-functionality

To build a reliable indicator of cross-functionality, we began by taking five items from the questionnaire and using a five-point attitude scale, ranging from *"Completely agree"* to *"Completely disagree"*. 'The topic addressed is the change in user opinion as perceived by the respondent.

- Item 49 *"In your opinion, ERP users have a more global overview of their department"*,

- Item 50 *"In your opinion, ERP users have a more global overview of their company"*,

- Item 51 *"In your opinion, ERP users are more aware of the concept of cross-functionality"*.

- Item 52 *"In your opinion, ERP users are more aware of the effect their actions may have on the work of others"*

- Item 53 *"In your opinion, ERP users believe that they have a single system of reference"*.

[5] Accountancy/finance, production, purchasing, management control, sales management, human resources and Others (project management, logistics, maintenance, etc.).

A reliability analysis of the first three items was then made using Cronbach's alpha coefficient. The result obtained was 0.9232. The alpha coefficient values obtained from the other combinations of these items, i.e. groups of 3, 4 and 5, ranged from 0.40 to 0.80. Given the number of items (3) and scales (5) used, we have retained only items 49, 50 and 51 in constructing the cross-functionality indicator (ITRANSVE).

The cross-functionality indicator therefore groups the values (*0* to *4*) for each item and may assume values of between *"0"* (low level of cross-functionality) to *"12"* (high level of cross-functionality).

Items	Total explained variance (eigen values)			Quality of opinion
	Total	% var	Cumulative %	Extraction
49	2.733	54.657	54.657	0.867
50	1.274	25.484	80.141	0.822
51	0.630	12.605	92.746	0.862
52	0.214	4.289	97.035	0.691
53	0.148	2.965	100	0.766

Table 1: Total explained variance (ITRANSVE)

Extraction method: Analysis of the main components.

Examination of the factor analysis (table 1) shows us that the first three items explain over 90% of the variance seen in the five items used to construct ITRANSVE.

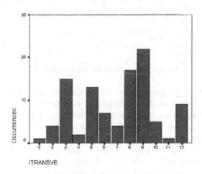

Diagram 2: Frequency diagram for the ITRANSVE indicator

The mean obtained for the cross-functionality indicator (ITRANSVE) amongst the one hundred companies in our sample is 6.99, with a standard deviation of 2.94, a minimum score of *"0"* (one response only) and a maximum score of *"12"* (nine responses). We also note a modal value for the indicator of 9 and a median of 8.

II.2 Independent variables

At this level, we present the independent variables obtained from the results of single criterion breakdown, which enable us to test the scope of change within company functions and the degree of cross-functionality brought about by the introduction of an ERP system.

II.2.1 Process re-engineering (variable: REDE)

Item 16 *"Have you redefined your processes to adapt them to those offered by your ERP system?"*

REDE	Frequency
Completely	1
Widely	62
Moderately	28
Slightly	8
Not at all	0
No response	1
Total	100

Table2: Frequencies of the REDE variable

We would observe that approximately two thirds of respondents said that they had undertaken a widespread redefinition of processes. In most cases, this reconfiguration of processes was undertaken as part of aligning the company's processes with the organisational model offered by the ERP system. Other companies were obliged to redefine their processes given the nature of the way ERP works and the interdependence of the modules installed.

II.2.2 The organizational vision (variable: CIBL)

Item 11 "Was the implementation of your ERP system preceded by the definition of an organizational vision by senior management?

CIBL	Frequency
Yes	61
No	39
Total	100

Table 3: Frequencies of the CIBL variable

Nearly two-thirds (61%) of companies had defined an organizational vision in advance. This task was the main preoccupation of senior management and its form differed depending on the context: companies decided to centralise or decentralise their organisational structures as part of harmonising their processes.

TOTMOD	Frequency
1	7
2	10
3	17
4	13
5	13
6	11
7	16
8	6
9	2
Total	95

Table 4: Frequencies of the TOTMOD variable

II.2.3 Functional coverage (variable: TOTMOD)

Item 2 "Which are the main modules already installed?", from which we have calculated the number of modules installed (TOTMOD).

At the time of the survey, five companies had yet to complete their ERP implementation, which explains the size of the sample (95) tested in respect of this variable (cf. Table 5).

This variable is distributed relatively evenly, with an average of 4.62 modules installed.

II.2.4. Implementation strategy (variable: DEPL)

Item 8 "Which method was used to deploy your ERP?"

DEPL	Frequency
Big-bang	47
Progressive	47
No response	6
Total	100

Table 5: Frequencies of the DEPL variable

The companies in our sample opted in equal measure for one of the two-implementation strategies.

II.2.5 Specific developments (variable: DESP)

Item 37 "Have you opted for specific developments in order to respond to your company's management problems?"

The companies surveyed had made recourse to specific developments. However, the degree to which this option was taken up varied from company to company.

DESP	Frequency
Not at all	19
To a limited degree	17
In several cases	36
In many cases	20
No response	8
Total	100

Table 6: Frequencies of the DESP variable

Before progressing to the results of the tests conducted on our hypotheses, we would like to present some single criterion breakdown results relating to the process of ERP adoption and implementation in France in order to enable comparison with other countries. The organisational changes brought about by information technology can only be interpreted in a socio-economic and temporal context (Carlson et al., 1999), linked to a greater or lesser degree with the intentions of those involved.

II.3 ERP adoption and implementation in France

Several studies and surveys have been conducted in an attempt to understand the nature of projects implemented in French companies. The first trade survey was undertaken by CIGREF in 1999 and addresses the reasons why major French companies felt obliged to adopt ERP and the impact of that decision on their organisations. Stressing the importance of the formulation phase and the problems of selecting the right ERP solution, Besson and Rowe (2001) demonstrated that, over and above purely financial and functional motives, there were five significant reasons behind the decision of major companies to adopt ERP: the ideology of BPR, the desire for complete control over the organisation, the desire to reduce the power of Information Systems Departments (ISD), cost reduction and the conscious or unconscious need to mimic competitors.

II.3.1 The motivation behind ERP projects

In our monographs, we have observed the following motives (amongst others): SNECMA decided to implement an ERP solution to optimise job function-based processes, whilst Renault and Air France opted for ERP to cover support functions. Our quantitative survey reveals that the three leading reasons why major companies adopt ERP systems are: to modernise their information systems (46%), reorganise their processes (25%) and improve the flexibility of the company (12%). The three most important reasons amongst SMEs are: improving the flexibility of the company (32%), reorganising processes (12%) and modernising information systems (8%). The Euro and Year 2000 transitions proved to be turning points which focused companies' attention on the development of their information systems.

II.3.2 The timing of ERP projects

The companies we surveyed began to use their ERP modules in the mid-1990s after an initial period of hesitation. The rate of project implementation accelerated from 1995/1996 and peaked in 1998/1999. With the exception of the selection phase, which took rather longer, there was a constant and relatively even sequence in which more or less one year passed between each of the four stages. Generally speaking,

approximately three years were required for installation.

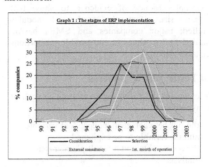

II.3.3 Functional coverage and the distribution of the number of modules

Financial modules were the most frequently deployed, followed by purchasing, sales and production management. It seems likely that the Year 2000 and euro transition processes created the opportunity to replace financial applications, since these events coincided with the installation of a high number of accounting modules. Human Resources modules were rarely implemented. The first implementations in major companies involved chiefly financial, accounting and management control modules, followed by purchasing and supply modules. Amongst SMEs, the modules installed included support modules alongside strategic modules (production and logistics modules for transport companies). This feature can be partly explained by the relatively less complex organisations seen in SMEs.

	Major companies			SMEs		
Number of modules	1-3	4-7	8-10	1-3	4-7	8-10
Frequency (%)	37	59	4	39	52	9

Table 7: Functional coverage of ERP / Comparison between Major Companies/SMEs

Lastly, we observe that when French companies say they have adopted an ERP solution, they often mean that they have adopted only a few of the modules involved (4 modules on average[6]). It should be stressed in this context that there is a remarkable absence of evidence to show that company size affects the number of modules installed: major companies and SMEs having installed ERP modules in comparable proportions (see table above).

II.4 Testing our hypotheses

We examined the following in relation to each of our hypotheses:

- the link between each independent variable and the variable to be explained
- the results obtained by multiple regression analysis
- the results obtained by a stepwise regression analysis.

The presentation of the statistical tests validating or not the hypotheses will be illustrated by examples pulled from the monographs realized during our research project DARES.

II.4.1 Testing hypothesis 1

Table 8 shows the correlation between the redefinition of processes (independent variable REDE), the scope of change in functions and the cross-functionality indicator (the CHFTOT and ITRANSVE variables). The values obtained are significant to 0.01 (bilateral).

REDE	
0.612**	CHFTOT
0.279**	ITRANSVE

Table 8: (Pearson) correlation between reengineering, change indicators and cross-functionality

Hypotheses H1a and H1b are proven:

- The greater the degree of process re-engineering, the more profound the change.

- The greater the degree of process re-engineering, the more cross-functional the company is seen to be by users (as

perceived by respondents).

This statistical result is clearly supported by the outcome pulled from the case of French company Salins du Midi that have engaged, when adopting SAP package, a large redefinition of her organizational processes. The result of this operation was the adoption of a new mode of management supported by a new organizational structure conceived around the Autonomous Strategic Units (USA) by sector. The adoption of the process vision favored also the decompartmentalization of the organizational structure and the institution of a transverse vision. The SAP users have now a better visibility of the work of other members of the firm. Moreover, even within the competence center, a transverse structure was adopted, including operational managers and members of the IS function, and organized to maintain this logic of cross-functionality and handle the necessary improvements for the future flows.

II.4.2 Testing hypothesis 2

Table 9 shows the results obtained by analysing the variance of the organizational vision (nominal independent variable CIBL) with the scope of change in functions and the cross-functionality indicator (the CHFTOT and ITRANSVE variables).

	Sum of squares	DF	Mean of squares	F	Significance
CHFTOT					
Inter-groupes	68,166	1	68,166	1,975	,163
Intra-groupes	3382,344	98	34,514		
Total	3450, 510	99			
ITRANSVE					
Inter-groupes	69,322	1	69,322	8,625	,004
Intra-groupes	787,668	98	8,037		
Total	856,990	99			

Table 9: Analysis of the variance of the organizational vision overview and the change and cross-functionality indicators

---

[6] The breakdown has a statistical basis. The mean has been obtained by dividing the total number of installed modules by the number of companies making up our sample.

Hypothesis H2a is not proven: the definition of a vision organization does not directly promote more profound change. In fact, it seems that other decisions concerning process redefinition and the enlargement of functional cover are taken between the time when the vision organization is defined by senior management and the time at which the ERP system comes into operation. This introduces change into the functions. So, for example, one of our monographs (Air France Company) contains the case where, having encountered problems in interfacing the ERP finance module with specific manufacturing logistics applications, the company decided to enlarge coverage by implementing the ERP manufacturing accounting module, which brought about major changes in the function concerned. The vision initially defined by senior management had not envisaged such profound change. Thus, defining the organizational vision provided a clearer and more cross-functional overview and confirmed senior management's support for faster successful change, but not necessarily more profound change.

On the other hand, **Hypothesis H2b is proven:** where senior management defines an organizational vision, users have a more cross-functional overview of the company. In practice, this means that senior management has set out its vision of the future organisation. This definition is put into practice during the parameterization undertaken by the project team during the engineering phase in the form of ERP parameterization and configuration. It is during this phase of ERP that users begin to perceive greater cross-functionality.

II.4.3 Testing hypothesis 3

Table 10 shows the correlation between functional coverage (the independent variable TOTMOD), the scope of change in functions and the cross-functionality indicator (the CHFTOT and ITRANSVE variables). The values obtained are significant to 0.01 (bilateral).

Hypotheses H3a and H3b are proven:

- The greater the number of modules installed, the greater the degree of change brought about in the functions.

TOTMOD	
0.450**	CHFTOT
0.288**	ITRANSVE

Table 10: (Pearson) correlation between functional coverage and the change and cross-functionality indicators

- The greater the number of modules installed, the more cross-functional the overview perceived by users.

The implementation of principals SAP modules in Salins du Midi produced an important organizational change and allowed the users to have a better vision of the workflow and of the interdependence created by the ERP (sequential, pool and reverse (Geffroy-Maronnat, 2002)), favoring a more transverse vision. For example, one user of the logistic module can ask easily the products inventory in the SAP system, without appealing to production department, to know if he is able to answer or not customer's orders. This operation was long and difficult in the earlier system and mobilized more than two persons. We noted also in others monographs that this transverse vision is translated by an increased attentiveness of the users. Beyond the cross-functionality between departments, the trace back functionality conveyed by the ERP can explain also this redoubling attentiveness.

II.4.4 Testing hypothesis 4

Table 11 shows the results obtained by analysing the variance of the implementation strategy (nominal independent variable DEPL) with the scope of change in functions and the cross-functionality indicator (the CHFTOT and ITRANSVE variables).

Hypotheses H4a and H4b are proven:

- The big-bang (fast) implementation strategy brings about a more profound change

- The big-bang (fast) implementation strategy promotes a more cross-functional overview amongst users

	Sum of squares	DF	Mean of squares	F	Significance
CHFTOT					
Inter-groupes	182,564	1	182,564	5,897	,017
Intra-groupes	2848,426	92	30,961		
Total	3030,989	93			
ITRANSVE					
Inter-groupes	58,255	1	58,255	7,245	,008
Intra-groupes	739,745	92	8,041		
Total	798,000	93			

Table 11: Analysis of the variance of the implementation strategy and the change and cross-functionality indicators

As the *"big-bang"* implementation strategy is significantly and positively linked to the change and cross-functionality indicators, this produces a more profound degree of change.

This report is very obvious when we compare changes produced at Renault and Salins du midi. By opting to Big-Bang implementation, les Salins du Midi show clearly her attention to work officially with the new organizational structure. On the other hand, a progressive implementation of three SAP modules by Renault, a project that started in 1998, did not produce the expected changes and upset the organization, which continues until today arranging its local processes and structures.

A Big Bang rather than progressive implementation favors more easily the transverse appropriation of the ERP. Indeed, the monographs show that in the progressive implementation, users have more difficulties to appropriate this transverse vision as far as the ERP environment is not stabilized. This instability compels users to revise their interactions with other functions at every new implementation. This implementation strategy can deform any interest of integration benefits if there is no global follow-up and a project management mode.

II.4.5 Testing hypothesis 5

Table 12 shows the correlation between the size of specific developments (independent variable DESP), the scope of change in functions and the cross-functionality indicator (the CHFTOT and ITRANSVE variables). The values obtained are significant to 0.01 (bilateral) for CHFTOT and ITRANSVE.

DESP	
- 0.285**	CHFTOT
0.270**	ITRANSVE

Table 12: (Pearson) correlation between specific developments and the change and cross-functionality indicators

Hypothesis H5a is proven: The negative correlation with CHFTOT is in accordance with our hypothesis. The more specific applications the company develops, the narrower the scope of change seen in the functions.

On the other hand, **hypothesis H5b is not proven:** Specific developments do not restrict users gaining a cross-functional overview. The positive correlation between the "DESP" variable and the "ITRANSVE" cross-functionality indicator is unexpected and contrary to our initial hypothesis.

There are two possible explanations for this unexpected result. According to the IS managers and project managers interviewed at the time of writing our monographs, users do not differentiate between specific applications and standard ERP modules. For these users, specific developments are "transparent" and form part of a shared information system. It may also be that respondents have interpreted the term "specific developments" in a wider sense than we anticipated. Such a wide interpretation could include all developments other than ERP modules, thus including truly specific developments alongside interfaces with parts of the information system other than the ERP package. In this latter case, there would be improved IT cross-functionality and therefore a positive correlation between DESP and ITRANSVE. A significant correlation of 0.277 between the DESP variable and the variable concerned with the change in the sharing of tasks between departments would seem to corroborate our argument.

II.4.6 The main factors contributing to change inside functions (CHFTOT)

We began with a multiple regression using the TOTMOD (functional coverage), DEPL (implementation strategy), REDE (process re-engineering) and DESP (specific development) variables. We obtained an adjusted R2 value of 0.593, with 000 significance. In order to take account of the links between the various independent variables, we then conducted a stepwise regression. All four stages of the model produced the same result.

Thus:

- the greater the number of modules installed,

- the greater the extent of process re-engineering,

- the fewer specific developments undertaken

- combined with "big-bang" implementation strategy,

the greater the change brought about by ERP within the functions of the company.

II.4.7 The main factors contributing to change in opinions (ITRANSVE)

We began with a multiple regression using the TOTMOD (functional coverage), DEPL (implementation strategy), REDE (process re-engineering) and CIBL (organizational vision) variables. We obtained an adjusted R2 value of 0.163, with 00 significance. In order to take account of the links between the various independent variables, we then conducted a stepwise regression. The two stages of the model led to the exclusion of two independent variables: process re-engineering (REDE) correlated with CIBL, whilst the implementation strategy (DEPL) correlated significantly with TOTMOD. Adjusted R2 = 0.146, significant to .001.

Thus:

- the greater the number of modules installed,

- in combination with the definition of a vision organization by senior management

the greater the cross-functional overview amongst users.

III. Discussion and general conclusion

We make a distinction between the results relating to change and those relating to cross-functionality.

In terms of **change**, all our hypotheses are proven, except the one based on the prior definition of a vision organisation. We believe that this promotes faster change, but not necessarily more profound change. Moreover, the regression coefficients of the multivariable analyses are high and retain all the variables. This demonstrates that approaching change in terms of a lifecycle and preparing for it by defining a vision organization (for speed), introducing process re-engineering and opting for speed (through choice of implementation strategy) and scope (through functional coverage) is pertinent. The dialectic approach taken by others has already demonstrated the relevance of taking account of resistance to change. We have interpreted the creation of specific developments as evidence of such resistance, which occurs during the engineering phase and sometimes even prior to that. This interpretation remains to be assessed accurately from the viewpoint of other participants, but does not detract from the fact that the existence of specific developments holds back change. From this perspective, specific developments are a factor in the lifecycle of management and company information systems in as much as they are taken into account during the development of new versions and/or have a direct effect on the strategic flexibility of the company (El Amrani et al., 2002).

In terms of **cross-functionality**, all our hypotheses are proven, except that based on specific developments. However, when examined using stepwise regression, only functional coverage and the definition of a vision organization explain the emergence of a cross-functional overview of the company.

Finally, all the tests demonstrate that functional coverage is a factor that should be taken into account in ERP research and, more especially, by those seeking to understand change. This may enable us to go further in analysing the contribution these systems make to financial performance. Another outcome of this research involves exploring the concept of cross-functionality and its measurement.

However, some limitations and reservations relating to this study can be grouped together under two headings. The size of our sample (100 companies) is of average size when compared with the quantitative work published internationally on the subject of ERP. Its structure favoured those responses coming from medium-sized companies. The non-random selection of the individuals concerned causes a bias in the analysis of responses (individualised requests to participate in the survey according to previously defined and validated criteria). However, given the context of this study, it is fair to consider the size of this sample to be sufficient since this is a difficult area given the sensitivity of the issues addressed and the difficulty to gain access to respondents, who are difficult to identify since their occupation is not a traditional company appointment.

These very clear-cut contributions and results require greater explanation in a number of respects:

1- Cross-functionality is examined in this research from the point of view of a single participant and merits being examined in greater detail from the user viewpoint.
2- The purpose of specific developments should be investigated in order to address any remaining speculation as to their final influence based on the observations of the cases we have studied.
3- The longitudinal approach taken here is restricted purely to the overall description of ERP issue and should be developed and carried forward as a basis for future research into the progressive effects of increasing functional coverage, thus taking account of version upgrades.

REFERENCES

Adam, F., O'Doherty, O. (2000). "Enterprise Resource Planning: Myth and Reality" *5ème colloque de l'AIM, Montpellier, France.*

Al-Mashari, M., Zairi, M. (2000), "Revisiting BPR: a holistic review of practice and development", *Business Process Management Journal*, Vol 6, n°1, pp 10-42.

Alsène, E. (1994), « L'intégration informatique et la transformation de l'organisation », *Revue Internationale du travail*, vol. 133, n° 5-6, pp 719-739.

El Amrani R., Geffroy-Maronnat B., Marciniak R., Rowe F., Bidan M., (2002), « PGI, flexibilités, organisation du travail et représentations dans les moyennes et grandes entreprises », rapport DARES-Ministère du Travail.

Bachelard, G. (1938), *La formation de l'esprit scientifique*, Paris : Vrin, (réédition, 1993).

Bancroft, N. (1996). *Implementing SAP/R3: How to introduce a large system into a large organization*, London: Manning/Prentice Hall.

Beath, C. A. (1991) : "Supporting the Information Technology Champion", *MIS Quarterly*, 15, 3, pp 355-372.

Beretta S., (2001), "Unlashing the Integration Potential of ERP Systems : the Role of process based performance measurement systems", *3rd Workshop on Management accounting Change*, Siena, 17-19 May.

Besson, P. (1999). " Les ERP à l'épreuve de l'organisation ", *Systèmes d'Information et Management*, vol.4, n°4, pp 21-52.

Besson, P., Rowe, F. (2001), "ERP project dynamics and enacted dialogue : perceived understanding, perceived leeway, and the nature of task-related conflicts", *Database for Advances in Information Systems*; Vol. 32, n° 4; pp 47-66.

Bingi P., Sharma M. K., Golda J.K., (1999), "Critical issues affecting an ERP implementation", *Information Systems Management*, pp.7-14.

Boudreau, M-C., (1999), "ERP Implementation and Forms of Organizational Change", working paper, Georgia university.

Bouillot, C. (1999). " Mise en place de Progiciels de Gestion Intégrée à l'occasion de fusions et cessions d'entreprises dans un contexte international ", *Systèmes d'Information et Management*, vol.4, n°4, pp 91-106.

Bourdieu, P (1994), *Le sens pratique*, les éditions de Minuit.

Brehm L., Heinzl A., Markus M. L., (2001), "Tailoring ERP systems : a spectrum of choices and their implications", *Proceedings of the 34th Hawaii International Conference on System Sciences*.

Carlson P.J., Khan B.K., Rowe F., (1999), « Organizational Impacts of New Communication Technology : A Comparison of Cellular Phone adoption in France and the United States », *Global Information Management*, Vol.7, n°.3

CIGREF (1999) : Club Informatique des Grandes Entreprises Françaises : «Retours d'expériences ERP », rapport consultable sur www.cigref.com

Coat F., Favier M., (1999), « Passage à l'ERP et refonte du système d'information : le cas des ASF», *Systèmes d'Information et Management*, vol.4, n°4.

Crozier M., Friedberg E., (1977), *L'acteur et le système*, Paris, Seuil.

Davenport T.H. (1998) «Putting the Entreprise in the Entreprise system », *Harvard Business Review*. Jul-Aug.

Davenport T.H., Short J.E. (1990), « The new industrial engineering information technology and Business Processus Redesign», *Sloan management Review*, Summer.

Davenport, T. (1993), *Process Innovation : Re-engineering work through information technology*, Harvard Business School Press, Moston, MA.

Esteves, J., Pastor, J. (2001). "Entreprise Resource Planning Sysytems Research : an annotated bibliography", *Communications of the Association for Information Systems*, Vol.7.

Forest, G.,(1999), « Généalogie des ERP et gestion des flux physiques », *Systèmes d'Information et Management*, vol.4, n°4.

Fulk J., DeSanctis G., (1995), "Electronic Communication and Changing Organizational Forms", Organization Science, Vol.6, N°.4, July-August.

Galbraith, J. (1977), *Organization Design*, Addison-Wesley

Gallivan M., Hofman D., Orlikowski W., (1994), "Implementing radical change: gradual versus rapid pace", *XVth International Conference on Information Systems*, Vancouver, pp 325-40.

Geffroy-Maronnat, B., (2002), « Intégration informationnelle et formes d'interdépendances : quels enjeux organisationnels ? le cas de l'ERP dans une PME », *7ème colloque de l'AIM*, Hammemet, Tunisie

Grover, V. Jeong, S. Kettinger, W. Teng, J.(1995). "The implementation of Business Process Reengineering", *Journal of Management Information Systems*, vol.12, n°1, pp 109-144.

Hammer M., Champy J. (1991), *Reengineering the corporation*, Haper Business, New York.

Hanseth, O., Braa, K.,(1999), " SAP as Emergent Infrastructure in a Global Organization", *Systèmes d'Information et Management*, vol.4, n°4.

Hong K. K., Kim Y. G., (2002), "The critical success factors for ERP implementation: an organizational fit perspective", *Information & Management*, 40, pp. 25-40.

Jarvenppa S. L., Ives B. (1991) : « Executive Involvement and Participation in the Management of Information Technology", *MIS Quarterly*, 15, 2, pp 205-227.

Lawrence, P.R., Lorsch J.W. (1973), *Adapter les structures de l'entreprise, intégration et différenciation*, Les Ed. d'Organisation – Paris.

Leonard-Barton D., (1988). « Implementation characteristics of organizational innovations », *Communication Research*, October, pp 603-631.

Lesuisse R., (2002), «De la spécificité à la généricité des logiciels », in Rowe F (ed.), *Faire de la recherche en systèmes d'information*, Paris, Vuibert.

Lorino P. (1995), « Le déploiement de la valeur par les processus », *Revue Française de Gestion*, N°104, pp 55-71.

Lozzi, M., Maggiolini, P., Migliarese, P., (2000), « Joint design of organization processes and information system : a methodology based on action theory », *5e Colloque de l'AIM*, Montpellier, France.

Marciniak, R. (1996), «Management des projets informatiques : complexité et gestion des conflits », *Systèmes d'Information et Management*, vol. 1, n°1, pp 27-50.

Marciniak, R., Rowe, F. (1997). *Systèmes d'information, dynamique et organisation*, Paris: Economica.

Markus M. L., (1983), "Power, politics, and MIS implementation", *Communication of the ACM*, 26, 6, pp. 430-444.

Markus M.L., Tanis C. (2000). The Enterprise System Experience: from adoption to success, in *Framing the domains of I.T. management*, Zmud R. (ed.), Cincinnati: Pinnaflex, pp 173-208.

Markus M.L., Tanis C., Van Fenema P. (2000), "Multisite ERP implementations", *Communications of the ACM*, vol.43, n°4, pp 42-46.

Nelson K., Somers T. M. (2001), "The Impact of Critical Success Factors across the Stages of ERP Implementations", *Proceedings of the 34th Hawaii International Conference on System Sciences*.

Noble, D.F., (1979) : "Social choice in machine design : The case of automatically controlled machine tools" in *Case studies on the labor process*, Monthly Review Press, New York, pp 18-50.

Orlikowski, W. (1992), "Learning from Notes : organizational issues in Groupware Implementation" Technical Report, Center for coordination Science, MIT, Cambridge, MA.

Orlikowski, W. (1996), "Improvising organizational transformation over time: a situated change perspective", *Information Systems Research*, vol.7, n°1, pp 63-92.

Parr A. N.,(2000), « A Taxonomy of ERP Implementation Approches", *Proceedings of the 33rd Hawaii International Conference on System Sciences*.

Poston R., Grabski S. (2001), "The impact of Entreprise Resource Planning Systems on firm performance", *XXIInd International Conference on Information Systems*, New Orleans.

Ravarini, A., Tagliavini, M., Pigni, F., Sciuto, D. (2000), "A Framework for Evaluating ERP Acquisition within SMEs", *5ème colloque de l'AIM, Montpellier, France.*

Robey, D., Ross, J. W., and Boudreau, M.-C., (A venir) "Learning to Implement Enterprise Systems: An Exploratory Study of the Dialectics of Change," *Journal of Management Information System.*

Robey D., Boudreau M.-C. (2000), "Organizational consequences of information technology : dealing with diversity in empirical research", in *Framing the domains of I.T. management*, Zmud R. (ed.), Cincinnati: Pinnaflex, pp 51-64.

Rockart J.F., Short J.E. (1995), « L'organisation en réseau et le management de l'interdépendance », in *L'entreprise compétitive au futur, Technologies de l'information et transformation de l'organisation*, de Michael S. Scott Morton, Les Ed. d'Organisation, chap. 7, pp 233-272.

Rowe, F. (1999), « Cohérence, intégration informationnelle et changement : esquisse d'un programme de recherche à partir des Progiciels Intégrés de Gestion », *Systèmes d'Information et Management*, vol.4, n°4, pp 3-20.

Saint-Léger, G., Nubert, G., Pichot, L., (2002), « Projet ERP : incidence des spécificités des entreprises sur les FCS », *7ème colloque de l'AIM*, Hammemet, Tunisie.

Scott, W. (1987). *Organizations: rational, natural, and open systems* (2nd Ed.), Englewood Cliffs, NJ: Prentice Hall.

Tarondeau, J.C. (1998), « De nouvelles formes d'organisation pour l'entreprise. La gestion par les processus », *Cahier Français, Management et organisation des entreprises*, n° 287. La Documentation Française, Paris.

Truex, D. (2001). "ERP Systems as facilitating and confounding factors in corporate mergers: the case of two Canadian telecommunications companies", *Systèmes d'Information et Management*, vol.6, n°1.

Urwin G., (2001), "Managing complexity in implementing ERP projects", *Proceeding of the Twelfth Australian Conference on Information Systems.*

Van de Ven, A. Scott Poole, M. (1995), "Explaining development and change in organizations", *Academy of Management Review*, vol.20, n°3, pp 510-40.

Van Everdingen, Y. Van Hillegersberg, J. Waarts, E. (2000), "ERP Adoption by European midsize companies", *Communications of the ACM*, vol.43, n°4, pp 27-31.

Yazici, H.J. (2002), « The role of communication in organizational change : an empirical investigation », *Information & Management*, Vol. 39, Issue 7, July, pp 539-552.

A MODEL-DRIVEN APPROACH FOR ITEM SYNCHRONIZATION AND UCCNET INTEGRATION IN LARGE E-COMMERCE ENTERPRISE SYSTEMS

Simon Cheng, Mathews Thomas
IBM Global e-business Solution Center, Dallas, TX, USA
Email: scheng@us.ibm.com

Santhosh Kumaran, Amaresh Rajasekharan, Frederick Wu, Yiming Ye, Ying Huang
IBM T. J. Watson Research Center, Yorktown Heights, NY, USA
Email: sbk@us.ibm.com

Keywords: Business Process Integration, artifacts, entities, large scale enterprise, item synchronization

Abstract: The pervasive connectivity of the Internet and the powerful architecture of the WWW are changing many market conventions and creating a tremendous opportunity for conducting business on the Internet. Digital marketplace business models and the advancement of Web related standards are tearing down walls within and between different business artifacts and entities at all granularities and at all levels, from devices, operating systems and middleware to directory, data, information, application, and finally the business processes. As a matter of fact, business process integration (BPI), which entails the integration of all the facets of business artifacts and entities, is emerging as a key IT challenge. In this paper, we describe our effort in exploring a new approach to address the complexities of BPI. More specifically, we study how to use a solution template based approach for BPI and explore the validity of this approach with a frequently encountered integration problem, the item synchronization problem for large enterprises. The proposed approach can greatly reduce the complexities of the business integration task and reduce the time and amount of effort of the system integrators. Different customers are deploying the described Item Synchronization system.

1 INTRODUCTION

The emerging growth of electronic commerce over the Internet is bringing exciting opportunities for companies. However, reaping the full potential of e-commerce will depend on achieving Business Process Integration (BPI) - with minimal cost and effort. A successful BPI strategy can bring the implementation of e-business systems to a whole new level of productivity. As a matter of fact, system integration is emerging as a key IT challenge. The Gartner Group estimates that 40% of the average IT budget is spent on Systems Integration http://www.eaijournal.com/Article.asp?ArticleID=29 5). Integration is a multi-faceted problem, spanning the whole IT spectrum. At the lower ends of the spectrum are device integration, OS integration, and middleware integration. At the higher levels are directory integration, data integration, information integration, and application integration. At the highest level is business process integration (BPI). The BPI typically entails all the other facets of the integration problem across the spectrum.

It is crucial in electronic commerce to explore new approaches, paradigms, languages, technologies, and tools to effectively address the integration challenge. Currently, organizations run the business by defining their own business processes. These business processes define the type of transactions and the handling of exceptions in the context of process execution. Examples of such business processes include processing of Purchase Orders, Sales Orders, Request for Quotes (RFQ), and Contracts. Typically these business processes are long running transactions with complex interaction among various disjoint software

O. Camp et al. (eds.), Enterprise Information Systems V, 77-84.

components. These transactions in reality are not fully automated and have to use diverse software components, legacy systems and possibly many databases and backend enterprise information systems (EIS). Most of these processes span intra- and inter-organization boundaries, which might involve the task of automating business processes both within the enterprise and also with suppliers, retailers and other partners. However, it is often necessary for businesses to alter their business processes to keep pace with changing requirements and market conditions. It is not uncommon in the industry to upgrade one or more existing applications to improve efficiency and increase resource utilization. Given the complexity in the business processes, these updates are seldom simple, and often trigger a ripple effect across various components. The goal of the integration effort is to make different components work together in a way that minimizes the changes required when the business process changes. The idea is to bring all these pre-fabricated pieces together and choreograph them to effectively automate the business process.

In this paper, we propose a model driven approach for business process integration. We argue that such an approach can reduce the complexity of BPI solutions in three ways. (1) It facilitates component reuse leading to reduced development time. (2) It enables architecture reuse leading to more repeatable solutions. (3) It enables the formalization of best practices into a well-defined methodology. We explore the validity of this approach using an integration problem frequently encountered in the retail industry. We present a case study in which we apply the model-driven business integration approach to address the item synchronization problem. Item Synchronization is the process by which a supplier introduces a new product to the market through retailers. A closely related process is used to update the attributes of an existing product. These processes are complex because a supplier's product identification code, associated attributes codes, and database structures are usually different from those of the retailers. Currently, much of the item synchronization process is accomplished manually. Expediting this process and reducing its cost has been a challenge for large enterprises. This is particularly true for enterprises with multiple divisions, which own and maintain their own divisional Item Databases. These enterprises not only need to synchronize their databases internally but also need to synchronize with their many trading partners through item updates.

This paper is organized as follows. We begin with a description of the model driven business integration approach. This is followed by the detailed definition of the item synchronization problem. Next we derive a "solution template" for item synchronization based on the principles of model driven business integration. We describe a concrete implementation of a solution for the item synchronization problem based on this solution template. We conclude with an analysis of this approach in the context of related work in this area.

2 MODEL DRIVEN BUSINESS INTEGRATION

There are two primary reasons that contribute to the complexity of BPI solutions: (1) The need for a multitude of applications and systems distributed over the network and across enterprise boundaries to work together and deliver new functionality (2) The variability of the solution requirements between customer instances. In the model-driven approach, a small number of arbitrary modeling elements are used to express a large number of solution instances. By tuning the model parameters, we customize a specific solution instance. The structure of these modeling elements and the relationships between them are formalized via a metamodel. The definition of this metamodel is a key aspect of our approach.

2.1 Metamodel for Business Process Integration

The metamodel defines a common architecture for all BPI solutions. The modeling elements generated from the metamodel may be partitioned into the following functional modules: Process choreography components that choreograph the execution of business processes, conversational adapters for B2B integration and enterprise application integration, and screenflows for user experience integration. The metamodel supports solution management and access control specifications by decorations of the model elements.

The metamodel is defined via compositions. We begin with the following three simple constructs as the building blocks of the metamodel:

Business Objects (BOs) model the business data. Examples include Purchase Order, Contract, and Advance Shipping Notice (ASN).

Connectors model the components used for protocol adaptation. Examples include IIOP Connector, MQ Connector, and SOAP Connector.

Commands model an abstract operation. Examples include Create PO, Send ASN, and Cancel Contract.

We compose a small set of higher-order modeling elements, called "modeling artifacts", using these basic building blocks. There are four such modeling artifacts: (1) Adaptive Documents (2) Flows (3) Screenflows and (4) Adapters. These compositions are driven by a set of organizational structures. There are three such organizational structures: (1) State machine (2) Flow composition model (3) Hierarchies. Below we discuss the modeling artifacts in detail.

Adaptive Documents (ADocs) are used to model the business artifacts of a solution. The business artifacts are different from business objects. The business artifacts are what the business process is all about. A business artifact could be "managing" a large number of business objects. A business artifact has a well-defined lifecycle, with a finite number of states. A business artifact is a semi-autonomous entity with state-dependent behavior. This behavior defines how the artifact responds to business events.

The ADoc metamodel is partitioned into two sections, a "controller" section that models the behavior of the business artifact and an "entity" section that models the business objects managed by the artifact. We model the behavior of a business artifact by means of a finite state machine and the Command design pattern (Alexander 1977). The entity section is merely an aggregation of the primary keys of the business objects. A complete description of the ADoc metamodel is given in (Kumaran).

A flow artifact models the flow of control or data as a directed graph. It consists of a set of "activity" nodes and a partial order among these activities. The activities may be a simple command, another flow, or a temporal ADoc. There are two types of flow artifacts, microflows and macroflows. The microflows are atomic and uninterruptible while the macroflows are long running and interruptible.

The ability to define flows as activities leads to hierarchical compositions of flows. All terminal activities of a microflow are commands. In a macroflow, there is at least one terminal activity that is a temporal ADoc. The structure of a temporal ADoc is exactly the same as a regular ADoc, except that it models the activity lifecycle.

The screenflows model the user interaction with the BPI solution. Screenflows are modeled as compositions of "views" using a state machine. The state machine defines the "controller" in the classic Model-View-Controller paradigm. The views are context-driven, implying that the views change based on the role of the user and the context in which the user is interacting with the system. The views define the data being presented to the user and a set of actions that can be taken by the user. A combination of commands and business objects can

be used to define a view. The state machine controller that choreographs the screenflow may use commands as part of state transitions to access the "model" in the MVC sense. This model could be an ADoc, an activity in a flow, or an adapter.

The adapters model the integration logic for B2B and EIS integration. It uses business objects, commands, and connectors. An adapter uses a connector for protocol adaptation. It uses a source business object, a target business object, and the mappings between them to define semantic adaptation. A command defines the abstraction of the action performed by an adapter.

Finally, a global composition model enables the synthesis of BPI solutions from the modeling artifacts discussed above. The global composition model provides a mechanism to compose screenflows with the ADocs, the ADocs with the activities, and the adapters with the activities or ADocs.

2.2 Solution Templates for Business Process Integration

A set of ADocs, flows, screenflows, and adapters may be defined for a specific solution domain. These artifacts may be composed into a BPI solution using the global composition model. The resulting composition of artifacts is called a "solution template". For example, we may define a global composition for the item synchronization problem to create a Solution Template for Item Synchronization.

A solution template may include prototypical implementations of the modeling artifacts. Thus a solution template can provide not merely the metamodel, but the initial solution implementation itself. The implementation team can customize this initial solution to create a final solution using business rules and policies specific to a customer. More details on the solution template design can be found in (Huang).

3 ITEM SYNCHRONIZATION PROBLEM

Designing and implementing solutions for item synchronization is challenging even with a very small number of internal item databases and trading partners, and is highly complex with multiple item databases and trading partners. The complexity arises from the fact that enterprises and the trading partners need to agree not only on the communication protocol, but also on the processes, message formats, message semantics, message contents, audit requirements, etc.

Traditionally the trading partners (suppliers and retailers) exchange the catalog information in a fairly proprietary way: The retailer checks the supplier catalogs periodically to learn of any changes, or the supplier publishes the catalog directly into the retailer's systems. Both approaches have serious shortcomings. In the first model where the retailer polls the supplier database, the problem is the polling interval. For example, a supplier who is offering a product may change its price or available quantity. This will not be communicated to the retailer until the retailer chooses to check the catalog again. In some cases this time lag could be large. If the time gap were large, the catalog databases at both ends would be out of synch for a long time. One way to solve this problem would be to use a "Supplier Push" model as opposed to a "Retailer Pull" model. In the supplier push model, it is the supplier who pushes the data into the retailer side systems whenever there is an update. While this reduces the risk of catalog items being out of synch, it introduces a significant burden on the supplier. Many small suppliers have limited resources and IT skills. Requiring the supplier to push the catalog to retailer systems means expecting the supplier to understand the retailer's systems and interfaces. The supplier needs to understand the schema, interfaces and the data of interest at the retailer side for each retail partner. This imposes a significant load on the supplier. Moreover, a change on the supplier side has to be triggered if one of the retailers changes its data format or interfaces. This makes the system difficult to maintain. In this supplier push model, the supplier needs to understand the following aspects of the retailer's systems:

Data format

Data compliance, validation

Publish / Search / Update capabilities

System connectivity

Application interfaces

Transport format (XML standard or business objects, etc.)

Keeping track of all the above factors for every retailer imposes a heavy workload on the supplier. Extending the scenario a little bit, if a new retailer wants to do business with the supplier, the supplier needs to learn the new retailer's systems and build the required infrastructure to handle the retailer's requirements. Clearly this model cannot be considered scalable. In the ideal world, the supplier-retailer interaction could be described as "plug & play". That means that the trading partners should be able to work together without needing to understand each other's systems and without needing to change each other's systems. Extending this model, it would

be ideal to isolate the supplier from any changes at the retailer side and vice versa. This brings us to a "hub and spoke" architecture. In this architecture, we have the hub in the center capturing information about all the trading partners. On one side we have the suppliers and on the other side we have the retailers. All the trading partners interact with the hub, remaining oblivious to the system intricacies on the other side of the hub.

In the hub and spoke architecture, we can get the best of both worlds viz., Retailer Pull and the Supplier Push. The idea is to have the supplier push the item information to the hub, which transfers the data to the retailer. The advantages of this architecture are as follows:

The supplier systems need interact only with the hub. As a consequence, the supplier does not need to have intelligence to transform the data into different formats. All that is required at the supplier side is the knowledge of hub side interfaces and data formats.

The retailer systems need not poll the supplier systems. The hub can transfer the item updates to the retailer side through a B2B transport.

The retailer can also "subscribe" to a set of items or a category of items and any changes to them can be "published" to the retailer side from the hub.

UCCnet is an example of such a hub, providing an industry-wide synchronization database of product information for the CPG Industries (www.uccnet.org). It has gained a lot of attention recently because of increasing industry support from major retailers such as Wal-Mart, Ahold, and Shaw's. UCCnet enables the participating trading partners, such as suppliers and buyers, to synchronize their item and related information via its portal and/or its machine-to-machine communication gateway.

Specifically, the UCCnet model has the following two key objectives:

To provide a shareable registry of basic data about Universal Product Code (UPC) encoded items and the businesses that use them. One could think of this as a list of registered UPC's, called Global Trade Item Numbers (GTIN), and a list of every member company and its locations, called the Global Location Numbers (GLN).

To publish and enforce standards, especially around processes (e.g., New Item Add) and transaction formats. This latter role is one that the UCCnet has borrowed from its parent company, the Universal Code Council, Inc. (UCC).

A supplier initiates UCCnet processes by adding the new product (item) information to UCCnet. Once the new item is in UCCnet, the supplier can publish the new item to selected retailers and their organizations. A retailer subscribes to UCCnet publications/notifications with user-defined filters.

When the retailer receives a new item publication from the supplier, the retailer responds with one of the possible UCCnet pre-defined responses: AUTHORIZE, PREAUTHORIZE, PEND, REJECT, and DE-AUTHORIZE. Updating item information in UCCnet and publishing the updates to retailers follows essentially the same flow.

It should be noted that UCCnet currently only edits/validates 60+ attributes for a product, whereas a product may have hundreds of attributes of interest to retailers. A supplier whose backend systems do not have all of the required UCCnet attributes would need to complete any missing attributes via automatic and/or manual data entry before adding the item information to UCCnet. Many retailers will also require the supplier to provide the additional non-UCCnet attributes before the retailer validates and accepts the data. Methods of receiving the attributes from a supplier, editing them, and storing them in the retailer's backend systems vary from electronic communication via EDI to manual data entry by the supplier and/or the retailer.

4 SOLUTION TEMPLATE DEFINITION

We use the item synchronization problem as one of the examples to validate the solution template approach for business process integration. A complete solution for item synchronization extends enterprise boundaries and will involve one or more hubs, several retailers, and a large number of suppliers. In this paper, we focus on the solution components that need to be deployed on the retailer side for item synchronization. We define a solution template for retailer-side item synchronization process.

4.1 Metamodel for Business Process Integration

The item synchronization process on the retailer side may be decomposed into the following stages: Initial Entry, Complete/Verify, Approval, Update Backends, and Acknowledgement. Initial Entry is the initial handling of the new item data from UCCnet. Complete/Verify is the step of completing missing attributes of the item required for a retailer's backend(s) but not provided by UCCnet. Approval is the step of approving the completed item data. Update Backends is the step of updating the retailer's backend(s) with the item data. Acknowledgement is the step of sending acknowledgement back to the supplier.

4.2 Process Choreography Components

The business artifact associated with the item synchronization process is "Item Data", which is modeled as an ADoc (Kumaran). The arrival of the Item Data message at the retailer side triggers the creation of the ItemData ADoc. The ADoc spawns a workflow for completion, inspection, verification, and approval of the item data. Once it is approved, the ADoc updates the backend systems and sends notifications as necessary.

The verification, completion, and approval of item data constitute a collaborative workflow process. The macroflow artifact of the metamodel may be used to model this workflow. The macroflow defines a set of activities and a partial order among them.

4.3 User Experience Components

The screenflow artifacts that make up the user experience components of the solution template are shown in Figure 1. Each screenflow artifact has an associated role property that determines the set of users who may interact with the system via that screenflow.

4.4 Adapters

The last set of components in the solution template consists of the B2B connectors and EIS adapters. Figure 1 shows the B2B connectors in the template. These artifacts are used to model the B2B integration of the item synchronization solution. In particular, this includes the integration of the retailer systems with the supplier systems and/or hub systems. The B2B connectors in the template stores information on the integration partner, integration protocol, purpose of integration, and the data being exchanged.

Figure 1 shows the adapters used for integrating the enterprise systems of the retailer with the item synchronization process. For each adapter, the template stores the target system, the data being integrated, and the purpose of the integration.

4.5 Putting It All Together

The final step in the definition of the solution template is the global composition of the solution artifacts into an end-to-end solution for item synchronization.

The Item Data ADoc provides the context for the activities in the Verify-Approve workflow. At execution time, when these activities become available, they dynamically bind with the Item Data ADoc. This implies that all business events directed to the Item Data ADoc are propagated to the temporal ADoc representing the activity that is bound to the ADoc. The global composition model facilitates the definition of this dynamic binding between ADocs and activities.

Each of the screenflows connects to the Item Data ADoc. The EIS adapters are connected to the ADoc via the command invocations in the state machine transitions. Certain B2B adapters can trigger business events that lead to the creation of an ADoc while others serve as the receivers for the commands that get executed by the ADoc controller. Figure 1 shows a complete solution template, albeit highly simplified.

4.6 Customization

We customize a solution template by tuning the model parameters to match the needs of a specific customer. For example, we can customize the ADoc behavior by changing the definition of the state machine, the commands that get executed as part of the state transitions, and/or the receivers of these commands. The macro and micro flow definitions can be changed as well. Screenflow definitions can be easily modified to suit the needs of a specific engagement. Adapters may be modified or new adapters may be added. These changes are done at the modeling level and very little, if any, code changes are needed.

5 CUSTOMER VALIDATION

This section discusses the validation of our approach by applying the item synchronization solution template to four retailers. Changing the definitions of the modeling artifacts and the global composition model easily accommodates the customization needs.

Various artifacts of the solution template orchestrate the execution of the item synchronization scenario for Retailer A, which is a UCCnet subscriber, as follows. In response to a query from Retailer A, UCCnet sends a New Item Message to the retailer through the UCCnet Connector. The UCCnet Connector immediately persists the message for audit purposes and sends it to process choreography engine resulting in the creation of an Item Data ADoc. The ADoc initiates a workflow process. The first step in the workflow is to notify (by e-mail) the Assistant Category Manager of the arrival of a new item. The Assistant Category Manager logs onto the system, views the UCCnet data for the new item, and adds attribute data specific to Retailer A, such as an internal product identifier. This interaction is modeled using the CompleteVerify screenflow. Upon completion of input by the Assistant Category Manager, the workflow notifies a user on the supplier side to add further data that is specific to Retailer A, such as the discounted cost based on a contract between the supplier and the retailer. When this step is complete, workflow notifies the Retailer's Category Manager, who verifies the complete set of item attributes and makes the decision to approve or reject the new item for the retailer's stores. Approval completes the workflow process, and initiates an update of the retailer's master catalog by the RETEK adapter. After the master catalog update is successful, the ADoc instructs the UCCnet Connector to send an approval message to UCCnet.

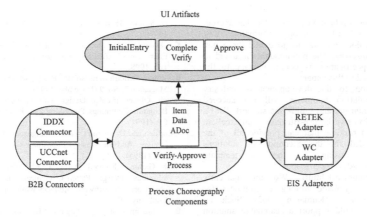

Figure 1: Item Synchronization Solution Template

6 ANALYSIS AND RELATED WORK

The fundamental driver behind our template-based approach for business process integration is the highly influential work on design patterns (Alexander 1977). Gamma et al define design patterns as "descriptions of communicating objects and classes that are customized to solve a general design problem in a particular context". Similarly, our metamodel describes communicating modeling objects that solve the business process integration problem in the context of a specific solution domain.

Most of the work in code reuse has been focused around object-oriented frameworks (Johnson 1998). An excellent example of an object-oriented framework targeted to business applications is the San Francisco project (Jaufman 2000, Arnold 1997, Bohrer 1998) . Our solution template approach differs from this and other frameworks in many ways:

- Solution templates are at a higher level of abstraction than OO frameworks. While OO frameworks can be embodied in code, only examples of solution templates can be embodied in code.
- Frameworks are more specialized than solution templates. For example, frameworks have been designed to help build graphical editors, compilers for different programming languages and target machines, and financial modeling applications. In contrast, we position our solution template metamodel as

a design pattern for business process integration.
- Primary mechanism for customization in OO frameworks is inheritance. Solution templates are customized by scripting behavior of the modeling artifacts.
- The OO frameworks are targeted primarily for solution development. Our work addresses the solution assembly and integration problem. They are complimentary in the sense that OO frameworks could be used for developing solution components and the solution template could be used to integrate these components with legacy applications and Web services to realize new business functions.

Standardization is key to the success of the solution template approach. Standardization can lead to the commoditization of the components consistent with our solution template metamodel. This could facilitate a "plug-and-play" paradigm for business process integration. The standardization work currently going on in Web Services and J2EE are encouraging developments in this area. For example, Web Services Flow Language (WSFL) (Leymann 2001) has been proposed as a standard for defining flow models. The flow models are merely a part of our BPI metamodel. There is a lot more work to be done in defining standards that cover the complete BPI spectrum.

Another encouraging development in the standardization area is the emerging OMG specification on UML Profile and Interchange Models for Enterprise Application Integration (OMG 2002). This specification defines two metamodels: (1) EAI Integration Metamodel. (2)

EAI Common Application Metamodel. The current version of our BPI metamodel externalizes EAI adapters and does not attempt to model the actual adapters themselves. The metamodels discussed in the OMG specification is complementary to the work discussed in this paper.

In addition to the development of industry standards, solution templates will not succeed without the runtime and build-time support. IBM's application framework for e-Business is an excellent example of a runtime that can provide all of the services needed for the execution of solutions generated using the template (www.ibm.com/developer/features/framework/framework.html). We are currently working on a holistic tooling environment for solution templates (Kumaran 2002). Such an environment should support a searchable solution template repository, provide tools to create and modify individual artifacts as well as the global compositions, and support verification and simulation of the solutions.

7 CONCLUDING REMARKS

Business process integration and automation has emerged as an important area in business computing. It is widely acknowledged that business process integration is an extremely complex problem. We use a model-driven approach to address the complexity of this problem. A model-driven approach is only as good as the model being employed. Thus the success of our approach hinges on the merits of our solution template metamodel. Our current work focuses on applying the solution template concept to as many customer problems as possible in order to validate the model.

REFERENCES

http://www.eaijournal.com/Article.asp?ArticleID=295

C. Alexander, S Ishikawa, M. Silverstein, M. Jacobson, S. Angel. A Pattern Language. Oxford University Press, New York, 1977

V.D. Arnold, R. Bosch, E. Dumstorff, P. Helfrich, T. Hung, V. Johnson, R. Persik, and P. Whidden, "IBM Business Frameworks: SanFrancisco Project Technical Overview". IBM Systems Journal 36, No. 3, 437-445, 1997.

K. Bohrer, "Architecture of the San Franscisco Frameworks", IBM Systems Journal 37, No. 2, 156-169, 1998.

K. Bohrer, "Middleware Isolates Business Logic," Object Magazine 7, No. 9 (November 1997)

Booch, Object-Oriented Design with Applications, The Benjamin/Cummings Publishing Co., Redwood City, CA (1991)

J. Coplien and D. Schmidt, Pattern Languages of Program Design, Addison-Wesley Publishing Co., Reading, MA (1995).

Erich Gamma, Richard Helm, Ralph Johnson, John Vlissides, Design Patterns, elements of reusable object-oriented software, Addison-Wesley Publishing Company, 1994)

E. Jaufmann, and D. Logan, "The use of IBM SanFrancisco core business process as accessors to Enterprise JavaBeans components", IBM Systems Journal 39, Vol. 39, No. 2, 2000.

T. W. Malone and K. Crowston, "The Interdisciplinary Study of Coordination," Computing Surveys 26, No. 1, 87-119 (1994)

D. A. Taylor, "The Use and Abuse of Reuse," Object Magazine 6, No. 2, 16-18 (April 1996)

K. Weick and K. Roberts, "Collective Mind in Organizations: Heedful Interrelating on Flight Decks," Administrative Science Quarterly, 357-381 (1993).

S. Kumaran, P. Nandi, K. Bhaskaran, T. Heath, R. Das, "ADoc-Oriented Programming", IBM Research Report.

Y. Huang, "Design of a Solution Template for Business Process Integration", IBM Research Report.

www.uccnet.org, "Universal foundation for electronic commerce."

R. E. Johnson and B. Foote, "Designing reusable classes", Journal of Object-Oriented Programming, June/July 1988.

F. Leymann, "Web Services Flow Language", IBM Corporation, 2001.

OMG, "UML Profile and Interchange Models for Enterprise Application Integration", January 2002.

www.ibm.com/developer/features/framework/framework.html, Application Framework for e-Business.

S. Kumaran, "End-to-end BPM Tooling", IBM Academy of Technology Business Process Integration Conference, May, 2002.

Douglas R. Hofstadter , "Godel, Escher, Bach: An Eternal Golden Braid".

EXTENDING GROUPWARE FOR OLAP
Where did my time go?

Stefan Edlund, Daniel Ford, Vikas Krishna

IBM Almaden Research Center, San Jose, CA 95120, USA
Email: {edlund, daford, vikas}@almaden.ibm.com

Sunitha Kambhampati

Computer Science and Engineering, Arizona State University, AZ, USA
Email: ksunitha@asu.edu

Keywords: Personal Information Management Systems, Groupware, Data Warehousing, OLAP, R-OLAP, XML, Information drilldown

Abstract: While applications built on top of groupware systems are capable of managing mundane tasks such as scheduling and email, they are not optimised for certain kinds of applications, for instance generating aggregated summaries of scheduled activities. Groupware systems are primarily designed with online transaction processing in mind, and are highly focused on maximizing throughput when clients concurrently access and manipulate information on a shared store. In this paper, we give an overview and discuss some of the implementation details of a system that transforms groupware Calendaring & Scheduling (C&S) data into a relational OLAP database optimised for these kinds of analytical applications. We also describe the structure of the XML documents that carry incremental update information between the source groupware system and the relational database, and show how the generic structure of the documents enables us to extend the infrastructure to other groupware systems as well.

1 INTRODUCTION

Electronic Personal Information Management (PIM) Systems have been available on the market for many years. They store and manage personal information, such as events, to-do items and address books either on a local system or by accessing a sever on the network. The Calendaring and Scheduling (C&S) aspect of these systems record where people are planning to go, whom they will meet and why and typically provide convenient reminders of upcoming events. A couple of the most popular products are Lotus Notes™ and Microsoft Exchange™. These systems are also categorized as groupware, in that they allow for people in a group to share documents and accomplish tasks (e.g. schedule a group meeting).

Groupware systems can potentially contain large amounts of data. Analysis of such data can yield useful results, for instance summaries of how much time an individual or group spent on a particular project during a year, or how much time was spent

meeting with a particular customer (see Figure 1 for an example). Up until now, C&S applications have primarily been focused on the planning aspects, ensuring that conflict free schedules are maintained and typically optimised for generating temporal planning views, such as a weekly or monthly calendar. Moving groupware data into data warehouses to allow for convenient analysis and decision support has largely been ignored.

While the dataset of an individual can be fairly small, an aggregation of groupware data from a set of people (e.g., employees) can quickly grow in size. Information hidden inside such large data sets can provide key insights into the dynamics of an organization and potentially be used to help improve efficiency. In addition, integration of data from a groupware system with other data marts, for instance sales data, can provide useful information on how customer interactions directly relates to revenues. Of course, there are privacy issues that must be addressed to ensure that sensitive personal information is not disclosed to unauthorized individuals, or better yet, not disclosed at all. Recent

O. Camp et al. (eds.), Enterprise Information Systems V, 85-92.
© 2004 *Kluwer Academic Publishers. Printed in the Netherlands.*

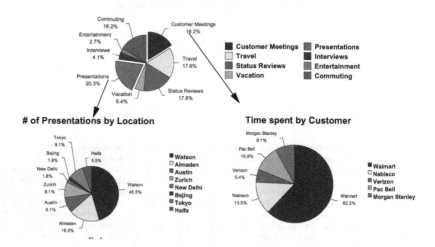

Figure 1: Analysis of Calendar & Scheduling data

work (Agrawal, 2000) shows how privacy-preserving data mining can be used to some extent to hide sensitive information during analysis while still producing useful results. This becomes ever more important as the range of potential users with data warehouse access is moving away from being the sole domain of executives and managers to almost anyone within an organization. A review of the security and design issues for data warehousing can be found in (Priebe, 2000).

OLAP (Online Analytical Processing) has found widespread use in business applications, enabling good analysis performance and ease-of-use. It was first introduced in 1993 by E.F. Codd (Codd, 1993), where he outlined a set of twelve rules for decision support systems. A key feature was multidimensional data analysis, i.e. the ability to consolidate and analyse data according to multiple dimensions in ways that make sense to a specific enterprise analyst at any given point in time. There are several variants of OLAP; MOLAP (multidimensional OLAP) systems store data in a

dedicated multidimensional database and often pre-consolidate data along certain dimensions to allow for very fast query response times. As a side effect, MOLAP databases can grow quickly in size for even a small input data set. ROLAP (Relational OLAP) stores business data in a relational database, typically organized as a star schema. ROLAP can handle very large data sets, but unless the relational database has built-in OLAP calculations, the analysis must be carried out on the client side or at an intermediary level, which can hamper performance. However, these days many relational database products have OLAP calculations integrated into the database engine (e.g. Informix, DB2).

Building a data warehouse traditionally comprises a three-step process of extraction, transformation and load (ETL). In the extraction step information is retrieved from an operational data store, e.g. a relational database optimised for OLTP. "Transformation" involves consolidation of the information into a multidimensional structure and conversion of data instances if necessary. "Load" means inserting the transformed data into the target OLAP system. In case of ROLAP, this means inserting data into tables organized as a star schema in relational database. To increase performance, incremental updates are typically supported.

The three steps can be a fairly intricate process, and to help manage the complexity a market for ETL tools has evolved, for instance the DB2 Warehouse Manager™. However, support for less traditional data sources, such as groupware systems, is to a large extent lacking.

Attempts to extend OLAP to include external data objects without requiring physical integration have been made (Pederson, 2000). They allow for "decorating" analysis results with pointers to external objects; however it is still necessary to integrate certain data items into the OLAP system to allow for efficient analysis performance. These systems are tailored towards object database systems, and are difficult to apply in a generic fashion.

Reviewing our requirements and existing groupware applications today, we determined that implementing an efficient toolkit for analysis of groupware information (and in particular C&S data) had to exhibit the following characteristics:

- **Data source abstraction.** A framework for abstracting any generic operational data store that could be used as an OLAP data source is difficult to realize. However, the smaller subset of groupware data stores allows us to make certain assumptions in the implementation to help abstract the source using a set of common interfaces. The goal is to be able to extend the infrastructure to additional groupware systems without too much effort.
- **Full OLAP Integration.** The groupware data source and the OLAP system should be kept separate, and no links maintained between them. By doing this, we avoid having to manage synchronization and maintain referential integrity between the OLAP database and a potentially large set of heterogeneous groupware systems. Also, groupware data replicated in the OLAP database can automatically be used for analysis and decision support without requiring access to proprietary groupware interfaces.
- **Ability to manage large data sets.** We see no restrictions in the amount of groupware data we need to manage. Using a ROLAP solution, we can take advantage of the scalable storage infrastructure implemented by the RDBMS.
- **Management tools.** To manage the ETL process, a set of tools is necessary. In particular,

in the transformation step groupware data is cleaned, filtered and converted into multi-dimensional OLAP structure. An administrator must be able to control aspects of the transformation. At minimum, the administrator should be able to specify how data items extracted from the groupware system are mapped to particular OLAP dimensions. The ability to manipulate the OLAP database and ETL process without system interruption (e.g. by adding, modifying or deleting dimensions) is also desirable.

- **Multi-user interface.** The analysis tool must be able to handle concurrent access by multiple users (actually, this is one of the key characteristics an OLAP system should exhibit, described in one of the twelve points by E.F. Codd in 1993). In addition, if we ensure that the tool is available from Web interface (Web-OLAP), deploying the tool within an organization becomes effortless.

The rest of this paper is organized as follows: In section 2, we give an overview of the characteristics of groupware data, and in particular data from the Calendaring and Scheduling (C&S) domain. Some of the issues with translating such data into a ROLAP store are discussed. In section 3, we describe the system architecture and implementation details of the C&S data analysis tool implemented, and in section 4 we give an overview of Sapient (Cody, 2002), a prototype OLAP toolkit used in the project. Finally, in section 5 give some conclusions and provide a discussion of potential future directions.

2 ANALYSING GROUPWARE DATA FOR CALENDARING AND SCHEDULING

As a first step, we looked at the properties of calendaring and scheduling objects in groupware applications attempting to compile a list of potentially useful OLAP dimensions. The iCalendar specification (Dawson, 1998) describes a standard set of C&S components such as events, to-do items and journal entries, and a common set of component properties. Most groupware systems support the standard in some way or another, ensuring that a pervasive set of properties was selected. They are:

- CATEGORIES. This property provides a component categorization. For calendar events, it can be used for classification into meetings,

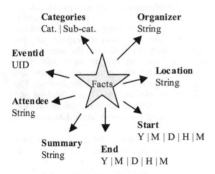

Figure 2: ROLAP star schema for a basic set of C&S dimensions.

anniversaries etc. It is a multi-valued property in iCalendar.

- LOCATION. The location where an event is taking place. In iCalendar, it is a simple text field with an additional URI qualifier.
- ATTENDEE. A multi-valued property containing event attendees. These are typically a set of invited people.
- ORGANIZER. Specifies the organizer of an event. Often (but not always), this is the same as the creator of the event.
- DTSTART and DTEND. The start- and end-times of scheduled events.
- SUMMARY. A brief description of the component. This is a free form text field.

This initial set of properties allows us to analyse when, where and with who time was spent. Each property is represented in a star schema, where a table of facts reference values in dimension tables using foreign keys. Figure 2 shows an overview of the star schema. Given the set of dimensions, we set out designing an ETL routine, keeping in mind that this initial set of dimensions should be customisable and extensible by an administrator.

Our initial target groupware system was Lotus Notes. In Lotus Notes data is organized as a set of documents in a document store. Layered on top of the store is a set of services provided, for instance the ability to visualize data in using different views, access control and workflow support. The organization of a document is simple; it consists of a flat structure of fields that hold data values. For instance, a calendar event is a stored as a document with fields for the start time, end time, a summary etc. Collections are typically represented in a single field using a comma-separated list of data values.

As it turns out, there are several issues translating such documents into a multi-dimensional OLAP structure. For instance, documents contain several properties holding collections of attendee information. A particular person can show up in any of those properties depending upon the person's attendee status, and it is also possible that the same person shows up in two of those properties at the same time. The extraction and transformation process must be able to aggregate such information if required into a single "Attendee" dimension. Another issue was the way categories are handled. No particular field holds a category value for an event. Rather, the presence of a given field in a document gives an indication of category membership.

In addition, the temporal aspects of scheduled events can become fairly complex, especially for repeating events. We had to make sure that the ETL routine was able to expand repeating events into facts about a set of isolated events.

DB2 UDB does not allow columns that store multi-valued information, for example a set of people representing the attendees of an event. Such information had to be flattened into several facts, each fact describing one of the attendees. To accomplish this, an additional dimension was necessary associating a given fact with a unique event identifier (represented as *Eventid* in Figure 2).

Information stored in calendars often has little context information associated with them. One example is the location property, commonly implemented as simply a free-form text string. Also, the classification of events is often limited to a small set of categories, e.g. a meeting or a conference call. There is parallel work attempting to automatically derive additional semantics from C&S data using data mining algorithms or semantic lookup techniques (reference can be provided). The ETL routine must be able to dynamically derive dimension data from such external algorithms, and we had to make sure our system was designed to handle this. For instance, if we can accurately determine where meetings take place, location can be implemented as a hierarchical dimension (e.g. country, state, city and address), allowing an analyst to precisely summarize data according to specific geographies.

To allow for optimal performance, it is sometimes useful to embed data directly into the facts table instead of referring to external dimensions. To analyse how duration of meetings correlate to productivity (most likely a negative correlation), the ETL routine can derive duration values from the start and end times of scheduled events and insert them as part of the load step into the fact table. This allows us to avoid a couple of

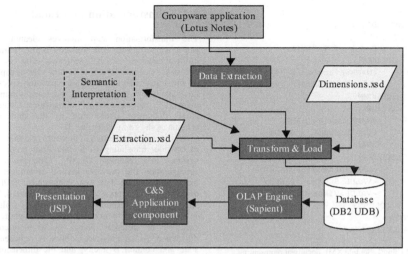

Figure 3: System Architecture of the Data Analysis Tool

extra levels of joins during analysis. We implemented a special "computed" dimension to ensure that we supported this scenario.

In section 3 we describe in detail how we solved these issues, and how the specifics of the groupware system was abstracted using an XML data layer between the extraction and transformation step.

3 SYSTEM ARCHITECTURE

The entire data analysis system is divided into five components: extraction, transformation & load, Sapient, C&S Application Component, and GUI (see Figure 3). In the extraction phase, data is extracted from a groupware system and abstracted into a common XML data layer. The transformation step takes as input a configuration file describing the dimensions of interest for analysis. During transformation, external routines can optionally derive additional semantics for the extracted calendar entries. Next, the extracted data is transformed into a star schema structure and loaded into the database. After transformation and load, the data is adapted for OLAP kind queries generated by the Sapient OLAP tool. The query results are fed to a GUI component that renders easy to understand graphical representations of analysis results. The system uses two XML schema definitions for generation and validation of XML documents. 'Extraction.xsd' in Figure 3 defines the structure of XML documents constructed from extracted C&S information in a groupware system.

'Dimensions.xsd' defines a valid dimension configuration file, containing mapping information between extracted C&S data and ROLAP dimensions. XML documents from these two schemas are used as input to the ETL process.

3.1 Extraction

Different groupware systems are proprietary in nature and expose native APIs to clients. Besides, the semantics of data values used in groupware are limited to the respective system and is not always universal in nature. We take advantage of the extensible nature of XML Schemas and propose an intermediary representation using an XML document capable of capturing the different data representations, while allowing for extensibility. The extraction step abstracts these details using a generic XML schema definition for extracted groupware data. The schema allows for representing extracted data items as XSD data type instances, and also defines a way of representing multi-valued attributes present in the data. The extracted data is stored in an XML document conforming to the schema. A sample is shown in Listing 1. The COLUMN tag contains information about the extracted column and the values correspond to the extracted values. The NAME tag contains the extracted column name. Each calendar entry is represented as an ENTRY tag with the ENTRYTYPE indicating whether it is new or modified calendar event. A COLUMN can map directly to a column in a ROLAP dimension table, or it can be filtered out in the transformation phase.

```
<CALENDARDATA>
<ENTRY>
<ENTRYTYPE>new</ENTRYTYPE>
    <COLUMN>
        <NAME>EventId</NAME>
        <VALUE>ADDDBSDFE</VALUE>
    </COLUMN>
    <COLUMN>
        <NAME>Chair</NAME>
        <VALUE>Stefan</VALUE>
    </COLUMN>
    <COLUMN>
        <NAME>Attendees</NAME>
        <VALUE>Stefan</VALUE>
        <VALUE>Vikas</VALUE>
    </COLUMN>
</ENTRY>
</CALENDARDATA>
```

Listing 1. Sample XML document representing extracted data.

The data extraction step uses an extractor driver to implement the common interface for extraction, allowing for easy plug-in of different extractors for different groupware systems. In the groupware that we have researched, the values for particular entries such as 'appointment type' are represented in proprietary format. For example, appointment type value of 1 implies that it is a meeting while appointment type value of 2 implies that it is a reminder. The necessary interpretation of these values is left to the extractor driver since it has the best knowledge about the particular groupware system. To help increase performance, the extractor driver interface supports incremental extraction, allowing the extractor class to return data as an XML document with the entries that have been modified or created after the last extraction time.

Calendar systems can represent repeating events, for instance weekly meetings that recur at some specific interval. Repeating events are expanded into a collection of single isolated calendar entries in the XML document. After extraction, the data is fed to the transformation step.

3.2 Transformation and Load

The transformation step involves cleaning the extracted groupware data and converting it into a multi-dimensional OLAP structure. Our system allows for an administrator to control various aspects of the transformation. The administrator specifies how data items extracted from groupware system are mapped to particular OLAP dimensions, using an XML document conforming to the dimension schema as shown in the Figure 3.

As discussed in Section 2, there are several issues to consider translating C&S data from groupware systems into relational OLAP. The dimension configuration file provides several techniques for mapping extracted data onto hierarchical ROLAP dimensions. An overview is shown in Figure 4. The simplest kind of mapping is represented by Column A and Column B, which are mapped to particular columns at different levels in a hierarchical dimension. As an example, Column A represents a state and column B a city, and the dimension is 'Location'.

To represent the fact that a given column is present in the input entry, a special mapping was introduced. In this case, the value of the column is unimportant but there is a need to record, as a fact, the existence of it. Column X in Figure 4 represents any column present in the entry matching a value in the third column (level 3) of the dimension. The dimension is "bootstrapped" by pre-initialising it with a set of tuples in the configuration file.

Many times, there is a need to aggregate several extracted columns into a single ROLAP dimension. In our initial implementation for Lotus Notes, attendee information was represented in multiple entry columns depending upon a person's role, and it was possible for a person to show up in two extracted columns in the same entry. To reduce redundancy and to optimally aggregate this kind of information, a new aggregated mapping type was introduced. It allows a ROLAP dimension column to derive values from multiple extracted data columns. For the case when extracted data contains multiple references to the same data item, it is necessary to optimally represent this information without redundancy. Figure 5 shows an overview of the aggregated dimension mapping.

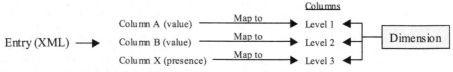

Figure 4: Mappings between extracted columns and columns in an ROLAP dimension table

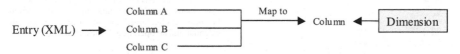

Figure 5: Aggregating multiple columns into a single ROLAP dimension column

To allow for optimal performance and to support a variety of derived data, a computed dimension type was defined. For instance, if the duration of a calendar event should be computed dynamically, it can be represented in the configuration file using the example in Listing 2.

```
<DIMENSION>
<NAME>Duration</NAME>
<COMPUTED>
    <CLASS>ComputeDuration</CLASS>
        <METHOD>compute</METHOD>
        <SQLTYPE>int</SQLTYPE>
        <PARAM>StartTime</PARAM>
        <PARAM>EndTime</PARAM>
</COMPUTED>
</DIMENSION>
```

Listing 2. Example of a computed dimension determining the duration of a calendar event

Duration is a computed dimension and the "ComputeDuration" class has the logic to compute the values given the parameters specified by the PARAM tags. At run time, when data is populated as facts in the fact table, the translator invokes the compute method passing the parameters corresponding to the 'StartTime' and 'EndTime' dimension values for the entry. By using a computed dimension we avoid a few extra joins necessary to compute the value from the dimension table values during analysis. Computed dimensions can also dynamically incorporate information computed by more advanced programs, such as a routine that automatically categorize calendar entries using data mining techniques.

A 'user' dimension in the ROLAP schema records the owner of a particular calendar entry, allowing us to implement additional services such as access control in the future. Currently, the toolkit allows an analyst to freely access information derived from a single user, a collection of users, or the data warehouse as a whole.

The data analysis tool also supports the dynamic management tasks of adding and deleting dimensions from the system. There is no disruption of the system during this process. To allow for consistent syntax, adding and deleting a dimension involves specifying the desired dimensions via an administration interface that accepts new dimension descriptions in a format matching the dimension schema.

The loader takes both the dimensions and the extracted data in XML format and populates the dimension tables and the facts. The dimension tables are populated first and then the fact table is populated after flattening of the facts for data containing multi-valued attributes.

In our implementation, the transformation step builds and populates the star schema in DB2 relational database. It generates dynamic SQL statements depending on the semantics of the mapping information in the configuration file, utilizing optimisation such as JDBC prepared statements.

3.3 Querying and GUI

After the transformation and load steps, we use the Sapient-OLAP tool to help generate the drill down queries. Details of the tool are discussed in Section 4. Sapient allows querying the system with analytical queries across multi-dimensions and even across separate warehouses using shared dimensions. The queries have been refined to allow for analysis over specific time ranges, thus giving a wide range of choices to the user.

The data analysis tool has been extended to enable Web access using Servlets and JSP technology. To allow for easy and dynamic configuration of the system, there is a dynamic setup file that specifies the database parameters and other details. The query interface exposes all the dimensions to the user and the user is free to query across multiple dimensions.

The results of the query and the graphical representation of the results are presented to the user using pie charts and bar graphs. An example is shown in Figure 6.

The unbundling of various conceptual steps allows for easy plug-in of different extractor classes, translator classes, and the query interface. The

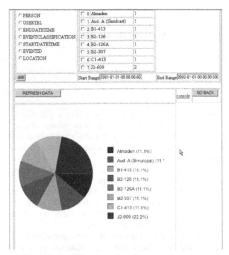

Figure 6: Web-based user interface. In this case, the location of meetings is being summarized

architecture supports modular updates and allow for extending the system to future query and GUI tools.

4 SAPIENT

Sapient is a system for analyzing multidimensional data. It allows the analyst to "slice and dice" the data by drilling along any number and combination of dimensions to arrive at a cell of interest in a data cube. The Sapient system consists of a software layer that can be used through an application programming interface to break down the data along the dimensions of interest. To use this software, the information about the star schema, such as the dimension names, their table structure outlining parent-child relationships in case of a hierarchy, and associated fact table(s) are stored in a metadata table used by the software to generate the appropriate queries. Once this is in place, information about the drill items and path selected by the analyst using the user interface are collected and sent to the Sapient system. An appropriate query is generated, executed against the database, and the resulting break down in a table-form is sent back to the reporting component of the user interface.

One unique feature of Sapient is its ability to perform analysis across warehouses, often greatly enhancing the decision support available. Two relational star schemas can be connected using a shared dimension, for instance the time dimension.

The shared dimension can be used to build queries that spans warehouse data from two separate business applications, for instance a groupware calendar and an operational sales database.

5 RESULTS AND CONCLUSION

In this paper, we have described a system for analysis of C&S data from a groupware application. Details on the extraction, transformation and load steps were discussed, and we showed the Web GUI used to analyse scheduled calendar events.

One important future direction is improving security by implementing some level of access control to the data warehouse. Such services can be implemented on either the application level or the database level using database infrastructure. We also plan to investigate techniques for integrating the analysis toolkits into existing groupware applications, such as Lotus Notes.

ACKNOWLEDGEMENTS

Thank you to everybody involved in the various calendaring projects in our team: Bill Cody, Jared Jackson, Joann Ruvolo, Yael Shaham-Gafni, and Sumit Taank.

REFERENCES

Agrawal, R. et al., 2000. Privacy-Preserving Data Mining. In *ACM SIGMOD 2000*, pg. 439-450.

Priebe, T. et al., 2000. Towards OLAP Security Design – Survey and Research Issues. In *ACM DOLAP 2000*, pg. 33-40

Codd, E.F. et al., 1993. Providing OLAP to User-Analysts: An IT Mandate, Arbor Software Corporation Whitepaper

Pederson, T. et al., 2000. Extending OLAP Querying To External Object Databases. In *ACM CIKM 2000*, pg. 405-413

Dawson, F. et al., 1998. Internet Calendaring and Scheduling Core Object Specification (iCalendar), RFC 2445, http://www.ietf.org/rfc/rfc2445.txt (current as of Aug. 2002).

Cody, W.F., et al., 2002. The integration of business intelligence and knowledge management, *IBM Systems Journal*, Volume 41, No 4

XML-BASED OLAP QUERY PROCESSING IN A FEDERATED DATA WAREHOUSES

Oscar Mangisengi, Wolfgang Essmayr, Johannes Huber, Edgar Weippl

Software Competence Center Hagenberg (SCCH), Hauptstrasse 99, A-4232 Hagenberg, Austria

Email: *oscar.mangisengi@scch.at, wolfgang.essmayr@scch.at, johannes.huber@scch.at, edgar.weippl@scch.at*

Keywords: Data warehouse, OLAP, XML, and federated data warehouse systems

Abstract: Today, XML is the format of choice to implement interoperability between systems. This paper addresses the XML-based query processing for heterogeneous OLAP data warehouses in a federated architecture. In our approach, XML, as an intermediary representation, can be used as a basis for federated queries and queries for local OLAP data warehouses, whereas XML DTD can be used for query language definition and validation of a XML federated query.

1 INTRODUCTION

Nowadays, data warehouses (DWHs) have become the enabling technology for supporting on-line analytic processing (OLAP) (Codd et al, 1993). The goal of a data warehouse is to integrate applications at the data level. The data is extracted, transformed, and integrated from multiple, independent data sources like operational databases or external systems. It is cleansed to conform to a standard understanding or definition of content and meaning, and optimized to support decision support systems, or business intelligence tools.

In classical data warehouse, data is stored in a centralized repository (i.e., star, snowflake schemas) for providing enterprise integration. A centralized repository has the advantage to manage and control data. However, building a centralized data warehouse is more expensive than building distributed or heterogeneous DWHs.

One of the problems with that centralized approach is that data in the warehouse is not synchronized with data residing in the underlying data sources. Although the goal of DWHs is to create a centralized and unified view of enterprise data holdings, this goal has not been fully realized (Kerschberg, 2001). Many factors contribute to this, e.g. semantic heterogeneity, terminology conflicts. Building a centralized data warehouse for an enterprise wide solution is always an extremely time and cost consuming effort that is improbable to be successful (Garber, 1999).

In fact, due to the life cycle for building data warehouse, distributed and heterogeneous DWHs are a more promising solution for many companies or organizations for resolving their own local business problems. As a consequence, organizations collect heterogeneous DWHs distributed into different locations. However, the issue emerges how to access DWHs islands into a unified view in order to provide useful information for OLAP data analysis for high-level decision maker. According to (Eckerson, 2000) enterprises increasingly end up with multiple islands of DWHs that are operated separately and cannot be accessed in a homogeneous way. In addition, extracting, transferring, and loading (ETL) heterogeneous DWHs sources from different locations into a central repository of DWH is an inadequate solution due to time consuming process. It is more flexible when heterogeneous DWHs are built in a federated architecture for providing interoperability. Trends indicate that federated data warehouse architectures are more practical, from political, operational, and technical points-of-view (Kerschberg, and Weishar, 2000) (Firestone, 1999). The benefit is that existing DWH resources can be used in this situation without extracting, transforming, and loading them together into a new set of common tables. Therefore, establishing federated architectures to accomplish this interoperability of heterogeneous DWHs systems for supporting unified access is necessary.

Extensible Markup Language (XML) has been proposed as data interchange formats (W3C, 1998) and has been used for many applications. The strength of XML is that it has some rather

O. Camp et al. (eds.), Enterprise Information Systems V, 93-100.

formalized ways of thinking about structure – with ideas, such as well-formedness, validity, and schemas. The usage of XML for supporting distributed data warehouse has been introduced by (Mangisengi et al, 2001) (Ammoura et al, 2001).

In this paper we focus on XML as a basis for querying OLAP data warehouses in the federated architecture. For supporting querying data in data warehouse, we approach XML DTD for query language definition.

The remainder of this paper is structured as follows: Section 2 presents related work. Section 3 illustrates our motivation of our work. An overview of the system architecture for supporting interoperability of heterogeneous data warehouses is presented in Section 4. Section 5 deals with XML-based OLAP query processing in the federated data warehouses. Finally, Section 6 present conclusion of our work.

2 RELATED WORK

There have already been done some approaches on DWH interoperability and distributed DWHs architecture: In (Mangisengi et al, 2001) the authors describe the usage of XML to enable interoperability of data warehouses by an additional architectural layer used for exchanging schema metadata. Distributed DWH architectures based on CORBA are introduced by (Hümmer et al, 2000). In (Ammoura et al, 2001) they introduce a centralized virtual data warehouses based on CORBA and XML. They construct a virtual data warehouse from a set of distributed DBMS systems. Information needed during a visualization session is communicated between the visualization module and the virtual data warehouse as XML documents using CORBA or SOAP technologies. The concepts of federated database management systems and mediator have been proposed by (Sheth and Larson, 1990) and (Wiederhold, 1992) respectively and those concepts have been applied for many applications.

In this paper we introduce XML as a basis for querying heterogeneous data warehouses in a federated architecture for supporting data analysis. We approach XML DTD as query language definition to build and validate a federated XML query.

3 MOTIVATION

The motivation illustrates examples taken from the *Upper-Austria Health Insurance Organization*, which is one of nine regional bodies of the *Austrian Social Insurance Federation*. Besides the enormous amount of extremely sensitive data handled within health insurances, the analytical potential of that data is the key to cost reduction and service improvement, which are usually two major goals of any organization. Due to the fact, that the social insurance protection in Austria is provided by 28 insurance organizations in total, centralized information systems are neither possible to develop nor desirable in the viewpoint of particular insurance organizations, since they want to remain autonomous in many respects. The organization usually merges and integrates results from heterogeneous DWHs to provide cost analysis for supporting decision-making for the highest-level management. The provider has different DWH-systems, from which several "DWH-instances" are deployed. All DWH-instances of one DWH-system are established on the same technologies and they manage data from different provinces.

Consider two similar star schemas (Kimball, 1996) for an OLAP warehouse for health insurance information systems, each consists of a fact table that contains tuples for each item in an health insurance transaction; and a set of dimensions. The star schemas are given in Figure 1.

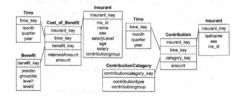

Figure 1: Two DWH star schemas

The first star schema (DWH1) is used to analyze the cost paid for medical treatment of the insurants analyzed across the *Time*, *Insurant*, and *Benefit* dimensions, whereas the other (DWH2) analyzes the contribution, which insurants have to pay analyzed across the *Time*, *Insurant*, and *Category* dimensions. A query is intended to calculate the difference between the sum of the contributions and the sum of the benefits, constrained and grouped by various attributes.

In our work we focus on the usage of XML and XML DTD for querying OLAP data in the federated

DWHs. In this approach we do not consider the performance – this is beyond our intention.

4 AN OVERVIEW OF THE SYSTEM ARCHITECTURE

In this section we introduce an overview of the architecture for supporting interoperability of distributed DWHs given in Figure 2. In detail the architecture and a framework can be shown in (Mangisengi et al, 2001). The architecture consists of the local, the mediation, the federated, and the client layers globally.

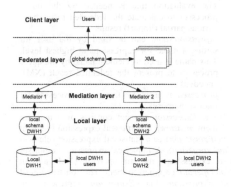

Figure 2: A layered architecture for federated data warehouses

4.1 Local Layer

The local layer provides local DWHs resources and its local DWH schemas. Local DWHs, which participate in the federation, use its local schema for describing their data. This local schema follows any local data model, which can provide a multidimensional view on data (star schema, snowflake schema or the like). Before local schemas can be integrated, they must be unified thus handling heterogeneity. In our work we apply XML for describing a local schema for supporting the local layer.

4.2 Mediation Layer

This mediation layer is an additional architectural layer in heterogeneous DHWs, which is used to bridge the gap between the federated layer and the local layer. The mediation layer facilitates exchanging schema metadata. The tasks of mediator are as follows:

- Translate the local query to the query language used by the local DWH.
- Transform the partial result, which is sent back from the local DWH in a proprietary format, to a unified format. In our implementation we use extensible markup language (XML).

The federated DWH is independent from underlying local DWHs. Thus, for the implementation, a particular mediator must be built to integrate a new DWH model with a different data model and query language.

4.3 Federated Layer

The federated layer hides the structure heterogeneity of DWHs and provides a unified view for users to access local DWHs. In this layer a federated (global) schema is created and it is a collection of attributes, cubes and measures of the integrated local schemas and notes, which instances of the local DWHs participate in the federated DWH. For this purpose, the federated layer consists of the following components:

- **Canonical Data Model**. The canonical data model serves for describing each local schema including cubes, measures, dimensions, dimension hierarchies, and dimension levels and it should be possible to describe any schema represented by any multidimensional data model, such as star schema model, snow-flake model, and the like. The CDM is used for creating a global schema in the federated layer. For this purpose, we apply the *Unified Modeling Language* (UML) notation for modeling the CDM given in (Mangisengi et al, 2001). To ensure the consistency of representing all local schemas in the global schema in the federated layer, we provide an XML DTD for the CDM. Thus, all local schemas - described in XML files - refer to this DTD. We have a relation between XML files and local schemas on the one side and the DTD and canonical data model on the other side.
- **Mapping**. A mapping file describes the mapping of schema objects of the federated schema to the schema of the local layer. Additionally information of the local schemas and DWHs is contained in the mapping. The mapping that is responsible for one federated schema consists of mapping information, such as schema, cube, and attributes. The mapping is represented using XML document.

4.4 Client Layer

The client layer is used for creating federated queries and sends them to the federated layer for analyzing data in heterogeneous DWHs. Also, it receives results from the federated layer.

5 XML-BASED OLAP QUERY PROCESSING

In this section we present XML-based query processing for heterogeneous OLAP data warehouses given in Figure 3. In our work the main usage of XML is intended for querying data in the OLAP data warehouses in a federated level and for querying data for each local DWHs. Figure 3 shows that users in the federated level create federated queries using a global query builder.

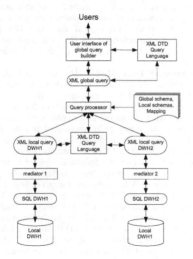

Figure 3: XML query processing

5.1 XML DTD for Federated Query

For analyzing data in the federated layer, users need to send federated queries. For this purpose, we provide a federated query language that consists of four parts, namely the *Select-*, an optional *Where-* and *GroupBy-* and a *ResultSet-*part. In order to present the federated query and ensure consistency of the query, we create an XML DTD for the

definition of the query. In our work, the federated queries are encoded in XML and are created by a program. The XML federated query refers to XML DTD for the validation. The XML DTD for representing federated queries is illustrated in Figure 4. The content of the XML DTD is given as follows:

5.1.1 The Select-Expression Element

The *Select*-element consists of one or more *expressions.* Element *expression* has the following XML-attributes:
- *belongsToResult* and *expressionIdentifier* are used for the construction of the evaluation tree during the decomposition of the federated query. The evaluation tree is needed by the query processor to calculate the federated result from various partial (import) results.
- *expressionName* can be used by the user for setting a name for expressions at highest level. This name is used as element name by the query processor to present the federated result (XML encoded)
- *processed* is used by the query processor for internal purposes.

The *Expression*-element consists of a measure (element *measure*), a numerical expression (element *NumExpression*) or a statistical expression (element *StatExpression*). A numerical expression comprises two expressions and an operator (XML-attribut *CalcOperator*) applied to them. The construction of *NumExpression* via *Expression* represents an indirect recursion. Therefore arbitrary nested expressions can be built. A statistical expression (element *StatExpression*) consists of a measure, to which a statistical operator (XML-attribut *StatOperator* of element *StatExpression*) is applied. The inner most expression of a nested expression always consists of the selection of a measure to which a numerical or statistical function is applied.

5.1.2 The Where-Element

In the *Where*-part the user defines the constraints on measures chosen in the Select-part, by providing values for attributes. Several constraints can be concatenated with *and* or *or* (element *and_or* respectively XML-attribute *type* of *and_or*). Element *PredicateWithComparison* consists of following three elements:
- *Attribute* (for a federated query) or *LevelAttribute* respectively *DimAttribute* (for an importQuery).
- *Operator* with XML-attribute *type* (denotes the kind of predicate – EQ, LT, GT etc.).

– *Value*, representing the value, to which the attribute should be restricted.

Unlike federated queries, local queries need the XML-attribute *belongsToDimension* for further describing the elements *LevelAttribute* and *DimAttribute*.

```
<!ELEMENT SelectStatement (Select, Where?, GroupBy?, ResultSet)>
<!ATTLIST SelectStatement
    queryName CDATA #REQUIRED
    againstSchema CDATA #REQUIRED
    againstInstance CDATA #IMPLIED
>
<!ELEMENT Select (Expression+)>
<!ELEMENT Expression (Measure | NumExpression | StatExpression)>
<!ATTLIST Expression
    belongsToResult CDATA #IMPLIED
    expressionIdentifier CDATA #IMPLIED
    expressionName CDATA #IMPLIED
    processed CDATA #IMPLIED
>
<!ELEMENT Measure (#PCDATA)>
<!ATTLIST Measure
    fromCube CDATA #REQUIRED
    fromInstance CDATA "OOE"
>
<!ELEMENT NumExpression (Expression, Expression)>
<!ATTLIST NumExpression
    CalcOperator (PLUS | MINUS | MULT | DIV) #REQUIRED
>
<!ELEMENT StatExpression (Measure)>
<!ATTLIST StatExpression
    StatOperator (SUM | AVG | MIN | MAX) #REQUIRED
>
<!ELEMENT Where ((PredicateWithComparison | PredicateWithIn), and_or?)+>
<!ELEMENT PredicateWithComparison ((Attribute | LevelAttribute | DimAttribute), Operator, Value)>
<!ELEMENT Attribute (#PCDATA)>
<!ELEMENT LevelAttribute (#PCDATA)>
<!ATTLIST LevelAttribute
    belongsToDimension CDATA #REQUIRED
>
<!ELEMENT DimAttribute (#PCDATA)>
<!ATTLIST DimAttribute
    belongsToDimension CDATA #REQUIRED
>
<!ELEMENT Operator EMPTY>
<!ATTLIST Operator
    type (EQ | LT | LTE | GT | GTE | NEQ) #REQUIRED
>
<!ELEMENT Value (#PCDATA)>
<!ELEMENT PredicateWithIn (#PCDATA)>
<!-- not implemented yet-->
<!ELEMENT and_or EMPTY>
<!ATTLIST and_or
    type (AND | OR) #REQUIRED
>
<!ELEMENT GroupBy (Attribute | LevelAttribute | DimAttribute)+>
<!ELEMENT ResultSet (Attribute | LevelAttribute | DimAttribute)+>
```

Figure 4: XML DTD for federated query

5.1.3 Other Elements

Other elements consist of the group-by and the result set element and they are as follows:

1. The *GroupBy*-element. The *GroupBy*-element is to group *attributes* (i.e., *LevelAttributes* and *DimAttributes*), when a statistical operation is applied to a measure. The *GroupBy*-element at the federated layer will be translated to SQL by the mediators. The federated layer needs to synchronize the GroupBy results from local DWHs.
2. The *ResultSet*-element. The element *ResultSet* is intended for specifying which *Attributes* (respectively *LevelAttributes* and *DimAttributes*) should appear in the federated result, additional to the measures and expressions specified in the Select-part.

5.2 XML Federated Query

Referring to the XML DTD shown in Figure 4, the user interface of federated query builder generates a XML federated query. An example of the federated query is given in Figure 5. Based on the federated query, our system generates one or more queries for local DWHs. Federated queries and local queries use the same language with the only difference that some XML elements and attributes are only used by local queries and not by federated queries and vice versa. With the aid of the query language the user can choose measures or facts, apply statistical operations and formulate arbitrary nested numerical expression on the basis of other expressions. A constraint of a query can be specified by constraining attributes.

```
<!DOCTYPE SelectStatement SYSTEM "Query.dtd">
<SelectStatement queryName="FedQuery4" againstSchema="FedDWH">
  <Select>
    <Expression expressionName=" Contribution-Benefit ">
      <NumExpression CalcOperator="MINUS">
        <Expression>
          <StatExpression StatOperator="SUM">
            <Measure fromCube="Contribution"
              fromInstance="UpperAustria">ContributionAmount</Measure>
          </StatExpression>
        </Expression>
        <Expression>
          <StatExpression StatOperator="SUM">
            <Measure fromCube="Benefit"
              fromInstance="UpperAustria">BenefitAmount</Measure>
          </StatExpression>
        </Expression>
      </NumExpression>
    </Expression>
  </Select>
  <Where>
    <PredicateWithComparison>
      <Attribute>Year</Attribute>
      <Operator type="EQ"/>
      <Value>2000</Value>
    </PredicateWithComparison>
    <and_or type="AND"/>
    ...
  </Where>
  <GroupBy>
    <Attribute>Year</Attribute>
    ...
  </GroupBy>
  <ResultSet>
    <Attribute>Year</Attribute>
    ...
```

Figure 5: An example of federated query in XML

At the federated level, there are some important operations, such as OLAP operations, and synchronization of aggregation operation. OLAP operations (i.e., drill-down, roll-up) can be virtually applied by building query particularly in the WHERE-element. To synchronize aggregation operation, the federated layer provides mapping between global dimension hierarchy and local DWHs dimension hierarchies.

5.3 Query Processing of Local DWHs

A federated query must be decomposed into various local queries for local DWHs. For this purpose, the federated layer provides a query processor for processing a federated query. In addition, the query processor calculates the federated result in XML representation from results sent back by the local DWHs via their mediators. First, the query processor parses the federated query and the parsed global query is represented as a tree. Second, the query processor must identify parts of the federated query, which belong completely to a local DWH. For decomposing the federated query into local queries, the query processor needs the mapping information of a federated schema to the local DWH schemas. Third, the query processor must gather the information (evaluation tree) it needs to calculate the federated result from import results of the local DWHs. Figure 6 shows the example of a local query in XML.

Figure 6: An example of a local query in XML

```
<SelectStatement againstInstance="UPPERAUSTRIA" againstSchema="DWH1"
                 queryName="FedQuery4~DWH1#UpperAustria">
  <Select>
    <Expression belongsToResult="DWH1#UPPERAUSTRIA" expressionIdentifier="E1"
                expressionName="BenefitAmount_UpperAustria" processed="yes">
      <StatExpression StatOperator="SUM">
        <Measure fromCubes
                 "COST_OF_BENEFIT" fromInstance="UpperAustria">AMOUNT
        </Measure>
      </StatExpression>
    </Expression>
  </Select>
  <Where>
    <PredicateWithComparison>
      <LevelAttribute belongsToDimension="TIME">YEAR</LevelAttribute>
      <Operator type="EQ"/>
      <Value>2000</Value>
    </PredicateWithComparison>
    <and_or type="AND"/>
  </Where>
  <GroupBy>
    <LevelAttribute belongsToDimension="TIME">YEAR</LevelAttribute>
    ...
```

The decomposition of a federated query yields two results:
− A set of local queries. Every local query is determined for a local DWH and must be handed over to the corresponding mediator.

An evaluation tree. This tree looks very similar to the select part of the federated query tree. The difference is that nested expressions of the federated query tree, which can be evaluated completely by a local DWH, are collapsed into one expression in the evaluation tree. The evaluation tree retains the operations, which must be applied to expression of the import results to gain the federated result. Expressions of the evaluation tree are marked with the XML-attributes *belongsToResults* and *expressionIdentifier* to identify to which import result and which expression within an import result they belong to. The example of evaluation tree is given in

Figure 7.

The local queries are passed to the mediators, which deliver the import results back - encoded in XML. After the query processor has received all import results, it must calculate the federated result.

For calculating the federated result, the query processor must perform two tasks:
1. Join operation. Equal rows – rows with same attribute values - of the import results must be found.
2. Calculation of federated expressions for equal rows.

After equal rows have been detected, federated expressions must be evaluated. The evaluation tree supplies the information the query processor needs to evaluate a federated expression. This information includes from which import result an expressions originates, the identification of that expression within the import result, and the operators, which must be applied to the expressions. For all equal rows of the import results the query processor writes a federated row with all attributes and federated expressions.

```
<EvaluationTree>
  <Expression belongsToResult="federated" expressionName="Contribution-Benefit">
    <NumExpression CalcOperator="MINUS">
      <Expression belongsToResult="DWH1#UpperAustria" expressionIdentifier="E1"
                  expressionName="ContributionAmount_UpperAustria" processed="yes">
      <Expression>
      <Expression belongsToResult="DWH2#UpperAustria" expressionIdentifier="E1"
                  expressionName="BenefitAmount_UpperAustria" processed="yes">
      <Expression>
    </NumExpression>
  </Expression>
</EvaluationTree>
```

Figure 7: Evaluation tree in XML document

5.4 Query Processing in Mediator

The query processor transfers the local queries to the mediators. The mediators translate their local queries to SQL and, send it to the local DWHs. The result of translation into SQL statement is given in Figure 8.

```
SELECT TIME.YEAR, TIME.QUARTER, INSURANT.CONTRIBUTIONGROUP, SUM(AMOUNT) AS E1
FROM INSURANT, TIME, COST_OF_BENEFIT
WHERE TIME.YEAR                      = '2000' AND
      TIME.QUARTER                   = '2000Q1' AND
      INSURANT.INSURANT_KEY          = COST_OF_BENEFIT.INSURANT_KEY AND
      TIME.TIME_KEY                  = COST_OF_BENEFIT.TIME_KEY
GROUP BY TIME.YEAR, TIME.QUARTER, INSURANT.CONTRIBUTIONGROUP
ORDER BY TIME.YEAR, TIME.QUARTER, INSURANT.CONTRIBUTIONGROUP
```

Figure 8: SQL-statement for DWH1

The local DWHs send their partial result back to the mediators. The mediators transform the results set into XML and the query processor calculates the federated result from all import results, by using the information from the evaluation tree.

5.5 XML Query Processing Results

In our work, we provide the results (i.e. local and federated query results) represented as XML document. For illustrating the result example, we populate the following example data for DWH1 of the prototype given in Figure 9. A query calculates the difference between the sum of the contributions and the sum of the benefits, constrained and grouped by various attributes.

BENEFIT

benefit_key	posdsc	grpdsc	level1	level2
5004	tooth extraction	dental treatment	specialist	A
5005	tooth sealing	dental treatment	specialist	A
.	.	.	.	.
8278	antibitic_nr1	antibiotic	medicament	D

COST_OF_BENEFIT

insurant_key	time_key	benefit_key	retainedamount	amount
1389657	45	5004	0	45
1389657	45	5005	3	28
.	.	.	.	.
1389659	45	8278	0	24

TIME

time_key	month	quarter	year
45	Jan	2000Q1	2000
46	Feb	2000Q1	2000
.	.	.	.
56	Dec	2000Q1	2000

INSURANT

insurant_key	ins_id	name	sex	salarylevel	agedecade	salary	contributiongroup
1389657	4875-030745	Huber	M	1002-2250	51-55	2178	B21D
1389658	2154-051278	Mayr	F	1501-1750	21-25	1800	A01D
.	.	.	.	.	.	.	.
1389659	2128-240862	Hofer	M	2251-2500	36-40	2289	A01L

Figure 9: Data example of DWH1

An example of the partial query result in XML for DWH1 is given in Figure 10. The first <row> element of the XML result for DWH1 shows that the <E1> element denotes the SUM of the attribute amount of the COST_OF_BENEFIT table. The SUM is analyzed according to the contribution group A01D of the INSURANT dimension given in the <contributiongroup> element and the quarter 2000Q1 in year 2000 of the time dimension.

```
<RowSet>
  <Row>
    <YEAR>2000</YEAR>
    <QUARTER>2000Q1</QUARTER>
    <CONTRIBUTIONGROUP>A01D</ CONTRIBUTIONGROUP >
    <E1>623919</E1>
  </Row>
  <Row>
    < YEAR >2000</ YEAR >
    < QUARTER >2000Q1</ QUARTER >
    < CONTRIBUTIONGROUP >A01L</ CONTRIBUTIONGROUP >
    <E1>400498</E1>
  </Row>
  ...
</RowSet>
```

Figure 10: Import result of DWH1

Figure 11 depicts an XML federated query result. The first <row> element contains the <Contribution-Benefit> element. This element calculates the difference between the sum of the contributions and the sum of the benefits analyzed according to the contribution group A01D of the

INSURANT dimension given in the <contributiongroup> element and the quarter 2000Q1 in year 2000 of the time dimension. In this paper, we do not show the partial result of DWH2, which present the sum of contribution.

6 CONCLUSION & FURTHER WORK

In this paper we have presented an XML-based query processing approach for DWHs in a federated architecture. We show the use of XML for querying federated OLAP data warehouses. The XML DTD is used for the federated query language definition and validation, whereas XML, as intermediate presentation facilitates creating and building queries for analyzing data in a federated architecture. In our approach the intermediate representation of both the import query and the results are coded in XML. The query results from local DWHs in XML facilitate merging and analyzing the results into one answer, as well as the usage of statistical analysis.

```
<RowSet>
  <Row>
    <Year>2000</ Year >
    <Quarter>2000Q1</ Quarter >
    <ContributionGroup>A01D</ ContributionGroup >
    <Contribution-Benefit>128354.0</ Contribution - Benefit >
  </Row>
  <Row>
    < Year >2000</ Year >
    < Quarter >2000Q1</ Quarter >
    < ContributionGroup >A01L</ ContributionGroup >
    < Contribution - Benefit >78965.0</ Contribution - Benefit >
  </Row>
  ...
</RowSet>
```

Figure 11: Federated query result

The important benefit of our approach is that local DWHs can continue working and deciding autonomously moreover, they can tailor the structure of their data warehouse to their particular needs without impacting the federated data warehouse. In addition, the federated queries from federated users are not dependent on the queries of the local users of local data warehouses. Based on our approach and the prototype, we believe that the use of XML for analyzing data in OLAP data warehouse, particularly in a federated architecture, is a very important approach in the near future.

ACKNOWLEDGEMENT

The authors gratefully acknowledge the support of the **Kplus** program, which is funded by the Austrian

Government, the province of Upper Austria and the Chamber of Commerce of Upper Austria. Furthermore, we would like to thank the *Upper-Austrian Health Insurance Organization (Oberösterreichische Gebietskrankenkasse - OÖGKK)* for sponsoring the project.

REFERENCES

Sheth, A.P., and Larson, J.A., 1990. Federated Database Systems for Managing Distributed, Heterogeneous, and Autonomous Databases. ACM Computing Surveys, Vol. 22, No. 3, September 1990.

Wiederhold, G., 1992. Mediators in the Architecture of Future Information Systems. The IEEE Computer Magazine, March 1992.

Codd, E.F., Codd, S.B., and Salley, C.T., 1993. Providing OLAP (On-Line Analytical Processing) to User-Analyst: An IT mandate. Technical Report, E.F. Codd & Associated, 1993.

Kimball, R., 1996. The Data Warehouse Toolkit, John Wiley & Sons, 1996.

Bauer, A., and Lehner, W., 1997. The Cube-Query-Language (CQL) for Multidimensional Statistical and Scientific Database Systems. *Proceedings of the 5th. International Conference on Database Systems for Advanced Applications (DASFAA)*, Melbourne, Australia, April 1-4, 1997.

W3C, 1998. Extensible markup language (XML) 1.0. http://www.w3.org/TR/1998/REC-xml-19980210 , 1998.

Garber, L., 1999. Michael Stonebraker on the Importance of Data Integration. IT Professional, Vol. 1, No. 3, pp. 80, 77-79, May, June 1999.

Hümmer, W., Albrecht, J., and Günzel, H., 2000. Distributed Data Warehousing Based on CORBA. *Proc. Of IASTED International Conference on Applied Informatics (AI'2000)*, Innsbruck, Austria, February, 2000.

Eckerson, W.W., 2000. Data Warehousing in the 21st. Century. The Data Warehousing Institute, 2000. http://www.dw-institute.com/

Mangisengi, O., Huber, J., Hawel., Ch., and Essmayr, W., 2001. A Framework for Supporting Interoperability of Data Warehouses Islands Using XML. *Proc. Of DAWAK 2001*, Springer LNCS 2114, pp. 328-338, Munich, Germany, Sept. 2001

Kerschberg, L., 2001. Knowledge Management in Heterogeneous Data Warehouse Environments. *Proc. Of DAWAK 2001*, Springer LNCS 2114, pp. 1-10, Munich, Germany, September 2001.

Ammoura, A., Zaiane, O., and Goebel, R., 2001. Towards a Novel OLAP Interface for Distributed Data Warehouses. *Proc. Of DAWAK 2001*, Springer LNCS 2114, pp. 174-185, Munich, Germany, Sept. 2001.

Gray, J., Bosworth, A., Layman, A., and Pirahesh, H. Data Cube: A Relational Aggregation Operator Generalizing Group-By, Cross-Tabs, and Sub-Totals. *Proceedings of ICDE'96*, New Orleans, February 1996.

Li, C. and Wang, X.S. A Data Model for Supporting On-Line Analytical Processing. *CIKM 1996*.

Meta Data Coalition. Metadata Interchange Specification (MDIS) Version 1.1, August 1997.

Meta Data Coalition. Open Information Model. Version 1.1, August 1999. http://www.mdcinfo.com/.

Agrawal, R., Gupta, A. and Sarawagi, A. Modeling Multidimensional Databases. IBM Research Report, IBM Almaden Research, September 1995.

Chaudhuri, S., and Dayal, U. An Overview of Data Warehousing and OLAP Technology. SIGMOD Record Volume 26, Number 1, September 1997.

Albrecht, J., Guenzel, H., and Lehner, W. An Architecture for Distributed OLAP. *Conference Parallel and Distributed Processing Techniques and Applications* (PDPTA), Las Vegas, USA, July 13-16, 1998.

Gyssens, M. and Lakshmanan, L.V.S. A Foundation for Multi-Dimensional Databases. *Proc. of VLDB'97*, 1997.

Albrecht, J., and Lehner, W. On-Line Analytical Processing in Distributed Data Warehouses. *International Databases Engineering and Applications Symposium (IDEAS)*, Cardiff, Wales, U.K., July 8-10, 1998.

Cabbibo, L., and Torlone, R. A Logical Approach to Multidimensional Databases. *EDBT*, 1998.

Lehner, W. Modeling Large Scale OLAP Scenarios. *6th. International Conference on Extending Database Technology (EDBT'98)*, Valencia, Spain, 23-27 March, 1998.

Garcia-Molina, H., Labio, W., Wiener, J.L., and Zhuge, Y. Distributed and Parallel Computing Issues in Data Warehousing. *In Proceedings of ACM Principles of Distributed Computing Conference*, 1999. Invited Talk.

Widom, J. Research Problems in Data Warehousing. Proceedings of the 4th. International Conference on Information and Knowledge Management (CIKM), November 1995.

EMPIRICAL VALIDATION OF METRICS FOR UML STATECHART DIAGRAMS

David Miranda, Marcela Genero and Mario Piattini

ALARCOS Research Group
Department of Computer Science, University of Castilla - La Mancha
Paseo de la Universidad, 4, 13071 - Ciudad Real, Spain
Email: dmiranda@proyectos.inf-cr.uclm.es, {Marcela.Genero, Mario.Piattini}@uclm.es

Keywords: Object Oriented Software Systems maintainability, UML behavioural diagrams, UML statechart diagrams, Structural complexity metrics, Empirical validation, Experiment replica

Abstract: It is widely recognised that the quality of Object Oriented Software Systems (OOSS) must be assessed from the early stages of their development. OO Conceptual models are key artifacts produced at these early phases, which cover not only static aspects but also dynamic aspects. Therefore, focusing on quality aspects of conceptual models could contribute to produce better quality OOSS. While quality aspects of structural diagrams, such as class diagrams, have being widely researched, the quality of behavioural diagrams such as statechart diagrams have been neglected. This fact leaded us to define a set of metrics for measuring their structural complexity. In order to gather empirical evidence that the structural complexity of statechart diagrams are related with their understandability we carried out a controlled experiment in a previous work. The aim of this paper is to present a replication of that experiment. The findings obtained in the replication corroborate the results of the first experiment in the sense that at some extent, the number of transitions, the number of states and the number of activities influence statechart diagrams understandability.

1 INTRODUCTION

Nowadays the idea that "measuring quality is the key to developing high-quality OO software" is gaining relevance (Schneidewind, 2002), and it is widely recognised that the quality of OOSS must be assessed from the early stages of their development. Conceptual modelling has become a key task of those early stages because it provides the solid foundation for OOSS design and implementation. The proof of this is that most of approaches towards OOSS development, like OMT, Catalysis, Rational Unified Process, OPEN, etc. have considered conceptual modelling as an integral part.

As early available, key analysis artifacts the quality of the conceptual models are crucial to the success of OOSS development. Therefore, the quality of conceptual models could have a significant impact on the quality of OOSS, which is ultimately implemented and must be evaluated, and if needed improved.

Modelling OOSS with the Unified Modeling Language (UML) (OMG, 1999) the static aspects at conceptual level are mainly represented in structural diagrams such as class diagrams, whilst dynamic aspects are represented in behavioural diagrams such as statechart diagrams, activity diagrams, sequence diagrams and collaboration diagrams. In this work we only focus on quality aspects of statechart diagrams.

Maintainability has become one of the software product quality characteristics (ISO 9126, 2001) that software development organisations are more concerned about since it is the major resource consumer of the whole software life cycle. But we are aware that maintainability is an "external quality attribute" that can only be evaluated once the product is finished or nearly finished. Therefore, it is necessary to have early indicators of such qualities based, for example, on the structural properties of statechart diagrams (Briand et al., 1999), such as their structural complexity.

Cant et al. (1995) have proposed a general cognitive model of software complexity that elaborates on the impact of structure on understandability. In the core of this model is a human memory model and there is some belief within the software engineering community that this model is a reasonable point of departure for

O. Camp et al. (eds.), Enterprise Information Systems V, 101-108.

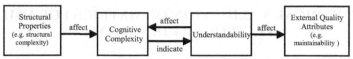

Figure 1: The complexity model for system development artifacts of (Briand et al., 1998).

understanding the impact of structural properties on understandability. The theoretical basis for developing quantitative models relating structural complexity and external quality attributes has been provided by (Briand et al., 1998). It is the basis for much empirical research in the area of software artifact structural properties (El-Emam and Melo, 1999; El-Emam, 2001; Poels and Dedene, 2000b). We assume in this work a similar representation to hold for statechart diagrams. We implement the relationship between the structural complexity on the one hand, and external quality attributes on the other hand (see figure 1). We hypothesized that the structural properties (such as structural complexity) of a UML statechart diagram have an impact on its cognitive complexity. By cognitive complexity we mean the mental burden of the persons who have to deal with the artifact (e.g. developers, testers, maintainers). High cognitive complexity leads to an artifact reduce their understandability and this conduce undesirable external qualities, such as decreased maintainability.

To assess the structural complexity of statechart diagrams in an objective and quantitative way it is necessary to dispose of metrics, avoiding thus bias in the quality evaluation process.

After having thoroughly reviewed existing works about metrics, which measure quality aspects, for UML diagrams we found several works related to metrics for structural diagrams such as class diagrams (Brito e Abreu and Carapuça, 1994; Chidamber and Kemerer, 1994; Fenton and Neil, 2000; Genero, 2002; Lorenz and Kidd, 1994; Marchesi, 1998). However, there is little reference to metrics for behavioural diagrams such as statechart diagrams in the existing literature. One of the first approaches towards the definition of metrics for behavioural diagrams can be found in (Derr, 1995), where metrics were applied to statechart diagrams developed with OMT (Rumbaugh et al., 1991). Yacoub et al. (1998) proposed structural complexity and coupling metrics for measuring the quality of dynamic executions. Metrics were defined basing in concepts as Petri Net and McCabe's cyclomatic structural complexity and were applied to simulated scenarios in Real-Time Object Modelling (ROOM) (Selic et al., 1994). Poels and Dedene (2000b) defined structural complexity metrics for event-driven OO conceptual models using MERODE

(Snoeck, 1995). These proposals of metrics have not gone beyond the definition step. As far as we know, there is no published works related to their theoretical an empirical validation (except Poels and Dedene who performed the theoretical validation). Therefore, and as was pointed out in (Brito e Abreu et al., 1999, 2000, 2002; Poels and Dedene, 2000b) the definition of metrics for diagrams that capture dynamics aspects of OOSS it is an interesting topic for future investigation. This fact motivated us to define metrics for behavioural diagrams, starting with metrics for measuring the structural complexity of UML statechart diagrams.

According some suggestions about "how to define valid metrics" (Briand et al., 1997; Calero et al., 2001) we have followed a process consisting of three main tasks: metric definition, theoretical validation and empirical validation.

For the definition and the theoretical validation of the metrics (Genero et al., 2002) we followed the DISTANCE framework (Poels and Dedene, 1999, 2000a) which assures the theoretical validity of the defined metrics, i.e., that they measure the attribute they intend to measure. By means of the usage of the DISTANCE framework we could also assure that the proposed metrics are characterised by the ratio scale type, which as Zuse (1998) pointed out it is a main concern when defining metrics for software artifacts.

Empirical validation is crucial for the success of any software measurement project (Basili et al., 1999; Fenton and Pfleeger, 1997; Kitchenham et al., 1995; Schneidewind, 1992). A proposal of metrics has not value if their practical use is not demonstrated empirically, either by means of case studies taken from real projects or by controlled experiments. Therefore, our main motivation is to investigate, through experimentation, if the metrics we proposed in (Genero et al., 2002) for UML statechart diagram structural complexity are related to statechart diagrams understandability. We performed a previous controlled experiment (Genero et al., 2002), pursuing a similar objective. However simple studies rarely provide definite answers and it is also necessary to accumulate the material of many studies (Basili et al., 1999; Miller, 2000), to obtain stronger findings. Following this purpose the main objective of this paper is to show how we carried out a replication of that previous experiment.

Table 1: Metrics for UML statechart diagram structural complexity.

Metric Name	Metric definition
NUMBER OF ENTRY ACTIONS (NEntryA)	The total number of entry actions, i.e. the actions performed each time a state is entered.
NUMBER OF EXIT ACTIONS (NExitA)	The total number of exit actions, i.e. the actions performed each time a state is left.
NUMBER OF ACTIVITIES (NA)	The total number of activities (do/activity) in the statechart diagram.
NUMBER OF STATES (NS)	The total number of simple states, considering also the simple states within the composites states.
NUMBER OF TRANSITIONS (NT)	The total number of transitions, considering common transitions (the source and the target states are different), the initial and final transitions, self-transitions (the source and the target state is the same), internal transitions (transitions inside a state that responds to an event but without leaving the state).

This paper is organized in the following way: Section 2 presents a proposal of metrics for the structural complexity of UML statechart diagrams.

A replication of a previous controlled experiment for empirically validating the proposed metrics is presented in section 3. The comparison of the results of the previous experiment with this replication is presented in Section 4. Finally section 5 shows the conclusions and some lines, which are still open for further investigation.

2 A PROPOSAL OF METRICS FOR UML STATECHART DIAGRAMS STRUCTURAL COMPLEXITY

The statechart diagrams structural complexity is determined by the different elements that compose it, such as states, transitions, activities, etc. As Fenton (1994) points, it is not advisable to define a single metric for the structural complexity of UML statechart diagrams since a single metric of structural complexity cannot capture all possible aspects or viewpoints of structural complexity. So

several metrics were defined (Genero et al., 2002), each one focusing on a different statechart diagram element (see table 1).

A relevant property of the proposed metrics is that they are simple and ease to automate, which are, as Fenton and Neil (2000) remark in a paper related to the future of software metrics, desirables properties for software metrics.

3 REPLICATION OF A CONTROLLED EXPERIMENT

In this section we describe a replication of an experiment we have carried out to empirically validate the proposed metrics as early understandability indicators (Genero et al., 2002). We have followed some suggestions provided in (Briand et al., 1999; Kitchenham et al., 2002; Perry et al., 2000; Wohlin et al., 2000) on how to perform controlled experiments and have used (with only minor changes) the format proposed by Wohlin et al. (2000) to describe it.

Analyse	UML statechart diagrams structural complexity metrics
For the purpose of	Evaluating
With respect to	The capability of being used as understandability indicators of the UML statechart diagrams
From the point of view of	OOSS designers
In the context of	Undergraduate students in the third year of Computer Science in the University of Castilla-La Mancha

Table 2: Goal of the experiment.

	NEntryA	NexitA	NA	NS	NT	Mean of the understandability time (seconds)
D01	1	1	0	3	7	129.8
D02	1	0	3	4	7	124.4
D03	2	0	2	4	7	261.7
D04	0	0	2	4	11	195.4
D05	3	2	2	4	13	129.4
D06	6	6	0	6	13	134.8
D07	1	0	1	5	11	169.6
D08	1	0	3	5	13	135.8
D09	0	1	4	5	10	155.4
D10	2	1	0	4	6	108.9
D11	1	2	1	6	17	185.7
D12	1	1	1	3	5	115.3
D13	2	1	0	2	4	93.3
D14	1	1	2	3	8	128.5
D15	1	0	4	9	13	181.3
D16	0	0	5	9	24	162.9
D17	2	0	1	5	8	149.4
D18	2	0	1	12	24	166.5
D19	0	1	0	2	6	108.9
D20	0	0	0	5	12	99.5

Table 3: Metric values for each UML statechart diagram.

3.1 Definition

Using the Goal-Question-Metric (GQM) template (Basili and Weiss, 1984; Basili and Rombach, 1988) for goal definition, the goal of the experiment is shown in table 2.

3.2 Planning

After the definition of the experiments (why the experiment is conducted), the planning took place. The planning is preparation for how the experiment is conducted and includes the following activities:

- **Context selection.** The context of the experiment is a group related to the area of Software Engineering at the university, and hence the experiment is run-off line (not in an industrial software development environment). The subjects were twenty students enrolled in the third-year of Computer Science at the Department of Computer Science in the University of Castilla-La Mancha in Spain. The experiment is specific since it focuses on UML statechart diagram structural complexity metrics. The ability to generalise from this specific context is further elaborated below when we discuss threats to the experiment. The experiment addresses a real problem, i.e., which

indicators can be used to assess the understandability of UML statechart diagram? To this end it investigates the correlation between metrics and understandability.

- **Selection of subjects.** The subjects are chosen for convenience, i.e. the subjects are students that have medium experience in the design and development of OOSS.
- **Variables selection.** The independent variable is UML statechart diagram structural complexity. The dependent variable is UML statechart diagram understandability.
- **Instrumentation.** The objects used in the experiment were 20 UML statechart diagrams. The independent variable was measured by the metrics presented in section 2. The dependent variable was measured by the time the subject spent answering the questionnaire attached to each diagram. We called that time "understandability time".
- **Hypothesis formulation.** An important aspect of experiments is to know and to state in a clear and formal way what we intend to evaluate in the experiment. This leads us to the formulation of the following hypotheses:

Null hypothesis, H_0: There is no significant correlation between the UML statechart diagrams structural complexity metrics and the understandability time.

Alternative hypothesis, H_1: There is a significant correlation between the UML statechart

diagrams structural complexity metrics and the understandability time.
- **Experiment design.** We selected a within-subject design experiment, i.e. all the questionnaires had to be solved by each of the subjects. The subjects were given the tests in different order.

3.3 Operation

It is in this phase where measurements are collected including the following activities:
- **Preparation.** At the time the experiment was done all of the students had taken a course on Software Engineering, in which they learnt in depth how to design OOSS using UML. Moreover, the subjects were given an intensive training session before the experiment took placing. However, the subjects were not aware of what aspects we intended to study. Neither they were informed about the actual hypotheses stated.

We prepared the material we handed to the subjects, which consisted of a guide explaining the UML statechart notation and 20 UML statechart diagrams. These diagrams were related to different universes of discourse that were easy enough to be understood by each of the subjects. The structural complexity of each diagram is different, covering a broad range of the metrics values (see table 3). Each diagram had a test enclosed, which includes a questionnaire in order to evaluate if the subjects really understand the content of the UML statechart diagrams. Each questionnaire contained exactly the same number of questions (four) and the questions were conceptually similar and were written in identical order. Each subject had to write down the time he started answering the questionnaire and at the time they finished. The difference between the two is what we called the understandability time (expressed in seconds).
- **Execution.** The subjects were given all of the material described in the previous paragraph. We explained to them how to carry out the experiment. Each subject had to carry out the test alone and there was a teacher supervising the execution of the experiment. We collected all of the data with the understandability time calculated from the responses of the experiments.

- **Data Validation.** Once the data were collected, we controlled if the tests were completed and if the questions have been answered correctly. All the tests were considered valid because all the questions were correctly answered.

3.4 Analysis and Interpretation

First we summarized the data collected for each diagram. We had the metric values and we calculated the mean of the subjects' understandability time for each statechart diagram (see table 3). We want to analyse these data in order to test the hypotheses formulated in section 3.2. For this purpose we used the Statistical Package for Social Science (SPSS).

We applied the Kolmogrov-Smirnov test to ascertain if the distribution of the data collected was normal. As the data were non-normal we decided to use a non-parametric test like Spearman's correlation coefficient, with a level of significance α = 0.05, which means the level of confidence is 95% (i.e. the probability that we reject H_0 when H_0 is false is at least 95%, which is statistically acceptable). Each of

the metrics was correlated separately to the mean of the subjects' understandability time (see table 4).

For a sample size of 20 (mean values for each diagram) and α = 0.05, the Spearman cut-off for accepting H_0 is 0.44 (Briand et al., 1997; CUHK, 2002). Because the computed Spearman's correlation coefficients for metrics NA, NS and NT (see table 4), are above this cut-off and the p-value < 0.05, the null hypothesis H_0, is rejected. Hence, we can conclude that there is a significant correlation between NA, NS and NT metrics and subjects' understandability time.

3.5 Validity evaluation

We will discuss the various issues that threaten the validity of the empirical study and the way we attempted to alleviate them:
- **Threats to Conclusion Validity.** The only issue that could affect the statistical validity of this study is the size of the sample data (20 values), which perhaps are not enough for both parametric and non-parametric statistic test

	NEntryA	NExitA	NA	NS	NT
Understandability time	- 0.046 p=0.85	- 0.346 p=0.14	**0.517 p=0.02**	**0.575 p=0.01**	**0.550 p=0.01**

Table 4: Spearman's correlation between metrics and understandability time.

(Briand et al., 1997). We are aware of this, so we will try to obtain bigger sample data through more experimentation.

- **Threats to Construct Validity.** The construct validity is the degree to which the independent and the dependent variables are accurately measured by the measurement instruments used in the experiment. For the dependent variable we use the understandability time, i.e., the time each subject spent answering the questions related to each diagram, that it is considered the time they need to understand it. It is an objetive measure so we consider the understandability time could be considered a measure constructively valid. The construct validity of the metrics used for the independent variable is guaranteed by Poels and Dedene´s framework (Poels and Dedene, 1999, 2000a), used for their theoretical validation (Genero et al., 2002).

- **Threats to Internal Validity.** The internal validity is the degree of confidence in a cause-effect relationship between factors of interest and the observed results. The analysis performed here is correlational in nature. We have demonstrated that several of the metrics investigated had a statistically and practically significant relationship with understandability. Such statistical relationship do not demonstrate per se a causal relationship. They only provide empirical evidence of it. Only controlled experiments, where the metrics would be varied in a controlled manner and all other factors would be held constant, could really demonstrate causality. However, such a controlled experiment would be difficult to run since varying structural complexity in a system, while preserving its functionality, is difficult in practice. On the other hand, it is difficult to imagine what could be alternative explanations for our results besides a relationship between structural complexity and understandability. The following issues have also been dealt with: Differences among subjects, Knowledge of the universe of discourse among class diagrams, Precision in the time values, Learning effects, Fatigue effects, Persistence effects, Subject motivation, Plagiarism and Influence between students.

- **Threats to External Validity.** External validity is the degree to which the research results can be generalised to the population under study and other research settings. The greater the external

validity, the more the results of an empirical study can be generalised to actual software engineering practice. Two threats to validity have been identified which limit the ability to apply any such generalisation: Materials and tasks used and Selection of subjects.

3.6 Presentation and Package

As the diffusion of experimental data is important for the external replication of the experiments (Brooks et al., 1996) we have put all of the material of this experiment onto the website http://alarcos.inf-cr.uclm.es.

4 COMPARISON WITH THE RESULTS OF A PREVIOUS EXPERIMENT

The most important difference between the previous experiment we carried out and this replication is the subjects who participate in them. In the first experiment the subjects were teachers and advanced students in the final year of computer science; whilst the subjects that performed this replication were third-year students.

Comparing the findings of both experiments (see tables 4 and 5) we realized that they are similar. This means that the metrics NA, NS and NT are to some extent correlated with the understandability time of UML statechart diagrams.

Nevertheless, despite the encouraging results obtained we still consider them as preliminaries. Further replication, both internal and external (Brooks et al., 1996), is of course necessary and also new experiments must be carried out with practitioners who work in software development organizations. Only after performing a family of experiments you can build an adequate body of knowledge to extract useful measurement conclusions regarding the use of OO design metrics to be applied in real measurement projects (Basili et al., 1999; Briand et al., 1998).

To improve our empirical studies it is necessary to increase the difference between the values of the metrics. This option could lead to more conclusive results about the metrics and their relationship with the factor we are trying to control.

Another way to enhance the validity of the

	NEntryA	NExitA	NA	NS	NT
Understandability time	0.215	0.285	**0.483**	**0.500**	**0.605**
	p=0.45	p=0.28	**p=0.03**	**p=0.02**	**p=0**

Table 5: Spearman's correlation between metrics and understandability time in the previous experiment.

results is by working with data obtained from industrial environments, for gathering real evidence that the metrics we presented can be used as early statechart diagram understandability indicators. However, the scarcity of such data continues to be a great problem so we must find other ways to tackle validating metrics. Brito e Abreu et al. (1999, 2000, 2002) suggested the necessity of a public repository of measurement experiences, which we think would be a good step towards the success of all the work done on software measurement. It will possible to do that when more "real data" on systems developed using UML is available, which is the challenge of most of the researchers in this area.

5 CONCLUSIONS AND FUTURE WORK

With the hypothesis that the structural complexity of UML statechart diagrams may influence their understandability (and therefore in their maintainability), we defined a set of metrics for the structural complexity of UML statechart diagrams (Genero et al., 2002). This hypothesis was empirically corroborated by a controlled experiment we carried out before. In order to emphasise these results we carried out a replication, which was thoroughly described in the current work.

As a result of all the experimental work, we can conclude that the metrics NA, NS and NT seem to be highly correlated with the understandability of UML statechart diagrams. Despite of this, we are aware that further empirical validation of these metrics would be necessary to assess if they could be really used as early understandability indicators of the UML statechart diagrams.

Once we obtained stronger results in this line, we think the metrics we proposed could also be used for allowing OOSS designers a quantitative comparison of design alternatives, and therefore, an objective selection among several statechart diagram alternatives with equivalent semantic content, and predicting external quality characteristic, like understandability in the initial stages of the OOSS life cycle and a better resource allocation based on these predictions. In this sense we plan to build a prediction model (based on the metrics values) using advanced techniques borrowed from artificial intelligence such as Fuzzy Classification and Regression Trees (Delgado et al., 2001) and Fuzzy Prototypical Knowledge Discovery (Olivas and Romero, 2000), which have been used for prediction purposes in others domains obtaining accurate predictions.

Finally, another research line of interest would be to evaluate the influence of the structural complexity of the UML statechart diagrams on other maintainability factors such as modifiability and analysability.

ACKNOWLEDGEMENTS

David Miranda is supported by a FPI grant. This research is part of the DOLMEN project supported by Subdirección General de Proyectos de Investigación - Ministerio de Ciencia y Tecnología (TIC 2000-1673-C06-06).

REFERENCES

Basili, V. and Rombach, H., 1988. The TAME project: towards improvement-oriented software environments. In *IEEE Transactions on Software Engineering 14(6) 758-773*.

Basili, V. and Weiss, D., 1984. A Methodology for Collecting Valid Software Engineering Data. In *IEEE Transactions on Software Engineering 10(6) 728-738*.

Briand, L., Arisholm, S., Counsell, F., Houdek, F. and Thévenod-Fosse, P., 1999. Empirical Studies of Object-Oriented Artifacts, Methods, and Processes: State of the Art and Future Directions. In *Empirical Software Engineering 4(4) 387-404*.

Briand, L., Bunse, C., Daly, J. and Differding, C., 1997. An Experimental Comparison of the Maintainability of Object-Oriented and Structured Design Documents. In *Empirical Software Engineering 2(3)*.

Briand., L., Wüst, J. and Lounis, H., 1998. A Comprehensive Investigation of Quality Factors in Object-Oriented Designs: an Industrial Case Study. In *Technical Report ISERN-98-29, International Software Engineering Research Network*.

Brito e Abreu, F. and Carapuça, R., 1994. Object-Oriented Software Engineering: Measuring and controlling the development process. In *4th International Conference on Software Quality*.

Brito e Abreu, F., Henderson-Sellers, B., Piattini, M., Poels, G. and Sahraoui, H., 2002. In *Quantitative Approaches in Object-Oriented Software Engineering. ECOOP'01 Workshop Reader*, LNCS Vol. 2323, Springer-Verlag 174-183.

Brito e Abreu, F., Poels, G., Sahraoui, H. and Zuse, H., 2000. In *Quantitative Approaches in Object-Oriented Software Engineering. ECOOP'2000 Workshop Reader*, LNCS Vol. 1964, Springer-Verlag 93-103.

Brito e Abreu, F., Zuse, H., Sahraoui, H. and Melo, W., 1999. In *Quantitative Approaches in Object-Oriented Software Engineering. ECOOP'99 Workshops Reader*, LNCS Vol. 1743, Springer-Verlag 326-337.

Brooks, A., Daly, J., Miller, J., Roper, M. and Wood, M., 1996. Replication of experimental results in software engineering. In *Technical report ISERN-96-10, International Software Engineering Research Network.*

Calero, C., Piattini, M. and Genero, M., 2001. Empirical validation of referential integrity metrics. In *Information and Software Technology 43 949-957.*

Cant, S., Jeffery, R. and Henderson-Sellers, B., 1995. A Conceptual Model of Cognitive Complexity of Elements of the Programming Process. In *Information and Software Technology 7 351-362.*

Chidamber, S. and Kemerer, C., 1994. A Metrics Suite for Object Oriented Design. In *IEEE Transactions on Software Engineering 20(6) 476-493.*

CUHK - Chinese University of Hong Kong - Department of Obstetrics and Gynaecology – http://department.obg.cuhk.edu.hk/ResearchSupport/M inimum_correlation.asp (Last visited on July 22nd, 2002).

Delgado, M., Gómez-Skarmeta, A. and Jiménez, L., 2001. A regression methodology to induce a fuzzy model. In *International Journal of Intelligent Systems 16(2) 169-190.*

Derr, K., 1995. *Applying OMT,SIGS Books*, Prentice Hall. New York.

El-Emam, K. and Melo, W., 1999. The Prediction of Faulty Classes Using Object-Oriented Design Metrics. In *NRC/ERB1064*, National Research Council. Canada.

El-Emam, K., 2001. Object-Oriented Metrics: A Review on Theory and Practice. In *NRC/ERB 1085*, National Research Council. Canada.

Fenton, N. and Neil, M., 2000. *Software Metrics: a Roadmap. Future of Software Engineering*, Anthony Finkelstein Ed., ACM 359-370.

Fenton, N. and Pfleeger, S., 1997. *Software Metrics: A Rigorous Approach*, Chapman & Hall. London, 2nd. edition.

Fenton, N., 1994. Software Measurement: A Necessary Scientific Basis. In *IEEE Transactions on Software Engineering 20(3) 199-206.*

Genero, M., 2002: Defining and Validating Metrics for Conceptual Model, *Ph.D. thesis*. University of Castilla-La Mancha.

Genero, M., Miranda, D. and Piattini, M., 2002. Defining and Validating Metrics for UML Statechart Diagrams. In 6th International ECOOP Workshop on Quantitative Approaches in Object-Oriented Software Engineering (QAOOSE'2002) 120-136.

ISO 9126, 2001. Software Product Evaluation-Quality Characteristics and Guidelines for their Use, ISO/IEC Standard 9126. Geneva.

Kitchenham, B., Pflegger, S. and Fenton, N., 1995 Towards a Framework for Software Measurement Validation. In *IEEE Transactions of Software Engineering 21(12) 929-943.*

Kitchenham, B., Pflegger, S., Pickard, L., Jones, P., Hoaglin, D., El-Emam, K. and Rosenberg, J., 2002. Preliminary Guidelines for Empirical Research in Software Engineering. In *IEEE Transactions of Software Engineering 28(8) 721-734.*

Lorenz, M. and Kidd, J., 1994. Object-Oriented Software Metrics: A Practical Guide, *Prentice Hall*. Englewood Cliffs, New Jersey.

Marchesi, M., 1998. OOA Metrics for the Unified Modeling Language. In 2nd Euromicro Conference on Software Maintenance and Reengineering 67-73.

Miller, J., 2000. Applying Meta-Analytical Procedures to Software Engineering Experiments. In *Journal of Systems and Software Vol. 54 29-39.*

Object Management Group, 1999. UML Revision Task Force, OMG Unified Modeling Language Specification, v. 1.3, document ad/99-06-08.

Olivas, J. and Romero, F., 2000. FPKD. Fuzzy Prototypical Knowledge Discovery. Application to Forest Fire Prediction. In *SEKE'2000, Knowledge Systems Institute, Chicago, Ill. USA 47-54.*

Perry, D., Porter, A. and Votta, L., 2000. Empirical Studies of Software Engineering: A Roadmap. In *Future of Software Engineering. Anthony Finkelstein Ed., ACM 345-355.*

Poels, G. and Dedene, G., 1999. DISTANCE: A Framework for Software Measure Construction. In *Research Report DTEW9937, Dept. Applied Economics, Katholiek Universiteit Leuven, Belgium.*

Poels, G. and Dedene, G., 2000a. Distance-Based software measurement: necessary and sufficient properties for software measures. In *Information and Software Technology 42(1) 35-46.*

Poels, G. and Dedene, G., 2000b. Measures for Assessing Dynamic Complexity Aspects of Object-Oriented Conceptual Schemes. In *19th International Conference on Conceptual Modelling (ER 2000) 499-512.*

Rumbaugh, J., Blaha, M., Premerlani, W., Eddy, F. and Lorensen, W., 1991. *Object- Oriented Modelling and Design*, Prentice Hall. USA.

Schneidewind, N., 1992. Methodology For Validating Software Metrics. In *IEEE Transactions of Software Engineering, 18(5) 410-422.*

Schneidewind, N., 2002. Body of Knowledge for Software Quality Measurement. In *IEEE Computer 35(2) 77-83.*

Selic, B., Gullekson, G. and Ward P., 1994. *Real-Time Object Oriented Modelling*, John Wiley & Sons, Inc.

Snoeck, M., 1995: On a process algebra approach for the construction and analysis of M.E.R.O.D.E. - based conceptual models, *Ph.D.* Katholieke Universiteit Leuven.

Wohlin, C., Runeson, P., Höst, M., Ohlson, M., Regnell, B. and Wesslén, A., 2000. Experimentation in Software Engineering: An Introduction, *Kluwer Academic Publishers.*

Yacoub, S., Ammar, H. and Robinson, T., 1998. Dynamic Metrics for Object Oriented Designs. In *Sixth IEEE International Symposium on Software Metrics.*

Zuse, H., 1998. A Framework of Software Measurement, Walter de Gruyter. Berlin.

ERP SYSTEMS IMPLEMENTATION DETERMINANTS AND SUCCESS MEASURES IN CHINA: A CASE STUDY APPROACH

Liang Zhang, Matthew K. O. Lee
Department of Information Systems, City University of Hong Kong, Hong Kong
Email: iszhang@is.cityu.edu.hk, ismatlee@cityu.edu.hk

Zhe Zhang
Faculty of Business Administration, Northeastern University, Shenyang, P.R.China
Email: zhang_zhe@neusoft.com

Christy M. K. Cheung
Department of Information Systems, City University of Hong Kong, Hong Kong
Email: iscc@is.cityu.edu.hk

Keywords: Enterprise resource planning, Implementation, Information systems success, User satisfaction, organizational impact

Abstract: With the growing intensive global competition and integration of the world economy, manufacturing firms have to reduce inventory level and operation costs, improve customer service to obtain competitive advantage against their competitors. Manufacturing companies are forced to adopt new methods to achieve the above objectives. Enterprise resource planning (ERP) system is one of the most widely accepted choices. Significant benefits such as improved customer service, better production scheduling, and reduced manufacturing costs can accrue from the successful implementation of ERP (Ang et al, 1995). However, the successful implementation rate is extremely low especially in China and many firms didn't achieve intended goals. Thus, it's necessary for ERP practitioners and researchers to investigate the reasons why the implementation success rate of ERP systems in China is so low. Prior studies mainly focus on critical success factors or single ERP implementation success measure without theoretical support. This study attempts to combine Ives, Hamilton, and Davis (1980) MIS research model and DeLone & McLean's (1992) IS success model to develop an ERP implementation success model, identifying both generic and unique factors that affect ERP systems implementation success in China and using multiple ERP implementation success measures to assess whether an ERP implementation is a success or failure.

1 INTRODUCTION

Enterprise resource planning (ERP) is probably the most rapidly growing system area in operations today. Thousands of companies have implemented or are in the process of implementing an ERP system. AMR predicts the total ERP market, estimated at $20.2 billion for 1999, will reach $66.6 billion by 2003, growing an estimated 32% annually over the next five years. Significant benefit such as improved customer service, better production scheduling, and reduced manufacturing costs can accrue from

successful implementation of ERP systems (Ang et al, 1995).

Kumar et al (2000) defined enterprise resource planning (ERP) systems as "configurable information systems packages that integrate information and information-based processes within and across functional areas in an organization". ERP systems are expensive and time-consuming, and once ERP systems are implemented, management should evaluate whether it is successful. Although ERP systems provides an integrated information

109

systems for the entire organization, limited empirical research has been conducted to evaluate implementation of complex organizational information systems or to identify critical factors which improve the probability of ERP systems implementation success. In information systems area, implementation is defined as "the process that begins with the managerial decision to install a computer-based organizational information system and is complete when the system is operating as an integral part of the organization's information system" (Burns & Turnipseed, 1991). A recent Standish Group report on ERP implementation projects reveals that these projects were, on average, 178% over budget, took 2.5 times as long as intended and delivered only 30% of promised benefit. According to the data of IDC (1998), foreign ERP vendors took up more than 90 percent ERP market share. Until now, nearly 1,000 companies in China have implemented MRP, MRP II or ERP systems since 1980. Among them the successful implementation rate is extremely low at only 10% (Zhu & Ma, 1999). The steep difference of ERP systems implementation success rate between Western countries and China produces a need of research to examine generic and unique factors that affect ERP implementation in China. Among the studies evaluating ERP success, mostly use a single measure such as user satisfaction, improved intended business performance, on-time delivery, within budget, etc. ERP related publications mostly concern the practices of ERP systems adoption, implementation, benefits, cost and risks analysis, lack of theoretical support. This study attempts to combine the Ives, Hamilton, and Davis (1980) MIS research model and DeLone and McLean (1992) IS success model, with adequate modification for the ERP field, to develop a conceptual ERP implementation success model.

The organization of this paper is as follows. First, literature on both determinants of ERP systems implementation success and success measures including IS literature is reviewed to facilitate understanding of current research status. Second, research design is developed to guide the research progress. Third, conceptual research framework is developed followed by data collection and analysis. Finally, the study concludes with a summary and an outlook to future directions of the research.

2 LITERATURE REVIEW

In this section, previous studies on ERP systems implementation and information systems (IS)

success measures are reviewed to search for theoretical support and research model development.

2.1 ERP Systems Implementation Literature

Limited studies have been conducted to identify critical factors affecting ERP systems implementation success with many of them focused on single-case study of how we implemented ERP systems in our company. Moreover, most of these studies overlooked how to measure the success of ERP implementation (Cox and Clark 1984; Wilson et al, 1994; Ang et al, 1995; Bingi et al, 1999; Holland and Light 1999). Most studies that have measured ERP implementation success used only one surrogate of ERP implementation success with user satisfaction (Ang et al 1994).

Cox and Clark (1984) conducted an extensive literature review and classified problems with ERP systems implementation into three categories: management, technical, and human problems. They argued that management and personnel problems are by far the most serious problems in terms of cost and source of system failure. Burns et al (1991) classified factors into two categories: environmental factors and methodological factors. The environmental factors include organization function, organization size, production process, product technology, process technology, and organizational willingness to change. The methodological factors include use of a project team, use of a project manager, use of a consultant, the consultant's involvement in the implementation, use of an implementation plan, the conversion approach, extent of hardware modification, the source of the software, the previous system's environment, and the extent of organizational modification required. Burns et al conducted a large-scale mail survey of organizations in the southeastern United States (n=1,544) to test their model. They included user satisfaction indicating the extent to which the ERP system had met the respondent's expectations and White's *ABCD* classification scheme (White 1984) that best described the organization's ERP implementation as surrogates of ERP implementation success.

Ang et al (1995) identified 13 critical success factors that affect MRP implementation success in Singapore: (1) top management support, (2) clear goals and objectives, (3) Inter-department cooperation, (4) Inter-department communication, (5) visibility of implementation, (6) staff training and education, (7) staff motivation and commitment, (8) staff's level of MRP knowledge prior to implementation, (9) vendor knowledge of MRP, (10) vendor support, (11) suitability of hardware and software, (12) data accuracy and integrity, and (13) company expertise in IT. According to Rockart (1979), critical success factors are defined as "those factors that determine success or failure for a business unit or organization". They represent those areas that management must carefully consider in order to bring about continued good performance (Ang et al 1995). Some of the CSFs identified by Ang et al (1995) cannot be said as CSFs including (8). Moreover, Inter-department cooperation and communication could be defined as one factor rather than two.

There is growing evidence that failures to adapt ERP packages to fit different organizational and national cultures leads to projects that are expensive and late. Unlike the traditional software development approach, which promotes building systems from scratch, ERP packages encapsulate reusable best business processes and software (Krumbholz and Maiden, 2001). Moreover, Chinese culture is far different from that of Western countries plus foreign ERP vendors play a dominant role in China ERP package market. Thus, it is necessary to investigate the impact of Chinese culture on ERP implementation.

The literature varies regarding which variables are required for implementation success or responsible for failure. A review of relevant literature suggests that problems with the implementation of ERP systems occur for a number of reasons. These include:

1) The need for business process change during the implementation of an ERP system is needed (Al-Mashari and Zairi, 2000; Bingi et al 1999; Motwani et al, 2002).

2) Lack of top management support, data accuracy, and user involvement can attribute to system implementation failures (Ang et al 1995 and 2002; Bingi et al 1999; Sum et al, 1997; Wilson et al 1994).

3) Education and training are frequently underestimated and are given less time due to schedule pressures, and less understanding of cross-functional business processes are often reported (Ang et al 1995; Markus et al, 2000).

4) When adopting an ERP system, there is a need to recognize the unique Asian context in that the embedded business models typically reflect Western practices (Soh et al, 2000).

As for how to define ERP systems implementation success, there is no agreed measures until now. Oliver White created *ABCD* Checklist that classified ERP implementations into four categories. User satisfaction is also used to serve as a surrogate for ERP implementation success (Burns et al 1991; Ang et al 1994 and 2002; White et al 1982). White et al (1982) defined successful ERP implementation along two dimensions: (1) improved performance, and (2) user satisfaction. Markus et al (2000) argue that the definition and measurement of ERP success are thorny matters and success depends on the point of view from which you measure it. People whose jobs are to implement ERP systems (e.g. project managers and implementation consultants) often define success in terms of completing the project plan on time and within budget. However, people whose jobs are to adopt ERP systems and use them in achieving business results tend to emphasize having a smooth transition to stable operations with the new systems, thereby achieving intended business improvements such as inventory reductions and gaining improved decision support capabilities.

From previous ERP implementation success literature review, there are several measures that can be used as surrogates of ERP implementation success:

(1) User satisfaction
(2) Intended business performance improvements
(3) Oliver White's *ABCD* Classification
(4) On-time go live
(5) Within-budget implementation
(6) System acceptance and usage

In the above 6 measures of ERP system implementation success, Oliver White's *ABCD* Classification is not suitable in nowadays ERP system implementation in that most firms implemented ERP systems could achieve rough integration among ERP system modules. Meanwhile, even if ERP system implementation exceeds contracted delivery time and budget, firms may still think their ERP implementation is a success. While system acceptance and usage are inappropriate once the use of an ERP system is required. Thus, only user satisfaction and intended business performance improvements could be used as success measures.

2.2 Information Systems Literature

A large number of studies have been conducted during the past two decades to identify those factors that contribute to information systems (IS) success. The Ives, Hamilton, and Davis (1980) MIS research model includes five environment variables (i.e., external environment, organizational environment, user environment, IS development environment, and IS operations environment) that interact with the information system variable. These interactions can be observed by three process variables or performance measures (i.e., use process, development process, and operation process).

However, the dependent variable of IS success is difficult to define and a cumulative research is not easy to come into being. Nearly for more than ten years, there are no concerted dependent variables for information systems success in the literature. Zmud (1979) used user performance, MIS usage, and user satisfaction as the dependent variables for information systems success. Ginzberg (1981) adopted system use and user satisfaction as the dependent variables to measure information systems success. Ives and Olson (1984) used system quality and system acceptance as the two dependent variables for information systems success. Lack of conclusive findings relating dependent variables of IS success can be attributed to many factors. Weill and Olson (1989) have stated that the concepts of information systems success and systems fit are ill-defined and more specifically, the scales which constitute the existing instruments for measuring user information satisfaction lack a theoretical basis (Shirani et al 1994). Not until ten years ago was the dependent variable—IS success identified by DeLone & McLean (1992) that has been considered a suitable foundation for further empirical and theoretical research, and has met with general acceptance as such (Ballantine et al, 1998).

DeLone & McLean's IS Success Model

DeLone & McLean (1992) based on the work of Shannon and Weaver (1949) and Mason (1978), conducted an extensive literature review on 180 empirical studies published in six top information systems journals and one of the most important information systems conference proceedings, classifying dimensions of information systems success into six categories (Figure 1 illustrates their IS Success Model): *System Quality; Information Quality; Use; User Satisfaction; Individual Impact; Organizational Impact.*

In Figure 1, system quality and information quality singularly and jointly affect both use and user satisfaction. While use and user satisfaction have positive or negative impact on the other. Use and user satisfaction are direct antecedents of individual impact. Lastly, this impact on individual performance should eventually affect organizational performance.

First, it's clear that actual use, as a measure of IS success, only makes sense for voluntary or discretionary users as opposed to captive users (Lucas 1978). Moreover, in an involuntary situation of using an information system, user satisfaction leads to use rather than use stimulating user satisfaction (Baroudi and Davis 1986). Thus, for DeLone & McLean (1992), when the use of information system is mandatory or required, the previous measures of system quality, information quality, and use become less useful.

Another problem with DeLone and McLean's IS success model is that they attempted to combine both process and causal explanations of IS success in their model (Seddon 1997). "Variance models assert that for some population of interest, if all other things are equal, variance in any one of the independent variables is necessary and sufficient to cause variance in the dependent variables. By contrast, process models (Newman and Robey, 1992) show how certain combinations of events, in a particular sequence, cause certain outcomes. Each event in the process model is necessary, but not sufficient, to cause the outcome" (Seddon 1997).

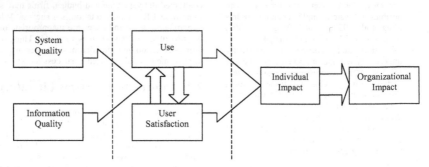

Figure 1: DeLone & McLean's IS Success Model

3 MULTIPLE-CASE STUDY RESEARCH DESIGN

Qualitative research involves the use of qualitative data, such as interviews, documents, and participant observation to explain social phenomena. As the focus of information systems research shifts from technological to managerial and organizational issues, qualitative research methods become increasingly useful (Myers 1997). Moreover, case studies are far from being only an exploratory strategy (Yin 1994) and collecting large sample size from organizations. Moreover, the availability of more detailed information from specific phenomena makes case study a viable research methodology for the ERP systems implementation research.

The literature review has shown that most case studies conducted on ERP implementation used a single case design focusing on "how an ERP system was implemented in my company". Such a single case study is frequently criticized for its descriptive and exploratory nature. However, the evidence from multiple cases is often considered more compelling, and the overall study is therefore regarded as being more robust (Herriott & Firestone, 1983). Contrary to common misconception that case studies provide little basis for scientific generalization, case studies are generalizable to theoretical propositions, not to populations or universes (statistical generalization) (Ang et al 2001; Lee 1989; Yin 1994). Moreover, generalizability is a quality describing a theory that has been tested and confirmed in a variety of situations, whether such testing is conducted through case research, laboratory experiment, statistical experiment, or natural experiments. As such, generalizability poses no more, and no less, of a problem for MIS case research than it does for the studies conducted in the natural sciences (Lee 1989). Taking my research objectives into consideration, a multiple-case study is an appropriate methodology.

Study Questions

Research questions of this study include "what," "why," and "how" questions as following:

❖ What are the critical factors that affecting ERP systems implementation success in China?

❖ Why are these factors critical for successful ERP implementation in China?

❖ How can ERP systems be implemented successfully in China?

❖ How can an ERP systems implementation be measured and defined as a success or a failure in China?

Validity and Reliability

One advantage of using multiple sources of evidence (documents, archive records, open-ended interviews, focused interviews, observations, and physical artifacts) lies in its capability of providing multiple measures of the same phenomenon in each setting resulting in the development of converging lines of inquiry, a process of triangulation. Thus, the construct validity of the case study could be more convincing and accurate. Moreover, by using replication logic of the same interview protocol in multiple case studies, the external validity of the information collected can be obtained. To increase the reliability of the information in the study, several methods or steps would be taken. First, sufficient citation to the relevant portions of the case study database will be made by citing specific documents, interviews, and/or observations; Second, the database would reveal the actual evidence and also indicate the circumstances under which the evidence was collected; Third, these circumstances would be consistent with the specific procedures and questions contained in the case study protocol, to show that the data collection followed the procedures stipulated in the protocol; Finally, a reading of the protocol should indicate the link between the content of the protocol and the initial study questions. Thus, the ultimate "chain of evidence" is built and the reliability of the information in the case studies can be increased.

Subjects of Case Study

❖ Criteria for Selection

The author defines an ERP company as one that has installed at least the basic modules of the three major integral part of an overseas' ERP system: manufacturing, distribution, and finance modules. Moreover, the ERP system installed should have gone live no more than two years for the reasons of difficulty in recalling past implementation process. At least four ERP companies based on the characteristics of firms (e.g. industry, company size, organizational structure, profit/non-profit status, ownership, and so on) will be interviewed. This study focuses on "literal" replications (similar results are predicted) rather than "theoretical" replications (contradictory results are predicted).

❖ Unit of Analysis

In each of these ERP companies, at least three persons serving as embedded units of analysis will be interviewed including: one member of the steering committee, the project manager, and one of the major end users who have gone through the whole ERP implementation process from start to end.

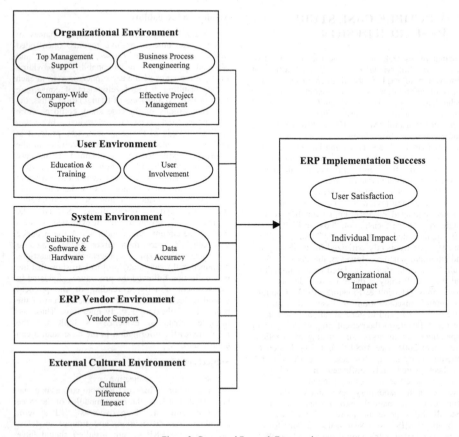

Figure 2: Conceptual Research Framework

4 RESEARCH FRAMEWORK

Based on the ERP literature and the MIS research model proposed by Ives, Hamilton, and Davis (1980), factors that affect successful ERP implementation in China have been identified. From the IS success model of DeLone and McLean (1992) the dependent variables that measure ERP implementation success are defined.

With specific objective in this study, through combining and adapting the Ives, Hamilton, and Davis model with ERP and IS success literatures, the research framework is depicted in Figure 2. The IS development environment and the IS operations environment are replaced with system environment and ERP vendor environment. Moreover, the three process measures are replaced by the three success measures (user satisfaction, individual impact, and organizational impact) from the DeLone and McLean model. The interactions among the three dependent variables are beyond the focus of this study and not studied.

Organizational Environment

❖ *Top Management Support*

Many studies have stressed the importance of top management support as a necessary ingredient in successful ERP implementation (Ang et al, 1995; Bingi et al, 1999; Duchessi et al, 1999; Sum and Yang, 1992; Thong et al, 1996). Since ERP is a highly integrated information system, its design, implementation, and operation require the complete cooperation of line and staff members from all segments of the business. Top management support can play a useful role in setting disputes and in providing clear signals to any doubts. Meanwhile, implementing an ERP system is not a matter of changing the software systems; rather it is a matter of reengineering the company and transforming the business practices to the best business practices.

❖ Re-engineering Business Process

Business process re-engineering (BPR) is defined by Hammer and Champy (2001) as "the fundamental rethinking and radical redesign of business processes to achieve dramatic improvements in critical, contemporary measures of performance, such as cost, quality, service and speed". Implementing an ERP system involves re-engineering the existing business processes to the best business process standard (Bingi et al, 1999; Burns and Turnipseed, 1991; Holland and Light, 1999; Motwani et al, 2002). One of the principal reasons why ERP and other large technologically sophisticated systems fail is that organizations simply underestimate the extent to which they have to change and re-engineering the existing business processes in order to accommodate their purchase.

❖ Effective Project Management

According to Dennis Lock (1996), "project management has evolved in order to plan, coordinate and control the complex and diverse activities of modern industrial and commercial projects." ERP systems implementation is a set of complex activities, involving all business functions and often requiring between one and two years of effort, thus companies should have an effective project management strategy to control the implementation process, avoiding overrun of budget and ensuring the implementation within schedule.

❖ Company-Wide Commitment

Since ERP systems are enterprise-wide information systems that integrate information and information-based processes within and across all functional areas in an organization, it's imperative to get support from all functional segments of the organization (Ang et al, 1995; Sum et al, 1997).

User Environment

People element is one of the most important factors affecting organizational information systems implementation and deployment. Lack of care about stakeholders within organizations will result in disaster. As such, lack of user education and training (Sum et al, 1997; Burns and Turnipseed, 1991; Bingi et al, 1999) and user involvement (Baroudi et al,

1986) in the process of ERP systems implementation also leads to failure.

System Environment

❖ Suitability of Software and Hardware

ERP packages provide generic off-the-shelf business and software solutions to customers. More or less they can't fully meet the company's needs, especially when the business processes of the company are unique. Thus, to increase the likelihood of success, management must choose the software/hardware that most closely fits its requirements.

❖ Data Accuracy

Since ERP system modules are intricately linked to one another, inaccurate data input into one module will adversely affect the functioning of other modules. If you lie to the ERP systems, then the ERP systems will lie to you and you will get inaccurate or misleading results. Thus, data accuracy is a major determinant of ERP success (Duchessi, 1999; Sum et al, 1997).

ERP Vendor Environment

Since most China's companies purchase ERP packages from foreign ERP vendors and use outside consultancy service, it's important to get the vendor support.

External Cultural Environment

Table 1: International Comparison Data on Cultural
Dimensions (Hofstede 2001)
Note: All index scores range from 1 to 100.

Country	Power Distance	Individualism	Masculinity	Uncertainty Avoidance
USA	40	91	62	46
Germany	35	67	66	65
Netherlands	38	80	14	53
China	80	20	66	30

Densley (1999) revealed that adapting the implementation to the prevailing cultural style was one important cause of project implementation failures. A company who implements an ERP system has to change its business processes to the ERP best-practice processes. The change both impacts on the customer's culture and is constrained by it (Krumbholz and Maiden, 2001). Since foreign ERP vendors took up more than 90 percent ERP market share in China, and Kumar & Bjorn-Anderson (1990) have concluded that information system design methodologies have built-in value biases reflecting the value priorities of the culture in which they are developed. Moreover, national cultures between China and Western countries are different according to Hofstede's dimensions of national culture (See Table 1). Therefore, there is a need to include the factor of cultural difference impact in this study and high-UAI societies' (USA, Germany, and Netherlands) culture values embedded in their ERP packages is hypothesized to be affected negatively when these ERP systems are deployed in low-UAI societies such as China.

According to Hofstede, the dimension of uncertainty avoidance concerns with use of technology most, thus in this study the researcher focuses only on this dimension. The inclination of members of a culture to avoid uncertainty and ambiguity profoundly affects the way in which institutions are organized and managed (Hofstede 1991). Based on Hofstede (2001), compared with lower uncertainty avoidance index (UAI) score, higher UAI score (USA, Germany, and Netherlands) tends to feel stress easier, then these lower UAI score holders try to find security through rule and stability. They tend to group decision and consultative management to avoid risk for the individual over individual decision and authoritative management, employ technology to assist decision, continue working for long time, structure activities including formalization, specialization, and standardization, focus much more on details and short-term feedback, task-oriented, beliefs in specialists and expertise rather than generalists and common sense, and top management tends to involve in operations rather than strategy. However, lower UAI score holders tend to welcome innovations a bit too easily but may not put enough energy into their application. In addition, the precision and punctuality needed to make an innovation work is likely to come more naturally in high-UAI societies; in low-UAI societies these have to be learned and managed.

ERP Implementation Success Measures

Based on DeLone & McLean's (1992) IS success model, user satisfaction, individual impact, and organizational impacts are selected as ERP systems implementation success measures (See Figure 2) at the individual and organizational levels. According to DeLone and McLean (1992), once mandatory use of information systems is required, system quality, information quality, and system use are inappropriate for measuring information systems success.

In the context of ERP system implementation, the user satisfaction measure concerns overall satisfaction and specifics satisfaction with the system implementation adapted from Doll and Torkzadeh (1988), DeLone and McLean (1992). The

individual impact variable could be divided into several dimensions to evaluate including improved individual productivity, task performance improvement, decision effectiveness and quality, and time to make decision. Intended business process improvement has been used as an ERP success measure and it could be combined into organizational impact of ERP system implementation on the organization. The measure of organizational impact includes the impacts of ERP implementation on the organization's operating cost, overall productivity gains, customer service level, and the realization of specific ERP implementation objectives.

Since a mix of measures is used to evaluate whether an ERP system implementation is a success, only when all the three measures are given positive answers by the organization can we call it a success. And when all the three measures are marked as negative, the implementation is defined as a failure. Otherwise, the implementation won't be defined either a success or a failure.

5 CONCLUSION

This work-in-progress study aims to improve understanding of critical factors affecting ERP implementation success in China and establish success measures to assess the extent to which an ERP system implementation can be defined as a success or a failure. The contribution of this study lies in the attempt to classify factors affecting ERP implementation success in China into five categories. Not limited to China's environment, findings of this research could also be applied to other countries in that the first four categories of factors are generic. Moreover, by considering the difference between domestic culture and other countries, this study could be adapted to find the impact of national culture on ERP implementation in specific, information technology in general. Thus, the inclusion of culture to this study could be a big contribution.

Moreover, this study is supported by DeLone & McLean' IS success model and Ives, Hamilton, and Davis' MIS research model. Comparing with previous studies on the ERP field, which lack of theoretical support, this study could be further developed to form academic accumulation.

REFERENCES

References will be available on request.

GLOBAL QUERY OPTIMIZATION BASED ON MULTISTATE COST MODELS FOR A DYNAMIC MULTIDATABASE SYSTEM*

Qiang Zhu   Jaidev Haridas
Department of Computer and Information Science
The University of Michigan - Dearborn, MI 48128, USA
Email: {qzhu,jaidev}@umich.edu

Wen-Chi Hou
Department of Computer Science
Southern Illinois University at Carbondale, IL 62901, USA
Email: hou@cs.siu.edu

Keywords: Multidatabase, query optimization, multistate cost model, multiple-version plan, dynamic environment

Abstract: Global query optimization in a multidatabase system (MDBS) is a challenging issue since some local optimization information such as local cost models may not be available at the global level due to local autonomy. It becomes even more difficult when dynamic environmental factors are taken into consideration. In our previous work, a qualitative approach was suggested to build so-called multistate cost models to capture the performance behavior of a dynamic multidatabase environment. It has been shown that a multistate cost model can give a good cost estimate for a query run in any contention state in the dynamic environment. In this paper, we present a technique to perform query optimization based on multistate cost models for a dynamic MDBS. Two relevant algorithms are proposed. The first one selects a set of representative system environmental states for generating an execution plan with multiple versions for a given query at compile time, while the second one efficiently determines the best version to invoke for the query at run time. Experiments demonstrate that the proposed technique is quite promising for performing global query optimization in a dynamic MDBS. Compared with related work on dynamic query optimization, our approach has an advantage of avoiding the high overhead for modifying or re-generating an execution plan for a query based on dynamic run-time information.

1   INTRODUCTION

A multidatabase system (MDBS) integrates data from multiple local (component) databases and provides users with a uniform global view of data. A global user can issue a (global) query on an MDBS to retrieve data from multiple databases without having to know where the data is stored and how the data is retrieved. How to process such a global query efficiently is the task of global query optimization.

There are a number of challenges for global query optimization in an MDBS. They are mainly caused by heterogeneity and local autonomy of the system. One major challenge is that some necessary local optimization information such as local cost models may not be available at the global level. Several methods to derive cost models for an autonomous local database system (DBS) at the global level have been proposed in the literature, including a calibration method (Du, 1992; Gardarin, 1996), a query sampling method

(Zhu, 1994; Zhu, 1996a; Zhu, 1998), a cost vector database approach (Adali, 1996), a fuzzy approach (Zhu, 1997), and a generic model approach (Naacke, 1998; Roth, 1999). Other multidatabase query optimization issues that have been studied in the literature include: join tree parallelism (Du, 1995; Evrendilek, 1997; Subramanian, 1998), entity joins (Tsai, 1997), outerjoins (Chen, 1990; Yu, 1998), schema level optimization (Lee, 1998), semantic query optimization (Goni, 1996; Lim, 1995; Zhu, 1996b), and query modification and decomposition (Yu, 1998).

It is noted that many factors (e.g., CPU load, I/O load, and available memory space) in an MDBS may change dramatically over time. These dynamic factors make query optimization in an MDBS even more challenging. A number of researchers have studied the issues on dynamic query optimization in an MDBS recently (Amsaleg, 1996; Bouganim, 2000; Ng, 1999; Urhan, 1998). All the dynamic techniques proposed so far have a common characteristic, that is, they modify or re-generate an execution plan for a given query based on dynamic information observed at run time. One shortcoming of such an approach is that the amount of work that needs to be done to

*Research supported by the US National Science Foundation under Grant # IIS-9811980 and The University of Michigan under OVPR and UMD grants.

O. Camp et al. (eds.), Enterprise Information Systems V, 117-128.
© 2004 *Kluwer Academic Publishers. Printed in the Netherlands.*

modify or re-generate an execution plan may be very significant, which directly affects the query response time.

We adopt an alternative approach to perform query optimization in a dynamic multidatabase environment. In our recent work (Zhu, 2000), we utilized a qualitative approach to build multistate cost models for dynamic local database systems in an MDBS. It has been shown that a multistate cost model can give a good cost estimate for a (component) query run in any contention state at a dynamic local site in an MDBS. In this paper, we present a technique to perform global query optimization for a dynamic MDBS based on multistate cost models. The basic idea is to select a set of representative system environmental states for a dynamic MDBS, generate an execution plan with multiple versions (corresponding to the representative system environmental states) for a given query at compile time, and then determine the best version to run for the query based on dynamic information at run time. Due to the limit on the number of versions allowed in an execution plan, an issue that needs to be addressed is how to choose a set of good representative system environmental states for generating versions for a query execution plan. Another issue is how to determine the best version of an execution plan for the running system environmental state at run time. Two algorithms to solve the above issues are proposed in this paper. Our simulation results demonstrate that the presented technique is quite promising in optimizing a global query in a dynamic MDBS.

One advantage of our optimization approach is that the amount of optimization work that needs to be done at run time is minimized and in the meanwhile the variation of dynamic factors affecting query performance at run time is taken into account. This is achieved by using the multistate cost models to estimate (component) query costs in a dynamic environment and shifting significant optimization work to the compile time, which does not affect the query response time.

The rest of the paper is organized as follows. Section 2 gives an overview of multistate cost models. Section 3 discusses the potential approaches for performing query optimization based on multistate cost models in a dynamic MDBS. Section 4 presents the details of a promising query optimization approach that employs a query execution plan with multiple versions for a dynamic multidatabase environment. We will discuss two algorithms: one is to select a set of representative system environmental states for generating multiple versions for a query execution plan at compile time, and the other is to determine the best version to invoke based on run-time information. Section 5 shows some experimental results. Section 6 summarizes the conclusions.

2 MULTISTATE COST MODEL

To incorporate the effect of dynamic factors on query performance into a cost model for an MDBS, we introduced an effective qualitative approach recently (Zhu, 2000).

This approach considers the combined effect of all the dynamic factors on a query cost together rather than individually. Although dynamic factors may change differently in terms of changing frequency and level, they all contribute to the contention level of the underlying system environment, which represents their net effect. Notice that the cost of a query increases as the contention level. The system contention level can be divided into a number of discrete states (categories) such as "$High\ Contention$" (H), "$Medium\ Contention$"(M), "$Low\ Contention$" (L), and "$No\ Contention$" (N). A qualitative variable can be used to indicate the contention states. This qualitative variable, therefore, reflects the combined effect of the dynamic environmental factors. A cost model including such a qualitative variable can capture the dynamic factors to a certain degree.

Since, for a given query, its cost increases as the system contention level, we can use the cost of a small probing query to gage the contention level and classify the contention states for the dynamic system environment. To obtain an appropriate classification of system contention states, we first partition the range of a probing query cost in the given dynamic environment into subranges (intervals) with an equal size. Each subrange represents a contention state. If some neighbor contention states are found to have a similar effect on the derived cost model, they are merged into one state. Such a uniform partition with merging adjustment procedure for a classification of contention states has been proven to be very effective in practice (Zhu, 2000).

A qualitative variable X with M possible system contention states $s_1, s_2, ..., s_M$ can be represented by a set of $M - 1$ indicator (binary) variables $Z_1, Z_2, ..., Z_{M-1}$. That is, $X = s_i$ ($1 \leq i \leq M - 1$) is represented by $Z_i = 1$ and $Z_j = 0$ (for any $j \neq i$); and $X = s_M$ is represented by $Z_k = 0$ (for any $1 \leq k \leq M - 1$). Including qualitative variable X in a cost model is equivalent to including indicator variables $Z_1, Z_2, ..., Z_{M-1}$ in the cost model.

To develop a cost model including the indicator variables, we extend the query sampling method (Zhu, 1998). More specifically, component queries that can be performed on a local DBS in an MDBS are grouped into homogeneous classes first, based on some information available at the global level in an MDBS such as the characteristics of queries, operand tables and the underlying local DBS. A set of sample queries are then drawn from each query class and run against the user local database in different contention

states. The observed costs of sample queries are used
to derive a regression cost model with indicator variables of the following form:

$$Y = \underbrace{(B_0^0 + \sum_{j=1}^{M-1} B_0^j Z_j)}_{intercepts} +$$

$$\sum_{i=1}^{n} \underbrace{(B_i^0 + \sum_{j=1}^{M-1} B_i^j Z_j)}_{slopes} X_i , \quad (1)$$

where Y is the query cost, X_i's are explanatory variables (such as the operand table cardinality(ies), result table cardinality, etc), Z_j's are the indicator variables, and B_i^j's are the regression coefficients. The intercepts and slopes of equation (1) change from one contention state to another, indicated by the values of Z_i's. Each query class has such a multistate cost model.

To estimate the cost of a query at run time, the query class to which the query belongs is first identified. The running system contention state is determined using the observed cost of a small probing query. The cost of the query is then estimated by using cost model (1). Studies have shown that a multistate cost model can give a good cost estimate of a query run in any contention state in a dynamic MDBS (Zhu, 2000).

To reduce the overhead of cost estimation, the running system contention state can also be determined by using an estimated cost (rather than observed cost) of a probing query Q_p. A regression equation between the probing query cost Y_{Q_p} and some major system contention parameters (such as CPU load ld_1, I/O load io, and size of used memory space um for a dynamic environment) is built first, i.e.,

$$Y_{Q_p} = E_0 + E_1 * ld_1 + E_2 * io + E_3 * um, \quad (2)$$

where E_i ($i = 0, 1, 2, 3$) are regression coefficients. Once such an equation is in place, every time we want to determine the system contention state in which a query is executed, we need to calculate the estimated cost Y_{Q_p} of probing query Q_p by using equation (2) without actually executing Q_p. The contention state is then determined using this estimated cost. Since obtaining the parameter values (ld_1, io, um) in equation (2) usually requires much less overhead than executing a probing query, using the estimated costs of a probing query to determine system contention states is usually more efficient.

Note that different query classes may classify contention states at the same local site differently in order to obtain a good cost model specifically tuned for the underlying query class. For example, assume the cost range (i.e., the range of contention level) of a probing query at a particular local site S_1 is [0,

90], namely[1], the minimum probing cost is (approximately) 0 second and the maximum probing cost is (approximately) 90 seconds. One query class G_{11} may use three contention states: $s_1^{(11)} = [0, 30]$, $s_2^{(11)} = (30, 60]$, $s_3^{(11)} = (60, 90]$ for its cost model, while another query class G_{12} may utilize four contention states $s_1^{(12)} = [0, 15]$, $s_2^{(12)} = (15, 35]$, $s_3^{(12)} = (35, 65]$, $s_4^{(12)} = (65, 90]$ for its cost model. Note that each contention state basically represents an interval (subrange) of contention level, which is called the representing interval of the state in the following discussion. The classification of contention states for a query class in a dynamic environment is automatically determined during its cost model building (Zhu, 2000).

On the other hand, for a probing query cost Y_0 (i.e., a contention level) gaged at a local site S_i ($1 \le i \le N$), there is a unique corresponding contention state $s^{(ij)}(Y_0)$, i.e., the representing interval contains Y_0, for each query class G_{ij} ($1 \le j \le K_i$) at the site. In other words, a unique (local) contention state vector $\vec{s}^{(i)}(Y_0) = < s^{(i1)}(Y_0), s^{(i2)}(Y_0), ..., s^{(iK_i)}(Y_0) >$ is determined by contention level Y_0 at site S_i. In general, when the component queries of a global query are to be performed at several sites, a (local) contention state vector can be determined by a gaged probing query cost at each site. The combination of all the (local) contention state vectors is called a (global) system environmental state in this paper, which reflects the running contention environment for the query.

3 QUERY OPTIMIZATION BASED ON MULTISTATE COST MODELS

Establishing cost models is not the ultimate goal of query optimization. The ultimate goal is to choose a good execution plan for a query on the basis of the cost estimates given by the cost models. How to make use of multistate cost models to choose a good execution plan for a given query in a dynamic environment is the issue to be studied in the rest of the paper.

3.1 Interpretation vs Compilation for Query Processing

In general, there are two approaches to processing a query. The first one is called the interpretation ap-

---

[1] In mathematical convention, a closed end (i.e., '[' or ']') of an interval indicates that the end point is included, while an open end (i.e., '(' or ')') indicates that the end point is not included.

proach. In this approach, simple query optimization is performed on the fly while a query is being executed. This approach is suitable for ad hoc/interactive queries, which are usually executed only once. The second one is called the compilation approach. In this approach, comprehensive query optimization is performed for a given query at compile time, resulting in an execution plan. The execution plan can then be executed repeatedly at run time as needed. This approach is more suitable for stored and embedded queries, which are usually executed repeatedly. In an MDBS environment, both stored/embedded queries and ad hoc/interactive queries are expected.

Using multistate cost models to perform query optimization in the interpretation approach is relatively easy. Since the multistate cost models give cost estimates that reflect the current running system environment, the global query optimizer can choose a good query execution plan for the current environment based on the cost estimates.

Using multistate cost models to perform query optimization in the compilation approach is more difficult. The main challenge is that it is not easy to predict the run-time system environment in which the query is to be executed when a query is optimized at compile time. Apparently, the traditional methods of using static cost models to perform query optimization are not acceptable since a system environment is dynamic rather than static. There are several potential ways to perform query optimization based on multistate cost models in the compilation approach, which are described in the following subsection.

3.2 Optimization Approaches Based on Multistate Cost Models

(A) Optimistic Approach. The idea of this approach is to simply choose an efficient execution plan using the query cost estimates given by multistate cost models for the current system environmental state at compile time. This approach works only under the assumption that the system environment changes slowly. Due to the slow change of the system environment, cost estimates given by a multistate cost model for the current system environment remain valid for a certain period of time. The execution plan chosen for a query on the basis of the cost estimates is also good for some time. Clearly, the applicability of this approach is quite restricted.

(B) Environment Predicting Approach. The idea of this approach is to predict/estimate the system environmental state in which a query is to be executed. The system environmental state in which a query is to be executed may be predicted/estimated by analyzing the application background. For example, system-administration-related queries are more likely to be

executed in evenings/weekends when system load is low, and business-related queries are more likely to be executed during business hours on working days when system load is high, etc. The usage (execution) pattern of user queries and the load pattern of a system environment can also be analyzed to improve the predication accuracy. In addition, users may be required to provide inputs about their queries usage to help the system to optimize the queries. Using multistate cost models based on a predicted run-time running system environmental state can usually provide better cost estimates than using traditional static cost models based on a static system environmental state or using multistate cost models simply based on a compile-time system environmental state. The degree of goodness of an execution plan based on a predicted running system environmental state depends on how accurate the prediction is. This approach works well when the user query usage and system load patterns are clear and stable. It would be difficult to deal with the situation in which a user changes his/her query usage pattern frequently.

(C) Lazy Approach. This approach generates an execution plan at compile time based on a static system environmental state or a typical system environmental state. At run time, unless the plan is found to be very inefficient, the query optimizer execute the query according to the execution plan. If the plan is found to be very inefficient, the query optimizer adaptively improves the execution plan. This approach is similar to the dynamic query optimization approaches mentioned in Section 1. As indicated, the overhead for adjusting an execution plan can be very high. An execution plan is adjusted only if the overhead is paid off by the benefits of the new execution plan. Note that it is usually very expensive and complicated to adjust an execution plan in the middle of an execution. Furthermore it is sometimes too late to find the current execution plan is very inefficient. Re-generating a brand new execution plan at run time is equivalent to the interpretation approach, which prohibits comprehensive query optimization since its overhead directly affects the query response time.

(D) Multiple Version Approach. The idea of this approach is to generate multiple versions of an execution plan for a query at compile time, one for each representative run-time system environmental state. When a user runs the query at run time, an appropriate version of the execution plan is invoked according to the actual running system environmental state. Note that the main aim for our query optimization technique is to take the dynamic behavior of the system environment into consideration when choosing an execution plan for a query and in the meantime reduce the optimization work performed at run time. This approach is very promising in achieving this aim. It is expected to provide a better plan/version than the one

generated by assuming a fixed environment (e.g., the static one), and also take much less work than that for conventional dynamic optimization at run time since most work is done at compile time. This approach makes the run-time algorithms simple, efficient and easy to implement. Since this approach is the most promising one, we will further discuss the relevant issues in the next section.

4 QUERY OPTIMIZATION VIA MULTIPLE PLAN VERSIONS

In this section, we address two key issues for the multiple version optimization approach, that is, what versions should be generated for an execution plan at compile time and which version should be invoked at run time.

4.1 Selecting Plan Versions at Compile Time

Assume that a given query Q involves N participating local sites (databases) in the MDBS: S_1, S_2, ..., S_N. The range of probing query cost $Y_{Q_p^i}$ (i.e., contention level) for site S_i is $[V_i, W_i]$ ($1 \leq i \leq N$). There are K_i query classes at site S_i. The number of (local) contention states used by the cost model for query class G_{ij} ($1 \leq j \leq K_i$) at site S_i is M_{ij}. Let $H_{ij} = \{s_1^{(ij)}, s_2^{(ij)}, ..., s_{M_{ij}}^{(ij)}\}$ be the set of the contention states for query class G_{ij} at site S_i, with $s_1^{(ij)}$ representing the lowest contention state and $s_{M_{ij}}^{(ij)}$ the highest one. Let $s^{(ij)}(Y_{Q_p^i}) \in H_{ij}$ be the unique contention state determined by probing query cost $Y_{Q_p^i} \in [V_i, W_i]$ for query class G_{ij} at site S_i.

Hence the set

$$H_i = \{ \vec{s}^{(i)}(Y_{Q_p^i}) = < s^{(i1)}(Y_{Q_p^i}), s^{(i2)}(Y_{Q_p^i}), ...,$$
$$s^{(iK_i)}(Y_{Q_p^i}) > where \ Y_{Q_p^i} \in [V_i, W_i] \}$$

contains all contention state vectors at site S_i, and

$$H = H_1 \times H_2 \times ... \times H_N$$

contains all possible system environmental states for query Q.

If the contention level (i.e., $Y_{Q_p^i}$) at each site is given, the contention state vector at each site is determined. The system environmental state is then also determined. In other words, there is a unique system environmental state corresponding to a point $< Y_{Q_p^1}, Y_{Q_p^2}, ..., Y_{Q_p^N} >$ in the N-dimensional region $D_0 = [V_1, W_1] \times [V_2, W_2] \times ... \times [V_N, W_N]$. We call $< Y_{Q_p^1}, Y_{Q_p^2}, ..., Y_{Q_p^N} >$ a system environmental

(contention) level, and $[V_i, W_i]$ the interval of region D_0 in the i-th dimension. Note that many system environmental levels may correspond to the same system environmental state.

For any given system environmental state, the multistate cost models can give good cost estimates for component queries run at local sites in the environment. When a user issues a global query to an MDBS, the global query optimizer needs to decide how to decompose it into component queries and where to execute the component queries. These decisions are specified in an execution plan. If the system environmental state is known, the query optimizer can generate an efficient plan for the query based on cost estimates of component queries as well as possible communication costs[2]. Unfortunately, what run-time system environmental state in which the query is to be executed is unknown at compile time when the query optimizer optimizes the query.

One solution to this problem is to generate multiple versions of the execution plan, one for each possible system environmental state, and run the right version corresponding to the system environmental state in which the query is executed at run time. If the number of (participating) sites and the number of contention states for each query class at all sites are small, which leads to a small number of system environmental states, this solution is feasible. Otherwise, the query optimizer may have to generate too many versions for a query execution plan. In practice, there is a limit on the number of versions we could generate for a query execution plan due to the space and time constraints. Thus the number of versions that can be generated may be less than the number of possible system environmental states (with respect to the query) in an MDBS. We therefore need a way to select an appropriate subset of system environmental states for which we generate multiple versions of a query execution plan.

Assume that each system environmental level, i.e., a point in region D_0, has an equal chance to occur at run time. If only one version is allowed for a plan, which system environmental state we should select? In principle, the selected system environmental state should be representative in the sense that the corresponding version of the plan will minimize the performance degradation when it is invoked in another system environmental state. A good choice in this case is to select the system environmental state corresponding to the center point $\vec{p}_0 = < (V_1 + W_1)/2, (V_2 + W_2)/2, ..., (V_N + W_N)/2 >$ in region D_0 since the sum of the distances between any

---

[2]A communication cost is usually proportional to the amount of data transferred. For simplicity, we consider a fast LAN in which the communication cost is negligible for the rest of the paper.

point in D_0 and $\vec{p}_0$ is minimized. In other words, the selected system environmental state is $s(\vec{p}_0) =<$ $\vec{s}^{(1)}((V_1+W_1)/2), \vec{s}^{(2)}((V_2+W_2)/2), ..., \vec{s}^{(N)}((V_N+W_N)/2) >$. Figure 1 shows an example in the two-dimensional case.

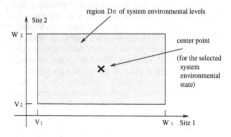

Figure 1: Selection of one representative system environmental state

If two versions are allowed for the plan, we can do the following. Let

$$A_i(D_0) = (\sum_{j=1}^{K_i} |H_{ij}(D_0)|)/K_i, \quad (1 \leq i \leq N) \quad (3)$$

where $|H_{ij}(X)|$ denotes the number of contention states for query class G_{ij} whose representing intervals have a non-empty intersection with the interval of region X in the i-th dimension. We call $A_i(D_0)$ the average number of contention states related to D_0 in the i-th dimension (site). Clearly, $A_i(D_0) \geq 1$ is always true. Let $A_k(D_0) = max\{A_1(D_0), A_2(D_0), ..., A_N(D_0)\}$. Since D_0 is related to more contention states on average in the k-th dimension, we divide D_0 into two half regions by splitting it along the k-th dimension as: $D_{01} = [V_1, W_1] \times ... \times [V_k, W_k'] \times ... \times [V_N, W_N]$ and $D_{02} = [V_1, W_1] \times ... \times (V_k', W_k] \times ... \times [V_N, W_N]$ where $V_k' = W_k' = (V_k + W_k)/2$. That is, D_0 is divided into two half regions along the dimension that has the maximum number of contention states (on average for all query classes) related to D_0. In this way, the maximum number of contention states (on average) that are covered (represented) by each sub-region (i.e., each chosen representative system environmental state) in any dimension is expected to be minimized. Hence the performance degradation caused by invoking a representative query plan version in a system environmental state other than the representative state can be reduced. If there is a tie for choosing such a dimension k, any of the tied dimensions can be used for splitting. The system environ- ment states corresponding to (i.e., containing) the center points of D_{01} and D_{02} are selected as the rep- resentatives for generating two versions[3] for the query

---

[3]Note that it is possible that the plan versions for two

execution plan. Figure 2 shows an example in the two-dimensional case.

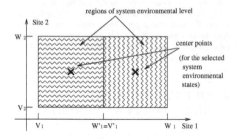

Figure 2: Selection of two system environmental states

In general, for any given number m, we can recur- sively apply this procedure to split a region into two until m representative system environmental states for generating m plan versions are selected. Note that the center point for a selected representative sys- tem environmental state is uniquely determined by a given region. It is sufficient to determine m re- gions in order to select m representative system en- vironmental states. A general region D is denoted by $\langle L_1, U_1] \times \langle L_2, U_2] \times ... \times \langle L_N, U_N]$, where '$\langle$' can be either closed '[' or open '('; L_i and U_i are the min- imum and maximum contention levels at site (dimen- sion) i for the region, respectively. $\langle L_i, U_i]$ is called the interval of D in the i-th dimension.

The following algorithm, for a given number m, se- lects m regions from which the m representative sys- tem environmental states are extracted from.

ALGORITHM 4.1 : Selecting regions for generating query plan versions
Input: (1) the number m of system environmen- tal states to be selected for generating multiple ver- sions of a query execution plan, (2) the region $D_0 = [V_1, W_1] \times [V_2, M_2] \times ... \times [V_N, M_N]$ for the system environmental level, and (3) the set H_{ij} of contention states, including their representing intervals, for ev- ery query class G_{ij} $(1 \leq j \leq K_i)$ at each site S_i $(1 \leq i \leq N)$.
Output: (1) a set of regions whose center points are used to determine the system environmental states for which query plan versions are to be generated, and (2) a data structure $SiteInfo$ that keeps the infor- mation about the current intervals for each dimension and their associated regions to facilitate the search for

---

representative system environmental states are identical, de- pending on the particular MDBS. Since this phenomenon does not degrade the representativeness of the versions for the regions, for simplicity, we consider plan versions as dif- ferent instances regardless of their contents in this paper.

a query plan version at run time.
Method:

1. **begin**
2. Let $R := \{D_0\}$,
   where $D_0 = [V_1, W_1] \times [V_2, M_2] \times ... \times [V_N, M_N]$;
   /* R keeps the current set of selected regions */
3. Initialize $SiteInfo$;
4. Let $j := 1$;
5. **while** $j < m$ **do**
   /* more regions to be selected */
6. Take one region $x \in R$; /* every region in R
   has one average number of contention states
   related to each dimension at this point */
7. Let k be a dimension such that $A_k(x) = max\{$
   $A_1(x), A_2(x), ..., A_N(x)\}$ where
   $$A_i(x) = (\sum_{j=1}^{K_i} |H_{ij}(x)|)/K_i;$$
   /* if there is a tie, choose any one of them */
8. Let $a := A_k(x)$;
9. **if** $a = 1$ **then break**; /* no need to further
   split the region */
10. **while** there exists a region:
    $D = \langle L_1, U_1 \rangle \times \langle L_2, U_2 \rangle \times ... \times \langle L_N, U_N \rangle$
    in R such that $A_k(D) = a$ **do**
11. Let $L'_k := U'_k := (L_k + U_k)/2$;
12. Let $D_1 := \langle L_1, U_1 \rangle \times \langle L_2, U_2 \rangle \times ...$
    $\times \langle L_k, U'_k \rangle \times ... \times \langle L_N, U_N \rangle$;
13. Let $D_2 := \langle L_1, U_1 \rangle \times \langle L_2, U_2 \rangle \times ...$
    $\times \langle L'_k, U_k \rangle \times ... \times \langle L_N, U_N \rangle$;
14. Replace D in R by D_1 and D_2;
15. j := j+1;
16. Update $SiteInfo$;
17. **if** j = m **then break**;
18. **end while**;
19. **end while**;
20. **return** R and $SiteInfo$;
21. **end.**

Algorithm 4.1 repeatedly splits a region along the dimension with the largest average number of contention states related to the region until the desired number of regions are obtained or every dimension has only one contention state related to the region. Thus the number of loops to be done is $O(m)$. Usually, m is much less than the total number of possible system environmental states.

If a region $D = \langle L_1, U_1 \rangle \times \langle L_2, U_2 \rangle \times ... \times \langle L_N, U_N \rangle$ is selected, its center point:

$$\vec{p} = < (L_1 + U_1)/2, (L_2 + U_2)/2,$$
$$..., (L_N + U_N)/2 > \in D$$

is used to determine a representative system environmental state:

$$s(\vec{p}) = < \vec{s}^{(1)}((L_1 + U_1)/2), \vec{s}^{(2)}((L_2 + U_2)/2),$$
$$..., \vec{s}^{(N)}((L_N + U_N)/2) > .$$

A version of the query execution plan is generated for each of such representative system environmental states for the selected regions.

To facilitate the search for an appropriate version of the query execution plan at run time, Algorithm 4.1 also maintains a data structure $SiteInfo$, which contains a substructure for each site (dimension) (see Table 1). The use of this data structure will be dis-

Site	Interval	Regions containing interval
Site 1	interval 1	regions containing interval 1
	interval 2	regions containing interval 2
	...	.....
Site 2	interval 1	regions containing interval 1
	interval 2	regions containing interval 2
...		
Site N	interval 1	regions containing interval 1
	interval 2	regions containing interval 2
	...	.....

Table 1: $SiteInfo$ data structure

cussed in the next subsection.

Example 4.1 Suppose we have 3 participating sites (dimensions) x, y, z for a given query. The entire region of contention levels is $D_0 = [0, 40] \times [0, 50] \times [0, 60]$. Each site has two query classes, whose contention states and their representing intervals are shown in Table 2. Using Algorithm 4.1, Figure 3 shows the regions selected when 5 versions are to be generated for a query execution plan. In the first iteration, region D_0 is split into two regions D_1 and D_2 along the y dimension (since it has the largest average number of contention sates related to D_0). In the next iteration, region D_1 is split into two regions D_3 and D_4 along z dimension and similarly region D_2 is split into two regions D_5 and D_6. In the final iteration, region D_3 is split along the x dimension to get regions D_7 and D_8. The final selected regions are D_4, D_5, D_6, D_7 and D_8 (i.e., the leave nodes of the tree in Figure 3). The center points of the selected regions are: $\vec{p}_4$ =<20, 12.5, 45>, $\vec{p}_5$ =<20, 37.5, 15>, $\vec{p}_6$ =<20, 37.5, 45>, $\vec{p}_7$ =<10, 12.5, 15>, and $\vec{p}_8$ =<30, 12.5, 15>. Then the selected representative system environmental states are:

$$s(\vec{p}_4) = << s_2^{(x1)}, s_2^{(x2)} >,$$
$$< s_2^{(y1)}, s_2^{(y2)} >, < s_3^{(z1)}, s_4^{(z2)} >>,$$
$$s(\vec{p}_5) = << s_2^{(x1)}, s_2^{(x2)} >,$$
$$< s_3^{(y1)}, s_3^{(y2)} >, < s_1^{(z1)}, s_2^{(z2)} >>,$$
$$s(\vec{p}_6) = << s_2^{(x1)}, s_2^{(x2)} >,$$
$$< s_3^{(y1)}, s_3^{(y2)} >, < s_3^{(z1)}, s_4^{(z2)} >>,$$
$$s(\vec{p}_7) = << s_1^{(x1)}, s_1^{(x2)} >,$$
$$< s_2^{(y1)}, s_2^{(y2)} >, < s_1^{(z1)}, s_2^{(z2)} >>,$$
$$s(\vec{p}_8) = << s_3^{(x1)}, s_3^{(x2)} >,$$
$$< s_2^{(y1)}, s_2^{(y2)} >, < s_1^{(z1)}, s_2^{(z2)} >> .$$

A version of the query execution plan is then generated for each of the selected system environmental

123

	States for query class 1	States for query class 2
Site x	$s_1^{(x1)} = [0,15], s_2^{(x1)} = (15,25], s_3^{(x1)} = (25,40]$	$s_1^{(x2)} = [0,10], s_2^{(x2)} = (10,20], s_3^{(x2)} = (20,30], s_4^{(x2)} = (30,40]$
Site y	$s_1^{(y1)} = [0,8], s_2^{(y1)} = (8,25], s_3^{(y1)} = (25,40], s_4^{(y1)} = (40,50]$	$s_1^{(y2)} = [0,10], s_2^{(y2)} = (10,20], s_3^{(y2)} = (20,30], s_4^{(y2)} = (30,40].$ $s_5^{(y2)} = (40,50]$
Site z	$s_1^{(z1)} = [0,20], s_2^{(z1)} = (20,40], s_3^{(z1)} = (40,60]$	$s_1^{(z2)} = [0,12], s_2^{(z2)} = (12,24], s_3^{(z2)} = (24,36], s_4^{(z2)} = (36,48].$ $s_5^{(z2)} = (48,60]$

Table 2: Contention states at local sites

Figure 3: Selection of one system environmental state

states. Data structure $SiteInfo$ for Sites x, y and z is shown in Table 3.

Site	Interval	Regions containing interval
Site x	[0,20]	D_7
	(20,40]	D_8
	[0,40]	D_4, D_5, D_6
Site y	[0,25]	D_4, D_7, D_8
	(25,50]	D_5, D_6
Site z	[0,30]	D_5, D_7, D_8
	(30,60]	D_4, D_6

Table 3: An Example of $SiteInfo$

Note that if the assumption that every system environmental level has an equal chance to occur is not true, the actual distribution of system environmental level can be analyzed. Based on the analysis, more regions could be selected for the space area in which a system environmental level has a higher chance to occur. Due to the length limitation of the paper, the details of such a distribution-dependent partition of the space will be discussed in a separate paper.

4.2 Determining an Appropriate Version at Run Time

When a user requests to execute a query at run time, the best version of the relevant query execution plan should be invoked. How to determine the best version of the plan at run time is the issue to be discussed in this subsection.

First of all, the (current) running contention level at each participating local site can be gaged by the (observed or estimated) cost of a small probing query at run time as described in Section 2. Hence we have the running system environmental (contention) level. The corresponding running system environmental state can also be determined.

If the system environmental state in which the query is running is one of the selected representative system environmental states for which the versions of the query execution plan are generated, the corresponding version should be invoked. However, in general, the running system environmental state may not be one of the selected states since the number of the latter is limited. In this case, the selected region that contains the running system environmental level needs to be identified. Since the set of selected regions form a partition of initial region D_0, there exists only one selected region containing the running system environmental level. The version of the execution plan generated for the representative system environmental state corresponding to the center point of the region should be invoked for the given query. Although this version was not generated exactly for the running system environmental state, it can usually yield a fair performance, compared with the single version (for a fixed static system environmental state) provided by a traditional static optimization approach. The more versions the query execution plan has, the better the query performance is expected.

Clearly, we need an efficient technique to search for the region that contains the running system environmental level. To do that, we make use of the data structure $SiteInfo$ maintained by Algorithm 4.1. In fact, $SiteInfo$ provides an index for relevant regions along each participating site/dimension. Note that it is possible that a running (local) contention level at a participating local site belongs to two region intervals. One is a sub-interval of the other (see intervals [0,20] and [0,40] in Table 3). The cause for this phenomenon is that the split of regions along one dimension may not be completely done before the sufficient number of regions have been selected. However, there is at most one such dimension along which intervals with different lengths may exist. Although the region to which the running (global) system environmental level belongs is unique, we may have to search two lists for a desired region at one site/dimension.

The following algorithm makes use of $SiteInfo$ to efficiently search for the relevant region to which a running system environmental level belongs and then returns the version of the execution plan for a query to be executed in the environment.

ALGORITHM 4.2 : Selecting a version of the execution plan for a given query at run time
Input: (1) the running (global) system environmental level $\vec{Y}_{Q_p} = <Y_{Q_p^1}, Y_{Q_p^2}, ..., Y_{Q_p^N}>$ at run time, where $Y_{Q_p^i}$ is a running (local) contention level at site i ($1 \leq i \leq N$), (2) data structure $SiteInfo$ maintained by Algorithm 4.1, and (3) the execution plan with multiple versions, one for each selected region, for a given query Q.
Output: The best version of the execution plan for query Q in the running system environmental state corresponding to $\vec{Y}_{Q_p}$.
Method:
1. **begin**
2.   Find an interval I_1 along dimension (site) 1 that contains local contention level $Y_{Q_p^1}$;
3.   Use $SiteInfo$ to get set R_{match} of regions containing interval I_1;
4.   **if** there exists another interval I_1' along dimension 1 that contains $Y_{Q_p^1}$
5.   **then** use $SiteInfo$ to get set R_{match}' of regions containing interval I_1';
6.   **else** let $R_{match}' := \emptyset$;
7.   Let $R_{sel} := R_{match} \cup R_{match}'$;
8.   **for** i = 2 to N **do**
9.   Find an interval I_i along dimension i that contains local contention level $Y_{Q_p^i}$;
10.   Use $SiteInfo$ to get set R_{match} of regions containing interval I_i;
11.   **if** there exists another interval I_i' along dimension i that contains s_i
12.   **then** use $SiteInfo$ to get set R_{match}' of regions containing interval I_i';
13.   **else** let $R_{match}' := \emptyset$;
14.   Let $R_{match} := R_{match} \cup R_{match}'$;
15.   Let $R_{sel} := R_{sel} \cap R_{match}$;
16.   **end for**
17.   Find the center point $\vec{p}$ of the final selected region in R_{sel};
18.   Find the representative system environmental state $s(\vec{p})$ for $\vec{p}$;
19.   **return** the plan version generated for $s(\vec{p})$;
20. **end.**

Algorithm 4.2 essentially utilizes indexes to locate the relevant regions without exhaustively checking all regions, when searching for a representative region for

a given running system environmental level.

Example 4.2 Let us consider the query execution plan with 5 versions generated in Example 4.1. Let the running system environmental level at which the query is executed at run time be $<25, 45, 50>$, that is, the probing query costs at sites x, y and z are 25 sec., 45 sec. and 50 sec., respectively. Now, we need to find a selected region that contains point $<25, 45, 50>$. Applying Algorithm 4.2, we first use $SiteInfo$ to find the interval(s) that contains 25 along dimension x. Once such intervals (20,40] and [0,40] are found, the regions associated with the intervals are saved in R_{sel}, namely, $R_{sel} = \{D_4, D_5, D_6, D_8\}$. We then use $SiteInfo$ to find the interval containing 45 along dimension y. Once such an interval [25, 50] is found, the regions associated with the interval is saved in R_{match}, namely, $R_{match} = \{D_5, D_6\}$. Then $R_{sel} = R_{sel} \cap R_{match} = \{D_5, D_6\}$. We finally use $SiteInfo$ to find the interval containing 50 along dimension z. Once such an interval (30, 60] is found, the regions associated with the interval is saved in R_{match}, namely, $R_{match} = \{D_4, D_6\}$. Calculating $R_{sel} = R_{sel} \cap R_{match}$, we get $R_{sel} = \{D_6\}$. Hence the desired region is D_6. The center point for D_6 is $\vec{p}_6 = <20, 37.5, 45>$. Its corresponding representative system environmental state is $s(\vec{p}_6) = << s_2^{(x1)}, s_2^{(x2)} >, < s_3^{(y1)}, s_3^{(y2)} >, < s_3^{(z1)}, s_4^{(z2)} >>$. Therefore, the version generated for $s(\vec{p}_6)$ is selected for executing the query.

5   EXPERIMENTS

To verify the effectiveness of our technique, we conducted some simulation experiments. In the experiments, global queries with 4 participating local database systems (sites) in an MDBS were considered. Two sites (Sites a and b) run Oracle 8.0 and the other two sites (Sites c and d) run DB2 5.0. Each site uses a SUN UltraSparc 2 workstation running Solaris 5.1.

An experimental database was created at each local site, with the same set of tables as those used in previous work (Zhu, 2000). More specifically, each local database has 12 tables $R_i(a_1, a_2, ..., a_j)$ ($i = 1, 2, ..., 12; j \in \{3, 5, 7, 9, 11, 13\}$) with cardinalities ranging from $3,000 \sim 250,000$. The data in the tables is randomly generated. Each table has a number of indexed columns and various selectivities for different columns.

Two query classes were considered at each local site: one for unary queries and the other for join queries. A multistate cost model was developed for each query class by applying the qualitative approach described in Section 2 based on the observed costs of sample queries run on the local database systems. Using the multistate cost models, we can estimate the cost of a (component) query run in any contention state at a local site. Since we focus on studying the effect of dynamic factors at autonomous local sites on query processing, we assume that the communication costs are negligible by using a high-performance local area network. For our simulation experiments, the costs of component queries obtained from decomposing a global test query are simulated by using the corresponding cost estimates given by the multistate cost models with a random error within 30%. From our previous empirical studies (Zhu, 2000), this simulation is reasonable.

The global queries tested in our experiments are of the following form:

$$(\pi_{\alpha^a}(\sigma_{F^a}(R^a))) \overset{\bowtie}{F^{ab}} (\pi_{\alpha^b}(\sigma_{F^b}(R^b)))$$

$$\overset{\bowtie}{F^{bc}} (\pi_{\alpha^c}(\sigma_{F^c}(R^c))) \overset{\bowtie}{F^{cd}} (\pi_{\alpha^d}(\sigma_{F^d}(R^d))) \quad (4)$$

where R^x is a table at local site x, α^x is a list of columns in R^x, F^x is a qualification condition on R^x, F^{xy} is a qualification condition on R^x and R^y, and $x, y \in \{a, b, c, d\}$.

There are a number of strategies to perform such a query. Figure 4 shows two of them. Given a system environmental level, we can determine the corresponding system environmental state. We can then use the cost estimates given by the multistate cost models in the system environmental state to determine a best execution strategy from many alternatives. Each chosen execution strategy for a given representative system environmental state yields a version in the corresponding query execution plan. If several representative system environmental states are considered, we have a query execution plan with multiple versions. At run time, the best version is chosen to run by the technique discussed in Section 4.2, based on the given running system environmental level.

Figure 5 shows the comparison of costs for a set of random global queries of form (4) run in system environmental states determined by some random system environmental levels. The following costs for each query were compared: (i) the cost following the best version of the execution plan with (a random number between 2 and 8) multiple versions generated by the technique discussed in Section 4.1; (ii) the cost following the execution plan chosen by the static cost models (i.e., the ones assuming a static environment without considering dynamic factors); and (iii) the cost following the optimal execution plan for the running system environmental state determined by a given system environmental level. The figure shows that the execution plans with multiple versions are more efficient than the static execution plans. The performance of the execution plans with multiple versions well approximates the performance of optimal

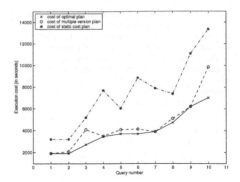

Figure 5: Costs of query execution plans

execution plans for the queries in the running system environmental states.

Figure 6 shows that the performance of a query execution plan with multiple versions is usually getting

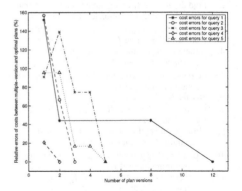

Figure 6: Performance improvement as number of versions increases

better and better as the number of versions allowed in the plan increases. In the experiment, we considered a number of global queries run in the system environmental states determined by some random running system environmental levels. As we increase the number of versions allowed in the execution plan for a query, the performance is usually getting better since a better version could be chosen to run the query. It is observed that the performance of the optimal plans for most queries in the experiment can be achieved without having to use a large number of versions. Besides, although in some cases the query performance

126

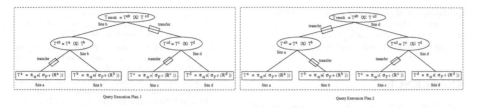

Figure 4: Examples of execution plan versions

may stay the same or even temporarily degrade, it always improves eventually as the number of versions in the plan increases. The figure demonstrates some typical types of query performance behavior in the experiment.

Figure 7 shows the results of another experiment, in which we assumed that only one version (i.e., the

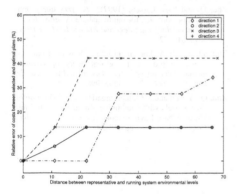

Figure 7: Effect of level distance on performance

one corresponding to the center point of the initial region) was allowed for the execution plan of a given query. We considered a number of running system environmental levels with various distances from the center point along different directions. The figure shows that the closer the running level is to the representative level (i.e., the center point), the closer the performance of the selected representative version is to the performance of the optimal plan. Therefore, when the representative regions are getting smaller and smaller (i.e., the maximum distance between the center and any point in the region is smaller), the better and better performance is expected for the execution plan with multiple versions.

Our experimental results demonstrate that the technique proposed in this paper is quite promising in performing global query optimization for a dynamic mul-

tidatabase environment.

6 CONCLUSIONS

The techniques proposed so far in the literature for global query optimization in multidatabase systems can be classified into static ones and dynamic ones. A static technique optimizes a query at compile time and does not consider the dynamically-changing environmental factors that may have a significant effect on the query cost at run time. Hence, the query execution plan generated with such a technique is often sub-optimal in a dynamic environment. However, the amount of work performed at run time for optimization in this case is negligible if not nothing as all the work for generating plans is done at compile time. A dynamic optimization technique on the other hand takes into consideration the dynamically-changing environmental factors and modifies or re-generates query execution plans at run time. Hence, the modified/re-generated plans are usually more efficient than the ones produced at compile time. However, the amount of work performed for such optimization is significant at run time, which directly affects the query response time and thus greatly reduces the benefits of an improved query execution plan.

The query optimization technique proposed in this paper overcomes the problems with the above two types of techniques. It takes into account the dynamically-changing environmental factors by adopting so-called multistate cost models for dynamic local sites. A multistate cost model can give a good cost estimate of a query run in any contention state at a dynamic local site. Based on the cost estimates, the technique generates an execution plan with multiple versions at compile time, one for each selected representative system environmental state. The algorithms to select a set of good representative system environmental states at compile time and to determine the best query execution plan version at run time are presented. Our experiments demonstrate that the proposed optimization technique is quite promising in

127

optimizing global queries in a dynamic multidatabase environment. However, our work is just the beginning of further research that needs to be done in the future in order to completely solve all relevant issues.

REFERENCES

Adali, S., *et al.* (1996). Query caching and optimization in distributed mediator systems. In *Proc. of ACM SIG-MOD Conf.*, pp 137–48.

Amsaleg, L., *et al.* (1996). Scrambling Query Plans to Cope With Unexpected Delays. In *Proc. of Int'l Conf. on Paral. and Distr. Inf. Syst.*, pp 208–19.

Bouganim, L., *et al.* (2000). Dynamic Query Scheduling in Data Integration Systems. In *Proc. of IEEE Int'l Conf. on Data Eng.*, pp 425–34.

Chen, A. L. P. (1990). Outerjoin optimization in multi-database systems. In *Proc. of Int'l Symp. on DB in Paral. and Distr. Syst.*, pp 211–18.

Du, W., *et al.* (1992). Query optimization in heterogeneous DBMS. In *Proc. of VLDB Conf.*, pp 277–91.

Du, W., M. C. Shan, and U. Dayal. (1995). Reducing Multidatabase Query Response Time by Tree Balancing. In *Proc. of ACM SIGMOD Conf.*, pp 293 – 303.

Evrendilek, C., *et al.* (1997). Multidatabase Query Optimization. In *Distributed and Parallel Databases*, 5(1): 77–113.

Gardarin, G., *et al.* (1996). Calibrating the query optimizer cost model of IRO-DB, an object-oriented federated database system. In *Proc. of VLDB Conf.*, pp 378–89.

Goni, A., *et al.* (1996). Using Reasoning of Description Logics for Query Processing in Multidatabase Systems. In *Proc. of 3rd Workshop on Knowl. Repres. Meets DB*, pp 1–6.

Lee, C. and C. J. Chen. (1998). Query Optimization in Multidatabase Systems Considering Schema Conflicts. In *IEEE Trans. on Knowledge and Data Eng.*, 9(6): 941–55.

Lim, E.-P., *et al.* (1995). An Algebraic Transformation Framework for Multidatabase Queries. In *Distributed and Parallel Databases*, 3: 273–307.

Yu, C.T. and W. Meng. (1998). Principles of Database Query Processing for Advanced Applications. *Morgan Kaufmann Publishers, Inc.*.

Naacke, H., G. Gardarin, and A. Tomasic. (1998). Leveraging mediator cost models with heterogeneous data sources. In *Proc. of IEEE Int'l Conf. on Data Eng.*, pp 351–60.

Ng, K. W., *et al.* (1999). Dynamic Query Re-Optimization. In *Proc. of Int'l Conf. on Sci. and Stat. DB Manag.*, pp 264–273.

Roth, M. T., *et al.* (1999). Cost models DO matter: providing cost information for diverse data sources in a federated system. In *Proc. of VLDB Conf.*, pp 599–610.

Subramanian, D. K., and K. Subramanian. (1998). Query optimization in multidatabase systems. *Distributed and Parallel Databases*, 6(3): 183 – 210.

Urhan, T., M. J. Franklin and L. Amsaleg. Cost-based Query Scrambling for Initial Delays. In *Proc. of ACM SIGMOD Conf.*, pp 130–141.

Tsai, P. S. M. and A. L. P. Chen. (1997). Optimizing entity join queries when data transmission cost dominates. In *Data & Knowledge Engineering*, 22, pp 283–308.

Zhu, Q. and P.-Å. Larson. (1994). A query sampling method for estimating local cost parameters in a multidatabase system. In *Proc. of IEEE Int'l Conf. on Data Eng.*, pp 144–53.

Zhu, Q. and P.-Å. Larson. (1996). Building regression cost models for multidatabase systems. In *Proc. of Int'l Conf. on Paral. and Distr. Inf. Syst.*, pp 220–31, 1996.

Zhu, Q. and P.-Å. Larson. (1996). Global Query Processing and Optimization in the CORDS Multidatabase System. In *Proc. of 9th Int'l Conf. on Paral. and Distr. Comp. Syst.*, pp 640–6.

Zhu, Q. and P.-Å. Larson. (1997). A fuzzy query optimization approach for multidatabase systems. *Int'l J. of Uncertainty, Fuzziness and Knowledge-Based Sys.*, 5(6):701 – 22.

Zhu, Q. and P.-Å. Larson. (1998). Solving local cost estimation problem for global query optimization in multidatabase systems. *Distributed and Parallel Databases*, 6(4): 373 – 420, 1998.

Zhu, Q., Y. Sun and S Motheramgari. (2000). Developing Cost Models with Qualitative Variables for Dynamic Multidatabase Environments. In *Proc. of IEEE Int'l Conf. on Data Eng.*, pp 413-24.

PART 2

Artificial Intelligence and Decision Support Systems

BUILDING INTELLIGENT CREDIT SCORING SYSTEMS USING DECISION TABLES

Bart Baesens, Christophe Mues, Manu De Backer, Jan Vanthienen

Catholic University of Leuven
Naamsestraat 69, B-3000 Leuven, Belgium
{Bart.Baesens;Christophe.Mues;Manu.Debacker;Jan.Vanthienen}@econ.kuleuven.ac.be

Rudy Setiono

National University of Singapore
Kent Ridge, Singapore 119260, Republic of Singapore
Rudys@comp.nus.edu.sg

Keywords: Credit scoring, decision tables, rule extraction, neural networks

Abstract: Accuracy and comprehensibility are two important criteria when developing decision support systems for credit scoring. In this paper, we focus on the second criterion and propose the use of decision tables as an alternative knowledge visualisation formalism which lends itself very well to building intelligent and user-friendly credit scoring systems. Starting from a set of propositional if-then rules extracted by a neural network rule extraction algorithm, we construct decision tables and demonstrate their efficiency and user-friendliness for two real-life credit scoring cases.

1 INTRODUCTION

Nowadays financial institutions see their loan portfolios expand and are actively investigating various alternatives to reduce the risk of credit loss due to defaulting loan applicants. With the emergence of large-scale data storing facilities, huge amounts of data have been stored regarding the repayment behaviour of past applicants. It is the aim of credit scoring to analyse this data and build models which aim at distinguishing good applicants from bad applicants using characteristics such as amount on savings account, marital status, purpose of loan, etc. Many machine learning and statistical techniques have been suggested in the literature to build credit scoring models (Thomas, 2000). Amongst the most popular are traditional statistical methods (e.g. logistic regression (Steenackers and Goovaerts, 1989)), nonparametric statistical models (e.g. k-nearest neighbour (Henley and Hand, 1997) and classification trees (Davis et al., 1992)) and neural network models (Desai et al., 1996). Currently, intensive research is conducted on further developing new, more powerful classification algorithms (e.g. support vector machines, bayesian network classifiers, ant colony algorithms, etc.). Although this is very interesting from a performance perspective, it has to be mentioned that credit scoring models should not only be accurate but also comprehensible and user-friendly. In other words, credit scoring models should be made white-box and transparent by explaining how the classifications are being made. Clearly, this plays a pivotal role in credit-risk evaluation as the evaluator may be required to give a justification why a certain credit application is approved or rejected. Furthermore, having simple and comprehensible credit scoring models will facilitate their successful adoption and integration in the credit granting process.

In this paper, we report on the use of decision tables to build explanatory and intelligent decision support systems for credit scoring. The decision tables are built using a set of propositional if-then rules previously extracted by a powerful neural network rule extraction algorithm. It is then investigated how these tables can be reduced in size using contraction and row-order minimisation routines. We also illustrate how the decision tables allow for easy and efficient consultation using the PROLOGA workbench. The experiments are conducted using a publicly available credit scoring data set and another obtained from a Benelux (Belgium, the Netherlands and Luxembourg) financial institution.

This paper is organised as follows. In section 2, we briefly elaborate on the topic of rule extraction for building intelligent credit scoring systems. Section 3 discusses the basic concepts of decision tables. Section 4 then illustrates how decision tables can be applied to represent propositional rules in a user-friendly and efficient manner. Section 5 concludes the paper.

131

O. Camp et al. (eds.), Enterprise Information Systems V, 131-137.
© 2004 *Kluwer Academic Publishers. Printed in the Netherlands.*

2 DEVELOPING INTELLIGENT SYSTEMS FOR CREDIT SCORING

For a successful adoption of automated credit scoring systems into the daily credit decision environment, two properties are essential. First, the systems should achieve a high performance in discriminating bad customers from good customers. In this context, several performance measures may be of interest, e.g. classification accuracy, sensitivity, specificity, receiver operating characteristic curves, etc. Furthermore, credit scoring systems should also be made explanatory in the sense that they should provide a clear insight to the expert about how and why a certain applicant is classified as good or bad. More and more, financial institutions are being legally obliged to justify their credit decisions. The Equal Credit Opportunities Act (1976) and regulation B in the US prohibit the use of characteristics such as gender, marital status, race, whether an applicant receives welfare payment, colour, religion, national origin and age, in making the credit decision (Crook, 1999). Hence, the issue of making credit-risk evaluation systems intelligent and explanatory is becoming more and more a key factor for their successful deployment and implementation.

When considering only the first objective, it is well-known that neural networks are amongst the best performing techniques for credit scoring because of their universal approximation property (Bishop, 1995). However, their complex mathematical internal workings essentially turn them into black box, opaque structures, which limits their comprehensibility and prohibits their practical use. In previous research (Baesens et al., 2003), we tackled this problem by extracting rule sets that mimic the decision process of the trained networks. To this end, we used a.o. the Neurorule method which is a neural network rule extraction technique originally proposed in (Setiono and Liu, 1996). Neurorule aims at extracting propositional if-then rules from trained neural networks with (approximately) the same predictive power as the networks. Figure 1 and 2 depict the rule sets which were extracted using Neurorule on two real-life credit scoring cases. Figure 2 concerns a real-life credit scoring data set obtained from a major Benelux financial institution (3123 obs., 33 inputs) whereas Figure 1 involves the well-known German credit data set (1000 obs., 20 inputs) which is publicly available at the UCI repository.

It was shown that both rule sets achieve a very high classification accuracy on independent test set data. The rule sets are both concise and easy to interpret and thus provide the credit scoring expert with an explanation facility to guide his/her credit decisions. However, while propositional rules are an intu-

If Checking account $\neq$ 4) And (Checking account $\neq$ 3) And (Term = 1) And (Credit history $\neq$ 4) And (Credit history $\neq$ 3) And (Credit history $\neq$ 2) And (Purpose $\neq$ 8) Then Applicant = bad

If (Checking account $\neq$ 4) And (Checking account $\neq$ 3) And (Credit history $\neq$ 4) And (Credit history $\neq$ 3) And (Credit history $\neq$ 2) And (Term = 2) Then Applicant = bad

If (Checking account $\neq$ 4) And (Checking account $\neq$ 3) And (Credit history $\neq$ 4) And (Purpose $\neq$ 5) And (Purpose $\neq$ 1) And (Savings account $\neq$ 5) And (Savings account $\neq$ 4) And (Other parties $\neq$ 3) And (Term = 2) Then Applicant = bad

Default class: Applicant = good

Figure 1: Rules Extracted by Neurorule for German credit.

If Term $>$ 12 months And Purpose = cash provisioning And Savings account $\leq$ 12.40 Euro And Years client $\leq$ 3 Then Applicant = bad

If Term $>$ 12 months And Purpose = cash provisioning And Owns property = No And Savings account $\leq$ 12.40 Euro Then Applicant = bad

If Purpose = cash provisioning And Income $>$ 719 Euro And Owns property = No And Savings account $\leq$ 12.40 Euro And Years client $\leq$ 3 Then Applicant = bad

If Purpose = second hand-car And Income $>$ 719 Euro And Owns property = No And Savings account $\leq$ 12.40 Euro And Years client $\leq$ 3 Then Applicant = bad

If Savings account $\leq$ 12.40 Euro And Economical sector = Sector C Then Applicant = bad

Default class: Applicant = good

Figure 2: Rules Extracted by Neurorule for Bene1.

itive and well-known formalism to represent knowledge, they are not necessarily the most suitable representation in terms of structure and efficiency of use in every day business practice and decision-making. Recent research in knowledge representation suggests that graphical representation formalisms can be more readily interpreted and consulted by humans than a set of symbolic propositional if-then rules (Santos-Gomez and Darnel, 1992). In the following section, we will discuss how the extracted sets of rules may be transformed into decision tables which facilitate the efficient classification of applicants and at the same time provide adequate explanations for the classifications being made (Vanthienen, 1994).

3 BASIC CONCEPTS OF DECISION TABLES

Decision tables provide an alternative way of representing data mining knowledge extracted by e.g. neural network rule extraction in a user-friendly way (Wets, 1998). Decision tables (DTs) are a tabular representation used to describe and analyze decision situations (e.g. credit-risk evaluation), where the state of a number of conditions jointly determines the execution of a set of actions. In our neural network rule extraction context, the conditions correspond to the antecedents of the rules whereas the actions correspond to the outcome classes (Applicant = good or bad). A DT consists of four quadrants, separated by double-lines, both horizontally and vertically (cf. Figure 3). The horizontal line divides the table into a condition part (above) and an action part (below). The vertical line separates subjects (left) from entries (right). The

condition subjects	condition entries
action subjects	action entries

Figure 3: DT quadrants.

condition subjects are the criteria that are relevant to the decision making process. They represent the attributes of the rule antecedents about which information is needed to classify a given applicant as good or bad. The action subjects describe the possible outcomes of the decision making process (i.e., the classes of the classification problem). Each condition entry describes a relevant subset of values (called a state) for a given condition subject (attribute), or contains a dash symbol ('-') if its value is irrelevant within the context of that column. Subsequently, every action entry holds a value assigned to the corresponding action subject (class). True, false and unknown action values are typically abbreviated by '×', '-', and '.', respectively. Every column in the entry part of the DT thus comprises a classification rule, indicating what action(s) apply to a certain combination of condition states. If each column only contains simple states (no contracted or irrelevant entries), the table is called an expanded DT, whereas otherwise the table is called a contracted DT.

Table contraction can be achieved by combining logically adjacent (groups of) columns that lead to the same action configuration. For ease of legibility, only contractions are allowed that maintain a lexicographical column ordering, i.e., in which the entries at lower rows alternate before the entries above them; see Figure 4 (Figure 5) for an example of an (un)ordered DT, respectively. As a result of this ordering restriction, a tree structure emerges in the condition entry part of the DT, which lends itself very well to a top-down evaluation procedure: starting at the first row,

and then working one's way down the table by choosing from the relevant condition states, one safely arrives at the prescribed action (class) for a given case. The number of columns in the contracted table can be further minimised by changing the order of the condition rows. It is obvious that a DT with a minimal number of columns is to be preferred since it provides a more parsimonious and comprehensible representation of the extracted knowledge than an expanded DT. This is illustrated in Figure 4.

1. Owns property?	yes				no			
2. Years client	<3		>3		<3		>3	
3. Savings amount	low	high	low	high	low	high	low	high
1. Applicant=good	-	×	×	×	-	×	-	×
2. Applicant=bad	×	-	-	-	×	-	×	-

(a) Expanded DT

1. Owns property?	yes			no	
2. Years client	<3		>3		
3. Savings amount	low	high	-	low	high
1. Applicant=good	-	×	×	-	×
2. Applicant=bad	×	-	-	×	-

(b) Contracted DT

1. Savings amount	low			high
2. Owns property?	yes		no	-
3. Years client	<3	>3	-	-
1. Applicant=good	-	×	-	×
2. Applicant=bad	×	-	×	-

(c) Minimum-size contracted DT

Figure 4: Minimising the number of columns of a lexicographically ordered DT (Vanthienen and Wets, 1994).

1. Savings amount	high	-	low	low
2. Owns property?	-	yes	no	-
3. Years client	-	>3	-	<3
1. Applicant=good	×	×	-	-
2. Applicant=bad	-	-	×	×

Figure 5: Example of an unordered DT.

Note that we deliberately restrict ourselves to single-hit tables, wherein columns have to be mutually exclusive, because of their advantages with respect to verification and validation (Vanthienen et al., 1998). It is this type of DT that can be easily checked for potential anomalies, such as inconsistencies (a particular case being assigned to more than one class) or incompleteness (no class assigned). The decision table formalism thus facilitates the verification of the knowledge extracted by e.g. a neural network rule extraction algorithm. What's more, inspecting and validating a DT in a top-down manner, as suggested above, should prove more intuitive, faster, and less prone to human error, than evaluating a set of rules one by one. Then, in a final stage, once the decision table has been approved by the expert, it can be incorporated into a deployable decision support system (Vanthienen and Wets, 1994).

We will use the PROLOGA[1] software to construct the decision tables for the rules extracted in section 2. PROLOGA is an interactive design tool for computer-supported construction and manipulation of DTs (Vanthienen and Dries, 1994). With PROLOGA, knowledge is acquired and verified in the form of a system of DTs. A powerful rule language is available to help specify the DTs, and automated support is provided for several restructuring and optimisation tasks. Furthermore, to assist in the implementation and integration of the modeled knowledge into various types of application settings, a range of import / export interfaces is included (e.g., code generation utilities), as well as a standard consultation environment, which allows the user to apply the knowledge to a given problem case by means of a targeted question / answer dialog, similar to that offered in a typical rule-based KBS shell.

4 USING DECISION TABLES TO BUILD INTELLIGENT SYSTEMS FOR CREDIT SCORING

Table 1 presents the properties of the DTs built for the rules extracted by Neurorule on both credit scoring data sets. For the German credit data set, the fully expanded decision table contained 6600 columns, enumerating every possible combination of distinct attribute values ($= 4 \times 5 \times 2 \times 11 \times 5 \times 3$). For the Bene1 data set, the expanded table consisted of 192 columns. Though hardly suitable for visual inspection at this point, both descriptions proved computationally tractable given the input space reduction achieved in the preceding stages of the knowledge discovery process. Subsequently, we converted each of these expanded DTs into a more compact DT, by joining nominal attribute values that do not appear in any rule antecedent into a common 'other' state, and then performing optimal table contraction. Considering the limited number of inputs, we adopted a simple exhaustive search method (requiring only a few seconds on a Pentium 4); a branch- and-bound approach to find the optimal condition order is described elsewhere (Vanthienen and Dries, 1996). As a result of this reduction process, we ended up with two minimum-size contracted DTs, consisting of 11 and 14 columns for the German credit and Bene1

[1]http://www.econ.kuleuven.ac.be/tew/academic/infosys/research/Prologa.htm

data sets, respectively (cf. right column of Table 1). Figures 8 and 9 depict the resulting decision tables. Clearly, their relative conciseness, combined with their top-down readability, is what makes them a very attractive visual representation of the extracted knowledge.

Data set	Columns in expanded DT	Columns in minimised DT
German credit	6600	11
Bene1	192	14

Table 1: The number of columns in the expanded and minimised DTs.

Interestingly, the size gains achieved by the DT contraction mechanism were, in both cases, substantial, even with non-optimal condition orders. For example, for the Bene1 credit set, the maximum (average) contracted DT size amounted to 48 (26), respectively, which is still well below the theoretical worst-case of 192 (non-contractable) columns. Figures 6 and 7 show a bar plot of which the Y-axis depicts the number of condition orders leading to the DT size indicated on the X-axis.

Also, it is important to note here that transforming a set of propositional rules into a DT does not entail any loss of predictive accuracy; i.e., the decision tables depicted in Figures 8 and 9 have exactly the same classification accuracy as the rules of Figures 1 and 2 from which they were generated. Hence, as no anomalies are indicated in the DT, the completeness and consistency of the extracted rules are demonstrated.

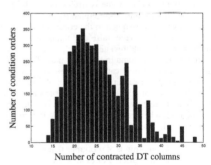

Figure 6: Bene1; DT size distribution

Decision tables allow for an easy and user-friendly consultation in every day business practice. Figure 10 presents an example of a consultation session in PROLOGA. Suppose we try to work ourselves towards column 12 of the decision table for Bene1 depicted

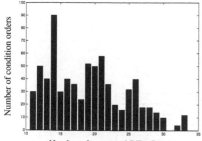

Figure 7: German credit; DT size distribution

in Figure 9. We start by providing the system with the following inputs: Savings account $\leq$ 12.40 Euro, Economical sector = other and Purpose = second-hand car. At this point, the Term input becomes irrelevant (indicated by '-') and hence, the system prompts for the next relevant input which is the number of years the applicant has been a client of the bank. We then indicate that the applicant has been a client for more than three years. The other remaining inputs (Owns Property and Income) then become irrelevant, which allows the system to draw a conclusion: Applicant = good. This is illustrated in Figure 11. For this particular applicant, the system needed only 4 of the 7 inputs to make a classification decision. This example clearly illustrates that the use of decision tables allows to ask targeted questions by neglecting the irrelevant inputs during the decision process. It is precisely this property that makes decision tables interesting tools for decision support in credit scoring.

5   CONCLUSIONS

In this paper, we have illustrated the potential of decision tables to build intelligent systems for credit scoring. Using two real-life cases, it was shown how a set of propositional if-then rules, extracted by a neural network rule extraction algorithm, can be represented as a decision table. The constructed decision tables were then reduced in size using lexicographical order-preserving contraction and condition row order minimisation routines which in both cases yielded a parsimonious representation of the extracted rules. It was also demonstrated that the use of decision tables allows to ask targeted questions by neglecting the irrelevant inputs during the decision process. Hence, using decision tables in combination with a sophisticated rule extraction algorithm provides an interesting approach for building powerful and intelligent credit scoring systems.

REFERENCES

Baesens, B., Setiono, R., Mues, C., and Vanthienen, J. (2003). Using neural network rule extraction and decision tables for credit-risk evaluation. *Management Science*. forthcoming.

Bishop, C. (1995). *Neural networks for pattern recognition*. Oxford University Press.

Crook, J. (1999). Who is discouraged from applying for credit ? *Economics Letters*, 65:165–172.

Davis, R., Edelman, D., and Gammerman, A. (1992). Machine learning algorithms for credit-card applications. *IMA Journal of Mathematics Applied In Business and Industry*, 4:43–51.

Desai, V., Crook, J., and Overstreet Jr., G. (1996). A comparison of neural networks and linear scoring models in the credit union environment. *European Journal of Operational Research*, 95(1):24–37.

Henley, W. and Hand, D. (1997). Construction of a k-nearest neighbour credit-scoring system. *IMA Journal of Mathematics Applied In Business and Industry*, 8:305–321.

Santos-Gomez, L. and Darnel, M. (1992). Empirical evaluation of decision tables for constructing and comprehending expert system rules. *Knowledge Acquisition*, 4:427–444.

Setiono, R. and Liu, H. (1996). Symbolic representation of neural networks. *IEEE Computer*, 29(3):71–77.

Steenackers, A. and Goovaerts, M. (1989). A credit scoring model for personal loans. *Insurance: Mathematics and Economics*, 8:31–34.

Thomas, L. (2000). A survey of credit and behavioural scoring: forecasting financial risk of lending to customers. *International Journal of Forecasting*, 16:149–172.

Vanthienen, J. (1994). A more general comparison of the decision table and tree. *Communications of the ACM*, 37(2):109–113.

Vanthienen, J. and Dries, E. (1994). Illustration of a decision table tool for specifying and implementing knowledge based systems. *International Journal on Artificial Intelligence Tools*, 3(2):267–288.

Vanthienen, J. and Dries, E. (1996). A branch and bound algorithm to optimize the representation of tabular decision processes. research report 9602, K.U.Leuven.

Vanthienen, J., Mues, C., and Aerts, A. (1998). An illustration of verification and validation in the modelling phase of kbs development. *Data and Knowledge Engineering*, 27:337–352.

Vanthienen, J. and Wets, G. (1994). From decision tables to expert system shells. *Data and Knowledge Engineering*, 13(3):265–282.

Wets, G. (1998). *Decision Tables in Knowledge-Based Systems: Adding Knowledge Discovery and Fuzzy Concepts to the Decision Table Formalism*. PhD thesis, Department of Applied Economic Sciences, Catholic University of Leuven, Belgium.

1. Checking account	1 or 2										3 or 4
2. Credit History	0 or 1			2 or 3						4	-
3. Term	1		2	1	2					-	-
4. Purpose	1 or 5	8	other	-	-	1 or 5	8 or other			-	-
5. Savings account	-	-	-	-	-	-	1 or 2 or 3	4 or 5		-	-
6. Other parties	-	-	-	-	-	-	1 or 2	3	-	-	-
1. Applicant=good	-	×	-	-	×	×	-	×	×	×	×
1. Applicant=bad	×	-	×	×	-	-	×	-	-	-	-
	1	2	3	4	5	6	7	8	9	10	11

Figure 8: Decision table for the rules extracted by Neurorule on German credit.

1. Savings Account	≤12.40 Euro												> 12.40 Euro
2. Economical sector	Sector C	other											-
3. Purpose	-	cash provisioning					second-hand car					other	-
4. Term	-	≤ 12 months			> 12 months		-						
5. Years Client	-	≤ 3		>3	≤ 3	>3	≤ 3			>3			
6. Owns Property	-	Yes	No		-	-	Yes	No	Yes	No		-	-	-
7. Income	-	-	≤ 719 Euro	> 719 Euro	-	-	-	-	-	≤ 719 Euro	> 719 Euro	-	-	
1. Applicant=good	-	×	×	-	×	-	×	-	×	×	-	×	×	×
2. Applicant=bad	×	-	-	×	-	×	-	×	-	-	×	-	-	-
	1	2	3	4	5	6	7	8	9	10	11	12	13	14

Figure 9: Decision table for the rules extracted by Neurorule on Bene1.

136

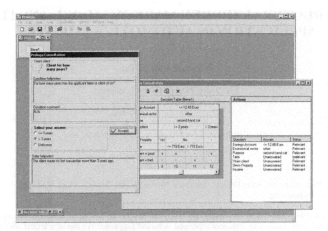

Figure 10: Example consultation session in PROLOGA.

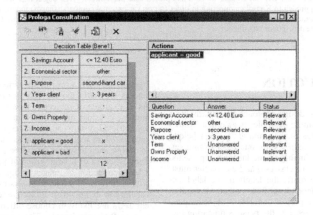

Figure 11: Classifying an applicant in PROLOGA.

STRUCTURAL HIDDEN MARKOV MODEL AND ITS APPLICATION IN AUTOMOTIVE INDUSTRY

D. Bouchaffra, J. Tan

Department of Computer Science & Engineering
131 Dodge Hall, Oakland University
Rochester, MI, 48309, USA
Telephone: (248)370-2242
Fax: (248)370-4625
Emails: dbouchaffra@ieee.org, jtan@oakland.edu

Keywords: User Perceptions, Engineer Designs, Structural Hidden Markov Models, Shape Modeling, Kansei Engineering.

Abstract: We have introduced a new methodology that maps designs to human perceptions. Perceptions are adjectives/adverbs, phrases or sentences expressed in natural language. We used the lexical database WordNet to compute semantical relationships (or distances) between these perceptions. We partitioned the set of perceptions into k clusters that represent the classes for a further classification task. We have developed a new classifier called "structural hidden Markov model" (SHMM) that combines probability and distances in a seamless way. SHMM enables to learn and predict user perceptions given object designs. We have applied this approach to Kansei engineering in order to map car external contours (shapes) to customer perceptions. The accuracy obtained using the SHMM is 90%. This model has outperformed the neural network and the k-nearest-neighbor classifiers.

1   INTRODUCTION

In the traditional design approach for pattern classifiers, a set of training examples is assumed. Some times, the examples in the training set are labeled. Each example is assigned only one label from a set of labels. The cardinality of the label set represents the distinct number of classes that the classifier must deal with. Furthermore, the labels in the label set are considered independent of each other. Generally, the pattern classes represent concrete or objective patterns and the labelers, i.e. the persons preparing the training examples, agree on labels assigned to different examples. A number of powerful methodologies currently exist to deal with the design of pattern classifiers under the above scenario, which can be termed *the expert labeling of training examples (Duda et al., 2001; Ripley, 1996).*

With increasing proliferation of hand-held computers and Internet in almost every human endeavor, another pattern classifier design scenario is emerging where the training examples are not labeled by experts but by non-experts. Furthermore, each of these non-experts may use a different set of labels to mark the same set of examples. This may happen because of their different backgrounds, for example cultural and educational. We term this scenario of classifier design as *the subjective labeling of training examples.* As an example of subjective labeling of training examples, consider the design of a content-based image retrieval system capable of responding to queries such as "show me pictures that exude joy". One way to design such a system would be to collect subjective responses of a large group of potential users to a large collection of images to link image attributes with emotions. If we let the users use their own vocabulary to express their subjective responses, different users are likely to choose different labels to assign to the same image. There are several reasons for this. First, the variation in the labeling occurs because the emotional response to an image is subjective, and depends upon the environment and the current emotional state of the viewer. Second, the different users may choose different words or descriptors to describe their responses to an image even when the image appeals to their same emotion. This issue is best summed up by Keister (Keister, 1994) who states: "[it] is not so much that a picture is worth a thousand words, for many fewer words can describe a still picture for most retrieval purposes, the issue has more to do with the fact that those words vary from one person to another..." The scenario for content-

O. Camp et al. (eds.), Enterprise Information Systems V, 138-145.

based image retrieval described above has been argued as a way of enhancing the capabilities of current system by Brown (et al., 1996) who terms it image retrieval by *democratic indexing*.

Another example of the subjective labeling of training examples can be found in the practice of *Kansei engineering* where the goal is to design products that not only satisfy the physical needs but also lead to a target set of emotions in their intended audience, the consumers (N. Enmoto and Sawada, 1993; K. Kashiwagi and Nagamachi, 1994; Lee and Harada, 1998; Nagamachi, 1999; Nagamachi, 1995). Kansei in Japanese means a consumer's psychological feeling and image regarding a product. An important component of Kansei engineering consists of collecting users' impressions on a range of products to find the latent relationships between different product features and feelings. When the response data is collected through an open-ended questionnaire survey, we realize the scenario of subjective labeling of training examples.

The current methods for classifier design are not adequate to deal with pattern classification tasks involving subjectively labeled training examples. The main reasons for inadequacy are as follows. First, the current methods do not incorporate any processing to relate the subjective responses of the labelers. Second, the current methods generally assume the existence of one or more prototypical patterns for each class; however, there are no easy prototypical patterns for subjectively defined classes. For example, an object may be "beautiful" for one group of labelers but not so for another group. Thus, the same label in the subjective labeling scenario may stand for a wide collection of patterns. Third, the different aspects of a pattern might invoke different subjective responses. In other words, a pattern might be composed of several sub-patterns that might invoke different subjective perceptions. For example, the soundtrack of a movie clip might be "annoying" but the visuals may be "pleasing". Similarly, the front of an automobile might be "attractive" whereas the rear or the side might be "ugly". The classification methodology should be able to integrate or differentiate such different aspects of a pattern depending upon a given application. Finally, the nature of subjective responses is such that a small change in one of the attributes of a pattern can lead to a significant change in its subjective labeling.

The goal of this paper is to present a pattern classification methodology suitable for dealing with problems involving the subjective labeling of training examples or patterns. The organization of this paper is as follows: in section 2, we state the problem. In section 3, we introduce our methodology by addressing three main issues: (i) how to measure similarity between different designs and divide them into equiva-

lent groups; (ii) how to relate subjective impressions of a design provided by a group of potential users using the electronic lexical database WordNet; and (iii) how to link the aspects of a design with different classes of subjective judgments using a novel classifier called structural hidden Markov model (SHMM). The SHMM classifier relates observations in each hidden state through a proximity measure or an equivalence relation to make the final classification decision. The application and experiments are discussed in section 4. Finally, the conclusion and future work are laid out in section 5. To show how our approach works, we present the results of an automotive design application related to external contours of an automobile.

2 PROBLEM STATEMENT

Let $\mathcal{X}$ be the design vector space and Ω be the set of perceptions. The problem that we are trying to solve is threefold: (i) extract information that represents a design, (ii) extract the global perception $\omega \in \Omega$ assigned to a design $x \in \mathcal{X}$ based on subjective responses from users, and (iii) classify an input design into a predefined set of user perception, i.e., subjective response categories. Analytically, this third subproblem can be expressed in the following way: determine a mapping f from $\mathcal{X}$ to Ω such that: $\forall x_i \in \mathcal{X}, \exists! \omega_j \in \Omega$ with: $f(x_i) = \omega_j$ and $dist(\omega_j, \omega^*)$ is minimum. The class ω^* is the true perception. In other words, we attempt to predict the optimal perception ω^* assigned to the design x_i through the function f using the distance metric $dist$.

3 PROPOSED METHODOLOGY

Before providing the details of our proposed methodology, we first introduce some definitions.

3.1 Object Design and Perception

Three principal elements which are "design", "perception" and "classification" (or mapping) form the core of this research. Let's first define them:

Definition 3.1 *A design (representation of an object)* $x \in \mathcal{X}$ *is a vector defined by a pair* $(\mathcal{F}, n)$ *where:*

- $\mathcal{F}$ *is a set of features that characterizes the design,*
- n *is the dimension of the design feature space, (* $|\mathcal{F}| = n$ *).*

We focus in this paper on physical designs such as an automobile. Physical designs are represented by their external shapes. Techniques of shape modeling such as Fourier descriptors, wavelet descriptors,

139

chain codes, polygons and B-splines are being investigated (Li and Hero, 2002; Chang and Kuo, 1996; Pratt, 1996; Rachidi and Spacek, 1994). However, the challenge is to determine the one that "best" maps shapes to user perceptions.

Definition 3.2 *A perception graph $P \in \mathcal{P}$ is a triplet $(\mathcal{V}, \mathcal{U}, \mu)$ where:*

- $\mathcal{V}$ *is a collection of vertices,*
- $\mathcal{U}$ *is a collection of edges that link each pair of vertices,*
- μ *is a proximity measure that computes the strength of association between a pair of vertices.*

3.2 Context and Perception Graph

3.2.1 Perception Context

Perception attributes mean different things for different individuals and can change as a function of the following variables: "the age", "the gender", and "the socio-professional category" (SPC)[1]. Since the application domain is emphasized during the survey itself, therefore it is not a part of the context information. These criteria constitute the *perception context*. A vector concept that assigns a digit to each variable is computed in the following way:

- if age ≤ 30 then age = 1 ; else if ($31 \leq age \leq 50$) then age =2 ; else age =3.
- if male then gender = 0 ; else gender = 1.
- if senior executive then SPC = 0 ; else if middle manager then SPC = 1 ; else if student then SPC = 2 ; else SPC = 3

Therefore, there is a need to consider the context within which we make our survey. For example, if we collect opinions (using adjectives) of cars from young male students, then the context vector is $[1, 0, 2]^T$. Thus, the same adjectives used during the survey have the same meaning. Otherwise, the meanings of one word may differ subjectively if it comes from people of different age, gender, and socio-professional category.

In this way, we can compare a pair of perception attributes through a suitable similarity measure.

3.2.2 Perception Graph and Survey

We present two different ways that enable to build the perception graph, they are:

- **Open verbal perception graph**: users are asked to give their opinions on a design such as a car or on

---

[1]Other variables such as "cultural background" might affect human perceptions.

---

a sub-design such as a car front. Their feelings regarding such a design are described verbally during a survey. These verbal responses could be words, phrases or sentences. In this paper, we focus only on adjectives contained within a phrase or a sentence. A speech recognizer is used in order to transcribe the uttered input into ASCII strings. A part of speech tagger is invoked in order to extract all word-forms with their respective syntactical categories. In this case, the speaker can be in a remote client site and her uttered opinion about the design is transmitted (via Internet) to a server site where the perception graph is built (see Figure 1).

- **Closed perception graph**: in this case, predefined perceptions are used to collect responses. Each participant ranks the responses using some suitable scale. The vertices of the graph are the perception attributes that have been selected by all persons that have participated in the survey.

We have developed a similarity measure between pairs of vertices based on the electronic lexical database WordNet. WordNet accepts one word p (or perception attribute) and searches for its *synset* (set of synonyms) $W(p)$ with respect to a specified usage and context. The following describes this similarity measure:

3.2.3 Similarity Measure between Perceptions

Here we consider how to compute a similarity between two perception attributes (words) within a specific perception context. This measure will apply when the word is an adjective representing a vertex of the perception graph.

Definition 3.3 *The similarity measure μ of order k between two vertices p_i and p_j in a perception graph is defined as:*

$$\mu^k(p_i, p_j) = \frac{|W^k(p_i) \wedge W^k(p_j)|}{|W^k(p_i) \vee W^k(p_j)| \times k}, \quad (1)$$

where $W^k(p) = W \circ W \circ ... \circ W(p)$ is a synset assigned to x using the WordNet operator k times.

The division by k is performed in order to reduce the similarity values between perceptions that are far apart (k large!). As an example, let's assume that $k = 2$, p = "attractive" and let's compute $W^2(p)$. Invoking the online lexical database WordNet, we obtain the following synset assigned to the perception attribute "attractive": W("attractive") = {gorgeous, captivating, handsome, beautiful, exquisite}, therefore: W^2("attractive") = W[W("attractive")]=W{gorgeous, captivating, handsome, beautiful, exquisite} = W(gorgeous) $\vee$

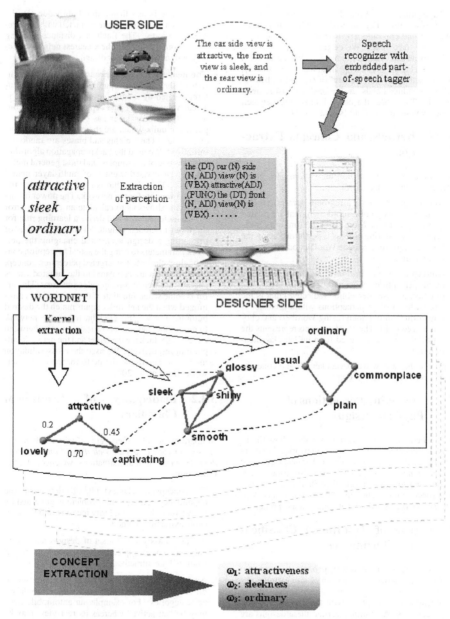

Figure 1: Three kernels and three concepts are extracted from a perception graph after a survey on "fronts" (sub-designs) of 11 different cars. The same procedure is performed for the "sides" and "rears". Through a majority vote, only one perception is assigned to a car view.

W(captivating) ∨ W(handsome) ∨ W(beautiful) ∨ W(exquisite). For the sake of illustration, let's take k=1 and compute μ^1 ("*attractive*", "*elegant*") given the fact that: W("elegant") = {handsome, neat, exquisite, refined, smart}. W("attractive") ∧ W("elegant") = {handsome, exquisite}, W("attractive") ∨ W("elegant")= {gorgeous, beautiful, captivating, handsome, refined, exquisite, neat, smart}. Therefore, the order 1 proximity between these two user perceptions is equal to 1/4.

3.2.4 Kernels and Concepts Extraction

We introduce in this section the notions of a graph perception kernel and its concept.

- **Kernel:** is a cluster that regroups perceptions (assigned to a design or a sub-design) that are related with respect to the Wordnet-based similarity measure. The clustering process is performed using the k-means algorithm and the WordNet-based similarity measure.

- **Concept:** is the *central meaning* that is conveyed by all perceptions contained in a same kernel. In practice, the user perception (adjective) that is the closest to all other perceptions within a cluster is transformed into a noun (using Wordnet) and chosen as a concept. The set of concepts represents the set of classes that are used for a further classification task.

Figure 1 shows how we extract kernels and concepts from a verbal perception graph.

3.3 Predicting Perceptions of Physical Designs

In the first part of this section, we show how the k-nearest neighbors, and the neural networks classifiers can be used to predict the optimal concept assigned to a design (or input pattern). We also discuss their inadequacy to solve this problem. In the second part, we propose a novel classifier called *structural Hidden Markov model* (SHMM) that is more appropriate.

3.3.1 Use of Traditional Classification Techniques

- **The k-nearest neighbor approach**: we compute a distance between the design of an incoming object and the set of reference object designs stored during a training phase with their respective user perceptions. As outlined earlier, these designs are vector representation of contours of physical objects. Once a match is found (i.e., distance between

two vectors is less than a threshold value ϵ!), the perception concepts $\omega_i's$ are extracted with their respective scores. The Euclidean distance is being used in order to extract the k nearest neighbor vectors assigned to the input design.

- **The neural network approach:** the network consists of three layers: input, hidden and output, interconnected by modifiable weights. The input is a real valued vector that captures the object contour. The hidden layer has 5 units and the output has c units which are the perception concepts $\omega_1, \ldots, \omega_c$. The weights and biases are randomly initialized. We used the backpropagation algorithm which is one of the simplest and most general methods for supervised training of multi-layer neural network. This algorithm is used to determine the optimal weights for the network. The power of this algorithm allows us to calculate an effective error for each hidden unit, and derive a learning rule for the input-to-hidden weights. This rule consists of presenting a design vector and changing the network parameters to bring the actual perception concept class closer to the targeted perception concept class. Outputs are compared to the targeted values and any difference corresponds to an error. This error is some scalar function of the weights. It is minimized when the network outputs match the desired outputs. The weights are adjusted by the network to reduce the measure of the training error between ω_k^* and ω_k which are the target and the network output unit respectively. We used the cross-validation method to determine the performance of the network (Duda et al., 2001).

3.3.2 Inadequacy of Traditional Classifiers

Nonparametric classifiers are efficient when the classes (or categories) are *well defined and independent*. However, in many situations, we encounter the following:

1. The concepts (or classes) might be dependent, the dependency notion in this problem is governed by the Wordnet-based similarity measure and the concepts extraction method.

2. A class is assigned to a set of designs and not to only one. For example, there are more than one car front that are attractive.

3. An input pattern (design) might be composed of different sub-designs which are assigned to different categories. For example, an automobile front may be "attractive" whereas its rear view may be "ugly". Similarly, the visuals in a video may not be "pleasing" but the background music may be

"soothing". In such cases, we would like to combine different aspects of the object in order to target a specific design.

4. A small variation of the input pattern (design) changes the class decision drastically. For example, a small deformation of a car external shape has a big impact on customer perceptions. Traditional classifiers tend to assign a same class to two "similar" input patterns.

Therefore, we introduce a novel classifier called "structural hidden Markov model" (SHMM) that takes into account the first three issues. The fourth issue is beyond the scope of this current paper.

3.3.3 The Concept of Structural HMM's

Let's consider $\omega = \omega_1, \omega_2, ..., \omega_T$ a concept sequence and $x = x_1, x_2, ..., x_T$ a design sequence. Each concept ω_i is assigned to one design x_i. For example, if the design is a car, then there are three concepts which are assigned to the car front, car side and the car rear respectively. Our problem consists of determining the optimal sequence of concepts $\omega^* = \omega_1^*, \omega_2^*, ..., \omega_T^*$ from which we can "better" observe the sequence of designs $x = x_1, x_2, ..., x_T$. Mathematically, this is written as: $\max_{\omega} P(x, \omega | \lambda_\mathcal{R}) = \max_{\omega} P(x | \omega, \lambda_\mathcal{R}) \times P(\omega | \lambda_\mathcal{R})$, where $\lambda_\mathcal{R}$ is the model that contains all terms involved in this computation. The equivalence relationship $\mathcal{R}$ gathers designs (or patterns) that are very similar in some sense. Therefore, $\mathcal{R}$ induces a distance (or similarity measure) in the design space. This problem is viewed as a *Structural Hidden Markov Model* (SHMM) because observations (or clusters of designs) within a hidden state (a concept) are related through a proximity measure (or an equivalence relation). In classical HMM's, the computation of the probability of an observation sequence requires the proportion of each observation within a hidden state and the state distribution (Rabiner and Juang, 1993; Bouchaffra et al., 1999). However, in our approach the notion of concept cannot be mapped to only one single design but to a cluster of designs that share common features. The clustering of designs is performed through the k-means algorithm on the design representation vectors. Therefore, we can write:

$$P(x_1, x_2, ..., x_T | \omega_1, \omega_2, ..., \omega_T, \lambda_\mathcal{R}) \equiv P(\dot{x}_1, \dot{x}_2, ..., \dot{x_T} | \omega_1, \omega_2, ..., \omega_T, \lambda_\mathcal{R}), \qquad (2)$$

Let's assume as in classical HMM's that the observations are *state conditionally independent*. Hence, we finally state our problem as: determine the optimal concept sequence $\omega_1^*, \omega_2^*, ..., \omega_T^*$ such that $P(\dot{x}_1, \dot{x}_2, ..., \dot{x_T} | \lambda_\mathcal{R})$ is maximum. Mathematically,

this can be expressed as:

$$< \omega_1^*, \omega_2^*, ..., \omega_T^* > = \arg \max_{\omega_1, ..., \omega_T} [$$
$$\prod_{i=1}^{i=T} P(\dot{x}_i | \omega_i) \times \pi_{\omega_1} \prod_{i=2}^{i=T} P(\omega_i | \omega_{i-1}, \omega_{i-2}, ..., \omega_1)].$$

Therefore, we introduce the SHMM concept as follows:

Definition 3.4 *A structural Hidden Markov Chain is a quadruplet* $\lambda = (\pi, \mathcal{A}, \mathcal{B}, \mathcal{R})$, *where:*
- π *is the state initial probability vector,*
- $\mathcal{A}$ *is the state transition probability matrix,*
- $\mathcal{B}$ *is the state conditional probability matrix of the visible observations,*
- $\mathcal{R}$ *is an equivalence relation that captures structures of the visible observations. The equivalence relation* $\mathcal{R}$ *controls the clustering process which has an impact on the matrices* $\mathcal{A}$ *and* $\mathcal{B}$ *and the initial vector* π.

Because of a psycho-linguistic aspect involved in the user perception process, we believe that the concept of SHMM is more adequate to solve this mapping problem. The output of the SHMM is a sequence of T concepts corresponding to each element of the whole design. A *majority vote*-based technique (Ho et al., 1994) is used in order to derive the unique optimal concept assigned to the whole design x.

3.3.4 SHMM Parameters Estimation

The structural information is embedded within the SHMM through the relation $\mathcal{R}$. As outlined above, the three parameters π, $\mathcal{A}$, and $\mathcal{B}$ are related to the clustering process created by $\mathcal{R}$. We first provide the maximum likelihood (ML) estimation of the concept conditional probability of an input design $P(\dot{x}_i | \omega_i)$. We replace each neighbor of x_i with x_i itself and each user perception (adjective) by the concept that represents it. We finally compute the number of times the design x_i was assigned to the concept ω_i divided by the number of times the concept ω_i was present in the training sample. This computation assumes that the set of designs and the set of user perceptions have already been clustered. However, the concept transition probability is ML estimated as the number of times the i-grams $< \omega_i, \omega_{i-1}, \omega_{i-2}, ..., \omega_1 >$ was present in the training sample divided by the number of times the $(i-1)$ grams $< \omega_{i-1}, \omega_{i-2}, ..., \omega_1 >$ was present in the training sample, after all the user perceptions in the training sample have been replaced by their concepts. Finally, the initial probability vector can be estimated as: the number of times the concept ω_i was assigned to an instance of x_1, divided by the total number of instances of x_1. By adding more data in the training sample, the precision of the SHMM parame-

143

ters will improve. The following algorithm illustrates the parameter variation:

```
Begin
    Initialize:  k = 0; i = 0;
        ε small (closeto 0) fixed value;
        T[i] = M (large number)
    Repeat
    ++k; ++i;
    Cluster the set of perceptions
        and the set of designs:  R^k
    Compute the model λ^k = (π^k, A^k, B^k, R^k)
    Compute the design maximum
        likelihood  P^k = P(x_1, x_2, ..., x_T|λ^k) =
        P(x|ω, λ^k) × P(ω|λ^k);
        assign T[i] = P^k;
    Add more designs in training sample;
    Until |T[i] - T[i - 1]| ≤ ε
    Store the optimal model λ^k*
End.
```

4 APPLICATION AND EXPERIMENTS

We have applied this research in order to predict customer perceptions given car designs. We collected 114 images of regular cars (no trucks or vans!) with their three views (i.e., 342 images). During our survey, we have presented these images to 100 students (all young females) of Oakland University. Therefore the perception context was specific. We used the closed perception graph method described in section 3.2. We extracted the contour x of three sides: "front (f)", "side (s)", and "rear (r)" and represent a car design as: $x = (x_f, x_s, x_r)$. In this current stage of research, we are experimenting Fourier descriptor for contour extraction. Because Fourier descriptors are not powerful enough to capture the high frequency properties (representing sharp edges), therefore other shape modeling techniques will be invoked later in this ongoing research. We have used 7 pairs of Fourier descriptors to capture the front and the rear contours and 15 pairs to describe the side contour. A feature vector is obtained through this contour extraction phase. The k-nearest neighbors, the neural networks classifiers and the SHMM have been experimented. Preliminary performance results are depicted in Table 1. SHMM outperformed the two traditional classifiers since its accuracy is 90%.

This optimal prediction of user perceptions within a context is fed to the design engineer before the object (car in this application) is put into making. ¿From the economical standpoint, our model saves a lot of money to several industrial companies.

Precision in % Sample Size	k-NN	NN	SHMM
70 cars	52.1	54.2	66.7
114 cars	73.2	78.6	90

Table 1: Performances obtained using the k-nearest neighbors, the neural network and the SHMM classifiers.

5 CONCLUSION AND FUTURE WORK

We have presented in this paper a novel approach that maps physical objects to user perceptions. Our methodology goes beyond Kansei-engineering since (i) the classes which are the concepts are built automatically from the user perceptions, they are not given *a-priori*, (ii) the mapping between perceptions and designs is nonlinear, thus more general. We have introduced the concept of Structural HMM as a nonlinear mapping between designs and perceptions. SHMM embeds a similarity measure (or a distance) within HMM's. However, as outlined in section 3.3.2, a small deformation of a design impacts user perceptions. As a future work, we plan to develop a more robust clustering by discovering the best partitioning of the data (in terms of preserving the pairwise similarity in the raw data). However, this investigation opens a door to category theory (Hahn and Ramscar, 2001). As for application, we plan to build an intelligent shape synthesis system that a designer is able to use and manipulate to produce automotive contours by giving commands in the form of adjectives. We believe such a system plugged into a virtual reality display will truly showcase the potential of creating designs by transforming qualitative descriptors into prototypical designs.

REFERENCES

Bouchaffra, D., Govindaraju, V., and Srihari, S. N. (1999). Postprocessing of recognized strings using nonstationary markovian models. *IEEE Transactions: Pattern Analysis and Machine Intelligence, PAMI*, 21(10).

Chang, C. and Kuo, C. (1996). Wavelet descriptor of planar curves: Theory and applications. *IEEE Trans. Image Processing*, 5:56–70.

Duda, R., Hart, P., and Stork, D. (2001). *Pattern Classification*. Wiley, New York.

et al., P. B. (1996). The democratic indexing of images. *New Review of Hypermedia and Multimedia: Applications and Research*, (2):107–120.

Fellbaum (1998). *WordNet: an electronic lexical database*. Bradford Book.

G. Miller, R. Beckwith, C. F. D. G. and Miller, K. (1990). Introduction to wordnet: An online lexical database. *Journal of Lexicography*, (3(4)):235–244.

Hahn, U. and Ramscar, M. (2001). *Similarity and Categorization*. Oxford University Press, New York, 279.

Ho, T., Hull, J., and Srihari, S. N. (1994). Decision combination in multiple classifier systems. *IEEE Transactions: Pattern Analysis and Machine Intelligence*, 16(1).

K. Kashiwagi, A. M. and Nagamachi, N. (1994). A feature detection mechanism of pattern in kansei engineering. *Human Interface*, (9(1)):9–16.

Keister, L. H. (1994). User types and queries: Impact on image access systems in challenges in indexing electronic text and images (fidel, r et al., eds). *ASIS*, pages 7–22.

Lee, S. and Harada, A. (1998). A pattern approach by objective and subjective evaluation of kansei information. *Proceedings Int'l Workshop on Robot and Human Communication (RoMan'98), Hakamatsu, Japan*, pages 327–332.

Li, J. and Hero, A. O. (2002). A spectral approach to statistical polar shape modeling. *ICIP 2002*.

N. Enmoto, M. Nagamachi, J. N. and Sawada, K. (1993). Virtual kitchen system using kansei engineering, in: G. salvendy and mj smith (eds.), human-computer interaction: Software and hardware interfaces. *Elsevier, Amsterdam*, pages 657–662.

Nagamachi, M. (1995). Kansei engineering: A new ergonomic consumer-oriented technology for product development. *Int'l Journal of Industrial Ergonomics*, 15:3–11.

Nagamachi, M. (1999). Kansei engineering and its application in automotive design, in human factors in audio, interior systems, driving, and vehicle seating. *Proceedings of 1999 SAE, International Congress and Exposition, Detroit, MI, SEA*, (1):1265.

Pratt, I. (2-7-1996). Shape representation using fourier coefficients of the sinusoidal transform. *Technical Report Series, University of Manchester*.

Rabiner, L. and Juang, B. (1993). *Fundamentals of Speech Recognition*. Prentice Hall.

Rachidi, T and Spacek, L. (1994). Boundary-based correspondence computation using the topology constraint. *5th British Machine Vision Conference*.

Ripley, B. D. (1996). *Pattern Recognition and Neural Networks*. Cambridge University Press.

PARTIAL ABDUCTIVE INFERENCE IN BAYESIAN NETWORKS BY USING PROBABILITY TREES

Luis M. de Campos[1], José A. Gámez[2], Serafín Moral[1]

[1]*Departamento de Ciencias de la Computación e I.A.*
Universidad de Granada.
Granada - 18071 - Spain
Email: lci@decsai.ugr.es

[2]*Departamento de Informática*
Universidad de Castilla-La Mancha.
Albacete - 02071 - Spain
Email: jgamez@info-ab.uclm.es

Keywords: Abductive inference, Bayesian networks, junction/join trees, probability trees, approximate propagation.

Abstract: The problem of partial abductive inference in Bayesian networks is, in general, more complex to solve than other inference problems as probability/evidence propagation or total abduction. When join trees are used as the graphical structure over which propagation will be carried out, the problem can be decomposed into two stages: (1) to obtain a join tree containing only the variables included in the explanation set, and (2) to solve a total abduction problem over this new join tree. In De Campos et al. (2002a) different techniques are studied in order to approach this problem, obtaining as a result that not always the methods which obtain join trees with smaller size are also those requiring less CPU time during the propagation phase. In this work we propose to use (exact and approximate) *probability trees* as the basic data structure for the representation of the probability distributions used during the propagation. ¿From our experiments, we observe how the use of exact probability trees improves the efficiency of the propagation. Besides, when using approximate probability trees the method obtains very good approximations and the required resources decrease considerably.

1 INTRODUCTION

A *Bayesian network (BN)* (Pearl, 1988; Jensen, 2001) is a directed acyclic graph (DAG) where the nodes $X_\mathcal{U} = \{X_1, \ldots, X_n\}$ represent random variables, and the topology of the graph shows the (in)dependence relations among the variables. A set of parameters is also stored for each variable in $X_\mathcal{U}$, which are usually conditional probability distributions $P(X_i|pa(X_i))$, where $pa(X_i)$ contains the parents of X_i in the DAG. Figure 1.(a) shows a Bayesian network with 8 variables. From this set of conditional probability distributions, and due to the probabilistic independences induced by the graphical model (DAG), we can recover the joint probability over $X_\mathcal{U}$ as:

$$P(X_1, \ldots, X_n) = \prod_{i=1}^{n} P(X_i|pa(X_i)), \quad (1)$$

Once we have specified our knowledge base as a Bayesian network, we can use it to perform any kind of probabilistic reasoning. Inference or reasoning in a Bayesian network is carried out by means of propagation algorithms. These algorithms proceed by sending flows of messages (potentials[1]) through the nodes of a graphical structure called *join tree* (JT). A *join tree* (Jensen, 2001) is a higher level graphical structure, obtained from the original BN by means of a process called *compilation*. The use of this secondary graphical structure (JT) as the inference engine, instead of using directly the initial one (the BN) avoids to introduce restrictions about the topology of the BN. Figure 1.(b) shows a JT for the BN represented in the left side of the same figure.

In the context of probabilistic reasoning, abductive or diagnostic inference corresponds to finding the maximum 'a posteriori' probability state of the system variables given some observed evidence. Thus, if X_O is the set of observed variables, $X_O = x_O$ is the observed evidence and X_U is the set of unobserved variables, the goal is to obtain the configuration x_U^* of X_U such that:

$$x_U^* = \arg\max_{x_U} P(x_U|x_O). \quad (2)$$

Usually, x_U^* is known as the *most probable explanation* (MPE) (Pearl, 1988).

---

[1]A potential is a non negative function defined over a set of variables. No additional assumption (conditional probability, normalization, etc, ...) is considered

O. Camp et al. (eds.), Enterprise Information Systems V, 146-154.
© 2004 *Kluwer Academic Publishers. Printed in the Netherlands.*

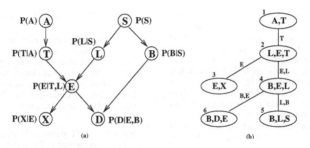

Figure 1: (a) *Asia* Bayesian network. (b) A join tree for *Asia*

In (Dawid, 1992) an efficient algorithm to calculate the most probable explanation (MPE) in a join tree is developped. The algorithm is based on the probability propagation algorithm (Andersen et al., 1989) but replacing summation by maximum in the calculation of the messages. However, in general we are interested not only in the MPE, but in the K MPEs, and (Nilsson, 1994) proved that for $K \geq 4$ Dawid's algorithm is not valid. In this case more sophisticated methods have to be used. (Nilsson, 1998) has developed an efficient method for finding the K MPEs for every K. The method is based in the combination of Dawid's algorithm with a divide and conquer technique which iteratively identified the remaining $K-1$ explanations without carrying out more propagations. Besides, in that paper Nilsson also proved that only the first (upward) phase of Hugin's message passing is actually necessary in order to solve the MPE problem.

Sometimes we are interested in obtaining the K MPEs only for a subset of the network's variables called *explanation set* (Neapolitan, 1990). This problem is known as *Partial Abductive Inference* and we think that in practical applications is more interesting than the classical abductive inference problem, because we can select as the explanation set the variables representing diseases in a medical diagnosis problem, the variables representing critical components (starter, battery, alternator, ...) in a car diagnosis problem, ...

Now, if we denote by $X_E \subset X_U$ the explanation set, then the goal is to obtain the configuration x_E^* of X_E such that:

$$x_E^* = \arg \max_{x_E} P(x_E|x_O) = \arg \max_{x_E} \sum_{x_R} P(x_E, x_R|x_O),$$

(3)

where $X_R = X_U \setminus X_E$. In general, x_E^* is not equal to project the configuration x_U^* over the variables of X_E. So, we need to obtain x_E^* directly (eq. 3).

From the study or Equation 3 the problem of partial abductive inference in BNs can be solved in two steps:

1. Eliminate (by summation) the variables not in X_E.

This process will yield a junction tree containing only the variables in the explanation set (X_E). Formally this process is known as a marginalization of the join tree; thus, if $\mathcal{T}$ is the intial JT, i.e., the JT obtained from the BN, we obtain a new JT $\mathcal{T}_E$ by means of the marginalization $\mathcal{T}^{\downarrow X_E}$.

2. Apply an algorithm of *total* abduction (Nilsson, 1998; Seroussi and Goldmard, 1994) over $\mathcal{T}_E$.

However, this process is more complex than it looks, because summation and maximum have to be used simultaneously and these operations do not have a commutative behaviour. This problem is studied in (de Campos et al., 2002a) by revising existing methods, adding some improvements to them, and proposing and alternative method, always working with tabular representation of the potentials involved in computations. Our proposal for this work is to show how the algorithms for solving partial abductive inference in BNs can take advantage of using potentials represented as probability trees (Cano and Moral, 1997). The paper is organised in 5 sections including this introduction. In Section 2 we revise the methods studied/proposed in (de Campos et al., 2002a). The third section is devoted to a brief introduction of probability trees and to an empirical analysis of the results obtained when comparing partial abduction in BNs by using probability trees vs probability tables. In Section 4 we propose to approach the partial abductive problem in an approximate way by using probability trees. Finally, Section 5 contains our concluding remarks.

2   EXACT PARTIAL ABDUCTIVE INFERENCE IN BNS BY USING JT-BASED PROPAGATION ALGORITHMS

The main problem we face when dealing with partial abductive inference is the non commutative behaviour of summation and maximum as marginalization operators. Because of this, not all join tree obtained from the original BN is *valid* to solve partial abductive inference for a given explanation set X_E. In fact, the two-stages algorithm cited in the previous section, can be only directly applied over a join tree $\mathcal{T}$ such that no marginalization by summation has to be carried out over a potential obtained as a result of a marginalization by maximum. This condition has the following topological equivalence: *a join tree $\mathcal{T}$ is valid for a given explanation set X_E, if and only if there is a sub-tree $\mathcal{T}_E \subset \mathcal{T}$ containing only the variables belonging to X_E.*

Therefore, the problem is how to obtain a valid join tree for a given explanation set X_E. We can distinguish two different approaches:

- *Adaptation of a general (unconstrained) join tree.* (Xu, 1995) gives a method for transforming any join tree into another one containing a node C_i in which all the variables in X_E are included. The problem of this method is that if X_E contains many variables, then the size[2] of the potential associated with that node C_i will be too large. (Nilsson, 1998) outlines how to slightly modify Xu's algorithm in order to allow (when possible) that the variables of X_E constitute a sub-tree and not a single node, reducing in this way the size of the potentials attached to those nodes. The method consists in

  1. Identify the smallest sub-tree $\mathcal{T}'$ of the initial join tree $\mathcal{T}$, such that, X_E is contained in $\mathcal{T}'$.
  2. Marginalize out by summation in $\mathcal{T}$ the variables not included in $\mathcal{T}'$. In this way a factorisation of $P(X_{\mathcal{T}'})$ is obtained.
  3. Start a fusion process in which those neighbour nodes in $\mathcal{T}'$ which share variables not in X_E are fused by eliminating (by summation) those variables (for details and some additional improvements to this method see (de Campos et al., 2002a)).

- *Searching for an specific join tree.* In this approach, instead of taking an unconstrained join tree and try to adapt it for a given explanation set X_E, the idea is to directly search for a join tree specifically thought to perform partial abductive inference over a given explanation set X_E (de Campos et al., 1997; de Campos et al., 2002a).

This task can be achieved by taking advantage of the available degrees of freedom in the compilation process. Concretely, during the triangulation we can use constrained deletion sequences, in such a way that we start to delete the variables of X_E

only when all the variables not in X_E have been deleted.

Using the degrees of freedom available in the process of building a join tree from a BN, constrained deletion sequences are used during the compilation process, by forcing the elimination of all the variables not included in the explanation set before than eliminating any variable of X_E. The result is a join tree in which the fusion process is not already necessary.

We will use AJT to denote the method (with the improvements presented in (de Campos et al., 2002a)) which uses an Adapted Join Tree, and SJT to denote the method which uses an Specific Join Tree. Experiments with the these two approaches and, using probability tables as the potential representation, are carried out in (de Campos et al., 2002a). After the experimentation with several networks carried out in that paper, the following general conclusion can be drawn: the problem of partial abductive inference is, in general, much more complex than the one of total abductive inference. This is due to the (sometimes enormous) difference between the size of the join tree over which the inference has to be carried out. With respect to the use of AJT and SJT, the conclusion is that in most of the cases the size of the JTs obtained when using SJT is smaller than the size of the JTs obtained by AJT; this conclusion is, in general, valid with respect to the size of the whole JT (size of the initial JT plus size of the cluster created during the fusion process) and also with respect to the final JT ($\mathcal{T}_E$) over which abductive inference will be carried out. However, this gain in the size of the join tree, not always is translated to a gain in running CPU time.

In order to explain this *surprising* fact, we have studied it detecting that the greater difference in CPU time is due to the initial stage of the process. Thus, while the construction of the graphical part of a JT is a symbolic process and so it consumes little CPU time, the creation and initialisation of the potentials is a highly-demanding CPU time when the size of the JT nodes is large, as occurs in the case of using SJT. The same happen with the process of entering evidence [3] because it is necessary to run over all the configurations in the potential to set its probability to 0.0 for those which disagree with the observed evidence.

Let us to analyse a concrete and representative case [4]. In this case the obtained JTs have size 217749 and 188907 when using AJT and SJT respectively, and the size of the JT, $\mathcal{T}_E$, is the same for both methods. Table 1 shows the CPU time required by both algorithms,

---

[2]In this paper by *size* of a potential or JT node, we refer to the state space size necessary to store the potential as a probability table. By *size* of a JT we refer to the sum of the sizes of all the nodes it contains.

[3]In our experiments we have generated a different evidence with 5 observed variables for each generated explanation set.

[4]This case corresponds to one of the experiments carried out in the next section, and denoted as Alarm.14.9.

but detailed for each of the following stages:

1. *Construction of the JT $\mathcal{T}$ and entering of evidence*: The CPU time spent in this first stage by AJT is less than the 1% of the CPU time spent in the whole process. However, for SJT this stage represents the 62% of the total CPU time!. Remark that the process of initialising and entering evidence in large potentials is expensive, because in both operations the whole potential/table has to be visited.

2. *Identification of $\mathcal{T}'$ and obtaining $P(X_{\mathcal{T}'})$*: Also in this stage the difference between both methods is quite significant. A possible reason for this difference can be the following: when using SJT it is quite frequent the presence of a large node/cluster in $\mathcal{T}'$, so, the process of eliminating variables by addition from this node is costly. However, this difference on CPU time with respect to AJT can be compensated because there is no need of carrying out the fusion process (stage 4).

3. *Computing $P(X_O = x_O)$ (upward evidence propagation in the current JT $\mathcal{T}'$)*: In this case as SJT operates over a large join tree, it is clear that it consumes more CPU time than AJT. In these case a possible alternative could be to construct a general JT and to use it for computing $P(X_O = x_O)$, because as we can see from table 1 the total amount of time spent by AJT in stages 1, 2 and 3 is smaller than the amount of time spent by SJT in this stage.

4. *Fusion process and obtaining $\mathcal{T}_E$* (this stage is only necessary when using AJT): It is clear that is in this stage where AJT consumes the greatest amount of CPU time.

5. *Obtaining the 10 MPEs over $\mathcal{T}_E$*: As in this case (Alarm.14.9) both final JTs have the same size (which does not imply that they are equals), the amount of CPU time required by both methods is almost the same.

Table 1: Partial CPU time for Alarm.14.9 (seconds)

Method	stage1	stage2	stage3	stage4	stage5	total
AJT	0.167	0.027	0.041	38.038	7.252	45.545
SJT	102.106	47.948	6.789	0.0	7.237	164.080

From these results, we think that the main disadvantage of SJT resides on the fact of dealing with large potentials since the beginning of the process. However, as the initial data (network's probability families) is the same for both methods, it is quite probable the presence of many regularities in the potentials associated to the JT nodes built by SJT. Because of this we think that by using an alternative representation for the potentials, it is quite probable to improve the efficiency of SJT, although AJT could be also benefited.

3 JT-BASED EXACT PARTIAL ABDUCTIVE INFERENCE IN BNS BY USING PROBABILITY TREES

We think that an alternative representation to probability tables that can exploit the presence of such regularities in the data is the use probability trees. In this section we briefly revise this representation and present our results when using it instead of probability tables.

3.1 Probability trees

A *Probability Tree* (Cano and Moral, 1997; Boutilier et al., 1996; Salmerón and Moral, 2000) is a directed labeled tree, where each inner node represents a discrete variable and each leaf represents a probability value. Each inner node will have as many children as different states the variable it represents has. A probability tree represents a potential, and the probability value for a given configuration, $X_I = x_I$, of the variables in that potential is the real number associated to the leaf we achieve after starting in the root node and selecting at each inner node/variable the path corresponding to the value taken by that variable in given configuration.

Probability trees are an appropiate tool for dealing with *context specific independence* (Boutilier et al., 1996), and, in general, to efficiently represent regularities in potentials (Cano and Moral, 1997). Figure 2.(b) shows a probability tree for the potential ψ whose tabular representation is given in the same figure (left side). As we can see in Figure 2.(c) the use of probability trees is specially advantageous when evidence has been entered (in this case we assume that $X_2 = 2$, by multiplying by the indicator of this function).

In this paper we will follow the methodology proposed by (Cano and Moral, 1997) to build a probability tree from a probability table. This methodology it is based on methods for inducing decision trees from examples. Concretely Quinlan's ID3 algorithm (Quinlan, 1986) is used but considering a different information measure, because now each leaf represents a probability value and not classes as in decision trees. In the methodology proposed by Cano and Moral, also operations for summation-based marginalization and combination of probability trees are provided.

X_1	X_2	X_3	$\psi(.)$	$\psi'(.)$
1	1	1	0.2	0.0
1	1	2	0.5	0.0
1	2	1	0.7	0.7
1	2	2	0.7	0.7
2	1	1	0.3	0.0
2	1	2	0.5	0.0
2	2	1	0.6	0.6
2	2	2	0.6	0.6

(a) Tabular representation.

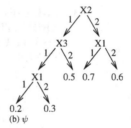

(b) ψ

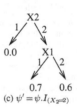

(c) $\psi' = \psi.I_{(X_2=2)}$

Figure 2: Tabular and (a possible) tree-shaped representation of two potentials (ψ, ψ').

3.2 Results obtained when using probability trees

As Cano and Moral probability trees are implemented in the Elvira[5] software (Elvira Consortium, 2002), we have used its own implementation, but adding some abduction specific methods (marginalization by maximum, getting the i-th configuration of maximum probability from a tree, etc, ...).

After finishing the implementation, our first experiment is the repetition of the experiment commented on Section 2 but using probability trees instead of tables when applying AJT and SJT. The results are shown in table 2.

Table 2: Partial CPU time for Alarm.14.9 when using probability trees.

Method	stage1	stage2	stage3	stage4	stage5	total
AJT/ Trees	0.170	0.015	0.017	28.587	5.664	34.453
SJT/ Trees	0.375	13.870	1.039	0.0	5.201	20.485

As we can see CPU time have decreased for both methods, but being drastic the reduction obtained for SJT, where the amount of CPU time required in stage 1 has been reduced from 102.1 to 0.375 seconds.

Once we have confirmed our expectations about the advantage of using probability trees in our problem, we have tested the behaviour of both methods (AJT and SJT) by carrying out the set of experiments described below.

We have used the *Alarm* (Beinlich et al., 1989) Bayesian network, which has 37 variables and has been frequently used in the BN scientific literature. Besides, in this network evidence or probability propagation and total abduction can be solved in a very efficient way (join tree of size $\simeq$ 1000 and less than 1 second of CPU time per propagation), while solving complex problems of partial abductive inference can

---
[5]http://leo.ugr.es/~elvira

require too much CPU time and space. We have randomly generated 50 different scenarios (explanation sets + evidence), 10 with 9 variables, 10 with 14, 10 with 19, 10 with 24 y 10 with 29. We will refer to these cases as Alarm.X.Y, where X denotes the explanation set size and Y=1..10 the identification number for this case (given the value of X).

The results of these experiments can be seen in Figure 3, where different comparisons are carried out by considering AJT or SJT and tables or trees as potential representation. In the X axis we represent the 50 cases, thus from 1 to 10 we have the cases with 9 variables in the explanation set, from 11 to 20, the cases with 14 variables in the explanation set, and so on. In the Y axis we represent CPU time in seconds in logarithmic scale. From these results, we can see how the use of probability trees is (almost) always beneficial with respect to the use of tables, over all in the more complex cases. Furthermore, when probability trees are used SJT works better than AJT, except when there are few variables in the explanation set, because in these cases both algorithms yield similar results.

4 JT-BASED APPROXIMATE PARTIAL ABDUCTIVE INFERENCE IN BNS BY USING PROBABILITY TREES

As the size of the join trees obtained for partial abductive inference is, in general, larger than the size of those obtained for evidence propagation or total abduction (de Campos et al., 2002a), and as these tasks are NP-hard (Cooper, 1990; Shimony, 1994; Park, 2002), it is obvious that very often approximate methods will be necessary to solve partial abductive inference. In this paper we propose to approximate partial abductive inference, not by using approximate propagation methods or search-based methods (de Campos et al., 2002b; de Campos et al., 2002c; Park, 2002),

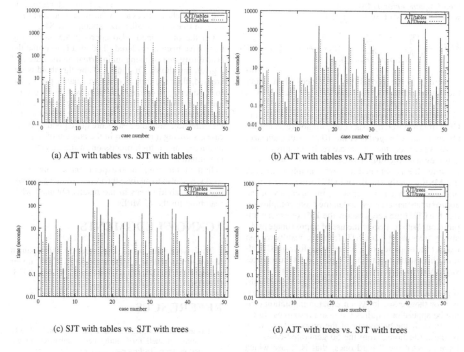

Figure 3: CPU time for the experiments with the Alarm Bayesian network

but by using approximate probability trees.

4.1 Approximate probability trees

Probability trees represent a useful tool for approximate inference (Cano and Moral, 1997; Salmerón and Moral, 2000; Cano et al., 2000), because exact propagation algorithms can be applied, but using an approximate (and smaller) representation of the potentials. This approximation consists in to set up an upper limit for the size (number of leaves) of the probability tree. The following procedure can be used to approximate a potential represented as a probability tree (Cano and Moral, 1997):

- **Pruning**(T,T',ϵ). This method returns an approximation T' of probability tree T by using a threshold ϵ. The idea is to (recursively) select a node such that all its children are leaves and to replace it and its children by one node containing the average of the values of the leaf nodes being removed. In the methodology proposed in (Cano and Moral, 1997), such a node is pruned only when

an information measure $I(\cdot,\cdot)$ (defined in terms of Kullback-Leibler's divergence) is lower than a given threshold depending on ϵ.

4.2 Results obtained when using approximate probability trees

Now, we have experimented with the same 50 cases previously generated for the *Alarm* Bayesian network, but using approximate probability trees and considering different values for ϵ. Furthermore, in this series of experiments we have focused our analysis in the case of looking for the best MPE, although the method is valid for looking for the K MPEs.

Table 3 shows the results (on the average) for each of the five different sizes considered for the explanation set. For each case: the first row refers to the required CPU time; the second row refers to the number of times in which the obtained MPE ($\hat{x}_E$) coincides with the true MPE x_E (obtained in the experiments of the previous section); and the third row shows the *mean square error* (MSE) (only for those cases in which the true MPE was obtained):

$$MSE = \sqrt{\frac{1}{N} \sum_{\{i:1..10 \ ; \ x_E^i = \hat{x}_E^i\}} (\hat{p}(\hat{x}_E^i | x_O) - p(x_E^i | x_O))^2},$$

(4)

where $\hat{p}$ is the probability obtained when using the approximate method and $N = |\{\hat{x}_E^i \ ; \ i : 1..10 \wedge x_E^i = \hat{x}_E^i\}|$.

Finally, in the last row of the table we can see the CPU time required by exact computation (exact probability trees), averaged over the 10 cases of each size.

As we can see, the results are really promising, because even for the higher values of ϵ, 10^{-3} and 10^{-4}, the true MPE is obtained in a great number of cases, the MSE is really small, and CPU time is less than one second. When ϵ decreases, the accuracy of the approximation increases, and in the more complex series the CPU time keeps below the 10% of exact computation. With respect to the use of approximate probability trees in AJT and SJT, from the results we can extract the tendency of a better behaviour of SJT, although in some cases (the simplest ones) it requires slightly more time.

Although we can always use approximate methods, it is clear that this approach will be specially interesting for those cases in which exact computation cannot be applied or requires too much resources. In order to study the behaviour of the proposed approach in these situations, from the 50 generated cases, we have selected the 5 hard ones, that is, those which require more than 100 CPU seconds when applying AJT (with probability trees). The results for these cases are shown in Table 4, while for each case we show the CPU time and the probability of the best MPE when using approximate probability trees. Besides, the first row of the table shows the same values but for exact probability trees.

In all the cases except but in Alarm.29.4, the best explanation found when using $\epsilon = 10^{-3}$ was the true MPE. In the difficult case Alarm.29.4, the MPE found by the approximate algorithm only differs from the true MPE in one literal, and coincides with the second MPE found by the exact algorithm, which has similar probabiltiy (0.009466) to the true MPE. As we can see, the use of approximate probability trees is of great interest in complex problems.

5 CONCLUDING REMARKS

In this work we have introduced the use of probability trees in the task of solving partial abductive inference in Bayesian networks. From our experiments, we can say that when potentials are represented by using probability trees instead of tables, then, both algorithms (AJT and SJT) become more efficient, because they require less CPU time and space. Moreover, the use of probability trees allows us to take advantage of the join tree with smaller size obtained by SJT.

On the other hand, also approximate probability trees have been considered. The idea is to prune the probability tree by using an information measure and a given threshold. Of course, if the threshold is decreased, then the tree receives an smaller prune, and so a better approximation is achieved, but more resorces are required during the propagation. In our experiments we have considered different values for that threshold, and the results are quite good in all the cases, showing a reduction in the amount of required resources, and a high precission in the obtained approximation.

In the future we plan to experiment with more networks, and also to analyse the impact of using approximate probabiltiy trees in the results obtained when searching for the K MPEs.

ACKNOWLEDGMENTS

This work has been supported by the Spanish Ministerio de Ciencia y Tecnología (MCyT), under projects TIC2001-2973-C05-01 and TIC2001-2973-C05-05.

REFERENCES

Andersen, S., Olesen, K., Jensen, F., and Jensen, F. (1989). Hugin: a shell for buiding belief universes for expert systems. In *Proceedings of the 11th International Joint Conference on Artificial Intelligence*, Detroit.

Beinlich, I., Suermondt, H., Chavez, R., and Cooper, G. (1989). The ALARM monitoring system: A case study with two probabilistic inference techniques for belief networks. In *Proceedings of the Second European Conference on Artificial Intelligence in Medicine*, pages 247–256. Springer-Verlag.

Boutilier, C., Friedman, N., Goldszmidt, M., and Koller, D. (1996). Context-specific independence in Bayesian networks. In *Proceedings of the Twelfth Annual Conference on Uncertainty in Artificial Intelligence (UAI–96)*, pages 115–123, Portland, Oregon.

Cano, A. and Moral, S. (1997). Propagación exacta y aproximada con árboles de probabilidad. In *Actas de la VII Conferencia de la Asociación Española Para la Inteligencia Artificial*, pages 635–644.

Cano, A., Moral, S., and Salmerón, A. (2000). Penniless propagation in join trees. *International Journal of Intelligent Systems*, 15:1027–1059.

Cooper, G. (1990). Probabilistic inference using belief networks is NP-hard. *Artificial Intelligence*, pages 393–405.

Dawid, A. (1992). Applications of a general propagation algorithm for probabilistic expert systems. *Statistics and Computing*, 2:25–36.

de Campos, L., Gámez, J., and Moral, S. (1997). Un método exacto para realizar abducción parcial en redes Bayesianas. In Botti, V., editor, *Actas de la VII Conferencia de la Asociación Española para la inteligencia artificial*, pages 621–633, Málaga.

de Campos, L., Gámez, J., and Moral, S. (2002a). On the problem of performing exact partial abductive inference in Bayesian belief networks using junction trees. In Bouchon-Meunier, B., Gutierrez-Rios, J., Magdalena, L., and Yager, R., editors, *Technologies for Constructing Intelligent Systems 2: Tools*, pages 289–302. Physica-Verlag.

de Campos, L., Gámez, J., and Moral, S. (2002b). Partial Abductive Inference in Bayesian Belief Networks: An Evolutionary Computation Approach by Using Problem Specific Genetic Operators. *IEEE Transaction on Evolutionary Computation*, (6):105–131.

de Campos, L., Gámez, J., and Moral, S. (2002c). Partial Abductive Inference in Bayesian Belief Networks by using Simulated Annealing. *International Journal of Approximate Reasoning*, (27):263–283.

Elvira Consortium (2002). Elvira: an environment for creating and using probabilistic graphical models. In Gámez, J. and Salmerón, A., editors, *Proceedings of the First European Workshop on Probabilistic Graphical Models (PGM'02)*, pages 222–230.

Jensen, F. (2001). *Bayesian Networks and Decision Graphs*. Springer Verlag.

Neapolitan, R. E. (1990). *Probabilistic Reasoning in Expert Systems. Theory and Algorithms*. Wiley Interscience.

Nilsson, D. (1994). An algorithm for finding the M most probable configurations of discrete variables that are specified in probabilistic expert systems. *MSc. Thesis*, University of Copenhagen.

Nilsson, D. (1998). An efficient algorithm for finding the M most probable configurations in Bayesian networks. *Statistics and Computing*, 9:159–173.

Park, J. (2002). Map complexity results and approximation methods. In *Proceedings of the 18th Conference on Uncertainty in Artificial Intelligence (UAI 02)*. Morgan Kaufmann Publishers.

Pearl, J. (1988). *Probabilistic Reasoning in Intelligent Systems*. Morgan Kaufmann, San Mateo.

Quinlan, J. (1986). Induction of decision trees. *Machine Learning*, 1:81–106.

Salmerón, A. Cano, A. and Moral, S. (2000). Importance sampling in bayesian networks using probability trees. *Computational Statistics and Data Analysis*, 34:387–413.

Seroussi, B. and Goldmard, J. (1994). An algorithm directly finding the K most probable configurations in Bayesian networks. *International Journal of Approximate Reasoning*, 11:205–233.

Shimony, S. (1994). Finding maps for belief networks is NP-hard. *Artificial Intelligence*, 68:399–410.

Xu, H. (1995). Computing marginals for arbitrary subsets from marginal representation in markov trees. *Artificial Intelligence*, 74:177–189.

Table 3: Results of using approximate probability trees.

					$|X_E|$					
	9		14		19		24		29	
ϵ	AJT	SJT	AJT	SJT	AJT	SJT	AJT	SJT	AJT	SJT
10^{-3}	0.199	0.185	0.330	0.366	0.311	0.260	0.333	0.308	0.305	0.215
	10/10	9/10	9/10	8/10	9/10	6/10	10/10	7/10	8/10	7/10
	0.00816	0.03038	0.00899	0.02864	0.00740	0.01600	0.00492	0.00974	0.00352	0.00159
10^{-4}	0.343	0.360	0.868	0.800	0.853	0.564	0.759	0.518	0.814	0.323
	10/10	10/10	7/10	8/10	10/10	9/10	9/10	9/10	10/10	9/10
	0.00513	0.01094	0.00417	0.00391	0.00140	0.00302	0.00055	0.00247	0.00070	0.00062
10^{-5}	0.533	0.601	1.992	1.722	2.226	1.024	1.354	0.772	1.914	0.402
	10/10	10/10	9/10	10/10	10/10	10/10	9/10	10/10	10/10	9/10
	0.00058	0.00253	0.00181	0.00366	0.00037	0.00259	0.00018	0.00031	0.00002	0.00011
10^{-6}	0.744	0.882	4.228	2.927	4.602	1.755	2.059	1.056	3.658	0.590
	10/10	10/10	10/10	10/10	10/10	10/10	10/10	10/10	10/10	10/10
	0.00016	0.00021	0.00010	0.00065	0.00002	0.00027	0.00002	0.00006	0.00000	0.00001
Exact	2.284	2.082	45.205	10.506	41.571	4.988	13.335	2.356	49.143	1.111

Table 4: Analysis of the results obtained for the 5 more difficult cases when using AJT and probability trees

		Alarm.14.5	Alarm.19.3	Alarm.19.7	Alarm.29.4	Alarm.29.8
Exact	time (secs.)	296.645	125.995	190.993	322.670	110.134
	$p(EMP)$	0.078661	0.157274	0.025734	0.009563	0.031036
$\epsilon = 10^{-3}$	time (secs.)	1.02	0.747	0.734	0.741	0.579
	$\hat{p}(EMP)$	0.079294	0.153401	0.023270	0.009263	0.028687
$\epsilon = 10^{-4}$	time (secs.)	3.13	1.995	1.971	2.368	1.17
	$\hat{p}(EMP)$	0.0774822	0.156857	0.025170	0.009511	0.030169
$\epsilon = 10^{-5}$	time (secs.)	7.77	5.07	6.268	6.427	3.097
	$\hat{p}(EMP)$	0.078578	0.157267	0.025954	0.009558	0.031027
$\epsilon = 10^{-6}$	time (secs.)	18.601	12.31	13.804	16.483	5.415
	$\hat{p}(EMP)$	0.078661	0.157274	0.025734	0.009563	0.031036

EVALUATION OF AN AGENT-MEDIATED COLLABORATIVE PRODUCTION PROTOCOL IN AN INSTRUCTIONAL DESIGN SCENARIO

Juan Manuel Dodero
Paloma Díaz Pérez
Ignacio Aedo Cuevas

Departamento de Informática, Universidad Carlos III de Madrid
Avda. de la Universidad 30, 28911 Leganés, Madrid, Spain
Email: dodero,pdp@inf.uc3m.es, aedo@ia.uc3m.es

Keywords: Knowledge management, Multi-agent coordination, Learning objects

Abstract: Distributed knowledge creation or production is a collaborative task that needs to be coordinated. A multiagent architecture for collaborative knowledge production tasks is introduced, where knowledge-producing agents are arranged into knowledge domains or *marts*, and a distributed interaction protocol is used to consolidate knowledge that is produced in a mart. Knowledge consolidated in a given mart can be in turn negotiated in higher-level foreign marts. As an evaluation scenario, the proposed architecture and protocol are applied to facilitate coordination during the creation of learning objects by a distributed group of instructional designers.

1 INTRODUCTION

Knowledge production or generation is the process supporting the creation of new knowledge (Davenport and Prusak, 1998; Nonaka and Takeuchi, 1995), both externally acquired and also developed within the bosom of a workgroup. Such generated knowledge is the result of the social interaction process between actors, according to their interests and the regulations that apply in the group. When a group of people is collaboratively creating a complex object, the establishment of a set of coordination rules is needed.

This situation happens, for instance, when several people are building a software component. Let's suppose two developers who are designing respective modules, which will be part of the same software component. During the design, the need to develop two sub-elements for the same purpose can be detected by both developers. Each one usually has her own pace of work in developing the common element. As well, they can be differently skilled in that work. If the development process is not appropriately coordinated, the following problems can arise:

- A developer could get her work crushed, depending on the required speed and quality of the design, in comparison to her partner's competency.

- When speed is more important than quality, a more elaborated and reusable product can be readily thrown away.

- In the best of cases, effort will be duplicated in several phases of the project.

Therefore, the coordination of knowledge production should meet the following objectives:

- Bring together participants' different pace of creation.

- Take advantage of participants' different skills in the problem domain and the tools that are managed.

- Reduce the number of conflicts provoked by interdependencies between in-production knowledge components.

- In a more general sense, avoid duplication of effort.

Coordination is a key pattern of interaction needed to obtain a good quality knowledge that has been validated by means of contrast and/or consensus in the group. Although knowledge acquisition and sharing efforts are worth to be considered, distributed knowledge production still lacks interaction models and methods to coordinate a group of autonomous, distributed users during the collaborative generation of knowledge.

In the rest of the paper we present an agent-mediated solution for knowledge production (2), together with an evaluation scenario of learning objects design (3), including the results obtained from that evaluation (4) and, finally, some conclusions and future work (5).

155

2 AGENT-MEDIATED KNOWLEDGE PRODUCTION

Multiagent systems have been successful in the distributed implementation of knowledge management processes. Knowledge acquisition agents have been one of the most successful applications of software agents (Etzioni and Weld, 1995), were knowledge-collector agents operate within available information resources, and validate them in accordance with the users' interests. On the other hand, knowledge delivery lies in an end-to-end routing of knowledge that is generated by some actor. This is a task that has been typically realized by software agents (Genesereth and Tenenbaum, 1991). Therefore, it is reasonable to approach the multiagent paradigm for knowledge production. Knowledge-producing agents need to do formulations that keep with a validation scheme supporting the knowledge construction. Since agents have been proven as a helpful tool for the coordination of people who are performing a given task (Maes, 1994), multiagent systems can support the coordinated interaction needed to achieve an agreement on the knowledge that is eventually generated, and even on the validation scheme.

Agent interaction protocols govern the exchange of a series of messages among agents, i.e. a conversation. There are some popular interaction protocols, used heavily by multi-agent systems, like contract protocols (Smith, 1980) and computational economies (Wellman, 1997). These approaches tackle rather general aspects of agent interactions, usually characterized as competitive, cooperative or negotiative. During knowledge production, agents try to convince each other in a group to accept a given knowledge in some domain, so building the corpus of shared knowledge. The aim is to allow agents to consolidate knowledge that is continuously produced. Consolidation in a group of producers is to establish a given knowledge as accepted by the group as a whole, with every member knowing about that circumstance. Agents can reach a consensus on the knowledge that is consolidated by the exchange of messages, using a consolidation protocol described below.

The working hypothesis is that a group of agents can help to coordinate the distributed production of knowledge, acting as representatives of knowledge-producing actors, according to the following principles:

- Agents can be structured into separable knowledge domains of interaction. This structuring reflects the knowledge differences between producers.

- A dynamic re-thinking of the structure of interactions in different domains can help to reduce the inter-dependencies during the process.

2.1 A Multi-agent Architecture for Knowledge Production

In our architecture, knowledge-producing agents can operate within the boundaries of a specific domain or knowledge mart. Nevertheless, interaction among different domains is also supported. Tightly-coupled interaction domains are modelled as separate knowledge marts for agents. A knowledge mart is a distributed group of agents that is trying to produce a piece of knowledge in a given domain.

In order to facilitate interaction between domains, marts can be structured in a hierarchical way. Knowledge produced in a mart can be merged in a structured fashion, by using representatives in a common higher-level mart. When knowledge produced in a mart can affect performance in some other domain, special proxy agents act as representatives in foreign marts, so that interaction between separate marts is not tightly coupled.

Interaction between agents is carried out by exchanging proposals in a FIPA-like common language (FIPA, 1997) that is driven by participants' goals and needs, so shaping a social interaction-level knowledge (Jennings and Campos, 1997). With *proposal* we mean each formulation act of an agent that intends to consolidate a given knowledge in its group. Since a proposal exhibits an intentional nature, we will not refer to it as fully produced knowledge until it becomes consolidated. The following basic types of messages can be exchanged between producing agents:

proposal(k, n)**:** Given an interaction process n, agents send a *proposal* message when they want a piece of knowledge k to be consolidated in the mart.

consolidate(k, n)**:** Agents send a *consolidate* message when they reach a given state in the interaction protocol, and they want a previously submitted proposal k to be accepted in an interaction process n.

Both types of message can be respectively identified with `propose` and `inform` declaratives from FIPA ACL specification (FIPA, 1997). Nevertheless, since FIPA ACL provides them with a well-defined semantics —especially different in the case of `consolidate`— we prefer to use the types of message recently described.

A proposal reflects the intention of an agent to produce a given knowledge. The *attributes* of a proposal are elementary criteria that may be considered when comparing it to another in a mart. Some examples of proposal attributes are:

- The submitter's hierarchical level, useful when agents present different decision privileges in the mart about the acceptance of proposals.

- The degree of fulfilment of a set of goals. For instance, before the development of a learning content, a set of educational objectives or corporate training needs should be defined.

- A time-stamp of the moment when a proposal was firstly submitted in the mart.

Agents' rationality needs to be modelled in terms of preference relations or relevance functions, in order to allow them to evaluate and compare proposals. The relevance of a proposal is defined as the set of proposal attributes considered when interacting, while the preference relationship denotes which of two proposals is preferred. We define the *relevance* of a proposal as the set of proposal attributes that are considered during a message interaction. The relevance function $u(k)$ of a proposal k in a mart returns a numerical value, dependent on attributes of k, in such a way that if $k_i \neq k_j$, then $u(k_i) \neq u(k_j)$. Another way to express the relevance is by means of *preference relationships*, where a proposal k_1 is preferred to another k_2 in a mart, denoted as $k_1 \succ k_2$, if $u(k_1) > u(k_2)$.

2.2 Knowledge Consolidation Protocol

The function of the protocol executed by agents is to consolidate knowledge that is created in a mart. By *consolidation* we mean the establishment of knowledge as accepted by every agent in the mart, in such a way that every member agent eventually know about it. The consolidation protocol (Dodero et al., 2002) is a two-phase process:

- The distribution phase begins when an agent submits a proposal, i.e. when the agent starts the protocol. A given timeout t_0 is defined to set the end of this phase.

- The consolidation phase begins if there is a proposal waiting to be consolidated. This event can occur whether the distribution timeout t_0 expired or a t_0-waiting agent received a proposal that was evaluated as preferred. A distinct timeout t_1 is used for the consolidation phase.

An agent can participate in several interaction processes. Each interaction process is handled separately, by initiating a new execution thread of the protocol. Two different timeouts are used over the course of the protocol. Timeout t_0 is used for the distribution phase, that occurs after an agent submits a $proposal(k,n)$ message, where n represents an interaction process and k is a piece of knowledge that wants to be consolidated in the mart. During t_0, messages can arrive from any other agent, consisting in new proposals, referring to same interaction process.

The message used to consolidate a proposal has the form $consolidate(k,n)$, and its aim is to establish a previously submitted proposal k as consolidated in an interaction process n.

At any moment, the reception of a message from another agent may provoke a momentary retraction from a previously submitted proposal, until a counter-proposal is elaborated. An agent that has not reached this state will be waiting for t_0 timeout. Then, if the agent receives a proposal that is evaluated as preferred, a new timeout t_1 is set to give it a chance. But if the preferred proposal is not eventually ratified, then the agent goes on about its aims and will try again to consolidate its own proposal.

3 COLLABORATIVE PRODUCTION OF LEARNING OBJECTS

A concrete case of a system for the shared creation of knowledge is that dedicated to the instructional design (Merrill, 1994) of learning objects (Farance and Tonkel, 2001; ADL, 2001). During the process, a number of instructional designers may wish to contribute, for example, making some modification to the structure of a course or adding some learning resource to the course contents. Interaction between authors should be coordinated by issuing and consolidating proposals to extend or modify the educational material. Authors are undertaken to meet a protocol that reflects their different interaction styles —i.e., cooperation, competition, negotiation, etc.

Evaluation scenario. The evaluation scenario consists of a set of agents representing different roles of docent coordinator (C_1), instructors (I_1 and I_2), and students (S_1, S_2 and S_3). The goal of agents in the mart is the development of a learning object —a course named "XML Programming"— that fulfills a set of educational objectives.

Learning objects packaging complies with SCORM/IMS standards (IMS, 2001a; IMS, 2001b), which are used as a simple reference ontology for learning objects development. Since these standards have room for describing each part of the learning object —v.g., table of contents (TOC), resources, metadata, etc.—, there may be several interaction processes initiated, each one affecting a section of the learning object that should be dealt with. Nevertheless, we will restrict our discussion to the TOC structure, and assume that the interaction process n is devoted to it.

When authors submit proposals, they will include the differences between both TOCs and referred to the same interaction. The interaction protocol is executed by every receiving author, until the proposal is eventually accepted, or substituted by a further elaborated proposal. This process continues until some proposal wins all evaluations, an agreement is reached, or some degree of consensus is achieved (depending on the kind of interaction, i.e., competitive, negotiating or cooperative). Although authors' behavior is an asynchronous process, agents interaction protocol helps to synchronize their operations.

Objectives. These are the educational objectives that define the preference relation used to evaluate proposals about the TOC of the course: (1) Ability to program XHTML (i.e., XML-generated HTML) web applications; (2) ability to program server-side web applications; and (3) ability to program XML data exchange applications.

The degree of fulfillment of educational objectives is modeled as a three-component vector $\mathbf{x} = (x_1, x_2, x_3)$, with $x_k \in I = [0,1]$ for $k = 1, 2, 3$. Let $f : I^3 \to I$ be a numerical measure of how well a proposal meets the objectives.

Evaluation criteria. The relevance of a proposal is graded by the fulfillment of the educational objectives described above. All objectives being equally satisfied, the rank of the agent will decide —coordinator's rank is higher that instructor, and instructors' rank is higher than students'—. If ranks are the same, the instant when the proposal was issued decides, which is determined by a time-stamp included with each proposal.

Each proposal $\mathbf{p}$ is described by a three-component vector (p_1, p_2, p_3), where $p_1 = f(\mathbf{x})$ is a numeric measure of the degree of fulfillment of educational objectives $\mathbf{x}$; p_2 is the numerical rank held by the submitter agent; and p_3 is a time-stamp.

Sequence of events. To clarify the operation of the protocol, a snapshot of it is depicted in figure 1. Therein, success in the execution of the consolidation protocol is marked with a circle ($\bigcirc$), whilst failure is indicated with a cross ($\times$). The sample sequence of events can be traced as follows:

I. I_1 starts by sending a proposal $\mathbf{i}_{11}$. When $\mathbf{i}_{11}$ is about to be consolidated, I_2 agent will issue a better evaluated proposal $\mathbf{i}_{21}$. C_1 does nothing and silently will accept every proposal that comes to it.

II. I_1 and I_2 elaborate two respective proposals $\mathbf{i}_{12}$ and $\mathbf{i}_{22}$, approximately at the same time during the distribution phase. The proposal from I_2 has a better evaluation than I_1's, and both are better than those in the first act.

III. C_1 builds and sends the best-evaluated proposal of this scene, which will eventually win the evaluation.

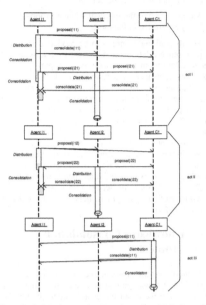

Figure 1: A sample snapshot sequence of events in the evaluation scenario.

4 EXPERIMENTAL EVALUATION

In order to evaluate the collaborative production system, tests were formulated as experiments that examine how far the multiagent architecture facilitates the coordination of a group of instructional designers that are cooperating to produce a learning object. The objectives for this evaluation were to prove the following hypothesis:

1. The quality of produced objects (i.e., their grade of fulfillment of educational objectives) is increased over the course of the interaction.

2. Conflicts that may occur during the interaction decrease and tend to be avoided.

3. The interaction offers stability in the development, without missing a chance for further evolution of developed material.

4.1 Settings and measurements

In order to accomplish evaluation goals, a number of
measurements were collated in the instructional settings described above, both dividing up actors in two
separate marts (cf. figure 2, left side) and putting them
together (cf. figure 2, right side). Their purpose is
to collate different results that measure the evaluation
objectives.

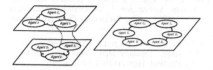

Figure 2: Two different arrangement of agents for the evaluation in a two-mart scenario (left side) and one-mart scenario (right side).

During the interaction process, quantitative measurements on throughput and performance were taken
in both scenarios, concerning observable actions and
behaviors about the following issues:

- Grade of fulfilment of previously defined educational objectives (cf. figure 3).

- Number of conflicts occurred per time unit (cf. figure 4).

- Lifetime of each consolidated object, before it is
  overruled by another consolidation process (cf. figure 5).

4.2 Experimental results

With regard to the first evaluation objective, figure 3
represents a plot of issued proposals in two-mart and
one-mart scenarios. Since I_2 is acting as a proxy
agent in the two-mart scenario, a slightly greater
number of proposals are generated than in the one-
mart scenario, though the excess in the former carry
the same contents than those submitted in the latter.
Moreover, some consolidations can be actually repeated, since they occur in different marts. In both
cases, the series of consolidated proposals —those labelled with a numeric percentage— are ascendant.

As for the second objective, figure 4 depicts the reduction in the number of conflicts occurred per time
unit from one-mart to two-mart scenario.

Finally, in figure 5 we can see how lifetime of consolidations progressively increases in both scenarios.
Notice that, though the tendency curve is ascendant,
in the two-mart scenario it is not monotonously increasing. The explaining to this event comes from the
fact that a group of agents collaborating in the subordinated mart can generate better quality objects that

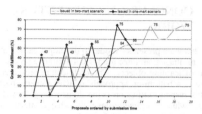

Figure 3: Grade of fulfillment of educational objectives for
issued and consolidated proposals in two-mart and one-mart
scenarios.

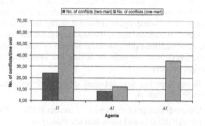

Figure 4: Number of conflicts occurred in both scenarios.

an only agent would do. When that better-quality object that is consolidated in the subordinated mart is
sent up to the higher-level mart, the chance that it cuts
off a previous consolidation is higher, and its consolidation lifetime may fall down earlier than if an only
agent had tried it.

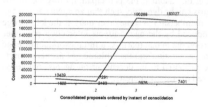

Figure 5: Consolidation lifetime for proposals that become
consolidated in both scenarios.

159

5 CONCLUSIONS AND FUTURE WORK

This work presents a model to develop a participative multiagent architecture for collaborative production of learning objects. The architecture presented here is a bottom-up approach to, where every mart holds responsibilities on some domain-level knowledge, while coordination-level knowledge interfaces to other domains are well-defined.

The participative approach presented in this work has been successfully applied to the constructivist, participative development of learning objects. Results obtained from a single-mart evaluation scenario have turn out that the coordination protocol improves conflict-solving and coordination during the shared development process. Moreover, the absence of participation of some agent does not delay the overall process. In sum, the agent-mediated solution has been found to facilitate the following aspects of distributed creation of learning objects during the instructional design process:

- Bring together instructional designers' different pace of creation.

- Take advantage of designers' different skills in the overall domain and tools that are managed.

- Reduce the number of conflicts provoked by inter-dependencies between different parts of the learning objects.

- In a general sense, avoid duplication of effort.

In order to test the multilevel architecture, these results need to be confirmed in more complex scenarios, consisting of more groups of participative agents working in different knowledge marts. We are also conducting tests on the impact of the number of agents and marts for the scalability of the architecture.

A dynamic re-thinking of the structure of interactions in different domains can help to reduce the inter-dependencies during the production process. Since interaction processes are not completely independent from one another, the participation of agents in the marts can be dynamic, such that an agent can change its membership to some other mart, if the knowledge produced by the agent affects interaction processes carried out in that mart. As a future work, knowledge mart generation and the affiliation of agents to marts are proposed to be dependent on agents' ontology-based expressed interests.

REFERENCES

ADL (2001). SCORM specifications. Technical report, Advanced Distributed Learning.

Davenport, T. H. and Prusak, L. (1998). *Working Knowledge: How Organizations Manage What They Know.* Harvard Business School Press.

Dodero, J. M., Aedo, I., and Díaz, P. (2002). Participative knowledge production of learning objects for e-books. *The Electronic Library*, 20(4):296–305.

Etzioni, O. and Weld, D. S. (1995). Intelligent agents on the internet: Fact, fiction, and forecast. *IEEE Expert*, pages 44–49.

Farance, F. and Tonkel, J. (2001). Learning Technology Systems Architecture (LTSA) Draft 8. Technical report, IEEE Learning Technology Standards Committee (LTSC).

FIPA (1997). Specification part 2 – Agent Communication Language. Technical report, Foundation for Intelligent Physical Agents (FIPA), Geneve.

Genesereth, M. and Tenenbaum, J. (1991). An agent-based approach to software. Technical report, Stanford University Logic Group.

IMS (2001a). IMS Content Packaging Information Model, version 1.1.2. Technical report, IMS Global Learning Consortium.

IMS (2001b). IMS Learning Resource Meta-Data Information Model, Version 1.2.1. Technical report, IMS Global Learning Consortium, Inc.

Jennings, N. R. and Campos, J. R. (1997). Towards a social level characterisation of socially responsible agents. *IEEE Proceedings on Software Engineering*, 144(1):11–25.

Maes, P. (1994). Agents that reduce work and information overload. *Communications of the ACM*, 37(7):31–40.

Merrill, M. D. (1994). *Instructional design theory.* Educational Technology Publications, Englewood Cliffs, NJ.

Nonaka, I. and Takeuchi, H. (1995). *The Knowledge-Creating Company.* Oxford University Press, New York.

Smith, R. G. (1980). The contract net protocol: High-level communication and control in a distributed problem solver. *IEEE Transactions on Computers*, 29(12):1104–1113.

Wellman, M. P. (1997). A computational market model for distributed configuration design. In Huhns, M. N. and Singh, M. P., editors, *Readings in Agents*, pages 371–379. Morgan Kaufmann, San Francisco, California.

SYMBOLIC MANAGEMENT OF IMPRECISION

Mazen El-Sayed, Daniel Pacholczyk

University of Angers, 2 Boulevard Lavoisier, 49045 ANGERS Cedex 01, France
Email: {elsayed,pacho}@univ-angers.fr

Keywords: Knowledge representation and reasoning, Imprecision, Vagueness, Many-valued logic, Multiset theory.

Abstract: We study knowledge-based systems using symbolic many-valued logic and we focus on the management of knowledge through linguistic concepts characterized by vague terms or labels. In previous papers we have proposed a symbolic representation of nuanced statements. In this representation, we have interpreted some nuances of natural language as linguistic modifiers and we have defined them within a multiset context. In this paper, we continue the presentation of our symbolic model and we propose new deduction rules dealing with nuanced statements. We limit ourself to present new *generalizations of the Modus Ponens rules* dealing with nuanced statements.

1 INTRODUCTION

The developement of knowledge-based systems is a rapidly expanding field in applied artificial intelligence. The knowledge base is comprised of a database and a rule base. We suppose that the database contains facts representing *nuanced statements*, like "Jo is very tall", to which one associates truth degrees. The *nuanced statements* can be represented more formally under the form "x is m_α A" where m_α and A are labels denoting respectively a nuance and a vague or imprecise term of natural language. The rule base contains rules of the form *"if x is m_α A then y is m_β B"* to which one associates truth degrees.
Our work presents a symbolic-based model which permits a qualitative management of vagueness in knowledge-based systems. In dealing with vagueness, there are two issues of importance: (1) how to represent vague data, and (2) how to draw inference using vague data.
When the imprecise information is evaluated in a *numerical way*, fuzzy logic which is introduced by Zadeh (Zadeh, 1965; Zadeh, 1979), is recognized as a good tool for dealing with aforementioned issues and performing reasoning upon common sense and vague knowledge-bases. In this logic, "x is m_α A" is considered as a fuzzy proposition where A is modeled by a fuzzy set which is defined by a membership func-

tion. This one is generally defined upon a numerical scale. The nuance m_α is defined such as a *fuzzy modifier* (Bouchon-Meunier and Yao, 1992; Pacholczyk, 1992; Zadeh, 1979) which represents, from the fuzzy set A, a new fuzzy set "m_α A". So, "x is m_α A" is interpreted by Zadeh as "x is (m_α A)" and regarded as many-valued statement.
A second formalism, refers to a symbolic many-valued logic (De-glas, 1989; Pacholczyk, 1992), is used when the imprecise information is evaluated in a *symbolic way*. This logic is the logical counterpart of *multiset theory* introduced by De Glas (De-glas, 1989). In this theory, the term m_α linguistically expresses the degree to which the object x satisfies the term A. So, "x is m_α A" means "x (is m_α) A", and then regarded as boolean statement. In other words, "m_α A" does not represent a new vague term obtained from A.
In previous papers (El-Sayed and Pacholczyk, 2002a; El-Sayed and Pacholczyk, 2002b), we have proposed a symbolic-based model to represent nuanced statements of natural language. This model is based on the many-valued logic proposed by Pacholczyk (Pacholczyk, 1992). Our basic idea has been to consider that some nuances of natural language can not be interpreted as satisfaction degrees and must be instead defined such as *linguistic modifiers*. Firstly, we have proposed a new method to symbolically represent vague terms of natural language. The basic idea

O. Camp et al. (eds.), Enterprise Information Systems V, 161-168.
© 2004 *Kluwer Academic Publishers. Printed in the Netherlands.*

has been to associate with each vague term a new *symbolic* concept called *"rule"*. This symbolic concept is equivalent to the membership function within a fuzzy context. By using the new concept, we have defined *linguistic modifiers* within a multiset context.

In this paper, our basic contribution has been to propose deduction rules dealing with nuanced information. For that purpose, we propose deduction rules generalizing the *Modus Ponens* rule in a many-valued logic proposed by Pacholczyk (Pacholczyk, 1992). Note that the first version of this rule has been proposed in a fuzzy context by Zadeh (Zadeh, 1979) and has been studied later by various authors (Baldwin, 1979; Bouchon-Meunier and Yao, 1992; Lascio et al., 1999):

Rule	:	if "X is A" then "Y is B"
Fact	:	"X is A'"
Conclusion	:	"Y is B'"

Where X and Y are fuzzy variables and A, B, A' and B' are fuzzy concepts.

This paper is organized as follows. In section 2, we present briefly the basic concepts of the M-valued predicate logic which forms the backbone of our work. Section 3 introduces briefly the symbolic representation model previousely proposed. In section 4, we study various types of inference rules and we propose new *Generalized Modus Ponens* rules in which we use only simple statements. In section 5, we propose a generalized production system in which we define more Generalized Modus Ponens rules in more complex situations. In section 6, we study the problem of graduality of inference and we demonstrate the types of graduality satisfied by our GMP rules.

2 M-VALUED PREDICATE LOGIC

Within a multiset context, to a vague term A and a nuance m_α are associated respectively a multiset $\mathbb{A}$ and a symbolic degree τ_α. So, the statement "x is m_α A" means that x belongs to multiset $\mathbb{A}$ with a degree τ_α. The M-valued predicate logic (Pacholczyk, 1992) is the logical counterpart of the multiset theory. In this logic, to each multiset $\mathbb{A}$ and a membership degree τ_α are associated a M-valued predicate **A** and a truth degree τ_α−true. In this context, the following equivalence holds: x is m_α $\mathbb{A} \Leftrightarrow x \in_\alpha \mathbb{A} \Leftrightarrow$ "x is m_α A" is true $\Leftrightarrow$ "x is A" is τ_α−true. One supposes that the membership degrees are symbolic degrees which form an ordered set $\mathcal{L}_M = \{\tau_\alpha, \alpha \in [1, M]\}$. This set is provided with the relation of a total order: $\tau_\alpha \le \tau_\beta \Leftrightarrow \alpha \le \beta$, and whose smallest element is τ_1 and the largest element is τ_M. We can then define in

$\mathcal{L}_M$ two operators $\wedge$ and $\vee$ and a decreasing involution $\sim$ as follows: $\tau_\alpha \vee \tau_\beta = \tau_{max(\alpha,\beta)}, \tau_\alpha \wedge \tau_\beta = \tau_{min(\alpha,\beta)}$ and $\sim \tau_\alpha = \tau_{M+1-\alpha}$. One obtains then a chain $\{\mathcal{L}_M, \vee, \wedge, \le\}$ having the structure of De Morgan lattice (Pacholczyk, 1992). On this set, an implication $\to$ and a T-norm T can be defined respectively as follows: $\tau_\alpha \to \tau_\beta = \tau_{min(\beta-\alpha+M,M)}$ and $T(\tau_\alpha, \tau_\beta) = \tau_{max(\beta+\alpha-M,1)}$.

Example 1 *For example, by choosing M=9, we can introduce:* $\mathcal{L}_9$=\{not at all, little, enough, fairly, moderately, quite, almost, nearly, completely\}.

In the following of this paper we focus our intention on the management of statements which are nuanced by linguistic modifiers. So, we consider that m_α A represents a multiset derived from A, and "x is m_α A" is a many-valued statement.

3 REPRESENTATION OF NUANCED STATEMENTS

Let us suppose that our knowledge base is characterized by a finite number of concepts $\mathcal{C}_i$. A set of terms P_{ik}[1] is associated with each concept $\mathcal{C}_i$, whose respective domain is denoted as X_i. The terms P_{ik} are said to be the *basic terms* connected with the concept $\mathcal{C}_i$. As an example, basic terms such as *"small"*, *"moderate"* and *"tall"* are associated with the particular concept *"size of men"*. A finite set of *linguistic modifiers* m_α allows us to define *nuanced terms*, denoted as *"$m_\alpha P_{ik}$"*.

In previous papers (El-Sayed and Pacholczyk, 2002a; El-Sayed and Pacholczyk, 2002b), we have proposed a symbolic-based model to represent nuanced statements of natural language. In the following, we present a short review of this model. We have proposed firstly a new method to symbolically represent vague terms. In this method, we suppose that a domain of a vague term, denoted by X, is not necessarily a numerical scale. This domain is simulated by a *"rule"* (cf. Figure 1) representing an arbitrary set of objects.

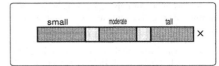

Figure 1: Representation with *"rule"* of a domain X

---

[1]In the following, we use the same notation P_{ik} to represent either a vague term P_{ik}, the multiset $\mathbb{P}_{ik}$ and the predicate $\mathbf{P}_{ik}$ associated with it.

Our basic idea has been to associate with each multiset P_i a symbolic concept which represents an equivalent to the membership function in fuzzy set theory. For that, we have introduced a new concept, called "rule", which has a geometry similar to a membership L-R function and its role is to illustrate the membership graduality to the multisets. In order to define the geometry of this "rule", we use notions similar to those defined within a fuzzy context like the core, the support and the fuzzy part of a fuzzy set (Zadeh, 1979). We define these notions within a multiset theory as follows: the core of a multiset P_i, denoted as $Core(P_i)$, represents the elements belonging to P_i with a τ_M degree, the support, denoted as $Sp(P_i)$, contains the elements belonging to P_i with at least τ_2 degree, and the fuzzy part, denoted by $F(P_i)$, contains the elements belonging to P_i with degrees varying from τ_2 to τ_{M-1}. We associate with each multiset a "rule" that contains the elements of its support (cf. Figure 2). This "rule" is the union of three disjoined subsets: *the left fuzzy part, the right fuzzy part* and *the core*. For a multiset P_i, they are denoted respectively by L_i, R_i and C_i.

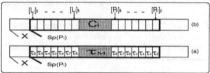

Figure 2: a *"rule"* associated with a multiset P_i

We suppose that the left (resp. right) fuzzy part L_i (resp. R_i) is the union of M-2 subsets, denoted as $[L_i]_\alpha$ (resp. $[R_i]_\alpha$), which partition it. $[L_i]_\alpha$ (resp. $[R_i]_\alpha$) contains the elements of L_i (resp. R_i) belonging to P_i with a τ_α degree. In order to keep a similarity with the fuzzy sets of type L-R, we choose to place, in a "rule" associated with a multiset, the subsets $[L_i]_\alpha$ and $[R_i]_\alpha$ so that the larger α is, the closer the $[L_i]_\alpha$ subsets and $[R_i]_\alpha$ are to the core C_i (cf. Figure 2). That can be interpreted as follows: the elements of the core of a term represent the typical elements of this term, and the more one object moves away from the core, the less it satisfies the term. Finally, we have denoted a multiset P_i with which we associate a "rule" as $P_i = (L_i, C_i, R_i)$, and we have introduced symbolic parameters which enable us to describe the form of the "rule" and its position in the universe X. These parameters have a role similar to the role of numerical parameters which are used to define a fuzzy set within a fuzzy context.

3.1 Linguistic modifiers

By using the "rule" concept we have defined the linguistic modifiers. We have used two types of linguistic modifiers.

- *Precision modifiers*: The precision modifiers increase or decrease the precision of the basic term. We distinguish two types of precision modifiers: contraction modifiers and dilation modifiers. We use $\mathbb{M}_6 = \{m_k | k \in [1..6]\}$ ={*exactly, really, $\emptyset$, more or less, approximately, vaguely*} which is totally ordered by $j \leq k \Leftrightarrow m_j \leq m_k$ (Figure 3).

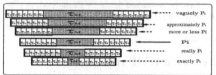

Figure 3: Precision modifiers

- *Translation modifiers*: The translation modifiers operate both a translation and precision variation (contraction or dilation) on the basic term. We use $\mathbb{T}_9 = \{t_k | k \in [1..9]\}$ ={*extremely little, very very little, very little, rather little, $\emptyset$, rather, very, very very, extremely*} totally ordered by $k \leq l \leftrightarrow t_k \leq t_l$ (Figure 4). The translation amplitudes, the precision variation amplitudes are calculated in such a way that the multisets $t_k P_i$ cover the domain X.

Figure 4: Translation modifiers

In this paper, we continue to propose our model for managing nuanced statements. In the following, we focus our intention to study the problem of exploitation of nuanced statements.

4 EXPLOITATION OF NUANCED STATEMENTS

In this section, we treat the exploitation of nuanced information. In particular, we are interested to propose some generalizations of the Modus Ponens rule within a many-valued context (Pacholczyk, 1992). We notice that the classical Modus Ponens rule has the following form: If we know that $\{If "x is A"$ then $"y is B"$ is true$\}$ and $"x is A"$ we conclude that $"y is B"$ is true. Within a many-valued context, a generalization of Modus Ponens rule has one of the following forms:

F1- If we know that $\{If "x is A"$ then $"y is B"$ is τ_β-true and $"x is A'"$ is τ_ϵ-true$\}$ and that $\{A'$ is more or less near to A$\}$, what can we conclude for $"y is B"$, in other words, to what degree $"y is B"$ is true?

F2- If we know that *{If "x is A" then "y is B" is τ_β-true* and *"x is A'" is τ_ϵ-true}* and that *{A' is more or less near to A}*, can we find a B' such as *{B' is more or less near to B}* and to what degree *"y is B'"* is true?

These forms of *Generalized Modus Ponens* (GMP) rule have been studied firstly by Pacholczyk in (Pacholczyk, 1992). In this section, we propose new versions of GMP rule in which we use new relations of nearness.

4.1 First GMP rule

In Pacholczyk's versions of GMP, the concept of nearness binding multisets A and A' is modelled by a similarity relation which is defined as follows:

Definition 1 *Let A and B be two multisets. A is said to be τ_α-similar to B, denoted as $A \approx_\alpha B$, if and only if:* $\forall x | x \in_\gamma A$ *and* $x \in_\beta B \Rightarrow min\{\tau_\gamma \to \tau_\beta, \tau_\beta \to \tau_\gamma\} \geq \tau_\alpha$.

This relation generalizes the equivalence relation in a many-valued context as the similarity relation of Zadeh (Zadeh, 1979) has been in a fuzzy context. It is (1) reflexive: $A \approx_M A$, (2) symmetrical: $A \approx_\alpha B \Leftrightarrow B \approx_\alpha A$, and (3) weakly transitive: $\{A \approx_\alpha B, B \approx_\beta C\} \Rightarrow A \approx_\gamma C$ with $\tau_\gamma \geq T(\tau_\alpha, \tau_\beta)$ where T is a T-norm.

By using the similarity relation to model the nearness binding between multisets, the inference rule can be interpreted as: *{more the rule and the fact are true}* and *{more A' and A are similar}*, more the conclusion is true. In particular, when A' is more precise than A ($A' \subset A$) but they are very weakly similar, any conclusion can be deduced or the conclusion deduced isn't as precise as one can expect. This is due to the fact that the similarity relation isn't able alone to model in a satisfactory way the nearness between A' and A. For that, we add to the similarity relation a new relation called *nearness relation* whose role is to define the nearness of A' to A when $A' \subset A$. In other words, it indicates the degree to which A' is included in A.

Definition 2 *Let A and B be two multisets such that $A \subset B$. A is said to be τ_α-near to B, denoted as $A \sqsubset_\alpha B$, if and only if* $\{\forall x \in F(B), x \in_\beta A$ *and* $x \in_\gamma B \Rightarrow \tau_\alpha \to \tau_\beta \leq \tau_\gamma\}$.

The nearness relation satisfies the following properties: (1) Reflexivity: $A \sqsubset_M A$, and (2) Weak transitivity: $A \sqsubset_\alpha B$ and $B \sqsubset_\beta C \Rightarrow A \sqsubset_\gamma C$ with $\tau_\gamma \leq min(\tau_\alpha, \tau_\beta)$. In the relation $A \sqsubset_\alpha B$, the less the value of α is, the more A is included in

B. We can notice that the properties satisfied by the nearness relation are similar to those satisfied by the resemblance relation proposed by Bouchon-Meunier and Valverde (Bouchon-Meunier and Valverde, 1997) within a fuzzy context. Finally, by using similarity and nearness relations, we propose a first *Generalized Modus Ponens* rule.

Proposition 1 *Let A and A' be predicates associated with the concept $\mathcal{C}_i$, B be predicate associated with the concept $\mathcal{C}_e$. Given the following assumptions:*

1. it is τ_β-true that if "x is A" then "y is B"

2. "x is A'" is τ_ϵ-true with $A' \approx_\alpha A$.

Then, we conclude :

"y is B" is τ_δ-true with $\tau_\delta = T(\tau_\beta, T(\tau_\alpha, \tau_\epsilon))$.

If the predicate A' is such that $A' \sqsubset_{\alpha'} A$, we conclude:

"y is B" is τ_δ-true with $\tau_\delta = T(\tau_\beta, \tau_{\alpha'} \longrightarrow \tau_\epsilon)$.

Example 2 *Given that "really tall" $\approx_8$ "tall" and "really tall" $\sqsubset_8$ "tall", from the following rule and fact:*
- if "x is tall" then "its weight is important" is true[2]
- "Pascal is really tall" is quite-true,
we can deduce: "Pascal's weight is really important" is almost-true.

4.2 GMP rules using precision modifiers

In the previous paragraph we calculate the degree to which the conclusion of the rule is true. In the following, we present two new versions of GMP rule in which the predicate of the conclusion obtained by the deduction process is not B but a new predicate B' which is more or less near to B. More precisely, the new predicate is derived from B by using precision modifiers[3] ($B' = mB$). The first version assumes that the predicates A and A' are more or less similar. In other words, A' may be less precise or more precise than A. The second one assumes that A' is more precise than A.

Proposition 2 *Let A and A' be predicates associated with the concept $\mathcal{C}_i$, B be predicate associated with the concept $\mathcal{C}_e$. Let the following assumptions:*

1. it is τ_β-true that if "x is A" then "y is B"

2. "x is A'" is τ_ϵ-true with $A' \approx_\alpha A$.

---

[2]In our many-valued logic, "completely true" is equivalent to "true" in classical logic.

[3]The definitions of these are presented in appendix A.

Let $\tau_\theta = T(\tau_\beta, T(\tau_\alpha, \tau_\epsilon))$. If $\tau_\theta > \tau_1$ then there exists a $\tau_{n(\delta)}$–dilation modifier m, with $\tau_\delta \leq T(\tau_\alpha, \tau_\beta)$, such that:

"y is mB" is $\tau_{\epsilon'}$-true and $\tau_{\epsilon'} = \tau_\delta \longrightarrow \tau_\theta$.

Moreover, we have: $B \subset mB$ and $mB \approx_\delta B$.

This proposition prove that if we know that A' is more or less similar to A, without any supplementary information concerning its precision compared to A, the predicate of the conclusion obtained by the deduction process (mB) is less precise than B (i.e. $B \subset mB$) and which is more or less similar to B. In the following proposition, we assume that A' is more precise than A.

Proposition 3 *Let A and A' be predicates associated with the concept C_i, B be predicate associated with the concept C_e. Let the following assumptions:*

1. it is τ_β-true that if "x is A" then "y is B"

2. "x is A'" is τ_ϵ-true with $A' \sqsubset_\alpha A$.

Let $\tau_\theta = T(\tau_\beta, \tau_\alpha \longrightarrow \tau_\epsilon)$. If $\tau_\theta > \tau_1$ then there exists a $\tau_{n(\delta)}$–contraction modifier m, with $\tau_\delta \geq \tau_\beta \longrightarrow \tau_\alpha$, such that:

"y is mB" is $\tau_{\epsilon'}$-true and $\tau_{\epsilon'} = T(\tau_\delta, \tau_\theta)$.

Moreover, we have: $mB \sqsubset_\delta B$.

This proposition prove that from a predicate A' which is more or less near to A we obtain a predicate mB which is more or less near to B. More precisely, if A' is more precise than A then mB is more precise than B. The previous propositions (2 and 3) present two general cases in which we consider arbitrary predicates A'. In the following, we present two corollaries representing special cases of propositions 2 and 3 in which we assume that the rule is completely true and that A' is obtained from A by using precision modifiers.

Corollary 1 *Let the following rule and fact:*

1. it is true that if "x is A" then "y is B"

2. "x is $m_k A$" is τ_ϵ-true where m_k is a τ_{γ_k}–dilation modifier.

If $T(\sim \tau_{\gamma_k}, \tau_\epsilon) > \tau_1$ then we conclude:

"y is $m_k B$" is $\tau_{\epsilon'}$-true, with
$\tau_{\epsilon'} = \sim \tau_{\gamma_k} \longrightarrow T(\sim \tau_{\gamma_k}, \tau_\epsilon)$.

Example 3 *Given the following data:*
- if "x is tall" then "its weight is important" is true,
- "Jo is more or less tall" is moderately-true.
Then, we can deduce:
"Jo's weight is more or less important" is moderately-true.

Corollary 2 *Let the following rule and fact:*

1. it is true that if "x is A" then "y is B"
2. "x is $m_k A$" is τ_ϵ-true where m_k is a τ_{γ_k}–contraction modifier.

Then, we conclude that: "y is $m_k B$" is τ_ϵ-true.

Example 4 *Given the following data:*
- if "x is tall" then "its weight is important" is true,
- "Pascal is really tall" is moderately-true.
Then, we can deduce:
"Pascal's weight is really important" is moderately-true.

These two corollaries present a particular form of graduality of inference. This form is known as graduality by means of linguistic modifiers (Delechamp and Bouchon-Meunier, 1997). It enables us to obtain, from a fact whose predicate A' is nuanced by linguistic modifiers, a conclusion whose predicate is also nuanced by linguistic modifiers.

4.3 Other inference rules

In the previous paragraphs, we presented GMP rules in which we can either (1) calculate the degree to which the conclusion of the rule is true, or (2) to obtain a new conclusion which is more or less near to the rule's one and to calculate the degree to which it is true. In this paragraph, we present new inference rules in which the predicate of the conclusion obtained by the deduction process is a new predicate B' which is more or less near to B. The new predicate is choosen from the set of nuanced predicates associated with a concept. The existence of such a predicate is not always sure and is depending on the predicate B and on the other predicates associated with the same concept. We notice that these forms of inference rules can be used to evaluate the truth of a statement by using rules and facts which are available in the knowledge-based system. In other words, if we know that $\{$If "x is A" then "y is B" is τ_β-true and "x is A'" is τ_ϵ-true$\}$ and that $\{A'$ and B' are respectively more or less near to A and $B\}$, can we calculate the degree to which "y is B'" is true?

We present below two inference rules. The first version assumes that the predicates A and A' are more or less similar. The second one assumes that A' is more precise than A.

Proposition 4 *Let A and A' be predicates associated with the concept C_i, B and B' be predicates associated with the concept C_e. Let the following assumptions:*

1. it is τ_β-true that if "x is A" then "y is B"

2. "x is A'" is τ_ϵ-true with $A' \approx_\alpha A$.

Let $\tau_\theta = T(\tau_\beta, T(\tau_\alpha, \tau_\epsilon))$. If $\tau_\theta > \tau_1$ and if there exists a predicate B' such that $B' \approx_\delta B$, then we can conclude that:

"y is B'" is $\tau_{\epsilon'}$-true and $\tau_{\epsilon'} = T(\tau_\delta, \tau_\theta)$.

If the predicate B' is such that $B \sqsubset_{\delta'} B'$, we conclude:

"y is B'" is $\tau_{\epsilon'}$-true with $\tau_{\epsilon'} = \tau_{\delta'} \longrightarrow \tau_\theta$.

Proposition 5 Let A and A' be predicates associated with the concept $\mathcal{C}_i$, B and B' be predicates associated with the concept $\mathcal{C}_e$. Let the following assumptions:

1. it is τ_β-true that if "x is A" then "y is B"

2. "x is A'" is τ_ϵ-true with $A' \sqsubset_\alpha A$.

Let $\tau_\theta = T(\tau_\beta, \tau_\alpha \longrightarrow \tau_\epsilon)$. If $\tau_\theta > \tau_1$ and if there exists a predicate B' such that $B' \approx_\delta B$, then we can conclude that:

"y is B'" is $\tau_{\epsilon'}$-true and $\tau_{\epsilon'} = T(\tau_\delta, \tau_\theta)$.

If the predicate B' is such that $B \sqsubset_{\delta'} B'$, we conclude:

"y is B'" is $\tau_{\epsilon'}$-true with $\tau_{\epsilon'} = \tau_{\delta'} \longrightarrow \tau_\theta$.

Example 5 Given that "very important" $\sqsubset_6$ "important", "really tall" $\approx_8$ "tall" and "really tall" $\sqsubset_8$ "tall", and let our knowledge-based system contain the following rule and fact:
- if "x is tall" then "its weight is important" is true,
- "Jo is really tall" is quite-true.
Then, we want to know the truth degree of the statement "Jo'weight is very important". By applying the proposition 5, we can deduce:
"Jo's weight is very important" is fairly-true.

5 GENERALIZED PRODUCTION SYSTEM

In this section, we present some generalizations of Modus Ponens rule in more complex situations. More precisely, we study the problem of reasoning in 4 situations:

1. When the antecedent of the rule is a conjunction of statements.

2. When the antecedent is a disjunction of statements.

3. In presence of propagation of inferences. In other words, when the conclusion of the first rule is the antecedent of the second rule, and so on.

4. When a combination of imprecisions is possible. In other words, when we have some rules which have the same statement in their conclusion parts.

So, we present the following 4 propositions representing inference rules in these situations.

Proposition 6 (Antecedent is a conjunction) Let A_i and A'_i be predicates associated with the concept $\mathcal{C}_i$, B be predicate associated with the concept $\mathcal{C}_e$. Given the following assumptions:

1. if "x_1 is A_1" and ... and "x_n is A_n" then "y is B" is τ_β-true,

2. for $i = 1..n$, "x_i is A'_i" is τ_{ϵ_i}-true,

3. for $i = 1..n$, $A_i \approx_{\alpha_i} A'_i$.

Then, we can deduce: "y is B" is τ_δ-true with $\tau_\delta = T(\tau_\beta, T(\tau_{\alpha_1}, \tau_{\epsilon_1})) \wedge ... \wedge T(\tau_\beta, T(\tau_{\alpha_n}, \tau_{\epsilon_n}))$.

If, for $i = j .. k$, the predicates A'_i are such that $A'_i \sqsubset_{\alpha'_i} A_i$, we can deduce: "y is B" is τ_δ-true with $\tau_\delta = \tau_{\delta_1} \wedge ... \wedge \tau_{\delta_n}$ and $\tau_{\delta_i} = T(\tau_{\alpha'_i} \longrightarrow \tau_{\epsilon_i}, \tau_\beta)$ if $i \in [j,k]$ and $\tau_{\delta_i} = T(\tau_\beta, T(\tau_{\alpha_i}, \tau_{\epsilon_i}))$ if not.

Proposition 7 (Antecedent is a disjunction) Let A and A' be predicates associated with the concept $\mathcal{C}_i$, B be predicate associated with the concept $\mathcal{C}_e$. Given the following assumptions:

1. if "x_1 is A_1" or ... or "x_n is A_n" then "y is B" is τ_β-true,

2. for $i = 1..k$, "x_i is A'_i" is τ_{ϵ_i}-true,

3. for $i = 1..k$, $A_i \approx_{\alpha_i} A'_i$.

Then, we can deduce: "y is B" is τ_δ-true with $\tau_\delta = T(\tau_\beta, T(\tau_{\alpha_1}, \tau_{\epsilon_1})) \vee ... \vee T(\tau_\beta, T(\tau_{\alpha_k}, \tau_{\epsilon_k}))$.

If, for $i = j .. L$, the predicates A'_i are such that $A'_i \sqsubset_{\alpha'_i} A_i$, we can deduce: "y is B" is τ_δ-true with $\tau_\delta = \tau_{\delta_1} \vee ... \vee \tau_{\delta_k}$ and $\tau_{\delta_i} = T(\tau_{\alpha'_i} \longrightarrow \tau_{\epsilon_i}, \tau_\beta)$ if $i \in [j,L]$ and $\tau_{\delta_i} = T(\tau_\beta, T(\tau_{\alpha_i}, \tau_{\epsilon_i}))$ if not.

Proposition 8 (Propagation of inferences) Let A and A' be two predicates associated with the concept $\mathcal{C}_i$, B and C be two predicates associated respectively with the concepts $\mathcal{C}_j$ and $\mathcal{C}_e$. Given the following assumptions:

1. if "x is A" then "y is B" is τ_β-true,

2. if "y is B" then "z is C" is τ_γ-true,

3. there exists $\tau_\epsilon > \tau_1$ such that "x is A'" is τ_ϵ-true,

4. there exists τ_α such that $A \approx_\alpha A'$.

Then, we can deduce:

"z is C" is τ_δ-true, with
$$\tau_\delta = T(T(\tau_\beta, \tau_\gamma), T(\tau_\alpha, \tau_\epsilon)).$$

If the predicate A' is such that $A' \sqsubset_{\alpha'} A$, then we can deduce:

"z is C" is τ_δ-true, with
$$\tau_\delta = T(T(\tau_\beta, \tau_\gamma), \tau_{\alpha'} \longrightarrow \tau_\epsilon).$$

Proposition 9 (Combination of imprecisions) *Let A_i and A'_i be predicates associated with the concept C_i, B be predicate associated with the concept C_e. Given the following assumptions:*

1. for $i = 1..n$, if "x_i is A_i" then "y is B" is τ_{β_i}-true,

2. for $i = 1..n$, "x_i is A'_i" is τ_{ϵ_i}-true,

3. for $i = 1..n$, $A_i \approx_{\alpha_i} A'_i$,

then we can deduce that: "y is B" is τ_δ-true with $\tau_\delta = T(\tau_{\beta_1}, T(\tau_{\alpha_1}, \tau_{\epsilon_1})) \vee ... \vee T(\tau_{\beta_n}, T(\tau_{\alpha_n}, \tau_{\epsilon_n}))$.

If, for $i = j .. k$, the predicates A'_i are such that $A'_i \sqsubset_{\alpha'_i} A_i$, then we can deduce: "$y$ is B" is τ_δ-true with $\tau_\delta = \tau_{\delta_1} \vee ... \vee \tau_{\delta_n}$ and $\tau_{\delta_i} = T(\tau_{\alpha'_i} \longrightarrow \tau_{\epsilon_i}, \tau_{\beta_i})$ if $i \in [j, k]$ and $\tau_{\delta_i} = T(\tau_{\beta_i}, T(\tau_{\alpha_i}, \tau_{\epsilon_i}))$ if not.

We present below an example in which we use the GMP rules presented in this section. In this example, we use index cards written by a doctor after his consultations. From index cards (IC_i) and some rules ($\mathcal{R}_j$), we wish deduce a diagnosis.

Example 6 *Let assume that we have the following rules in our base of rules.*

$\mathcal{R}_1-$ *"If the temperature is high, the patient is ill" is almost true,*

$\mathcal{R}_2-$ *"If the tension is always high, the patient is ill" is nearly true,*

$\mathcal{R}_3-$ *"If the temperature is high and the eradrum color is very red, the disease is an otitis" is true,*

$\mathcal{R}_4-$ *"If fat eating is high, the cholesterol risk is high" is true,*

$\mathcal{R}_5-$ *"If the cholesterol risk is high, a diet with no fat is recommended" is true.*

Let us assume now that we have an index card for a patient and we want to deduce a diagnosis.

$\mathcal{F}_1-$ *"the temperature is rather high" is nearly true,*

$\mathcal{F}_2-$ *"the tension is always more or less high" is almost true,*

$\mathcal{F}_3-$ *"the eradrum color is really very red" is quite true,*

$\mathcal{F}_4-$ *"the fat eating is very very high" is moderately true.*

Using the GMP rules previously presented, we can deduce the following diagnosis:

$\mathcal{D}_1-$ *"the patient is ill" is almost true,*

$\mathcal{D}_2-$ *"the disease is an otitis" is almost true,*

$\mathcal{D}_3-$ *"the cholesterol risk is high" is true,*

$\mathcal{D}_4-$ *"a diet with no fat is recommended" is true.*

Let us assume that we have the following relations: "rather high" $\sqsubset_7$ "high", "more or less high" $\approx_8$ "high", "really very high" $\sqsubset_4$ "high", "very red" $\sqsubset_5$ "red" and "very very high" $\sqsubset_2$ "high". Then, the diagnosis ($\mathcal{D}_1 - \mathcal{D}_4$) are obtained as follows.

- $\mathcal{D}_1$ *is obtained by applying proposition 9 to $(\mathcal{F}_1, \mathcal{F}_2)$ and $(\mathcal{R}_1, \mathcal{R}_2)$,*
- $\mathcal{D}_2$ *is obtained by applying proposition 6 to $(\mathcal{F}_1, \mathcal{F}_3)$ and $\mathcal{R}_3$,*
- $\mathcal{D}_3$ *is obtained by applying proposition 1 to $\mathcal{F}_4$ and $\mathcal{R}_4$,*
- $\mathcal{D}_4$ *is obtained by applying proposition 8 to F_4 and $(\mathcal{R}_4, \mathcal{R}_5)$.*

6 GRADUALITY OF INFERENCE

In this section, we are interested to investigate the graduality of inference verified by our GMP rules. We distinguish mainly five types of gradual rule involving graduality: (1) on the truth value, (2) on inclusion between multisets, (3) by means of linguistic modifiers, (4) or dealing with the degree of similarity or the proximity of multisets, (5) or graduality on terms associated with a concept. In this section, we are limited to study the graduality based on the truth value and on inclusion between multisets. Other forms of graduality will be investigated in next papers.

In the following, we study the graduality verified by the GMP rules proposed in paragraphes 4.1 and 4.2. The following proposition prove the form of graduality underlying by the first GMP rule (proposition 1).

Proposition 10 *Let A and A' be predicates associated with the concept C_i, B be predicate associated with the concept C_e. Given the following assumptions:*

1. it is τ_β-true that if "x is A" then "y is B"

2. "x is A'" is τ_{ϵ_1}-true,

then, we can conclude:

$$\text{"y is B" is } \tau_{\epsilon'_1}\text{-true.}$$

If we have the fact "x is A''" is τ_{ϵ_2}-true such that $\{A'' \subset A'$ and $\tau_{\epsilon_2} \geq \tau_{\epsilon_1}\}$, we can conclude:

$$\text{"y is B" is } \tau_{\epsilon'_2}\text{-true with } \tau_{\epsilon'_2} \geq \tau_{\epsilon'_1}.$$

In other words, the GMP rule in the proposition 1 satisfies the following gradual rule:

- the more (the less) the proposition "x is A'" is true and the more (the less) A' is included in A ($A' \subset A$), the more (the less) the proposition "y is B" is true.

The following proposition prove the graduality underlying by the GMP rules in the propositions 2 and 3.

Proposition 11 *Let A and A' be predicates associated with the concept C_i, B be predicate associated with the concept C_e. Given the following assumptions:*

1. it is τ_β-true that if "x is A" then "y is B"

2. "x is A'" is τ_{ϵ_1}-true,

then, there exists a precision modifier m_1 such that:
"y is $m_1 B$" is $\tau_{\epsilon'_1}$-true.

If we have the fact "x is A''" is τ_{ϵ_2}-true such that $\{A'' \subset A'$ and $\tau_{\epsilon_2} \geq \tau_{\epsilon_1}\}$, then we can find a precision modifier m_2 such that:
"y is $m_2 B$" is $\tau_{\epsilon'_2}$-true, with
$\{m_2 B \subset m_1 B$ and $\tau_{\epsilon'_2} \geq \tau_{\epsilon'_1}\}$.

This proposition is valid if either $A'' \subset A' \subset A$ or $A \subset A'' \subset A'$. In the first case, we have the following form of gradual rule which is verified by the GMP rule in proposition 3:

- the more the proposition "x is A'" is true and the more A' is included in A, the more the "y is mB" is true and the more mB is included in B.

In the case of $A \subset A'' \subset A'$, we have the following form of gradual rule which is verified by the GMP rule in proposition 2:

- the less the proposition "x is A'" is true and the less A' is included in A (i.e. the more A is included in A'), the less the proposition "y is mB" is true and the less mB is included in B.

7 CONCLUSION

In this paper, we have proposed a symbolic-based model dealing with nuanced information. This model is inspired from the representation method on fuzzy logic. In previous papers, we have proposed a new representation method of nuanced statements. In this method, we have defined a vague term by symbolic parameters given by an expert in a qualitative way. By using this representation, we have defined some linguistic modifiers in a purely symbolic way. In this paper, we proposed some deduction rules dealing with nuanced statements and we presented new *Generalized Modus Ponens* rules. In these rules we can use either simple statements or complex statements. Finally, we have studied the problem of graduality of inference and we demonstrate the types of graduality satisfied by our GMP rules. Other types of graduality of inference are under investigation and the results will be presented in next papers.

REFERENCES

Baldwin, J. F. (1979). A new approach to approximate reasoning using fuzzy logic. *Fuzzy sets and systems*, 2:309 - 325.

Bouchon-Meunier, B. and Valverde, L. (1997). A ressemblance approach to analogical reasoning function. *Lecture notes in comp. sc.*, 1188:266–272.

Bouchon-Meunier, B. and Yao, J. (1992). Linguistic modifiers and imprecise categories. *Int. J. of intelligent systems*, 7:25–36.

De-glas, M. (1989). Knowladge representation in fuzzy setting. Technical Report 48, LAFORIA.

Delechamp, J. and Bouchon-Meunier, B. (1997). Graduality by means of analogical reasoning. *Lecture notes in computer science*, 1244:210 – 222.

El-Sayed, M. and Pacholczyk, D. (2002a). A qualitative reasoning with nuanced information. *8th European Conference on Logics in Artificial Intelligence (JELIA 02), 283 - 295, Italy.*

El-Sayed, M. and Pacholczyk, D. (2002b). A symbolic approach for handling nuanced information. *IASTED International Conference on Artificial Intelligence and Applications (AIA 02), 285 - 290, Spain.*

Lascio, L. D., Gisolfi, A., and Garcia, U. C. (1999). Linguistic hedges and the generalized modus ponens. *Int. J. of intelligent systems*, 14:981–993.

Pacholczyk, D. (1992). *Contribution au traitement logico-symbolique de la connaissance*. PhD thesis, University of Paris VI.

Zadeh, L. A. (1965). Fuzzy sets. *Information and control*, 8:338–353.

Zadeh, L. A. (1979). A theory of approximate reasoning. *Int. J. Hayes, D. Michie and L. I. Mikulich (eds); Machine Intelligence*, 9:149–194.

Appendix A: Definitions of precision modifiers

We distinguish two types of precision modifiers: contraction modifiers and dilation modifiers. A contraction (resp. dilation) modifier m produces nuanced term mP_i more (resp. less) precise than the basic term P_i. In other words, the "rule" associated with mP_i is smaller (resp. bigger) than that associated with P_i. We define these modifiers in a way that the contraction modifiers contract simultaneously the core and the support of P_i, and the dilation modifiers dilate them. The amplitude of the modification (contraction or dilation) for a precision modifier m is given by a new parameter denoted as τ_γ. The higher τ_γ, the more important the modification is.

Definition 3 *m is said to be a τ_γ-contraction modifier if, and only if it is defined as follows:*

1. if $P_i = (L_i, C_i, R_i)$ then $mP_i = (L'_i, C'_i, R'_i)$ such that $L'_i \trianglelefteq_M L_i$ and $R'_i \trianglelefteq_M R_i$

2. $\forall x, x \in_\alpha P_i$ with $\tau_\alpha < \tau_M \Rightarrow x \in_\beta mP_i$ such that $\beta = max(1, \alpha - \gamma + 1)$.

Definition 4 *m is said to be a τ_γ-dilation modifier if, and only if it is defined as follows:*

1. if $P_i = (L_i, C_i, R_i)$ then $mP_i = (L'_i, C'_i, R'_i)$ such that $L'_i \trianglelefteq_M L_i$ and $R'_i \trianglelefteq_M R_i$

2. $\forall x, x \in_\alpha P_i$ with $\tau_\alpha > \tau_1 \Rightarrow x \in_\beta mP_i$ such that $\beta = min(M, \gamma + \alpha - 1)$.

A WEB-BASED DECISION SUPPORT SYSTEM FOR TENDERING PROCESSES

N. M. Mohamad Noor [1] , K.N. Papamichail [2], B.Warboys [1]

[1]Department of Computer Science, Oxford Road, University of Manchester, Manchester M13 9PL, UK.
Email: noor@cs.man.ac.uk, brian@cs.man.ac.uk
[2]Manchester Business School, Booth Street West, Manchester, M15 6PB, UK.
Email: nadia.papamichail@mbs.ac.uk

Keywords: Decision-making; process modelling; process support technologies, tendering processes; Web-based DSS.

Abstract: A decision support system (DSS) is an interactive computer-based system that helps decision makers utilise data and models to solve complex and unstructured problems. Procurement is a decision problem of paramount importance for any business. A critical and vital procurement task is to select the best contractor during the tendering or bidding process. This paper describes a Web-based DSS that aids decision makers in choosing among competitive bids for building projects. The system is based on a framework of a generic process approach and is intended to be used as a general decision-making aid. The DSS is currently being implemented as a research prototype in a process-support environment. It coordinates the participants of tendering processes and supports the submission, processing and evaluation of bids. A case study is drawn from the construction business to demonstrate the applicability of our approach.

1 INTRODUCTION

Decision Support Systems (DSSs) are computer programs that aid users in a problem solving or decision-making environment. These systems employ data models, algorithms, knowledge bases, user interfaces, and control mechanisms to support a specific decision problem (Bhargava et al, 1995). A Decision Support System (DSS) does not simply provide direct solutions, but it rather gives a recommendation based on the input of the decision makers.

Traditional DSSs have been developed for single users. This requires data and model bases, and user interface components to reside in the same machine (Bhargava and Tettelbach, 1997). With the advent of the Internet, Web-based DSSs have been established. Web–based DSSs retain and extend the advantages of single-user DSSs. Benefits include accessibility, efficient distribution, effective administration, and cross-platform flexibility. While traditional DSSs require software or installation on individual workstations or computers, Web-based DSSs are easily accessible to users with Internet connection (Klercker and Klercker, 1998).

This paper discusses the design of a Web-based DSS which is based on a framework of a generic process approach and is intended to be used as a general decision-making aid. The system, which is currently under development as a research prototype, facilitates the management of tendering processes. The principal aim of such processes is to select contractors that offer best value for money. The winner of a tender is the one who makes the best offer based on the evaluation criteria under consideration.

The specific tender analysis procedure to be studied will be based on the Malaysian standard (Department of Work, 2001). The role of the DSS is to help construction managers or other chief decision makers choose a successful bid. The DSS uses process-support technologies to coordinate all the actors that are involved in the decision-making process. As it operates over the Web, it has all the advantages of Web-based technologies that were mentioned above. An additional benefit is that it allows tenderers or bidders to register their details, submit their bids and if needed check on the status of their bid, which makes the process more transparent.

The structure of this paper is as follows. Section 2 reviews the literature on Web-based DSS technologies. Section 3 states the aims and

O. Camp et al. (eds.), Enterprise Information Systems V, 169-176.
© 2004 Kluwer Academic Publishers. Printed in the Netherlands.

objectives of this work. Our research approach is discussed in section 4. Section 5 describes a framework for supporting tendering processes. Finally, section 6 gives the conclusions of our study.

2 PROBLEM DOMAIN

The Fifth International Conference on Decision Support Systems (ISDSS'99, 2000), held on July 20-24, 1999 in Melbourne Australia had a clear focus on DSS practice. This was encouraging since it showed that in the past two decades, DSSs have progressed from advancements of theory to serious application. These include management and planning (Bhat and Zaberi, 2002), command and control (Andriole and Halpin, 1991), system design (Nemati *et al*, 2002), and health care and operation management. Most of these DSSs have been tailored to either a specific application, for example financial planning or water management, or particular decision-making phases such as problem framing or impact assessment.

Research in the area of competitive bidding/ tendering strategy models has been in progress since the 1950s (e.g., Friedman, 1956). Numerous models have been developed, some of which are designed specifically for the construction industry (Stark and Rothkopf, 1979). Despite the number of competitive bidding strategy models that have been developed, few of these are used in practice, largely because they do not meet the needs of construction contractors (Ahmad and Minkarah, 1988, Hegazy and Moselhi, 1995, Shash, 1995, Ting and Mills, 1996).

The Internet and the World Wide Web are rapidly evolving. Less than five years ago, the Web was primarily used to post documents for review. Emerging Web-based application technologies create a new environment for DSSs. An electronic tendering system will allow clients and contractors to download documents via the Web. Completed forms can also be submitted electronically (Green Paper, 1999). Each year the procedures of awarding construction work contracts produce a huge mass of documents, which is enormous to handle and quite costly. Therefore, this work is an attempt to enable the transition from the costly traditional manual processes currently being employed by (paper-based) procurement management to a cost-effective and independent (Web-based) platform.

The rise of Internet-based technology initiatives makes the exchange of information simple, fast, accessible and accurate (Seneviratne and Schexnayder, 1999; Bodamer, 1999). In the past few years research on the adoption and use of information technology integrated with the Internet in the construction industry, such as work by Zift, (2000); Hudgins and Chang, (2000); Ahmad, (1999) has emphasised the potential of Web technologies and highlighted their usefulness for managing project performance, simplifying operations process and document management, as well as organizing communication and coordination between project participants.

Kumaraswamy and Dissanayaka (2000) have proposed a DSS model for managing project procurement but they did not focus on tender evaluation or tender analysis. Research on Internet-based electronic purchasing, such as the research report on procurement practices and trend by Segev *et al* (1998), which covered the results from surveys and interviews from over 80 companies, has included such topics as Internet-based procurement technological processes, technology, and utilisation. There are only a few bid analysis products currently available from companies such as Emptoris (www.emptoris.com), and Frictionless Commerce Perfect (www.perfect. com).

All of these products are based on the single user decision analysis method and are limited in their capabilities for supporting decision-making processes and obviously they are not focusing on analysing tenders for construction work. They have in no way been undertaken with the specific needs of the construction industry in mind regarding Web-based tender evaluation. Apart from merely transmitting online documents or announcing tenders, the proposed Web-based DSS is specially designed for evaluating or analysing tender documents specific for construction works and choosing the successful tenderers. Besides, the system facilitates real-time communication between clients/owners, consultants and contractors.

3 AIM AND OBJECTIVES

The aim of the research is to propose a framework for supporting decision-making in tendering processes. The proposed framework assists decision makers in the formulation, evaluation and appraisal stages (Holtzman, 1989) of the decision analysis process.

The objectives of this research are:

1. To develop a framework of generic decision support for complex and unstructured tendering processes in the construction industry.

2. To use the concept of D2P (Oquendo *et al*, 2000), an architecture for modelling and coordinating decision-making activities, in the implementation of tendering processes in order to

provide a basis for subsequent generalisation of the approach.

3. To demonstrate the applicability of the approach using a real-world scenario by developing an efficient Web-based management system for tendering processes. The system supports procurements, consolidates and analyses tender information from government, semi-government and the private Central Tender Repository of Malaysia.

4 RESEARCH APPROACH

The need for a more effective analysis and improvement of procurement processes provides the starting point for this research. There are many approaches to developing DSSs, such as knowledge-driven, document-driven, communication-driven and model-driven methods (Powel, 2000). In this work, we have combined model-driven and communication-driven methods to develop a hybrid DSS. A model-driven DSS places emphasis on statistical analysis, financial optimisation or simulation. It uses data and parameters provided by decision makers in analysing and choosing the best alternative. A communication-driven DSS supports communication, collaboration and coordination among multiple users.

The proposed DSS will offer prescriptive advice i.e. its recommendation will be based on the input of the decision makers. Other DSS applications, for example Molenaar and Songer, (2001), Thomas and Smith, (1998) and Moselhi et al, (1993), have supported decision-making activities. The Web-based DSS however, will support the process of decision-making.

The adopted approach is to use a real case study to demonstrate the complexity of decision-making. The plan is to exploit a particular concept of D2P, which is an implementable framework for supporting the process of decision-making. Unlike other proposed DSS design approaches such as prototyping (Angehrn and Luthi, 1990; Gottler, 1989) and others (Bonczek et al, 1981; Hopcroft and Ullman, 1979), this approach includes a rigorous yet evolvable step-by-step procedure to be implemented in this work. The aim of the chosen case study is to select the best contractor for certain construction

projects or in other words to analyse and evaluate tender forms submitted by contractors. This application uses a generic model and is designed in a flexible manner so that it is possible to run tender analysis for various construction projects.

5 A FRAMEWORK FOR SUPPORTING DECISION MAKING IN TENDERING PROCESSES

The generic definition of a DSS is 'an interactive computer based system that helps decision makers utilise data and models to solve unstructured problems' (Sprague, 1980). During the decision-making process, input information is of vital importance. The primary source of information is raw data, which is converted to information by utilising relevant methodologies. Both data and models are necessary resources that need to be managed efficiently to improve the efficiency and effectiveness of the overall decision-making process.

The architecture of the generic DSS in tendering processes is depicted in Figure 1. There are six major components in this architecture, which are database, model-base, Internet user interface, input, output and registered user(s). A database is one of the three fundamental components of a DSS. The central component of the software system is a relational database, implemented using MySql. The database resides at the Web-server and so is available to all the registered users of the system via their Web-browsers. The database contains data about the tendering processes such as clients, contractors and project details, various forms such as financial capability and adjustment price forms.

Models are an integral part of any DSS. They are employed to support individual semi-structured decisions. Mathematical calculations are used for the structured parts, leaving the decision-makers to exercise judgment in handing the unstructured parts. The main model in this Web-based DSS for tendering processes is the analysis model, which is developed by using a model-driven DSS approach.

ENTERPRISE INFORMATION SYSTEMS V

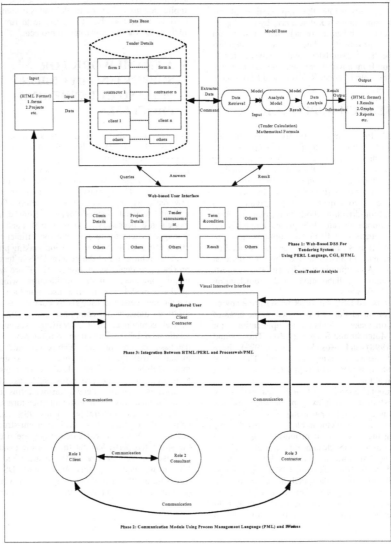

Figure 1: A Proposed Generic Web-Based DSS Architecture and Communication Module in Tendering Process

172

Since this DSS is intended for use over the Web, the user interface makes use of a Web-browser. It uses the concept of the visual interface and dynamically generates HTML documents. It is an effective communication medium that allows clients (e.g. procurement managers) to view, explore, navigate, search, compare and classify submitted bids. Information is delivered to the user via the produced HTML and related files, which are displayed by the Web-browser.

Data entry or the input of files in HTML format can be completed by decision-makers and the contractors via password-protected Internet-based forms. Output files can also be generated for input to statistical analysis software. The gateway is implemented using the common gateway interface (CGI), enabling functioning with any Web-browser. To minimize typing by the end user, pull down menus will enable the user to select items from a list.

As mentioned by Etter (1988), any methodology that facilitates information flow and the associated decision analysis reduces risk. The DSS will use a decision analysis model in order to process and evaluate the submitted tenders. The system will offer functionalities similar to other bid evaluation

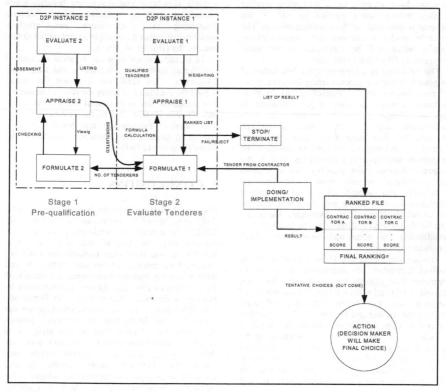

Figure 2: A Generic Tender Process

systems that employ multi-criteria decision analysis methods to rank criteria by score (Carlos *et al*, 2002). However this system is unlike other traditional DSSs; it will also facilitate a real-time communication between users for example clients, consultants and contractors (communication-driven DSS). The system will operate on Process*Web*, a process support system for managing complex software engineering problems (Warboys *et al*, 1999). Process*Web* enables the real-time communication between the client, contractor and consultant roles. As mentioned above, D2P is a generic model that represents decision-making processes (Papamichail and Robertson, 2002). We have adapted D2P to reflect the properties of the tendering process (see Figure 2). The specialised D2P model is enacted by using PML (process management language). This model is evolvable in the sense that it recurses i.e. it instantiates another decision process when needed to address the changing requirements of the tendering process. The enactable model constitutes the communication module, which will be connected to the other components of the Web-based DSS.

The following is a (step-by-step) description of the generic tendering process using the concept of the meta-process D2P. Regarding the problem resolution strategy, a two stage procedure is proposed: Stage 1 (D2P instance 2): pre-qualification, Stage 2 (D2P instance 1): evaluate tenderers. The first stage is to check and screen tenderers. Tenderers are required to complete the compulsory and supporting documents (such as the company's balance sheet, monthly bank statements and confidential reports from bank/ financial institutions) and submit copies of completed certificates for each of the projects. If a tenderer fails to submit all the above documents, the tender shall be disqualified and shall not be given further consideration. This means that this tenderer will not be considered in stage 2.

Pre-qualification (stage 1) is a process which involves screening of contractors, in order to determine their competence to execute the work (Russell, 1992) and provides clients some degree of confidence that the chosen contractor will meet project needs (Baker and Orsaah, 1985). Screening in this case is the process of selecting pre-qualified contactors. A pre-qualified contractor must be capable to carry out the planned project as the client wishes. The aim of pre-qualification is mainly to reject clearly unsuitable contractors and shortlist bids that are worthy of further analysis and evaluation.

The criteria for the tender evaluation include financial capacity, technical capability, past performance, past experience and availability of technical staff. Stage 2 involves the use of mathematical models and calculations for the evaluation of tenders. As a means of reflecting the different degrees of importance attached to different criteria in a complex tender analysis, the decision-makers will assign weights (in the form of points or percentages) to important measurable criteria before tenders are received. Each tender is then assessed against these criteria, and is assigned scores reflecting how well it satisfies each of them. The weighted scores for each criterion are calculated and aggregated.

Studies confirm that 87 percent of clients (procurement managers) consider price to be their main criterion and 84 percent of contractors consider price as the most important factor in winning a contract (Baker and Orsaah, 1985; and Latham, 1994). However, decision-makers should choose a suitable contractor that maximises benefits while minimising costs by weighting selection criteria concerning skill, experience and previous performance, rather than simply accepting the lowest tender offer (Holt et. al, 1993).

In practice, a few bids are rejected because of insufficient compulsory documents and supporting documents. The DSS will document the reason behind the decision and notify the rejected tenderers. The feedback for unsuccessful contractors could include reasons that lead to the rejection of their bids, thereby encouraging rectification of such failings to increase their chances of success in the future (Holt et. al., 1995).

6 CONCLUSIONS

DSSs are becoming increasingly more critical to the daily operation of the organisations (Nemati *et al*, 2002). In general the tendering processes have become very complex, so that it is no longer possible to use traditional methods for tendering process management. Clients and contractors who wish to actively manage their tenders are faced with the problem of choosing among the contractors by employing the most efficient tools. As Tserng and Lin (2002) point out it is crucial to select appropriate contractors to implement the specific project. Therefore, the ultimate goal of this study is to develop a Web-based DSS for tendering processes that facilitates real time communication and coordination between clients, contractors and consultants using process support technologies. This interactive Web-based DSS, which is currently under development as a research tool, will assist procurement managers in evaluating tenders in a systematic way and contractors in submitting bids and checking on the status of their tenders. Adding transparency into the tendering process can improve understanding and acceptance of the decisions taken.

REFERENCES

Ahmad, I., (1999), "Managing, Processing and Communication Information: What A/E/C Organisation Should Know?" *Journal of Management Engineering*, ASCE 154: 33-36.

Ahmad, I. and Minkarah, I., (1988), "Questionnaire Survey on Bidding in Construction." *Journal of Management in Engineering*, ASCE, 4(3): 229-243.

Andriole, S.J., and Halpin, S.M., (1991), "Special Issues on Information Technology for Command and Control." *IEEE Transaction on Systems, Man and Cybernetic.* 16(6).

Angehrn, A.A., and Luthi, H.J., (1990), "Intelligent Decision Support Systems: A Visual Interactive Approach." *Interfaces*, 2(6): 17-28.

Baker, M., and Orsaah, S., (1985). "How Do the Customers Choose a Contractor?" *Building Magazine*, May: 30-31.

Bhargava, H.K., and Tettelbach, C., (1997), "A Web-based Decision Support System for Waste Disposal and Recycling." *Computer, Environment and Urban System.*, 21(1): 47-65.

Bhargava, H.K., King, A.S., and McQuay, D.S., (1995), "DecisionNet An Architecture for Modelling and Decision Support over the World Wide Web." *Proceeding, 3rd International Conference on Decision Support System*, International Society for Decision Support Systems. Austin, Texas: 499-506.

Bhatt, G.D., and Zaveri, J. (2002). "The Enabling Role of Decision Support Systems in Organizational Learning." *Decision Support System*, 32: 297-309.

Bodamer, D., (1999), "The New Perspective on IT." *Civil Engineering Management*, ASCE 69(5): 52-55.

Bonczek, R.H., Holsapple, C.W., and Whinston, A.B., (1981), *Foundations of Decision Support Systems.* Academic Press, New York.

Carlos, A.B., Emerson, C.C., Jean-Marie, D.C., and Jean-Claude, V., (2002), "Facilitating Bid Evaluation in Public Call for Tenders: A Social-Technical Approach." *Omega (The International Journal of Management Science)*, 30: 227-242.

Department of Work, (2001), "Guidance for Tender Evaluation" (in Malay), Malaysia.

Etter, W.E., (1988), "Investment by Design." *Real Estate Centre Journal*, 3(1): 16-19.

Friedman, L., (1956), "A Competitive Bidding Strategy." *Operations Research*, 4 June 104-112.

Gottler, H., (1989), "Graph-Grammars, A New Paradigm for Implementing Visual languages." Lecture Notes in Computer Science, vol. 355, Springer-Verlag, Berlin.

Green Paper, (1999), "Communication on Public Procurement in the European Union" *EU Official Journal.*

Hegazy, T., and Moselhi, O., (1995), "Elements of Cost Estimation: A Survey in Canada and the United States." *Construction Engineering*, 37(5): 27-33.

Holt, G.D., Olomolaiye, P.O., and Hariss, P.C., (1993), "Factors Influencing U.K. Construction Clients' Choice of Contractor." *Building and Environment*, 26: 241-248.

Holtzman, S., (1989), *Intelligent Decision Systems.* Addison-Wesley Publishing Company, INC, Reading, MA.

Hopcroft, J.E., and Ullman, J.D., (1979), *Introduction to Automata Theory, Languages, and Computation*, Addison-Wesley, Reading, MA.

Hudgins, S., and Chang, K.L., (2000), "Information Technology in the Construction Industry: Managing Projects in the Age of the Internet." *Proceeding of the 17th International Symposium on Automation and Robotics in Construction (ISARC)*, Taipei, pp: 1177-1181.

ISDSS'99, (2001), "Decision Support System in the New Millennium." *Decision Support System.* 31:163-164.

Klercker, T., and Klercker, M., (1998), "Decision Support System for Primary Health Care in an inter/intranet Environment." *Computer, Methods and Programs in Biomedicine*, 55(1): 31-37.

Kumaraswamy, M.M., and Dissanayaka, S.M., (2000), "Developing The Decision Support System for Building Project Procurement." *Building and Environment* 36: 337-349

Latham, M., Sir, (1994), "Joint of Government Industry Review of Procurement and Contractual Arrangement in the UK Construction Industry." *Interim Report* H.M.S.O., London.

Molenaar, K.R., and Songer, A.D., (2001), "Web-Based Decision Support Systems: Case Study in Project Delivery." *Journal of Computing in Civil Engineering*. 5(4): 259-267.

Moselhi, O., Hegazy, T., and Fazio, P., (1993), "DBID: Analogy-Based DSS for Bidding in Construction." Journal of Construction Engineering and Management. 119(3): 467-479.

Nemati, H.R., Steiger, D.M., Iyer, L.S., and Herschel, R.T., (2002). "Knowledge Warehouse: An Architectural Intergration of Knowledge Management, Decision Support, Artificial Intelligence and Data Warehousing." *Decision Support System*, 33: 143-161.

Oquendo, F., Papamichail, K.N., and Robertson, I., (2000), "Overcoming In-adequacies Modelling: The Need for Decisioning be a First-Class Citizen." *7th European Workshop Software Process Technology (EWSPT 2000)*, Lecture Notes in Computer Science, Vol. 1780, Berlin Heidelberg, New York: Spring Verlag, pp: 84-89.

Papamichail, K.N. and Robertson, I., (2002), "Supporting the Decision Process using an Evolution Model", *16th Triennial Conference of the International Federation of Operational Research Societies, IFORS 2002*, Edinburgh.

Powel, D. J., (2000), "Web-Based and Model Driven Decision Support Systems: Concepts and Issues." *AMCIS2000*, Americas Conference on Information Systems, Long Beach California.

Russell, J., (1992), "Decision Models for Analysis and Evaluation of Construction Contractors." *Construction Management and Economics*, 10,: 185-202.

Segev, A., Gebauer, J., and Bean, C. (1998). "Procurement in the Internet Age-Current Practices and Emerging Trends." Fisher Center for Management and Information Technology, Hass School of Business, U.C. Berkeley, *CMIT Working Paper* WP-98-1033.

Seneviratne, I., and Schexnayder, C., (1999), "A Wisely, Establishing a World Wide Web Presence." *The Practice Period of Structure Construction*, 4(2): 69-74.

Shash, A., (1995), "Bidding Strategies: An Overview." *Construction Engineering Journal*, 37(2): 19-20.

Simon H.A., (1977), *The New Science of Management Decision*, Englewood Cliffs, New Jersey Prentice - Hall, Inc.

Sprague, R.H., (1980), "A Framework for Development of Decision Support Systems." *MIS Quarterly*, 4(4): 1-26.

Stark, R.M., and Rothkopf, M.H., (1979), "Competitive Binding: A Comprehensive Bibliography." *Operation Research*, 27(2): 364-390.

Thomas, S. Ng., and Smith, N.J., (1998), "Verification and Validation of CASE-Based Pre-qualification System." *Journal of Computing in Civil Engineering*. 12(4): 215-216.

Ting, S.C., and Mills, A., (1996), "Analysis of Contractors: Bidding Decisions." *Proceeding in CIB W92 Int. Symposium on Procurement System*, University of Natal, Duban, South Africa, 53-65.

Tserng, H.P., and Lin, P.H., (2002), "An Accelerated Subcontracting and Procuring Model for Construction Projects." *Automation in Construction*, 11: 105-125.

Warboys, B.C., Kawalek, P., Robertson, I., and Greenwood, R.M., (1999) *Business Information Systems: A Process Approach*, London.

Zift, P.J., (2000), "Technology-Enhanced Project Management." *Journal of Management Engineering*. ASCE 16(1): 34-39.

MINING VERY LARGE DATASETS WITH SUPPORT VECTOR MACHINE ALGORITHMS

François Poulet, Thanh-Nghi Do

ESIEA Recherche, 38 rue des Docteurs Calmette et Guérin, 53000 Laval, France
Email: poulet@esiea-ouest.fr, dothanh@esiea-ouest.fr

Keywords: Data mining, Parallel and distributed algorithms, Classification, Machine learning, Support vector machines, Least squares classifiers, Newton method, Proximal classifiers, Incremental learning.

Abstract: In this paper, we present new support vector machines (SVM) algorithms that can be used to classify very large datasets on standard personal computers. The algorithms have been extended from three recent SVMs algorithms: least squares SVM classification, finite Newton method for classification and incremental proximal SVM classification. The extension consists in building incremental, parallel and distributed SVMs for classification. Our three new algorithms are very fast and can handle very large datasets. An example of the effectiveness of these new algorithms is given with the classification into two classes of one billion points in 10-dimensional input space in some minutes on ten personal computers (800 MHz Pentium III, 256 MB RAM, Linux).

1 INTRODUCTION

The size of data stored in the world is constantly increasing (data volume doubles every 20 months world-wide) but data do not become useful until some of the information they carry is extracted. Furthermore, a page of information is easy to explore, but when the information becomes the size of a book, or library, or even larger, it may be difficult to find known items or to get an overview. Knowledge Discovery in Databases (KDD) can be defined as the non-trivial process of identifying valid, novel, potentially useful, and ultimately understandable patterns in data (Fayyad et al., 1996).

In this process, data mining can be defined as the particular pattern recognition task. It uses different algorithms for classification, regression, clustering or association. Support Vector Machine (SVM) algorithms are one kind of classification algorithms. Recently, a number of powerful support vector machine (SVM) learning algorithms have been proposed (Bennett and Campbell, 2000). This approach has shown practical relevance for classification, regression or novelty detection. Successful applications of SVMs have been reported for various fields, for example in face identification, text categorization, bioinformatics (Guyon, 1999).

The approach is systematic and properly motivated by statistical learning theory (Vapnik, 1995). SVMs are the most well known algorithms of a class using the idea of kernel substitution (Cristianini and Shawe-Taylor, 2000). SVMs and kernel methodology have become increasingly popular tools for data mining tasks. SVM solutions are obtained from quadratic programming problems possessing a global solution, so that, the computational cost of an SVM approach depends on the optimization algorithm used. The very best algorithms today are typically quadratic and required multiple scans of the data. Unfortunately, real-world databases increase in size: according to (Fayyad and Uthurusamy, 2002), world-wide storage capacity doubles every 9 months. There is a need to scale up learning algorithms to handle massive datasets on personal computers. We have created three new algorithms that are very fast for building incremental, parallel and distributed SVMs for classification. They are derived from the following ones: least squares SVMs classifiers (Suykens and Vandewalle, 1999), finite Newton method for classification problems (Mangasarian, 2001) and incremental SVMs classification (Fung and Mangasarian, 2001). Our three new algorithms can classify one billion points in 10-dimensional input space into two classes in some minutes on ten computers (800 MHz Pentium III, 256 MB RAM, Linux).

O. Camp et al. (eds.), Enterprise Information Systems V, 177-184.

We briefly summarize the content of the paper now. In section 2, we introduce least squares SVMs classifiers, incremental proximal SVMs, and finite Newton method for classification problems. In section 3, we describe our reformulation of the least squares SVMs algorithm for building incremental SVMs. In section 4, we propose the extension of the finite Newton algorithm for building incremental SVMs. In section 5, we describe our parallel and distributed versions of the three incremental algorithms. We demonstrate numerical test results in section 6 before the conclusion in section 7.

Some notations are used in this paper. All vectors will be column vectors unless transposed to row vector by a t superscript. The 2-norm of the vector x will be denoted by $\|x\|$, the matrix $A[mxn]$ will be m trained points in the n-dimensional real space R^n. The classes +1, -1 of m trained points are denoted by the diagonal matrix $D[mxm]$ of +1, -1. e will be the column vector of 1. w, b will be the coefficients and the scalar of the hyperplane. z will be the slack variable and v is a positive constant. I denote the identity matrix.

2 RELATED WORKS

We briefly present a general linear classification task of SVMs and then we summarize three algorithms: least squares SVM, incremental proximal SVM and finite Newton SVM algorithm.

Incremental learning algorithms (Syed et al., 1999), (Cauwenberghs and Poggio, 2001) are a convenient way to handle very large data sets because they avoid to load the whole data set in main memory: only subsets of the data are to be considered at any one time.

2.1 Linear SVMs Classification

Let us consider a linear binary classification task, as depicted in figure 1, with m data points in the n-dimensional input space R^n, represented by the mxn matrix A, having corresponding labels ±1, denoted by the mxm diagonal matrix D of ±1.

For this problem, the SVMs try to find the best separating plane, i.e. furthest from both class +1 and class -1. It can simply maximize the distance or margin between the support planes for each class ($x^t w = b+1$ for class +1, $x^t w = b-1$ for class -1). The margin between these supporting planes is $2/\|w\|$. Any point falling on the wrong side of its supporting

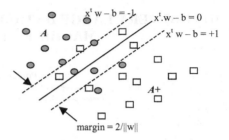

Figure 1: Linear separation of the datapoints into two classes

plane is considered to be an error. Therefore, the SVMs have to simultaneously maximize the margin and minimize the error. The standard SVMs with linear kernel is given by the following quadratic program (1):

$$\min f(z,w,b) = ve^t z + (1/2)\|w\|^2$$

$$\text{s.t. } D(Aw - eb) + z \geq e \quad (1)$$

where the slack variable $z \geq 0$ and v is a positive constant.

The plane (w,b) is obtained by the solution of the quadratic program (1). And then, the classification function of a new data point x based on the plane is:

$$f(x) = \text{sign}(wx - b) \quad (2)$$

2.2 Least squares SVM classifiers

A least squares SVMs classifier has been proposed by (Suykens and Vanderwalle, 1999). It uses an equality instead of the inequality constraints in the optimization problem (1) with a least squares 2-norm error into the objective function f. Least squares SVMs are the solution of the following optimization problem (3):

$$\min f(z,w,b) = (v/2)\|z\|^2 + (1/2)\|w\|^2$$

$$\text{s.t. } D(Aw - eb) + z = e \quad (3)$$

where the slack variable $z \geq 0$ and v is a positive constant.

Thus substituting z into the objective function f we get an unconstraint problem (4):

$$\min f(w,b) = (v/2)\|e - D(Aw - eb)\|^2 + (1/2)\|w\|^2 \quad (4)$$

For least squares SVMs with linear kernel, the Karush-Kuhn-Tucker optimality condition of (4) will give the linear equation system of (n+1) variables (w,b). Therefore, least squares SVMs is very fast to train because it expresses the training in terms of solving a set of linear equations instead of quadratic programming.

2.3 Proximal SVM classifier and its incremental version

The proximal SVMs classifier proposed by (Fung and Mangasarian, 2001) also changes the inequality constraints to equalities in the optimization problem (1). However, besides adding a least squares 2-norm error into the objective function f, it changes the formulation of the margin maximization to the minimization of $(1/2)\|w,b\|^2$. Thus substituting for z from the constraint in terms (w,b) into the objective function f we get an unconstraint problem (5):

$$\min f(w,b) = (v/2)\|e - D(Aw - eb)\|^2 + (1/2)\|w,b\|^2 \quad (5)$$

Setting the gradient with respect to (w,b) to zero gives:

$$[w_1\ w_2\ ..\ w_n\ b]^t = (I/v + E^tE)^{-1}E^tDe \quad (6)$$

where $E = [A\quad -e]$

This expression for (w,b) requires the solution of a system of linear equations. Proximal SVMs is very fast to train.

Linear incremental proximal SVMs is extended from the computation of E^tE and $d = E^tDe$ from the formulation (6). Let us consider the small blocks of data A_i, D_i, we can simply compute $E^tE = \Sigma E_i^tE_i$ and $d = \Sigma d_i = \Sigma E_i^tD_ie$. This algorithm can perform the linear classification of one billion data points in 10-dimensional input space into two classes in less than 2 hours and 26 minutes on a 400 MHz Pentium II (Fung and Mangasarian, 2002). About 30% of the time was spent reading data from disk. Note that all we need to store in memory between two incremental steps is the small (n+1)x(n+1) matrix E^tE and the (n+1)x1 vector $d = E^tDe$ although the order of the dataset is one billion data points.

2.4 Finite Newton SVMs Algorithm

We return to the formulation of the standard SVMs with a least squares 2-norm error and changing the

margin maximization to the minimization of $(1/2)\|w,b\|^2$.

$$\min f(z,w,b) = (v/2)\|z\|^2 + (1/2)\|w,b\|^2$$

$$\text{s.t.}\quad D(Aw - eb) + z \geq e \quad (7)$$

where the slack variable $z \geq 0$ and v is a positive constant.

The formulation (7) can be reformulated by substituting for $z = (e - D(Aw - eb))_+$ (where $(x)_+$ replaces negative components of a vector x by zeros) into the objective function f. We get an unconstraint problem (8):

$$\min f(w,b) = (v/2)\|(e - D(Aw - eb))_+\|^2 + (1/2)\|w,b\|^2 \quad (8)$$

If we set $u = [w_1\ w_2\ ..\ w_n\ b]^t$ and $H = [A\ -e]$ then the formulation (8) will be rewritten by (9):

$$\min f(u) = (v/2)\|(e - DHu)_+\|^2 + (1/2)u^tu \quad (9)$$

O. Mangasarian has developed the finite stepless Newton method for this strongly convex unconstrained minimization problem (9). This algorithm can be described as follows:

Start with any $u^0 \in R^{n+1}$ and $i = 0$.
Repeat
1) $u^{i+1} = u^i - \partial^2 f(u^i)^{-1}\nabla f(u^i)$
2) $i = i + 1$
Until $(\nabla f(u^{i-1}) = 0)$

where the gradient of f at u is:

$$\nabla f(u) = v(-DH)^t(e - DHu)_+ + u,$$

and the generalized Hessian of f(u) is:

$$\partial^2 f(u) = v(-DH)^t diag(e - DHu)'(-DH) + I,$$

with $diag(e - DHu)'$ denotes the (n+1)x(n+1) diagonal matrix whose j^{th} diagonal entry is subgradient of the step function $(e - DHu)_+$.

The sequence $\{u^i\}$ of the algorithm terminates at the global minimum solution as demonstrated by (Mangasarian, 2001). In almost all the tested cases, the stepless Newton algorithm has given the solution with a number of Newton iterations varying between 5 and 8.

179

3 INCREMENTAL LS-SVMs

We return to the least squares SVMs algorithm with linear kernel as in section 2.1 by changing the inequality constraints to equalities, and substituting for z from the constraint in terms (w,b) into the objective function f. Least squares SVMs involve the solution of the unconstrained optimization problem (4):

$$\min f(w,b) = (v/2)\|e - D(Aw - eb)\|^2 + (1/2)\|w\|^2 \quad (4)$$

Applying the Karush-Kuhn-Tucker optimality condition of (4), the gradient with respect to w,b is set to zero, we obtain the linear equation system of $(n+1)$ variables (w,b):

$$vA^tD(D(Aw - eb) -e) + w = 0$$

$$-ve^tD(D(Aw - eb) -e) \quad = 0$$

We can reformulate the linear equation system given above as (10):

$$[w_1\ w_2 .. w_n\ b]^t = (I'/v + E^tE)^{-1}E^tDe \quad (10)$$

where $E = [A\ -e]$, I' denotes the $(n+1)x(n+1)$ diagonal matrix whose $(n+1)^{th}$ diagonal entry is zero and the other diagonal entries are 1.

The solution of the linear equation system (10) will give (w,b). Note that least squares SVMs solving by (10) is very similar to the linear system (6) of the linear proximal SVMs, furthermore, setting to zero the $(n+1)^{th}$ diagonal entry of I in the system (6) gives I' in (10). Therefore, we can extend the least squares SVMs to build the incremental learning algorithm in the same way as the incremental proximal SVMs with linear kernel. We can compute $E^tE = \Sigma E_i^tE_i$ and $d = \Sigma d_i = \Sigma E_i^tD_ie$ from the small blocks A_i, D_i. We can see that the incremental least squares SVMs algorithm has the same complexity as the incremental proximal SVMs. It can handle very large datasets (at least 10^9 points) on personal computers in some minutes. And we only need to store the small $(n+1)x(n+1)$ matrix E^tE and the $(n+1)x1$ vector $d = E^tDe$ in memory between two successive steps.

4 INCREMENTAL FINITE NEW-TON SVMs

The main idea is to incrementally compute the generalized Hessian of $f(u)$ and the gradient of f $(\partial^2 f(u)$ and $\nabla f(u))$ for each iteration in the finite Newton algorithm described in section 2.3.

Suppose we have a very large dataset decomposed into small blocks A_i, D_i. We can simply compute the gradient and the generalized Hessian of f by the formulation (11) and (12):

$$\nabla f(u) = v(\Sigma(-D_iH_i)^t(e - D_iH_iu)) + u \quad (11)$$

$$\partial^2 f(u) = v(\Sigma(-D_iH_i)^t\text{diag}(e-D_iH_iu)'(-D_iH_i)) + I \quad (12)$$

where $H_i = [A_i\quad -e]$

Consequently, the incremental finite Newton algorithm can handle one billion data points in 10-dimensional input space on personal computer. Its execution time is very fast because it gives the solution with a number of Newton iterations varying from 5 to 8. We only need to store a small $(n+1)x(n+1)$ matrix and two $(n+1)x1$ vectors in memory between two successives steps.

5 PARALLEL AND DISTRIBUTED INCREMENTAL SVM ALGORITHMS

The three incremental SVMs algorithms described above are very fast to train in almost cases and can deal with very large datasets on personal computers. However they run only on one single machine. We have extended them to build incremental, parallel and distributed SVMs algorithms on a computer network by using the remote procedure calls (RPC) mechanism. First of all, we distribute the datasets (A_i, D_i) on remote servers.

Concerning the incremental proximal and the least squares SVMs algorithms, the remote servers compute independently, incrementally the sums of $E_i^tE_i$ and $d_i = E_i^tD_ie$, and then, a client machine will use these results to compute w and b. Concerning the incremental finite Newton algorithm, the remote servers compute independently, incrementally the sums of:

$$(-D_i H_i)^t (e - D_i H_i u), \text{ and}$$

$(-D_i H_i)^t \text{diag}(e - D_i H_i u)'(-D_i H_i)$.

Then a client machine will use these sums to update u for each Newton iteration.

The RPC protocol does not support asynchronous communication. A synchronous request-reply mechanism in RPC requires that the client and server are always available and functioning (i.e. the client or server is not blocked). The client can issue a request and must wait for the server's response before continuing its own processing. Therefore, we have created a child process for parallel waitings on the client side.

The parallel and distributed implementation versions do have significantly speeded up the three incremental versions.

6 NUMERICAL TEST RESULTS

Our new algorithms are written in C / C++ on personal computers (800 MHz Pentium III processor, 256 MB RAM). These computers run on Linux Redhat 7.2. Because we are interested in very large datasets, we focus numerical tests on datasets created by the NDC program from (Musicant, 1998). The first three datasets contain two millions data points in 10-dimensional, 30-dimensional and 50-dimensional input space. We use them to estimate the execution time for varying the number of dimensions.

Table 1- CPU time to classify one billion 10-dimensional data points on ten machines

Block size	Proximal SVM (mn hh:mn:ss) 90.803 %		LS-SVM (mn hh:mn:ss) 90.803 %		Newton-SVM (mn hh:mn:ss) 90.860 %	
100	00:07:05		00:07:05			00:39:14
500	00:07:20		00:07:20			00:40:03
1000	00:07:20		00:07:20		61	01:00:43
5000	00:20:40		00:20:40		101	01:40:49
10000	00:28:10		00:28:10		103	01:42:33
50000	00:28:15		00:28:15		105	01:44:58
100000	00:28:15		00:28:15		105	01:45:03
500000	00:28:30		00:28:30		105	01:45:24
1000000	00:28:30		00:28:30		109	01:49:09

Table 2 - CPU time to classify one billion 30-dimensional data points on ten machines

Block size	Proximal SVM (mn hh:mn:ss) 90.803 %		LS-SVM (mn hh:mn:ss) 90.803 %		Newton-SVM (mn hh:mn:ss) 90.860 %	
100	50	00:49:50	50	00:49:50	208	03:28:19
500	74	01:13:45	74	01:13:45	281	04:40:49
1000	82	01:21:40	82	01:21:40	371	06:10:49
5000	175	02:55:00	175	02:55:00	442	07:22:30
10000	180	03:00:00	180	03:00:00	453	07:27:30
50000	181	03:00:50	181	03:00:50	453	07:33:19
100000	181	03:00:50	181	03:00:50	453	07:33:19
500000	181	03:00:50	180	03:00:50	477	07:56:39
1000000	189	03:09:10	189	03:09:10	N/A	

Table 3 - CPU time to classify one billion 50-dimensional data points on ten machines

Block size	Proximal SVM (mn hh:mn:ss) 90.803 %		LS-SVM (mn hh:mn:ss) 90.803 %		Newton-SVM (mn hh:mn:ss) 90.860 %	
100	130	02:10:00	130	02:10:00	508	08:28:19
500	152	02:32:30	152	02:32:30	737	12:16:39
1000	185	03:05:50	185	03:05:50	982	16:21:39
5000	430	07:10:00	430	07:10:00	1004	16:44:09
10000	483	08:03:20	483	08:03:20	1012	16:51:39
50000	487	08:06:40	487	08:06:40	1021	17:00:49
100000	486	08:05:50	486	08:05:50	1024	17:04:09
500000	487	08:07:30	487	08:07:30	N/A	

The last dataset consists of twenty millions 10-dimensional data points, its purpose is to estimate how the execution time varies according to the size of tested datasets and the size of small blocks for each incremental step. Thus, we have measured computational time of our new algorithms to classify one billion data points in 10, 30, 50-dimensional on ten machines as shown in table 1, 2 and 3.

Note that on these tables, the N/A results are used to indicate that the Newton-SVMs does not support the given block size for the incremental step. We have only measured the computational time without the time needed to read data from disk. The algorithms have linear dependences on the number of machines, size of datasets and a second order of the number of dimensions. Concerning the communication cost, they take about one second when the dataset dimension is less than 100.

The first part of the curve is an increasing part up to a nearly constant one. It corresponds to an increasing block size with the lowest values, the block is completely in main memory, then an increasing part of the block must be swapped on the secondary memory (on the hard disk) and finally the whole swap space is used (the time does not vary any more). For the highest block sizes in 30 and 50 dimensional data sets, there is no result: the data block is too large to fit in memory, the program is always swapping parts of the block between main memory and secondary memory and does not perform any more calculation.

Whatever the data dimension and the block size are, we can see that the Newton-SVM is very slower than the two other ones. In fact, this algorithm is

algorithms are exactly the same as the original ones, they can be found in (Fung and Mangasarian, 2002) for the incremental PSVM, in (Mangasarian, 2001) for the finite Newton method and in (Suykens and Vandewalle, 1999) for the least squares SVM.

The results obtained have demonstrated the effectiveness of these new algorithms to deal with very large datasets on personal computers.

7 CONCLUSION

We have developed three new SVMs algorithms able to classify very large datasets on standard personal computers. We have extended three recent SVMs algorithms to build incremental, parallel and distributed SVMs: least squares SVMs classifiers, finite Newton method and incremental proximal SVMs classifiers. Our new algorithms can perform the classification of one billion data points into two classes in 10-dimensional input space in some minutes on ten machines (800 MHz Pentium III, 256 MB RAM, Linux).

A forthcoming improvement will be to extend these algorithms to the non-linear kernel cases. Another one could be to use the XML-RPC

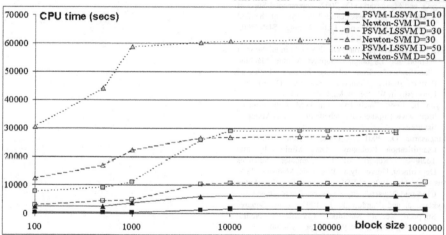

Figure 2: CPU time for the classification according to the block size

designed for the particularly case of the multicategory classification and it gives significantly better results (concerning the accuracy) than the PSVM and the LS-SVM (but with a higher computation cost). The accuracy of the distributed

mechanism for the parallel and distributed implementation to operate over any XML-capable transport protocol, typically over HTTP. The software program could then be distributed on different kind of machines, for example on a set of various remote PCs, Unix stations or any other computer reachable via the web.

REFERENCES

Bennett K. and Campbell C., 2000, "Support Vector Machines: Hype or Hallelujah?", in SIGKDD Explorations, Vol. 2, No. 2, pp. 1-13.

Cauwenberghs G. and Poggio T. 2001, "Incremental and Decremental Support Vector Machine Learning", in Advances in Neural Information Processing Systems (NIPS 2000), MIT Press, Vol. 13, 2001, Cambridge, USA, pp. 409-415.

Cristianini, N. and Shawe-Taylor, J., 2000, "An Introduction to Support Vector Machines and Other Kernel-based Learning Methods", Cambridge University Press.

Fayyad U., Piatetsky-Shapiro G., Smyth P., Uthurusamy R., 1996, "Advances in Knowledge Discovery and Data Mining", AAAI Press.

Fayyad, U., Uthurusamy R., 2002, "Evolving Data Mining into Solutions for Insights", in Communication of the ACM, 45(8), pp.28-31.

Fung G. and Mangasarian O., 2001, "Proximal Support Vector Machine Classifiers", in proc. of the 7th ACM SIGKDD Int. Conf. on KDD'01, San Francisco, USA, pp. 77-86.

Fung G. and Mangasarian O., 2002, "Incremental Support Vector Machine Classification", in proc. of the 2nd SIAM Int. Conf. on Data Mining SDM'2002 Arlington, Virginia, USA.

Fung G. and Mangasarian O., 2001, "Finite Newton Method for Lagrangian Support Vector Machine Classification", Data Mining Institute Technical Report 02-01, Computer Sciences Department, University of Wisconsin, Madison, USA.

Guyon I., 1999, "Web Page on SVM Applications", http://www.clopinet.com/isabelle/Projects/SVM/app-list.html

Mangasarian O., 2001, "A Finite Newton Method for Classification Problems", Data Mining Institute Technical Report 01-11, Computer Sciences Department, University of Wisconsin, Madison, USA.

Musicant D., 1998, "NDC : Normally Distributed Clustered Datasets", http://www.cs.cf.ac.uk/Dave/C/

Suykens, J. and Vandewalle J., 1999, "Least Squares Support Vector Machines Classifiers", Neural Processing Letters, Vol. 9, No. 3, pp. 293-300.

Syed N., Liu H., Sung K., 1999, "Incremental Learning with Support Vector Machines", in proc. of the 6th ACM SIGKDD Int. Conf. on KDD'99, San Diego, USA.

Vapnik V., 1995, "The Nature of Statistical Learning Theory", Springer-Verlag, New York.

THE DESIGN AND IMPLEMENTATION OF IMPROVED INTELLIGENT ANSWERING MODEL

Ruimin Shen, Qun Su

Computer& Tech Department,Shanghai Jiaotong University,Shanghai,China
Email: rmshen@sjtu.edu.cn, qsu@sjtu.edu.cn

Keywords: Generalization, Data Preprocess, Pattern, Intelligent Answering

Abstract: Based on the analysis of the main technical problems in the designs of the Intelligent Answering System, the traditional Answering System Model and its working mechanism is provided. Based on the analysis of the model, a Improved Intelligent Answering Model based on the data generalization based on the patterns tree, association rule mining of patterns, and the mergence and deletion of the rules based on the knowledge tree is come up with and implemented. In the end, the improvement of this model in intelligence is analyzed and proved with some data in a experiment.

1   INTRODUCTION

The teaching environment based on the network provides for the birth of automatic and intelligent answering system. At the same time, in this environment, the participation in study of so many students require the answering system should have more intelligence(Renzi 2000). From the analysis of the current main answering system, such as FAQ of the Microsoft Product, the tech forum based on keywords search of the hottest programming developer web site (WWW.CSDN.NET) and the intelligent answering system of Shanghai Jiaotong University Distance Learning Center Lab based on the related keywords search based on the primary understanding of the semantic of words of the language and the knowledge point data mining and so on. To improve the intelligence of the Answering System, two main technical problems should be resolved: How to understand the question asked and found the related questions from the database? And how to calculate the degree of relativity of the questions and sort them so as to provide the most related questions and their answers to the asker.

After the analysis of these answer systems, we find the traditional answer model is like figure 1, and   the following is its structure:

1.1   Definition

The questions asked by the students is   "To be Answered" Q; After the analysis of the "To be Answered" Q, the questions that are related to Q are called "Related Questions" ($Q_1..Q_n$).

1.2   Answering Process

The answering process of the traditional model consists of the following: (1) The decomposition of the question Q to get its knowledge points and their interrogative words; (2) Finding the related questions(Q1..Qn); (3) The calculation and sorting of the related questions(Q1..Qn).

1.3   The shortcomings of the traditional answering model

Although the traditional answering model is able to come out with an effective answer, there still exists three shortcomings:

(1) The decomposition of the question is too slow, because it has to do a lot of matching calculations; and when it come to the professional questions, the result is not effective.

(2)The intelligence is too low. Because the uniform function is taken to calculate the relativity, the suitable function is too hard to be made.

(3)No self-accommodation exists. Because once the function is made, the order of the questions that is used to answer the question Q is determined and can't be adjusted with the decision of the users. But in general, the order in which the student browses the questions that are submit is the order of the relativity of the questions by the student. It's a piece

O. Camp et al. (eds.), Enterprise Information Systems V, 185-191.
© 2004 *Kluwer Academic Publishers. Printed in the Netherlands.*

of important information. But it isn't made full use of.

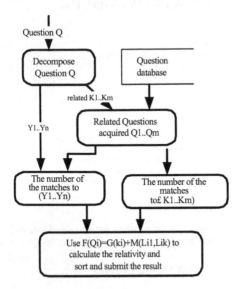

Figure 1 traditional answering model

2. THE THEORETIC BASIS - THE ASSOCIATION MINING OF THE PATTERNS RESULTED FROM THE GENERALIZATION OF THE DATE WITH THE COMBINATION OF THE KNOWLEDGE POINT TREE

2.1 The premise of the data mining

In the system, the way to answer the asker is to summit several related questions that have been sorted and the asker chooses to read the most related question. There is a default premise: in general, the first question that is selected by the user is the most related to the "To be Answered" Q; And the order to browse the questions is similar to the order of the relativity.

2.2 Association Mining

Let $I=\{i1, i2, \ldots, im\}$ be a set of items. Let D, the task relevant data, be a set of database transactions where each transaction T is a set of items such that $T\subseteq I$. Each transaction is associated with an identifier, called TID. Let A be a set of items. A transaction T is said to contain A if and only if $A \subseteq T$. An association rule is an implication of the form $A\Rightarrow B$, where $A \subseteq I$, $B\subseteq I$ and $A\cap B= \varnothing$. The rule $A \Rightarrow B$ holds in the transaction set D with support s, where s is the percentage of transactions in D that contain $A \cup B$. The rule $A \Rightarrow B$ has confidence c in the transaction set D if c is the percentage of transactions in D containing A which also contain B. That is $support(A\Rightarrow B) = Prob(A \cup B)$ and $confidence(A \Rightarrow B)= Prob(B\cap A)$. Rules that satisfy both a minimum support threshold (min sup) and a minimum confidence threshold (min conf) are called strong.

2.3 The data preprocess of the answering resource mining----The transformation from the related questions to the related pattern

To answer the "To Be Answered" Q, the system will produce a series of related questions, then the student will choose to see some questions$(Q_1..Q_k)$ so as to find the answer. Apparently, we can conclude that the question Q is related with the set of the questions$(Q_1..Q_k)$. Therefore, we can in turn decompose the question Q and the related question Qp into their own series of knowledge points and interrogative word word$(K_1..K_m$, $Y_1..Y_n)$ and $(K_{p1}.. K_{p(mi)}$, $Y_{p1}..Y_{p(ni)})$. Turn the series of $(K_1..K_m$, $Y_1..Y_n)$into m*n patterns$(K_i$, $Y_j)$that is composed of knowledge point and interrogative word word. This leads to the related patterns transactions set T, in which T_i is composed of two parts that is $\{(K_i$, $Y_j)$, $(K_{pi}, Y_{pj})\}$. This is what we are going to mine.

But, we find that the data is too large, for example in one question Q, there are m*n patterns and in its related questions there are K*m*n patterns, therefore there are around $O(K*m^2*n^2)$ transactions. Firstly, because the number of the questions that are asked is too large, so the calculation will be large if we apply the algorithm Apriopri to mine the data. Secondly, after the decomposition, the probability of the occurrence of a pattern in several questions is so small that the results mined are scarce. Finally, if the concept of the results is too small, then the probability that they are be made use of is small. So, before the mining process, we use the preprocessing of concept generalization.

2.4 Patten tree combined by the knowledge point tree and the interrogative word tree

The structure of the knowledge point tree is tree-like network structure. As the node of the knowledge network---the relationship of the knowledge points is very complex. In(Jian 1998), there are 4 kinds of relationship: (1)prior/ subsequence (2)include and be included (3)sibling (4)refer and be referred . In the patterns generalization, the relationship used is the "include and be included" relationship of the knowledge point. Similarly, the relationship used of the node of the interrogative word tree is the same of that of the knowledge point tree.

In the construction of the patterns tree, the partial order of one pattern and another one is determined by the following rule: if in $M_1(K_1 , Y_1)$and $M_2(K_2,Y_2)$, $K_1 \subseteq K_2$ and $Y_1 \subseteq Y_2$, then $M_1 \subseteq M_2$, verse visa. But if $K_1 \subseteq K_2$,but not $Y_1 \subseteq Y_2$, then there is only the relationship of the level between M_1 and M_2 .This is determined by the comparison of the sum of K_1 andY_1 and that of K_2 与Y_2 .

2.5 The second preprocess of the related patterns---the concept generalization based on the knowledge point tree

Concept generalization: Basing on the concept tree, use the high level concept to take the place of the low level concept to preprocess the primary data. For example, the classified concept, the knowledge of "os", one kind of knowledge classification, can be generalized to the higher level concept---the knowledge of "software" of the knowledge of "system"; Similarly, numerical concept, for example, the visiting times can be generalized to the higher level concepts such as "often", "usually" and "seldom" and so on.

Traditional concept hierarchies consist of concept hierarchies for numeric data and categorical data(Han, et al. 2001). The ways to get the concept hierarchies for numeric data are composed by:

binning, histogram analysis, clustering analysis, entropy-based discretization, segmentation by natural partitioning. The ways to get the concept hierarchies for categorical data are composed by : specification of a partial ordering of attributes explicitly at the schema level by users or experts, specification of a portion of a hierarchy by explicit data grouping, specification of a set of attributes but not of their partial ordering, specification of only a partial set of attributes.

The pattern transactions gotten from the answering resource include two kinds of information: corresponding of patterns and the relativity of the corresponding. Firstly, in the calculation of the degree of the relativity, we apply entropy-based discretization to the data to get the information of the relativity. Apply the predigestion of "$I(S,T)= |S_1|/|S|*Ent(S_1)+|S_2|/|S|*Ent(S_2)$, $Ent(S_1)= -\sum_{i=1}^{n} (pi * log(pi))$ " ----$Ent(S)= -\sum_{i=1}^{n} (pi * log(pi))$ to calculate the relativity. After deciding how to transform the order to the relativity, we can realize the generalization of the relativity of the questions.

Then in the generalization of the related patterns, we use the knowledge point tree and interrogative word tree to process the transactions. For example, ("Router", "Why") can not only be generalized to("Network device", "Why"), but also be generalized to ("Router", "Reasoning"). It can make the similar information in the low level integrate to high level and is easy to be understood. At the same time, it can also lessen the noise and the exception data in the data mining. The degree of generalization can be controlled by the experimental coefficient set before the mining. Once the number of the different sorts in a level of one attribute is less than or equal to this coefficient, we stop the concept generalization in this attribute.

2.6 The multi-level association mining in the related patterns based on the pattern tree (Jiawei, et al. 1995)(Figure 2)

After generalizing all the patterns to a level using the pattern tree, we got the generalized related patterns. Because the visiting order of the question that all the patterns exist is different and for any kind of the relativity, there is a corresponding categorical coefficient, we get a series of patterns that include the categorical coefficient. In the mining, the process of the coefficient is taking the similar process of the number of the product in the shopping association mining, which means we think there are several similar patterns.

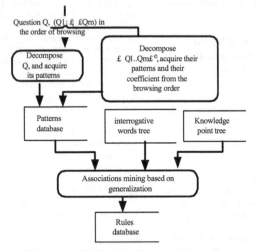

Figure 2 Multi-level mining model based on the preprocess of the generalization that combined with the patterns tree

3. IMPROVED INTELLIGENT ANSWERING MODEL BASED ON ASSOCIATION MINING ON THE GENERALIZED RELATED PATTERNS

3.1 Improved intelligent answering model

To the shortcoming that the traditional answering model has in the calculation of the relativity, we put forward a new intelligent answering model, which makes use of the results that was multi-levelly mined from the patterns after the generalization and is the adjustment of the traditional answering model. The new model is described in figure 3. We adjust the traditional model in two aspects:

(1) Pick up the knowledge points part from some good rules and insert them in to the database as the related knowledge points. When discomposing the sentence, use the related knowledge points first. It makes the speed of the decomposition quicker and has higher ratio correctness, especially when the question is a professional one.

(2) In the calculation of the relativity, after the decomposition of the question Q, match the keyword q with the left part or the right part of the associations in the database. If there are more than or equal to one match $(R_1..R_i)$, then the related matches$(R_1..R_n)$ will be calculated. Then all the related matches would be I=($R_1..R_i$) $\cup$ ($R_1..R_n$). Then analyze in the related questions how many matches to the set I and acquire the number of the matches$(r_1..r_p)$. And adjust the relativity calculation function from $F(Q_i)=G(k_i)+M(L_{i1},L_{ik})$ to $F(Q_i)=G(k_i)+M(L_{i1},L_{ik})+N_{(ri)}$.

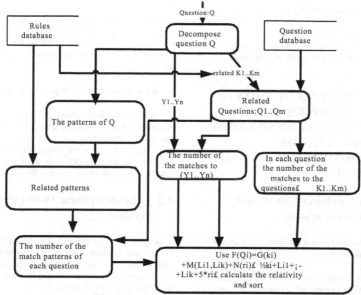

Figure 3 Improved Answering
Model

3.2 The effect of the improved model

e.g. "To Be Answered" Q: how many kinds of transmitting media are used in the computer network.

Apply the old model:

The knowledge points gotten from the decomposition: Computer, Network, transmitting media.

The related knowledge points: Computer, Network, transmitting multimedia (Supposed to be the same as the above).

The interrogative word words: how many

The related questions found (only list three questions):

Q_1: In order to reduce the noise, how many ways to connect the lines in the network?

Q_2: How many kinds of the transmitting media?

Q_3:List the difference of the transmitting medias in the computer network?

The related knowledge points matched: Q_1 (Network)Q_2(Transmitting media)Q_3(Computer, Network, transmitting media)

The related interrogative word matched: Q_1(how many, weight 1), Q_2(how many, weight 1) Q_3(NULL, weight 0)

Supposed a very simple relativity calculation function $F(Q_i)=k_i+L_{i1}+...+L_{ik}$

Then, the relativity of the $F(Q_1)=2$, $F(Q_2)=2$, $F(Q_3)=3$.

Now, the system thinks Q_3 is the more related question than Q_1, Q_2. But we know Q_2 is most related question.

Apply new model:

If in the database there are these mining rules mined: pattern ("How many", "kind") .

As for question Q: Match pattern ("How many", "kind").

Related Pattern: ("How many", "kind")

As for Q_1 (no match pattern), Q_2(1 match pattern),Q_3(no match pattern).

The related knowledge points matched: Q_1 (Network), Q_2 (Transmitting media), Q_3(Computer, Network, transmitting media)

The related interrogative word matched: Q_1(how many, weight 1), Q_2(how many, weight 1) Q_3(NULL, weight 0)

Suppose the adjusted function $F(Q_i)=G(k_i)$

$+M(L_{i1},L_{ik})+N(r_i)=k_i+L_{i1}+...+L_{ik}+5*r_i,$

Then: the corresponding relativity of Q_1、Q_2、Q_3:

$F(Q_1)=2$, $F(Q_2)=7$, $F(Q_3)=3$.

Then the system will think Q_2 is the most related question. It is a more satisfying result.

4. THE IMPLEMENTATION OF THE IMPROVED INTELLIGENT ANSWERING MODEL AND THE EXPERIMENT TO TEST THE SYSTEM

4.1 Construction of improved answering system

4.1.1 The preprocess module based on the patterns tree

Create a data warehouse of answering data of the user. During the process of answering, we save the question of the user and the question-browsing order to the database. We preprocess the data by generalizing the data with the patterns tree and save the result to the data warehouse.

4.1.2 Multi-level association mining module

Apply association mining on the data of the information of the asker in the data warehouse. Then combined with the knowledge points tree and the interrogative word tree, merge or delete the redundant associations. Then user adds or the system automatically add them to the related pattern database.

4.1.3 Question-Preprocess Module

Combined with the dictionary、the professional word in the question related field and interrogative word database, using the KMP to decompose the question into a series of knowledge points and interrogative word.

4.1.4 Related question producing module

Uses the knowledge points and interrogative word words to look for the related questions. After finding the related questions, combine with the related knowledge points tree and interrogative word tree to calculate the relativity of the question, and sort these questions and submit the result to the asker.

4.2 The experiment to test the system

In general, after the question is submitted, the system will produce a group of questions, the first question that the asker browses relate most to the "To Be Answered" question. So, in the experiment, we do the following experiment:

50 students ask questions in the lesson of Computer Network. The system would produce two questions. One is produced by the traditional model and the other is produced by the improved model. The order of these two questions is random. These students will select the more related one. And the system calculates the count of the questions chosen of each system. The calculation abides by the rule: if two questions are the same, then two systems would be added by one and the student can choose to select none. The rule allows for the situation in which the students are satisfied with either choice. Each student will ask 10 questions. And we do the experiment for 10 times. Each time, the number of the related pattern would be different in the improved mode, from 20, 40 , , , to 200. And figure 4 describes the result of our experiments.

the ratio
of
correctness

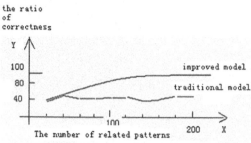

Figure 4 The comparison of these two modles

We find that when we don't use the result of the data mining, the ratio of the correctness is around 41%, and with the number of the related patterns increases, the ratio of the correctness is increasing to around 87%. So, our model is flexible in find the suitable related question.

5. CONCLUSION

The improved model is based on the analysis of traditional answering model. Considering the characteristics of the data of the answering system, apply the generalization and multi-level mining to improve the intelligence of the answering system. But in the determination of the function to calculate the relativity can be improved when we do more experiments. And in the preprocess of the generalization, multi-level mining and the merge and deletion of the redundant associations must be improved through research.

REFERENCES

Stefano Renzi, Steps toward computer-supported collaborative learning for large classes, Educational Technology & Society 3(3) 2000

SRIKANT RAGRAWAL R. Mining generalized association rules[A]. VL DB 9 5[C] .Zurich:[n s] ,1995

Yunfei Jian. Intelligent Teaching Plan based Knowledge Structure Graphic [J].Computer Research and Development, 1998(9):787—792

HAN Jiawei, FU Yongjian. Discovery of multiple level association rules in large databases [A]. VL DB 9 5[C] .Zurich:[n s] , 19 9 5.1

Micheline Kamber,Lara Winstone. Generalization and Decision Tree Induction:Efficient Classification in Data Mining. 7th International Workshop on Research Issues in Data Engineering (RIDE '97) High Performance Database Management for Large-Scale Applications 1997(4):111-120

Jiawei Han and Yongjian Fu . Dynamic Generation and Refinement of Concept Hierarchies for Knowledge Discovery in Databases. KDD Workshop 1994 : Seattle, Washington, USA 1994:157-168

JiaWei Han, Micheline Kamber. Data Mining Concepts and Techs. Morgan Kaufmann Press. 2001.150-183

PART 3

Information Systems Analysis and Specification

THE RELEVANCE OF A GLOBAL ACCOUNTING MODEL IN MULTI-SITE ERP IMPLEMENTATIONS

Ksenča Bokovec

Sapphir Management Consulting d.o.o, Ul. Malci Beliceve 46, Ljubljana, Slovenia
Email: ksenca.bokovec@sapphir.si

Talib Damij

Faculty of Economics, University of Ljubljna, Slovenia
Email: talib.damij@uni-lj.si

Keywords: Enterprise resource planning, global implementation, accounting

Abstract: ERP systems and their processes are cross-functional. They transform companies' practice from traditional functional and local oriented environments to global operations, where they integrate functions, processes and locations. They can support company-specific processes in the framework of globally defined organisational structures and procedures if properly implemented. This paper seeks to contribute to the area of multi-site ERP implementations. A case study from several companies in a large retail corporation is presented, focusing on the global accounting model from the perspective of an ERP implementation project. This case study analyses the most important elements of a globally designed financial and management accounting model and their 'translation' to the structures and processes of the ERP system. Moreover, It demonstrates the importance of the application methodology in early project phases. Central standardisation and maintenance issues of the global accounting model are also outlined.

1 INTRODUCTION

Enterprises are nowadays moving away from nationally oriented businesses to international, dispersed patterns of work and co-ordination. This new business environment necessarily brings many changes not only to the way companies operate but also to the information technology which supports the enterprises. A modern enterprise today is a global corporation and it needs an up-to-date technology to support its multi-site operations.

Historically, international firms have managed their business on a country level with different, non-integrated information systems. There were a few exceptions like Hewlett Packard (Lee and Billington, 1995) and Ford (Treece et al., 1995). On the other hand, such a high level of international co-ordination was not necessary, because companies were mostly nationally oriented and innovative supply chain strategies had not yet been in place.

To improve the management of global operations and assure better co-ordination of a firm's internal and external activities across the world, legacy information systems have been replaced by modern Enterprise Resource Planning systems designed to support global corporations. ERP systems have become the de facto standard for international organisations (Holland and Light, 1999). SAP for example supplied 60% of the ERP used by multinational companies (Bowley, 1998). ERP systems are a corporate marvel with a huge impact on both the business and information technology worlds (O'Leary, 2000).

In this article we are going to focus primarily on the globalisation of financial and management accounting models in a multinational corporation. The implementation of an integrated ERP system in an international multi-site environment is a highly complex activity. Globalisation requires tight co-ordination of activities, standardisation and the setting of a common strategy in all parts of the organisation. One of the primary areas in an organisation where these guidelines need to be followed is financial and management accounting. Therefore it is particularly important to recognise those features and capabilities of ERP systems

O. Camp et al. (eds.), Enterprise Information Systems V, 195-203.

which can support a multi-site environment from the financial and management accounting point of view. The characteristics which ensure the development of a multi-national accounting system are:

- multi-lingual environment,
- multi-currency environment,
- flexible organisational structures and
- country specific-solutions.

The objective of this study was to present those elements of a global accounting system which would enable a multi-national corporation to support:

- a common accounting system on the corporate reporting level,
- country-specific accounting systems on a country/company reporting level and
- synergy of the country specific and global accounting systems.

2 THE RESEARCH METHOD

The research method employed was a case study, since ERP systems are a modern information technology concept where qualitative research methods can be effectively applied. Multiple case design is an intensive empirical research approach suited to the study of emerging and complex phenomena (Yin, 1994). Case study research is also the most common qualitative method used in information systems (Orlikowski and Baroudi, 1991). Researching the globalisation of accounting models is primarily an organisational issue, which has to be supported by the appropriate information technology in order to yield the expected results. The case study research method is particularly well-suited to IS research, since the object of our discipline is the study of information systems in organisations and - according to Benbasat – interest has shifted to organisational rather than technical issues (Benbasat et al., 1987).

The major research questions were:

1. How should the global organisational structure ensuring a global accounting system be implemented in the ERP system?
2. Which accounting elements should be globalised to ensure common corporation-wide reporting?
3. How to ensure simultaneously that the legal country- specific accounting requirements can be followed?

For this research we chose five companies from the retail industry. In accordance with the objectives of this study a multi-site case approach was used in order to understand the nature and complexity of the processes taking place (Benbasat et al., 1987, Eisenhardt, 1989).

All chosen retail firms, which belonged to the same multi-national corporation, were in different countries to respect the truly multi-site and multi-national basis of this research. In order to understand the importance of a global financial and management accounting system for a multi-national corporation, companies were selected which had large differences in their national accounting systems and were undergoing one of the phases of a common corporate-wide ERP implementation project. The main facts underpinning this case study were:

- The chosen ERP system was SAP R/3 with industry solution 'Retail'.
- All five companies at the time of this study were engaged in one of the phases of the ERP implementation project.
- All five companies had their own more or less sophisticated legacy accounting systems, which were partially or non- integrated with their retail POS and back-office systems.
- All five companies used their national accounting standards and kept local books only.
- Country-specific reporting was prepared in their legacy accounting systems and partially in Excel.
- Corporate-wide reports were prepared manually in Excel on the basis of data extracted from the legacy accounting systems.

The implementation approach used was the roll-out approach. The roll-out approach creates a model implementation at one site, which is then rolled out to other sites (Welti, 1999). However, in this common roll-out approach in four of the chosen companies we used a big-bang approach implementing all modules of IS Retail at once using a pilot retail store, and in one company a phased approach starting with financials and partially controlling modules without a pilot store. The roll-out approach was thus used on 2 levels:

- The roll-out of a certain number of retail stores in each company.
- The roll-out of the model company to other companies in other countries.

2.1 Data collection

We used qualitative open-ended interviews, as well as quantitative response forms with quantified responses, from multiple respondents in each company and in the corporation's headquarters. We grouped interviews in two groups: (1) representing country views, (2) representing corporate-wide views. We analysed them separately to be able to find the main problem areas between national and global accounting approaches. This enabled us to achieve the triangulation of data and insights (Broadbent et al., 1999).

We also analysed the organisational documentation, internal reports and accounting standards of each country. Of particular importance was the analysis of the legacy accounting systems which gave us insight into the practices and results of their accounting procedures and reporting. In this way we were able to estimate the effort necessary to produce country-specific legal and corporate-wide reports. This would give us a certain comparison with the effort expected after the implementation of the new ERP global accounting system.

We also analysed in depth the global corporate-wide accounting practice designed to enable production of common consolidated balance sheets and P&L statements.

2.2 Case data

In the framework of our research we included five companies of a multi-national corporation. For the purpose of this study we named this corporation ReCor. ReCor is a US based global corporation with affiliates in over 100 countries all over the world. Its business is divided into two main sectors – (1) the wholesale sector, which includes some production companies and (2) the retail sector. Our case study companies belonged to the retail sector. In each country there was typically one retail company which had stores all over the country. We named these companies RC1 through RC5.

All retail companies sell convenience products in their shops. They purchased goods from two sources: 80% of the articles were purchased directly from the ReCor wholesale companies (we named them WHC) while 20% of the articles were purchased from other national suppliers, which had to be chosen from the ReCor list of preferred suppliers for each country. There was a WHC company in each country. The national RC company(ies) directly traded with the WHC company from the same country. The business of each pair of wholesale and retail national companies

was tightly connected. The hierarchically structured reporting relationship is shown in Figure 1.

First each retail company reported its financial, purchase and sales figures periodically to the wholesale company from the same country. The wholesale company prepared a consolidated financial, purchase and sales report and sent it to the next level, the corporate information system, where global consolidated reports were produced.

In parallel consolidated reports associating data from all world RC companies were also produced in ReCor headquarters (these were rather summary reports since RC companies do not trade with each other).

3 THE ERP PROJECT

When we started our research the ERP implementation project had already been under way for some time. It began in 1997 in one of the countries in the European Union. The reason for starting the project on an 'ad hoc basis' was to ensure the replacement of the old legacy system with a new information system which would ensure a smooth transition to the Y2K and Euro conversion. Therefore the project was not prepared in a globally strategic way from the very beginning which later caused numerous problems, particularly in the financial and accounting area. The ERP system was implemented based only on country-specific requirements, although ReCor financial guidelines had been already in use in certain WHC companies. The resulting strategic response often requires new ways of work and new organisational forms which are underpinned by information systems (Holland and Light, 1999). It is necessary that business and IT strategies should be aligned (Henderson and Venkatraman, 1991; Reich and Benbasat, 1996). We had to align the project with the global perspective to fulfil ReCor's requirements and assure appropriate reliability, comparability and controllability of RC companies' data. We started this case study research at the end of 2000. Our aim was to determine global financial and accounting elements and translate them into appropriate ERP structures and functions in order to use them in the subsequent country roll-outs. We took ReCor strategic financial and management accounting guidelines and rules as a basis.

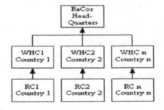

Figure 1: Reporting structure in ReCor

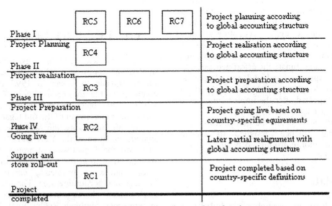

Figure 2: ERP implementation project development

Figure 2 shows the development of the ERP project in RC companies during the start-up in 1997 and the adoption of the case study research. In the meantime the results of the case study research were successfully applied and incorporated in the relevant phases of RC3 and RC4 projects as further roll-outs.

We found it particularly important for project success in which phase the new global approach in the accounting model was introduced. Most projects fail in the definition phase, since concepts are usually a bit fuzzy at the beginning (Lewis, 2001). The planning phase, where the concepts were developed, proved to be the most decisive phase for the success of the project. We measured its success by the extent to which it met the planned objectives, time frame and budget. At the moment of writing this paper, companies RC3 and RC4 have gone live successfully in line with the new global accounting model. In all other planned project roll-outs we also adopted the new design from the planning phase on. Company RC2 was later partially adjusted to the new design, which proved to be a tiresome and time consuming process causing substantial additional

costs. Company RC1 is still running in the framework of its country-specific design. Its accommodation to the new global design will require substantial additional effort and costs. However, there is a corporate requirement that companies RC1 and RC2 become global accounting model compliant in the next two years, because their data lack reliability and comparability.

4 THE ELEMENTS OF A GLOBAL ERP ACCOUNTING MODEL

The main processes in the RC companies researched were sales and purchase. Both processes needed to be redesigned to a certain extent during the ERP implementation to be in line with ERP best practice solutions for retail companies. Some BPR is inevitable, particularly when legacy systems are involved (Parr and Shanks, 2000).

Financial values flowing into and out of these processes always resulted in financial accounting.

In the legacy system work was mostly done manually or by means of interfaces, which updated financial ledgers in certain predefined time intervals. With the usage of the new highly integrated ERP system the accounting system was updated on-line. Since one of the objectives of the ERP project was to unify the processes in all RC companies, this also had impact on the accounting systems.

Table 1 demonstrates the common global accounting elements which were evaluated as decisive for ERP implementation. The implementation of global accounting elements ensured the interconnectivity of specific financial and management accounting systems of RC and WHC companies, as well as corporate main headquarters accounting system.

4.1 Organisational Structure

The organisational structure in terms of entities used in an ERP system reflecting the company's organisation was the basis for the implementation of the global accounting system. As our ERP system was SAP R/3 we used its internal enterprise structures to depict different levels of the corporate organisation, ensuring comparability of different business sectors and departments across the whole corporation and its constituent companies.

Table 1 - Global accounting system elements

ERP accounting element	Global element	Local element	Remark
Organisational Structure			
Company code		Local	Used for each legal entity
Business area	Global		Global list of business areas was defined
Functional area	Global		Global list of functional areas was defined
Controlling area	Global		One controlling area was defined for all RC companies
Profit centres	Global		One structure of profit centres was defined for all RC companies
Operating concern	Global		One operating concern was defined for all RC companies
Chart of Accounts			
Common corporate accounts	Global		Defined in the corporation headquarters
Local accounts		Local	Defined in the corporation headquarters
Corporate accounts	Global		Defined in the corporation headquarters
Currency and Foreign Exchange			
Company (country currency)		Local	Local currency used for statutory reports in each country
Parallel currency	Global		Corporation currency (USD)
Valuation methods	Global		Used for realised and unrealised gains and losses in all countries
Valuation procedures	Global		Depending on the company's local currency
Language			
Primary ERP language	Global		English
Country language		Local	Used only for statutory reporting

Each of the six elements was used for a particular reporting purpose:

- Company code: used for legal statutory reporting,
- Business area: used for reporting by main business lines (wholesale, production, retail),
- Functional area: used for cost-of-sales accounting method,
- Controlling area: used for management accounting and cost allocations,
- Profit centres: used for internal profitability reporting,
- Operating concern: used for external, market oriented profitability reporting.

This approach also allowed us to report in the general corporate consolidated reporting system alongside different business lines, companies, and internal and external profitability segments, since they were clearly identified by means of ERP enterprise structure entities.

4.2 Chart of Accounts

Each chart of accounts should be a detailed and ordered list of value categories in which the economic situation of a company can be recorded. Most legal systems insist on being able to scrutinise a set of financial documents for the group as a whole and for each of the constituent companies (ASAP World Consultancy, 1998).

It was therefore necessary to set-up a global chart of accounts which would ensure statutory and corporate-wide reporting on several levels:

- Global, group level (common, group accounts),
- Local, country level (local accounts in accordance with the legal requirements of different countries),
- Headquarters level (headquarters accounts according to US legal requirements).

Some of the countries (e.g. companies RC2 and RC3) had no special legal requirements regarding accounts, meanwhile others (e.g. companies RC4 and RC5) were obligated to use country-specific accounts. Figure 3 shows different combinations of accounting ledgers for multi-level reporting.

All RC companies in our case study had to use the global set of accounts, which contained all the necessary accounts. Company RC2 used only global accounts and did not have to make double postings. Companies RC3 and RC4 used global and some local accounts for statutory reporting

purposes and in these cases performed double postings to corporate only and local ledgers (this approach was used for certain concepts like legal reserves, payroll taxes and fixed assets where the corporate headquarters used different calculation methods according to US law).

Applying this kind of chart of the accounts structure, we ensured consistent reporting on a country level as well as on a corporate wide level, respecting different accounting standards. After month-end or year-end closure no re-postings, aggregations or mapping of accounts was needed. The companies' books were simply incorporated in the corporate-wide accounting system, since the principle of account, concept and organisational structure match was respected from the lowest level on.

4.3 Currency and Foreign Exchange

In a global corporation companies usually operate in different monetary environments. On one hand there are companies with stable currencies and on the other there are companies in countries where the inflation rate can be relatively high. Moreover, there are often requirements to show corporate books in a common corporate currency valid for the whole group.

In our case study research four companies were from the European Union, while one was from Latin America. We had two kinds of foreign exchange environments.

1. EUR → stable environment (companies RC1, RC2, RC4, RC5)
2. LAC[1]→ unstable environment (company RC3)

Since SAP R/3 is designed to handle a multi-currency environment it was possible to establish several currency levels:

- Transaction currency (document currency),
- Local currency (in which company books were managed),
- Group currency (USD).

---

[1] LAC stands for a fictitious Latin America currency

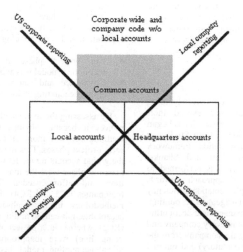

Figure 3: Reporting views in the global accounting system

By setting a group currency in USD every posting in the system was reflected simultaneously in local and group currencies, translated at the current exchange rate between the local currency and USD. As result of the multi-level currency design and stable versus unstable monetary environments, a complex global foreign exchange model was defined with the following elements:

- Accounts to be translated,
- Valuation methods for different monetary environments,
- Posting procedures for valuation results,
- Usage of different exchange rate lists (average rate, month-end rate etc.).

At month end after the automatic valuation process was performed all accounts were reflected in the group currency with respective exchange rates depending on the monetary environment. Using this global foreign exchange model USD ledgers were prepared for corporate reporting without major effort.

4.4 Language

All major ERP systems support a multi-language environment. SAP R/3 for example supports an increasing number of languages. Global corporations usually decide to use one language only.

Corporation ReCor decided to use English as the main operational language in all constituent companies. This means that system customising was done in English and that the logon language was also English. The method is based on a set of standard texts assigned to reports, screen displays and printed documents (ASAP World Consultancy, 1999). Every company had to use SAP functionality in the English language. In general there were two issues influencing language usage:

- The level of English knowledge in different countries and
- The requirement to produce statutory reports in the country-specific language.

The decision to use English was based on the fact that many ERP settings would have to be customised in both, the corporate and country-specific languages in order to function correctly. This would incur additional costs and ReCor decided to allow only one language – English. There was however still the problem with the statutory reporting which was solved by introducing an alternative chart of accounts for each country, where the global accounts in English had a description in the domestic language. All corporate-wide reporting was however performed in English (logon language) using standard SAP functionality.

In certain countries (companies RC2, RC3 and RC4) the knowledge of English among users was at a pretty low level and therefore we experienced a certain language barrier which influenced training and work. But, on the other hand, many consulting days were saved, since customising and master data definition was prepared in only one language.

5 CONCLUSION

Since there is evidence that the overwhelming majority of ERP implementations exceed their budget and their time allocations, research has begun to analyse ERP implementation in Case Studies in order to provide an implementation framework which maximises efficiency (Parr and Shanks, 2000). Our case study research was performed to contribute a methodological approach towards maximising global ERP implementation efficiency in the field of financial and management accounting. Nevertheless, financial and management accounting underpins the overall business in every company and is a key function in managing the company from the point of view of its external (statutory) and internal relationships. For our case study research this was the guideline which led us to start our research in the accounting field.

We came to the conclusion that there were four global accounting elements which were decisive for successful ERP implementation in a global multi-national corporation. These four elements – organisational structure, chart of accounts layout and usage, currency model and language – played the key role in the global standardisation and unification of corporate business procedures. Not only that they unified and standardised organisational entities throughout the corporation and its constituent companies, but they also allowed the usage of a common chart of accounts independent of the country-specific and legal requirements. Using this methodology companies could avoid double work in preparing corporate and company specific reports. No mapping of specific and corporate accounts was necessary as was usually the case in legacy systems, as well as some modern ERP implementations. By means of a global accounting model we managed to use one global chart of accounts and one global organisational structure for several reporting levels – global, local and corporate-only, which significantly reduced the implementation and maintenance complexity.

Using this methodology we could significantly reduce the time and costs of every further roll-out implementation. We calculated that the implementation time for companies RC3 and RC4 was reduced by 30% in comparison with companies RC1 and RC2. With continuous refinement of this model we expect even bigger time and cost savings in future implementations (RC5, RC6 and RC7).

However we have to mention two issues which we found extremely important for the successful application of this methodology:

- The project phase in which the global accounting model was applied and
- Centralised and standardised maintenance of global accounting elements.

By assessing the implementation time of each RC project it became obvious that the use of this methodology was more efficient if applied in the early project phases. This means that projects where the global accounting model was already used in the planning phase were the most successful in terms of time and effort needed for their completion (companies RC3 and RC4). The application of the methodology in the realisation phase was still acceptable, but caused additional effort and changes (RC2), whereas later project phases (preparation and going live) were inappropriate for applying the global accounting model, because the system was based on other design principles. The transition to the global accounting model (company RC1) would require a whole new project due to the significant changes in the ERP design in a company with a 'live' system. Every change has to be done without influencing daily operational work.

We also have to stress the importance of the central maintenance of global accounting elements. Using a global model means that all its elements have to be centrally defined and maintained. For this purpose a special support group was established in the ReCor headquarters which managed the global accounting model. Countries had to adhere to these standards. Organisational entities in SAP R/3 and their purpose was strictly defined and numbered by the central support group. The basic set of global and corporate accounts was also prepared centrally. Every new account request which was of a local nature had to be forwarded to the central support group for approval. A common chart of accounts and an organisational structures database was managed which contained global, local and corporate accounts as well as predefined organisational structures with comprehensive explanations. Countries could then choose accounts and other elements from the central database. Sometimes we experienced long response times from the central support group, but on the other hand there were many advantages in the central management of global accounting elements.

The globalisation of ERP implementation had a broad impact on corporate processes in the field of financial and management accounting, at the same time influencing all other business functions as well.

ERP embodies the essence of organisation, its structures, processes and the roles of individuals (Holland and Light, 1999).

REFERENCES

ASAP World Consultancy, 1998. *Administering SAP R/3: The FI-Financial Accounting and CO-Controlling Modules,* Que Corporation. USA.

ASAP World Consultancy, 1999. *Using SAP R/3,* Que Corporation. USA, Special Edition.

Benbasat I., Goldstein D.K., Mead M., 1987. *The Case Research Strategy in Studies of Information Systems,* MIS Quarterly (11:3). Pp. 369-386.

Bowley G, 1998. *Silicon Valley's Transplanted Sapling,* Financial Times, March 27, 1998.

Broadbent M., Weill P., St. Clair D., 1999. *The Implications of Information Technology Infrastructure for Business Process Redesign,* MIS Quarterly (23:2). Pp. 159-182.

Eisenhardt K.M., 1989. *Building Theories from Case Study Research,* Academy of Management Review (14:4). Pp. 532-550.

Henderson J.C., Venkatraman N., 1991. *Understanding Strategic Alignment,* Business Quarterly, Winter, 1991. Pp. 72-78.

Holland C.P., Light B.,1999. Global Enterprise Resource Planning Implementation. In *Proceedings of the 32nd Annual Hawaii International Conference on System Sciences IEEE.* Computer Society Press. Los Alamitos, CA.

Lee H.L., Billington C., 1995. *The Evolution of Supply-Chain Management Models and Practice at Hewlett-Packard,* Interfaces, Vol.25, No. 5. Pp.42-63.

Lewis J.P., 2001. *Project Planning Scheduling and Control: A Hands-on Guide to Bringing Projects in on Time and on Budget,* McGraw-Hill. New York.

O'Leary D.E., 2000. *Enterprise Resource Planning Systems: Systems, Life Cycle, Electronic Commerce, and Risk,* Cambridge University Press. Cambridge, UK.

Orlikowski, W.J., Baroudi, J.J., 1991. *Studying Information Technology in Organisations: Research Approaches and Assumptions,* Information Systems Research (2). Pp. 1-28.

Parr A.N., Shanks G., 2000. A Taxonomy of ERP Implementation Approaches. In *Proceedings of the 33rd Hawaii International Conference on System Sciences.* Computer Society Press. Los Alamitos, CA.

Reich B.H., Benbasat I., 1996. *Measuring the Linkage between Business and Information Technology Objectives,* MIS Quarterly, May, 1996. Pp. 55-81.

Treece J.B., Kerwin K., Dawley H., 1995. *Alex Trotman's Daring Global Strategy.* Business Week, 3 April, 1995. Pp. 36-44.

Yin, R., 1994. *Case Study Research: Design and methods,* Sage Publications.., Newbury Park, CA, 2nd edition.

TOWARDS THE ENTERPRISE ENGINEERING APPROACH FOR INFORMATION SYSTEM MODELLING ACROSS ORGANISATIONAL AND TECHNICAL BOUNDARIES

Remigijus Gustas, Prima Gustiené

Information System Department, Karlstad University, Sweden
Email: Remigijus.Gustas@kau.se, Prima.Gustas@kau.se

Keywords: Enterprise engineering, semantics, pragmatics, technical and organisational system components

Abstract: Enterprise Engineering proved to be useful when a generally accepted intentional description of information system is not available. A blueprint of enterprise infrastructure provides a basis for system analysis of the organizational and technical processes. It is sometimes referred as enterprise architecture. The major effort of this paper is the demonstration of how to bridge a gap among various levels (syntactic, semantic and pragmatic) of enterprise engineering. Most information system engineering methodologies are heavily centred on system development issues at the implementation level. Thus, such methodologies are restrictive in a way that a supporting technical system specification can not be motivated or justified in the context of organizational process models. Enterprise models provide a basis for gradual understanding of why and how various technical system components come about. Some undesirable qualities of enterprise engineering are sketched in this paper.

1 INTRODUCTION

Business process improvement is a major concern for today's organisations. The interorganisational parts of businesses are particularly problematic for change management. Enterprise engineering deals with modelling and integration (Vernadat, 1996) of various organisational and technical parts of business processes. The concept of enterprise in the context of information system development denotes a limited area of activity in the organisation (Bubenko, 1993) that is of interest by a system analysis expert. At the same time, enterprise engineering can be viewed as an extension and generalisation of the system analysis and design phase. Enterprise modelling should take place during the early, middle and late information system development life cycle. The most difficult part of enterprise modelling is to convert fuzzy requirements into a coherent, complete and consistent specification of the desired information system.

Traditional methods of information system analysis and design are based on the idea of a separation of concerns, which are represented by using various static and dynamic diagrams. Although there is a great power of traditional approaches, there is also a deep fallacy in this orientation. Semantic diagrams of traditional methods usually do not take into account interdependencies of various diagrams as well as the communication dependencies among organisational and technical system components. In industry, this often results in huge financial resources being wasted for IT system development without a significant impact. One of the major reasons of such failures is a communication gap between the management and IT development personnel. Many software maintenance problems arise because every enterprise has to survive a systematic change when new software is introduced.

Various studies of change management problems in different companies and in the public sector have demonstrated that an explicit representation of the organisational and technical system infrastructure is necessary to understand orderly transformations of existing work practices. If the initial software requirements are presented without taking into consideration a context of the organisation, then the requirements engineering approach can not be considered as viable, because it is not able to address the issues of software quality and IT fitness. A blueprint of the enterprise infrastructure provides a basis for the organization's information technology planning. It is referred to as enterprise architecture (Zachman, 1996). Just as the complex buildings or

204

O. Camp et al. (eds.), Enterprise Information Systems V, 204-215.
© 2004 *Kluwer Academic Publishers. Printed in the Netherlands.*

machines require explicit representations of design structures, so does an invisible enterprise infrastructure. It needs to be captured, visualised and agreed upon (Gustiene & Gustas, 2002). There is no way to study the fitness of the organizational and technical process without taking into account an infrastructure of the existing system prior to the designing a new one.

R. L. Ackoff has identified various causes of misunderstanding (Ackoff, 1989) among information system developers and system users. The condition, under which an information system developer knows what information is needed for the user, is when he has a complete understanding of how an overall system is functioning. It is not so easy to attain such understanding, if developers do not know what organisational and technical system components are and how they are supposed to interact. The trouble is that without complete understanding of organisational architecture, stakeholders have no criteria for determination the irrelevance or ambiguity of the information flows. That is why users frequently are misunderstood or they are provided by ambiguous, incomplete and inconsistent solutions.

Misunderstanding between information system users and designers is a common problem. Precondition of a successful requirement engineering process is a mutual understanding. It can not be achieved without close cooperation of both parties. The problem is that the users do not want to be the software engineering experts. On the other hand, the designers have difficulties to understand the organizational system requirements in which the supporting software system is supposed to operate. According to the enterprise modelling approach (Gustas, 2000), one of the problems in most of conventional software development approaches is that the implementation level requirements can not be represented without taking into consideration the organisational requirements, because they are not able to address some extremely important issues of software quality and IT fitness.

Organisational systems must adopt to fast changing conditions of environment in order to survive. Thus, they are in the process of permanent change. One of the common software development failures is that, by the time the information system application is produced, quite often it is no longer relevant to the existing work practices (Zachman, 1996). Software system problems very often occur for a simple reason that various applications do not fit or they can not support the organisational components as it was anticipated. There are some important attempts to overcome the software component fitness and integration problems by designing software in a non traditional way. The Lyee methodology (Negoro, 2001) is a way for building software on a basis of various logical structures of layouts (Gustas & Gustiene, 2002) by which information system users are supported in performing their tasks.

Every enterprise has to survive a systematic change at a time when the new software is introduced. Various studies of change management problems in different companies have demonstrated that the explicit representation of the business infrastructure is a necessary condition to understand orderly transformations of their work practices. They need to be guided to achieve a mutual agreement on how the logical design should look like. Such agreement can not be reached without a complete understanding of how overall information system is working.

Many customer organisations have information technology (IT) experts that are able to present various screen, printout and data file layouts to be implemented. Nevertheless, in many cases logical design structures can not be identified without a complete understanding of how an overall information system is working. A long list of software system development failures demonstrates that in many cases such understanding is not available. Furthermore, the customers have great difficulties to capture and to communicate unambiguously (Gustiene & Gustas, 2002) information system requirements by using natural language.

The paper is organised as follows. In the next section three levels of enterprise engineering are shortly introduced. The third, fourth and the fifth section defines the basic elements and dependencies that are used at the pragmatic, semantic and syntactic level. The desirable qualities of enterprise engineering are discussed in the sixth section. The conclusion section outlines the perspective of enterprise engineering approach and the future work.

2 THREE LEVELS OF ENTERPRISE ENGINEERING

Small changes in the organisational infrastructure are sometimes introduced so fast that software system components tend to become obsolete very quickly. One of the major problems of enterprise engineering is that comprehensible analysis methods across organisational and technical system boundaries are not available. If the requirement engineers would like to understand why a technical system component is useful and how it fits into the overall organisational system, then at least three levels of information system models are necessary for maintenance of a systematic change:

- The pragmatic level,

- The semantic level,
- The syntactic level.

These levels can be viewed as three dimensions of requirements engineering (Pohl, 1993). The agreement dimension is dealing with the pragmatic aspects of change analysis, the representation dimension – with the semantic aspects of system analysis and the specification dimension – with the implementation oriented system design aspects.

The most abstract is the strategy-oriented business process analysis level, which sometimes is referred to as pragmatic level. Strategic models are useful for illustration of the actual architectural solutions and general communication infra structure. They are necessary to provide motivation behind new business solutions that can be expressed in qualitative and quantitative terms. The semantic level must have a capacity to describe clearly the static and dynamic structures of business processes across organisation and technical system boundaries. The syntactic level should define implementation-oriented details, which explain the data processing needs of a specific application (Davis & Olson, 1985) or software component.

Most software methodologies are heavily centred on the implementation level. Thus, they are restrictive in a way that a supporting system specification can not be motivated or justified in the context of organizational process models. The consequence is that to apply these approaches in some areas such as electronic commerce is not so simple. One of the problems is that business processes are spanning across organisational and technical system boundaries. These boundaries are not always clear. They are changing over time. If boundaries are not clearly identified and mutually agreed, then the result would be a misunderstanding (Gustiene & Gustas, 2002) between system users and designers.

The pragmatic level concentrates on a strategic description, i.e. it is supposed to give a definition of the "why" - a long term intention or a vision of the enterprise under development. A pragmatic description motivates various enterprise components at the semantic level. Sometimes, desired software components can be easily described before the goals are well understood. Elaboration of the objectives is then done backwards, by asking for the reason for existence of the introduced components. Information system methodologies recognise that it is not enough to concentrate distinctly on one of the levels.

The qualitative criteria of enterprise engineering are essential for understanding various issues of the organisational fitness. Nevertheless, it is rather unusual to see the quantitative aspects taken into account in the traditional approaches of information system analysis and design. The quantitative criteria

play an important role in order to assess the pragmatic value of a new organisational solution. The quantitative terms such as such as cost, revenue and profit are used in PENG method (Dahlgren et al., 2000). These notions are important to understand the economic value of the new business process. It should be noted that the foundation for system assessment in qualitative terms in PENG is missing.

In the enterprise engineering approach a communication paradigm-based modelling foundation (Gustas, 1997), (Gustas, 2000) is used that has been proved to be useful for representation of the qualitative aspects of business processes across technical and organisational boundaries. Currently, we are aiming at the extended enterprise modelling approach with an engineering process that is similar to what architects use when constructing buildings. The graphical models at various levels of abstraction are used for visualising and reasoning about information system quality. The ultimate goal of the enterprise modelling is to introduce a common basis for integration of various dependencies (Gustiene & Gustas, 2002) that are used in requirements engineering and conceptual modelling (Roland & Prakash, 2001) at the syntactic, semantic (Storey, 1993) and pragmatic level.

One of the most important problems of software engineering is to maintain the existing software. This problem is due to the fact that software development methods have adopted a purely process-driven or purely data-driven approach. During the last years a number of new methods have been developed, but still all these methods suffer from several drawbacks. Most of the methods use a mix of the natural language and semiformal graphical notations for the purposes of software requirement specification. The natural language comments quite often appear ambiguous. It causes semantic problems of misunderstanding (Gustiene & Gustas, 2002) among system users and system developers. Even though these problems were taken into consideration by the more powerful modelling techniques (Yourdon, 1989), (Booch at al, 1999), it did not help to control the integrity and consistency of specifications that are presented on various levels of abstraction.

Another big problem is the implementation bias of many information system modelling techniques. The same concepts have been applied to the design and analysis stages, without rethinking these concepts fundamentally. Modelling at the semantic level should follow the basic conceptualisation principles (Griethuisen, 1982). Only conceptually relevant aspects, both static and dynamic, should be included, thus excluding aspects of physical implementation.

Many methodologies lack a systematic approach to the assessment of software quality and change management. The idea of model-driven approach (Snoeck et al., 1999) is to provide solutions for solving such problems. Model-driven software development follows the idea, pioneered by Jackson, that the complexity of information system is driven by the complexity of the underlying world (Jackson, 1983). By analysing and modelling a so called enterprise infrastructure, not concentrating on the specification of the desired functionality, information system developers are able to better manage the complexity of a developed system.

Similarity of model-driven approach to most classical development methods is that the enterprise model, which is constructed in the early stage of software development, is an abstraction of what the desired system must do, but not how (Snoeck et al., 1999). Most current software development methods are centred on how a software application needs to be implemented. The separation between the pragmatic, semantic and syntactic - implementation based model leads to a natural division of enterprise engineering products into three different representations. It is more reasonable to conceptualise enterprise architecture and business processes before supporting software system is defined (Checkland, 1981). It seems not useful to model the real world having no functionality in mind. Hence, all three levels of models should contribute to the extended methodology of enterprise-wide engineering technique.

Information system semantics can be defined by using the static and dynamic dependencies of various kinds. Most of the semantic diagrams are based on the entity notations that are provided by several links. Links are established to capture semantic detail about various relationships among concepts. The ability to describe information system in a clear and sufficiently rich way is acknowledged as crucial in many areas. Typically semantic dependencies are defining semantics in different perspectives such as the "what", "who", "where", "when" and "how" (Zachman, 1996). For instance, in the object oriented approach (Martin & Odell, 1998) the "what" perspective is defined by using the class diagram, the "how" perspective can be defined by using the activity diagrams and the "when" perspective can be described by the state-transition diagrams.

3 PRAGMATIC LEVEL

Humans, technical systems or organisations can be thought as actors. Communication dependencies between actors involved describe the "who" perspective. Dependency link between two actors (agent and recipient) indicate that one actor depends on another actor. An agent can be an actor who is

able to initiate an action to achieve his goal. A recipient is an actor, who is dependent on the action performed by an agent. An instance of actor can be an individual, a group of people, an organisation, a machine, a software component, an information system, etc. The dependent actors in a diagram can be related by the actor dependency link (·····▶). The actor dependency is usually seen as a physical, information or a decision flow between two participants of a business process. Graphical notation of the actor dependency between an agent and a recipient is presented in Figure 1.

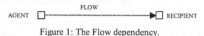

FLOW

AGENT □————————————————▶□ RECIPIENT

Figure 1: The Flow dependency.

If an actor B is dependent on A on some flow, then such dependency is represented as A ·····▶ B. A dependency link denotes that a recipient depends on an agent for some information, physical flow or an action. If actor B is dependent on A for a flow F, then this dependency is specified by the following expression: **A ·····▶ (F) ·····▶ B**. The flow dependency represents a communication channel for transferring of information or physical flow between agent and recipient.

A typical action workflow loop (Action Technologies, 1993) includes two communication flows sent into opposite directions. An agent is an actor who initiates the work flow loop to achieve his goal. A recipient of a communication flow can be viewed as an agent in the next communication action. Actor dependencies in two opposite directions imply that certain contractual relationships are established. For instance: If Person ·····▶ (Trip Requirements) ·····▶ Travel Agent then Travel Agent ·····▶ (Trip Reservation) ·····▶ Person. Various actor communication dependencies at a strategic level are illustrated in Figure 2.

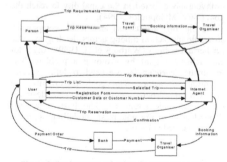

Figure 2: Basic communication flows among actors.

In this example, we can see various information flows among the actors such as User, Internet Agent, Bank and Travel Organiser. The middle part of this diagram illustrates the basic communication flows between User and Internet Agent in the process of making trip reservation by using the Travel Agent's web site. This part represents a simplified process of buying trips on the Internet. A lower part of the diagram demonstrates that the Bank is involved to handle a payment. A Travel Organiser delivers the actual Trip when the payment for the trip is made. A higher part of the diagram demonstrates the core communication loops in the traditional business process. This part represents a non-electronic way of buying trips. It can be overridden by the more specific interactions, should a person take a more specific role of a user or an agent would play a role of Internet Agent. It is not clear at this moment what kind of organisational or technical components in reality can be used to carry out this business process. This diagram represents just the actors involved and strategic dependencies among them. In general, the actor dependency links describe various ways of how agents can affect the recipients. At the semantic level, the actors can be decomposed or specialised by using dependencies of other kinds. For instance, the inheritance link was used to indicate that a User is more specific than Person and a Travel Agent is more general than Internet Agent.

If the communication flow is represented by a material object, then such dependency represents changes of the ownership right for this specific instance of a flow. Before sending it, an AGENT owns the FLOW and later, dependent on whether the flow would be accepted, the ownership right is transferred to a RECIPIENT. Recipient by depending on agent is able to achieve his goals. It should be noted that very often he is not able to achieve them alone. At the same time, a recipient becomes vulnerable to the failure of agent. If agent fails to deliver the flow, then a recipient would be unfavourably affected in the capability to reach the goal (Yu & Mylopoulos, 1994).

Goals of various organisational components stimulate interaction among actors, leading to some further interactions (Warboys et al, 1999). Any actor can achieve a goal by avoiding a problem. The pragmatic dependencies are used to define various intentions of actors. The goal, opportunity and problem dependencies can be used to refer desirable or not desirable situations. The basic pragmatic dependencies of the enterprise modelling approach are represented in Figure 3.

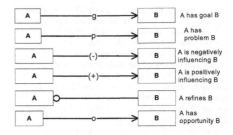

Figure 3: Notation of the pragmatic dependencies

Goals or problems can be decomposed by using a refinement link. It should be noted that the interpretation of some software requirement or situation as a problem, opportunity and goal is relative. The achievement of some goal by one actor can be regarded as a problem for another actor. Negative influence dependency (-) and positive influence dependency (+) are used to indicate influences. Negative influence dependency from situation A to B indicates that A can be regarded as a problem, because it hinders the achievement of goal B. The positive influence dependency from A to B would mean that A can be viewed as an opportunity in the achievement of goal B. A small example of the pragmatic dependencies is illustrated in Figure 4.

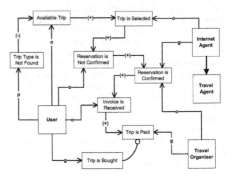

Figure 4: Illustration of the pragmatic dependencies.

The illustrated pragmatic dependencies were defined for the same process of buying trips on the Internet. These dependencies demonstrate how actors can affect each other by using their opportunities or achieving some goals. For instance, if Travel Organiser could reach the goal 'Trip is Paid', then it would automatically cause the achievement of User's goal 'Trip is Bought'. The 'Trip is Paid' state is positively influenced (+) by 'Invoice is Received', which is viewed as an opportunity for User.

The Internet Agent box at the syntactic level will play a role of software component. We are not going into details of some pragmatic dependencies, because of the space limitations. A discussion on this issue can be found at (Gustas, 1997), (Gustas, 1998).

4 SEMANTIC LEVEL

The semantic dependencies in the enterprise modelling are of two kinds: static and dynamic. Descriptions of organisational *activities* as well as *actors* involved in these activities are based on the dynamic dependencies. So, the dynamic part of the enterprise model can be represented by actions that are using and producing various communication flows and by actors that are responsible for initiation of those actions. The dynamic relations are state dependencies and communication dependencies. The communication dependencies among enterprise actors are relevant for description of the "who" perspective. It is based on the communication action tradition in information system development that is stemming from the Scandinavian approaches. During enterprise engineering process, the actor dependencies at the semantic level are refined into the action and state transition links.

Any flow dependency at the semantic level should be described in a more detail by using a communicative action. Therefore, the actor dependency is considered to be an action and a communication flow (Goldkuhl, 1995). Cohesion of action and communication flow at the semantic modelling level results into a more complex abstraction, which is entitled to as a communicative action (Gustas, 20000). In such a case, the flow dependency link between two actors specifies that the recipient depends on the agent not just only by the specific flow, but by the action as well. Actions will be represented by ellipse. Graphical notations of dynamic constituents in the extended communication flow and action dependency are represented in Figure 5.

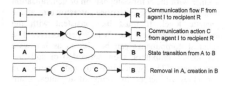

Figure 5: Graphical notation of the dynamic dependencies.

State dependencies define semantic relationships between states of actions. They are normally considered as the "how" perspective. Both state transition and communication dependencies describe a very important part of knowledge about business processes. Unfortunately, many communication approaches often neglect some behavioural aspects of the state transition and vice versa, many software engineering approaches disregard the dependencies of communication.

The static concept dependencies are used for the specification of attributes for various states of processes. They define the "what" perspective. These dependencies are stemming from various semantic models that are introduced in the area of information system analysis and design (Martin & Odell, 1998). Graphical notations of static dependencies are represented in Figure 6.

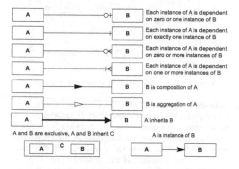

Figure 6: Graphical notation of the static dependencies.

The similarities can be shared between concepts by extracting and attaching them to a more general concept. In this way, all kinds of static and dynamic dependency links can be inherited by several concepts. Composition or aggregation dependency is useful for formation of a new concept as a whole from other concepts that might be viewed as parts.

Dynamic semantic dependencies are used to define relations between different actors, their actions and communication flows. If concept A is connected to B by a communication dependency, then A is an agent and B is a recipient. Depending on whether there is or there is no physical flow component in the action, the communication flows can be information, material or decision. The extended communication loops between User and Internet Agent in the initial part of process of buying trips on Internet are represented in Figure 7.

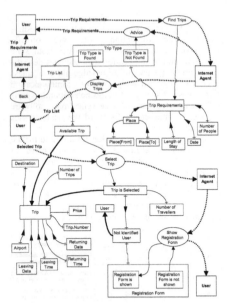

Figure 7: Reservation process at the semantic level.

It should be noted that the presented diagram is incomplete, but its communication dependencies and states are consistent with the previously defined basic constraints (see the diagrams at the pragmatic level). When Find Trips action is executed, then two outcomes are possible. If the desired 'Trip Type is Found', then a 'Trip List' object is created. It consists of 1 or many available trips (see the state 'Available Trip' at the semantic level and the opportunity of user at the pragmatic level). The trip list will be displayed in the next action. If the desired 'Trip Type is Not Found', then User is advised to start the process from the beginning and initial Trip Requirements are displayed. An available trip should satisfy the specific constraints (they are not presented in this paper). If trip is available, then a user can select a trip. If so, then the registration form will be shown to enter or verify user's identity data.

Any communication loop is able to change the static associations between instances. State changes are important to both actors. Without the ability to represent noteworthy state changes, we would have difficulties to understand the rational and effect of every communication loop. Actions express the permissible ways in which state changes may occur. These changes are specified by using the integrated dependency of communication and state transition (Gustas, 2000).

5 SYNTACTIC LEVEL

The enterprise modelling language should be able to represent graphically business processes across the organisational and technical (hardware and software) system boundaries. The outcome of the enterprise modelling effort can be defined in terms of components and their interfaces with the structural definition of the printout, message, screen and file layouts. These layouts can be viewed as syntactic elements of the actor oriented diagrams that define existing or expected communication infrastructures to support various actors involved. Enterprise models suggest a different way of defining the collaboration infrastructures that is based on an intentional way of thinking and on a new constructive way of reasoning.

Modelling primitives of the syntactic level are dependent on the tools, which are used in the software development process. For instance, the enterprise modelling approach that was specially designed for the Lyee methodology (Gustas & Gustiene, 2002) was build on the basis of syntactic elements that are represented in Figure 8.

Figure 8: Basic syntactic elements.

These syntactic elements are considered as the implementation perspective or CASE tool dependent. For example, database relations are typical representatives of the syntactic level. File or database layouts can be defined by using the conventional programming languages or traditional database definition languages. Almost the same set of syntactic elements could be used for the object-oriented approach. In this case, the notion of a file layout should be replaced by the notion of class layout (it would contain the operations as well).

Enterprise actors, which at the semantic level are represented by square boxes, at the syntactic level can be thought as humans or technical components. Communication flow dependencies among actors together with the actor composition or generalisation links might describe enterprise infrastructure at the syntactic level. It must be consistent with the previously described the "who" perspective. The technical components can be viewed as hardware (machines, computers, their networks) or software components. The generalisation and aggregation hierarchies of actors in terms of technical components that are used in different communication loops would motivate a relevant hardware or software system architecture. Typical instances of the actors in the area of information system development are represented by Figure 9.

Figure 9: Human and technical system components.

The presented list of the component classes is not exhaustive. Other types of icons such as fax machines, phones, computer networks, etc., can be introduced on demand. These components in combination with the basic layouts can be used as the main building blocks for representation of the technical deployment architecture, software component infrastructure or organisational dependency structure.

From the software component designer perspective, the definition of the software system architecture is not sufficient. The designers need to understand a technical system architecture and organizational infrastructure, where application is going to be installed. Therefore, the enterprise modelling approach focuses not just on the pragmatics and semantics, but also on the software deployment architecture. A small example for illustration of technical deployment details of two software components in the first interaction loop (see semantic level) is represented in Figure 10.

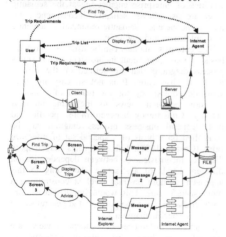

Figure 10: Human and technical system components.

This diagram illustrates that the Internet Agent software component is deployed on the Server and

the Internet Explorer will be used as a client. They are supposed to communicate via screen and message layouts that must have the identical underlying semantic structure as information flows such as Trip Requirements and Trip List. The deployment diagram represents a very important technical system requirements that should be communicated to a software engineer (designer as well as software builder) before a specification of the represented software system components commits.

The communication flow structures with the action names and the generalised state structures define a foundation for a specification of file and screen layouts. For instance, the concepts that are dependent of Trip (see the semantic diagram) constitute the foundation of the file layout that can be represented by the following relation:

TRIP (Trip Number, Destination, Airport, Leaving_Date, Leaving_Time, Returning_Date, Returning_Time, Number_of_Trips, Price).

When Find Trip action is receiving 'Trip Requirements' from a User, a Trip List object may be created, which consists of 1 or many available trips. If the desired 'Trip Type is Found', then the Trip List can be displayed. The flow of 'Trip Requirements' with all possible action names that could affect a course of the illustrated process, constitute the basis for definition of the first screen layout. It will be identified by Screen 1. Representation of the first screen layout at the syntactic level is represented in Figure 11.

Figure 11: Screen layout (Screen 1) of Trip Requirements.

The set of the enterprise modelling dependencies at the semantic level is a subject to the refinement into the implementation dependent structures. It should be noted that the syntactic diagrams are constrained by the dependencies at the semantic and pragmatic levels. The implementation dependent file, message, printout or screen layouts are supposed to define the operating infrastructure of software components. The example of syntactic diagram that is defined for the Internet Agent (IA) software component is represented in Figure 12.

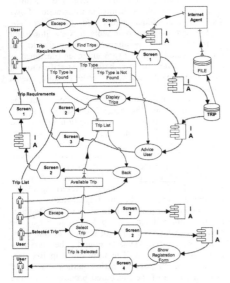

Figure 12: A syntactic diagram of the IA (Internet Agent) software component.

This diagram illustrates how the enterprise model at the semantic level is going to be implemented. Various previously defined semantic dependencies have to be taken into account by a more specific level. It means that the syntactic dependencies must be consistent with the higher levels of abstraction. A special inference rules can be defined in order to validate the semantic consistency. Thus, the enterprise engineering approach can be used as a uniform basis of reasoning about modelling quality at the pragmatic, semantic and syntactic quality.

6 DESIRABLE QUALITIES OF REPRESENTATIONS

Various diagrammatic constructions that humans employ for representation of information system solutions on different levels of abstraction can be evaluated by certain criteria. It means that 'good' diagrams should posses some important qualities. Such qualities are still poorly understood in the area of information systems. Nevertheless, these qualities are essential when the enterprise engineering

product is intended for effective communication of various architectural solutions among system designers and system users.

Lindland, Sindre and Solvberg (Lindland et al., 1994) has proposed a framework for understanding the syntactic, semantic and pragmatic quality. The syntactic quality can be characterised by correctness of modelling language. All constructions of diagrams have to be defined according to the syntax. Two characteristic features of the semantic quality are validity and completeness. Validity means that all statements in the model are relevant to the problem. Completeness means that the model contains all relevant statements. It is not easy to satisfy these two requirements, because we do not know how the semantic quality can be measured. A better pragmatic quality of system specification would mean that all concerned participants understand how the intended system is going to function and all stakeholders agree on what is going to be achieved. Misunderstanding and disagreement on some issues would automatically imply a lower pragmatic quality.

Identification of undesirable characteristics is critical at the semantic level. Semantic representations are defining and constraining the diagrams at the syntactic level. They should also support the diagrams that are defined on the pragmatic level. On the other hand, pragmatic representations should justify enterprise models at the semantic and syntactic level. The undesirable qualities of enterprise engineering at the semantic level are as follows: semantic inconsistency, semantic incoherence, semantic redundancy, semantic incompleteness and ambiguity.

The enterprise models can be used as a uniform basis of reasoning about inconsistency of business process diagrams that are defined on the various levels of abstraction. It is not so easy to attain semantic consistency for the reason of a natural variation between views to the same business activity. Consistency between more specific and more general business process diagram can be controlled on a basis of a special set of inference rules (Gustas, 1997). Inference rules may help to discover inconsistencies between dependencies on different levels of abstraction. According to this approach, a more abstract level is constraining a more specific one. This would imply that a more abstract diagram is a composition and generalisation of a more specific diagram.

Semantic differences of conceptual views are typically introduced by different visions of stakeholders. Inconsistencies between constructs of diagrams that are represented on two neighbouring levels of abstraction indicate that two diagrams are incompatible. This situation is referred to as inconsistent. Inconsistency demonstrates that the semantic descriptions of enterprise components are contradictory. Consistency issues have to be resolved before the engineering of any software component commits. Introduction of new organisational or technical component might be a reason of the new consistency problems that need careful analysis. Software component fitness to the existing work practices is one of the main issues that can be studied by using enterprise modelling.

Semantic incoherence can be defined as opposed to minimality (Weber, 2001). Minimality means that at some time during the life cycle of subsystem, all state variables are 'used'. Incoherence analysis in the enterprise engineering is questioning the integrity between computerised information system state change and communication flow internal structure. Any parameter of a communication flow is supposed to be used for some purpose. It might be a creation of object or deletion of object in some state. A communication action of removal in a specific state must destroy all association that are relevant for this state. A creation action must establish all relevant associations that are specified in the diagram, otherwise the action is rejected. Some actions can create and destroy associations at the same time. Such internal changes can be followed according to the static dependencies that are defined in various states (Gustas, 1998).

Communication flow parameters can be consumed or emitted by a predefined action. A consumption action is supposed to allocate parameter values into the correspondent state attributes. Every consumed parameter has to be defined in a postate of action. If a flow parameter is matching different name of the attribute, then an explicit computation rule for the attribute must be defined. Usage of any attribute should be questionable with respect to an overall structure of incoming flow. If an attribute is irrelevant for the action, then it should be removed. Any object can be terminated by a removal action. If so, then no attributes should be specified. Termination process can be represented by an action without a resulting state. In this case, no commitments of actors should be pending in connection to this state. A properly designed termination action should always emit information flow that is resulting from the deleted attributes values. Such flow can be viewed as a confirmation message to the initiator of action.

Semantic completeness of actions in all resulting branches is always relative. It is difficult to specify all imaginable alternatives of business process chains. However, it is rather easy to control a set of all final (desired) states for each actor. Each final state must be consistent with respect to some actor's goal. Goals define system boundary and therefore

may help designers to control a relative pragmatic completeness of a specific business process. A complete business process should consist of coherent actions and all interaction loops in a complete process must terminate. All final states must be desired by at least one of the actors. Besides that, all communication flow parameters should be consumed in action, otherwise they are not useful. If the final states are not desired by any actor or initial states are not problematic to any actor, then this would indicate overspecification or redundancy.

Semantic redundancy in general terms would mean that two different sets of semantic dependencies are used at the same time to express the same meaning. A special set of inference rules (Gustas, 1997) can be used to discover redundancy. If the inferred dependencies are represented in a same diagram, then they would indicate a situation of semantic redundancy. Semantic redundancy creates unnecessary 'noise', which is hindering effective communication among the members of enterprise engineering team. In traditional methods of information system development, structurally different, but semantically equivalent representations (Batini et al, 1986) is a reason of painful problems (Gustiene & Gustas, 2002)

Semantic incompleteness can be opposed to the characteristics of losslessness (Weber, 2001) and cohesion (Amber, 2001). Higher quality of semantic representation should preserve all emerging state dependencies and relevant heritable dependencies. Semantically incomplete representations of business processes can be characterised by the presence of semantic holes (Gustas, 1994). The semantic holes typically appear when a so called not totally applicable dependency is used. A totality of the static dependency would indicate that for any instance of one concept there is always an association to an instance of the dependent concept. Totality of the state transition dependency means that any object, which belongs to a current state, is applicable for the specified transition link. The totality of the actor dependency would mean that any instance, which is classified as an actor, is privileged to affect a dependent actor by initiation of the specified action, if certain preconditions and postconditions hold.

Ambiguity of concepts in the enterprise models indicates a low semantic quality of system specification. Very often it is the reason of incompleteness and poor understanding of what is going on in the business process. Sometimes, experienced system analysts can reason about concept dependencies even when various static and dynamic constraints are not precise. They also play out scenarios with the objects of ambiguous concepts and actively engage in analysis of semantic dependencies between actions and actors involved.

Some conceptual operations (Gustas, 1997) that are introduced in the enterprise modelling can be used as a means for clarification of meaning. These operations are useful to refine semantics of the compound natural language expressions. Compound concepts are introduced by different stakeholders in various stages of information system analysis. Very often ambiguous concepts contain semantic holes, which can be eliminated by using a special set of conceptual operations.

7 CONCLUDING REMARKS

We expect that the enterprise models can be used as a core method to analyse the rationale of the new organisational solution prior a new supporting IT system is introduced. It might help managers and IT experts to define, visualise and to assess various organisational changes by using a fully graphical approach to business process reengineering. This would in turn facilitate justification and motivation of software components that are used to support work of organisational actors involved in various business processes. Enterprise models can be considered as a corporate resource in diagnosing potential problems, these models are crucial to enable reasoning about business process integrity and the purposeful implications of an organisational change.

Analysing systems means creation of the shared set of concepts. Concepts must form a basis of communication among system analysts. To communicate effectively in a process of enterprise engineering, the experts must agree on mutually acceptable concepts that can be shared. A common situation in system engineering is one that refers to the semantically similar concepts. Similar concepts are represented by the same class of objects, yet these concepts do not share the same meaning. Typically, ambiguous concepts are represented by the long natural language expressions. Refinement of ambiguous concepts during the enterprise modelling process might help to sort out some problems of misunderstanding (Gustiene & Gustas, 2002). One simple approach to identify ambiguity problems in the enterprise models is based on the examination of semantic holes. Ideally, the analysts should insist on knowing the complete dependency set of every concept that is used in a semantic diagram.

System analysts in the area of enterprise engineering define first a very general and ambiguous business process scenario at the pragmatic level. Later, they gradually extend it by making a whole lot of assumptions into a well-defined and well-understood information system representation on the semantic level. On a way to unambiguous business process description, the analysts integrate various parts of specifications and play scenarios with objects of various types in order to validate and justify technical system components at the syntactic level. Semantically clean process description should consist of actions that are defined in terms of unambiguous concepts. The ultimate goal of the described ways for semantic quality improvement is to facilitate a process of enterprise engineering.

Enterprise models can be used for change analysis in a systematic way on a basis of the graphical representations that are defined for both traditional and electronic business. Our expectation is that enterprise modelling might help us to find solutions for the following difficult problems:

1) Ambiguity problem. Systems are spanning across organisational and technical system boundaries. These boundaries are changing over time and not always clear. That is why sometimes requirements specifications are ambiguous.

2) Integration problem. Various models are used for representation of static and behavioural system aspects. A clear way of integration between these models is missing. Enterprise models provide a very comprehensible foundation to understand the interplay between various syntactic, semantic and pragmatic dependencies.

3) Consistency problem. The same reality can be perceived in a number of ways and therefore intentions can be objectified on the various levels of abstraction. Consistent way of dealing with the pragmatic, semantic and syntactic representations of requirements is missing in most information system methodologies.

4) Completeness problem. There are no stopping rules for a process of information system requirement analysis. Pragmatic descriptions might suggest a way of dealing with the over specification at the semantic and at the syntactic level.

5) Change problem. Every new solution can be considered to be a symptom for a new problem. Change management problems can be tackled in a systematic way by using the extended approach.

Software systems should support business processes and software should be regarded as a value-added technology. If so, the technical processes must fit various organisational processes. Change management in the organisational part or in the technical (software) part of the system is a big challenge, because even a simple deviation from the traditional business practice may be considered as a symptom for a new problem. The key issue is determination of the true IT needs and how these needs are integrated into the overall organisational system.

Underlying communication dependencies between various actors play an important role in understanding of various e-business processes on a pragmatic level. A similar view is taken in some business process modelling approaches that are based on the communication paradigm (Winograd & Flores, 1986). A prerequisite of understanding between different groups of people and organisations is that business process components are structured on a basis of viable communication activities. Information system development methods that are able to adopt the communication paradigm can revolutionary change a way in which systems are analysed today. The new principles can not only improve communication between information system developers and users, but also might facilitate a mutual understanding among various stakeholders.

REFERENCES

Ackoff, R. L. (1989) "From Data to Wisdom: Presidential Address to ISGSR, June 1988", Journal of Applied System Analysis, Vol. 16, 3-9.

Action Technologies. (1993) Action Workflow Analysis Users Guide, Action Technologies.

Ambler (2001) The Object Primer – The Application Developer's guide To Object Orientation and UML, Cambridge University Press.

Booch, G., Rumbaugh, J. & Jacobsson, I. (1999) The Unified Modelling Language User Guide, Addison Wesley Longman, Inc., Massachusetts.

Bubenko, J. A. (1993) "Extending the Scope of Information Modelling", Fourth International Workshop on the Deductive Approach to Information Systems and Databases, Polytechnical University of Catalonia, 73-97.

Checkland, P. B. (1981) Systems Thinking, System Practice, Wiley, Chichester.

Dahlgren, L E, Stigberg, L and Lundgren, G (2000), Öka Nyttan av IT, Ekelids förlag (in Swedish).

Davis, G. B. & Olson, M. (1985) Management Information Systems, McGraw Hill, New York.

Griethuisen, J. J. (1982) Concepts and Terminology for the Conceptual Schema and Information Base, Report ISO TC97/SC5/WG5, No 695.

Gustas, R. (1997) Semantic and pragmatic dependencies of information systems, Monograph, Technologija, Kaunas.

Gustas, R. (1998) "Integrated Approach for Modelling of Semantic and Pragmatic Dependencies of Information Systems", Conceptual Modelling - ER'98, Springer, pp. 121-134.

Gustas, R. (2000) "Integrated Approach for Information System Analysis at the Enterprise Level", Enterprise Information Systems, Kluwer Academic Publishers, pp. 81-88.

Gustas, R. and Gustiene, P. (2002), "Extending Lyee Methodology using the Enterprise Modelling Approach", Frontiers in Artificial Intelligence and applications, IOS Press, Amsterdam, pp. 273-288.

Gustiene, P. & Gustas, R. (2002) "On a Problem of Ambiguity and Semantic Role Relativity in Conceptual Modelling", Proceedings of International conference on Advances in Infrastructure for e-Business, e-Education, e-Science, and e-Medicine on the Internet, ISBN 88-85280-62-5, L'Aquila, Italy.

Goldkuhl, G. (1995) "Information as Action and Communication", The Infological Equation, Goteborg University, Sweden, pp. 63-79.

Jackson, M. A. (1983) System Development, Prentice Hall, Englewood Cliffs, N.J.

Lindland, O. I., Sindre, G. and Solvberg, A. (1994) Understanding Quality in Conceptual Modelling, IEEE Software, (11, 2).

Martin, J. & Odell, J. J. (1998) Object-Oriented Methods: A Foundation (UML edition), Prentice-Hall, Englewood Cliffs, New Jersey.

Negoro, F. (2001) "Methodology to Define Software in a Deterministic Manner", Proceedings of ICII2001, Beijing, China.

Pohl, K. (1993) "The three Dimensions of Requirements Engineering", International Conference on Advanced Information System Engineeering – CAiSE'93, Springer Verlag.

Roland, C. & Prakash, N. (2001) From Conceptual Modelling to Requirements Engineering, Annuals of Software Engineering (to be published).

Snoeck, M., Dedene, G., Verhelst, M. & Depuydt, A. M. (1999) Object-Oriented Enterprise Modelling with MERODE, Leuven University Press.

Storey, V. C. (1993) "Understanding Semantic Relationships", VLDB Journal, F Marianski (ed.), Vol.2, pp.455-487.

Vernadat, F. B. (1996) Enterprise Modelling and Integration: Principles and Applications, Chapman & Hall, London.

Warboys, B., Kawalek, P., Robertson, I. & Grenwood, M. (1999) Business Information Systems: A Process Approach, McGraw-Hill Co., London.

Winograd, T. & Flores, R (1986) Understanding Computers and Cognition: A New Foundation for Design, Ablex Norwood, N.J.

Weber, R. (2001) Comprehending Decompositions: A Theory and Two Empirical Tests, unpublished manuscript.

Yourdon, E. (1989) Modern Structured Analysis, Prentice-Hall, Englewood Cliffs, N.J.

Yu, E. & Mylopoulos, J. (1994) "From E-R to 'A-R' - Modelling Strategic Actor Relationships for Business Process Reengineering", 13th International Conference on the Entity - Relationship Approach, Manchester, U.K.

Zachman, J. A. (1996) "Enterprise Architecture: The Issue of the Century", Database Programming and Design Magazine.

STRUCTURAL CONFLICT AVOIDANCE IN COLLABORATIVE ONTOLOGY ENGINEERING

Ziv Hellman, Amit Gal
Unicorn Solutions, Inc., New York City, USA
Email: *ziv@unicorn.com* , *amitg@klassi.org*

Keywords: collaborative ontology engineering, dependencies, dependency graphs

Abstract: Given the increasing importance of ontologies in enterprise settings, mechanisms enabling users working simultaneously to edit and engineer ontologies in a collaborative environment are required. The challenges that may arise in attempting to prevent structural conflicts when several users edit ontologies simultaneously are not trivial, given the high level of dependencies between concepts in ontologies. In this paper we identify and classify these dependencies. Sophisticated ontology locking mechanisms based on a graph depiction of the dependencies that are sufficient for preventing structural conflicts arising in collaborative settings are proposed. Applications of this research to the Semantic Web are also considered.

1   INTRODUCTION

Ontologies have served as major subjects of academic research for well over a decade (Smith and Welty, 2001). Two main developments – the increasing use of ontologies in industrial settings for semantics-based operations and data interoperability, along with the central role for ontologies identified by the Semantic Web developer community (Berners-Lee, Hendler and Lassila, 2001) (McGuinness 2001) – indicate they are poised to be of interest to wider audiences. Ontologies are increasingly being viewed in enterprise settings as providing, beyond data integration and interoperability, *semantically-rich central models* through which data rationalization, unification, and understanding throughout the enterprise may be achieved.

As pointed out by several researchers (Noy and Klein, 2002) (Klein, 2001) the main focus of ontology research has over time covered numerous topics. Ontology-related topics that occupied researchers in the past have included formal representation, ontology reusability, content development, and applying logic to ontologies.

It is now becoming increasingly clear that the distributed ontology authoring environments emerging in both industrial and Semantic Web developer communities are posing new challenges for researchers. A particularly pressing need in this regard centres on maintaining the consistency of ontologies in distributed authoring environments. Many of the widely available ontology authoring tools, such as Protégé and OilEd, are currently stand-alone systems that do not contain mechanisms for serious collaborative ontology editing. One exception to this is Unicorn Systems™ (Unicorn and Unicorn Systems are trademarks of Unicorn Solutions, Inc.) a product of Unicorn Solutions, which has sophisticated features enabling collaboration in ontology authoring and merging of ontology versions diverging from a common source.

Evolution and versioning challenges in ontologies are not trivial. Ontology authors wishing to collaborate on editing one and the same ontology are likely to create conflicting versions within a short space of time. Several authors (Heflin and Hendler, 200) (Klein, 2001) (Stojanovic et. al., 2002) have listed numerous divergences that may be expected to develop between versions of ontologies edited by disparate authors. These include problems stemming from the use of different names for the same concept, the opposite problem of using similar names for different concepts, the mismatch of intended scopes of classes, the application of different scales for numerical-valued properties, the granularity divergence in describing similar domains, and the logical contradictions in axioms.

All of these issues are difficult to handle. Many of them involve matters ultimately relating to semantics, intended meanings, and assumptions. Systems such as OntoMorph (Chalupsky, 2000) and ONION (Mitra, Wiederhold and Kersten, 2000) have been suggested for semi-automatic treatment of some of the semantic differences between ontology

O. Camp et al. (eds.), Enterprise Information Systems V, 216-225.
© 2004 *Kluwer Academic Publishers. Printed in the Netherlands.*

versions, combining statistical guesses of appropriate mappings between different versions with user-input.

There are, however, several difficulties in merging diverging ontology versions stemming solely from *syntactic* and *structural* conflicts, as explained in detail below. Even at this level, challenges must be resolved in any system built for collaborative ontology versioning and evolution. An example of a system designed to handle such structural conflicts is PROMPT (Noy and Musen, 2000). This paper will concentrate on that level of analysis, but differs from PROMPT, which emphasizes merging disparate ontologies and therefore relies on heuristic-type analyses.

In contrast, we will suppose that users are working from a single ontology that may diverge into different versions as users work simultaneously on editing them. Despite this, their goal all along is to end up with a single ontology. Emphasis is placed on the question of how structural conflicts can be avoided in the first place. Applications of some of the ideas presented here to what is expected to be a gargantuan and fully distributed ontology defining the future Semantic Web are also considered.

2 COLLABORATIVE ONTOLOGY AUTHORING IN ENTERPRISES

For the purposes of this paper, an ontology will be understood to be any formal structure that includes classes, properties, property constraints (also known as restrictions or business rules), and instances (Chaudhri et. al., 1998) (Noy and Klein, 2002).

Classes refer to collections of objects with similar properties and may participate in a subclass-superclass hierarchy with multiple inheritance. As with OO programming, the inheritance feature is a crucial characteristic of ontologies; it gives the ontology the flexibility to model the world with different levels of granularity and alternative classifications. It is one of the main elements in distinguishing ontologies from other data formats such as relational databases and entity-relationship diagrams.

Properties are partial functions whose domains and co-domains are classes. The properties that contain a particular class in their respective domains are naturally considered to be the properties *associated* with the class. A sub-class inherits all the properties associated with a super-class in the inheritance hierarchy.

Constraints (or *restrictions*) may be imposed on properties, specifying such details as their cardinalities, whether they are necessarily injective or not, a range of values they may take, how their values when applied to an instance compare with the values of other properties applied to the same instance, and so forth.

Instances are individual members of classes, and *instance data* refers to data about the instances and their property values.

These elements – classes, properties, instances, etc. – are termed *concepts* or *elements* in this paper.

2.1 Collaborative Ontology Authoring Scenario

The main example scenario of collaborative ontology authoring that illustrates the potential difficulties involved is the following:

An enterprise stores its ontologies in a central repository (CR) that functions also as a version-control system. Alice and Bob intend on editing the same ontology simultaneously. They do so by making local copies from the CR, implementing their edits, and then merging their edited copies with the CR copy. In the scenario, Alice begins editing a local copy on Day 1. Bob only starts editing on Day 2. Bob can know that Alice has begun editing the ontology at a prior time because the server stores such knowledge (though he would not know the nature of changes she has made), but Alice may be remote from the central server and have no knowledge that Bob has also decided to edit the same ontology. The separate copies of the ontology worked on by the users now evolve along different branches into distinct versions while a third unchanged version remains on the CR. On Day 3, the users wish to have their respective versions stored or merged together in the CR into a new single master copy of the ontology. The main challenge then becomes whether or not some form of merging algorithm can be fashioned to enable a valid and coherent ontology to be created out of the disparate versions of the users.

2.2 Ontology Authoring Collaboration versus Other Collaborative Environments

If at first glance it appears a straightforward sourcing and locking system – as familiar from many code-production and database systems – would suffice for collaborative ontology authoring, a careful look at the structure of ontologies and in particular their high density of inter-concept dependencies reveals that matters are not so simple.

To take just one example of a simple action that can cause widespread problems due to dependencies, imagine that Alice decides to delete a class called (A). This may affect the inheritance structure such that another class called (B) no longer inherits a certain property called (C). Bob, on the other hand is currently working to define a constraint on a different concept called (D). However, this constraint may depend heavily on the property (C). Imagine now that Alice and Bob try to merge their ontologies with the CR copy. Although Alice and Bob were working on distinct concepts, the effect of their operations inevitably creates an ill-defined state in the ontology.

3 ONTOLOGY DEPENDENCIES AND CONFLICTS

3.1 Contents and Dependent Roles in Ontologies

Each concept within an ontological system can be presumed to have a clearly defined "content". Intuitively, the term "content" is intended to capture all the fields that are needed for a full and valid expression of the concept in, for example, a mark-up serialization of the ontology such that a full listing of the concepts and contents of an ontology should suffice to reconstruct the ontology. Again, the details of what counts as the content of a concept will depend on the particular format of a given ontological system. One point that is critical here is that the content of a concept in an ontology will often include a reference or a pointer to another concept, such as when a property references its co-domain or an expression of inheritance references the subclass and superclass involved.

Delineating the content of concepts in an ontology is but the first step in analysing the potential conflicts that may arise in ontology versioning and ontology merging. The next step is working out how changes in the status or content of concepts can impact *other* concepts – what will be termed here dependency. Concepts may play different roles with respect to dependencies. A concept that potentially may be affected by editing performed on another concept is said to have a *dependency* and termed a *dependant*. The concept at the other end of the dependency is then an *impactor*, from the idea that changes to an impactor can impact other concepts. Because dependencies are of high

importance in determining the behaviour of concepts in ontologies, dependencies and the associated list of impactors will be considered part of the content of a concept, alongside its internal fields and definitions. Many of the difficulties of ontology versioning stem from the fact that editing an impactor may leave it with perfectly valid content but could result in ill-defined content for a *dependant*.

Editing will be understood as any change performed on the content of a concept. However, it should be noted that deleting a concept is considered here a separate action, not an act of editing.

In general, a concept's content is *ill-defined* at a given time if under current conditions the underlying system would flag an error. For the purposes of this paper, a concept will be considered to have ill-defined content for any one of the following reasons:

a) The content includes reference to another non-existent (or deleted) concept (termed "dangling references" by (Noy and Klein, 2002));

b) A formula in the content is non-sensible because operators within it are applied to objects outside their domain of definition;

c) The state of the system is such that the concept should be deleted (usually applied to second-class concepts whose existence is dependent on other concepts).

3.1.1 Examples

1) A property called *supervisor* is defined on a domain class called *Employee*. Some time later, the domain class *Employee* is deleted. This results in property *supervisor* lacking a well-defined domain. *Supervisor* is a dependant with a dependency on the domain class Employee, here playing the role of an impactor.

2) *Supervisor* also has a co-domain class *Manager*. The deletion of the class *Manager* could leave the property supervisor with a dangling reference to a non-existent class.

3) A property called *vacant_seats* with a domain class called *Airflight* and co-domain *Integer* has imposed upon it a business rule *vacant_seats = total_seats – reserved_seats*, where *total_seats* and *reserved_seats* also have domain *Airflight* and co-domain *Integer*. The co-domain of *total_seats* is subsequently redefined to be *String* rather than *Integer*, thus rendering the business rule unintelligible, as the '-' operator is not defined on strings. The content of the constraint is therefore ill defined. Here, the business rule is the dependant, and the impactors are the properties *vacant_seats*, *total_seats* and *reserved_seats*, as editing performed on any one of them could impact the business rule.

3.2 Classification of Ontology Dependencies

Each of the above examples serves as motivation for distinguishing between different types of dependencies:

1) Existential Dependency: Concept A will be said to have existential dependency on concept B if the deletion of B entails the deletion of A, i.e. A is a second-class object.

2) Referential Dependency: Concept A is said to have referential dependency on concept B if the deletion of B causes A to have ill-defined content, but does not necessarily cause the deletion of A.

3) Content Dependency: Concept A has content dependency on concept B if changes to the content of B can cause A to have ill-defined content.

4 DEPENDENCY GRAPHS

Depicting dependencies in graph format can serve as a useful tool for the analysis of efficient locking mechanisms and merging strategies.

Given an ontology **O**, as determined by the sum total of its concepts and their contents, create an associated directed "dependency graph" G_O as follows:

1) Each distinct concept of **O** becomes a node of the graph G_O.

2) For each dependency, construct an arrow with its tail anchored at the dependant and its head ending at the impactor in G_O. (Due to the fact that more than one type of dependency may exist between two concepts, the dependency graph could well be a "multi-edged graph" in some cases).

Readers familiar with graph depictions of ontologies, as appearing in (McGuiness, 2001) for example, should note that dependency graphs are different. In contrast to graph depictions of ontologies, a dependency graph does not record semantic information on ontologies; its arcs only indicate dependency between concepts/nodes.

This very general description already suffices to allow a positive statement on the subject of merging to be made. Any change implemented on a concept necessitates propagating impact analysis in only one direction, from an impactor to its dependants, "backwards" against the directionality of the graph. Unicorn Systems, a semantic data management product of Unicorn Solutions, Inc., which includes an ontology authoring environment, makes use of this type of dependency-graph analysis for the efficient calculation and presentation to users of the impacts that changes introduced to ontologies may have on the structural validity of the ontology. The dependency graph is again taken into account in Unicorn Systems during the merging of ontology versions for maximum efficiency.

5 LOCKING MECHANISMS IN COLLABORATIVE ONTOLOGY EDITING ENVIRONMENTS

Following a traditional – and sensible – approach common to computer versioning systems, one way to prevent conflicts is to enable users to "check out" concepts of an ontology that they wish to edit and in the process impose various locks on the actions that other users may perform, until such time as the user checks-in again.

Check out will be defined here as a comprehensive "locking policy" in a collaborative system. This means that a user wishing to edit an ontology located in the CR must first specify the exact set of concepts within the ontology he or she intends on editing – that set will be termed here a *packet*. Based on the check out policy and actions performed previously by other users, the system may reject or accept the user's check out request. Once a packet has been checked-out, the policy then further determines which *locks* will be imposed – that is, which actions will be permitted or forbidden until check in occurs. In general, the locks may impact a variety of possible editing actions in different ways, and locks may be imposed on concepts inside and outside of the packet specified by the user. What is sought now is a *check out* (alternatively called *locking*) *policy* that will prevent conflicts from arising when ontology versions are merged.

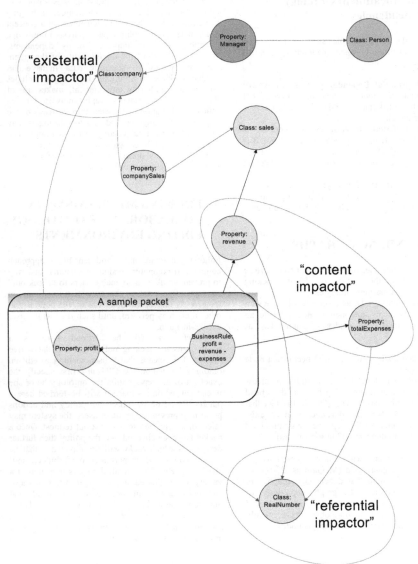

Figure 1: An example of a dependency graph

5.1 What to Lock: The Impactor

A packet may be depicted graphically in the dependency graph by a boundary being drawn around the nodes included in the packet, and only those nodes. The nodes included in the packet are then internal to the boundary of the packet, while those in the complement of the packet are external to the boundary.

Obviously, a user checking out a packet is mostly concerned with the concepts internal to the boundary of the packet. There is, however, associated with each packet a very important collection of concepts outside the boundary: concepts that are targets of the external dependency arcs/outgoing edges of a packet form its impactor set.

The motivation for these definitions is the idea that any editing changes a user performs within a checked out packet are his or her responsibility and presumably any internal conflicts can be corrected locally prior to check in and merging. Potential conflicts at merge time will arise either due to editing changes performed on concepts in the impactor set of P (i.e. outside the checked-out package) or to edits performed inside the packet to concepts that are impactors of concepts outside the packet. Borrowing a phrase from physics, it is only the *flux* of the dependency arrows crossing the boundary of the packet that is of interest for merge conflict-avoidance and resolution.

The impactor set can be sub-divided into the content impactor set, the existential impactor set, and the referential impactor set, in line with the types of dependency arcs connecting concepts inside the boundary with their impactors outside the boundary.

Figure 1 above depicts an example of a dependency graph, along with a packet and its impactor sets.

Concepts are depicted as coloured node circles, with dependencies presented as coloured arcs. The colours indicate different types of concepts and dependencies. A concept with valid content is in yellow. If it has ill-defined content it is coloured orange, and a concept deleted by a user is in grey.

The arc colours follow the rule that referential dependencies are in red, existential dependencies in blue and content dependencies are black.

In the figure, the user-defined packet contains a property *profit* and a business rule. The content impactor contains the properties *revenue* and *totalExpenses* because there are content dependencies between the business rule and these properties. The existential impactor contains the class *company*, because the property profit is assumed to depend on the existence of the class.

Finally, the class *RealNumber* is in the referential impactor because the properties profit, revenue and totalExpenses all referentially depend on this class.

5.2 Choosing Appropriate Locks for Collaborative Ontology Authoring

For the purposes of this paper, we assume that a user wishing to perform an action must obtain permission to perform it from the CR. Some systems do that implicitly. For each action that the user performs, the system connects to the CR and gets the relevant permissions. Other systems may request the user to explicitly "check out" the concepts he wishes to edit. The explicit "check out" process is especially needed if the system allows users to work "offline." Usually, those "permissions" are implemented as different types of *locks,* and the CR, besides keeping the main copy of the ontology, also keeps a list of locks that have been granted for users, thereby enabling them to perform various actions. In this way the CR has the power to minimize the chances of conflicts that may arise from simultaneous editing of the same ontology. Below we define the types of locks needed for collaborative ontology authoring, and the methods in which the CR grants them to users.

Locks in most systems are generally limited to "read" or "write" locks. A write lock is then a record of whether a particular concept may be edited or deleted. The subtleties of dependencies in ontologies, however, dictate finer locking considerations that distinguish between the different actions that are permitted or forbidden. Locks on ontology concepts will therefore relate to particular concepts and actions, specifying further whether the actions involved are blocked from all users, and whether a particular user has reserved the rights to perform the action.

Most structural conflicts in collaborative ontology environments will arise due to two particular actions performed on impactors: deleting an impactor, or editing its internal content. The relevant locks for the analysis in this paper will therefore be:

Block Delete Lock: When imposed on a concept, this prevents any user from deleting the concept.

Reserve Delete Lock: The user imposing the lock prevents any other user(s) from deleting the concept, while maintaining the right to deletion.

Block Edit Lock: When imposed on a concept, this prevents any user from editing the content of the concept.

Existing lock on concept / Request for lock on same concept	Block Delete	Reserve Delete	Block Edit	Reserve Edit
Block Delete	Approved	Denied	Approved	Approved
Reserve Delete	Denied	Denied	Denied	Denied
Block Edit	Approved	Denied	Approved	Denied
Reserve Edit	Approved	Denied	Denied	Denied

Table 1

Reserve Edit Lock: The user imposing the lock prevents any other user(s) from editing the content of the concept, while maintaining the right to editing.

In a very general analysis, it is possible to conceive of systems in which a user granted permission to perform an action on a concept does not necessarily also block others from receiving permission to perform that same action. This sort of system, however, may be highly counter-intuitive. **It will therefore be assumed here that a reserve lock subsumes a blocking lock**, in the sense that a user given a reserving lock with respect to a concept C and action A automatically imposes a blocking lock with respect to the same concept and action, whilst maintaining the right to perform the action himself.

The order in which reserving and blocking locks are imposed can be significant. For example, if user Alice has reserved permission to delete a concept, user Bob cannot impose a blocking lock on deletion of that concept. On the other hand, if Alice has imposed a blocking lock on deletion of a concept, Bob is prevented from taking a reserving lock on that same action on the concept.

Table 1 above summarizes the way locks are granted.

6 HOW TO PREVENT CONFLICTS IN ONTOLOGY MERGING

Locking policies are intended to avoid conflicts. The following is a listing of the types of conflicts that might be expected, and for each type of conflict, an associated "sufficient" locking policy meant to prevent it.

6.1 Preventing Direct Conflicts in Contents of Concepts

Direct conflict is understood as a type of ill-defined state arising from the internal content of a concept.

Claim: A locking policy that permits check out only if a user may take "reserve edit" locks on all the concepts with the scope of the checked-out packet is sufficient for preventing direct conflicts in contents of concepts.

How the proposed locking mechanism works: On Day 1 Alice checks-out a packet and imposes "reserve edit" and "reserve delete" locks on the concepts within the packet. On Day 2, Bob is prevented from checking out any of the concepts in Alice's packet due to the locks imposed on them, and therefore the concepts in Alice's packet are disjoint from Bob's. At check in, therefore, no user has edited concepts that another user has simultaneously edited, and there is no ambiguity in what the internal content of all concepts should be upon merge.

6.2 Preventing Ill-Defined Content Due to Content Editing of Impactors

Claim: A locking policy that imposes the rules:

- Check out is permitted only if a blocking edit lock can be imposed on the content impactor set;

- In addition, once check out has occurred, no new outgoing content dependencies may be added to concepts in the checked-out packet, unless communication has been re-established with server and a Blocking Edit Lock may be imposed on the new impactors

is sufficient for preventing ill-defined content due to content editing of impactors.

How the proposed locking mechanism works: On Day 1 Alice checks-out a packet and imposes a "block edit" lock on all concepts in the content impactor set of the packet she is checking-out.

On Day 2, Bob wishes to check out a packet. If any of the concepts in the packet he is requesting have been edit-blocked by Alice, he is not allowed to edit those concepts' content or Bob's impactors are reserved by Alice. This prevents Bob from impacting Alice's concepts. At the same time, Bob imposes a "block edit" lock on the impactor set of his packet – to prevent any other users from negatively impacting his concepts. If, however, concepts in Bob's impactor set have already been edit reserved by Alice, Bob may not check out the entire packet– this is for Bob's protection to avoid a situation in which Alice's edits have negative impact on Bob's packet.

If either Bob or Alice wishes to add new content dependencies to concepts in his or her packet, he or she must re-establish contact with the server and ensure that a block edit lock may be imposed on the new impactors. If the rights to edit the new impactors have already been reserved by another user, they cannot add a new dependency.

Upon check in, there can be no ill-defined content due to content editing of impactors.

6.3 Preventing Ill-defined Content Due to Deletion of Impactors

Claim: A locking policy that imposes the rules:

- Check out is permitted only if a block deletion lock can be imposed on all concepts in the existential and referential impactor set and a block deletion lock can be imposed on all concepts in the existential dependency transitive closure of the latter set;
- In addition, no new outgoing referential or existential dependencies may be added to concepts in the checked-out packet unless communication has been re-established with the server and a block deletion lock can be imposed on the new impactors and all the concepts in their existential dependency transitive closure.

is sufficient to prevent ill-defined content due to deletion of impactors.

Note: Following traditional terminology, the transitive closure of dependencies will be understood here being determined by beginning with any set P of nodes in the graph and then including the set of nodes P' that are impactors of concepts in P, and the set P'' of nodes that are impactors of concepts in P', and so forth by iteration.

How the proposed locking mechanism works: On Day 1 Alice checks-out a packet and imposes a "block deletion" lock on all concepts in the existential and referential impactor set of the packet she is checking-out, with the lock also propagating to the existential dependency transitive closure.

On Day 2, Bob wishes to check out a packet. If any of the concepts in the packet he is requesting have a block delete lock imposed as a result of Alice's previous actions, he is not allowed to delete them, although there is nothing preventing him from editing their contents. This prevents Bob from impacting Alice's concepts by deleting impactors. At the same time, Bob imposes a block deletion on existential and referential impactors of the packet he is interested in, also propagating along the existential transitive closure – assuming, of course, that Alice has not already reserved deletion rights for any of the concepts therein.

If Bob or Alice wishes to add new existential or referential dependencies to concepts in his or her packet, he or she must re-establish contact with the server and ensure that a block deletion lock may be imposed on the new impactors and their existential dependency transitive closure. If the rights to delete any of the concepts in this set have already been reserved by another user(s), then that other user(s) cannot add a new dependency.

Upon check in, there can be no ill-defined content due to the deletion of impactors, due to the locks.

Why the existential dependency transitive closure must be taken into account: Imposing a block deletion lock on the impactor set is not sufficient. Imagine a dependency graph A --> B --> C --> D, where the first arrow, from A to B, is referential, and the rest of the arrows are existential. Suppose a user checks-out A and imposes a block-deletion lock on B in order to avoid a structural conflict. Another user, however, could check out D with deletion permission. Upon deleting D, the existential dependant C must be deleted, followed in turn by B – leading to a conflict. Avoiding this situation

223

requires locking the existential dependency transitive closure.

7 APPLICATIONS TO THE SEMANTIC WEB

The above analysis is centred around versioning and merging issues in enterprise ontology editing environments in central repositories. The Semantic Web is envisioned as a different type of environment, being a far more distributed and decentralized arena for ontology usage and linking, with ontologies stored in Web documents and sites (similar to World Wide Web sites), each with clearly defined authors but with highly interlinked and dependent documents owned by others. "Existential dependency" between concepts in different documents is unlikely to be part of the architecture. Nevertheless, much of the above analysis remains applicable to the Semantic Web.

In particular, ill-defined content can be expected to be a familiar experience for Semantic Web users. In the World Wide Web of HTTP sites, users have become accustomed to the fact that they may receive a "404 Page Not Found" error message due to the actions of others such as deleting a page that is linked to. Links to sites frequently become obsolete, as the sites to which they point are modified or updated with completely different information. For most of the purposes of the World Wide Web, these real-world facts of life are annoying but tolerable.

If the Semantic Web develops to the point at which logical inference is implemented on distributed ontologies, the implications of such behaviour could be far more serious. If classes supposed to serve as property ranges in linked documents are deleted without warning or editing of property attributes in remote documents renders local constraints unintelligible, logical inferencing could grind to a halt or, even worse, arrive at widely incorrect conclusions. Locks are inconceivable in as distributed a system as the Semantic Web. The price to be paid will likely be ill-defined content, as defined above, plaguing the Semantic Web with costly, painful, and detrimental implications for business users and enterprises.

In situations where the cost of potentially corrupted inferencing due to ill-defined content is prohibitively high, one would imagine it likely that some enterprises offering services on the Semantic Web would hold local caches of all the ontological structure they need for their inference engines in order to avoid broken connections and ill-defined content. A new kind of service offering to keep track of links between ontologies following both "forward and backward" arcs in dependencies graphs may also develop, in order to inform users of modified, deleted, or broken links between linked impactors and dependants on an "asynchronous notification" basis. In the past, developers have proposed parallel ideas regarding services that would trace hyperlinks and "backward hyperlinks" on the WWW, subsequently informing users about broken links on a regular basis; apparently, there was never enough of a need for the idea to take off. As part of the Semantic Web vision, the need is much more pressing and obvious. The Semantic Web's builders might do well to consider whether infrastructural forethought will be needed to accommodate anticipated demand of such a feature.

When Semantic Web intranets or private Semantic Webs between enterprises are created, internal mechanisms for preventing ill-defined content arising from collaborative efforts, as detailed above, will be needed.

8 CONCLUSION

Due to the high-density and nature of dependencies between elements in ontologies, ensuring the stability of ontologies authored in collaborative environments requires novel approaches. In this paper, the concept of "dependency graph" is introduced as a tool for analysing potential conflicts in complex collaborative ontology engineering environments. This sort of analysis is useful for defining strategies for systems that facilitate collaborative ontology engineering while avoiding detrimental conflicts.

REFERENCES

Berners-Lee, T., Hendler, J. & Lassila, O., 2001. The Semantic Web: A new form of Web content that is meaningful to computers will unleash a revolution of new possibilities. In *Scientific American* May 2001.

Chalupsky, H., 2000. OntoMorph: A translation system for symbolic knowledge. In: *Principles of Knowledge Representation and Reasoning: Proceedings of the Seventh International Conference* (KR2000). Cohn, A.G., Giunchiglia, F. & Selman, B., editors. San Francisco, CA, Morgan Kaufmann Publishers.

Chaudhri, V.K., Farquhar, A., Fikes, R., Karp P.D. & Rice, J.P., 1998. OKBC: A programmatic foundation for knowledge base interoperability. In: *Proceedings of the Fifteenth National Conference on Artificial Intelligence (AAAI-98)*, Madison, Wisconsin, AAAI Press/The MIT Press.

Heflin, J. & Hendler, J. 2000. Dynamic Ontologies on the Web. In: *Proceedings of the Seventeenth National Conference on Artificial Intelligence (AAAI-2000)*, Austin, Texas.

Klein, M., 2001. Combining and relating ontologies: an analysis of problems and solutions. In: *Proceedings of the IJCAI-2001 Workshop on Ontologies and Information Sharing*, Seattle, Washington.

McGuinness, D.L., 2001. Ontologies Come of Age. *The Semantic Web: Why, What, and How*. Fensel, D., Hendler, J., Lieberman, H., & Wahlster, W., editors, MIT Press.

Mitra, P., Wiederhold, G. & Kersten, M., 2000. A Graph-Oriented Model for Articulation of Ontology Interdependencies. In: *Proceeding of the Conference on Extending Database Technology 2000* (EDBT '2000), Konstanz, Germany.

Noy, N.F., & Klein, M., 2002. SMI technical report SMI-2002-0926 (2002)

Noy, N.F. & Musen, M.A., 2000. PROMPT: Algorithm and Tool for Automated Ontology Merging and Alignment. In: *Proceedings of the Seventeenth National Conference on Artificial Intelligence (AAAI-2000)*, Austin, Texas.

Louis, R., 1999. Software agents activities. In *ICEIS'99, 1st International Conference on Enterprise Information Systems*. ICEIS Press.

Smith, B. & Welty, C., 2001. Ontology: Towards a New Synthesis In: *Proceedings of the International Conference on Formal Ontology in Information Systems – Volume 2001 Ogunquit, Maine, USA*. ACM Press New York, New York

Stojanovic, L., Maedche, A., Motik, B, & Stojanovic, N., 2002. User-Driven Ontology Evolution Management In: *Proceedings of the 13th European Conference on Knowledge Engineering and Knowledge Management EKAW, Madrid, Spain, 2002*.

TOWARDS ADAPTIVE USER INTERFACES GENERATION
One Step Closer To People

Víctor López-Jaquero, Francisco Montero, Antonio Fernández-Caballero, María D. Lozano

Laboratory on User Interaction & Software Engineering (LoUISE), University of Castilla-La Mancha, Albacete, Spain
Email: victor@info-ab.uclm.es, fmontero@info-ab.uclm.es ,caballer@info-ab.uclm.es, mlozano@info-ab.uclm.es

Keywords: Human Computer Interaction, model-based design, connectors

Abstract: User interface generation has become a Software Engineering branch of increasing interest, probably due to the great amount of money, time and effort used to develop user interfaces and the increasing level of exigency of user requirements for usability (Nielsen, 1993) and accessibility (W3C, 2002) compliances. There are different kinds of users, and that is a fact we cannot ignore. Human society is full of diversity and that must be reflected in human-computer interaction design. Thus, we need to engage users in a new kind of interaction concept where user interfaces are tailored-made, and where user interfaces are intelligent and adaptive. A new generation of specification techniques is necessary to face these challenges successfully. Model-based design has proved to be a powerful tool to achieve these goals. A first step towards adaptive user interface generation is introduced by means of the concept of connector applied to model-based design of user interfaces.

1 INTRODUCTION

Many things about computers are not changing at all (Dourish, 2001). Our basic idea about what a computer is, what it does, and how it does it, for instance, has hardly changed for decades. The increase in computational power and the expanding context, in which we put that power on, suggest that we need new ways of interacting with computers, ways that are better tuned to our needs and abilities.

In the last few years, a new conceptualization of computational phenomena has placed the emphasis not on procedure but on interaction (Wegner, 1997). Human-computer interaction in traditional application development is focused on the interaction between tasks and a single user interface designed for a single kind of user. Application user mass is treated as a single entity, making no distinction between the different user stereotypes included in that user mass (figure 1a). A logical evolution should lead interaction to a development model where these stereotypes are taken into account. There are different kinds of users, and that is a fact we cannot ignore. Human society is full of diversity and that must be reflected in human-computer interaction design (figure 1b).

However, one step forward in interaction design is required in order to translate this diversity into application development. Adding support for different user profiles is, of course, more accurate than development for a single kind of user, but the real thing is that we are all a little bit different. We might match a user profile, but with our own particularities, leading to the concept of specialization (figure 1c). Thus, we need to engage users in a new kind of interaction concept where user interfaces are tailored-made for each user, and where user interfaces are intelligent and adaptive.

From business point of view, HCI is becoming more and more important, because of the high cost associated to user interface construction for applications. Different studies have shown that 48% of an application code is dedicated to user interface development, and that 50% of implementation stage time is dedicated to user interface construction (Myers, 1992).

These facts have motivated the creation of different research projects (Elwert, 1995; Vanderdonckt, 1996; Lozano, 2001) that face these problems from an automatic user interface generation point of view. These projects try to fill the gap in Software Engineering between functional modelling and user interface development.

226

O. Camp et al. (eds.), Enterprise Information Systems V, 226-232.
© 2004 *Kluwer Academic Publishers. Printed in the Netherlands.*

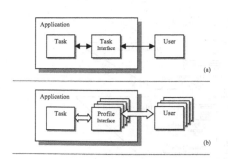

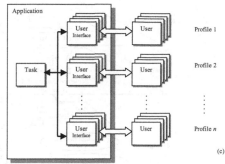

Figure 1: (a) Unity, (b) Diversity, and (c) Specialization in interaction design.

Among these projects, model based approaches (Paternò, 1999) arise as a useful and powerful tool to develop user interfaces. These approaches take as input a requirements specification that is converted into different declarative models. The most widely used are the task, the user, the domain, the dialogue and the presentation models. These declarative models are used to generate automatically a user interface compliant with the requirements captured in these models. Within these methodologies, user-centred design must be taken into account, so we are able to build *usable* (Nielsen, 1993) and *accessible* (W3C, 2002) user interfaces.

User-centred design implies studying the final user that will use the application that it is being created and make user take part in a interactive manner through all development stages.

In the next sections the connector concept is introduced applied to user interface generation and we will show how it actually makes easier adaptive and portable user interface generation.

2 USER INTERFACE DESIGN IN IDEAS

There are different proposals for model-based user interfaces design, *IDEAS* is one of those proposals (Lozano, Ramos & González, 2001). *IDEAS* is a methodology for user interfaces development within the framework of an automatic software production environment. This environment is supported by the object-oriented model *OASIS* (Letelier, 1998).

Abstraction is one of the basic principles needed to understand and model the reality. The object oriented paradigm favours this principle as it conceives the object oriented development process as an iterative and incremental approach that progressively allows a detailed specification of the system to be obtained.

The user interface development process within *IDEAS* is tackled following this principle. This process is not flat, but it is structured in multiple levels and multiple perspectives. The vertical structuring shows the reification processes followed from the first and most abstract level passing through the following levels to finally reach the system implementation, which constitutes the last level. On the other hand, the horizontal structuring shows the different perspectives offered by the different models developed in every one of the vertical levels. Thus, different models are used at the same abstract level to describe the different aspects of the graphical user interface.

Following these ideas, we propose the user interface development process depicted in figure 2. Due to space constraints, we cannot detail the different models proposed, so we will briefly describe this process showing some examples of the implemented tool which, interactively and automatically, supports this methodological approach.

At requirements level three models are created: the *Use Case Model*, the *Task Model* and the *User Model*. The *Use Case Model* captures the use cases identified within the information system. Then, for every one of the use cases there will be one or more tasks which the user may perform to accomplish the functionality defined by the use case.

227

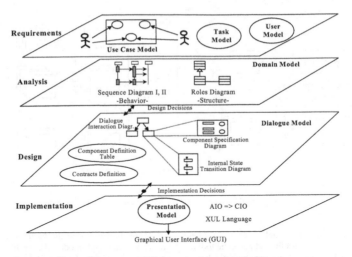

Figure 2: *IDEAS* user interface development methodology.

These tasks will be modelled in the task model. The *Task Model* defines the ordered set of activities and actions the user has to perform to achieve a concrete purpose or goal. We propose a template based on the one proposed by Cockburn (Cockburn, 2001) to describe in natural language all these issues. The *User Model* describes the characteristics of the different types of users. The purpose of this model is to support the creation of individual and personalized user interfaces. At analysis level the *Domain Model* is generated. This model consists of two diagrams. The first one is the Sequence Diagram, which defines the system behaviour. The second one is the *Role Model*, which defines the structure of the classes that take part in the associated sequence diagram together with the relationships among these classes, specifying the role of each one of them.

At design level the *Dialogue Model* is developed. All the models that have been generated up to now do not contain any graphical aspect of the final user interface. It is from now on that these issues start to be addressed and the way in which the user-system interaction will be performed is especially important.

The purpose is to describe the syntactic structure of the user-computer interaction. It establishes when the user can invoke commands, select or specify the input data and when the computer can require data from the user or display the output data. These items are modelled by means of Abstract Interaction Objects (AIO) (Vanderdonckt & Bodart, 1993).

At implementation level the *Presentation Model* is created. The Presentation Model describes the concrete interaction objects (CIO) composing the final graphical user interface, its design characteristics and visual dependencies among the objects. This model leads to the visualization of the final graphical user interface according to the final platform style guides. The final graphical user interface generation is performed by using XUL (Boswell, 2002), an XML based language, in order to make it as independent as possible from the final platform where the application is going to run.

The starting point for generating the graphical user interface in XUL is the Dialog Model developed at design level, which, as stated before, models the structure and the behaviour of the graphical user interface by means of AIOs. These AIOs are translated into the CIOs offered by XUL. Therefore, the graphical user interface structure is generated automatically from the Component Specification Diagram created at design level.

As a result of *IDEAS* methodology applied to an application three different societies of objects will appear: (1) the functional domain object society, that represents the objects that perform the functionality required in order to achieve the identified tasks, (2) the abstract interaction object society, that includes the objects that represent graphical user interface in an abstract manner, and finally (3) the concrete interaction object society, that will contain the objects that represent the graphical user interface in a specific platform.

228

Therefore, user interface operation will consist on the interaction between the objects included in the same society (intra-society interaction), the interaction between functional domain objects and abstract interaction objects, and the interaction between abstract interaction objects and concrete interaction objects (intersociety interaction) (see figure 3a).

Originally in *IDEAS* methodology interaction between functional domain objects and abstract interaction objects was specified using a modification of the principles about *contracts* between objects proposed by Andrade and Fiadeiro (Andrade & Fiadeiro, 1999).

3 INTERCONNECTING OBJECTS IN IDEAS: CONTRACTS

A contract describes interaction between objects creating an association between the objects involved in the interaction act. Business rules determine the policy that will rule the communication process and the coordination between objects, where that coordination will not be included in the definition of the interacting objects, but into contracts, because of the nature inherent to business rules. Business rules are associated to the tasks performed using the user interface, and not to the interacting objects.

Including this communication process into the contract definition will allow us to adjust business

rules according to the possible changes in system requirements in a transparent manner for the objects involved in the interaction act.

Figure 3b shows an excerpt of a contract specification using the template in *OASIS* language proposed in *IDEAS* methodology for this purpose.

To make easier understanding the mechanism described we have chosen a well-known interaction act: the interaction between a *Main Window* (belonging to abstract interaction object society - AIO), and a functional domain object that represents the global configuration for an application. The objects interacting will be described in the *partners* section of the specification. This interaction is included into a task we have called *Window_Management*. When *Main Window* tries to close - maybe because the user has ask the system to do so – the request will be captured by the contract according to the guard conditions specified in *when* clauses. The contract will check whether precondition is satisfied or not for that action. Precondition is specified in *with* clause. In our example, coordination event *CW* models this interaction as specified in *when* clause. First, it will check precondition. In this case it checks whether configuration has changed or not. If it has not changed it is not necessary to save data. Second, if the pre-condition is satisfied the actions in *do* clause will be executed. If the pre-condition is not satisfied the coordination event ends.

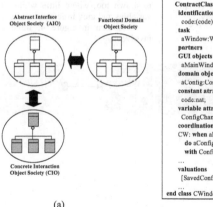
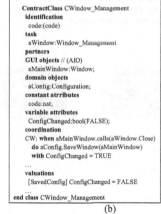

(a)   (b)

Figure 3: (a) User interface operation. (b) Contract class according to the template proposed in *IDEAS*.

Contracts provide a mechanism for object coordination where interacting objects are treated as black boxes.

Although this artefact greatly improves system flexibility, as long as it supports the modification of changes in business rules quite easily, it still introduces some drawbacks for adaptive and portable user interfaces generation. In contracts coordination between objects is specified explicitly inside the contract, so it makes hard to use "plug and play" coordination components according to different users (maybe profiles) or target platforms. It takes one step beyond so that we are allowed to switch between different components easily, even at run time. Connectors (Allen, 1997) provide a powerful tool to support this software coordination "plug and play" component paradigm.

4 ONE STEP BEYOND: CONNECTORS

A connector consists of a set of roles and the specification of glue to keep them together. Roles model the behaviour for each part involved in interaction. Glue, on the other hand, provides the coordination between instances for each role (Wermelinger, 2000).

Connectors where originally proposed for software architecture specification to provide a mechanism for software components interconnection. To use connectors in the construction process of a specific system, roles will be instantiated. Nevertheless, a component will not be able to instantiate the role if it doesn't comply with the specified service that role should play.

A connector is specified describing: (1) input variables that will be used as input ports, (2) output variables that will be used as output ports, and (3) a set of actions, which will be fired according to a guard condition. Both, variables and actions can be declared as public or private items. Private items are only available to the connector where they have been declared.

Communication between components is achieved in two different ways. On one hand, input and output variables from different components are interconnected, and on the other hand methods from several components may be synchronized.

When applying connectors to our object societies (Functional domain object society, Abstract interaction object society and Concrete interaction object society) we will need to encapsulate interacting objects within component interfaces, interconnected using connector paradigm. We will exemplify how to use connectors in user interface design by specifying the same scenario we described for contracts before.

Now we have a CIO for the AIO that represents the window. When the CIO wants to close, it will notify to the AIO component its intentions so it can react and perform any required action before it actually closes. In the example, *AIOWindow* should notify *Config* component. Then *Config* component will check whether the configuration for that window has changed or not, and if so it will ask the right object (*oConfig*) to save window information.

The communication protocol between the components and the objects involved in this coordination process is depicted in figure 4. Notice interconnection between input and output variables is shown too, where little white squares are input variables and grey little squares are output ones.

As shown in figure 4, three components are involved:

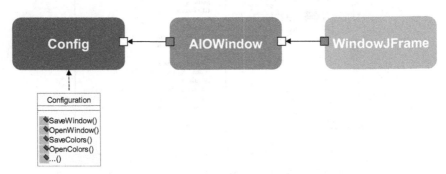

Figure 4: Connector and classes involved in *Window_Management* scenario.

```
Component Config                         Component AIOWindow                  Component WindowJMainFrame
   IN Cstatus: {open, close, …}             IN status: {open, close, …}          IN status: {open, close, …}
   PRV ConfigChanged:boolean               OUT AIOstatus: {open, close, …}      OUT AIOstatus: {open, close, …}
   PRV oConfig: Configuration
   do eCLOSE: if (Cstatus = Close) and    End Component                        …
              (ConfigChanged = TRUE) then                                      End Component
              oConfig.SaveWindow(AIOWindow);
              ConfigChanged := FALSE;
           end if;
   …
End Component
```

Figure 5: Connector components specification (excerpt).

(1) *WindowJFrame*, that models the CIO – a Java language frame -, (2) *AIOWindow*, which models the AIO that represents an application window, and finally (3) *Config*, which represents application configuration. This component makes use of an instance *oConfig* from *Configurator* class, and will do the real job. This class belongs to functional domain object society.

Next we will specify those depicted components, according to the semantics we have already described - input variables, output variables and actions. A specification of all three components involved in the coordination process in the example scenario is shown in figure 5.

So, what makes it different from contracts? The main difference is that involved components are specified separately and that they are interconnected through their interfaces. Therefore, it makes it possible for us to replace one component with another one whenever we may find it necessary. The only thing we should take into account is that the new brand component is compliant with the service requested and offers the same interface to the environment. Therefore, this will support cross platform development, as long as we can connect AIO components to any CIO (maybe CIOs for different platforms) which is able to offer the required functionality and interface to AIO component. For instance, in our window management example we could have components representing CIOs for XUL (Boswell, 2002) windows, Java[tm] (Java, 2002) windows or Microsoft Windows[tm]. Thus, our design process will boost portability and cross platform development with all the advantages it provides – above all reduced costs.

But this ability to switch between different components not only supports portability and cross platform design, it supports adaptive user interfaces specification to greatly improve overall user interface quality. AIO components are the traders between functional domain objects and CIO components, but we propose "intelligent" AIOs which are able to process the information to be presented, so they can choose between different CIOs to meet user preferences or device dependent features. For instance, a menu for an application could be presented in different ways depending on the number of options available for selection, as proposed in (Vanderdonckt, 1993). Thus, if there are just two options available a simple *checkbox* could do the work. If the available number of options is three, a set of grouped *radiobuttons* will be an interesting choice, while if there are more than three options available; a *listbox* could be used for this purpose.

Designing both CIO and AIO once we are able to achieve two great features: (1) we really boost portability and cross platform development, and (2) we generate automatically adaptive interfaces for all the applications using the designed AIO and CIO sets of components.

5 CONCLUSIONS

User interface generation has become a Software Engineering branch of increasing interest, probably due to the great amount of money, time and effort used to develop user interfaces and the increasing level of exigency of user requirements for usability (Nielsen, 1993) and accessibility (W3C, 2002) compliance interfaces. Besides the kind of users engaged in HCI is becoming more and more heterogeneous, and that is a fact we can not ignore.

In this paper we have proposed a first step towards user interface design and generation with some adaptive features by means of connectors in a model based user interface design methodology: *IDEAS*. We have shown how connectors can be used to introduce a high degree of portability and cross platform design, and how connectors can support adaptive user interfaces generation.

ACKNOWLEDGEMENTS

This work is supported in part by the Spanish CICYT TIC 2000-1673-C06-06 and CICYT TIC 2000-1106-C02-02 grants.

REFERENCES

Allen, R., Garlan, D. 1997. A Formal Basis for Architectural Connectors, *ACM TOSEM*, 6(3), pg. 213-249, July.

Andrade, L.F., Fiadeiro, J.L. 1999. Interconnecting Objects via Contracts. In: UML'99. *Proceedings of the International conference on the Unified Modeling Language.*

Boswell, D., King, B., Oeschger, I., Collins, P., Murphy, E. 2002. Creating Applications with Mozilla. O'Reilly. 0-596-00052-9.

Cockburn, A. 2001. *Writing Effective Use Cases.* Addison-Wesley.

Dourish, P. 2001.Where the Action Is: The Foundations of Embodied Interaction. Massachusetts Institute of Technology.

Elwert, T., Schlungbaum, E. 1995. Modelling and Generation of Graphical User Interfaces in the TADEUS Approach. In: *Designing, Specification and Verification of Interactive Systems.* Wien: Springer, 193-208.

Java. Sun Microsystems. 2002. http://java.sun.com.

Letelier, P., Ramos, I., Sánchez, P., Pastor, O. 1998. OASIS version 3: A Formal Approach for Object Oriented Conceptual Modeling. SPUPV-98.4011. Edited by Universidad Politécnica de Valencia, Spain.

Lozano, M. 2001. Entorno Metodológico Orientado a Objetos para la Especificación y Desarrollo de Interfaces de Usuario. Ph.D. Thesis. Supervisors: Dr. Isidro Ramos / Dr. Pascual Gonzalez. UPV. Valencia, 2001.

Lozano, M., Ramos, I., González, P. 2001. User Interface Specification and Modelling in an Object Oriented Environment for Automatic Software Development. IEEE 34th International Conference on TOOLS, USA.

Myers, B. A., Rosson, M. B.. 1992. Survey on User Interface Programming. In Striking a Balance. *Proceedings CHI'92.* Monterey, May 1992, New York: ACM Press, 195-202..

Nielsen, J. 1993. Usability Engineering. Academic Press.

Paternò, F. 1999. Model-Based Design and Evaluation of Interactive Applications. Springer.

Puerta, A.R. 1997. A Model-Based Interface Development Environment. IEEE Software, pp. 40-47.

Vanderdonckt. J.; Bodart, F. 1993. Encapsulating Kwowledge for Intelligence Interaction Objects Selection. Proceedings of Inter-CHI'93. ACM Press, 424-429.

Vanderdonckt, J. 1993. A Corpus of Selection Rules for Choosing Interaction Objects, Technical Report TR 93/3, University of Namur.

Vanderdonckt, J. 1996. Knowledge-Based Systems for Automated User Interface Generation: the TRIDENT Experience. Institut d'Informatique, Facultés Universitaires Notre-Dame de la Paix. Namur, Belgica.

Vanderdonckt, J. 1996. Knowledge-Based Systems for Automated User Interface Generation: the TRIDENT Experience. Institut d'Informatique, Facultés Universitaires Notre-Dame de la Paix. Namur, Belgica.

W3C. 2002. WAI. http://www.w3.org/WAI/

Wegner, P. 1997. Why interaction is more powerful than algorithms. Communications of the ACM, Vol. 40, No. 5 (1997) 80-91.

Wermelinger, M., Lopes, A., Fiadeiro, J.L. 2000. Superposing connectors, *in Proc. 10h International Workshop on Software Specification and Design*, IEEE Computer Society Press, 87-94

ANALYSING REQUIREMENTS FOR CONTENT MANAGEMENT

Virpi Lyytikäinen

Department of Computer Science and Information Systems, University of Jyväskylä, P.O. Box 35, 40014 Jyväskylä, Finland
Email: lyviau@cc.jyu.fi

Keywords: Document, Genre, Requirements analysis, Content management, Metadata

Abstract: The content to be managed in organisations is in textual or multimedia formats. Major part of the content is, however, stored in documents. In order to find out the needs of the people and organisations producing and using the content a profound requirements analysis is needed. In the paper, a novel method for the requirements analysis for content management purposes is introduced. The method combines different techniques from two existing methods, which were used in various content management development projects. The paper also describes a case study where the new method is exploited.

1 INTRODUCTION

The content to be managed across and between enterprises resides in both textual and multimedia objects. *Content management* concerns definition, creation, storage, organisation, transmission, retrieval, manipulation, update, and disposition of these objects. The major part of the organisations' content is stored in documents. If a *document* is defined according to Sprague (1995) as "... a set of information pertaining to topic, structured for human comprehension, represented by a variety of symbols, stored and handled as a unit", then methods for document management can be applied to content management problems in general (Boiko, 2002).

The concept of *genre* can also be used to comprehend the variety of content in enterprises. Yates and Orlikowski (1992) define genres as socially recognised types of communicative actions of organisational communication. The genres have content and form, and in digital environments also functionality (Shepherd & Watters, 1999). The genres can also be categorised into soft and hard genres according to extent and explicitness of their features (Schulze & Boland, 1997). Hardening of the genres can be achieved by extending their familiarity in the organisation and by defining more explicit rules for their use and structure (Karjalainen & Salminen, 2000).

In order to improve content management in enterprises, user requirements analysis is needed. Improvements may be implemented in various ways: for example, by planning and implementing new information system or buying one from the shelf, by developing work practices or by distributing work load differently. In the analysis, the requirements of all groups either producing or using the content in their work need to be elicited. The variety and multitude of the groups brings pressures on the requirements elicitation method, requiring it to be efficient yet simple to use.

The requirements analysis method for content management purposes should give answers to following questions:

- Where to start the improvements?
- What are the content units that are important to store and manage as documents?
- What are the current systems and techniques used in the content management of the domain?
- Is a new software system needed?
- What are the work processes in the content creation and usage?
- What are the organisations or organisational units involved in the creation and use of the content?
- What are the roles of people in content management?
- What are the problems in the current content management?

Answers to some of these questions can be reached by any requirements analysis method. There are also methods especially developed and tailored to give answers to questions like these. For example, RASKE is a methodology intended especially for content management development purposes, in par-

O. Camp et al. (eds.), Enterprise Information Systems V, 233-240.

ticular for the management of content by document standardisation (Salminen, Kauppinen & Lehtovaara, 1997; Salminen, 2000). It includes methods also for eliciting user requirements (Tiitinen, et al., 2000).

Organisational communication is the starting point for requirements analysis in the genre-based method described in (Karjalainen et al., 2000). The method offers tools especially for analysing the information flow between producers and users of information in an organisation.

The above mentioned requirements analysis methods have their strengths in content management development, but they also have their limitations. In this paper, the strengths and limitations are analysed and a new method exploiting techniques from the earlier methods is introduced. The new method has been tested in a case of a medium sized church (1,700 members, 9 employees), which needs to develop its practices of planning and informing its services.

The rest of the paper is organised as follows. The following section gives an overview of the related research of the requirements analysis. In Section 3 the unified requirements analysis method is described. Section 4 contains the description of the case where the method was used. In Section 5 the experiences of the case have been discussed, and Section 6 concludes the paper.

2 RELATED RESEARCH

Comprehensive reviews of requirements analysis or specification methods were introduced during the 1990s (Byrd, et al., 1992, Agarwal, et al., 1996, Zmud, et al., 1993, Vessey & Conger, 1994). Direct user interviews have been considered as the primary means for obtaining the requirements data (Agarwal & Tanniru, 1990; Holtzblatt & Beyer, 1995). User interviews have been recognised as a potentially rich method for requirements elicitation, but in practice, difficulties easily arise from its use (Moody et al., 1998). One reason for the difficulties is in the commonly occurring vocabulary difference between the analysts and the interviewees (e.g. Agarwal, & Tanniru, 1999; Byrd et al., 1992). Thus, Byrd et al. (1992) conclude that unstructured or open ended interviews are certainly useful for discovering global information specifications, but not appropriate for gathering detailed information requirements. As a solution, Alvarez and Urla (2002) suggest interview-generated narratives, which could provide data about "work practices and individual worker perspectives, as well as the larger organisational, political and cultural contexts".

Requirements analysis methods directed towards developing document management in organisations have also been introduced. To gather organisational metadata for electronic document management purposes, a genre-based metadata gathering method was designed (Karjalainen et al., 2000). In the method, communication genres together with their producers and users are first identified in group sessions using the diagonal matrix technique (Saaren-Seppälä, 1997). The technique allows the experts in the groups to use the vocabulary they are familiar with. The analysts need not to be familiar with the language of the domain in advance, nor need the experts spend much time to learn new notations for the group sessions. The groups also build up commitment of the participants to support the development by allowing the participants to express their opinions in the group discussions with co-experts of the domain. After the group sessions, metadata concerning the identified genres is gathered individually from the experts of the domain. The form based inquiry used has, however, been considered inefficient (Karjalainen et al., 2000).

In the RASKE methodology the requirements analysis is tied to the identification of work tasks involving documents in organisations. The methodology was initiated in a project where the needs for the management of the Finnish Parliamentary documents were investigated and major changes in the document management practices were implemented (Salminen, 2000; Tiitinen, et al., 2000).

In the RASKE methodology the user requirements are elicited by multiple methods: by informal interviews of experts, studying literal sources, direct semi-structured interviews, and by the work of a project council consisting of experts of the domain. The interviews are accompanied by predefined models of the domain. The models have been found important in helping the analysts to understand the language of the interviewees and in guiding the interviewees in orienting their thoughts to the domain in question (Tiitinen et al., 2000). While the genre-based method essentially relies on the utilisation of group work sessions for finding the requirements and getting the members of the domain involved with development, the RASKE methodology combines the use of multiple methods. User involvement is taken into account by other means.

The RASKE methodology has been used in situations where the identification of the development domain has not caused major problems. The methodology has been used in environments where work is document-centric (as it is in many public administration organisations). The genre-based method, on the other hand, has been especially designed for situations where the development domain and its content units are more vague. The following section describes how the requirements analysis methods of the RASKE methodology and genre-based method were unified to obtain a method better suited for purposes where the development domain may initially be vague but where well-defined descriptions of the chosen development area are expected as analysis products.

3 METHOD FOR REQUIREMENTS ANALYSIS

In order to efficiently and yet as simply as possible elicit user requirements for content management, a unified method was developed where capabilities offered in the RASKE methodology and the genre-based method were utilised. The process of the unified method is described in graphical format in Figure 1. In the figure, the analysis phases are depicted by ellipses, a dashed arrow pointing to an ellipse shows the input needed for that phase, and a dashed arrow pointing from the ellipse indicates the output of the phase. The solid arrows define the starting order of the phases. To get the work of a phase finished and to provide the results often requires work from the subsequent phases. This means that there is a lot of iteration in the process not explicitly indicated in the graph. The fifth and sixth phases of the method originate from the genre-based method while the others have their bases in the RASKE methodology. In the following, the phases are described in more detail. Section 4 contains a case description where the use of the method is explained with examples.

Establishing a steering committee

The steering committee should include the analysts and representatives from different interest groups. The purpose of the committee is to act as an organ for providing information to the analysts and coordinating the whole analysis.

Defining the domain

The steering committee should strictly define the domain to be analysed to limit the material of further study and also the number and size of group sessions. The domain definition can be based on organisational structure, process structure, type of content included as well as for a specific purpose.

Collecting literal sources and interviewing experts

After the domain has been defined the analysts get acquainted with existing literature sources over the domain. The material can be, for example, reports of earlier development projects, example documents, instructions, standards, and manuals. Also informal interviews and discussions with domain experts are a valuable source of information.

Modelling

Three kinds of models are used to illustrate the domain: organisational frameworks, document models, and process models. The models provide *contextual metadata* over the domain. The input for the models originates from the literal sources and expert interviews. However, the models are further refined during the later phases of the method.

Organisational framework describes the actors of the domain, especially organisational units and persons. The actors can form groups, which denote their hierarchical relationships. In the framework also the roles of the actors in the domain are shortly described.

One or more of the processes where the content is created in the domain are modelled as *process models*. To express both the information and control flows of the process, and yet keep the process model as simple as possible, a variant of the Information Control Nets (ICNs; Ellis, 1979) is used as the modelling technique (Salminen, Lyytikäinen & Tiitinen,

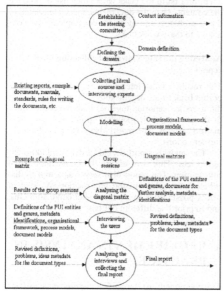

Figure 1: Overview of the requirements analysis method

2000). With ICN variants both the content used and produced during the process can be modelled.

The content of the domain is modelled on two levels. An overview of the important documents with their relationships can be observed from the *document-relationship diagram* (Salminen, 2000). The model is a simplification of the information structure diagram of the Object-Oriented Analysis methodology (OOA; Shlaer & Mellor, 1992). More detailed description of the life-cycles of the document types can be seen from *state transitions diagrams*, the technique introduced in OOA.

Group sessions

The communicative genres, i.e. information flows between the producers and users of information (PUI entities) are identified in group sessions using diagonal matrix technique (Saaren-Seppälä, 1997). The PUI entities form the diagonal of the matrix, and the genres are placed around the PUI entities in a clockwise manner: all genres produced by one entity are situated on a same horizontal level as the entity itself, and the genres used by the entity can be seen on the same vertical axis as the entity itself.

The phase of constructing the matrix has two main steps:
1. *Identify the PUI entities*. The names of the actors, organisational units, or processes producing or using content on the domain should be written on cards and placed on the wall. The kinds of PUI entities selected depend on the organisation, on its way to structure its functions.
2. *Identify content units* (genres). Either the group members themselves write the names of the genres on the cards and place the cards on the wall, or the facilitator fills the cards according to the information given by the group. Especially in the first case the final matrix should be cooperatively checked to ensure that all members have equal understanding over the matrix.

Analysing the diagonal matrix

As a result of the group sessions several diagonal matrixes may exist. For the analysing purposes the matrixes should be combined. A description of each of the objects in the matrix should be separately written. Especially those genres which can be considered as hard, i.e. they are produced according to formal rules, should be included in the focus of analysis. Also, if there are such soft genres which are considered so important that they should be hardened, they too should be included in the analysis. From this point forward the genres to be further analysed are referred to as documents.

The analysis of the diagonal matrix includes also a task of identifying the kinds of metadata to be collected during the interviews. All metadata concerns the document types, not the individual instances of the documents. The metadata can be, for example, format and media, medium size, number of versions and copies, aggregations or security class.

Interviewing the users

A representative sample of the members of the group sessions are selected to participate in interviews. In addition, other producers or users of the identified document types can be asked for the interviews, if the members of the group sessions or members of the steering committee so desire.

Before the interviews, each interviewee shall receive the models drawn in the modelling phase of the analysis. With the models the interviewees can orient themselves to the analysis domain. During the interview the models are also checked and revised according to the interviewee's opinions, if needed.

The interviews are intended to collect metadata and to help in finding needs and problems not revealed in the group sessions. Based on the sensemaking theory (Derwin, 1992) and on the use cases of Jacobson et al. (1994), the questions in the semi-structured interview questionnaire draw the users' attention first to the tasks where they use or produce the content. Then the documents, metadata related to them, problems and ideas for development are connected to these work tasks.

Analysing the interviews and collecting the final report

The results of the interviews are analysed and reported back to the organisation. The requirements of the users are reported together with the descriptions of documents, their metadata, processes and information systems. The report also gives guidelines for further actions.

The analysis report should be delivered to the interviewees. This is to ensure the correctness of the information. The report also serves as a tool to distribute information in the organisation. As such it offers possibilities to evaluate alternative solutions, and to prioritise different options.

4 REQUIREMENTS ANALYSIS IN PRACTICE

The components of the unified requirements analysis method have been tested separately in several cases. The unified method as such was tested for two different cases. In this paper, a case of a church of 1,700 members is described: The church wants to improve their planning of services as well as their communication about the services both to its members and outsiders. Currently, a major part of the information needed in the domain resides in documents, but, in the future solution, database support for the content management will be considered. Along with nine employees the church has hundreds of volunteers who actively participate in the services both as an audience and as performers. A challenge to the operational management of the church is to allocate the volunteers, musicians for example, to the services. In the following, the phases of the requirements analysis at the church are described.

Establishing a steering committee and defining the domain

The steering committee in this relatively small case consists of three persons: an analyst, an associate pastor, who is in charge of the operational functions of the church, and the chair of the management group of the church (also called the elders). The domain was defined and named as "Planning and communicating of services". Strategic planning and information flows related to administrative tasks were left out of the domain.

The relevant interest groups for the group sessions were defined to be the elders, the board of the church, different kinds of pastors, clerks, volunteers, team leaders, a web administrator, and the church members in general.

Collecting literal sources and interviewing experts

The members of the steering committee collected different kinds of communicative documents used in the church. Along with monthly service calendar, distributed in the web and in a paper to the service participants, the church communicates its services by announcements at the front door of the church and at the local newspaper. For internal use, the pastors and other employees use calendars covering different periods from one week to six months. The elders and the board of the church make plans for the whole year and strategic plans covering five years.

Modelling

The content management environment was described by an organisational framework model and a process model shown in Figures 2 and 3 respectively. The process model shows the major content units on the domain. Both of the models also provide contextual metadata related to the management of the units.

Preliminary models were created on the basis of the information gathered from the experts of the domain. Group sessions and user interviews provided additional information needed to create the final models shown in the figures.

Group sessions

Construction of the diagonal matrixes in group sessions was started in a group consisting of five persons from the church and three members of the analysis team. The participants identified altogether 13 PUI entities. After the PUI entities were in place,

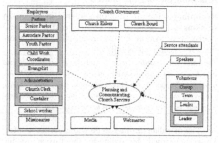

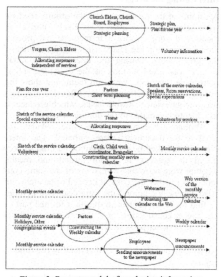

Figure 2: Organisational framework of the church

Figure 3: Process model of producing information about the church services

237

the participants identified 34 different genres, several of which flowed from or to multiple entities. The matrix was completed in the following three sessions where different interest groups were represented. The amount of identified genres rose to 54.

For the participants it was an educating experience to see the diverse items they spent their time with. It was found, for example, that not all the participants got all the information they needed in the most efficient way. The problems identified were written down and placed on the wall.

Analysing the diagonal matrix

According to the information gathered in the group sessions definitions of the entities of the diagonal matrix were written. For example, child work coordinator was defined as follows:

> *The child work coordinator is responsible for developing and coordinating the activities with children and teenagers. In her turn, she also participates in administrative tasks of the church, producing the monthly service calendar and newspaper advertisements, as well as gives speeches to the congregation.*

The metadata defined to be gathered in the interviews concerned, for example, the format, media, versioning, and archiving of documents.

Interviewing the users

A sample of the participants of the groups sessions were selected to the interviews. Each interviewee received the organisational framework and process model along with the matrix showing the results of the group work. During the interview, the interviewee was asked to look at the drawings, tell if there were something wrong in them, and show the phases he or she participated in. After this introduction, the interviewee's work tasks, which produce or use documents related to the domain, were listed.

Within each encountered task the metadata related to the documents were gathered. The interviewee was asked how often she or he used or produced the content, in which format and media, whether there were many versions of the same content, and whether the content needed to be archived. Also aggregate relationships were discussed in order to find out if the content in question formed part of any bigger construction, or if the interviewee could name any smaller parts which the content included.

Analysing the interviews and collecting the final report

After the interviews were completed, a report of the requirements analysis was prepared. The report contains information about the requirements analysis

method, the domain in general, producers and users of information, processes, information systems and documents. The problems found during the analysis were categorised into three classes: information systems, documents and work processes. The report ends with a recommendation for the further activities.

The analysis resulted in lots of detailed information about the content of the domain. Based on the interview it was possible to model the state transition diagrams for the most important documents concerning both the current situation and possible future scenarios. Also, problems of the domain were identified and discussed. The discussion about the future solution may continue after the report has been distributed to all interest groups including the interviewees themselves. The report can be used, for example, as a basis for inviting tenders to implement a new content management system.

5 EXPERIENCES

The components of the unified method complemented each other in the requirements analysis of the case organisation. The diagonal matrix technique in the group sessions helped to explore the whole domain while the techniques originating from the RASKE methodology shed light on the relevant details. Iteration in collecting the requirements with different means from the same persons was also found valuable. The people in the church did not have any previous experience in defining their needs, so they appreciated the chance to do so.

According to the analysis of the diagonal matrix, the central document related to the case domain in the church was the monthly service calendar. It was also the document related to most of the problems and development ideas. Therefore it was quite natural to start the improvements from developing the structure, layout, and production process of the calendar. Other important documents included different kinds of plans as well as announcements, which have a lot of the same content as the monthly service calendar. The information about the volunteers was a genre that needed hardening. Currently the information is more or less stored in the heads and private files of the team leaders.

The current systems and techniques for content management of the domain were examined first in informal expert interviews. The examination went further during the semi-structured interviews of the actors on the domain. New software was found to be needed, because currently there are no special tools for assisting in the production process of the documents.

The discussions with the experts, group members and the interviewees assisted in finding out the processes where the content of the domain is created and used. Similarly, the organisations, organisational units, as well as the roles of the people participating in the domain content management were defined.

The group sessions in the beginning of the analysis project clearly helped the users to focus on the domain in question. For those participants who had not previously been in contact with the project, the group session served as an informative tool to get to know the domain and some of its problems. It also revealed that even in such a small organisation, there is no single person who could know all the details related to the content of the domain. The sessions also helped the analysts to familiarise themselves with the organisation, its people, work, and vocabulary. Therefore, it was easier to discuss the matters in the interviews, since the participants had, at least at some level, a common language.

The contextual metadata illustrated by graphical models, was useful both to the analysts and the case organisation alike, because in the church they had not previously defined any formal graphs concerning their organisation. The graphs inspired discussions and ideas about improvements in the operative functions of the church. For the analysis point of view the contextual metadata gave valuable information about the context where the documents are produced and used.

The messiness and unfocused discussion was avoided in the interviews by concentrating from the beginning to the domain in question. Even though the interviews were intentionally quite informal, the semi-structured questionnaire helped in analysing the answers and ensuring that all the important details were covered. The interviewees also had a chance to contact the analysts later in case they remembered something important afterwards.

6 CONCLUSION

The requirements analysis forms the basis for building a usable information system. Varying methods have been introduced to elicit the requirements, but yet the old interviewing technique has remained as the primary means for the purpose. Despite its deficiencies – laborious, possibly messy and uncodeable data – its benefits make it a recommendable technique, especially if supplemented with other techniques that help to focus on the domain in question.

The method described in the paper has been combined from two formerly defined and tested methods: the RASKE methodology and a genre-based method. Due to the unification of the methods the content management domain, on the one hand, could be viewed as a whole, on the other hand, relevant details for developing the current practises could be found. The group sessions were realized as an important technique in addition to the multiple methods already in use in the RASKE methodology.

In the future, the method needs to be further tested up to the implementation and evaluation of the information systems built according to the gathered requirements. The method introduced in the paper is currently in use in a much bigger project in a more technical environment. The purpose of the project is to plan a data warehouse for strategic management in the organisation. With the requirements analysis in the complex organisation the requirements and ideas of various user groups are elicited and as a result the organisation will be able to place a call for tenders to build the data warehouse for their managers.

REFERENCES

Agarwal, R. & Tanniru, M. R., 1990. Knowledge acquisition using structured interviewing: An empirical investigation. *Journal of Management Information Systems*, 7 (1), 123-140.

Agarwal, R., Sinh, A. P., & Tanniru, M., 1996. Cognitive fit in requirements modeling: A study of object and process methodologies. *Journal of Management Information Systems*, 13 (2), 137-162.

Alvarez, R., & Urla, J., 2002. Tell me a good story: Using narrative information requirements interviews during an ERP implementation. *ACM SIGMIS Database*, 33 (1 Winter 2002), 38-52.

Boiko, B., 2002. *Content Management Bible*. New York, U.S.A: Hungry Minds, Inc.

Byrd, T. A., Cossick, K. L., & Zmud, R. W., 1992. A synthesis of research on requirements analysis and knowledge acquisition techniques. *Management Information Systems Quarterly*, 16 (1), 117-138.

Dervin, B., 1992. From the mind's eye of the user: the sense-making qualitative-quantitative methodology. In J. D. Glazier & R. R. Powell (Eds.), *Qualitative Research in Information Management* (pp. 61-84). Englewood (CO): Libraries Unlimited, Inc.

Ellis, C. A., 1979. Information Control Nets: A mathematical model of office information flow. In *Proceedings of the Conference on Simulation, Measurement and Modeling of Computer Systems, ACM SIGMETRICS Performance Evaluation Review*, 8 (3), 225-238.

Holtzblatt, K. & Beyer, H. R., 1995. Requirements gathering: The human factor. *Communications of the ACM*, 38 (5), 30-32.

Jacobson, I., Ericsson, M., & Jacobson, A., 1994. The *Object Advantage: Business Process Reengineering with Object Technology.* Addison-Wesley.

Karjalainen, A., Päivärinta, T., Tyrväinen, P., & Rajala, J., 2000. Genre-based metadata for enterprise document management. In R. H. Sprague (Ed.), *Proceedings of the 34th Annual Hawaii International Conference on System Sciences (HICSS)* (CD-ROM ed.). Los Alamitos CA: IEEE Computer Society.

Karjalainen, A., & Salminen, A. (2000). Bridging the gap between hard and soft information genres. In M. Khosrowpour (Ed.), *Challenges of Information Technology Management in the 21st Century. Proceedings of 2000 Information Resources Management Association International Conference* (pp. 92-95). Anchorage, Alaska, U.S.A: Idea Group Publishing, Hershey, U.S.A.

Moody, J. W., Blanton, J. E., & Cheney, P. H., 1998. A theoretically grounded approach to assist memory recall during information requirements determination. *Journal of Management Information Systems*, 15 (1), 79-98.

Päivärinta, T., Halttunen, V., & Tyrväinen, P., 2001. A genre-based method for information systems planning. In M. Rossi & K. Siau (Eds.), *Information Modelling in the New Millenium* (pp. 71-94). Hershey PA: Idea Group.

Päivärinta, T., & Peltola, T., 2001. Engineering of a genre-based method for developing electronic document management: The consultant's viewpoint. In J. Krogstie & K. Siau & T. Halpin (Eds.), *Proceedings of the Sixth CAiSE/IFIP8.1 International Workshop on Evaluation of Modeling Methods in Systems Analysis and Design (EMMSAD'01)* (pp. XIII 1-14).

Saaren-Seppälä, K., 1997. *Seinätekniikka prosessien kehittämisessä. (Using the wall-chart technique in process development, in Finnish), Kari Saaren-Seppälä Ltd.,* Finland (Technical report/ manual.).

Salminen, A., 2000. Methodology for document analysis. In A. Kent (Ed.), *Encyclopedia of Library and Information Science* (Vol. 67 (Supplement 30), pp. 299-320). New York: Marcel Dekker, Inc.

Salminen, A., Kauppinen, K., & Lehtovaara, M., 1997. Towards a methodology for document analysis. *Journal of the American Society for Information Science*, 48(7), 644-655.

Salminen, A., Lyytikäinen, V., & Tiitinen, P., 2000. Putting documents into their work context in document analysis. *Information Processing & Management 36* (4), 623-641.

Salminen, A., Lyytikäinen, V., Tiitinen, P., & Mustajärvi, O., 2001. Experiences of SGML standardization: The case of the Finnish legislative documents. In J. R. H. Sprague (Ed.), *Proceedings of the Thirty-Fourth Hawaii International Conference on System Sciences* (file etegv01.pdf at CD-ROM). Los Alamitos ,CA: IEEE Computer Society.

Salminen, A., Tiitinen, P., & Lyytikäinen, V., 1999. Usability evaluation of a structured document archive, In *Proceedings of the 32nd Annual Hawaii International Conference on System Sciences*: IEEE Computer Society Press.

Schulze, U., & Boland, R., Jr., 1997. Hard and soft information genres: An analysis of two Notes databases. In R. H. Sprague (Ed.), *Proceedings of the 30th Annual Hawaii International Conference on System Sciences. Digital Documents Track.* (Vol. VI, pp. 40 - 49). Maui (HA): IEEE Computer Society Press.

Shepherd, M., & Watters, C., 1999. The functionality attribute of cybergenres. In R. H. Sprague (Ed.), *Proceedings of the 32th Annual Hawaii International Conference on System Sciences. Digital Documents Track.* (pp. CD-ROM). Maui (HA): IEEE Computer Society Press.

Shlaer, S., & Mellor, S., J., 1992. *Object Lifecycles: Modeling the World in States.* Englewood Clisffs (NJ): Yourdon Press.

Sprague, R. H., 1995. Electronic document management: challenges and opportunities for information systems manager. *MIS Quarterly*, 19(1), 29-49.

Tiitinen, P., Lyytikäinen, V., Päivärinta, T., & Salminen, A., 2000. User needs for electronic document management in public administration: a study of two cases. In H. R. Hansen & M. Bichler & H. Mahler (Eds.), *Proceedings of the 8th European Conference on Information Systems* (Vol. 2, pp. 1144-1151). Wien: Wirtschaftsuniversität Wien.

Vessey, I. & Conger, S., 1993. Learning to specify information requirements: The relationship between application and methodology. *Journal of Management Information Systems*, 10 (2), 177-201.

Vessey, I. & Conger, S., 1994. Requirements specification: learning object, process, and data methodologies. Communications of the ACM, 37 (5), 102-113.

Yates, J., & Orlikowski, W. J., 1992. Genres of organizational communication: A structurational approach to studying communication and media. *Academy of Management Review*, 17(2), 299-326.

Zmud, R. W., Anthony, W. P., & Stair, R. M. J., 1993. The use of mental imagery to facilitate information identification in requirements analysis. *Journal of Management Information Systems*, 9(4), 175-191.

REUSING A TIME ONTOLOGY

Duarte Nuno Peralta and H. Sofia Pinto
Grupo de Inteligência Artificial, Departamento de Engenharia Informática
Instituto Superior Técnico
Av. Rovisco Pais, 1049-001 Lisboa, Portugal
Email: {duarte,sofia}@gia.ist.utl.pt

Nuno J. Mamede
L²F INESC-ID/IST - Spoken Language Systems Laboratory
Rua Alves Redol 9, 1000-029 Lisboa, Portugal
Email: Nuno.Mamede@inesc-id.pt

Keywords: Ontology Engineering, Ontology Building, Evolving Prototyping, Ontology Reuse, Knowledge Representation Translation, Reverse Engineering, Technical Evaluation, Knowledge Acquisition.

Abstract: Ontologies are becoming crucial in several disparate areas, such as the Semantic Web or Knowledge Management. Ontology building is still more of an art than an engineering task. None of the available methodologies to build ontologies from scratch has been widely accepted. One cost effective way of building ontologies is by means of reuse. In this article we describe the development of an ontology of Time by means of reuse, following an evolving prototyping life cycle. This process involved several complex subprocesses: knowledge acquisition and requirement specification using Natural Language techniques, reverse engineering, knowledge representation translation, technical evaluation. As far as we know, this is the first time that all these processes have been combined together. We describe the techniques and best practices that were successfully used.

1 INTRODUCTION AND MOTIVATION

Nowadays ontologies are becoming crucial in several disparate areas, such as the Semantic Web (Berners-Lee et al., 2001) or in Knowledge Management. In the Semantic Web, they will be one of its building blocks, improving conventional information retrieval technologies. In Knowledge Management, they support interoperability (easing knowledge sharing) and organization of information.

Ontology building is still more of an art than an engineering task. None of the available methodologies to build ontologies from scratch has been widely accepted. In the Ontology Engineering area several processes to ease the time consuming and complex task of ontology building have been proposed.

In this article we describe the ongoing ontology building process of ONTO-SD. This ontology will be organized in several sub-ontologies in different domains related to traveling, for instance commercial transactions (buying and selling), geographical information and time. The emphasis of this article is the development of the Time sub-ontology.

Reuse processes are a cost effective way of building ontologies. The Time ontology was built by means of reuse, following an evolving prototyping life cycle.

The process described in this article involved several complex subprocesses: knowledge acquisition and requirement specification using Natural Language techniques, reverse engineering, knowledge representation translation, technical evaluation. As far as we know, this is the first time that all these processes have been combined together. We describe the techniques and best practices that were successfully used.

We start by explaining the context of our experiment, Section 2. Then, we describe the ontology building process, Section 3. We discuss the most interesting features of our experiment, Section 4. Finally, we analyze related work, Section 5, and present our conclusions and future work, Section 6.

2 CONTEXT OF THE EXPERIMENT

We are involved in the development of ontologies to be used in a Natural Language dialogue system. This dialogue system will be placed in a bus terminal, as a ticket-vending/information machine.

An important requirement of this application is that the language must be Portuguese (although the concepts represented in an ontology are, in general, lan-

O. Camp et al. (eds.), Enterprise Information Systems V, 241-248.
© 2004 *Kluwer Academic Publishers. Printed in the Netherlands.*

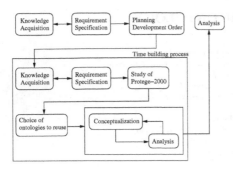

Figure 1: Building process of ONTO-SD

User:	To Oporto, at **17 hours**, in front.
Employee:	17 ?
User:	Yes.
Employee:	12 Euro.
User:	And for the boy ?
Employee:	8.

Figure 2: Example of real (translated) dialogue

guage independent,[1] the terms used to refer to those concepts are not).

We began the development of this ontology with the sub-ontology of time. At the moment, the several modules of the final ontology have been identified and the sub-ontology of time has been developed.

3 THE ONTOLOGY BUILDING PROCESS

When compared with typical software engineering processes, ontology building processes are less straight-forward. Typically, an ontology building process involves several iterations, most of them not a-priori planned. That is, ontology building processes follow an evolving prototyping life cycle.

In this section we describe the ONTO-SD building process performed so far (Pinto et al., 2002; Peralta, 2002), Fig. 1. Some parts of this process are rather complex and can be considered subprocesses on their own. We describe them in detail in appropriate subsections. Not only do we describe the activities that were performed - in *italics* - but also how they were performed.

Knowledge acquisition We began the whole process by going to a bus terminal in Lisbon and taping the dialogues that took place between users and the ticket booth employee. We will further describe this part of the process in Section 3.1.

Requirement specification/Conceptualization
First we looked for the most common terms in the transcription of the dialogues. With this information we identified the several sub-domains

---
[1]In Portuguese there is a concept that finds no parallel in other languages: "Saudade", which is a kind of nostalgia, home sick, is a genuine Portuguese concept.

that are involved, and the relations between them. Then, we structured the ONTO-SD ontology. We will further describe this part of the process in Section 3.1.

Planning development order Based on the structure found for ONTO-SD, an order was established for the development of the sub-ontologies. We will further describe this part of the process in Section 3.2.

Building the Time sub-ontology Building this sub-ontology is a sub-process of the overall building process. It was divided into:

Knowledge acquisition To represent and process the knowledge in the dialogues one needs a large corpus of knowledge, ontologies. We found that most of the terms in the dialogues require implicit knowledge in order to be represented. We *searched* for sources of knowledge, mostly ontologies, that contain the knowledge that cannot be extracted from the blind analysis of the texts corresponding to the transcription of the dialogues. The *chosen* source was Allen's time theory (Allen, 1984).

Requirement specification In this stage we *refined* the requirement specification stage of ONTO-SD for this particular sub-ontology. Mainly, we *identified* all terms related to time in the dialogues. One of the shortest and easiest dialogues that took place is shown in Fig. 2. It must be possible to represent the concepts referred by these terms using only the Time sub-ontology. This list of terms allows us to evaluate whether the final ontology meets its requirements.

Study of Protégé-2000 At this stage we started to *study* Protégé-2000 (Noy et al., 2001), since it was the chosen development tool. However, the learning process was continuous, and it stretched throughout the entire process. This tool was chosen because (1) it is locally installed, which is one of the a-priori requirements that was imposed, (2) it has a large community of users and (3) it has a very good and efficient technical support.

Choice of ontologies to reuse We *looked for* ontologies that could be reused both in libraries, such as the Ontolingua Server[2] (Farquhar et al., 1996), and in large ontologies, in particular WordNet[3], upperCyc[4] and SUMO.[5] We did a *preliminary analysis* and found out that most of the available ontologies about time were implementations of Allen's time theory. We decided to reuse the Simple-Time ontology, which is kept in the Ontolingua Server. The reasons for this *choice* were:

- This ontology is an implementation of the chosen time theory.
- Protégé-2000 has a plug-in to import ontologies kept in the Ontolingua Server, which eases the translation task.
- In large ontologies, such as WordNet, SUMO and upperCyc, knowledge about time is scattered throughout the ontology. Since these large ontologies are not organized in sub-ontologies it is difficult to extract all the knowledge about a specific domain.
- In the Ontolingua Server the Simple-Time ontology is one ontology, an unique object, with well defined boundaries, so it is easier to reuse.

Conceptualization/Analysis/Revision Cycle
During this stage of the process, the sub-ontology of time went through several iterations. This cycle consisted in: (1) make an initial conceptualization, (2) analyze the ontology and driven by this analysis, (3) revise the ontology, changing the conceptualization. We will further describe this part of the process in Section 3.3.

3.1 Knowledge Acquisition & Requirement Specification/Initial Conceptualization of ONTO-SD

We decided not to separate the descriptions of the knowledge acquisition and requirement specification/conceptualization stages, because we were constantly interchanging between the two. The knowledge acquisition and requirement specification/conceptualization stages of ONTO-SD can be divided into three steps:

- **Collect dialogues** We started by *taping* real dialogues in a bus terminal in Lisbon. We left the recorder in a ticket booth for one hour. The users were not warned of the presence of the recorder, so the dialogues were not biased by its presence.

- **Statistical analysis of dialogues** Using the *transcription* of these dialogues, we used a simple computer program[6] to count the number of occurrences of each term. In the first frequency analysis of the dialogues only individual terms were considered. However, we found that in some cases we should consider groups of terms instead of individual terms. For instance, we should consider the expression "Cartão Jovem" (Youth Card), and not "Cartão" and "Jovem". Therefore, we changed the transcription of the dialogues, so that those groups of terms would appear as one term only. Part of those results is presented in Fig. 3.

This simple *analysis* can only help us in: (1) getting an idea of the most important concepts that will have to be appropriately represented[7] and (2) identifying the domains involved.

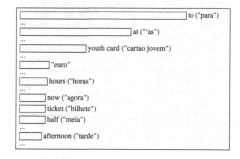

Figure 3: Frequency analysis of terms in the dialogues

- **Identification of domains** Using the results of the statistical analysis, we *identified* the most important domains that are a part of our ontology. To identify the relations between the several domains, we *analyzed* the most complex dialogues, that involved all domains.

The most common term used is "para",[8] Fig. 3. This means that the users identify the tickets they want to buy by stating their traveling destination. Another set of words often used is "Cartão Jovem", which refers to one available discount. This means the final ontology needs to have knowledge about possible discounts. There are also many words related to time. Sometimes a simple term analysis is not enough. We have to analyze the dialogues

---

[2] http://ontolingua.stanford.edu:5915
[3] http://www.cogsci.princeton.edu/~wn/
[4] http://www.cyc.com/cyc-2-1/cover.html
[5] http://ontology.teknowledge.com

[6] Program WordCount available at http://www.intellij.com as a sample of IDEA IDE for JAVA, from IntelliJ.

[7] Its aim is not to provide us with the required Time ontology.

[8] "Para" is the Portuguese word for "to", as in "ticket *to* the Algarve".

in detail and use abstraction to extract the concepts to be represented in the ontology. For instance, we will need to represent the concept destination, although the dialogues only refer specific locations.

All the domains and relations between them were identified, and the *structure* of ONTO-SD was established. This structure is shown in Fig. 4. There are five modules. The Time module defines concepts that are strictly related to time, for instance "hour". The module Time-Order, will define concepts like "next", "first", etc. The reason why we chose not to represent these concepts also in the Time module is that not only they are used in the dialogues to express a relation order between time points and time ranges, but also they can be used to express order between other concepts, in a different domain. For instance, related to trips, we have the concepts of "first bus stop", "last bus stop", etc. By separating the modules, we can later reuse the Time-Order module to represent those concepts. Another module is Spatial-Information. It will define concepts such as origin, destination, stop, all possible stops for all buses, and other spatial concepts, such as the position of seats inside a particular bus, or the exact location inside the bus terminal from which the bus will depart. The Travel module will define the concepts related to traveling, for instance, "bus stop", or "bus ticket". The Commerce module will define the concepts related to buying and selling, for instance, "Euro".

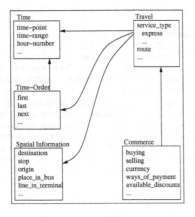

Figure 4: ONTO-SD structure

Trying to find the structure of the ontology and the relations between these modules is already a part of conceptualization activities.

3.2 Planning the Development Order

Before knowledge acquisition and requirement specification stages we had already decided to start the process by the sub-ontology of Time. Empirically, we could foresee that ONTO-SD would have a sub-ontology about time and this module would be independent from the rest of the ontology. Having established the final structure, our idea was confirmed. There are two modules in ONTO-SD that do not include any others. These modules are Time and Spatial-Information. The Time module is a better place to start than the Spatial-Information module because (1) it involves common sense knowledge about time, and (2) we would not need an expert in the domain to perform acquisition.

The established development *order* is: (1) Time, (2) Time-Order, (3) Spatial-Information, (4) Travel and (5) Commerce.

3.3 Conceptualization/Analysis/Revision Cycle of Time ontology

In this subprocess, Fig. 5, the ontology went through several iterations:

- **Reverse Engineering of Simple-Time** At this stage we *obtained a possible conceptual model* for the Simple-Time ontology. Part of this conceptual model is shown in Fig. 6. This subprocess was divided into three stages:

  - **Identify classes** We analyze the source code, Fig. 7, searching for definitions of classes. We link each class (in **bold**) to its super/subclasses establishing the taxonomy of classes for the ontology.

  - **Identify instances** We analyze the source code one more time searching for definitions of instances and link them (in *italics*) to the appropriate classes in the conceptual model.

  - **Identify relations and functions** We analyze the source code searching for definitions of relations and functions, and add them to the conceptual model. In the case of binary relations we link the appropriate origin and target concepts. The label of these links is the name of the relation.

- **Import from Ontolingua** To *import* the Simple-Time ontology from the Ontolingua Server into Protégé-2000 we used the OKBC (Chaudri et al., 1998) tab plug-in.[9]

---

[9]http://protege.stanford.edu/plugins/okbctab/okbc_tab.html

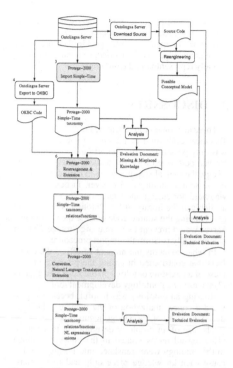

Figure 5: Conceptualization/Analysis/Revision cycle of Time ontology

Figure 6: Part of Simple-Time conceptual model

- **Analysis - identification of missing and misplaced knowledge** At this stage, we *compared* the conceptual model obtained earlier for the Simple-Time ontology with the translated version of the ontology. We *found* that the taxonomy was correctly imported. However, all relations and some functions were lost. All the axiomatic definitions of these relations were also lost. Although relations and axioms are outside to OKBC knowledge model, the OKBC export translator of the Ontolingua Server translated these relations as slots.[10] Moreover, some functions were misplaced.

- **Revision - rearrangement and extension of knowledge** The knowledge we found misplaced in the ontology was *relocated*. In what concerns missing knowledge, we *introduced* the relations and functions.

---

[10]The OKBC knowledge model only allows binary relations, which are represented as slots.

- **Analysis - technical evaluation of source ontology** Having the taxonomy, relations and functions, we *evaluated* the Simple-Time ontology in the Ontolingua Server according to the criteria proposed in (Gómez-Pérez et al., 1995). For that we used both the source code and the conceptual model. The reasons why we used both were: (1) if we only use the conceptual model we are not able to analyze the syntactical errors[11] (language conformity) and (2) if we only use the source code we loose the overall perspective of the ontology which is crucial to perform a thorough analysis.[12]

- **Revision - correction, Natural Language translation and extension** The problems found in the source ontology were *corrected* in the version kept in Protégé-2000. Then, we *translated* all the names of the knowledge pieces represented in the ontology into Portuguese. Finally, the *axioms* were *added* to our ontology using Protégé Axiom Language (PAL). The axioms were only introduced at this stage because in the documentation of the tool it is recommended that the axioms should be written only after the taxonomy is defined. Moreover, some of the *concepts* that we found during the requirement specification stage of Time, were *added*. For instance, half an hour.

- **Analysis - technical evaluation of Time ontology** Finally, we *technically evaluated* our ontology, again using the criteria proposed in (Gómez-Pérez et al., 1995), and also *comparing* the final result with the original Simple-Time ontology.

One of the differences is that the Time ontology introduces a new concept, representacao-

---

[11]For instance, the equals relation in Ontolingua is defined for both time-points and time-ranges (polymorphic refinement). However, there is an error, since the definition for time-ranges introduces two variables that are not declared.

[12]For instance, without the conceptual model, we could miss the fact that functions month-of and month-name-of are the same function.

245

```
(Define-Class Calendar-Date (?T)
"a specification of a point in absolute calendar time,
 at the resolution of one day."
:Def (And (Time-Point ?T)
          (Has-One ?T Day-Of)
          (Has-One ?T Month-Of)
          (Has-One ?T Year-Of))) ...

(Define-Frame Time-Point
:Own-Slots
 ((Arity 1)
  (Documentation
      "A time-point is a point in real, historical time
      (on earth). It is independent of observer and
      context. A time-point is not a measurement of
      time, nor is it a specification of time.
      It is the point in time. The time-points at which
      events occur can be known with various degrees of
      precision and approximation, but conceptually
      time-points are point-like and not interval-like.
      That is, it doesn't make sense to talk about what
      happens during a time-point, or how long the
      time-point lasts.")
  (Domain-Of Day-Of Minutes-Of Month-Of Seconds-Of
  Year-Of)
  (Instance-Of Class)
  (Subclass-Of Individual))) ...

(Define-Relation Equals (?Time-Point-1 ?Time-Point-2)
 " a time point ?time-point-1 is equal to a time point
 ?time-point-2. a time range ?time-range-1 is
 identical to a time range ?time-range-2."
:Axiom-Def
  ((=> (And (Time-Point ?Time-Point-1)
            (Time-Point ?Time-Point-2))
      (<=> (Equals ?Time-Point-1 ?Time-Point-2)
           (And (= (Year-Of ?Time-Point-1)
                   (Year-Of ?Time-Point-2))
                (= (Month-Of ?Time-Point-1)
                   (Month-Of ?Time-Point-2))
                (= (Day-Of ?Time-Point-1)
                   (Day-Of ?Time-Point-2))
                (= (Hour-Of ?Time-Point-1)
                   (Hour-Of ?Time-Point-2))
                (= (Minute-Of ?Time-Point-1)
                   (Minute-Of ?Time-Point-2))
                (= (Second-Of ?Time-Point-1)
                   (Second-Of ?Time-Point-2)))))

   (=> (And (Time-Range ?Time-Range-1)
            (Time-Range ?Time-Range-2))
      (<=> (Equals ?Time-Range-1 ?Time-Range-2)
           (And (Equals (Start-Time-Of ?Time-Range-1)
                (Start-Time-Of ?Time-Range-2))
                (Equals (End-Time-Of ?Time-Range-1)
                (End-Time-Of ?Time-Range-2))))))) ...
```

Figure 7: Example of Ontolingua source code

-numerica,[13] which is a function. It relates each temporal entity with the corresponding integer which is normally used to represent it.[14] It also introduces the concept numero-tempo,[15] which is a superclass of all classes that can be characterized using the representacao-numerica slot.

In order to *test the expressivity requirements* of the ontology, we also *represented* the concepts identified in the dialogues during the requirement specification stage. We *found* that some of these con-

---

[13]"Representacao-numerica" is the Portuguese word for "numeric representation".

[14]For instance, the numeric representation of the instance 1-the-month-number of the class month-number would be the Integer 1.

[15]"numero-tempo" is the Portuguese word for "time-number".

cepts cannot be represented directly in the ontology. For instance, the concept of amanha ("tomorrow") depends on the specific date on which the knowledge base is queried, so it cannot be statically represented in the ontology.

4 DISCUSSION

There are some unique features in this experience. Technical evaluation of the chosen source ontology was only performed after importing the ontology. If we had performed it before actually reusing the ontology, the logical step would be to correct the errors in the source ontology. However, in our case: (1) we could not change the source ontology, since it is available at the library of the Ontolingua Server, and (2) changing the source code outside the Ontolingua Server would prevent us from using Protégé-2000 to automatically perform the import procedure.

In what concerns the amount of effort, there two facts that contributed in easing the process: (1) the reuse of an existing ontology on the same domain and (2) the use of an ontology development tool.

Reusing an ontology was helpful, because it provided a conceptualization of the domain, which reduced the effort of knowledge acquisition.

The use of an ontology development tool helped (1) when all terms related to the concepts defined in the ontology were translated into Portuguese, because each knowledge piece only had to be translated once and all references to it were automatically changed, (2) when misplaced knowledge was rearranged in Protégé-2000, since we used drag&drop operations, and (3) when the Simple-Time ontology was automatically imported from the Ontolingua Server. Even with the conceptual model, which is the main advantage of reusing the Simple-Time ontology, if we had manually inserted the whole ontology from scratch into Protégé-2000, the effort would be much greater.[16]

5 RELATED WORK

There are several ways of building ontologies. Ontologies can either be built from scratch or by means of reuse. There are two different kinds of reuse processes: merge and integration (Pinto et al., 1999). The process described in this article is a typical integration process.

Although there are several methodologies proposed in the literature to build from scratch, none has been

---

[16]The Simple-Time ontology defines 14 classes, 209 instances, 17 relations and 14 functions.

accepted as standard. Some ontology reuse processes are described in the literature, but there are very few methodologies proposed for each kind of reuse process.[17]

Reuse processes are described in (Gangemi et al., 1998; Chaudhri et al., 2000; Pinto, 1999). The process described in (Gangemi et al., 1998) is a typical merge process. The one described in (Chaudhri et al., 2000) combines both merge and integration subprocesses. This particular reuse process combines automatic translation, analysis, slicing, reformulation, merging and extension. Comparing this process with our experience, both involved automatic translation. Moreover, they both have involved OKBC translators. Both processes involved analysis, although at different levels. While we have extensively and successively performed analysis activities, to choose the adequate ontologies, to structure the final ontology and to perform quality verification, the analysis described in the merge/integration experience was for comprehension purposes only. Slicing "involves selecting a portion of an input ontology for use in a new application", because one may not need the whole ontology. For instance, if we had chosen to reuse WordNet we would just need the concepts related to time. In our experience we could avoid slicing because the reused ontology is a unique object with well defined boundaries. In our case, we did not need to perform reformulation since the Protégé-2000 knowledge model is OKBC compliant (which was not the case in the merge/integration experience where a more expressive final knowledge model was used). Both processes involved extension activities. In our case, we performed extension to both (1) recover knowledge that was lost in the automatic translation and (2) to introduce knowledge missing in the source ontology that was found important for our application. In the merge/integration experience knowledge was introduced because it was missing.

Finally, the processes described in (Pinto, 1999) are also integration experiences that have led to a methodology (Pinto and Martins, 2001). One of the aims of our experiment was to test how natural this methodology is. For that, we deliberately prevented the actual person performing this process from knowing beforehand the actual details of this methodology. Comparing both experiences, we can see that our process closely follows the proposed methodology. However, there are some differences. We performed evaluation of the reused ontology after importing, while the methodology proposes that evaluation should be performed while choosing the source ontology to be reused. Another difference, was the fact that the actual experiments described in (Pinto, 1999) have not

involved such a large variety of subprocesses, namely they avoided translation (although this subprocess is referred in the methodology).

A manual reengineering process is described is (Blázquez et al., 1998). This process involves three steps: (1) abstract a conceptual model of an ontology given its implementation, (2) modify the conceptual model according to some criteria, and (3) implement the new conceptual model. In our case, we only extracted (step 1) the conceptual model of the Simple-Time ontology kept in the Ontolingua Server because we wanted to compare it with the conceptual model of the ontology obtained after the knowledge representation translation subprocess.

A translation process involving the Simple-Time ontology in the Ontolingua Server is described in (Russ et al., 1999). In this case, the export translator of Ontolingua into Loom was used. The authors identified two problems that make the automatic translation process difficult: (1) a mismatch of modeling styles between Ontolingua and Loom and (2) an inference engine bias. In our case, there was no mismatch in modeling style, but there was an inference engine bias, since PAL is a constraint checking mechanism rather than a theorem proving mechanism.

There is an evaluation methodology, OntoClean (Welty and Guarino, 2001), and criteria for evaluation (Gómez-Pérez et al., 1995). OntoClean is a method to correct taxonomies according to notions such as *rigidity*, *identity* and *unity*. These are philosophical notions that are difficult to understand at first. Therefore, in our experience, we performed two technical evaluations according to the criteria proposed by Gómez-Pérez. There are already some tools which automate the evaluation activity, like WebODE (Fernández-Lopéz and Gómez-Pérez, 2002) and the Analyzer of the Ontolingua Server. However, we did not use WebODE because it is not freely available and we did not use the Analyzer of Ontolingua because it only performs a syntactical analysis.

6 CONCLUSIONS AND FUTURE WORK

Ontology building is still an open area of Ontology Engineering. We followed an integration methodology that is general enough to be used in different integration processes. In our experience, we (1) used Natural Language techniques to help knowledge acquisition, (2) used tools to perform automatic translation of an ontology, (3) performed part of a manual reengineering process and (4) performed manual ontology evaluation. Although in the literature there are descriptions of the several subprocesses that were performed in this experience, they have never been all

---

[17] As far as we know, there is only one methodology proposed for each one of the reuse processes.

combined in one particular ontology building process. One of the aims of this article is to show how they can all be combined. Even the more complex reuse experiences described in the literature only involve some of these subprocesses.

The reuse of an ontology and the use of a development tool were crucial in reducing the amount of effort required to build the Time sub-ontology. The main advantage of reusing an existing ontology was that it gave us an initial conceptualization, which eased the knowledge acquisition stage. As for the tool, the main advantage was the automation of some of the subprocesses, namely knowledge representation translation.

At the moment only one of the modules of ONTO-SD is complete. We plan to proceed with the development of ONTO-SD. We are also going to improve Protégé-2000 OKBC tab plug-in.

REFERENCES

Allen, J. (1984). Towards a General Theory of Action and Time. *Artificial Intelligence*, 23:123–154.

Berners-Lee, T., Hendler, J., and Lassila, O. (2001). The Semantic Web. *Scientific American*, 284.

Blázquez, M., Fernández, M., García-Pinar, J. M., and Goméz-Pérez, A. (1998). Building Ontologies at the Knowledge Level Using the Ontology Design Environment. In *Proceedings of the Knowledge Acquisition Workshop, KAW98*.

Chaudhri, V., Stickel, M., Thomere, J., and Waldinger, R. (2000). Using Prior Knowledge: Problems and Solutions. In *AAAI2000 Proceedings*, pages 436–442. AAAI Press.

Chaudri, V., Farquhar, A., Fikes, R., Karp, P., and Rice, J. (1998). Open Knowledge Base Connectivity 2.0.3. Technical Report KSL-98-06, Knowledge Systems Laboratory, Stanford University.

Farquhar, A., Fikes, R., and Rice, J. (1996). The Ontolingua Server: A Tool for Collaborative Ontology Construction. In *Proceedings of the Knowledge Acquisition Workshop, KAW96*.

Fernández-Lopéz, M. and Goméz-Pérez, A. (2002). The integration of OntoClean in WebODE. In *Proceedings of EKAW2002 Workshop on Evaluation of Ontology-based Tools*. also alvailable as CEUR Proceedings, Volume 62, http://SunSITE.Informatik.RWTH-Aachen.DE/Publications/CEUR-WS/Vol-62/.

Gangemi, A., Pisanelli, D. M., and Steve, G. (1998). Ontology Integration: Experiences with Medical Terminologies. In Guarino, N., editor, *Formal Ontology in Information Systems*, pages 163–178. IOS Press.

Gómez-Pérez, A., Juristo, N., and Pazos, J. (1995). Evaluation and Assessment of the Knowledge Sharing Technology. In Mars, N., editor, *Towards Very Large Knowledge Bases*, pages 289–296. IOS Press.

Noy, N., Sintek, M., Decker, S., Crubézy, M., Fergerson, R., and Musen, M. (2001). Creating Semantic Web Contents with Protégé-2000. *IEEE Intelligent Systems*, 48.

Peralta, D. N. (2002). Desenvolvimento de ontologias. Trabalho Final de Curso, Departamento de Eng. Informática, Instituto Superior Técnico.

Pinto, H. S. (1999). Towards Ontology Reuse. In *Proceedings of AAAI99's Workshop on Ontology Management, WS-99-13*, pages 67–73. AAAI Press.

Pinto, H. S., Gómez-Pérez, A., and Martins, J. P. (1999). Some Issues on Ontology Integration. In *Proceedings of IJCAI99's Workshop on Ontologies and Problem Solving Methods: Lessons Learned and Future Trends*, pages 7.1–7.12.

Pinto, H. S. and Martins, J. P. (2001). A Methodology for Ontology Integration. In *Proceedings of the First International Conference on Knowledge Capture, K-CAP'01*, pages 131–138. ACM Press.

Pinto, H. S., Peralta, D. N., and Mamede, N. J. (2002). Using Protégé-2000 in Reuse Processes. In *EON2002, Evaluation of Ontology-based Tools*, pages 15–26. CEUR-WS.

Russ, T., Valente, A., MacGregor, R., and Swartout, W. (1999). Practical Experiences in Trading Off Ontology Usability and Reusability. In *Proceedings of the Knowledge Acquisition Workshop, KAW99*.

Welty, C. and Guarino, N. (2001). Supporting Ontological Analysis of Taxonomic Relationships. *Data and Knowledge Engineering, September 2001*.

DERIVING USE CASES FROM BUSINESS PROCESSES
The advantages of DEMO

Boris Shishkov, Jan L.G. Dietz

Faculty ITS, Delft University of Technology, 4 Mekelweg, Delft, The Netherlands
Email: Shishkov@IS.TWI.TUDelft.nl, j.l.g.dietz@its.tudelft.nl

Keywords: Use Cases; Business Process Modeling; DEMO; Norm Analysis; Petri Net

Abstract: The mismatch between the business requirements and the actual functionality of the delivered software application is considered to be a crucial problem in current software development. Solving this problem means to find out how to consistently place the software specification model on a previously developed business process model. If considering in particular the UML-based software design, we need to answer in this regard a fundamental question, namely – how to find all relevant use cases, based on sound business process modeling? Adopting the business process modeling as a basis for identification of use cases has been studied from three perspectives – Language/Action Perspective, Organizational Semiotics and Petri Net. The goal of the current paper is to study and analyze the strengths of DEMO concerning the derivation of use cases. This could be helpful not only for the investigation of DEMO but also for the further activities directed towards finding out the most appropriate way(s) of identifying use cases from business processes.

1   INTRODUCTION

The mismatch between the business requirements and the actual functionality of the delivered (software) application is considered to be an actual research problem in current software development (Shishkov & Dietz, 2002). In order to solve this problem, it is necessary to find out how to consistently place the specification of software on a business process model. It is worthwhile addressing these issues from the perspective of the Unified Modeling Language – UML (OMG, 2000) not only because of its completeness and wide applicability but also because UML turns out to be *de facto* the standard language for designing software, widely accepted by both researchers and practitioners.

Considering the mentioned problem from the perspective of UML leads directly to the notion of use case because, as it is well known, use cases are modeling constructs that serve to link the application domain (the business world) to the software domain, regarding the UML-based software development.

Ivar Jacobson introduced use cases in 1986, to be applied to requirements analysis (Jacobson et al, 1992). This was an essential contribution to UML where the use case concept plays a fundamental role. According to the concept, in a use case, a user performs a behaviorally related sequence of transactions in a dialogue with the (software) system (Fowler & Scott, 2000). Thus, a use case is a typical user / computer system interaction. A use case captures some user-visible function. This view suggests that developers of good use cases identify the users' goals, not the system functions. Based on these UML-related concepts, Alistar Cockburn further studies them, discussing how use cases should be developed and documented. Cockburn discusses the way in which use cases can be represented with varying levels of formality (Cockburn, 2001). The concepts of Jacobson and Cockburn were thoroughly investigated by Shishkov and Dietz (2001) from the point of view of their actuality for the development of UML. In UML, use cases (representing text documents) are implemented through the use case diagram which shows actors and use cases together with their relationships (OMG, 2000). The diagram itself is a graph of actors, a set of use cases, and the relationships between these elements (associations, generalizations, etc.). It might include also some interfaces. By representing the potential use cases for the system to be built and relevant actors, the diagram provides the starting point in system modeling. Therefore, the proper derivation of use cases and the construction of use case diagram are crucial concerning the task to place consistently the (UML-based) specification of software on prior

O. Camp et al. (eds.), Enterprise Information Systems V, 249-257.
© 2004 *Kluwer Academic Publishers. Printed in the Netherlands.*

business process modeling. Hence, it is essential to know how to derive use cases based on a sound business process model. We take into consideration that the software community still misses consistent guidance for the use case identification. Sound and complete methods for construction of UML use case diagram (Jacobson et al, 1992; Fowler & Scott, 2000; Shishkov & Dietz, 2001) on the basis of business process modeling are still needed.

This paper reports further results of a study directed towards derivation of use cases from business processes. Adopting the business process modeling as a basis for the identification of use cases has been studied (Shishkov & Dietz, 2002; Shishkov et al, 2002; Shishkov & Barjis, 2002) from three perspectives, namely: Language/Action Perspective and the DEMO theory in particular (Dietz, 1999), Organizational Semiotics and Norm Analysis in particular (Stamper, 1997), and Petri Net (Aalst, 1998). The goal of the current paper is, by considering the mentioned achieved results, to study and analyze the strengths of DEMO concerning the derivation of use cases. This could be helpful not only for the investigation of DEMO but also for the further activities directed towards finding out the most appropriate way(s) of identifying use cases from business processes.

Further on in this paper: The basic concepts regarding DEMO, Norm Analysis and Petri Net as well as the theoretical background for relating them to use cases are considered in Sections 2, 3, and 4, respectively. Section 5 illustrates through a case example how use cases could be derived, based on each of these tools. On this foundation, Section 6 studies which are the particular advantages of DEMO in deriving use cases, comparing this way of derivation to the Norm Analysis and Petri Net – based ones. Section 7 contains the conclusions.

2 DEMO

Dynamic Essential Modeling of Organizations - DEMO is a methodology for understanding, analyzing, (re)designing and (re)engineering business processes. Its underlying theory about organizations is rooted in the Language/Action Perspective (Flores & Ludlow, 1980), Organizational Semiotics (Liu, 2000) and Philosophical Ontology (Bunge, 1979). DEMO reveals the "construction" and "operation" of an organization, contrary to the current function and behavior-oriented approaches. It is characterized by three major features: 1) a white-box architecture of actors, production and coordination, 2) the

extraction of the essence of business processes from their realization, 3) the transaction pattern.

Actors, production, coordination. Like every other system (e.g. an alarm clock or a racing car), the functional behavior of an organization is brought about by the collective working of the constructional components. The construction and the working of a system are most near to what a system really is, to its ontological description (Bunge, 1979). An organization is defined as a (discrete dynamic) system in the category of social systems. This means that the elements are social individuals or actors, each of them having a particular authority to perform production acts (P-acts) and a corresponding responsibility to do that in an appropriate and accountable way. The structure of an organization consists of coordination acts (C-acts), i.e. the actors enter into and comply with commitments regarding the performance of P-acts. The generic white-box organizational model (Figure 1) consists of: the actors, the P-world, and the C-world (Dietz, 1999).

Figure 1: The white-box model of an organization

By performing P-acts, the organization does what it is supposed to do according to its function. C-acts serve to coordinate and control the performance of P-acts.

Essence, realization. Three perspectives on an organization are distinguished in DEMO: essential (the organization viewed as a system of authorized and responsible actors that create new original facts), informational (the organization viewed as a system of information processors that remember facts and derive new facts from existing ones), documental (the organization viewed as a system of formal operators that collect, transport, store, copy, destroy representations of facts) (Dietz, 1994).

Take for example the process of withdrawing money from a bank account using an ATM machine. Think of observing this process through essential, informational or documental "glasses" as a metaphor. Looking through documental "glasses" we see someone inserting a card into a machine, pushing buttons on a keyboard and finally getting out the card and other pieces of paper. Nothing with respect to the information on it or the purpose for which they are used, is seen. Looking at the same process through informational "glasses", we see someone providing information to an ATM system: a PIN code and specification of an amount of money. Also, the machine provides information if withdrawal is possible to the customer. We see that the machine outputs money and receipts. Looking through essential "glasses" shows responsible actors, their actions and interactions. A customer requests a bank to withdraw money from an account. The bank decides to do this and states that the money is withdrawn. Further on, the customer accepts it.

The transaction pattern. P-acts and C-acts appear to be performed in particular sequences that can be viewed as paths through a generic pattern called the (business) *transaction* (Dietz, 1999). A transaction is a finite sequence of C-acts between two actor roles, the customer and the producer. It takes place in three phases: the order phase (O-phase), the execution phase (E-phase), and the result phase (R-phase). O-phase is a conversation that starts with a request by the customer and that, if successful, ends with a promise by the producer. E-phase basically consists of the performance of the P-act by the producer. R-phase starts with the statement by the producer that the requested act is performed and ends, if successful, with the accept by the customer. The whole pattern of a transaction is represented by one symbol in the so-called Coordination Structure Diagram (CSD). Fig. 2 exhibits CSD for the money withdrawal example. The two boxes represent the two actor roles involved: A0(A1) is the customer(producer). The small black box indicates that A1 is the producer of T1 (and consequently A0 is the customer). The successful result of a transaction T1 is the P-fact "withdrawal W is performed" where W is constituted by the account, the amount and the time.

Figure 2: CSD of the money withdrawal example

Deriving Use Cases

A use case model can be consistently derived based on a DEMO business process model, as it has been studied in (Shishkov & Dietz, 2002). Applying DEMO, developers could provide a sound business process model for the software design, a clear model that captures the features which remain unchanged from realization. Such a model could be a proper basis for improving the delimitation, identification and the specification of the modeled software system (Dietz, 1994). Hence, DEMO possesses completeness and capability of capturing the essence of business processes. Therefore, if the developed software model stems from a DEMO business process model, the software designer would have the right (re)design freedom (Dietz, 1999). All this makes a DEMO model to be a sound basis for

further software specification activities. For this reason, we consider it worthwhile exploring the use case derivation based on DEMO business process modeling. In this regard, it has been studied that DEMO transactions are straightforwardly relatable to the pieces of functionality concerning the software (further specified). Thus, deriving use cases based on DEMO is well founded theoretically. Next to that, the actors associated with the identified use cases would be a reflection of the DEMO actors because they concern these same transactions. All this makes the reflection of a DEMO business process model in a use case model complete, consistent and well founded theoretically.

3 NORM ANALYSIS (NA)

When studying organizations from the perspective of agents' behavior it is necessary to specify the norms based on which this behavior is realized. Norms (Stamper et al, 1997) are the rules and behavior patterns - formal or informal, explicit or implicit, existing within a society, an organzation, or even a small group of people working together to achieve a common goal (Liu et al, 2001).

Norms are determined by Society or collective groups, and serve as a standard for coordination of actions. If the norms can be identified, individuals' behaviors, hence their collective behaviors, are mostly predictable. From this perspective, to specify an organization can be done by specifying the norms (Stamper, 1992).

Four types of norms exist: evaluative, perceptual, cognitive and behavioral norms. Each type of norms governs human behavior from different aspects. In business process modeling, most rules and regulations fall into the category of behavioral norms. They prescribe what people must, may, and must not do, which are equivalent to three deontic operators "is obliged", "is permitted", "is prohibited". Hence, the following format is considered suitable for specifying behavioral norms:
   whenever <condition>
   if <state>
   then <agent>
   is <deontic operator>
   to <action>

It is essential to recognize that norms are not as rigid as logical conditions. If a person does not drink water for certain duration of time he cannot survive. But an individual who breaks the working pattern of a group does not have to be punished in any way. For those actions that are "permitted", whether the agent will take an action or not is seldom deterministic. This elasticity characterizes the business processes, therefore is of particular value to understand the organizations.

A NA is normally carried out on the basis of the results of the Semantic Analysis (for information on Semantic Analysis interested readers are referred to (Liu, 2000)). The semantic model delineates the area of concern of an organization. The patterns of behavior specified in the semantic model are part of the fundamental norms that retain the ontologically determined relationships between agents and actions without imposing any further constraints. However, NA could be successfully related also to other modeling tools, e.g. Activity diagram, Petri net.

In general, a complete NA can be performed in four steps: 1) **Responsibility analysis** – it enables one to identify and assign responsible agents to each action, focusing on the types of agents and types of actions. 2) **Proto-norm analysis** – it helps one to identify relevant types of information for making decisions concerning a certain type of behavior; the aim of this analysis is to facilitate the human decisions without overlooking any necessary factors or types of information. 3) **Trigger analysis** – it is to consider the actions to be taken in relation to the absolute and relative time, the absolute time means the calendar time, the relative time makes use of references to other events; the results of trigger analysis are specifications of the schedule of the actions. 4) **Detailed norm specification** - it concerns the specification of norms in a natural and a formal language versions; the goals of this are to capture the norms as references for human decision and to perform actions in the automated system by executing the norms in the formal language.

For those norms identified in the business processes, some refer to the major authorities and responsibilities of the major figures in the organizations. These norms govern some trivial, relatively less important norms or those of lower priorities, from the perspective of organizational functionalities. This strongly suggests the possible hierarchies exist not only in the organization structure, but also in the norms. Liu et al (2001) use the terms framing norms, contractual norms, etc. to express the hierarchies.

Deriving Use Cases

As studied in (Shishkov et. al, 2002), NA can be useful in creating a business process model to be reflected into a use case one. NA has widely been used as an effective and proven tool for investigation (in combination with Semantic Analysis) of business processes. Regarding a business system under study, NA specifies the rules according to which agents' behavior is realized. This is a potential link to use cases which represent functionality of a system, by defining its behavior. Hence, deriving use cases from a NA model would be useful and is put on

sound theoretical foundation, since both modeling tools reflect behavior within business/software systems (norms describe rules of behavior; use cases represent pieces of functionality). Thus these could be methodologically related.

4 PETRI NET (PN)

Petri Net (PN) is a well known and widely used modeling technique (Aalst, 1998) that allows for consistent investigation of business systems by consideration of processes. Any business can be viewed as a collection of processes, where a process can be described as "a set of identifiable, repeatable actions, which are ordered in some way and contribute to the fulfilment of an objective". These processes change as organizations evolve over time in response to their business environments. The focus on the business processes is important in order to design, maintain and improve the way businesses work, effectively and efficiently.

PN could be very useful in supporting software specification activities. As it is well known, in the modeling of software systems, it is essential to model consistently the system itself, eliciting precisely all the necessary static and dynamic issues as well as to reflect the requirements in the designed functionality. As already stated, all this needs to be based on business process modeling, represented through a sound graphical tool. This is in order to capture the system dynamics, to represent processes in time sequence, etc. It is claimed that PN could be successfully used for this purpose, including in the cases in which we consider UML as a system elicitation environment. Combining UML and PN has been studied by Shishkov & Barjis (2002).

PN have well supported tools to allow modeling, analysis, and, if necessary, simulation (execution) of systems. PN are formalism and a graphical language for the design, specification, and verification of systems. In order to better understand PN, there are some typical examples of PN depicted in Figure 3. These examples are especially chosen to demonstrate PN application and way of modeling, while dealing with processes in series, parallel, and conditional or alternative processes. It should be noted that rectangles coloured in grey indicate that these transitions are enabled.

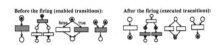

Figure 3: Typical PN examples

In Figure 3, there are the following situations represented before and after the firing of transitions, from the left to the right. The first example shows an ordinary process having one transition. The second example represents parallel processes. When the enabled transition fires, it enables two other transitions in parallel. The third example represents alternative processes. This example shows that only one of the two processes, for which the condition is true, will be undertaken. The fourth example shows synchronization or AND-join processes. In this situation it is necessary to finish both processes completely before starting the following one.

Deriving Use Cases

It was studied and demonstrated (Shishkov & Barjis, 2002) that a PN process/transition could be used as a consistent basis for use case derivation. We consider useful in this regard that PN is easily readable, simple and adapted to capture the dynamics of systems and processes; and next to that – there are many available tools supporting PN models of place transition type, e.g. simulation tools. All this is a guarantee that the use case model would stem from a consistently developed and verified business process model. Regarding the PN - use case mapping, it is well founded theoretically because PN models the dynamics of a business system, elaborating on the concrete business processes that reflect a particular behavior. As for use cases, they reflect the pieces of functionality concerning the designed system that is to support these same business processes.

5 THE HRB CASE

In this section, as said in the introduction, we will illustrate, through a case example, the three studied ways of deriving use cases from business processes, namely: based on DEMO, NA and PN. A system, representing a Hotel Reservation Broker (HRB) is modeled in order to illustrate this.

HRB matches the data about clients' required accommodation and hotel offers. Both the hotels and clients need to register in order to use the service for a selected period of time. The subscription fees for hotels are fixed depending on the chosen period and the hotel size; the fees are fixed for clients also, depending on the chosen period. Besides these subscription fees, both clients and hotels pay fixed fees when a match-making is realized. Further on, we refer to these fees as: a "reservation fee" (paid by a client) and a "hotel fee" (paid by a hotel). HRB accepts accommodation requirements from clients (e.g. check in/out dates, place, type of

accommodation, price, etc) and accommodation information from hotels (e.g. number and type of rooms/beds available, etc.). Once HRB has received requirements from a client, if requested, it performs match-making on a real time basis. HRB provides the client with a list of available accommodation (all of them meeting the client's requirements) to select from. Once the client has accepted one of the offers, he pays the reservation fee. He has to pay also the cost of the selected accommodation. Then, HRB is obliged to guarantee the accommodation. HRB should contact the selected hotel and realize the actual booking of a particular room/bed. Then, the hotel must pay to HRB the hotel fee, and will be paid (by HRB) the cost of the reserved accommodation. Once this is done, the reservation is actually completed. The service is considered finished.

Further on in this section, we will illustrate how the use case model for HRB could be built based on DEMO, and what alternative ways for use case derivation are offered by NA and PN.

5.1 Deriving the use case model based on DEMO

We will first consider issues concerning the building of the DEMO model itself and afterwards – its reflection in the derivation of the use case model.

Table 1 - Business Transactions List

transaction type	result fact type
T1 *match-making*	F1 *match <M> is made*
T2 *subscription*	F2 *subscription <S> is arranged*
T3 *subscr. payment*	F3 *the fee for period <P> by <Cl./Hotel> is paid*
T4 *reserv. payment*	F4 *the fee for reserv. <R> by <Cl./Hotel> is paid*
T5 *accom. payment*	F5 *the cost for accom. <A> by <Cl.> is paid*
T6 *accom. compens.*	F6 *<Hotel> is compensated for ac. <A>*
T7 *refund*	F7 *refund <RE> for violation <V> is arranged*
T8 *reservation*	F8 *reservation <R> by <Hotel> is arranged*

After delimitation of the domain, the business processes to be supported by HRB are explored with DEMO. The eight identified business transactions (transaction types) are listed in Table 1 together with their corresponding resulting fact types.

The focus is only on transactions on the essential level, in order to keep the business model abstract enough so that it should remain unchanged during (eventual) re-design of its realization.

Based on the transactions and result facts, the system(s) to be investigated should be selected, relevant DEMO actor(s) – identified, and their roles – determined (as customer and producer). Once this is done, all interaction relationships are determined. All this is depicted in Fig. 4, representing the Coordination Structure Model – CSM (it is

253

incomplete, since the goal is only to illustrate the usage of DEMO for use case derivation).

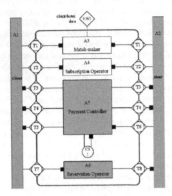

Figure 4: HRB – DEMO Coordination Structure Model

The system under study (HRB) is considered as well as the Client and Hotel (as actors). Regarding the system under study, it is represented on the figure in more detail: actors A3 and A4 (they are represented in white boxes, because they are elementary actors – involved in just one transaction each) are depicted as well as actors A5 and A6, whereas Client and Hotel are actors outside the system. The transaction types are represented by a symbol combining a disk and a diamond symbol. The small disk C3 represents a so-called conversation for initiation. It models the periodic activation of A5 to issue payment requests. The system boundary is represented by a grey round angle. There is a so-called external bank (EB1) which contains the accommodation data provided by hotels. The dotted line between EB1 and A3 means that actor A3 is allowed to inspect the contents of EB1. In other words, actor A3 is allowed to know the information provided by hotels. The reason for this allowance is that A3 needs to know the provided information. How A3 gets access and also how hotels add and remove data is not shown. These matters are considered to belong to the information and documental perspective and thus are not represented in the CSM.

As already stated, the DEMO transactions are straightforwardly mappable into use cases. The derived use case model is depicted on Fig. 5. The use cases are given numbers in order to trace directly from which DEMO transactions they are derived. This is illustrated in Table 2.

Table 2 - DEMO transactions and derived use cases

Source transaction (s)	Derived use case(s)
1	0; 1
2	2
3	3
4	4.1; 4.2
5	5
6	6
7	7
8	8

As seen from Figure 5 and Table 2, it is possible that more than one use case is derived from one DEMO transaction. Transaction 4, for example, has the same essence no matter who the actor is. As for the use case model, it should clearly distinguish the cases in which the Client pays reservation fee from the cases in which the Hotel does this. The reason is that the realization issues are different in these two situations. Thus, two use cases are needed. As for Transaction 1, it is reflected in the use case "Perform Match-making", but in order for this functionality to be realized it is necessary the data accuracy to be checked first. However, this is not an essential business transaction, it is just information checking. For this reason, the use case "Check Data Accuracy", being related to the use case "Perform Match-making", is also derived from Transaction 1.

Most of the derived use cases reflect essential behavior, as opposed to some use cases that reflect, for example, information update, like the use cases – "Check Data Accuracy" and "Add data in DBC" (the abbreviation "DBC" will be explained below). As already discussed, although these use cases are not directly derivable from DEMO transactions (as the use cases that reflect essential behavior), the DEMO theory helps developers clearly understand their role and thus – precisely identify them. As far as actors are concerned, the DEMO CSM offers methodological guidance for determining (DEMO) actors that are further reflected in the use case model.

The diagram on Fig. 5 shows use cases and actors typical for such a HRB. Since the purpose is just illustrative, only some of the use cases and actors typical for such a system are considered. Regarding the diagram, the abbreviation "DB" stands for the database, used by HRB. For convenience, DB is virtually divided into DBC and DBH (containing data of offered and searched accommodation, respectively). The diagram shows 2 actors: *Client* & *Hotel*. Concerning Client (Hotel) – he takes the decision, has the responsibility, has the goal to add request (offer) in DBC (DBH), and/or remove it from DBC (DBH), and have his data matched up with relevant data from DBH (DBC). There are 16 use cases: "Add Data in DBC", "Check User's Inf.", etc. There are 3 <<include>>

relationships ("Perform Match-making" requires "Check Data Accuracy"; "Add Data in DBC" & "Add Data in DBH" require "Check User's Inf.") and two <<extends>> relationships (in some cases, before adding their data to DBC/DBH, the system might request from Client/Hotel additional inf., so the basic use cases are "Add Data in DBC" and "Add Data in DBH", and they are extended with "Request Additional Inf.").

Figure 5: Use case diagram of HRB

As seen from this example, a DEMO business process model can be used as a consistent basis for derivation of a use case model. The DEMO transactions are straightforwardly mappable into use cases that reflect essential behavior. The DEMO theory offers methodological knowledge and guidance for clearly understanding and distinguishing between essential business transactions and transactions representing information update, for example. This could be useful as sound guidance in identifying further on the use cases that reflect information-related operations. As for actors, they directly reflect the DEMO actors which are consistently modelled based on the DEMO theory. Regarding the graphical representation, as seen from the example, the graphical notations of the DEMO CSM are very suitable from the point of view of use case derivation activities – the derivation process is easily visible and understandable. Next to these considerations it should be noted that a major advantage of this way of use case derivation is the consistency and completeness of DEMO as a business process modeling tool as well as the wide consideration and applicability of this tool.

5.2 Deriving use cases based on NA

Starting from the textual description concerning HRB, it is necessary to build a NA model on which to base use case derivation. In order to realize this, it is necessary, after delimitation of the domain, to draw an Ontology chart, as discussed in (Shishkov et. al, 2002). The norms are to be identified based on the Ontology chart. Because of the limited scope of this paper we are not going to depict the Ontology chart. Conducting Semantic Analysis and producing an Ontology chart, on the basis of textual description, is well studied and demonstrated in (Liu et al., 2001). It is also well studied how norms could be composed based on an Ontology chart. We will stress upon the issues connected with the derivation of use cases based on already constructed norms.

The following norms are chosen (depicted in Table 3) to illustrate the use case derivation.

Table 3 - Four norms concerning HRB

NORM: Matchmaking	NORM: Subscr. Payment
Whenever <The subscr. fee is paid by the Client/Hotel> **If** <The Client initiates the match-making> **Then** <HRB> **Is** <Obliged to> **To** <Perform the match-making>	**Whenever** <Client/Hotel has decided to use HRB> **If** <The Client/Hotel initiates subscription> **Then** <the Client/Hotel> **Is** <Obliged to> **To** <Pay the subscr. fee>
NORM: Cost Payment	NORM: Hotel Fee Payment
Whenever <The match-making is completed successfully> **If** <An accommodation is selected by the Client> **Then** <the Client> **Is** <Obliged to> **To** <Pay the ac.cost to HRB>	**Whenever** <An accommodation is selected by the Client> **If** <HRB has triggered booking procedure with a hotel> **Then** <the Hotel> **Is** <Obliged to> **To** <Pay hotel fee to HRB >

Based on these norms as well as on the theoretical foundation from Section 3, we derive the use case model, as shown on Figure 6 (only some of the use cases are depicted, for illustrative purpose).

It is easily seen from Figure 6 which are the norms each of the use cases is derived from (dotted line). The set of high-level norms (like the ones mentioned above) identified based on an Ontology chart is not enough to derive a complete use case model. Some use cases are to be derived, based on lower level norms (as "behavior" norms, for example). These lower level norms should be first identified based on relevant higher-level norms. Due to the limited scope of this paper we are not going in more detail concerning these issues which are well studied and demonstrated in (Shishkov et. al, 2002). The use case "Arrange Refund" (Fig. 5) is an example of a use case that comes from a lower level norm. It should be about the refund to be paid back to Client if a guaranteed accommodation is refused later for any reason. The norm should be identified based on a higher-level one concerning HRB's obligation to guarantee a reserved accommodation.

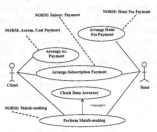

Figure 6: HRB – from NA to use cases

A great advantage of this way of use case derivation is that the high level norms complemented by lower level ones are a consistent basis for constructing a complete use case model. Concerning the use case model actors – they are not directly and formally identifiable from the NA model, although the contents of the norms make it clear which the actors are. A disadvantage of this way of use case derivations is that producing norms requires Semantic Analysis (or other business process investigation) to be conducted beforehand. This makes the modeling process more complicated.

5.3 Deriving use cases based on PN

Since it is considered well known how to derive a PN model based on textual description, we will start directly from the derivation of a use case model based on PN. Our constructed PN model is depicted on Fig. 7, the left side. To the right are several derived use cases (those same ones, considered in the previous sub-section). The PN and use case models are incomplete, because the purpose is just illustrative. It has only been demonstrated how the use cases considered in the previous subsection have been derived, now – based on PN.

It is seen that the use cases are straightforwardly derived from the PN model. For example, the use case "Perform Match-making" directly reflects the process/transition "HRB searches for matches" (the dotted line in Fig. 7 shows the connection between processes and corresponding use cases). As for the actors, they are derived indirectly, not as straightforwardly as e.g. from the DEMO model.

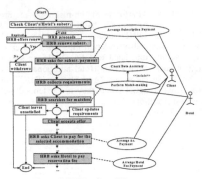

Figure 7: HRB – from PN to use cases

A significant advantage of this kind of derivation is the great popularity of PN models and the ease of building such models based on textual description. PN models are also well supported by relevant simulation tools that could be useful in some cases.

6 THE ADVANTAGES OF DEMO

Based on the realized theoretical and case study, some strengths of DEMO will be outlined, regarding the derivation of use cases from business processes.

A definite strength regarding DEMO is that its models are essential, fully abstracted from all realization issues. The completeness of the models is guaranteed by the DEMO theory that provides methodological knowledge on understanding and identifying essential business transactions as well as on distinguishing them from the realization issues. All this allows us to develop a sound and complete essential business process model. Placing the use case derivation on such a model, developers could be sure that the software specification activities are put on sound theoretical foundation.

Another strength of DEMO is the possibility (illustrated in Section 5) to straightforwardly derive: **1) use cases** that reflect essential behavior (from the DEMO transactions) **2) actors** in the use case model (from the DEMO actors). As for the rest of the use cases, the DEMO theory offers methodological knowledge (as stated), helpful for their derivation.

Regarding the ease and understandability of the derivation process, the used graphical notations are of significant importance. As seen from the example, the graphical notation of DEMO CSM is suitable with respect to the derivation of a use case model. The DEMO actors and transactions are depicted graphically in a very convenient way for their reflection into actors and use cases, in a use case model. This adds value to the derivation mechanism, making it easily understandable and illustratable.

Thus, use case derivation based on DEMO is well theoretically founded and easily implementable.

7 CONCLUSION

Our goal in this paper, as stated in the introduction, was to contribute to the knowledge on use case derivation based on business process modeling. We further continue the investigations in this direction that approach the use case derivation from three perspectives, namely – Language/Action Perspective (considering DEMO in particular), Organizational Semiotics, and Petri Net. Considering these alternative ways of use case derivation, we have studied and analyzed the advantages of DEMO in this regard. The study was supported by a case example.

It has been concluded, based on the conducted study, that the DEMO transactions and actors can be used as a consistent basis for deriving a use case model: in particular, use cases and actors, respectively. It is of particular importance that DEMO models consistently and completely the business reality, and guarantees in this way the soundness of the derived use case model. Regarding the derivation itself – the DEMO transactions are straightforwardly mapped into use cases that reflect essential behavior. The DEMO theory provides methodological guidance (by clearly distinguishing between essential and non-essential transactions) also concerning the identification of the rest of the use cases. All this contributes to the possibility to build a complete use case model. Next to that, the graphical notation of DEMO is suitable with respect to the derivation of a use case model. This makes the derivation process easy to understand and illustrate. For all these reasons, the DEMO-based use case derivation is claimed to be useful. There are issues however that are considered a subject of further study, in this regard, e.g. suggesting a more concrete guidance for identification of those use cases which do not reflect essential behavior.

The other two studied ways of use case derivation have also their advantages, as demonstrated in Section 5. However, this paper considers only the strengths of DEMO in this respect, identifying them from the perspective of the conducted study. It would be of benefit to further explore how the three considered tools could complement each other in deriving use cases.

The conducted study is expected to be helpful for current software development.

REFERENCES

Aalst, W.M.P. van der. Finding Errors in the Design of a Workflow Process: A Petri-net-based Approach. Proc: *19th Int. Conf. on Applications and Theory of Petri Nets – WFM*, 1998, Lisbon, Portugal.

Bunge, M.A. *Treatise on basic philosophy* (vol.4, D. Reidel Publishing Company, Dordrecht, NL, 1979).

Cockburn, A., 2001. *Writing Effective Use Cases*. Addison-Wesley, USA.

Dietz, J.L.G. Understanding and Modelling Business Processes with DEMO, Proc. *ER*, Paris, FR, 1999.

Dietz, J.L.G. Business Modelling for Business Redesign, Proc. *27th IEEE Hawaii Int. Conference on System Sciences*, Los Alamitos, CA, 1994.

Flores, F. and Ludlow, J.J. *Doing and speaking in the office* (G. Fick and H. Sprague, Decision Support Systems: Issues & Challenges. NY, Perg. Press, 1980).

Fowler, M. and Scott, K. 2000. *UML Distilled, Second Edition – a Brief Guide to the Standard Object Modeling Language*. Addison-Wesley, USA.

Jacobson, I., Christenson, M., Jonsson, P., Overgaard, G., 1992. *Object-Oriented Software Engineering: A Use Case Driven Approach*.

Liu, K., Sun, L., Dix, A., Narasipuram, M. *Norm-based Agency for Designing Collaborative Information Systems*. Info Systems Journal, 11, 2001.

Liu, K. 2000. *Semiotics in information systems engineering*. Cambridge University Press.

OMG, 2000. *Unified Modeling Language (UML)*, Version 1.3, www.omg.org.

Shishkov, B. and Barjis, J. Modeling of e-Business Brokerage Systems Using UML and Petri Net. Proc: *17th edition of the IFIP World Computer Congress*, August 25-30, 2002, Montreal, Quebec, Canada.

Shishkov, B. and Dietz, J.L.G. Integrated Methodology Allowing Design of ICT Applications Based on Bus. Process Investigation. Proc: *IASTED Int. Conf. Applied Simulation & Modelling*, June 25-28, 2002, Crete, GR.

Shishkov, B. and Dietz, J.L.G. Analysis of Suitability, Appropriateness and Adequacy of Use Cases Combined with Activity Diagram for Business Systems Modeling. Proc: *3rd Int. Conference on Enterprise Inf. Systems (ICEIS)*, July 7-10, 2001, Setubal, Portugal.

Shishkov, B., Xie, Z., Liu, K., Dietz, J.L.G. Using Norm Analysis to Derive Use Cases from Business Processes. Proc: *5th Workshop On Organizational Semiotics*, June 14-15, 2002, Delft, The Netherlands.

Stamper, R., Liu, K., Hafkamp, M., Ades, Y. 1997. Signs Plus Norms – One Paradigm for Organizational Semiotics. Proc: *1st Int. Workshop on Computational Semiotics*, Paris, France.

Stamper, R., 1992. *Language and computer in organised behaviour*. In Riet, R.P.v.d. and Meersman, R.A., (eds.), Linguistic Instruments in Knowledge Engineering. Elsevier Science, The Netherlands.

HOW DIGITAL IS COMMUNICATION IN YOUR ORGANIZATION?
A Metrics and an Analysis Method

Pasi Tyrväinen

Faculty of Information Technology, University of Jyväskylä, P.O.Box 35 FIN-40014, University of Jyväskylä, Finland
Email: Pasi.Tyrvainen@jyu.fi

Tero Päivärinta

Department of Information Systems, Agder University College, Serviceboks 422, 4604 Kristiansand, Norway
Email: Tero.Paivarinta@hia.no

Keywords: Categories of communication forms, CCF, taxonomy of communication media, digital media, metrics, measuring organizational communication, genre theory, measures for digitalisation, IT investment paradox

Abstract: Novel innovations in the area of digital media are changing the ways we communicate and organize. However, few practical measures exist for analysing the digitalisation of organizational communication as an intermediate factor in the initiatives to adopt new information and communication technologies (ICT). Building upon the genre theory of organizational communication, a categorization of communication forms, and quantitative measures we suggest such metrics and a measurement method. A case study applying them in an industrial organization suggests the method and metrics to be applicable for quantifying how new information systems affect to organizational communication as well as for anticipating their digitalisation impact prior to the implementation. The metrics provide a basis for further work on analysing correlation between organizational performance and adoption of information and communication technology.

1 INTRODUCTION

Digital media have increasingly reshaped organizational communication and the whole concept of organizing throughout the 20th century (Yates, 1989). Digital convergence and development in information and communication technology (ICT) will continue to bring novel means for organizational communication. Empirical research suggests that the adoption of ICT would appear economically valuable when complemented with changes in organizational design and work practices, such as increasing use of teams, redesigned business processes, and broader decision-making authority (Brynjolfsson, Hitt, and Yang, 1998, Dans 2002, Francalanci and Maggiolini 2002). However, the justification and evaluation of ICT investments has emerged as a complex issue often labeled as the "IT investment paradox" (van Grembergen, 2002).

The literature proposes a plethora of methods and techniques for the evaluation of ICT investments in organizations. Renkema and Berghout (1997) divided the methods into the financial, multi-criteria, ratio, and portfolio approaches. All of these aim at evaluating the expected financial and non-financial benefits of an investment. The methods vary in the degree, to account for the non-financial benefits and non-ICT investments. Methods of the popular ratio approach have proposed such ratios as ICT expenditures against total turnover and all yielding that can be attributed to ICT investments against total profits. According to Renkema and Berghout (1997), the available non-financial evaluation methods are hardly underpinned by a theoretical basis. Furthermore, the available methods tend to focus on the evaluation criteria and to pay less attention on the evaluation process.

The convergence of ICT remained somewhat absent in the methods reviewed by Renkema and Berghout (1997) - the term 'communication' was not mentioned. In general, among the various evaluation methods of the adoption of ICT in organizations, the traditional "black box" analysis relates the amount

258

of such investments straightforwardly to the performance measures of the organization (Soh and Markus, 1995; Berghout and Renkema, 2001, Francalanci and Maggiolini, 2002). However, according to Soh and Markus (1995) and Bakos and Kemerer (1992) it would be more relevant to examine **intermediate outputs directly linked to IT** than profit or other financial measures of performance.

We hypothesise that organizational communication represents an intermediate output that should be measured. The more the organization invests on ICT technology, the more digital organizational communication is likely to get, which will furthermore impact organizational performance. This hypothesis is often motivating the development of IS in general, as we speak of e-"everything" (e-government, e-business, e-learning), mainly focusing nothing but organizational communication.

This paper pursues a **metrics for measuring adoption of ICT in organizational communication,** according to the following criteria:
1. **Organizational communication**. It should conceptualise and measure organizational communication throughout the organization.
2. **Quantify for humans** the amount of information exchanged in organizational communication in units relevant for human perception rather than units relevant for computers. I.e. we should not measure bits rather than information exchanged in the organizational processes enabling evaluation of impacts of ICT on specific organization units or business processes in the future.
3. **Categorize for computer support** for analysing ability of computers to support the communication. If we wish to be able to evaluate the benefits of using computers we must be able to distinguish such communication that can be aided by computers from such that cannot, preferably in an ordinal scale.
4. **Measurable** with a reasonable effort whereas the level of detail should still be elaborate enough, though, to analyse organizational communication in context.

In the future, we wish to investigate with the metrics developed, how the digitalisation of organizational communication will impact performance. This involves such research questions as: how much does the adoption of ICT change organizational communication or does this greater utilization of ICT correlate with business results?

In the remainder, Section 2 reviews the theories of media use in organizational communication, especially the genre theory and taxonomies of media, needed to satisfy criterion 1. Section 3 represents the categorization of communication

forms and quantitative metrics, conforming criteria 2 and 3. Section 4 illustrates the measures by using them for an analysis of communicative practices in an industrial target organization. Section 5 discusses the contribution of the developed measures. Section 6 concludes and suggests tracks for subsequent research efforts with remarks of the applicability of the measures in light of criterion 4.

2 THEORETICAL BACKGROUND

2.1 Theories of Media Use in Organizational Communication

According to two literature reviews (Carlson and Zmud, 1999, Ngwenyama and Lee, 1997) the influential theories of media use in organizational communication since the mid-1980s include media / information richness theory (Daft and Lengel, 1986) elaborated in media synchronicity theory (Dennis and Valachich, 1999), critical mass theory (Markus, 1990), social influence model (Fulk, Schmitz and Steinfield, 1990), the "emergent network perspective" (Contractor and Eisenberg, 1990), channel expansion theory (Carlson and Zmud, 1999), critical social theory (Ngwenyama and Lee, 1997), and the genre theory of organizational communication (Orlikowski and Yates, 1994).

The seminal media/information richness theory (Daft and Lengel, 1986, Daft et.al. 1987, Trevino, Daft and Lengel 1990) discussed the equivocality of communication to be linked directly with the medium used. The social definition theories of the 1990s highlighted the idea that the properties of a medium alone explained the relationship between organizational communication and media use insufficiently. The phenomenon should be regarded, instead, as complex interaction between technology, people, and organizational context (Markus 1994, Ngwenyama and Lee, 1997). The most radical standpoint even stated, "There is no such thing as pure technology." (Contractor and Eisenberg, 1990 p. 143) - technology and media without a particular socio-organizational context. Our basic standpoint, however, is that communication technology can exist independent of a particular organization in which it will be applied. To establish the measures for digitalisation we need analytical concepts for structuring both such generic features of media and the socio-organizational contexts of communication, and to be able to connect these in a meaningful way. The media-attributes and design-choices theory (Sillince, 1997) introduces 17 generic media attributes and attempts to connect (two of) them directly to the choices of organization design affecting communication.

However, none of the above-mentioned theories alone proved straightforwardly useful for conceptualising simultaneously communication media and their application context for our research goals. We thus elaborated a framework, in which the socio-organizational side of organizational communication is conceptually structured by genre theory and merged with a categorization of communication media.

2.2 Genre Theory of Organizational Communication

A genre of organizational communication represents a typified and recurrent communicative action that can be identified by its communicative purpose(s) and, to some extent, by its form(s) (Yates and Orlikowski, 1992). The communicative purpose refers to social motives and topics expressed in a recurrent communicative context and the form includes certain structural features, communication media, and a symbol system to represent information, which all should be commonly recognized in the community in question (Yates and Orlikowski, 1992). A genre can be more or less widely enacted within the community (Yates, Orlikowski, and Okamura, 1999) or in other words, genres can be put on a scale from hard to soft (Schultze and Boland, 1997). From our point-of-view, a soft genre involves the use of varying communication forms for communicating instances of that genre thus affecting the heterogeneity of forms within the genre and its enactment.

Each community, an organization for example, has a repertoire of genres that can be identified with it (Orlikowski and Yates, 1994). For instance, a software development organization typically communicates through a set of genres: requirements specification documents, project plans, project meetings, budget documents. A set of genres can also interrelate within a wider communicative process thus forming genre systems (Bazerman, 1994, Yates, Orlikowski, and Rennecker, 1997).

Since the 1990s, genre theory has invoked increasing interest to guide research efforts on information systems (Päivärinta, 2001). Empirical efforts to identify organizational genre repertoires have reported hundreds of genres that can be found in organizations, denoting that this approach would provide a detailed, yet comprehensive and comprehensible, view on organizational communication (Karjalainen, Päivärinta, Tyrväinen, and Rajala, 2000, Tyrväinen and Päivärinta 1999).

At least one practical method to identify and analyse genre repertoires has been established by Päivärinta, Halttunen, and Tyrväinen (2001), with promising practical experience of its usefulness in efforts for information systems development (Päivärinta and Peltola, 2001). Genre taxonomies have recently been suggested as a conceptual basis to benchmark communication practices between organizations (Yoshioka, Herman, Yates, and Orlikowski, 2001). Hence, we regarded genre theory as a suitable conceptual basis to start with for our research purposes.

2.3 Taxonomies for Communication Media

The concept of genre structures organizational communication, and declares that certain media can be characteristic for certain genres (Yates and Orlikowski, 1992). The literature provides taxonomies for classifying media, which could be linked with genre analysis. Zmud, Lind, and Young (1990) studied organizational communication channels that managers and professional staff used for their work in the corporate headquarters of a manufacturing firm. The researchers and the sponsors of the study selected 14 communication channels within 5 categories jointly (table 1). Although being a step to the direction of our needs, this taxonomy does not provide sufficient detail for analysing various ICT media from the viewpoint of computer support or automation. For example, it does not separate XML-based e-business formats enabling semi-automated or fully automated (communicative) business transactions from less automated digital media, such as e-mail.

Table 1 - Communication channels of Zmud et al. (1990)

face-to-face	one-to-one consultations (formal) one-to-one chats (informal)
Group	group meetings (formal) group gatherings (informal)
Written	handwritten notes typed or printed memos or letters printed documents or reports charts and graphics computer reports
traditional communication technologies	phone voice conferencing facsimile
computer-mediated communication technologies	electronic mail voice messaging

Daft and Lengel (1986) argued that media richness represents the means to resolve equivocal communication tasks, in which the volume of information is the traditional means for managing uncertainty. In decreasing order of equivocality and uncertainty of the communicative task in question, preferred media is face-to-face, telephone, personal documents, impersonal written documents and numeric documents (Daft and Lengel, 1986). Or listed by the structural characteristics, one could relate these categories from group meetings, integrators in between organizational boundaries, direct contacts, planning, special reports, to formal information systems and rules and regulations, respectively. For our purposes this classification (as well as a later work on media synchronicity theory by Dennis and Valacich (1999)), however, lacks detail in distinguishing between various ICT-supportable media.

Yoshioka et. al. (2001) proposed use of taxonomic categories on the dimensions for genres and genre systems reflecting the questions why, what, how, when, where, and how (5W1H). Out of these, the question "How" addresses the form of a genre/genre system referring to observable features including structural elements, medium, and linguistic features, but does not construct a categorization for them. They have also implemented a prototype of genre taxonomy with 14-15 generic genres: such as business, letter, memo, expense form, report, face-to-face meeting genre system, personal homepage. This kind of taxonomy matches with hard genres (Schulze and Boland, 1997) that have only a single form, while a soft genre - such as a customer complaint – may be communicated verbally, by phone, by fax, via e-mail, and via a customer complaint database system. We wish to separate the communication forms – such as face-to-face meetings and fax – from the communicative purpose of a genre. Thus neither the dimension "How" nor the prototype taxonomy matches the goals of this study.

Slywotzky and Morrison (2000) suggest one of the few operationalized measures for adoption of digital media in organizational communication and business processes in their book "How DIGITAL Is Your BUSINESS?". They define the estimated Digital Ratio of a business based on a profile of percentages of the functions of an organization. The Digital Ratio of each function (e.g. selling, delivery, supply chain...) is defined by manager judgement on scale of 0%, 10%, 20%, ... (Slywotzky and Morrison, 2000 pp.15-16). However, due to a low level of detail in data collection and the subjective nature of analysis, the approach of Slywotzky and

Morrison is rather unlikely to produce accurate estimates on the issue. A case study related to this issue (Tyrväinen and Päivärinta, 1999) suggests it rather difficult to produce a consistent overview of the situation in a large organization with hundreds of genres without a more structured approach and a participation of several stakeholders. I.e. relying on simplified estimates based on manager judgement produces highly error-prone results. Further, as the classification used by Slywotzky and Morrison (2000) was simply digital vs. analogue, this approach is not able to make difference in between e-business media and digital images, for example.

3 A METRICS AND AN ANALYSIS METHOD

3.1 A Categorization of Communication Forms

We pursued measures for the ability to use computers to manage and automate communication in organizations. Thus, our categories try to reflect increasing ability to utilize the benefits of computers starting from non-mediated communication, through communication mediated by computers, until the extreme of formal data structures processed, analysed, filtered, restructured and interpreted by computers. Figure 1 represents the categories and their mutual inclusion on the left. On the right, there are some typical examples of ICT tools and technologies used for the upper categories as well as examples included in the non-mediated categories.

In addition to the basic distinction between analogue and digital communication, we elaborate the media categories further by separating stored communication from non-stored, permanently stored from transient communication, and one-to-one from group communication. Table 2 contains descriptions of the categories of communication forms (CCF) in increasing order of formality, i.e. ability to computers to interpret the contents of the communication form. Increasing formality matches roughly to the amount of metadata available for computers for interpretation of the actual data related to communication in the medium in question, as well as decreasing granularity of digital communication, i.e. size of managed content objects.

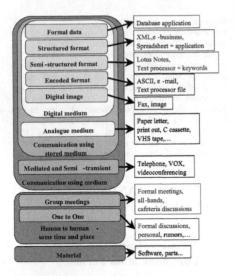

Figure 1: Taxonomy of categories of communication forms and examples of communication forms.

Table 2 - Descriptions of the categories of communication forms.

CCF	Description
Material	Information objects exchanged in between organizational entities, that cannot be classified as information exchange in between humans, although were identified as "information objects" important for the organization. For example, software distribution media, products and parts.
1-to-1, f-to-f	Personal face-to-face meetings in the same place and time include both formal person-to-person meetings and informal, casual meetings, such as discussions in cafeteria, etc.
Group Meeting	Formal group meetings and informal, spontaneous face-to-face meetings. Memorandums composed /distributed are classified to other categories.
Mediated / Semi-Transient	Mediated communication used for emulating face-to-face communication. Data is transmitted by computers or by other ICT equipment. Examples: phone calls, teleconference and videoconference. Mediated communication captured and stored temporarily is called here semi-transient communication. Typical examples include answering machine messages and VOX.

	Description
Analogue	This category includes data stored on some analogue medium, typically paper, microfilm, or VRC/audio tapes. Machines can copy this data, but storage and distribution requires manipulation and transportation of the physical media. Data management is based on metadata (reference) information stored separate from the data.
Digital Image	Digital data with no or minimal encoding of semantic information. Data can be stored, copied and transmitted by computers, but operations cannot make use of the meaning of the content. Examples: fax, bitmap images scanned from paper or used for storing digitised documents, and graphical encoding formats (e.g. GIFF, JPEG).
Encoded	Digital data intended for human use with encoding applicable for simple generic tools, e.g. by searching strings. Typical formats and tools include ASCII, UNICODE, mail messages, and word processor files.
Semi-Structured	Digital data containing both large bodies of natural language interpreted only by humans and sufficient structured (meta-)data for major computer applications, e.g. for workflow control and sophisticated data manipulation and retrieval. Examples: Lotus Notes databases with applications, spreadsheet applications, document templates with applications assuming procedural interpretation for the fields.
Structured	Digital data presented through displays or forms for humans. The content can be interpreted both by humans and specific computer applications without human intervention. Examples include RosettaNet applications, eBusiness messages, XML documents, and pre-defined spreadsheet sheets used for collecting data for computerised applications, such as collecting customer orders.
Formal	Digital data intended for computer use and interpreted by computers. The context needed for interpretation is predefined by a database schema or similar means. No common sense nor world knowledge of humans is needed for this process.

3.2 Measures Used

We use two basic quantities for communication: count of communication instances and volume of the instances. We further separate unique communication entities (Unique Instances, and Unique Volume) from the quantities including also copies of unique communication entities - Instances or Copies and Volume or Copy Volume, respectively. To be more specific, Unique instances (UI) refer to the distinct instances of a genre communicated excluding duplicates, e.g. a single mail message sent to several recipients or a broadcast is considered to be a single unique instance. A single annual report is being produced per year, whereas several invoices can be produced daily. Copies refer to the average number of copies delivered to distinct receivers of the UI. A project status meeting is the only copy of the communication act whereas the corresponding digital document - the memorandum – can be copied by e-mail and sent to tens of persons.

Size of instances refers to the average amount of information per instance of a genre. This varies from multi-volume contracts and manuals to acknowledgement notes or "Please call ..." notes. The size of an UI (being equal to the size of instance) is measured in Pages that refer to amount of information equal (for a human being) to view the size of a visual letter / A4 page. For the stored forms of communication this matches the number of printed pages in a paper version of a typical instance of a genre. A Page is considered to be roughly equivalent to 1-3 kilobytes of plain ASCII encoded text or about a megabyte of bits of a digital image. This approach aims at filtering out the physical size, size in bytes, and other medium-dependent aspects as technical details. Moving over from ASCII text to bitmap increases the amount of bits by factor of 100 or 1000 but does not affect the amount of information communicated nor the size of instances when measured in Pages. (For further discussion on quantitative metrics on information see (Landauer, 1986, Lesk, 1997, and Lyman, Varian, Dunn, Strygin, and Swearingen, 2000))

To sum up, the calculation process described next involves three orthogonal dimensions:
1. **Genres**, i.e. calculations per one genre or summaries of all genres.
2. **Categories of communication forms (CCF)**, i.e. calculations per one CCF, per a group of CCFs (such as Stored or Digital communication forms only), or per all communication forms.
3. **Measurement units** are further composed out of 3 dimensions:
   a) **UI** or **Copies**, i.e. whether all copies of genre instances are calculated.
   b) **Instances** or **Pages**, i.e. counting items and measuring their volumes.
   c) **Absolute** or **proportional**, i.e. absolute values or percentages against organizational totals, such as all / all stored communication.

3.3 Genre Identification and Calculation Process

The analysis method consists of three main processes: 1) genre identification, 2) metadata annotation, and 3) calculation. We adopted a previously suggested genre identification process (Päivärinta et.al. 2001) and tailored the associated metadata collection process for our purposes. The basic concepts of this method are:
- **Stakeholders** having interests to participate in the analysis.
- **PUI entities** producing or using information in the domain of interest (PUI = Producer or User of Information), including both external organizations and the internal entities of the organization, such as business processes, departments, functions, roles, or individuals.
- **Genres** in the domain of interest.
- **Properties** of the identified genres defining the metadata gathered about the genres from the stakeholders for the analysis.

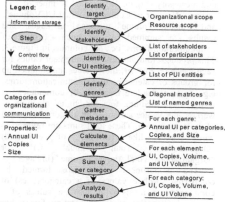

Figure 2: Phases of the analysis process for genre identification, metadata annotation, and calculation

Figure 2 depicts our analysis process as a data flow diagram. After defining the domain of interest, the stakeholders of data collection are identified. A number of group meetings are conducted to identify PUI entities and the genres emerging between them. From this on we diverge from the original method (Päivärinta et. al. 2001). Instead of defining the properties to be identified for further analysis we make use of a fixed set of genre properties based on our metrics. For each genre (each row in Figure 3), we collect the following metadata:
- Category or categories of communication forms used by the genre.
- Number of annual unique instances (UI).
- Copies (instances) per UI.
- Average size of instances.

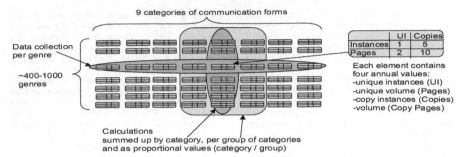

Figure 3: Data elements of the calculation.

The subsequent step calculates four values for each element, i.e. for each combination of a genre and a category (Figure 3): "Annual Number of UI", "Annual Number of Copies", "Annual UI Volume", and "Annual Volume" measured in Pages. The results are summed up per each category of communication forms, i.e., per columns in Figure 3. This produces four absolute measurement values for each category. Further, these values are summed up for groups of categories of communication forms, e.g., to four absolute measures of communication using Stored medium, four for Digital medium, as well as four values summing up all communication of the organization. These total sums are referred to with names like (number of estimated) "Organizational Total Annual UI" or "Organizational Total Annual Volume" (in Pages).

The proportional values are formed by comparing absolute values of a category(-ies) of communication forms with absolute values of a group of categories of communication forms. For example, "Organizational Stored UI Volume Percentage of Semi-structured communication forms" is calculated as "Organizations Annual UI Volume of Semi-structured communication forms" divided by "Organizations Annual UI Volume of Stored communication forms". As the applicability of the measurement unit "Page" is somewhat contradictory with the communication forms that do not use a tangible medium, we limit the use of the volume measures to the forms using medium. In the end, the results are analysed in relation to the meaningful decisions of the organization at hand (examples in the discussion section).

4 A CASE STUDY

The target organization to test the metrics was an independent unit of a multinational corporation, involving c. 400 employees in Finland. The genre identification process, performed in fall 1999 in connection to an organizational development initiative, included 8 sessions with 3-5 participants, lasting 3 hours each, with a total of 3,5 person weeks of effort from the target organization and 8 person weeks from the researchers, including the problem analysis. 744 genres were identified and named altogether.

Two persons, P1 and P2, participated in the analysis of the previously identified genres for our research purposes. Both of them have several years of experience with core processes, process development, and information systems of the organization. P1 can be best characterized as a manager of a central process while P2 carries the overall responsibility for the information systems of the target organization and has somewhat more overall knowledge over the genres in the target organization. The effort spent on the analysis of genres totalled five person days from P1 and P2.

Out of the over 700 genres originally identified, a subset of 10% was analysed both by P1 and P2 in order to save time and effort by picking up every 10th genre from the full list of genres. This is referred to as the "Subset" in later diagrams. As P1 and P2 were not familiar with all the genres, the unknown ones were filtered out from both of the data sets. Also the genres categorized as "Material" were filtered out. The "Full" filtered data set included 598 genres and the subset includes 54 genres. Some examples of the genres and metadata collected are presented in Table 2. Later on, the metadata was updated twice by P1 to conform to two changes in the ICT, concerning two genre systems: the adoption of a labour and travel cost tracking system and a new sales order processing system.

On an average, a genre used communication forms from 1,77 CCFs. Most of the 598 genres (about 60%) used Encoded communication forms, while only about 30% of the genres used Analogue communication forms (e.g. paper). However, when using the volume measures, the Encoded communication form was second to the Analogue CCF. The calculation process resulted in c. 49'000 annual unique instances for the 54 genres implying organization's total annual UI to be about 680'000.

Table 4 presents the figures calculated for the subset of 54 genres as well as the figures extrapolated to the organization's total 744 genres identified.

Table 3 - Examples of metadata collected in the case study.

Producer	Genre	User	Categories of communication forms	Annual UI	Copies	Size in Pages
Sales	Request for support	Project organization	Personal, Mediated / Semi-Transient, Encoded	hundreds	some	2
Dept 1	Internal training	Dept 2	Group meeting	some	1	100
Purchasing	Order for work	Contractors	Mediated, Digital image, Encoded, Structured (60%)	thousands	1	1
Project dept	Schedule changes	Project dept	One-to-one, Group meeting, Encoded (dominating)	hundreds	tens	1
Sales	Permission to tender	Sales	Encoded	hundreds	1	1
Project dept	Project plan	Sales	Encoded	hundreds	some	3

Table 4 - Organization's total Annual Volumes

	Subset (54 genres)	Estimated organization's total
Annual Unique Instances	49'000	680'000
Annual UI Volume / Pages	103'000	1'400'000
Annual Copies	170'000	2'300'000
Annual Volume / Pages	590'000	8'100'000

as well as average number of copies per UI were smaller for the changed genres than the average ones. The second change (from State 2 to State 3) had less impact. Detailed analysis based on distribution of measures per categories of communication forms performed in the target organization is not reported here due to space restrictions.

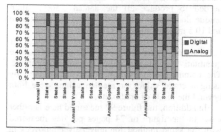

Figure 4: Analogue versus digital ratio for the subset for Stored information before, in between, and after two changes in information systems.

The digitalisation percentage of all Stored information was calculated three times - with respect to the original status of the organization as well as in between and after digitalisation of the two genre systems. Figure 4 represents the distribution of Annual UI, Copies, UI Volume, and Volume for the Subset in proportional values. From the two leftmost bars we can see that the first change (from State 1 to State 2) transformed over 60% of Annual UI from paper to digital communication formats. The changes in Annual UI Volume and Annual Volume were smaller implying that average size of instances

5 DISCUSSION

We illustrated a genre-based analysis method for analysing the adoption of ICT in organizational communication quantitatively. The metrics used in the case study were able to quantify the impact of two technology changes on the digitalisation of two genre systems. With the suggested metrics, it seems relatively simple to simulate adoption of new technology by manipulating the data collected and reading the expected impact from the resulting metrics values – categories of communication forms of the genres to be managed by the new technology are simply changed from previous values (e.g. "Analogue / Paper") to new values (e.g. "Structured / XML") and the answer is read as the change of resulting metrics values.

The results presented here measure simply the degree of digitalisation of stored information, while use of the full categorization will give more accuracy for analysing technology adoption. For example, adoption of e-business standards requires use of Structured or Formal communication forms. A recent focused study (Tyrväinen 2003) estimated quantitatively the applicability of mobile content formats (MMS, SMS, XHTML, and XML) to organizational use by matching the properties of these formats with characteristics of the categories of communication forms. Assuming contemporary communication practices of the target organization to set upper limits for each format as well as some other assumptions of the study, the use of multimedia messaging (MMS) was estimated to be

at the level of 5% of the use of SMS text messages. Also other similar applications are possible.

Table 5 - Alternative estimates of the total annual volumes of the target organization.

	Average		Genre-based		Median	
	Subset	Total	Subset	Total	Subset	Total
Number of genres	54	744	54	744	54	744
Annual unique instances	941				30	
Instances per UI	22				3	
Size of UI	20				2	
TOTAL pages / Thousands	22 400	308 000	586	8 100	10	134
Pages per person day		3 500		92		2

In our case, the data was collected bottom-up using the processes of the organization as the baseline for the analysis of the genres. In Table 4 we estimated the total communication activity related with all processes of the target organization. If we divide the total figures with the number of employees and the number of working days per year (400 and 220, respectively), we end up with an average of 26 instances and 92 Pages per day. Are these figures realistic? Did it pay off to go through a relatively elaborate data collection and calculation genre by genre instead of using, e.g., average or median values? Table 5 compares the daily information exchange figures per person with our metrics and in relation to two alternative approaches.

Using the average figures of 941 annual unique instances per genre, average 22 instances per UI, each on average 20 Pages, we end up with on an average 3'500 Pages of information sent or received per person per day. With the median values the result is 2 Pages per person per day.

Landauer (1986) estimated that people take in and remember only about a byte in a second. But they read about 3 to 5 words per second i.e. about 600 KBytes or 300 Pages per day during office hours. Thus the magnitude of 90 Pages per day seems realistic as it excludes verbal communication and not all of the 90 Pages are read or written rather than just skimmed and forwarded. Further, this figure includes all the communication related with the business of the organization, but excludes private communication.

In the project "How Much Information?" at Berkeley, Lyman et. al. (2000, Executive summary, table 6. p.6) estimated about 7'500 million titles of unique office documents to be produced worldwide annually, adding up to 19 Terabytes - or 7'500 million pages, each containing 2,5 Kbytes of plain

text per page (Lyman et. al. 2000, Print, table 1, p.2), i.e. one page per title. These accounted for 81% of all printed material produced in the World. In the target organization, the results suggested that each person sent and received annually total 335 unique Encoded and Analogue communication instances and 1760 Pages. Assuming half of them to be sent and half received and further, 81% of the sent ones to be produced using word processors, we can calculate back-wards the number of employees needed to produce all the annual 7'500 million unique documents and pages. These are 55 million and 10,5 million employees, respectively.

The comparison of the three approaches for verifying the figures support the assumption that the quantitative results are within a sensible magnitude. The communication volume estimates resulted by using average values or median values were both beyond the limits of credibility.

In addition, the figure 92 measured here is rather close to the figure or 74 pages per day measured with the same method for university employees in another case study (Tyrväinen et. al. 2003). Thus we can state that a sensible approximation for a method to quantify the adoption of digital media and ICT in organizational communication has been found.

6 SUMMARY AND FURTHER RESEARCH

A novel metrics and an analysis method for categorizing and quantifying the adoption of ICT in organisational communication were introduced. In the case study we demonstrated the capability of the metrics to quantify the digitalisation of two genre systems. Majority of stored information in the target organization used to be distributed on paper while after the two changes the majority was manipulated in digital formats. With the data collected by the genre identification method and the subsequent analysis according to the metrics established, we expect to be able to estimate the organizational impact of adopting a new ICT in the future in a focused way, as we can connect the analysis to focused organizational processes and units related to the analysed genres in context.

Further research is needed to promote the calibration, elaboration, and use of the analysis method and metrics. In the case study, the detailed analysis of every 10th of all genres minimized the effort needed from participants, being already able to capture the impact of both of the changes in ICT. Manipulation of the identified genres in an organization by harmonizing the genres and genre systems before their detailed analysis in order to reduce the number of genres for analysis would also aid the re-engineering or refinement of business processes.

Other extensions of the metrics and the method need to be tested in the future. First, empirical research on the correlation between organizational performance and the degree of digitalisation of communication is needed to verify the common hypothesis of ICT being beneficial. This work is already under way with some other organizations and will be reported in the near future.

Although our analysis process to test the metrics in the target organization was rather laborious pursuing an in-depth view on the reliability of the metrics, future research efforts could focus on a limited sets of genres and genre systems. A focus on certain generic genre taxonomies, e.g. such described by Yoshioka et al. (2001), could most probably produce quantitatively relevant research results on estimating the impact of digitalization across organizations with a modest effort. Organization-wide in-depth efforts, although more laborious, might produce additional qualitative understanding to the issue and to provide yet undiscovered research directions, as well.

REFERENCES

Bacos, J.Y. and Kemerer, C.F., 1992. Recent applications of economic theory in Information Technology Research, *Decision Support Systems*, 8, 365-386.

Bazerman, C., 1994. Systems of Genres and the Enactment of Social Intentions, in Freedman, A. and Medway, P. (ed.) *Genre and the New Rhetoric* London, Taylor & Francis, 79-101.

Berghout, E. and Renkema, T., 2001. Methodologies for IT investment evaluation: a review and assessment, in van Grembergen, W. *Information Technology Evaluation Methods and Management*, Hershey, PA : Idea Group Publishin, 78-97.

Brynjolfsson, E., Hitt, L.M. and Yang, S., 1998 Intangible Assets: How the Interaction of Computers and Organizational Structure Affects Stock Market Valuations. In *ICIS-98, 9th International Conference on Information Systems*: ICIS, 8-29.

Carlson, J.R. and Zmud, R.W., 1999. Channel Expansion Theory and the Experiential Nature of Media Richness Perceptions. *Academy of Management Journal*, 42, 2, 153-170.

Contractor, N.S. and Eisenberg, E.M., 1990. Communication Networks and New Media in Organizations. *Organizations and Communication Technology*: Newbury Park, Sage, 143-172.

Daft, R.L. and Lengel, R.H., 1986. Organizational Information Requirements, Media Richness and Structural Design. *Management Science*, 32, 5, 554-571.

Daft, R.L., Lengel, R.H. and Trevino, L.K., 1987. Message Equivocality, Media Selection, and Manager Performance: Implications for Information Systems. *MIS Quarterly*, 11, September, 355-366.

Dans, E., 2001. IT Investment in Small and Medium Enterprises: Paradoxically Productive? *Electronic Journal of Information Systems Evaluation*. 4, 1.

Dennis, A.R. and Valachich, J.S., 1999. Rethinking Media Richness: Towards a Theory of Media Synchronicity. In HICSS-32, *32nd Annual Hawaii International Conference on System Sciences*. Los Alamitos CA, IEEE Computer Society.

Francalanci, C. and Maggiolini, P., 2002. Measuring the Financial Benefits of IT Investments on Coordination, in *Information Systems Evaluation Management*, IRM Press, 54-74.

Fulk, J., Schmitz, J. and Steinfield, C.W., 1990. A Social Influence Model of Technology Use. In *Organizations and Communication Technology*: Newbury Park, Sage. 117-140.

Karjalainen, A., Päivärinta, T., Tyrväinen, P., and Rajala, J., 2000. Genre-Based Metadata for Enterprise Document Management, in *33rd Annual Hawaii International Conference on System Sciences*: Los Alamitos CA, IEEE Computer Society.

Landauer, T. K., 1986. How much do people remember? Some estimates on the quantity of learned information in long-term memory, *Cognitive Science*, 10 (4) Oct-Dec. 477-493.

Lesk, M., 1997. How much information is there in the world? Technical report, lesk.com, available at http://www.lesk.com/mlesk/ksg97/ksg.html.

Lyman, P. Varian, H.R. Dunn, J. Strygin, A. and Swearingen K., 2000. How Much Information? School of Information Management and Systems at

University of California at Berkeley, PDF report available at http://www.sims.berkeley.edu/how-much-info/summary.html and related pages. 10.11. 2000.

Markus, M.L., 1990. Toward a "Critical Mass" Theory of Interactive Media. In *Organizations and Communication Technology*: Newbury Park, Sage. 194-218.

Markus, M.L., 1994. Electronic Mail as the Medium of Managerial Choice. *Organization Science*, 5, 4. 502-527.

Ngwenyama, O.K. and Lee, A.S., 1997. Communication Richness in Electronic Mail: Critical Social Theory and the Contextuality of Meaning. *MIS Quarterly*, 21, 2, 145-167.

Orlikowski, W.J. and Yates, J. 1994. Genre repertoire: The structuring of Communicative Practices in Organizations. *Administrative Science Quarterly*, 39, 4, 541-574.

Päivärinta, T., 2001. The Concept of Genre within the Critical Approach to Information Systems Development. *Information & Organization*, 11, 3, 207-234.

Päivärinta, T., Halttunen, V., and Tyrväinen, P., 2001. A Genre-Based Method for Information Systems Planning, in *Information Modelling in the New Millennium*: Hershey PA, Idea Group, pp. 70-93.

Päivärinta, T. and Peltola, T., 2001. Engineering of a Genre-Based Method for Developing Electronic Document Management: The Consultant's Viewpoint. In 6th CAiSE/IFIP8.1 Interlaken, Switzerland, XIII 1-14.

Renkema, T.J.W. and Berghout, E.W., 1997. Methodologies for information systems investment evaluation at the proposal stage: a comparative review, *Information and Software Technology*, 39, 1, 1-13

Schultze, U. and Boland, R., 1997. Hard and Soft Information Genres: An Analysis of two Notes Databases. In HICSS-30, *30th Hawaii International Conference on System Sciences*: Los Alamitos CA, IEEE Computer Society Press, 40-49.

Sillince, J.A.A., 1997. A Media-Attributes and Design-Choices Theory of the Information Technology-Organization Relation. *Journal of Organizational Computing and Electronic Commerce*, 7, 4, 279-303.

Slywotzky, A.J. and Morrison, D.J., 2000. *How DIGITAL is Your BUSINESS?* New York, Crown Business.

Soh, C. And Markus, M.L., 1995. How IT Creates Business Values: A Process Theory Synthesis. In ICIS-16, *16th International Conference on Information Systems*. December 10-13, Amsterdam, 29-41.

Strassmann, P.A., 1990. *Information Payoff*, New York, Free Press.

Trevino, L.K., Daft, R.L., and Lengel, R.H., 1990. Understanding Managers' Media Choices: A Symbolic Interactionist Perspective. In *Organizations and Communication Technology*: Newbury Park, Sage, 71-94.

Tyrväinen, P., 2003, Estimating Applicability of New Mobile Content Formats to Organizational Use, In *HICSS-36, 36rd Annual Hawaii International Conference on System Sciences*, IEEE Computer Society.

Tyrväinen, P., Järvenpää, M., and Sievänen, A. 2003, On Estimating the Amount of Learning Materials, A Case Study. In *ICEIS'03, 5th International Conference on Enterprise Information Systems*, ICEIS Press.

Tyrväinen, P. and Päivärinta, T., 1999. On Rethinking Organizational Document Genres for Electronic Document Management. In *HICSS-32, 32nd Annual Hawaii International Conference on System Sciences*: Los Alamitos CA, IEEE Computer Society.

van Grembergen, W., 2002 *Information Systems Evaluation Management*, IRM Press, 2002. 322 p.

van Nievelt, M.C.A., 1992. Managing with information technology, a decade of wasted money? *Compact* Summer 1992, 15-24.

Yates, J., 1989. *Control through Communication: The Rise of System in American Management*. Baltimore, Johns Hopkins University Press.

Yates, J. and Orlikowski, W.J., 1992, Genres of Organizational Communication: A Structurational Approach to Studying Communication and Media, *Academy of Management Review*, 17, 2, 299-326.

Yates, J., Orlikowski, W.J. and Okamura, K., 1999 Explicit and Implicit Structuring of Genres in Electronic Communication: Reinforcement and Change of Social Interaction, *Organization Science*, 10, 1, 83-103.

Yates, J., Orlikowski, W.J. and Rennecker, J., 1997. Collaborative Genres for Collaboration: Genre Systems in Digital Media. In *HICSS-30, 30th Annual Hawaii International Conference on System Sciences*: Los Alamitos CA, IEEE Computer Society Press, 50-59.

Yoshioka, T., Herman, G., Yates, J., and Orlikowski. W., 2001. Genre taxonomy: A knowledge repository of communicative actions, *ACM Transactions on Information Systems*, 19, 4, 431-456.

Zmud, R.W., Lind, M.R. and Young, F.W., 1990. An Attribute Space for Organizational Communication Channels, *Information Systems Research*, 1, 4, 440-457.

PART 4

Software Agents and
Internet Computing

SOMEONE
A cooperative system for personalized information exchange

Layda Agosto,
FranceTelecomR&D, Technopole Anticipa, 2 avenue Pierre Marzin, 22307 Lannion, France
Email: Layda.Agosto@rd.francetelecom.com

Michel Plu
FranceTelecom R&D, Technopole Anticipa, 2 avenue Pierre Marzin, 22307 Lannion, France
Email:michel.plu@francetelecom.com

Laurence Vignollet
University of Savoie-Syscom, Université de Savoie, Campus Scientifique, F-73376 Le Bourget du Lac, France
Email: Laurence.Vignollet@univ-savoie.fr

Pascal Bellec
FranceTelecom R&D, Technopole Anticipa, 2 avenue Pierre Marzin, 22307 Lannion, France
Email:pascal.bellec@francetelecom.com

Keywords: Intranet information services, knowledge management, Internet and Collaborative Computing, Semantic Web Technologies, social media, social networks analysis, social capital, human web.

Abstract: This paper presents a user-centric, social-media service: SoMeONe. Its goal is to build an information exchange network using Web informational networks. Itshould   allow the construction of personal knowledge bases whose quality is improved by collaboration. It tries to increase the user's commitment by helping him to establish and to maintain interesting interactions with enriching people. Although many users are individualist, the rules we define for this media should encourage a cooperative behaviour. The functionalities it offers are between a bookmark management system and mailing lists. With SoMeONe users exchange information with semantic addressing: they only need to annotate information for being diffused to appropriate users. Each user interacts only through a manually controlled contact network composed of known and trusted users. However, to keep his contact network open, SoMeOne helps each user to send information to new appropriate users. In return, the user expects these users to send him new information as well. In companies, where the Intranet is composed of huge amounts of heterogeneous and diverse information, such collective behaviour should increase the personal efficiency of each collaborator. Thus, SoMeONe provides some solutions to some knowledge management problems particularly for companies aware of the value of their social capital.

1   MOTIVATION

Today, the World Wide Web is getting essential, but the problem is that it is just becoming so overwhelmed that, instead of satisfying the user, it frustrates him and can be a source of time waste. Of course, many services are developed to help the user to navigate in this magma of information. The most famous are search engines[1] and portals[2] including information directories. Others, more sophisticated, like recommendation systems (Delgado et al, 2001), (Popescul et al, 2001) are under development.

---

[1]   cf. http://www.searchenginewatch.com/
[2]   See   for   example: http://www.wanadoo.fr   , http://www.voila.fr ,or http://www.yahoo.fr

O. Camp et al. (eds.), Enterprise Information Systems V, 271-278.

However, all these tools are generally thought for creating centralized intelligent systems. Our approach is different. We use the distributed intelligence of the users that handle the information. We help users to exploit their relationship exchange networks to find and filter information between each other. By doing this, we develop a kind of new network where information navigates from users to users instead of having users navigate through information; we call this network the "human web". As with push technologies, information goes directly to the user. Nevertheless, instead of having channels controlled by information providers, we manage networks of human channels. With our system, a user from trustworthy relationships becomes a Third Party Confidence. We think that the selection made by these human channels can be much more personalized and adapted to users needs by using human faculties far beyond nowadays automatic indexing technologies. For example, how to identify, automatically, a document containing false information? How can software recognize that a level of document description is appropriate to a user's background knowledge, or to measure the clarity of the discourse, or the pedagogical qualities of the presentation? How can software model user's sensibilities in order to detect funny stories, beautiful pictures, dramatic movies that he/she will be sensible to and will certainly appreciate? The challenge is now to cope with the quantity of available information. But first, the goal is not to replace traditional search engines but it is to complement them for example with new ranking mechanisms. Second we hope to scale with the number of the users that will participate and will post new information in the network.

Many systems have been developed to take advantage of collaborative relationships. Newsgroups and mailing lists are the most famous ones. By using them, we are acquiring a new, social, cyber-behaviour that asks us to adopt new habits in working and even in thinking schemas. We call "social media" such systems where information comes from a network of users. These media support virtual communities, and deal more or less with social aspects of information exchange. Like many others, we call "virtual community", a group of people sharing common interests, ideas, opinions, and feelings over collaborative networks. Then a social media contributes to the creation and evolution of these communities and consequently helps people to establish relationships.

We present SoMeONe (Social Media using Opinions through a trust Network) a user-centric, social-media service that helps people to build efficient networks of relationships to exchange information. It is user-centric because users are the

source of qualified information and are assuming the main processes. The system only helps users. The quality of the exchanged information comes from our assumption that each user wants to send valuable information in order to confirm and maintain mutually enriching relationships. It is social because we take into account the social aspect of the analysis of relationship networks in order to regulate the media.

Compared to available social media, SoMeONe is first dedicated to information about information (meta-information). It can thus be seen as a media for the semantic web (Berners Lee 2001). Second, its operational rules are defined in order to stimulate cooperative behaviours. The following sections will develop these points.

2 TRADITIONAL MEDIA FOR INFORMATION EXCHANGE

Although the Internet was presented as an exchange and share support and although it has allowed the development of systems such as :
newsgroups,
mailing lists,
knowledge sharing systems (Bouthor, Dedieu, 1999) (Glance 1999), or
peer2peer systems (Adar and Huberman, 2000), (Adamic et Adar, 2000),
these collaborative systems still raise certain problems.

With newsgroups (1), the users receive a great amount of information because of the number of participants. The quantity of information could hide the interesting one. The number of participants makes it difficult to remember interesting people and to locate experts. The access to the published messages is public. As a result, the user who sends a message does not see the people who can read it. There is no control in the visibility of their publications. This is the typical source of spamming. This tendency seriously threatens the use of these community services.

Controlled sharing systems (2), like mailing lists, partially solve the problems listed above. Mailing lists allow the definition of the receiver of a sent message. However, they still contain inconveniences. A user receiving messages cannot filter them in another way than using the emitter's address (because he/she does not see the mailing list's name to use it as a filtering criterion). All the messages from this user are then filtered, whatever the subject. This can be a shame. When a list is personal, only the mailing list creator can send messages to this list. When a mailing list is public, everybody can send a message to this list, but if a message interests two groups of people corresponding to two different mailing lists, if one user belongs to both, he/she will receive this message twice. Notice that, whatever the privacy of lists, when we manually manage distribution lists, we only insert the people we know. It is true that users can sometimes ask to be registered. Nevertheless, how could a user know about an existing distribution list? Moreover, how can he/she know if the contents could interest him/her if he/she has no access to these contents already?

Knowledge sharing systems (3) store information to be shared among users. Information is usually classified in a collective taxonomy. Users can't access to information according to his own criterions. Users do not control information visibility. Without such control, some users are afraid and intimidated to participate.

Finally, new exchange systems are based on "peer to peer" (4) technologies. Their main problems are: the uncontrolled information search, the impersonality of the exchanges (although sometimes anonymity is appreciated) and, for most of them, the need for a specific client software installation.

Some systems try to handle some of those problems using collaborative techniques (Glance et al., 1999) (Good et al., 1999). However, this filtering process is limited by users' motivations to supply comments about the messages. Even if at the beginning the user is motivated to supply this information, the perceptible return on the quality of the obtained filtering is often long and can be disheartening.

Cockpit tries to take into account some subjective features in annotating information (Gräther and Prinz, 2001). However, Cockpit distinguishes between community and personal vocabulary, forcing users to add more information.

We also observe that whatever the exchange system, problems also arise from the user's behaviour (Adar and Huberman, 2000). One of the most observed behaviours is that more users are consuming rather than producing information. One consequence is that the quality and robustness of the system are dependent on these producers. Moreover, these users are powerful and can use this power in inadequate ways –like rumour diffusion, advertising, etc.

3 SOMEONE'S BASIC FUNCTIONALITIES

We try to deal with these problems in our system. SoMeONe's conception is influenced by ideas from mailing lists and personal bookmark managers

(Andrews, 2000), (Kanawati et Malek, 2000), (Trevor, 2001).

An online service. A difference between a traditional bookmark manager and SoMeONe, is that SoMeONe stores and manages all this information in an online server. There are two advantages of this network exchange solution. First, this very useful information can be accessed by the user from any terminal using a plain HTML browser. The increasing mobility of workers and the availability of multiple connected mobile devices is becoming crucial. Second, this information can be accessed and shared by several users.

Meta-information management. Each user can manage his/her own taxonomy to classify documents. Generally, 'shared workspace' systems require the definition of a common shared taxonomy (Gräther et al, 2001). We call each taxonomy element a topic. Each topic can be a specialization of a more general topic. Document references can be associated with several topics and can thus be found through each of those topics. Many bookmark managers do not allow this multiple access. Users can also associate textual description to references added to topics. This set of information is called "meta-information" (information about information). In the following, we call it "document reviews" or for short "reviews". It can be associated to any kind of documents available using http protocol (Berners-Lee and al., 1996). They can be mono or multimedia documents coming from the WWW or an enterprise Intranet, or an email in a web mail server, or any kind of personal file accessible by an http server. Their URL identifies them.

Communication functionality. Unlike general mailing systems, SoMeONe is dedicated to send information on information.

Indeed, we think that this specific kind of content needs a specific media to be distributed. The reasons are the following. First, several pieces of meta-information can be about the same document and specific treatments can then be applied in order to aggregate and filter them. For example when a review is seen or deleted by the user, any new review about the same document will be hidden; and all reviews about the same document are displayed grouped together showing the multiple topics the user can access that have been associated to the document. Second, the documents described by that meta-information may require availability of time, bandwidth, or display size to read it. This specific media is consulted when these appropriate resources are available.

Third, exchanged multimedia documents are increasing in size, in contrast, mobile devices are becoming smaller. By developing media that distribute documents by sending meta-information

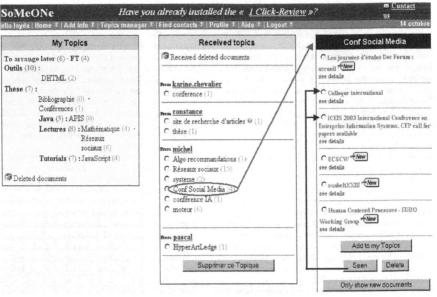

Figure 1: SoMeONe's home page.

and URLs, we want to encourage users to store documents on http servers and send URLs instead of sending huge attached files by email and copying them in each recipient's mailbox. Therefore, the disk space of mailboxes could be more efficiently used and the time to download communication messages significantly reduced. Users download voluminous contents only if they need it and when they have the appropriate connection. We are aware that users have to manage and control the accessibility of online documents on the http servers to the appropriate users, but easy solutions can be developed (see for example shared document functionalities associated with group or mailing list services on main Internet portals).

Finally, meta-information is a key issue for the famous Semantic Web and needs appropriate services to stimulate their production and use (Berners Lee 2001) .

Distribution list functionality. In SoMeONe as with mailing lists or personal email clients, users can manage distribution lists to send information.

To help the user, SoMeONe's interface shows the list to which he/she already sent or from which he/she received information. By doing this, SoMeONe reduces the possibility of spamming users who are not already known.

A user can also add new contacts corresponding to real people he/she already knows by asking them

their SoMeONe identifier using traditional media (email, phone, meeting, etc.). He/she can also add a new contact by only specifying an email address he knows. If this address corresponds to a subscribed user then SoMeONe will add the user identifier in the distribution list. If it is not the case, it will create automatically a new user subscription with a password and a user identifier computed from the email address. The new user identifier will then be added to the distribution list. SoMeONe proposes to the user to send an email to this newly created user displaying a mailto: hyperlink. When the user clicks on this link, his email client pops up with an automatically generated email. This mail tells the new user that some information is available for him by using SoMeONe. He has to follow an included URL, and use his/her generated password and identifier. He/she is also informed about the user who has made this information available (the sender of the e-mail) and the involved topic name. The new user will be able to change his identifier and password at anytime, and merge, if necessary, his multiple identities in SoMeONe(if he/she is already subscribed). This crafty feature lets the SoMeONe service to bootstrap and grow rapidly. Later, we will see how SoMeONe can help users to discover new interesting contacts.

To manage distribution lists, a user associates a list of users to each topic of his/her personal taxonomy.

274

Instead of having to manage as many distribution list as domains about which a user wants to exchange information, a SoMeONe user can reuse and specialize his/her distribution lists. A topic being a specialization of a more general topic can by default inherit the distribution list of its ancestor. A user can specialize this default list by adding or removing contacts. He can also declare that the topic is "secret". Any review with such a topic is only accessible from its author.

Then, to distribute a review on a document, a user only needs to add topics to the review for describing the document instead of having to precise physical mailing addresses. We distinguish this distribution process as "semantic addressing". According to the topics put together in a review, the distribution list will not be the same (for example if one topic is declared "secret" then the distribution list will be empty). Therefore, this semantic addressing process is also contextual.

Information access: These lists are used to compute information displayed to a user when he logs on to SoMeONe's home page (see screenshot on figure 1). This personal homepage is like the user's email clients. It shows the user's personal topics (left column of the screenshot) , and all the information a user has "virtually" received since all the information is in the server and no information is sent to any device or duplicated to any personal file folders (middle column of the screenshot). A user must belong to one of the distribution lists to be able to access a review of one of the topics. None of these topics should be declared "secret".

This new information is grouped by contact's identifiers and by topics. The displayed topics are those to which the user belongs to the distribution list. To limit spamming and information overload, the user can filter a topic of a specific user. This fine grain filtering allows a user to receive information from another user regarded as competent in these topics. To access the topic's contents -which are reviews that include this topic-, a user has to click on the topic name. A review is displayed if it is accessible (for example there is no "secret" topic) and if the user hasn't created any review on the same document. A user can declare any review as being seen or deleted (see buttons on right column of the screenshot). These two actions create specific reviews on the document associated to the user that will filter the review for the new displays. This precious personal information will also be used in the future to compute a personal profile of user interests. Documents being identified by their URL, we are aware that two documents having the same content but different URLs won't be filtered. We expect to download reviewed documents and to

compute a signature of them in order to identify that two URLs relate to the same document.

Thus, if a user "receives" several times the same document using reviews, he will consult its reviews only once.

Information propagation: For each displayed review, a user can create his own review on the same document with his own topic ("add to my topics" button of the screenshot). By doing so, the user will be able to retrieve this review using his own taxonomy criterion but he will also propagate the diffusion of the document to all his contacts in the distribution list of the topics in the new review.

When a user will access to the new review he will see his own review and all other review he can access on the same document. Only the topics of the reviews that contain the user in their distribution list are displayed.

4 SOMEONE SOFTWARE ARCHITECTURE

SoMeONe has been developed as a web application using Jalios content Management Suite[3]. Jalios provides a collaborative infrastructure that allows user groups to produce and publish information. Jalios architecture includes a light object-oriented database model entirely managed in memory, an external or internal web server (Apache, IIS), a performing jsp servlet engine (Resin), and a user directory (LDAP compatible) (see figure 2). This architecture is compliant to standards and multiple tools can be integrated. Scalability is handled by distributing servers with synchronised databases. Jalios has been implemented in Java.

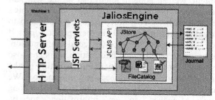

Figure 2: Jalios' architecture.

The whole administration is managed with a web interface. Default HTML templates are automatically generated for each managed information type and can be customized with classical graphical editors.

---

[3]http://www.jalios.com

5 ENCOURAGING COOPERATION

There is cooperation with SoMeONe when a user adds other users in the distribution list of one of his topics. Combining personal information management and information sharing functionalities in the same service reduces the extra cost of cooperation. Creating a document review has the same "cognitive cost" if the review is shared or not. The extra costs are in distribution list management. The reuse and specialization of distribution lists reduce the difficulty. Small lists are also easier to manage than long ones. Instead of having to manage long lists of users, these users can be distributed in small lists associated to different specific topics. Then adding several topics to the review can compose a long distribution list. To encourage cooperation, SoMeONe also needs to protect users who cooperate. We have already seen some features that reduce the possibility for spamming. A user sees another user's identifier only if the latter voluntarily sends him some information. This supposes that the user knows and trusts him. We will also see later that we plan to develop a recommendation system to motivate the sharing of information between two unknown users if they have valuable assets for each other. This feature has to be guaranteed by SoMeONe.

However, for the time being, cooperating only with known users is too restrictive. Users need to establish new relationships with others. To initiate those dynamics, motivated users can declare some of their topics as public. This means that any user can see the topic's name and add it's identifier to the distribution list. If this user is interested in the content, we can hope in return that he/she will add the owner of the public topic to one of his/her topic's distribution lists. Therefore, users are motivated to provide interesting contents in their public topics if they also want to receive good information. However, to receive new information users can also only wait for the availability of an interesting public topic without distributing back any information. We can expect that these users might wait for a long time. Moreover, in an information society, information is sometimes so crucial that users cannot afford waiting. Reluctant people might also be stimulated by their environment if for example, they see their nearest colleagues adopting a cooperative behaviour. So, they are better informed and have greater efficiency. Another stimulating factor is that a user can also decide, at any time, to stop having some of his topics being public. Then he can remove from the distribution lists those who did not provide him with interesting information. SoMeONe

offers facilities and encourages users to do this in order to improve global cooperation. For example, a user can display all the users that provide him with the most interesting reviews. By "interesting reviews" we mean those which have an associated review created or seen —and not deleted— by the user.

6 SOMEONE IN ENTERPRISE

The main application of SoMeONe is definitely in the enterprise. Intranet companies are getting bigger and bigger as companies grow. In addition, the biggest the company is, the more we find a large diversity of jobs, workers, and cultures. All this diversity hides differences in needs, backgrounds, and sensibilities. To face this diversity, only providing an access to information with some global indexing facilities is not always sufficient. To be efficient, collaborators need to access information relevant to their business and adapted to their personal capabilities and sensibilities. As an example, any industrial researcher knows that he/she will not present his work with the same slides to a scientific community or to marketers from a business unit. We believe that this level of adaptation can only come from people networks. These networks are open, flexible and dynamic. They cannot only rely on the enterprise organisation. Collaborators are increasingly working in teams belonging to multiple entities, inside or outside the company. Suppliers, technicians, engineers, marketers, even customers are getting closer relationships in information exchange networks.

For companies in the business of information society, communication is a key issue. In addition, the production of these companies is often based on the production of information and knowledge. For such companies, their need is to build valuable social capital, made of the knowledge of their employees and their mutually enriching relationships (Bourdieu, 1986). Here again, SoMeONe is particularly adapted to support and develop these valuable relationships.

Another application domain in enterprise is business intelligence. SoMeONe is a solution for distributing through the company the process of detecting important information and rapidly broadcasting it to appropriate audience with a validation and commenting process all along the chain that enriches the information.

7   PERSPECTIVES

The fundamentals of SoMeONe are based on users' willingness to cooperate. Like Hazel Hall (Hall, 2001), we agree on what economists already argue: individuals evaluate alternative courses of action so that they get best value at lowest cost from any completed transaction. But in social life, people (actors) can only obtain what they need and value (resources) through dependent relationships with others (structures) (Molm, 2001). Users need others to rapidly find relevant, up to date information for not becoming an outsider in the rapidly growing information society. We think that some participants can also be aware that the viability of their community depends on their commitment to it. This is "embodied in the willingness of individuals to share information and knowledge with other members of the community" (Merali, 2000). If no contributions are made the results are drastic: the community will not continue to exist. SoMeOne will stimulate this consciousness by showing users some viability indicators of his communities. These indicators will be computed using social network analysis techniques (Wasserman et al. 1994).

Anyway, we are aware that SoMeONe has to integrate regulation mechanisms to stimulate cooperative behaviours. The first mechanism we will implement is a recommendation system in order to propose users to exchange information. Nevertheless, the recommendation process will be completely different as traditional one (Glance et al 1994). Instead of directly proposing users to *receive* more information from a new contact and thus encouraging "free riders" (unproductive users) (Adar and Huberman, 2000), we will recommend users to *send* their information to carefully chosen users. Therefore, a user must have information to share for being able to receive, and it has to be valuable if he/she wants users to send him valuable information as well; but how will those users know what kind of information this user will find valuable? Being an expert in one topic, he can be disappointed to receive information on that topic. However, he can be interested in other topics. This is why our recommendation algorithm will try to couple users that have topics to exchange. It needs to search sets of four topics. Two of those topics ($u1$, $u2$) should belong to one user u, and the two others ($v1$, $v2$) should belong to another user v. Then we choose the sets of four topics that maximize the two of the following probabilities. If user v receives reviews from user u having the topic $u1$, he should review them with his topic $v1$, and if user u receives reviews from user v having the topic $v2$, he should review them with his topic $u2$. We are still working on the way we are computing those probabilities. This recommendation factor only takes into account the individual profile of users' interests. In order to augment global social optimisation of the exchange network, we think we also need to take into account other social criteria. For example, we will use structural social network analysis techniques to compute factors like: centrality, independence and solicitation (Wasserman, 1994). These factors will be stored in a social profile of each user and will be used in the choice of the sets of topics for making recommendations.

Finally, we need to validate our hypothesis, recommendation algorithm, and their multiple scaling factors. First, we need to identify the criteria of our social media we want to optimise. Then we need to find means to measure these criteria in the logs and SoMeONe's database. One of the problems is to compute global measures of a social system from individual indicators. How to evaluate global satisfaction, global noise, or silence? Having those measures defined, we then plan to use a simulation tool to test the influence of the regulation mechanism, algorithm options and scaling factors values. (Beugnard and Fan, 2002). To define and calibrate the model of the user's behaviour we will simulate and conduct some real experiments. One experiment will take place in a enterprise using its Intranet. Another one will be integrated into a larger project named "the Cartable Electronique"® (Martel and Vignollet, 2002).

8   CONCLUSION

We propose a social media to find and filter information in web-like networks. This service solves some of the main problems of traditional social media:

The service is available on line without any installation of dedicated software

Users visibility is managed and controlled.

The service develops personal relationships.

Information is classified with users own criterions, and can be aggregated and filtered according topics, users and novelty.

In order to receive valuable information, users are encouraged to send valuable one.

By combining a personal management information tool and a communication tool the cost of cooperation is reduced.

SoMeONe's main contributions are:

Using network of people as human information channels.

Information is successively filtered user after user and enriched with personal opinions.
The management of multiple personal taxonomies.
Message semantic addressing by automatic calculation of distribution lists according to document labelling
Easy management of distribution list using topics inheritance.
Tools to detect profiteers in order to remove them from the exchange networks.

This system should provide many users with a solution to take advantage of available information, mainly in companies. More generally, if some people see the power in knowledge, such system clearly set the power in personal networks.

The informational World Wide Web is an engine of the information society. The human web we have sketched in this system is it's dual space to complement it, where documents navigate from user to user instead of having users to navigate from document to document. It is also a source for the Semantic Web since it should stimulate the production of meta-information.

The main challenge is to develop a cooperative behaviour among users. To improve the efficiency of the system we have presented the future works we have planed. Experiments and simulations should confirm our expectations.

9 REFERENCES

Adamic Lada A. and Adar Eytan, 2000. Friends and neighbors on the web, Technical Report. http://www.hpl.hp.com/shl/papers/web10/

Adar Eytan and Huberman Bernardo, 2000.Free riding on Gnutella, First Monday, (October). http://www.firstmonday.dk

Berners-Lee, T., Fielding, R., and Frystyk H., 1996. Hypertext Transfer Protocol HTTP/1.0., RFC 1945 MIT/LCS, UC Irvine, May.

Berners-Lee , Hendler J and Lassila O. The Semantic Web. Scientific American, May 2001

Beugnard A and Phan D., 2002. Moduleco, a multi-agent modular framework for the simulation of network effects and population dynamics in social sciences, markets & organizations. http://www-eco.enst-bretagne.fr/~phan/moduleco/ModulecoGreyPaper.pdf

Bourdieu, P.,1986. The forms of capital. In J. Richardson (Ed.), Handbook of theory and research for the sociology of education (pp. 241-258). New York: Greenwood.

Bouthors Vincent, Dedieu Olivier, 1999. Pharos, a collaborative infrastructure for web knowledge. In proceedings of the third European Conference on Research and Advanced Technology for Digital Libaries, ECDL'99. Lecture Notes in Computer Science, 1696, pp. 215-233, Springer-Verlag Inc., (September).

Delgado Joaquin, Ishii Nohoiro,, 2001, multi-agent learning in recommender systems for information filtering on the internet, International Journal of Cooperative Information Systems, Vol. 10, Nos. 1 & 2 (2001), pp. 81 – 100.

Nathalie Glance, Damian Arregui, 1999. Manfred. Making Recommender Systems Work for Organizations Proceedings of PAAM'99, London, UK, (April 19-21).

Good Nathaniel, Shafer J. Ben, Konstan Joseph A., Borchers Al, Sawar Bradul, Herlocker Lon and Riedl John, 1999. Combining collaborative filtering with personal agents for better recommendations, AAAI/IAAI.

Gräther, W., Prinz, W., 2001.The social web cockpit: support for virtual communities. In ACM SIGGROUP Conference on Supporting Group Work, ACM Press, Boulder, Colorado, USA, 2001, pp. 252 - 259.

Kanawati Rushed and Malek Maria, 2000. Informing the design of shared bookmarks systems, In Proceedings of RIAO2000. Paris, France. Pp. 170-180.

Martel Christian, Laurence Vignollet, 2002. Educational Web Environment based on the metaphor of electronic schoolbag, ARIADNE 2002, Lyon, France.

Merali, Y., 2000. Self-organising communities. In S. Roc(Ed.), In Liberating knowledge (pp. 80-87). London: IBM/CBI.

Molm, L. D., 2001. Theories of social exchange and exchange networks. In G. Ritzer & B. Smart (Eds.), Handbook of social theory (pp. 260-272). London: Sage.

Popescul Alexandrin, Ungar Lyle H., Pennock David M., Steve Lawrence, 2001, Probabilistic models for unified collaborative and content-based recommendation in sparse-data environments, 17'th Conference on Uncertainty in Artificial Intelligence, pp. 437–444, 2001.

Trevor Robie, 2001.PageTracker: A Portable Bookmarking Tool Used for Fine-Grain Update Notification, 2001.

Wasserman Stanley and Katherine Faust, 1994. Social Network Analysis: Methods and Applications. Cambridge: Cambridge University Press.

ENGINEERING MULTIAGENT SYSTEMS BASED ON INTERACTION PROTOCOLS: A COMPOSITIONAL PETRI NET APPROACH

Sea Ling and Seng Wai Loke
School of Computer Science and Software Engineering
Monash University, Caulfield East, VIC 3145, Australia
Email:{sling,swloke}@csse.monash.edu.au

Keywords: Multiagent, Petri net, compositional, agent-based software engineering, AUML, interaction protocols

Abstract: Multiagent systems are useful in distributed systems where autonomous and flexible behaviour with decentralized control is advantageous or necessary. To facilitate agent interactions in multiagent systems, a set of interaction protocols for agents has been proposed by the Foundation of Intelligent Physical Agents (FIPA). These protocols are specified diagramatically in an extension of UML called AUML (Agent UML) for agent communication. In this paper, we informally present a means to translate these protocols to equivalent Petri net specifications. Our Petri nets are compositional, and we contend that compositionality is useful since multiagent systems and their interactions are inherently modular, and so that mission-critical parts of a system can be analysed separately.

1 INTRODUCTION

Multiagent systems are useful in distributed systems where autonomous and flexible behaviour with decentralized control is advantageous or necessary such as in supply-chain automation, distributed information retrieval and factory automation systems. In a multiagent system, agents communicate with each other via some interaction protocol. The protocol typifies a set of message passing communications to be executed by the agents in some correct order. A number of interaction protocols have been proposed by the organization FIPA (The Foundation for Intelligent Physical Agents) [1], whose purpose is to provide software standards for interacting agents for agent-based systems. Examples of interaction protocols are the contract net protocol, the English auction protocol and the Dutch auction protocol. The protocols have been specified in AUML (Agent UML) (Bauer et al., 2001), an extension of the Unified Modelling Language (UML). The notation used in the specification document thus far is a variant of UML's sequence diagram developed for agent-based systems, as shown in Figure 1. The figure reproduces FIPA's Contract Net interaction protocol. It depicts the sequence of messages exchanged between two agents: an initiator and a participant.

[1] http://www.fipa.org/

It has been proposed that each interaction protocol can be viewed as a pattern to be used as a "reusable aggregate of processing" (Bauer et al., 2001). In different problem domains, the pattern becomes a template that can be reused in such a way that the basic interaction and message sequencing remain the same while the agent roles and the message details will be modified to adapt to a different scenario. Such templates can be used by programmers as reference when building their multiagent system.

However, it often requires clever and careful programming to ensure that agents built do implement a particular protocol. How do we guarantee that the agents built do indeed conform to a given interaction protocol? One approach is to code and fix: given an interaction protocol described in AUML, code the agents up and apply a debugging tool to see that the agents do indeed send the right messages at the right time. This approach has some virtue and is practical (e.g., (Poutakidis et al., 2002)).

Another approach is specify and derive, is to start from specifications whose correctness have been verified, and then carefully derive (perhaps semi-automatically) code from the specifications. Such specifications can also be analysed for correctness. We believe this would be more systematic and more likely lead to correct code if it can be effectively done.

In this paper, we apply the Petri net formalism,

O. Camp et al. (eds.), Enterprise Information Systems V, 279-285.

widely used as a process specification and verification language (Murata, 1989), to model interaction protocols, and show how our model can be used for analysing agent behaviours for correctness and for building agents that interact correctly. The use of Petri nets to model agent interaction protocols and conversations have been done in other work such as (Cost et al., 1999; Poutakidis et al., 2002). However, we believe our approach is novel in the use of compositional Petri nets that are analogous to workflow nets (Aalst, 1999), in clearly separating the pattern of interaction from agent behaviour that is induced by the interaction, and in our aim of engineering multiagent systems that conform to patterns of interaction.

Our work begins with the simple observation that a given interaction protocol imposes particular constraints on the behaviour of participating agents. Informally but intuitively, we show how an interaction protocol represented in AUML can be translated into a Petri net modelling the pattern of interaction, and Petri nets, each modelling the participant agents' (or agent roles') behaviour. The Petri net for each agent (or agent role) acts as a specification of the aspect of the agent's behaviour that is induced by their involvement in the interaction protocol. Such a specification is in the spirit of the agent skeletons proposed in (Singh, 2000), where a skeleton captures the interaction aspect of an agent (with respect to that protocol). Then, an implementation of the agent is said to implement the interaction protocol (i.e., the agent correctly assumes some role in the protocol) if it at least satisfies the minimal requirements in this specification. Also, we anticipate that the Petri net for each agent can then be semi-automatically translated into skeleton code which can then be fleshed out to implement the required application. Moreover, since we use Petri nets, existing Petri net analysis methods (Murata, 1989) can be used to analyse and verify the correctness of specifications.

Because we start from the interaction protocol, we can view our approach as being *interaction-oriented* (Singh, 2000), i.e. a multiagent system is constructed based on the interactions among agents.

The paper is organized as follows. Section 2 provides the brief preliminaries on AUML, interaction protocols and Petri nets. Section 3 shows how the interaction protocols can be represented in Petri nets. section 4 describes the application of the protocols (in Petri net) to a multiagent system and how the resulting Petri net model can be subject to Petri net analysis methods. Section 5 outlines our approach of developing multiagent applications based on Petri net specifications obtained from AUML interaction protocol descriptions. Section 6 is the conclusion.

2 PRELIMINARIES

2.1 AUML and Interaction Protocol

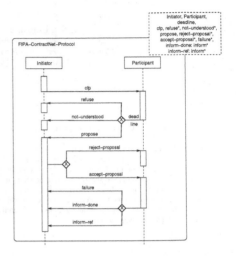

Figure 1: The Contract Net Protocol in AUML

For object-oriented software engineering, we have the de facto standard Unified Modelling Language (UML) for object-oriented analysis and design. For agent-oriented software engineering, an extension of UML called Agent UML (AUML) has been developed to cater for agent-based interaction analysis (Bauer et al., 2001). Some common interaction protocols between agents have been specified in AUML by FIPA and they are presented in an extension of UML's sequence diagram, as shown in Figure 1. The figure reproduces from FIPA specification of the Contract Net Interaction Protocol. It captures the chronological sequence of communications between two agents - the initiator and the participant. The dotted box in the upper right corner indicates that this is a template with unbound parameters divided by horizontal lines into three categories: role parameters, constraints and communication acts. The communication acts are represented by the arrows labelled with the names of the messages (instead of object-oriented style events in UML). To allow multiple threads of interaction, the AUML sequence diagram use three message passing structures, shown in Figure 2 which is reproduced from (Bauer et al., 2001). Figure 2(a) depicts all messages or communication acts (CA) sent concurrently, Figure 2(b) depicts zero or more are sent and Figure 2(c) only one of the messages is sent.

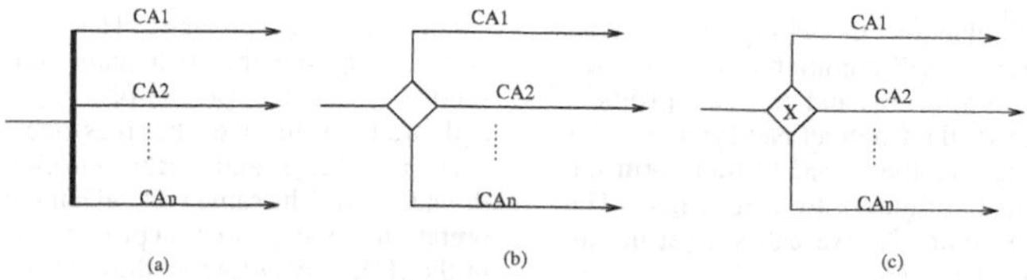

Figure 2: Multiple Message Threads

In the Contract Net protocol (Figure 1), a call-for-proposal (cfp) is sent by the initiator (the manager) to the participant (the contractor). Before some deadline, the participant can either refuse, claim not-understood or propose by generating a proposal to perform a task. If a proposal is received by the initiator, the initiator can either reject-proposal or accept-proposal. After the proposal is accepted, the participant will perform the task till the end when another message (failure, inform-done or inform-ref) is sent.

It should be noted that for each agent, there are a number of vertical activation bars. Each bar represents a different agent role or a different processing thread of the agent. Intuitively, the separation of these bars allows an agent to have different lifelines. For example, after sending cfp, the initiator may start a new role or lifeline to accept a return message (refuse, not-understand or propose) from the participant. For the participant, the reception of cfp must be followed by the sending of one message at the end of the deadline on the same lifeline because these activities occur in the same vertical bar.

2.2 PETRI NETS

Petri nets (Murata, 1989) have been widely used for process specification and verification. A standard Petri net graph consists of *places, transitions* and *arcs*. We can view places (represented graphically by circles) as describing the possible local system states or conditions, transitions (represented graphically by rectangles) are transition or events which may modify the system state and arcs (arrows) simply link a place to a transition or a transition to a place. In other words, an arc linking a place to a transition indicates which local state will cause the event to occur, and an arc linking a transition to a place indicates the local state transformation induced by the event occurrence.

Fundamentally, by connecting all places and transitions with arcs, we model the behaviour of a system in terms of its possible states and events. Different net structures can be drawn to exhibit different

behaviours, such as sequential, concurrency and non-determinism. At any time, a place may contain zero or more *tokens*, drawn as black dots. A token found in the place represents the current state at this moment in time. Examples of Petri net models are shown in Figure 5. The figure depicts the possible behaviour of two agents and their initial states in1 and in2.

The dynamic behaviour of a Petri net is controlled by the firing rule. A transition can *fire* (meaning an event can occur) if there is at least one token in each of the transition's preceding places (the event's pre-conditions are true). This transition is then said to be *enabled*. An enabled transition fires by removing one token from all of its input places (pre-conditions) and depositing one token in each of its output places (post-conditions). This movement of tokens from place(s) to place(s) indicates a change of system states after the occurrence of the event. In other interpretations, token flow from one place to another may also represent the flow of data item from one location to another.

Useful system properties have also been defined formally for Petri nets (Murata, 1989; Desel and Esparza, 1995). Two important properties are the liveness and the boundedness properties. To analyse the behavioural correctness of a system, Petri net analysis methods have been devised to check for these properties in the Petri net model of the system. In our previous work, (Ling and Loke, 2002), Petri nets have been used to model agent behaviour so that the appropriate analysis methods can be applied to provide a notion of behavioural correctness for mobile agent systems.

3 A PETRI NET TEMPLATE

Ultimately, the objective is to develop techniques to model interaction protocols in Petri nets so that together with Petri net models of individual agents, the entire multiagent system can be analysed for correctness. Individual mobile agent behaviour has been modelled in Petri nets (Ling and Loke, 2002). Specifically, a class of Petri nets called workflow net (Aalst, 1998) used in business process modelling has been adapted for agent behaviour modelling. It is envisaged that these agents will communicate with each other via interaction protocols and one such protocol is shown in Figure 1 - the Contract Net Protocol. For Petri net modelling, we then need to transform the AUML notation in the figure into a Petri net. The result is shown in Figure 3. We call such a net an Interaction Protocol (IP) net.

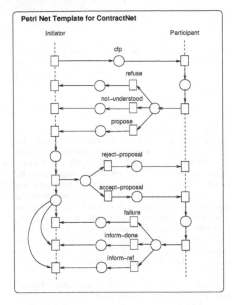

Figure 3: IP-net of the Contract Net Protocol

In Figure 3, for the initiator and the participant agents, the sending and receiving of messages are modelled by transitions or events. Intuitively, these events are activated by the respective agents. Multiple-threaded messages which may take any of the forms shown in Figure 2 can be replaced by the Petri net structures shown in Figure 4 respectively. As the Contract Net protocol exhibits only the multiple message threads of Figure 2(c), they are being replaced by the non-deterministic choice Petri net structure of Figure 4(c).

In the original interaction protocol (Figure 1), an agent can have multiple lifelines or processing threads denoted by separate vertical bars. Messages can be sent and received within the same thread or in different threads independently according to the specification. We model such independence by having individual send and receive transitions in Figure 3. In the IP-net, the initiator sends cfp independently of other events. However, if a proposal is received from the participant, the initiator must send reject-proposal or accept-proposal and wait to receive the message of failure, inform-done and inform-ref in the same thread (within the same vertical bar). This is the interpretation of the interaction protocol and it is reflected in the IP-net by enforcing these initiator events to be on the same processing thread.

It should be noted that the above translation is done from the viewpoint of the interaction protocol requirements. It is up to the agents to implement their own sequence of events and synchronise with the interaction protocol. The behavioural models of agents will need to synchronise with the IP-net. This is described in the next section.

4 MODELLING MULTIAGENT SYSTEMS

In (Ling and Loke, 2001; Ling and Loke, 2002), we modelled mobile agent itinerary with a type of Petri nets called Agent Itinerary (AI-) nets. An agent itinerary is a description of all the tasks to be performed by the agent in a designated order at different localities. In the current context, we can also use Petri nets to model agent behaviour. We call such a Petri net simply Agent net (A-net) since localities are no longer an issue here. An A-net models the interaction aspect of an agent (with respect to an interaction protocol) whereas an AI-net models the mobility aspect of an agent.

A-nets are similar to Workflow (WF) nets (Aalst, 1998) used to model business processes, in that the agent behaviour specification begins at a starting state and ends in a final state. This is analogous to a WF-net modelling a business process in which the process has a single entry point and a single exit point. One could view each A-net as a skeleton capturing the interaction aspect of an agent (with respect to that protocol).

Figure 5 shows the possible behaviours of the initiator agent (on the left) and the participant agent (on the right) with their initial states (places in1 and in2 respectively) marked with tokens. The agent behaviour is viewed as individual workflow with a collection of events (tasks) to be executed in the correct order. At the end of the execution, the final states are places out1 and out2. In order for both agents to communicate with each other, we use the IP-net in Figure 3 as a connecting net. The resulting two-agent system model is shown in Figure 6 and we call such a model a Multiagent Interaction Protocol net (MIP-net).

In the figure, each dotted line connects one transition from an A-net to another transition from the IP-

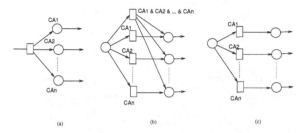

(a) (b) (c)

Figure 4: Petri Net Equivalence of Multiple Message Threads

net. Each line depicts a synchronous communication. It forces both transitions to be executed at the same time (as opposed to asynchronous communication). In Petri nets, such synchronous communication corresponds to a fusion or melting of a number of transitions. For example, transition send-cfp belonging to the Initiator is fused with t1 so that a cfp is sent to activate t2 which is fused with transition receive-cfp belonging to the participant. By executing the model, the agents are effectively satisfying the Contract Net interaction protocol and are able to reach the final states out1 and out2 respectively. As mentioned previously, the ability for any system to reach its final state is one of the criteria for correctness. In this example, the A-nets are correct in that the system does reach the final state. However, one could replace those A-nets with others (representing different specifications of agent interaction behaviours) to see if those A-nets would work together with other A-nets with respect to the IP-net.

We define the correctness criteria for multiagent system in a similar fashion as the notion of soundness for workflow business process systems (Aalst, 1998; Aalst, 1999). Informally, an agent system modelled by Petri nets is *sound* if and only if the following holds:

1. Starting from the initial state (in1 and in2), it is always possible to reach the final state (out1 and out2);

2. When the final state is reached, there should be no token in any other places. In other words, upon completion, there is no more work for agents to perform; and

3. It is always possible for an agent to perform any task specified in the model starting from the initial state.

As pointed out by Aalst (Aalst, 1999), the first two requirements ensure proper termination, in this instance, of agents. In order to "use" the interaction protocol or IP-net, the agent's A-net must:

1. provide the corresponding synchronous elements to synchronise with the template;

2. be sound; and

3. ensure that the entire multiagent system is *globally sound*.

The concept of global soundness has been introduced in (Aalst, 1999) for Interorganizational Workflow, in which multiple workflows from several organizations are involved in one "global" process. Individual workflows or WF-nets are connected to each other via synchronizing elements. Clearly, this can also be applied to multiagent systems. Essentially, we treat A-nets as individual WF-nets, and a multiagent system is a set of A-nets and a set of IP-nets.

The soundness properties are defined in terms of the liveness and the boundedness of the Petri net model (Aalst, 1999). Existing Petri net analysis methods can be used to check agent soundness and global soundness to ensure the multiagent system is implemented correctly.

5 DEVELOPING MULTIAGENT SYSTEMS FROM AUML DESCRIPTIONS

We outline how we can use AUML interaction protocol descriptions as a basis on which to develop multiagent applications.

1. From the AUML description of the interaction protocol, we manually derive the IP-net and the A-nets of the participating agent roles. Note that A-nets derived this way will be correct but tend to represent only the (intuitively) minimal interaction behaviour. The A-net might be expanded further according to the application being built at hand, or substituted by some other A-net reflecting application requirements. Also, although the process is done manually, it can be automated using

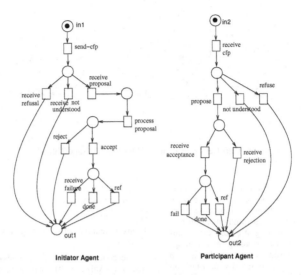

Figure 5: Agent Behaviour

a machine-readable representation of an AUML diagram.

2. If the A-nets are not the minimal ones, the IP-net and A-nets are composed as shown earlier and analysed for correctness. Note that if an agent is involved in multiple interactions (with different or same protocols), it would have its behaviour modelled by multiple A-nets, each A-net for one interaction. For example, an agent who is simultaneously a bidder in an English auction, a bidder in a different Dutch auction, and querying (using some protocol) a database would have its overall interaction behaviour represented by three A-nets. Each A-net represents a facet of interaction behaviour of the agent. The three A-nets would then need to be composed (according to the designer in an application-specific way) into a larger Petri net and analysed together with other A-nets and IP-nets of the protocols to see if the overall system will work.

3. The A-nets can be used to generate skeleton code in some preferred programming language (e.g., Java). Again, this can be done manually but we are investigating automation of this process.

4. Finally, the skeleton code derived from the A-nets are fleshed out with application-specific code.

6 CONCLUSION AND FUTURE WORK

We have informally introduced a method for engineering multiagent systems based on AUML interaction protocol descriptions using compositional Petri net specifications. Currently, we are in the process of formalising the definitions of A-nets, IP-nets and MIP-nets. We contend that compositionality is useful since multiagent systems and their interactions are inherently modular, and so that mission-critical parts of a large system can be analysed separately. The analysis aspects are being formalised too.

We point out that our work is different from Singh's work (Singh, 2000) which inspired our skeleton view of A-nets since he does not use Petri nets or AUML descriptions. Also, our work is different from (Xu et al., 2002) as they neither use compositional Petri nets (they use Predicate/Transition nets) nor AUML descriptions, and they involve domain-specific agent plans while our A-nets focus on only the interaction aspect of the agents rather than the agent's full internal reasoning. Certainly, Petri net descriptions of agent plans can be analysed together with A-nets and IP-nets.

Future work will involve developing a tool for our approach that will automate parts of our approach such as deriving Petri net specifications from machine-readable representations of AUML diagrams as well as deriving skeleton code from (enriched) A-

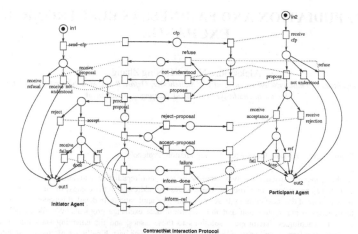

Figure 6: Two Agents Communicating via an Interaction Protocol

nets. We are also working towards analysis of non-functional properties such as performance and timing issues and agent commitments, using advanced Petri nets such as timed Petri nets.

REFERENCES

Aalst, W. v. (1998). The application of Petri nets to work-flow management. *The Journal of Circuits, Systems and Computers*, 8(1):21–66.

Aalst, W. v. (1999). Interorganizational workflows: An approach based on message sequence charts and Petri nets. *Systems Analysis - Modelling - Simulation*, 34(3):335–67.

Bauer, B., Müller, J. P., and Odell, J. (2001). Agent UML: A formalism for specifying multiagent interaction. In Ciancarini, P. and Wooldridge, M., editors, *Agent-Oriented Software Engineering*, pages 91–103. Springer-Verlay, Berlin.

Cost, R., Chen, Y., Finin, T., Labrou, Y., and Peng, Y. (1999). Modeling agent conversations with colored petri nets. In *Proc. 9th Int'l Joint Conference on Artificial Intelligence (IJCAI'99)*.

Desel, J. and Esparza, J. (1995). *Free Choice Petri Nets*. Cambridge University Press.

Ling, S. and Loke, S. (2001). Verification of itineraries for mobile agent enabled interorganizational workflow. In *Proc. 4th Int'l Workshop on Mobility in Databases and Distributed Systems*, pages 582–86.

Ling, S. and Loke, S. (2002). Advanced petri nets for modelling mobile agent enabled interorganizational work-

flow. In *Proc. 9th Int'l Conference on Engineering of Computer-Based Systems (ECBS2002)*, pages 245–52.

Murata, T. (1989). Petri nets: Properties, analysis and applications. *Proceedings of the IEEE*, 77(4):541–80.

Poutakidis, D., Padgham, L., and Winikoff, M. (2002). Debugging multi-agent systems using design artifacts: The case of interaction protocols. In *Proc. 1st International Joint Conference on Autonomous Agents and Multi-Agent Systems (AAMAS 2002)*.

Singh, M. (2000). Synthesizing coordination requirements for heterogeneous autonomous agents. *Autonomous Agents and Multi-Agent Systems*, 3(2):107–132.

Xu, D., Volz, R., Ioerger, T., and Yen, J. (2002). Modeling and verifying multi-agent behaviours using predicate/transition nets. In *Proc. of the Conference on Software Engineering and Knowledge Engineering*.

NON-REPUDIATION AND FAIRNESS IN ELECTRONIC DATA EXCHANGE

Aleksandra Nenadić, Ning Zhang

Department of ComputerScience, University of Manchester, Oxford Road, Manchester M13 9PL,UK
Email: anenadic@cs.man.ac.uk, nzhang@ cs.man.ac.uk

Keywords: E-commerce, Fair Data Exchange, Non-repudiation, Protocols

Abstract: In this paper we discuss the two security issues: non-repudiation and fairness in association with e-commerce applications. In particular, these issues are addressed in the context of electronic data exchange, which is one of the most commonly seen e-commerce applications. In detail, this paper gives a survey of the approaches to non-repudiation and fair electronic data exchange protocols. We additionally discuss the current technologies that propose solutions to these issues, and the emerging standards in the area of business data formats and protocols for the exchange of such data. Finally, we discuss the architecture layer at which to implement the protocols for non-repudiation and fair data exchange.

1 INTRODUCTION

The growing importance of e-commerce transactions has resulted in the need for adequate and secure solutions for reliable exchange of valuable electronic data. Creating a framework for secure and reliable e-commerce systems is currently one of the focal topics for the research community worldwide, and international technical and commercial groups and standardisation bodies. Several joint efforts have been undertaken to standardise document formats, business document libraries and messaging protocols.

Due to the fact that data exchanged in e-commerce transactions is usually valuable, and that business parties do not necessarily trust each other, adequate security measures are needed to ensure that the exchange is secure, fair and non-repudiable. Being *secure* means that an exchange process should be able to protect the exchanged data against unauthorised access, modification, deletion and replay. Being *fair* means that the exchange process should be able to avoid situations where one party has received the expected data, while the other has not. Additionally, commercial transactions have legal significance, and therefore the exchange process should have an embedded mechanism for the parties to gather sufficient evidence of the exchange/transaction. *Non-repudiation techniques* are used to gather such evidence for any possible dispute resolution, and to aid in achieving, restoring or retaining fairness of the exchange process.

In this paper, we address *fairness* and *non-repudiation* in the context of electronic data (document or information) exchange, such as exchanges of digital signatures on a contract, digital payments for e-goods, and a certified e-mail for its receipt/acknowledgements. Our current research on these issues is part of the FIDES (Fair Integrated Data Exchange Services) project, aimed at development of a complete end-to-end solution for automatic provision of non-repudiation and fair exchange services.

The paper is organised as follows. Definitions of non-repudiation and fairness, and examples of potential security risks in e-commerce caused by repudiation and unfairness are given in Section 2. In Section 3 we examine the existing work on non-repudiation and fair exchange protocols. A survey on currently emerging worldwide standards for the electronic business data formats and protocols for the exchange of such data is given in Section 4. In Section 5, we discuss appropriate architectural layer for positioning non-repudiation services in the context of security design, and propose architecture for non-repudiation and fairness services. The conclusion is outlined in Section 6.

O. Camp et al. (eds.), Enterprise Information Systems V, 286-293.
© 2004 *Kluwer Academic Publishers. Printed in the Netherlands.*

2 NON-REPUDIATION AND FAIRNESS AS SECURITY ISSUES

Security attacks, such as unauthorised access to resources or impersonation, mostly come from outside of a system. However, in an e-commerce system, security threats can also come from business partners (i.e. insiders), especially as, in such an environment, they do not conduct e-commerce activities in person. In the following, we give two such business scenarios to illustrate the threats imposed by insiders and the need for non-repudiation and fairness protections.

Example 1 - digital signing of a contract: Bob is selling a house and Alice would like to purchase it. They have agreed on a contract and decided to finalise the deal over the Internet. For signing this contract, each of them needs to generate a digital signature on the contract and send it to the other party. Let's assume that Bob follows the agreement and sends his signature to Alice straight away. However, without *fairness protection,* Alice may delay sending her signature to Bob while taking her time to look for a better house and later withdraw from the deal without making any compensation to Bob.

Example 2 – electronic purchase: Alice has sent a purchase order to Bob, the merchant, who, due to mismanagement, has failed to dispatch the goods to Alice as promised. To avoid paying compensation to Alice, Bob simply denies that he has ever received any purchase order from Alice. Without *non-repudiation protection,* Alice is left unguarded against this deception, and has no evidence to back herself up in this dispute.

2.1 Non-repudiation

Repudiation is denial of one of the entities involved in a communication of having participated in all or part of the communication. A non-repudiation security service does not eliminate repudiation, i.e. it cannot prevent a user from attempting to repudiate that a particular event has occurred, or prevent the user from denying previous commitments or actions. Instead, non-repudiation service counters repudiation by ensuring the availability of irrefutable evidence to support resolution of any disputes. Repudiation in electronic transactions can further be classified into repudiation of origin, (an originator of a message falsely denies that he has actually sent the message), and repudiation of receipt (a recipient falsely claims that he has never received the message).

Non-repudiation of origin service provides the recipient of a message with evidence of the origin of the message, which will protect the recipient against any attempt by the originator to falsely deny having sent the message. This service can be achieved by using a digital signature scheme. The originator generates a digital signature on the hash value of the message using his private key, and the public key corresponding to this private key is uniquely and legally bound to the originator through a trusted certificate issued by a trusted certification authority. The signature itself constitutes the evidence of the origin. This way, the message originator cannot later deny that he has sent the signed message, since he is the only one who could have produced the digital signature on the message.

Non-repudiation of receipt service provides the originator of the message with the evidence of the receipt of the message by the intended recipient, and this evidence will protect the originator against any attempt by the recipient to falsely deny having received the message. Non-repudiation of receipt is a security service that is more difficult to achieve than non-repudiation of origin. It may be achieved, for instance, by requiring the recipient to return an acknowledgement message containing the recipient's signature, if the two parties trust each other. However, this method offers no protection against repudiation of receipt if the communicating parties are not mutually trustful, or if the recipient chooses not to acknowledge the receipt of a message after seeing its content.

2.2 Fairness

The essence of a commercial transaction is usually an *exchange* of one item of value for another. An exchange of items is *fair* if, at the end of the exchange, either party receives the expected item, or neither party receives the expected item. The main objective of *fair (electronic data) exchange protocols* is to ensure that, at no point during the execution of a protocol, either party can gain any significant advantage over the other, even if the protocol is prematurely halted.

Depending on the types of business items exchanged, such as payments, valuable digital data, digital signatures, e-mails etc., the design and implementation of fair exchange protocols vary. Although there has not been much work yet in developing a generic approach, by which the exchange system can support secure and fair exchange of any business items, protocols for the exchange of some specific business items have been proposed in literature. Some specialised types of fair exchanges can be classified into the following three categories.

Electronic purchase (E-purchase). E-purchase is the exchange of an e-payment for purchased e-goods. The fair exchange in this application category has firstly to ensure that a payer receives the e-goods from a payee if and only if the payee receives the e-payment from the payer, and, secondly, that the e-goods delivered meet the expectation of the payer (i.e. that the payer had not received some junk document of no value). Additional form of e-purchase is the exchange of e-payments for their receipts. Some of the e-purchase protocols can be found in (Ketchpel, S., 1995), (Ray, I. & Ray, I., 2000), (Ray, I. & Ray, I., 2001), (Zhou, J. & Gollmann, D., 1997).

Contract signing. Fairness of the traditional (off-line) contract signing is achieved by having all the parties present at the time of signing, and signing the contract simultaneously. However, for on-line contract signing, the simultaneous binding is impossible as contracts are signed via sending messages over serial communication networks. Fair contract signing protocols ensure that either both parties are bound to the exchanged contract, or neither is. Some of the protocols in this category have been presented by Asokan, N., Shoup, V. & Wainder, M. (2000), Chadha, R., Kanovich, M. & Scedrov A. (2001), Chuan-Kun, W. & Varadharajan, V. (2001), Even, S., Goldreich, O. & Lempel, A. (1985).

Certified e-mail. In order for e-mail to be used for important communications, some notion of certified delivery must be provided to users. Certified e-mail is an exchange of an e-mail message for its receipt. A receiver gets the e-mail message if and only if a sender gets the receipt certifying the content of the e-mail. In other words, there must be a way for the sender to prove that the recipient has indeed received the e-mail, should the recipient falsely try to deny it. Likewise, there must be a way to protect the recipient against false denial, by the sender, of sending the e-mail. Some protocols for certified e-mail can be found in (Kremer, S. & Markowitch, O., 2000), (Riordan, J. & Schneier, B., 1998), (Zhou, J. & Gollmann, D., 1996), (Zhou, J. & Gollmann, D., 1997).

3 NON-REPUDIATION AND FAIR EXCHANGE PROTOCOLS

This section gives an overview of the existing work on non-repudiation and fair exchange protocols. Approaches used in the design of the protocols can be classified into two categories: two-party based

approach or third-party based approach, i.e. without or with the assistance of a trusted third party (TTP).

3.1 Two-Party Based Protocols

Two-party only protocols are usually carried out in the form of *simultaneous secret exchange*. Simultaneous secret exchange can be built by using two *gradual secret releasing protocols*, such that both parties release their secrets bit-by-bit in the interleaved manner. A party releases a bit of its secret (together with the zero-knowledge proof of correctness of the bit), and in return receives a bit of his counterpart's secret, and this interleaved bit releasing continues until both of them have received and released all the bits. An obvious constraint in this approach is that both secrets must be of the same length.

A major disadvantage associated with this class of protocols is that in order to achieve a stronger level of fairness, more rounds of exchanges are required for the zero-knowledge proving of correctness of every bit, which implies that more traffic would be generated and injected into the underlying network. Additionally, the participating parties are assumed to have equal computational power in order to achieve fairness. Otherwise, the computationally stronger party can launch a brute-force attack, after receiving the first several bits, and work out the remainder of his counterpart's secret.

The introduction of extra computational and communication overheads and strong assumption of equal computational power have made this approach impractical in distributed and heterogeneous network environments. Also, protocols of this kind provide no guarantees of the quality of secrets exchanged. In other words, there is no protection mechanism to prevent a party promising one thing, while in fact sending something else. Therefore, the application of these protocols is limited to the exchange of messages of known properties, such as in contract signing and certified e-mail. However, this approach does have one advantage - it makes no use of a third party. These protocols are sometimes also referred to as *probabilistic protocols*. The most notable protocols in this category are oblivious transfer protocols (Blum, M., 1983), (Even, S., Goldreich, O. & Lempel, A., 1985), and puzzle protocols (Merkle, R., 1978).

3.2 Third-Party Based Protocols

An alternative approach to the two-party based fair exchange protocols is through an assistance of a third party. Depending on the degree of its involvement in the exchange process, the third party needs to be either a fully trusted third party (TTP), or a semi-trusted third party (STTP). A TTP is expected to mediate all the exchanges and guarantee fairness, and all the parties involved in a fair exchange must place unconditional trust in it. STTPs need to meet fewer security requirements. General assumption about STTPs is that their own misbehaviour can be tolerated, but they are not expected to collude with other parties. The roles of the third parties in these protocols can be roughly classified into the following categories.

Notary. A notary helps participating parties by generating non-repudiation evidence and/or validating the exchanged documents. It may also generate, lodge and notarise encryption/decryption keys, and provide directory services for the evidences that can be retrieved by participating parties or adjudicator in the case of dispute. If keys or evidence are compromised then fairness and non-repudiation services are compromised. The level of security expected from the notary for the key and evidence protection is high. The notary needs to be on-line, and is actively involved in every exchange process. These two requirements make the notary a focal point for security and reliability concerns. Any security breach or system failure at the notary will paralyse the entire service. Finally, the level of trust on the notary is unconditional. Any collusion between the notary and the participating parties will lead to devastating security consequences. Some protocols with the third-party notary can be found in (Franklin, M. K. & Reiter, M. K., 1997), (Ray, I. & Ray, I., 2001), (Zhou, J. & Gollmann, D., 1996), (Zhou, J. & Gollmann, D., 1997).

Delivery authority. A delivery authority acts as an intermediary between an originator and a recipient, and is trusted to deliver messages and corresponding evidence from one party to another. It also has to be on-line and actively takes part in every exchange process. The weaknesses identified in the notary approach also apply here. In addition, this approach places heavier computational and communication overheads on the TTP in comparison with the notary approach, as exchanged messages (not only keys) actually go through the TTP. Protocols with the third-party delivery authority can be found in (Bürk, H. & Pfitzmann, A., 1990), (Ketchpel, S., 1995).

TTP as a public message board. In these protocols (Riordan, J. & Schneier, B., 1998), (Zhang, N. & Shi, Q., 1996), a TTP provides a central message server that serves as a public message board: everyone can look at the board for the messages designated to him or post messages for other recipients, but no one can erase or edit posted messages. In this approach, the TTP is not involved with the message delivery, rather it only publishes and maintains the public message board. However, a

disadvantage for this scheme is that the TTP needs to be on-line and participate in every execution of the protocol, and is susceptible to denial-of-service attacks.

TTP as a random beacon. In this protocol for signing contracts, Rabin (1983) employs a very simple form of intermediate third party called a random beacon, with purpose of broadcasting signals with encryption/decryption keys at regularly spaced time intervals Δ. The random beacon is considered as a STTP, as it just provides a reliable source of randomness. The correct operation of these protocols depends on tight synchronisation of all the parties' clocks. Time interval Δ must be chosen based on the lowest computational capacity among the parties, in order to allow all parties to meet the deadline for broadcasting messages in each transaction. In addition, this approach generates excessive traffic into the underlying network. Due to the nature of time deadline and broadcast requirement, the applicability of this mechanism in an internetworking environment is questionable.

Adjudicator (Arbitrator) - optimistic approach. This kind of TTP acts as an independent arbiter to help participating parties with possible dispute resolution. Under normal circumstances, where participating parties can come to a successful conclusion of an exchange process themselves, the TTP is not invoked. If any dispute arises during the protocol execution, the participating parties would first try to resolve it themselves. If not successful, they would then turn to the TTP for help. After examining the evidence of the exchange provided by the participating parties, TTP makes the decision and takes necessary steps to resolve the dispute and ensure fairness. In this way, the services of the TTP are not invoked if parties do not misbehave or are capable of and willing to resolve the dispute themselves. Protocols based on this approach are called *optimistic protocols*, and can be found in (Asokan, N., Shoup, V. & Wainder, M., 2000),(Bao, F., Deng, R.H. & Mao, W., 1998), (Boyd, C. & Foo, E., 1998), (Chuan-Kun, W. & Varadharajan, V., 2001), (Ray, I. & Ray, I., 2000), (Zhou, J. & Gollmann, D., 1997). In comparison with the protocols using an on-line TTP, the optimistic approach greatly reduces the involvement of the TTP, which in turn reduces the computational, communication and security requirements placed on the TTP.

4 E-COMMERCE FRAMEWORKS

A future e-commerce system is expected to be truly interoperable, global and automated, capable of supporting a range of e-commerce activities in various industries, geographical regions and legal environments, with different security and reliability requirements. Creating a framework for such a system is currently one of the focal research and working topics for the world's technical and commercial experts and standardisation bodies, such as the Organization for Advancement of Structured Information Standards (OASIS), United Nations Centre for Trade Facilitation and Electronic Business (UN/CEFACT), World Wide Web Consortium (W3C), etc. Their joint effort is in the area of standardising languages for describing document formats (e.g. XML), agreeing on standard and shared XML-based business libraries (e.g. UBL, ebXML), specifying standardised set of protocols for exchange of such business documents (e.g. ebXML Message Service), etc. They aim at making these proposals as the international standards for e-commerce.

It is widely agreed that eXtensible Markup Language (XML) can provide the basis for the development of technologies for business transactions over the Internet, as the format in which structured data is encoded and exchanged. From the e-commerce perspective, XML offers the following main benefits:

- XML provides standardisation in information representation and transfer;
- XML-encoded data is independent of any particular platform, application or vendor, and is transformable into different types of outputs for different media devices (Web browsers, mobile phones, paper, etc.);
- XML-encoded data will have a longer life span with future readability and reuse than data encoded in any of the proprietary or non-standard data formats;
- Support for language identification enables data to be encoded in any language;
- B2B communication and interoperability can be improved by using previously agreed business XML vocabularies (business languages based on XML syntax).

The first step towards achieving interoperable e-commerce is to standardise the format of information interchange, based on XML, and to agree on business libraries, which should contain standardised document formats needed for the business processes. OASIS has formed the Universal Business Language (UBL) Technical Committee, with the aim of developing a standardised library of XML business documents by modifying and incorporating the best features of already existing business libraries.

In addition to the standards for business documents proposed by the UBL, standardisation in the area of electronic contracts and other legal data is also important. These issues have recently been addressed by LegalXML eContracts Technical Committee, an OASIS Member Section formed in July 2002, with the aim of developing XML-based standards for the markup of contract documents. The committee's core activity is the creation of DTD(s) / Schema(s) that can be used by parties for negotiating and finalising contracts in an application neutral format and automated processing of contract contents.

Apart from the standardisation of business document formats, the second important issue in creating an e-commerce infrastructure is to specify services for reliable and secure exchange and delivery of business documents. The proposed standard for messaging service is ebXML Messaging Service (ebXML MS), which is specified by the ebXML Project jointly undertaken by UN/CEFACT and OASIS. ebMS defines an communication-protocol neutral way for exchanging ebXML messages and packaged payload data between parties, in a secure and reliable manner. ebMS is independent of both the underlying communication protocol and the message payload, and therefore is usable over a variety of network and application level protocols, such as HTTP, SMTP, FTP, IIOP, JMS, etc. It is defined as a set of extensions to the base of Simple Object Access Protocol (SOAP).

Clearly, e-commerce systems will need automated security provisions to facilitate secure e-commerce transactions, among which non-repudiation and fairness are of great importance. Currently, however, these issues are not being addressed in e-commerce systems, or are being addressed only partially and inconsistently.

5 NON-REPUDIATION AND FAIRNESS IN E-COMMERCE FRAMEWORKS

In a business process of an e-commerce system, there are different issues to which security characteristics can be applied, such as documents, transport channels, or a business process as a whole. For this reason, security requirements should be present at different levels, and offer a finer level of granularity for the security requirements. Depending on the type of the item that security services are applied to, they can be addressed on different levels – network, transport or application level. Sometimes

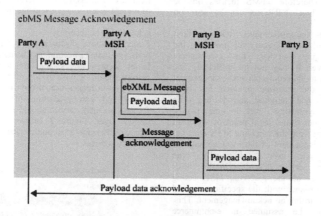

Figure 1: Acknowledgement of message, as provided by ebMS on the message-service level, and acknowledgement of a message payload on the application level.

application-layer security services duplicate the network- or transport-layer security services, as it may be necessary to address the same security issue on more than one level, depending on the need of an application. For instance, an encrypted e-mail has to be protected on a per-person basis (i.e. from person to person), regardless of whether additional network or transport encryption has already been applied.

According to the OSI Security Architecture Standard (ISO/IEC 7498-2), basic security services are authentication, access control, confidentiality, integrity and non-repudiation. Unlike non-repudiation, fairness is not a basic security property, as it is not an essential security service for all the applications (it is mostly needed only for e-commerce applications). Obviously, protocols to facilitate fair exchange should be built on the application layer of an e-commerce system.

On the other hand, it is not quite obvious where non-repudiation security service should be placed. The question is whether non-repudiation should be handled by the application or by the message-service layer.

In the following subsections, we will discuss how ebMS provides non-repudiation of receipt on a message-service level, and the need for the application level non-repudiation of receipt, in addition to the one provided by the ebMS. Then we propose a modular approach to non-repudiation and fairness with reference to basic security services.

5.1 ebMS: an XML-based Messaging Service

The general architecture of the ebMS is intended to support all basic security services - authentication, access control, confidentiality, integrity, non-repudiation of origin and reliability services, such as acknowledging messages (non-repudiation of receipt), avoiding duplicate messages and delivery of messages once-and-only-once. Combining these security features, different security profiles and policies can be created.

An ebXML message consists of two logical parts. The first part is referred to as Header Container (containing one SOAP compliant message), and is followed by zero or more additional parts, referred to as Payload Containers (containing application level payloads). In the ebMS infrastructure, there is a support for non-repudiation of receipt (NRR) in the form of a simple acknowledgement of message receipt by the message handler (MSH) receiving the message. However, the acknowledgment defined in this specification does not indicate that the payload of the ebXML message was syntactically correct, nor it acknowledges the accuracy of the payload information. It does not indicate the acceptance of the payload information, or agreement with the content of the payload by the endpoint recipient. The ebMS is designed to provide the sender with the confidence that the receiving MSH has received *the ebXML message* (not the message payload) securely and unaltered. Therefore, ebMS focuses on the message-service level NRR, as can be seen on Figure 1.

Although the message-service layer NRR is, without any doubt, useful and necessary for providing the reliable messaging service, for e-commerce purposes, however, it may not be sufficient. The business process might require an acknowledgement to certify that the *message payload* has been received securely and unaltered, and this has to be resolved at the application level. In other words, from the e-commerce and legal point of view, an acknowledgement from the receiving MSH does not mean an acknowledgement of the message payload by the endpoint user. Additionally, the acknowledgement service described in the ebMS specification relies on the receiving MSH acting correctly (in accordance with the specification) and its honesty in returning an acknowledgement. This, however, cannot be assumed in e-commerce applications where some of the parties might behave maliciously. Therefore advanced protocols at the application level are needed in order to achieve non-repudiation of receipt in the context of e-commerce.

To summarise the above discussion, security mechanisms of ebMS offer a non-repudiation protection at the message-service level. However, there is a need for the application level non-repudiation service, in addition to the one provided by the messaging services, for e-commerce related applications.

5.2 Incorporating Non-repudiation and Fairness in E-commerce Systems

We differentiate between two types of security services. *Message-level* services operate on single messages, while *message-exchange level* services operate on the exchange of the messages. For example, basic security services, such as authentication, access control, confidentiality and integrity, are message-level services, as they can be provided for a single message. On the other hand, fairness is a message-exchange level service, as it is a property of an exchange process.

Non-repudiation can be considered as a composite service, consisting of non-repudiation of origin and non-repudiation of receipt. Splitting a non-repudiation service into two is convenient when a recipient is concerned with repudiation of origin, but an originator is not concerned with non-repudiation of receipt. For instance, a merchant may send his e-catalogue over the Internet to a customer, and may only wish to have it protected from forgery, so that the customer can be assured of the origin of the catalogue. While non-repudiation of origin can be

treated as a message-level service, non-repudiation of receipt is a message-exchange level service, since there has to be the exchange of messages to acknowledge a receipt.

From the above discussion, we can conclude that non-repudiation of origin may better be positioned at lower security layers, and that non-repudiation of receipt should be built on top of non-repudiation of origin. As it makes use of both non-repudiation of origin and non-repudiaiton of receipt services, fairness security service should better be built at a higher layer. Figure 2 captures the relationship between message-level and message-exchange level security services.

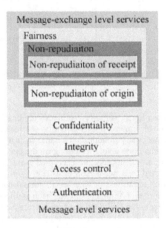

Figure 2: Message and message-exchange level security services.

6 CONCLUSIONS

In this paper we have presented non-repudiation and fairness security services, and discussed the technologies that may provide solutions to these services. These services are needed for reliable executions of business transactions and should be integrated in future e-commerce frameworks. We have also demonstrated the need for non-repudiation services at the application level, in addition to the message-service level non-repudiation services. In addition, we have proposed a modular approach to a security architecture, where non-repudiation of receipt and fairness are positioned at a higher level than non-repudiation of origin. Adopting this layered approach to non-repudiation and fairness services provides modularity, scalability and flexibility to an e-commerce system.

Non-repudiation and fairness security services are difficult to achieve between two mutually distrustful parties, without the assistance of a TTP. In two-party only scenarios, one of the parties has to make the first move by sending his item (or part of the item) to the other party, thereby getting into a disadvantageous position. Obviously, the third-party approach is more desirable. However, minimising the involvement of a TTP in the exchange process, as is done in the optimistic approach, should be the direction for the design of fair exchange solutions. This approach reduces the possibility for the TTP to become a performance and/or security bottleneck, and it reduces the level of trust placed upon the TTPs.

Our future work will be concentrated on the further design and development of a generic system architecture capable of supporting secure, but efficient non-repudiation and fair data exchange. Further, we will examine the ways to integrate fairness and non-repudiation protocols into emerging messaging standards and technologies.

REFERENCES

Asokan, N., Shoup, V. & Wainder, M. (2000) Optimistic Fair Exchange of Digital Signatures. *IEEE Journal on Selected Areas in Communications*, vol. 18, no. 4, pp. 593-610.

Bao, F., Deng, R.H. & Mao, W. (1998) Efficient and Practical Fair Exchange Protocols with Off-line TTP. In *Proceedings of IEEE Symposium on Security and Privacy*. pp. 77-85.

Blum, M. (1983) How to Exchange (Secret) Keys. *ACM Transactions on Computer Systems*. vol. 1, no. 2, pp.175-93.

Boyd, C. & Foo, E. (1998) Off-Line Fair Payment Protocol Using Convertible Signatures. In *Proceedings of ASIACRYPT '98. Lecture Notes in Computer Science*, vol. 1514, Springer-Verlag, pp. 271-85.

Bürk, H. & Pfitzmann, A. (1990) Value Exchange Systems Enabling Security and Unobservability. *Computers & Security*. vol. 9, pp. 715-21.

Chadha, R., Kanovich, M. & Scedrov A. (2001) Protocol Analysis: Inductive Methods and Contract-Signing Protocols. In *Proceedings of the 8th ACM Conference on Computer and Communications Security*, Philadelphia, USA. pp. 176-85.

Chuan-Kun, W. & Varadharajan, V. (2001) Fair Exchange of Digital Signatures with Offline Trusted Third Party.

In *Proceedings of International Conference on Information and Communication Security*. pp. 466-70.

Even, S., Goldreich, O. & Lempel, A. (1985) A Randomized Protocol for Signing Contracts. *Communications of the ACM*. vol. 28, no. 6, pp. 637-47.

Franklin, M. K. & Reiter, M. K. (1997) Fair Exchange with a Semi-Trusted Third Party (extended abstract). In *Proceedings of the 4th ACM Conference on Computer and Communications Security*. pp. 1-5.

Ketchpel, S. (1995) Transaction Protection for Information Buyers and Sellers, *In Proceedings of the Dartmouth Institute for Advanced Graduate Studies '95: Electronic Publishing and the Information Superhighway*, Boston, USA.

Kremer, S. & Markowitch, O. (2000) A Multi-Party Non-Repudiation Protocol. In *Proceedings of 16th Annual Working Conference on Information Security: Information Security for Global Information Infrastructures*, Beijing, China. pp. 271-80.

Merkle, R. (1978) Secure Communications Over Insecure Channels. *Communications of the ACM*, vol. 21, no. 4, pp. 294-99.

Rabin, M.O. (1983) Transaction Protection by Beacons. *Journal of Computer and System Science*, vol. 27, pp. 256-267.

Ray, I. & Ray, I. (2000) An Optimistic Fair Exchange E-commerce Protocol with Automated Dispute Resolution. In *Proceedings of EC-Web 2000, 1st Electronic Commerce and Web Technologies Conference, Lecture Notes in Computer Science*, Berlin, Germany, Springer-Verlag, vol. 1875, pp. 84-93.

Ray, I. & Ray, I. (2001) An Anonymous Fair Exchange E-Commerce Protocol. In *Proceedings of 15th International Parallel and Distributed Processing Symposium*. pp. 1790-7.

Riordan, J. & Schneier, B. (1998) A Certified E-Mail Protocol with No Trusted Third Party. In *Proceedings of 13th Annual Computer Security Applications Conference*, ACM Press, pp. 347-52.

Zhang, N. & Shi, Q. (1996) Security Issues in an EDI Environment. In *Proceedings of 12th Annual Computer Security Applications Conference*. Los Alamitos, USA, IEEE Comput. Soc. Press, pp. 129-36.

Zhou, J. & Gollmann, D. (1996) A Fair Non-Repudiation Protocol. In *Proceedings of IEEE Symposium on Security and Privacy*, Oakland, California, USA. pp. 55-61.

Zhou, J. & Gollmann, D. (1997) An Efficient Non-Repudiation Protocol. In *Proceedings of 10th Computer Security Foundations Workshop*. Los Alamitos, CA, USA, IEEE Comput. Soc. Press, pp. 126-32.

IMPLEMENTING AN INTERNET-BASED VOTING SYSTEM FOR PUBLIC ELECTIONS

Project Experience

Alexander Prosser, Robert Krimmer, Robert Kofler

Department Production Management
Institute for Information Processing and Information Economics
Vienna University of Economics and BA, Pappenheimgasse 35/5, A-1200 Vienna, Austria
Email: {alexander.prosser | robert.krimmer | robert.kofler} @wu-wien.ac.at

Keywords: Electronic voting, electronic democracy, Internet, public elections, national ID card

Abstract: Worldwide research groups have developed remote electronic voting systems using several different approaches with no legal basis. In 2001 the Austrian Parliament passed a law allowing electronic voting with digital signatures for public elections. Besides these legal requirements, an algorithm has to solve the basic technical problem, of how to identify the user uniquely with still guaranteeing the anonymity of one's vote and further not to allow fraud by the election administration. In this paper the authors give an experience report on the implementation of the first phase of an algorithm that fulfills these requirements by strictly separating the registration from the vote submission phase.

1 INTRODUCTION

A substantial decrease in voter participation, which has been observed worldwide, has led to various research projects in the field of remote electronic voting to enable secure and legally binding public elections over the Internet. With elections being the key element of a democratic system, the way they are held is determined by the political traditions, the social context and the legal system. However, most systems know the principles of free, equal, and secret elections, which result in the following basic problem to solve for every electronic voting system:

- the voter must be identified uniquely, but must still be able to
- cast her vote anonymously and
- even the administrators must not be able to change this vote.

In Austria, the voter turnout in nation-wide elections has been constantly above 90% until 1994 when it first dropped below that mark and reached an all time low of 80,4 % in 1999 (Die österreichischen Nationalratswahlen von einst bis heute, 2002). While this number is still high by international standards, first initiatives in favor of introducing means of distance (remote) voting for public elections came up (Weiss, J., 1999). So far only Austrians abroad are entitled to vote by mail in first-order elections, this being elections to the Parliament and to the Federal President (for further elaboration see Dujmovits, W., 2000).

In 2001 the Austrian Parliament passed two bills allowing electronic voting for elections of two organizations: the student union and the chamber of commerce. The laws also require the electronic voting system to use digital signatures and to be approved by Austria's data and privacy protection commission and by the national IT certification organization A-SIT.

In a research project funded by the City of Vienna a research group develops an electronic voting prototype in two development stages: First an electronic voting enabled registration is developed and based on this an electronic ballot box completes the prototype.

In this paper the authors first describe the algorithm used and then describe in a process model how the concept was implemented and which extensions were necessary due to further developments in the field of e-government. One example would be the concept of the Austrian national ID card that has not been available at the time the original algorithm was developed.

2 ALGORITHM

The algorithm under discussion was first proposed in (Prosser, A., Müller-Török, R., 2001) and then further

294

developed in the preparation of the implementation project. The basic characteristic of it is the strictly separation of registration and vote submission stage first identified by Nurmi et.al. in 1991 (Nurmi, H. et al, 1991):

— Registration phase: The voter's credentials are checked and the voter receives a blindly signed voting token, which is securely stored.
— Vote submission phase: The voter uses the voting token to obtain a ballot sheet and casts her vote.

Before we describe the process model, let us begin with some notation:

RS Registration Server
TC Trust Center
US Ballot Box Server
RegDB   Registration Database

pi Voter's personal identification file
c   Voter's constituency
e, d   Registration's public and private signature key
k, l Registration's public and private crypto key
ε, δ Trust Center's public and private signature key
κ, λ Trust Center's public and private crypto key

u, v   Voter's public and private signature key
w, z   Voter's public and private crypto key

u, ϖ Ballot box's public and private signature key
ω, ζ Ballot box's public and private crypto key

r, t Random numbers for voting token
ρ, τ Random numbers for validation token

x, ξ Blinded voting and validation token

m, m' Random asymmetric crypto key pair for voting process

2.1   Registration

Voters can register an arbitrary period of time before election day; since the ballot sheet is not handed out upon registration, voters can register even at a time when the list of candidates is not complete yet. As the first step the voter generates the random numbers for the voting token r, t and prepares it for the blind signature[1], adds a text where

she applies for electronic voting and signs: v(x, "I want to e-vote"). The message is encrypted with registration's public crypto key k and sent to the registration: k[v(x, "I want to e-vote")], which verifies the voter's credentials by resolving the public signature key of the voter. If the voter is entitled to vote, the registration signs x blindly giving x^d. After receiving x^d the voter can access the signed voting token t^d by dividing x^d by r.

The registration stores the electronic application and strikes the voter off the conventional voter's register. Also x^d is stored; if the original token is lost and the voter re-applies for another voting token, the registration will always respond with the original x^d to avoid the issue of multiple tokens.

In most elections, voters will be organized in constituencies c, this information is also sent back to the voter and has to be submitted on election day to indicate in which constituency the vote is to be counted. To avoid possible manipulation of c the blind signature keys used for x^d can be made specific to the constituency. Hence the clear-text c submitted on election day and the authentication token issued by the registration have to point to the same c.

A similar process is repeated with the Trust Center: The voter issues a second pair of random numbers ρ, τ and then prepares the blinded validation token ξ and obtains the blindly signed ξ^δ. By dividing again ξ^δ by ρ she gains the signed validation token τ^δ. This is required as it is the only way to make a collusion of the registration server and the ballot box server useless, as they always need the blind signature authentication of the Trust Center as well in order to forge a vote.

At the end of the registration phase, the voter holds two authentication tokens and her constituency information [t, t^d, τ, τ^δ, c], both voting and validation token are needed to cast a vote on election day.

2.2   Voting

On election day the voter sends the tokens to the ballot box server to obtain a ballot sheet. The voter does not sign this submission and the only means of authentication are the two tokens obtained earlier. The voter generates an asymmetric key pair m, m' to secure the communication (without disclosing the identity of the voters which would be case when using its crypto key pair on the signature smart card). The voter also adds the identification TC of the Trust Center used, which is not used to verify the voter's identity or to obtain any public crypto key, but to choose the right Trust Center key for resolving the blind

---

[1]   The blind signature model was developed by David Chaum in 1982 (Chaum, D., 1982). In general language it can be compared with the signature on a blue paper envelope.
(e, d) ... the server's blind signature pair according to the RSA system

$x = r^e * t$
$x^d = (r^e * t)^d$; which is then divided by r
giving $[(r^e)^d * t^d] / r = t^d$

signature. The message [TC, m, t, t^d, τ, τ^δ, c] is encrypted with ballot box's public crypto key ω and sent to the ballot box. After decrypting the ballot box resolves the signatures t^d and τ^δ and if the tokens can be authenticated the ballot box issues an empty ballot sheet and encodes it with the symmetric key $m(BS)$. The voter receives and decrypts it with m' and fills out the ballot sheet. This is then combined with the tokens, c and TC, encrypted again with the public crypto key of the ballot box and sent. After authentication of the tokens, the ballot box server stores the ballot sheet and the other information received from the voter.

Apart from the fact that anonymity can be guaranteed to the voter, if he uses different terminals (IP addresses) for registration and submission of vote, the server administration of the registration and the ballot box collude, votes cannot be forged, as a valid vote also has to be authenticated by a Trust Center.

3 IMPLEMENTATION

In Austria the concepts of e-Government and e-Administration have become an issue of high importance on the politicians' agenda. This resulted in the installation of the CIO (chief information office). The main task is to develop a coordinated strategy for e-Government in the Austrian administration (e-Austria in e-Europe, 2000). This strategy concentrates on issues of infrastructure and this makes the introduction of a national ID card based on the digital signature law an issue of high importance.

As described in the introduction, the digital signature on a smart card is one of the requirements for electronic voting by Austrian law[2]. When using smart cards to sign digital documents, everyone can access a public certificate server to verify the validity of the digital signature. But when one wants to uniquely identify a user, this is concept is not enough. Even if the user credentials comply with the person in the election register, one can not be sure that they are identical because only the name and date of birth are not enough to uniquely identify one user. This problem can be solved if either (i) the smart card issuing organization is the same as the election conducting body or if (ii) one uses a unique identifier like a citizen ID number that is stored in the personal identification file pi on the smart card.

While the first solution is useful for elections that have full control over the ID cards their voters use, it is not useable

for elections where the user may choose freely which ID card she may use. The second variant is a topic of infrastructure, as it requires a central register of all citizens. This central database not only involves problems of data acquisition and maintenance but also of data protection. That is why it is in most countries prohibited by law or by the constitutional court, such as in Germany. In Austria, this is not the case and the registration law 1995 installed such a Central Register (ZMR). It started public service on first of March 2001 and every Austrian citizen has been appointed one unique "ZMR-identification-number". However, in spite of its usefulness for electronic voting, it should be noted that critics like the data security specialists from *ARGEdaten* warned from misuse and called the system the first step to a surveillance state (2001).

With this ZMR-identification number stored in the personal identification file pi on the citizen's smart card it becomes a national ID card. In this way one can use it for the identification process for checking the citizen's eligibility to vote and the issuing of the voting token.

Another technical development very useful for e-voting is the "security layer" to be used with this card, which was developed by the Government's Chief Information Office (Hollosi, A., Karlinger, G., 2002). This software module is a standard application interface for signing and verification purposes in form of local http server installed on the user's computer. It handles all interactions between the users Internet browser and the smart card by using standard HTML forms, which enables interaction with the smart card without using Java.

These recent developments have now been implemented in the electronic voting prototype. This has led to a new five-step process in the first stage of the protocol, which is now described in detail:

1. Applet download
2. Preparation of the validation token
3. Authorization check, preparation of voting token
4. Blind signature of the validation token
5. Blind signature of the voting token

---

[2] The first larger number (approx. 20,000) of smart cards being rolled out is the student ID card of the Vienna University of Economics and Business Administration (WU) (Homepage der Wirtschaftsuniversität Wien, 2002)

3.1 Step One: Applet Download

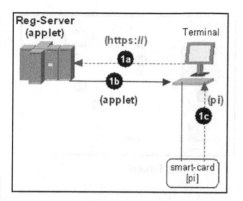

Figure 1: Download of the registration application

The voter starts the remote electronic voting process by entering the URL provided by the election administration (1a). Then the Web client of the voter downloads the registration java applet from the registration server (1b). The first action is the applet reading (1c) the personal identification file *pi* from the smart card (via a procedure call of the security layer) in preparation of the authorization check in step 3.

3.2 Step Two: Preparation of Validation Token

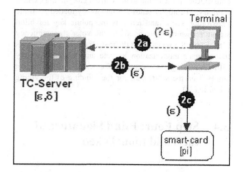

Figure 2: Preparation of the validation token

For the blinding process, random number r is chosen and signed with the public blind signature key of the server resulting in r^e. Afterwards the applet requests in (2a) this public key from the Trust Center, receives it in (2b) and stores it on the smart card for the blinding of the validation token (2c).

3.3 Step Three: Authorization Check and Preparation of Voting Token

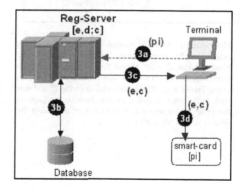

Figure 3: Authorization check and preparation of voting token

The third step is basically a repetition of step two but with the registration server, which checks the voter's eligibility. Hence, the citizen's right to retrieve an election token is checked here; also, the voter can be correctly assigned to constituency *c* according to her current entry in the Central Registry. The applet sends the previously loaded *pi* to the registration server and requests the public key for blind signature, which corresponds to the voter's constituency (3a). Using the registration database the server determines the citizen's authorization to vote and her constituency (3b). Following the reception of *e* and *c* (3c) the applet stores it on the smart card for the blinding of the voting token in (3d).

3.4 Step Four: Blind Signature of the Validation Token

Figure 4: Blind signature of the validation token

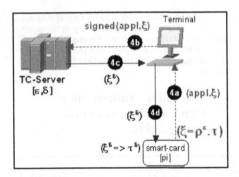

The validation token is blinded in (4a) by taking the random number ρ and signing it with ε resulting in the blinded token: $\xi = (\rho^\varepsilon \, \tau)$ and then sending it with the formal application ("I want to vote electronically") in (4b) to the Trust Center. This is then signed giving ξ^δ and sent back to the voter. In (4d) the voter stores the package on the smart card where it is then processed to receive the final validation token τ^δ (4e).

3.5 Step Five: Blind Signature of the

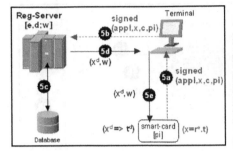

Figure 5: Blind signature of the voting token

Finally the voter applies for the voting token by first retrieving the blinded voting token *x* that consists of $(r^e * t)$ from the smart card (5a). It is then followed by sending it together personal identification file, the constituency and an application to the effect of "I want to vote electronically" to the registration server (5b). The registration is then again looking up the citizen's authorization to vote and checking the constituency using the personal identification (5c). If this is validated the registration server signs the blinded voting token. Further the server sends x^d with the constituency back to the voter and in case of success marks the citizen with a "has received voting token" tag (5d). In the final step (5e), x^d is stored in the smart card after t^d was calculated dividing x^d by *r*.

4 RESUME

The paper describes a protocol for public elections using remote electronic voting over the Internet. It not only solves the problem of casting a vote anonymously but also works under unfriendly conditions like when the registration server's and the ballot box server's administration are colluding. However, the implementation project also revealed the difficulties in implementing the algorithm:

- Unambiguous voter identification not only requires an electronic voters register, but also the link between the citizen's identity (number) and the digital certificate of the signature card being stored on the card.

Voting Token

◆ The OS of the signature card has to perform large parts of the algorithm, which means that the card OS has to provide the necessary service primitives in its application programming interface.

◆ The electronic voting token resides on the signature card between registration and voting stage of the protocol.

The last point imposes considerable restrictions on the signature card. On the one hand, the tokens have to be pin-protected to prevent third-party application from reading them. For most commercially available signature cards this means that a certain number of pin-protectable files in the file system of the card have to be pre-defined, which can then be used as "secure data containers" by the user.

On the other hand, the Java applet loaded from the electronic ballot box to cast the vote must not be able to ready any information from the card, which may identify the cardholder, even if the applet was fraudulently manipulated. This means that all files on the card containing such sensitive information have to be pin-protected, too. Examples would be (i) the unique card number (if the link to the card holder is stored when the card is issued), (ii) the digital certificate, (iii) the electronic link between the citizen's ID in the Central Register and the digital certificate issued by the Trust Centre (denoted as *pi* in the above protocol specification), (iv) and other information that may serve as a link to the cardholder (in the case of the above example of a students card, this would be the student ID or library access information).

It is of course possible to pin-protect all bits of sensitive information on the signature card, but this raises the question of the usability of a card, which contains information protected by 5-10 (different) PINs. The problem is a general one and can be expected to grow as new applications for smart cards emerge.

In our view, the only long-term solution to this problem is to extend the security layer, which was described above, to all card accesses. This means that any application, which requests information stored on the card, can only access the card via the security layer. The user visually sees the information retrieved from the card and releases it by a single access PIN. Fraudulent "exploration" of smart cards by external applications can thus be prevented.

In regards to e-voting itself, our further work will concentrate on the implementation of the second phase of the prototype (to cast a vote), in order to test the algorithm in a real- world (mock) election to gain further experience on how to improve it.

REFERENCES

ARGE Daten (2001), Überflüssiges Meldegesetz, http://www.ad.or.at/news/20010108.html accessed on 2002-08-15.

Chaum, David, Blind Signatures for Untraceable Payments, presented at: Advances in Cryptology, 1982.

Die österreichischen Nationalratswahlen von einst bis heute, (2002), http://www.modernpolitics.at/publikationen/jahrbuch/wahlergebinsse/wahlen_index.htm accessed on 2002-09-25.

Dujmovits, Werner (2000), Auslandsösterreicherwahlrecht und Briefwahl, Aufl., Verlag Österreich, Wien.

e-Austria in e-Europe, (2000), http://www.austria.gv.at/aktuell/database/topnews/german/20000414_713.html accessed on 2002-08-15.

Hollosi, Arno, Karlinger, Gregor (2002), Security-Layer für das Konzept Bürgerkarte, BMÖLS, CIO Unit, Wien.

Homepage der Wirtschaftsuniversität Wien, (2002), http://www.wu-wien.ac.at accessed on 2002-08-15.

Nurmi, H., Salomaa, A., Santean, L. (1991), Secret Ballot Elections in Computer Networks, in: *Computers and Security 36 (10)*, S. 553-560.

Prosser, Alexander, Müller-Török, Robert, Electronic Voting via the Internet, presented at: International Conference on Enterprise Information Systems ICEIS2001, Setùbal, 2001.

Weiss, Jürgen (1999), Gesetzesantrag >>Einführung der Briefwahl auf Landes- und Gemeindeebene<<, http://www.parlinkom.at/pd/pm/XXI/I/his/000/I00005_.html accessed on 2002-08-15.

THE RESOURCE FRAMEWORK FOR MOBILE APPLICATIONS
Enabling Collaboration Between Mobile Users

Jörg Roth

Computer Science Department, University of Hagen, 58084 Hagen, Germany
Email: Joerg.Roth@Fernuni-hagen.de

Keywords: Mobile Applications, Collaborative Applications, Application Framework, Development Platform

Abstract: Mobile devices are getting more and more interesting for several kinds of field workers such as sales representatives or maintenance engineers. When in the field, mobile users often want to collaborate with other mobile users or with stationary colleagues at home. Most established collaboration concepts are designed for stationary scenarios and often do not sufficiently support mobility. Mobile users are only weakly connected to the communication infrastructure by wireless networks. Small mobile devices like PDAs often do not have sufficient computational power to handle effortful tasks to coordinate and synchronize users. They have for example very limited user interface capabilities and reduced storage capacity. In addition, mobile devices are subject to other usage paradigms like stationary computers and often turned on and off during a session. In this paper, we introduce a framework for mobile collaborative applications based on so-called *resources*. The resource framework leads to a straightforward functional decomposition of the overall application. Our platform *Pocket DreamTeam* provides a runtime infrastructure for application based on resources. We demonstrate the resource concept with the help of two applications built on top of the Pocket DreamTeam platform.

1 INTRODUCTION

Software which enables collaboration between users, so-called *groupware*, allows users to cooperate even when they are geographically distributed. Groupware plays an essential role for shared document editing or cooperative software development. Field workers can use synchronous groupware to discuss shared documents such as manuals or service instructions with their colleagues at home. In this paper, we focus on *synchronous* collaboration, where users at different locations work together *at the same time*. Groupware platforms help to decrease the development costs for a synchronous groupware drastically as they take over a number of tasks of synchronous sessions. As a result, an application developer can concentrate on application-specific details. As development cycles are very short, we can apply rapid prototyping concept and involve the end-user very early in the design process.

A groupware platform usually covers three areas (Roseman & Greenberg, 1996; Dewan & Choudhary 1992):

- an application framework provides a frame for the application development;

- a runtime system offers services such as group, user and session management at runtime;
- a number of interfaces, abstractions and objects allow the developer to use platform services and hide implementation details.

If end-users are mobile, some established concepts of existing platforms are not longer applicable. Such concepts often depend on stationary workstations with high computational power, comfortable user interfaces and reliable, broad-banded networks. In this paper, we introduce an application framework, which was especially designed for mobile users in synchronous sessions. For our approach, we made the following assumptions:

- Synchronous sessions have both mobile as well as stationary participants.

- Mobile participants use mobile devices like PDAs or handhelds as shown in fig. 1. In principle, we could consider notebooks, but their computational power and interface capabilities can be compared to stationary PCs. Therefore notebook computers are not discussed here.

- The network connections of the mobile devices use wireless communication technologies. In our test environment, we use Wireless LAN (IEEE 802.11b) but also mobile phone networks such as GSM or UMTS as well as wireless personal

O. Camp et al. (eds.), Enterprise Information Systems V, 300-307.
© 2004 *Kluwer Academic Publishers. Printed in the Netherlands.*

area networks (e.g. Bluetooth, IrDA) are possible. We assume the existence of a stationary core network.

– The support of stream media (e.g. audio and video) is not object of this work. We assume that there is a corresponding communication channel for voice transmission, e.g. based on a mobile phone network.

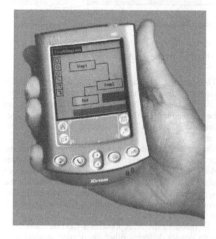

Figure 1: PDA with a Collaborative Application

2   RELATED WORK

Creating groupware platforms for synchronous teamwork has a long tradition. The platforms often are significantly different regarding the means of expression and abstractions for groupware tasks. *Habanero* (Chabert et al., 1998) for example distributes user events, synchronized by a central server. *Groupkit* (Roseman & Greenberg, 1996) uses a central server for the session management only, applications run replicated. The *ALV* model (Hill et al., 1993) allows the developer the express consistency conditions between the data model and the user interface. Many platforms base on multi-user variants of *MVC* (Graham, 1996; Schuckmann et al., 1996). A number of additional models, particularly *PAC**, are based on the *PAC* model (Coutaz, 1997).

All aforementioned models and platforms take an idealized view on networks and involved computer and concentrate on issues of user computer interaction. Mobility of users particularly remains unconsidered. Some newer platforms weaken the idea of

strong synchronous cooperation to express mobility issues. *QuickStep* (Roth & Unger, 2001) introduces the idea of *relaxed synchronous collaboration* when mobile participants are loosely coupled to the communication infrastructure and often disconnected from other participants. Further platforms like *Sync* (Munson & Dewan, 1997), *Coda* (Kistler & Satyanarayana, 1992) or *Rover* (Joseph et al., 1997) concentrate on conflict resolution of concurrent data accesses in mobile environments.

3   POCKET DREAMTEAM

To examine the consequences of end-user mobility in synchronous group environments, we extended our groupware platform *DreamTeam* (Roth, 2000) for mobile usage. DreamTeam first was designed for stationary users such as personal of a company, which either work at their office or are connected by modem connections from home. With the platform extension *Pocket DreamTeam,* we now want to support mobile users. Pocket DreamTeam extends the runtime system, the development environment and the application framework. Before we present the mobile extension, we briefly outline the stationary variant of DreamTeam.

DreamTeam is based on a completely decentralized architecture, i.e. apart from the users' workstations or PCs no further computers (e.g. servers) are needed. This architecture is ideal for a huge number of scenarios, where a central server is too cost-intensive or inappropriate for the intended task.

The runtime system of DreamTeam offers several services for the coordination of the participants, group and user profile management, session management and announcement services. Pre-defined elements to achieve group awareness (e.g. participant lists, distributed mouse pointers or overview windows) can be integrated into the application with view lines of code. DreamTeam applications are developed in Java. A class library of approx. 200 Java classes supports the developer.

3.1   The Stationary Application Model

Applications under DreamTeam are developed according to the *DreamTeam Resource Model (DRM).* Applications consist of an *application frame,* a set of *resources* and a *user interface.* The application frame links together all other components and provides an interface for the runtime system. With this interface, the runtime system can initialise, start and stop applications. In addition, the system can start

301

applications in private mode. A user can for example prepare documents for a collaborative session privately.

Resources represent the shared state of an application. Resources can for example be the content of shared web pages, shared paragraphs of text documents or diagram elements of a shared diagram. Resources both provide the data as well as the necessary functions for collaborative processing.

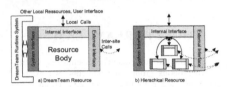

Figure 2: DreamTeam Resouces

Resources have three interfaces (fig. 2a):
- The *internal interface* is the method interface, which a resource provides by its implementation as a Java class. All application objects can use this interface according to traditional method call mechanisms of Java.
- An *external interface* is used to communicate to corresponding resources on other computers by so-called *inter-site calls*. These calls are method calls which are executed synchronously on all corresponding replicated resources. The developer indicates inter-site calls in the source code by a certain keyword. The runtime system uses the reflection API of Java to invoke replicated method calls.
- The *system interface*: a resource must offer services that make it possible for the runtime system to get control over the resource. The runtime system can transmit the status of a resource to latecomers automatically or maintain consistency during synchronous state changes initiated by different users.

Figure 3 presents the architecture of DreamTeam applications. This architecture has several advantages. On each site runs a complete set of application instances. All data is available locally, thus an application is still runnable in case of network problems. Inside a local application instance, resources can be used like other object, thus an application developer deals with established paradigms for software development. Not only several applications can be executed simultaneously. It is also possible to open more than one instance of a single application inside a session.

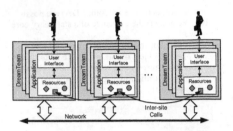

Figure 3: Stationary Applications with DreamTeam

The external interface connects a resource with its corresponding resources on other peers. Thus, a specific resource and its communication capabilities can be developed without the knowledge of other resource. This leads to a modular software architecture.

Via the system interface the runtime system gets the necessary control over the resources. The developer does not have to take care of the distribution of shared data, the support of latecomers, the synchronization of accesses etc. Particularly the complex area of communication is completely hidden from developer.

The resource model represents a flexible framework with covers different other application models such as MVC, PAC or ALV. Resources are not restricted by their complexity. Resources can be built up by other resources and thus represent small applications inside an application (fig. 2b). Hierarchically built resources form the basis of the component concept *TeamComponents* (Roth & Unger, 2000).

3.2 Mobile Users

The mobility of participants leads to a number of problems, which have far-reaching effects on the runtime environment, on the application framework and on the application development.
- Mobile devices have reduced capabilities regarding the user interface, have a low size and screen resolution and no or only a rudimentary keyboard. Usual interface paradigms of stationary environments cannot be transferred directly to mobile computers. Overlapping windows, icons, drag and drop, context menus etc., are not suitable for devices with small screens. Particularly the concept of direct manipulation is problematic (Kristoffersen & Ljungberg, 1999). To attain the overview on small displays, special dialog widgets and design guidelines were developed

Figure 4: The Distribution Architecture of Pocket DreamTeam

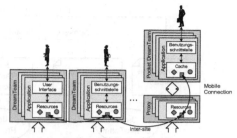

Figure 5: Applications with Pocket DreamTeam

which are significantly different from those of the traditional computers.

- Usually, mobile devices have a mobile power supply. Battery lifetime still is a limiting factor. If a device is continuously switched on, current batteries often only have power for some hours. The mobile device is therefore turned off most of the time or is in a power saving mode with reduced activity.
- Mobile devices are usually connected wirelessly to a network. Wireless networks have poor characteristics regarding bandwidth, latency time and reliability.
- Finally, technical properties of mobile devices have to be taken into account, which are low processor performances, small memory and no or only rudimentary file systems. Operating systems of mobile devices offer, compared to desktop operating systems, only a low amount of services.

Although mobile devices have limited capabilities, end-users expect very short response times of the applications, even shorter as for desktop applications. Bey et al. (2001) specify a maximum response time of one second for handheld applications. Furthermore, users expect to be able to turn the mobile device off any time and continue the work with the current state later. This usage is significantly different from usage of stationary computers: while a desktop computer is switched on for hours, mobile devices are frequently turned on and off, and sometimes run only for some seconds.

The restrictions on one hand and the high demands on the other hand lead to an architecture as represented in fig. 4.

Besides the mobile devices, we need additional computers called the *proxies*. A proxy executes computational expensive operations of the application. While the mobile device is turned off or the connection interrupted, the state of the session is updated by the proxy. For any stationary session participant, the proxy represents a permanently available contact point. A proxy runs without user invention, thus needs no user interface. With this architecture, arbitrary combinations of mobile and stationary users can cooperate inside a session. From the view of the network, both user types behave identically.

The general idea of a proxy is actually not very new. The first proxy architecture designed for networked applications was introduced by Shapiro (1986). Systems use Shapiro's proxy architecture whenever an application wants to use a specific service, but the actual service location and usage conditions may vary during runtime. Typical examples are CORBA and Jini. With the help of a proxy, a client can use a service without knowing the underlying protocol. However, this proxy resides on the client device, thus does not allow any load balancing between client and other computers.

An example, which is closer to our intended proxy architecture is the HTTP proxy (Fielding et al. 1997). HTTP proxies convey HTTP requests from a web browser to a web server and in turn transfer the requested data back to the client. As a benefit, a proxy can cache web pages, which speeds up access to frequently used pages. However, this kind of proxy only works in one direction, since clients do not offer any services themselves as in our framework. In addition, such proxies are intended to increase the network throughput, not to handle complete disconnections as our proxy. As clients cannot modify a shared state, the entire problem of consistency and coherence is not relevant for such service proxies.

At first sight, proxy computers are a break in the decentralized architecture of DreamTeam. However, there may be an arbitrary number of proxy computers in the architecture, thus the failure of a specific proxy computer particularly does not mean that a mobile user is disconnected from the session. Automatic recovery mechanisms switch a user to another proxy without interruption.

By the introduction of proxy computers, the application framework must be modified (fig. 5). A proxy computer maintains the resources for one or more

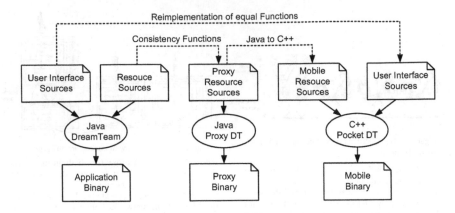

Figure 6: Steps to Develop Applications

mobile users. Inter-site calls are executed in the proxy. The state therefore remains up-to-date, even if the connection to the mobile computer is interrupted. The mobile computer stores a cache entry of every resource. The mobile application can access the data of the resources locally without executing long network transactions. As a result, the user can continue the work during interruptions for a limited time.

This comfort leads to more complex protocols for data distribution, cache coherence and consistency (Roth, 2002). Particularly the consistency control is crucial. Original DreamTeam uses pessimistic concurrency control procedures, which are suitable for optimally connected users in stationary networks. Pessimistic mechanisms lead to efficiently implementations and are easy to maintain by an application developer. Among mobile, weakly connected users however, pessimistic concurrency control mechanisms are not suitable any longer. As a solution, Pocket DreamTeam offers a combination of a pessimistic concurrency control for the stationary segment and an optimistic concurrency control for the mobile segment. The runtime system of Pocket DreamTeam keeps the problems of the consistency control away from the application developer as far as possible, but the developer has to program special procedures that support the runtime system performing the optimistic concurrency control.

3.3 The Development of Mobile Collaborative Applications

Software development for mobile devices is in principle more cost-intensive than the development for stationary computers. Developing groupware which shall run both on stationary and mobile computers another problem arises: both the operating system and the programming environment is differently. DreamTeam applications are developed under Java, Pocket DreamTeam applications run under C++. Cross-platform approaches (e.g. Java ME) are available in principle, but in reality not acceptable due to a number of technical limitations.

Despite these restrictions, rapid prototyping approaches should still be applicable with Pocket DreamTeam. This goal is accomplished by a strong reuse of source code.

Figure 6 shows the steps to develop Pocket DreamTeam applications. As a first step, a developer creates a stationary application variant. For this the source codes of user interface as well as the code for resources have to be generated.

In a second step, the developer derives the proxy variants of the resources. For this, the developer must generate code to support the optimistic consistency control.

In the third step, the mobile resources have to be generated. Since the mobile part is developed with another programming language, the syntax of the resources must be translated correspondingly. Usually, not the complete resource has to be ported - only the internal data structures and methods for reading the state are necessary. Inter-site calls are passed on to the proxy by the runtime system automatically, thus no porting costs arise here. Until now, the application developer derives the resource sources manually. This transformation should be done semi-automatically in future with the help of a tool. For this, we have to extend the syntax of the source to make use of a converter possible.

At present, the greatest overhead is arising by generating the user interface for the mobile device. User interfaces can be taken over only regarding content. A direct transfer is not reasonable since any target platform has its own optimised interface toolkit, widgets and design guidelines. Possible solutions may be approaches based on so-called *User Interface Plasticity* (Calvary et al., 2001), where a developer designs an interface once and derives the necessary realization for the target platforms automatically. Such approaches are object of intensive research and at present have not led to any usable tools.

3.4 Communication Issues

The communication between client and proxy plays an important role inside our architecture. We have to consider a number of issues:

- The communication link usually uses wireless technologies. As described in (Bakre & Badrinath, 1995), common transport protocols are optimised for wired links and often have poor performance over wireless links. In addition, wireless links do not offer the same variety of protocols. Actual implementations of IrDA, Bluetooth or GSM support the TCP/IP suite only with some serious drawbacks.
- A mobile device has to look up its corresponding proxy at runtime. The relation between proxy and client may change, when the client moves into another network. There exist a number of platforms to support service discovery in unknown environments such as SLP (Service Location Protocol) (Veizades et al., 1997) or Jini (Sun Microsystems, 2000). Some wireless network stacks provide their own discovery mechanisms, such as IAS (Information Access Service) in IrDA or SDP (Service Discovery Protocol) in Bluetooth.
- Client and proxy devices fundamentally differ regarding internal data representation. To exchange data between both devices, we need a machine- and language-independent encoding and decoding scheme. Data could be encoded using XML or Mime types.

As a communication basis for Pocket DreamTeam which addresses these issues, we use our own communication platform *NKF* (*Network Kernel Framework*) (Roth, 2002b). NKF is a middleware platform for small devices such as PDAs or digital cameras, as well as for traditional desktop systems. It is especially designed for supporting new devices, which do not come along with publicly available middleware platforms such as CORBA or RMI. In such cases, developers have to implement the middleware in addition to the actual application, thus NKF is easy to realize and does not make high demands on target platforms. Though we implemented NKF in Java and C, NKF does not rely on a specific programming language paradigm. NKF is based on network stacks such as IrDA or Bluetooth. Special features of a specific network stack such as service discovery or security functions can be accessed via NKF in a protocol-independent manner. Inside NKF, there exists a lookup and service discovery module, which allows an application to look up services

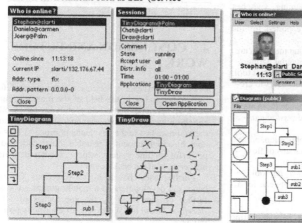
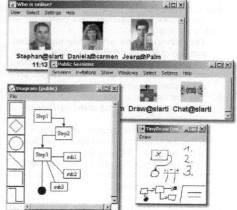

Figure 7: Pocket DreamTeam Windows (left) and DreamTeam Windows (right)

305

inside the network. If the underlying network stack comes along with its own service discovery mechanism, it is used by NKF. If not, NKF provides an own mechanism.

For encoding and decoding data, NKF offers a variety of so-called *codec* modules. NKF contains an XML codec to encode standard data types such as strings, numbers or dates. To transfer complex data such as the session profile, Pocket DreamTeam has to provide an additional marshalling/unmarshalling mechanism. For this, the Pocket DreamTeam development environment contains marshalling interfaces for both Java as well as C++, which are compatible to each other.

3.5 Sample Applications and Evaluations

To verify the concept, two core applications of DreamTeam as well as two cooperative applications were ported for mobile devices with the help of Pocket DreamTeam. It should particularly be verified, how far Pocket DreamTeam supports rapid prototyping.

For implementing the user interfaces, the capabilities of the different platforms were taken into account. While icons, overlapping windows, large menus etc. are common in desktop environments, the mobile variant was reduced to the essential functions. We avoid icons. Some functions of different dialog frames were integrated into a single frame to save time-consuming switches between windows.

The following applications were ported for the mobile platform (fig. 7):
— The *online list* shows, which group members are currently active, therefore are potential partners for sessions. This list represents an essential tool for group awareness and allows the users to create spontaneous sessions.
— The user can plan sessions, announce them and join sessions with the help of the *session management tool*.
— With a collaborative *diagram* application, entity relation ship diagrams, class diagrams or flow charts can be developed in the group.
— With a collaborative *free-hand drawing* tool users can create sketches in the group, e.g. for a brainstorming session.

Goal of these implementations was, besides testing the entire system, to assess the costs for application development. An experienced developer needed less

than two working weeks for all four applications in the sum. It is problematic to quantify the costs of the developments exactly, since these are very different from developer to developer. We present the numbers of the lines of code here. We know these represent only a trend and cannot be seen as an absolute measure.

Besides the four applications, the overhead of the development of the core platform is shown in table 1. The columns *Stationary*, *Proxy* and *Mobile* show the costs of the program parts of the respective computer category. The column *reused* shows the amount of code of the proxy application, which was reused from the stationary application. We see a very high ratio of at least 90%. In addition, only few lines of code are needed for mobile applications. The reason is that essentially the user interface had to be implemented here and complex functions of the functional core reside in the proxy. The usage of our middleware platform NKF leads to a very lean core platform for mobile devices.

Table 1: Implementation Costs

	Stationary (lines)	Proxy (lines)	re-used	Mobile (lines)
Core Platform	125000	110000	98 %	9500
Online List	4400	4000	95 %	930
Session Management	7100	6900	93 %	2100
Diagram	6900	5200	92 %	600
Draw	930	520	90 %	410

4 CONCLUSION AND FUTURE WORK

Pocket DreamTeam represents a starting point for further researches in the field of the mobile groupware. A developer can create prototypes for mobile collaborative applications economically and include the end-user fast in the development process. This is done by a high amount of reusable source code and a powerful runtime system, which executes demanding services in the background.

Further researches go in two directions. On one hand, the development of a mobile groupware shall further be simplified by the approaches of *User Interface Plasticity*. We expect an enormous potential here.

We will in addition investigate other aspects of mobility. Problem areas arise from the consideration of the spatial position or the current usage context. The complex area of the security in addition plays an important role for mobile users.

REFERENCES

Bakre, A.; Badrinath, R. R.; 1995. I-TCP: Indirect TCP for Mobile Hosts, *15th Internat. Conference on Distributed Computing Systems*, 1995

Bey, C.; Freeman, E.; Hillerson, G.; Ostrem, J.; Rodriguez, R.; Wilson, G.; Dugger, M.; 2001. *Palm OS Programmer's Companion, Volume I*, Palm Inc, July 2001

Calvary, J.; Coutaz, J.; Thevenin, D.; 2001. A Unifying Reference Framework for the Development of Plastic User Interfaces, *8th IFIP Working Conference on Engineering for Human-Computer Interaction (EHCI'01)*, Toronto, May 11-13, 2001, LNCS 2254, Springer, 173-192

Chabert, A.; Grossman, E.; Jackson, L.; Pietrowizc, S.; Seguin, C.; 1998. Java Object-Sharing in Habanero, *Communications of the ACM*, Vol. 41, No. 6, June 1998, 69-76

Coutaz, J.; 1997. PAC-ing the Architecture of Your User Interface, In Proceedings of the DSV-IS'97, 4. *Eurographics Workshop on Design, Specification and Verification of Interactive Systems*, Springer-Verlag, 1997, 15-32

Dewan, P.; Choudhary, R.; 1992. A High-Level and Flexible Framework for Implementing Multiuser Interfaces, *ACM Transactions on Information Systems*, Vol. 10, No. 4, Oct. 1992, 345-380

Fielding, R.; Gettys, J.; Mogul, J.; Frystyk, H.; Berners-Lee, T.; 1997. Hypertext Transfer Protocol - HTTP/1.1, *Request for Comments 2068*, January 1997

Graham, N.; 1996. *The Clock Language: Preliminary Reference Manual*, York University, Canada, 1996

Hill, R. D.; Brinck, T.; Patterson, J. F.; Rohall, S. L.; Wilner, W. T.; 1993. Rendezvous Language, *Communications of the ACM*, Vol. 36, No. 1, Jan. 1993, 62-67

Joseph, A. D.; Tauber, J. A.; Kaashoek, M. F.; 1997. Mobile Computing with the Rover Toolkit, *IEEE Transactions on Computers*, Vol. 46, No. 3, March 1997, 337-352

Kistler, J. J.; Satyanarayana, M.; 1992. Disconnected Operation in the Coda File System, *ACM Transaction on Computer Systems*, Vol. 10, No. 1, Feb. 1992, 3-25

Kristoffersen, S.; Ljungberg, F.; 1999. Designing Interaction Styles for a Mobile Use Context, *First International Symposion on Handheld and Ubiquitous Computing 1999 (HUC'99)*, Karlsruhe, Sept. 27-29, 1999, LNCS 1707, Springer, 281-288

Munson, J. P.; Dewan, P.; 1997. Sync: A Java Framework for Mobile Collaborative Applications, *Special issue on Executable Content in Java, IEEE Computer*, 1997, 59-66

Roseman, M.; Greenberg S.; 1996. Building Real-Time Groupware with GroupKit, a Groupware Toolkit, *ACM Transactions on Computer-Human Interaction*, Vol. 3, No. 1, 1996, 66-106

Roth, J.; 2000. DreamTeam - A Platform for Synchronous Collaborative Applications, *AI & Society* (2000), Vol. 14, No. 1, *Special Issue on Computer-Supported Cooperative Work*, Springer London, March 2000, 98-119

Roth, J.; 2002. Mobility Support for Replicated Real-time Applications (2001), *Innovative Internet Computing Systems (I2CS)*, Kühlungsborn (Germany), June 20-22, 2002, LNCS 2346, Springer-Verlag, 181-192

Roth, J.; 2002b. A Communication Middleware for Mobile and Ad-hoc Scenarios, *International Conference on Internet Computing (IC'02)*, June 24-27 2002, Las Vegas (USA), Vol. I, CSREA Press, 77-84

Roth, J.; Unger, C.; 2000. Developing synchronous collaborative applications with TeamComponents, in Dieng R. et al. (eds): *Fourth International Conference on the Design of Cooperative Systems*, Sophia Antipolis (France), May 23-26, 2000, IOS Press, 353-368

Roth, J.; Unger, C.; 2001. Using handheld devices in synchronous collaborative scenarios, *Personal and Ubiquitous Computing*, Vol. 5, Issue 4, Springer London, Dec. 2001, 243-252

Schuckmann, C.; Kirchner, L.; Schümmer, J.; Haake, J. M.; 1996. Designing Object-Oriented Synchronous Groupware With COAST, In: Proceedings of the *ACM Conference on Computer Supported Cooperative Work*, ACM Press, Nov. 1996, 30-38

Shapriro, M.; 1986. Structure and Encapsulation in Distributed Systems: the Proxy Principle, *Proc. of the 6th Internal. Conference on Distributed Computing Systems*, May 1986, 198-204

Sun Microsystems; 2000. *Jini Technology Core Platform Specification, Version 1.1*, Dec. 2000

Veizades, J.; Guttman, E.; Perkins, C.; Kaplan, S.; 1997. Service Location Protocol, *Request for Comments 2165*, June 1997

KNOWLEDGE CONSTRUCTION IN E-LEARNING: DESIGNING AN E-LEARNING ENVIRONMENT

Lily Sun, Shirley Williams and Kecheng Liu
Department of Computer Science, The University of Reading, UK
Email: {lily.sun, shirley.williams, k.liu}@reading.ac.uk

Keywords: e-Learning approach, courseware design, teaching and learning paradigms, knowledge construction model

Abstract   In the traditional classroom, students learned to depend on tutors for their motivation, direction, goal setting, progress monitoring, self-assessment, and achievement. A fundamental limitation is that students have little opportunity to conduct and manage their learning activities which are important for knowledge construction. e-Learning approaches and applications which are supported by pervasive technologies, have brought in great benefits to the whole society, meanwhile it also has raised many challenging questions. One of the issues that researchers and educators are fully aware is that technologies cannot drive a courseware design for e-Learning. An effective and quality learning requires an employment of appropriate learning theory and paradigms, organisation of contents, as well as methods and techniques of delivery. This paper will introduce our research work in design an e-Learning environment with emphases on instructional design of courseware for e-learning.

1 INTRODUCTION

An e-Learning approach has played a pivotal role in improving flexibility and quality of education and training by using the Internet and collaborative technologies (Schweizer 1999, Takacs *et al.* 1999, Gottfredson 2002). A number of specific applications, such as IBM Lutos LearningSpace, Blackboard, Microsoft Visual Studio, and Netware have been employed to support teaching and learning at universities. Evidence (Anderson 1998, Beller and Or 1998, Shank *el at.* 1994, El-Tigi and Branch 1997, Horton and Horton, 2002) show that these applications enable individual tutors to put teaching materials online, create discussion forums, organise assessments, and link with other sources. To a limited extent, these applications can support course design, but it is often up to the individual tutors to decide how the teaching materials should be organised. Researchers and educators are fully aware that technologies alone will not generate much benefit and are not the drive for courseware design. The most important aspects in e-learning are the employment of appropriate learning theory and paradigms, organisation of contents online, as well as methods

and techniques of delivery. So far there is little research for a development of suitable methods for online courseware design with the teaching and learning rooted in a sound educational theory embedded.

With this understanding, we base our work on the theories of constructivist and semiotics. These two theories encourage students to take responsibilities for the learning process. To acquire capability of deep learning, critical analysis and self-reflection is seen as more important and profund than acquring knowledge. Deep learning can only be realised by totally engaging the learners in knowledge construction as opposed to knowledge transfer. Constructivisit and semiotics guide us in devising a model for an e-learning environment and instructional design principles for courseware in this environment.

In this paper, we will first of all, critically assess the current practice of teaching and learning supported by technologies. Constructivist theory and semiotics are discussed in light of their relevance to e-learning. Components of a model for instructional design of courseware for e-learning are described based on our early work, followed by discussions on the current work and future research.

O. Camp et al. (eds.), Enterprise Information Systems V, 308-315.
© 2004 *Kluwer Academic Publishers. Printed in the Netherlands.*

2 CRITICAL ASSESSMENT OF CURRENT E-LEARNING

A body of knowledge with examplar practice shows promising results and a great potential in e-learning (Cunningham 1987, Uden *et al.* 2001, Liu and Sun 2002, Jona 2000, and Martinez, 2002). However, a large propotion of e-learning tends to be limited by only making contents available online together with assignments to set learning milestones. The online contents are normally orgainsed according to the functions encoded in the e-learning software. As a result, association between related contents and materials is not based on the ground of effective learning, but more due to the technical constraints or availabiliity of the software. The design of the courseware for e-learning is often driven by the technologies. The observation below summarises the issues, which require attention in future instructional design for e-learning.

- Learning is still pre-determined by instructional sequences and in a *push* manner. Students, therefore, are constrained to apply their prior knowledge to generate their mental models and to conceptualise various parts of information to form a whole within a given context.
- Students often find themselves in various situation and carry out multiple learning activities, which are hardly supported by the current course structure.
- Most computer assisted learning provides with customisation and personalisation machenisms, but little methodological guidance is provided for instructors to introduce the functions of the *social negotiation* on individual learning goals, learning content and learning methods into the courseware.

All these are due to the contents have been simply made eclectronically available. They are not organised in a manner for self-analysis and student-centred learning, and are also not presented to encourage students to seek knowledge independently and achieve their learning goals. There is therefore a need for a conceptual model underpinning the courseware for e-learning which is frimly rooted in a sound theoretical framework and teaching & learning paradigm. In this project,

we proposal an e-learning environment which enables students to construct knowledge and engage deep learning in a self-motivated and driected manner.

3 LEARNING AS KNOWLEDGE CONSTRUCTION

It is recognised in the education that learning is a process of knowledge construction. Constructivist claims that learners construct their own reality, or at least interpret it based upon their perceptions or experiences. According to constructivist (e.g. Savery & Duffy 1994, Honebein *et al.* 1993), knowledge is in our interactions with the environment. Learning is motivated by cognitive conflicts or puzzlements, which influences the organisation and nature of what is learned. Understanding is affected through the social negotiation of meaning. As the learner is the focus of the enterprise, they should be protected from potentially damaging instructional practices by promoting personal autonomy and control of learning. Support towards self-regulation should be provided by promoting the development of skills and attitudes that enable learners to take on increasing responsibility for their learning. Intentional learning and examination of errors should always be encouraged. Constructivists emphasise the role of the learners, who initiate the learning. The learners act and interact within the flux of events and actions. Through these acts they build their world and construct their knowledge.

Semiotics, as a discipline of the study of sign, has a strong influence on the way we understand the world which we live in and the way we conduct our work. The subjects of study of semiotics are all kind of signs. A sign is "something which stands for something else in some respect or capacity" (Peirce 1931-35). Signs can be a verbal language, pictures, literature, motion pictures, theatre, body language, and more. Semiotics has a strong relationship with understanding, as Peirce described in the key notion: semiosis (Figure 1). Semiosis is a process that involves an agent using a sign in understanding or interpreting something (Liu 2000). Understanding is a subjective process where the prior knowledge affects the interpretation of a given sign, and vice versa. It is difficult to assume for all agents involved to derive the same association between a given object and a sign, as it involves issues such as meaning,

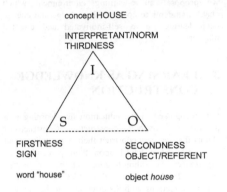

concept HOUSE

INTERPRETANT/NORM
THIRDNESS

FIRSTNESS   SECONDNESS
SIGN   OBJECT/REFERENT

word "house"   object *house*

Figure 1. Semiosis as a process of understanding.

cognition, behaviour, culture and social context. The learner, i.e. the agent, is in the centre of the semiosis process and has a control over it. Learning and understanding in this paradigm can be only realised by creation and use of signs.

Understanding the process of knowledge construction based on these two theories enables us to identify some important features of learning (Liu and Sun 2002, Uden *et al.* 2001).

1. Learning is a process of knowledge construction, rather than knowledge transfer or injection. Within semiotics the process of semiosis is deemed as a knowledge construction process whereby what we experience as reality is really prior cultural and personal codings - knowledge is not an entity to be acquired but a process of how we come to know. Within the constructivist realm, knowledge is constructed through interaction with the environment.

2. Learning is subjective. There is no single objective reality, knowledge construction is a process of personal interpretation of the perceived world and the negotiation of meaning. The process of semiosis enables us to structure our experiences and reveal the nature and culture of our understanding. Constructivism advocates that there are no cause-effect relationships between the world and the learner; learning to a large extent depends on the subjective view of the learner.

3. Learning should be collaborative - learning is negotiated from multiple perspectives.

Semiotics promotes educational strategies that emphasise many sign systems, or many ways of knowing. Constructivism emphasises that learning emerges from the human organism in ways which conserve adaptation and organisation - learning is to apply some sort of conceptual system upon the phenomena and to bring forth a world including those phenomena.

4. Learning is situated, and it should occur in realistic settings. Signs as codes of experience, according to semiotics, are related to social settings where learning takes place; learning is never a private act. The constructivist approach notes that living systems survive by fitting with one another and with other aspects of the surrounding medium.

These features can be incorporated in e-learning during the courseware design for e-learning.

4 IMPACT ON E-LEARNING

Knowledge, in semiotics, does not consist of objects or entities that we "acquire", but is better thought of as knowing, or a process. We build ways of knowing – abilities of understanding and interpreting, which is seen as an affordance. Gibson (1979) uses this term to describe biological patterns of behaviour. Stamper (1985) extends this further to denote social patterns of behaviour from the perspective of an organisational semiotics. The affordance acquired by a learner maps on to the process of knowledge construction which displays structures that determine his current understanding through his experience in the world. Through these structures, one literally constructs ones knowledge dynamically as one interacts in the world. Knowledge is not "out there" waiting to be discovered. The world as we know is culturally coded, relying on prior structures invented (not discovered) both collectively by our culture and individually by us. The refusal to accept the separation of knowledge from the knower is exactly what both constructivist and semiotics believe. An effective learning can only be realised through a highly interactive process in which the learner is totally engaged.

Another concept which is very relevant to learning from the theory of semiotics is that of *intertextuality*. It is argued that the meaning of a given text cannot be ascertained within that text itself, but only in relation to a broad spectrum of other texts or even social and culture context. This implies that all our knowledge is essentially intertextual, always embedded within a system of prior social and cultural codings and future possible codings. The concept of intertextuality has been most influential in theories of reading and writing. Meaning in reading is created by readers as they interact with the text. Texts only exist in reaction to what readers produce. Semioticians believe that the basic state of human consciousness is a state of belief. Beliefs can change through Abduction. Abduction is the inferential move where we, when confronted with some experience not accounted for by our existing beliefs, invent a new set of beliefs or revise an existing one. This new structure will provide a context within which the surprising experience is a matter of course (i.e., it makes sense). Teaching methods that promote abduction should be encouraged.

Semiotics theory also offers promise as a tool for understanding education as a social and cultural process. Inherent in semiotics is the notion of reflexivity, a reflection on our reflections, thinking about our thinking process, or knowing how we know. According to Cunningham (1987), "To be aware constantly of the assumptions guiding particular theory and method is to be free to examine alternatives, to invent different interpretative contexts and explore their consequences." The implications for learning and thinking are enormous. For one thing, knowledge would now be regarded as a process, not a static structure to be learned and remembered. There would be more emphasis put on how to think rather than what to think. Curriculum would be more interrelated. Teachers would become models of semiosis and monitors of the student's ongoing semiosis. Educational establishments would become places where appropriate contexts for knowledge are provided.

Adopting semiotics and constructivist paradigm would have a tremendous impact on designing of an e-learning environment. An e-learning environment should facilitate learners to interpret the multiple perspectives of domain context, guide learners to conduct and manage their personalised learning activities, and encourage collaborative and cooperative learning for critical thinking and problem-solving. A course should be designed in such way that participants can be facilitated and guided for their learning activities and empowered

to mediate and control their knowledge construction to achieve their learning goals. The collaborative learning environment will also offer other benefits. For example, there are quality teaching materials widely available from the internal source and the Internet. They can be selected and used as main teaching materials and auxiliaries, but there is no mechanism for sharing and reuse these materials. There is demand for reusing course contents and public available materials for tailoring course to meeting different target audience. This will save much time and cost to develop courses serving multi-disciplinary degree and training purposes. Knowledge transfer without constraints of geographic location and time difference is another area where the collaborative learning environment can help. It is possible to quickly package a course by using the sharable elements of the teaching materials in the repository.

5   A DESIGN OF AN E-LEARNING ENVIRONMENT

Based on the above principles, an e-learning environment has been designed for authoring and delivering modules for a university's degree course (Bachelor and Master level) (Figure 2). In this environment, students normally participate in learning as a personal and social construction of knowledge, and development of critical-thinking and problem-solving skills. A number of components have been defined that consist of the guidelines and templates:

1. *Course requirements*. This component enables an instructor to set an academic scope about a course that is derived to meet the needs of target learners. Requirements related to a course are categorised:

- **Learning goals** describe what subject knowledge students are expected to acquire and apply to situations. Learners can then set their learning activities to construct knowledge and develop skills.

- **Learning outcomes** specify expectations from the instructor and learners perspectives. The learning goals will be assessed by measuring the learning outcomes which should reflect the standards set by the academic institutes. The learning outcomes are described using quantifiable words/ontology so that learners follow them to plan their learning activities. The ontology (i.e., a conceptual map) is related to content objects and it can therefore assists the content selection.The learning outcomes should encourage students to develop the learning method on critical thinking, problem-solving, and decision-making for judging findings.

- **Transferable skills** are important for students to have for knowledge construction, extension, and self-reflective practices. These skills, e.g., independent learning, communication, presentation, writing, and team working, can be defined and embedded in the subject inquiries.

- **Assessment strategy** defines a suitable method of assessing learning outcomes to meet the learning expectations, e.g., replication, understanding and application of knowledge and skills. An assessment strategy is subject-dependent. Various assessment methods are available for choice, e.g., multiple choice test, continued assessment, examination, and coursework. A difficulty with some of these methods (e.g., continued assessment) is that the assessment content is not certain at the beginning of the course. It should in principle be developed and built as the course progresses, dependent on the understanding achieved by learners. In the meantime, assessment materials can be incorporated into the Specification Repository for future use (referring to Figure 2).

2. *Course configuration*. A course configuration is carried out based on a subject (or a module), which scopes the relevance of course content to meet the course requirements. This process should consider the selection of a suitable pedagogy for online course design.

There are two repositories which store course specifications and content objects respectively. The course specifications are instances of the course requirements with detailed description of topics, assessment method and criteria. The course specification and content are structured in a separate repository which comprises the sharable and reuseable objects. One object represents an "element" of the course specifications or subject content with granularities at different level of details.

Course content objects are identified to address subject issues (e.g. concepts, theory and principles) and will be structured as generic as possible so that their reuse between modules is possible, though sometimes customisation to suit a module's specific needs may be necessary. The course content can be internal sources from an institute as well as external sources, e.g., other universities, companies, and the Internet reposities. The contents embody a static view of a course. Delivery Strategy will provide a dynamic mechanism for instantiation (i.e., sequencing) of course contents for a particular class.

A process of the Course Configuration is one of a mapping between the Learning Specification and the Content Repository, which results in a course package. The Content Repository may grow rapidly and become complex as new content objects are created and existing ones are updated with input from the feedback from the learning process. The Course Configuration software will manage these changes.

3. *Course packaging*. A course package is created from the course configuration process based on the specified course requirements. The package is composed by *Course Content* and *Delivery Strategy*. The *Course Content* comprises:

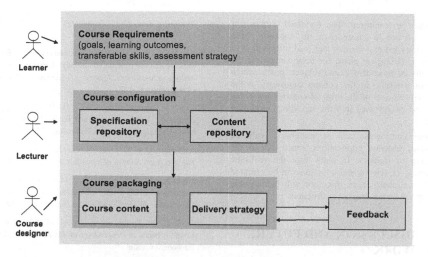

Figure 2. A methodology for instructional design of courseware and contents in e-learning.

- **Blocks**. The learning content is organised in manageable blocks which relate to the learning outcomes. This would give students support over their learning activities and progress. From the teaching point of view, the tutor can facilitate the learners to achieve their learning goals and also monitor teaching progress participated by the learners. Learning activities of students can be simulated into a Learning Pattern which can be fed back to the Course Configuration for improvements in the course construction.

- **Milestones**. Milestones are associated with the blocks. They allow tutors to know early enough whether the learning outcomes are likely to be achieved so that they can provide guidance to the students accordingly.

- **Assessment**. This is an ultimate learning measurement towards the achievement of learning outcomes and it performs two functions. Firstly, it provides an opportunity for instruction assessment design. Secondly, the actual assessment content and examination papers can be associated with the learning marerials.

The *Delivery Strategy* will support collaboration and interaction between tutors and students and also students and students:

- **Coordination** facilitates learners to carry out learning activities associated with the blocks subject content. During this dynamic process of teaching and learning, appropriate instructions should be provided when there is a need. The instruction should not only serve the purpose of explaining the materials, but also guide the students to develop additional skills such as critical thinking, problem-solving and decision-making.

- **Discussion forum** is where the students and tutors can post questions to and get answers from a shared space. This space encourages student-centred learning by engaging in the discussion to provide for alternative intepretation and understanding of the subject.

- **Personal profile** is used as a personalisation feature for individual learners. The students can be encouraged to participate in the course with initiative and self-management. It also stimulates the development of wider interests in the subject area. By doing so, students can apply their prior knowledge about experiencefor problem-solving. Meanwhile, their learning experiences can be captured and fed back to the *Course Configuration* phase for improvements.

4. *Feedback*. During the course's execution, the activities and experiences of students and tutors

should be monitored. The Feedback component can provide a mechanism to monitor these activities and experiences and feed information to *Course Packaging* phase for improvement of the quality of the course. Some subject content which wasot available in the content repository at the subsequent time of the original construction phase can be incorporated into the repository for future use.

These components can be integrated with the course execution applications which deliver the course to learners. In such way the real-time learning experience and activities can be captured and evaluated. These therefore will be valuable feedback for the course construction.

6 DISCUSSION AND FUTURE WORK

The teaching and learning theories and paradigms have been practised in the traditional education for long time. The evidence showed that the e-learning can be the innovative means to improve the efficacy and quality of teaching and learning. There are widely used applications in the universities for e-learning, but what is important for the design of the courseware for e-learning is the appropriate instruction and guidelines. This paper has illustrated the collaborative learning environment with its components and techniques to aid the e-learning courseware design. These components and techniques are being experimented in some of the degree courses in our department. A result will be critically analysed and refinements will be incorporated for improvement and enhancement.

ACKNOWLEDGMENT

The authors would like to thank the colleagues from the course team of BSc in Information Technology in the Department for their constructive comments and support.

REFERENCES

Anderson, M.D. (1998). Critical elements of an Internet based asynchronous distance education course. *Journal of Educational Technology Systems*, 26(4), pp. 383-388.

Beller, M., & Or E. (1998) The crossroads between lifelong learning and information technology: A challenge facing leading universities. *Journal of Computer Mediated Communication*, 4 (2).

El-Tigi, M. and Branch R.M. (1997) Designing for interaction, learner control, and feedback during web-based learning. *Educational Technology*, 37 (3), 23-29.

Cunningham, D. (1987) Outline of an Education Semiotic. *The American Journal of Semiotics*, 5(2), pp 201-216.

Gottfredson, C. (2002) Achieving Maximum Return on Instruction (ROi) with e-Learning, *The e-Learning Developers' Journal – Design Strategies*, September 24.

Jona, K. (2000) Rethinking the Design of Online Course, Keynote Paper, in *Proceedings of ASCILITE2000*, Coffs Harbour, Australia.

Honebein, P.C., Duffy T. and Fishman B. (1993) Constructivism and the Design of Learning Environment: Context and Authentic Activities for Learning, in T.M. Duffy, J. Lowyck and D. Jonassen (eds.), *Design Environments for Constructivist Learning*, Springer-Verlag, NY, pp. 87-108.

Horton, W. and Horton K. (2002) Bring Top Classroom Features Online – No more Boredom! *The e-Learning Developers' Journal – Design Strategies*, October 15.

Liu, K. and Sun L. (2002) Applying Semiotics in Constructivist Learning, International Conf on Teaching and English Translation in the 21st Century, Marco Politechnique Institute, Marco, 10-12 May 2002.

Martinez, M. (2002) What is Personalised Learning? *The e-Learning Developers' Journal – Design Strategies*, May 7.

Peirce, C.S., (1932-35) *Collected Papers of Ch.S, Peirce*, 1931 - 1935, edited by Hartshorne, C. & Weiss, P. (1960) Cambridge, Mass.

Savery, J.R. and Duffy T. (1994) Problem-based Learning: an Instructional Model and its Constructivist Framework, *Educational Technology*, 35(5), pp. 31-37.

Shank, G., Ross J.M., Covalt W., Terry S. and Weiss E. (1994) Improving Creative Thinking Using Instructional Technology: Computer-aided Abductive Reasoning, *Educational Technology*, 34(9), pp. 33-42.

Stamper, R., Liu K., Hafkamp M. and Ades Y. (2000) Understanding the Role of Signs and Norms in Organisations, - a semiotic approach to information systems design, *Behaviour and Information Technology*, 19(1), 15-27.Stamper, R. (1985) *Knowledge as Action: a Logic of Social Norms and Individual Affordances*, Gilbert G.N. and Heath C. (eds), Social Action and Artificial Intelleigence, GrowerPress, Aldershot.

Schweizer, H. (1999) *Designing and teaching and on-line course: Spinning your web classroom.* Needham Heights, MA: Allyn & Bacon.

Takacs, J., Reed W. M., Wells J. G., & Dombrowski, L. (1999) The effects of on-line multimedia project development, learning style, and prior computer experiences on teachers' attitudes toward the Internet and hypermedia. *Journal of Research on Computing in Education*, 31(4), pp. 341-355.

Uden, L. and Liu K. (2001) Linking Radical Constructivism and Semiotics to Design a Constructivist Learning Environment, *J. of Computing in Higher Education*, 12(2), 34-51.

315

A SURVEY OF KNOWLEDGE BASE GRID FOR TRADITIONAL CHINESE MEDICINE

Jiefeng Xu, Zhaohui Wu

Grid Computing Lab, College of Computer Science, Zhejiang University, Hangzhou, 310027, P.R.China
Email:xujf@cs.zju.edu.cn, wzh@cs.zju.edu.cn

Keywords: Knowledge Base Grid, Ontology, Semantic Browse, Knowledge Representation, Inference Service

Abstract: Knowledge base gird is a kind of grid, which takes many knowledge bases as its foundation and its knowledge sources. All these knowledge sources follow a public ontology standard defined by standard organization. Knowledge base grid has its own specific domain knowledge, and so can be browsed at semantic level. It also supports correlative browse and knowledge discovery. In this paper, we introduce a generic knowledge base grid for Traditional Chinese Medicine. Its framework consists of three main parts: Virtual Open Knowledge Base, Knowledge Base Index, and Semantic Browser. We anatomize the implementation in detail. Furthermore, knowledge presentation and services of knowledge base grid are discussed.

1   INTRODUCTION

1.1   Background

The term "the Grid" was coined in the mid 1990s to denote a proposed distributed computing infrastructure for advanced science and engineering (Ian, 1999). Now grid is regarded as the next generation of the Internet. It provides a series of protocols, APIs and SDKs to integrate services, share coordinated resource and solve problem across distributed, heterogeneous dynamic, multi-institutional virtual organizations formed from the disparate resources (Michel, 2001) (Ian, 2001).

Grid has solved the problem of resource sharing of the infrastructure and made computers change from single, isolated devices into entry points to a worldwide network of information exchange (Ying, 2002). Thus, support in data, information, and knowledge exchange has become a key issue in current computer technology. However, the web's phenomenal growth rate makes it increasingly difficult to locate, organize, and integrate the available information (Jeff, 2001).

Our knowledge base grid is built on the semantic web. It is an integration of semantic web and grid, and wants to provide people semantic browse by taking many distributed knowledge bases as its knowledge sources. We suppose that there are many knowledge bases on the Internet. Owning knowledge base on the Internet and building knowledge base grid on the semantic web, our purpose is to achieve the formal organization and easy management of knowledge, and provide personal service.

As an instance of knowledge base grid, we develop the Traditional Chinese Medicine (TCM) Knowledge Base Grid. As name implying, the TCM Knowledge Base Grid is domain-oriented. It gathers basic concepts, terms, rules and cases of TCM, etc. It also includes reference books of TCM, and comes into being Unified TCM Language System.

1.2 Terminology

– Metadata
    Metadata is "data about data", and it describes the content, quality, condition, and other characteristics of data. The distinction between "data" and "metadata" is not an absolute one; it is a distinction created primarily by a particular application. That is to say, maybe one application's metadata is another application's data.
– Ontology
    The proposed mechanism for realizing semantic web is to add semantic markup to web resources that describes their content and functionality. Ontologies will define the vocabulary for such markup; they consist of the domain of interest and giving meaning to the terms therein

316

(Ying, 2002). Therefore, ontology is a set of assertions specifying the concepts involved in the domain (Jeff, 2001).

– Semantic Web

To change the human-understandable data to machine-understandable semantic knowledge in the web storage, the Semantic Web (Jeen, 2001) occurs. The Semantic Web, which is based on RDF metadata techniques and XML data representation will bring structure to the meaningful content of Web pages, creating an environment where software agents roaming from page to page can readily carry out sophisticated tasks for users. Ontology engineering plays an important role in the semantic web. Various kinds of domain ontology construction and building are the basis of semantic web.

– Knowledge Base

In knowledge base grid, RDF is the model for the description of semantic information. The data in knowledge base is also expressed by RDF. An RDF knowledge base consists of domains and inference rules. RDF knowledge can be vast and defined according to different schemas. Since one knowledge base gird is corresponding to one domain, its RDF knowledge in knowledge bases is defined according to the same RDFS relying on the public ontology. Inference rules are the another component of the RDF knowledge base, that should contain only non-correlated information – all correlated knowledge should be inferred from ground facts in the knowledge base.

– Inference Engine

The RDF knowledge model defines only the structure of the knowledge base. Many pieces of information should be inferred from ground facts using inference rules. Inference engine stores generalized statements and inference strategies. It is the driver to trigger on the inference, who knows what kind of statements and strategies should be used under particular circumstance.

Inference Service is a knowledge service, which provides high-level intelligent services such as knowledge query and management service, backward-chaining inference service, forward-chaining inference service, subsumption and classification inference service, etc.

2 KNOWLEDGE BASE GRID FRAMEWORK

The knowledge base grid consists of three main parts: VOKBs, Knowledge Base Index (KBI), and Semantic Browser. Figure 1 shows the framework of our knowledge base grid.

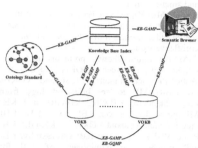

Figure 1: The framework of Knowledge Base Grid

– **VOKB:** Virtual Open Knowledge Base consists of many distributed knowledge bases, while knowledge base is made up of many knowledge sources. It stores the data of specific domain.

– **Knowledge Base Index:** Information repository of VOKBs. Every VOKB in the same knowledge base grid should register to the exclusive Knowledge Base Index, which is the linker between VOKB and Semantic Browser.

– **Semantic Browser:** The outward window of KB-Grid. Users explore the entire abundant and wonderful knowledge base grid world through it.

Furthermore, in the knowledge base grid framework, there is another entity: Ontology Standard. We suppose that there are many public ontology servers on the web. Since it is not particular for knowledge base grid, we do not list ontology standard in the main parts of the framework.

Each ontology standard is domain-specific. It well organizes the basic concepts, facts, rules, and meta-data of its domain, just like a dictionary. Depending on this ontology standard, different VOKBs can communicate each other expediently with heterogeneous information

Between the entities, four primary classes of knowledge base grid protocols can be distinguished:

– **KB-GIP:** Knowledge Base Gird Information Protocol is used to obtain information about the structure and state of a VOKB, for example, its configuration, current load, and usage policy (Ian, 2001).

– **KB-GRP:** Knowledge Base Gird Registration Protocol is used to register VOKBs with KBI, discussed in the next section. Together with KB-GIP, it provides knowledge discovery method.

– **KB-GAMP:** Knowledge Base Grid Acquisition and Management Protocol is used to acquire knowledge directly from VOKBs and manage it.

It mainly works during the ontology exploring and simple search.
- **KB-GQMP:** Knowledge Base Grid Query and Manipulation Protocol is used to complete deep search and inference. It mainly works during correlatively query.

As the figure shown, protocols make the communications between VOKBs, KBI and Semantic Browser smoothly. KBI and VOKBs follow KB-GAMP to get basic ontology from Ontology Standard. KB-GIP, KB-GRP and KB-GAMP are needed between KBI and VOKBs. KBI gets the information about VOKBs by KB-GIP. KB-GRP lets VOKB register to KBI successfully. KB-GAMP matches the requirement of KBI for knowledge acquisition and management. VOKBs use KB-GAMP and KB-GQMP to query and deeply infer between themselves. For Semantic Browser, it uses KB-GAMP to get common information, such as ontology and common search result from KBI, and uses KB-GQMP to get deep information, such inference result from VOKBs.

Basing on this framework, we develop the Traditional Chinese Medicine Knowledge Base Grid.

Figure 2 shows the architecture of the TCM Knowledge Base Grid.

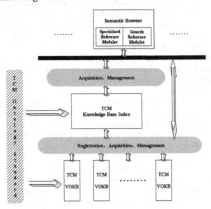

Figure 2: The architecture of the TCM KB-Grid

In this architecture, on the left side, a rounded rectangle means the TCM Ontology Standard, and the shadow means that this ontology standard does not grimly belong to our knowledge base grid. The ontology standard, just as mentioned above, can be a public reference.

At the bottom of the figure, the vertical boxes are knowledge sources of this grid: TCM VOKBs. Each of them may consist of DBs and KBs, or only

KBs. TCM VOKB maintains its own data according to the ontology standard. In addition, it registers to the TCM KBI.

In the middle part, one horizontal big box denotes TCM KBI. It acts as an adapter in this grid.

The top part shows the Semantic Browser, which consists of two reference modules: specialized one and generic one. At this level, we can develop other components, such as inference engine, search engine, etc.

Semantic Browser, TCM KBI and TCM VOKBs use protocols to communicate. There are Registration, Acquisition, and Management, three types between TCM KBI and TCM VOKBs while Acquisition and Management, two types between Semantic Browser and TCM KBI. Once TCM KBI builds the relationship between Semantic Browser and TCM VOKBs, they can also communicate directly using Acquisition and Management.

3 KNOWLEDGE REPRESENTATION

The Resource Description Framework is a foundation for semantic web and knowledge base grid. It provides interoperability between applets and applications that exchange machine- understandable information on the Web. The RDF Schema defines further modeling primitives in RDF (Jeen, 2001). It provides a mechanism to define domain-specific properties and classes of resources, to which you can apply those properties.

In knowledge base grid, RDF is the model for the description of semantic information. The data in knowledge base is also expressed by RDF. An RDF knowledge base consists of domains and inference rules. RDF knowledge can be vast and defined according to different schemas (Boris, 2000). Since one knowledge base gird is corresponding to one domain, its RDF knowledge in knowledge bases is defined according to the same RDFS relying on the public ontology. Inference rules are the another component of the RDF knowledge base, which should contain only non-correlated information – all correlated knowledge should be inferred from ground facts and rules in the knowledge base (Boris, 2000).

In the TCM Knowledge Base Grid, not only the KBI but also all the VOKBs are constructed based on the same public ontology. This component is the core part of TCM Knowledge Base Grid, which is constructed and built based on XML and RDF. Using XML and RDF metadata representation methods, we rebuild the TCM ontology (Figure 3

```
<?xml version='1.0' encoding='gb2312'?>
<!DOCTYPE rdf:RDF [
    <!ENTITY rdf 'http://www.w3.org/1999/02/22-rdf-syntax-ns#'>
    <!ENTITY a 'http://protege.stanford.edu/system#'>
    <!ENTITY xml_encoding 'http://protege.stanford.edu/xml_encoding#'>
    <!ENTITY rdfs 'http://www.w3.org/TR/1999/PR-rdf-schema-19990303#'>
]>
<rdf:RDF xmlns:rdf="&rdf;" xmlns:a="&a;" xmlns:xml_encoding="&xml_encoding;"
xmlns:rdfs="&rdfs;">
<rdfs:Class rdf:about="&xml_encoding;阴阳" rdfs:label="阴阳">
    <rdfs:subClassOf rdf:resource="&xml_encoding;阴阳五行"/>
</rdfs:Class>
<rdfs:Class rdf:about="&xml_encoding;五行" rdfs:label="五行">
    <rdfs:subClassOf rdf:resource="&xml_encoding;阴阳五行"/>
</rdfs:Class>
<rdfs:Class rdf:about="&xml_encoding;阴阳五行" rdfs:label="阴阳五行">
    <rdfs:subClassOf rdf:resource="&xml_encoding;中医人体基础"/>
</rdfs:Class>
<rdfs:Class rdf:about="&xml_encoding;中医人体基础" rdfs:comment="TA类与西医基
础解剖相关联"
    rdfs:label="中医人体基础">
    <rdfs:subClassOf rdf:resource="&xml_encoding;TCM"/>
</rdfs:Class>
<rdfs:Class rdf:about="&xml_encoding;TCM" a:role="abstract" rdfs:label="中国中医
药一体化语言系统">
    <rdfs:comment>This is an ontology of Traditional Chinese Medicine.中医总表
</rdfs:comment>
    <rdfs:subClassOf rdf:resource="&rdfs;Resource"/>
</rdfs:Class>
</rdf:RDF>
```

Figure 3: A simple RDFS of TCM Ontology class definition instance

shows a sample subpart of RDFS of TCM Ontology) and related data storages such as TCM terminology database, Controlled vocabularies (Disease database, Chinese Medical Formula database and Mesh database etc.) to provide a unified web-accessible knowledge sources.

All the VOKBs consist of knowledge sources in our architecture. They have their own data and rules. Maybe each of them covers one specific domain, and maybe all in one domain. In any case, their data formats all follow the public ontology, which is taken as standard. The VOKB uses RDF method to stores its data and rules. When one VOKB registers to the KBI and is accepted, it is one real part of the entire system. Then user can obtain data from it. Semantic Browser is bound with the KBI. It takes charge of drawing an ontology graph by getting part of ontology from the KBI. Users can select the concerned domain, which is represented as an ontology node. When one node is selected, the surrounding area is displayed in detail and users can select the sub node continuously. Semantic Browser also can send the search requirement and the selected ontology node to KBI, and show users the search result using "nodes and arcs diagrams". We

will explain it in detail when we introduce semantic browse service in the next section.

4 SERVICES OF KNOWLEDGE BASE GRID

In this section, we will introduce the services that knowledge base grid provides during it works. Figure 4 presents the hierarchy of services in the Knowledge Base Grid. This is discussed in detail in (Zhaohui, 2002) (Xuezhong, 2002). Based on the protocols, knowledge base grid provides four kinds of essential services.

Knowledge Base Gird Information Service (KB-GIS) provides the information about the structure and state of a VOKB. Knowledge Base Gird Registration Service (KB-GRS) is the easy way for VOKBs to register themselves with KBI. Together with KB-GIS, it provides knowledge discovery service. Knowledge Base Grid Acquisition and Management Service (KB-GAMS) is designed for simple knowledge access and management. During the ontology exploring and common search, we need this service. Moreover, Knowledge Base Grid Query and Manipulation Service (KB-GQMS) assists in completing deep search and inference. It mainly acts during correlative query.

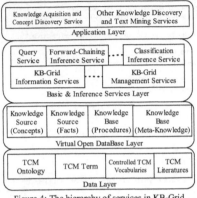

Figure 4: The hierarchy of services in KB-Grid

KB-GIS, KB-GRS, KB-GAMS, and KB-GQMS are the four basic key services provided by knowledge base grid. They are in the low level of the service architecture. Based on these basic services, knowledge base grid also provides some advanced services to form the high level.

– Registration Service

In our knowledge base gird, VOKBs are distributed over the whole Internet. What they must do is only to maintain their data according to the ontology standard. Any KB, which stores data following the ontology standard, can ask for joining to this grid. When one KB has prepared for joining, it sends a registration requirement to the KBI. This requirement is enveloped in the Registration protocol. Once received, KBI asks KB to send part of its data. After KB sends a part of data to it, KBI checks the data format to judge whether the KB can join in well.

The KBI checks the data from KB to judge whether it is following the ontology standard. Because the data from KB is defined by RDF, KBI translates the ontology standard to RDF pattern, and compares the ontology standard and the data from KB. If the data from KB is defined in the domain, which belongs to the ontology standard range, and its terms are some ontology standard's keywords, the KBI will accept the KB.

When it gets the result, KBI answers KB's requirement. If condition accordant, KB will receive the notice that it is accepted. Meanwhile, KBI needs

to write down the data information about this newly-accepted KB. The information written down includes KB's URI, KB's domain, etc. Owning this information, KBI can guide user exploring and search through Semantic Browser.

– Semantic Browse Service

Semantic Browse Service is one of the core services of TCM Knowledge Base Grid. Its aim is to let user explore the ontology and other knowledge at semantic level.

Semantic browser can be developed based on this service. When Semantic Browser starts up, it gets the corresponding services from Knowledge Base Grid, and the basic ontology is sent from KBI, which gets it from the Ontology Standard.

Semantic Browser draws ontology graph according to the basic ontology. The ontology graph is one kind of expressions of ontology; under some particular situations, it can be simplified to an ontology tree. In detail, classes and sub-classes defined in ontology is displayed as a node in the graph. Their affiliation is displayed as a vector arc between the nodes. The constraints are also marked on the vector arcs. Classes' and sub-classes' properties are displayed in the list beside the graph, just as Figure 5 shows.

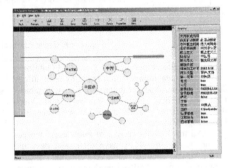

Figure 5: A snapshot of our Semantic Browser

When user selects one node, the Semantic Browser centralizes this node and draws its parent nodes and child nodes around it. Meanwhile, the sideward list shows its properties. Therefore, user can select node continuously to browse all the ontology. Once user focuses on a particular node, he can input what he wants into the property edit box, i.e. name, to trigger the search. Then, Semantic Browser drives KBI and correlative VOKBs to complete this job. When result returns, it draws "nodes and arcs diagrams" to show.

The entire browse process is independent on any URLs. Therefore, Semantic Browser releases users from more and more forgettable and fallible URLs.

Besides the basic concepts browsing and common search, the Semantic Browse Service contains correlative browse. It is aided by inference service

Figure 6: Nodes and arcs diagrams

Sometimes, user not only needs what they cared but also wants to get more correlative information. He can accomplish it recurring to inference service.
– Inference Service

Knowledge Base Grid provides some elementary inference services, such as forward-chaining (Stuart, 2002) inference service, backward-chaining (Stuart, 2002) inference service, forward-backward inference service and subsumption and classification (James, 1983) inference service.

After semantic search, user gets the result displayed by "nodes and arcs diagrams", which includes relationships between concepts and their properties. Since the ontology can be drawn as a graph, the relationships between nodes are very abundant. That is to say, the relationships between classes and sub-classes are very complex. Therefore, user can ask for correlative query based on these relationships.

For example, when user gets one concept's properties, he maybe want to see what else in this grid has the same properties; or he maybe want this concept's parents or children. According to the first circumstance, KBI provides the properties' ontologies and all the concepts that refer to them. Semantic Browser gets these concepts and their own properties to return. The second circumstance is simpler. KBI only needs to find the node in ontology graph which corresponding to this concept, and get its parent nodes, child nodes, and their properties to let Semantic Browser display.

During this process, Semantic Browser, KBI and VOKBs interact with each other several times. Semantic Browser finds the correct VOKBs through KBI, and then builds communication link to them directly.

5 CONCLUSIONS

We have described a computational framework for knowledge base grid. It merges the ideas of grid and semantic web. In the framework, Ontology Standard is a public knowledge reference, VOKBs construct the infrastructure and contain the domain-specific knowledge, Knowledge Base Index is an adapter of all the VOKBs and the linker of VOKBs and Semantic Browser, and Semantic Browser is a outward window of knowledge base grid. To provide normative organizing and convenient management of knowledge and personal service is our motivation to develop such kind of grid. In fact, knowledge base grid integrates the heterogeneous data on the Internet and provides uniform service depending on public ontology standard. Therefore, it has definitely and completely achieved our purpose.

The current implementation of knowledge base grid in Traditional Chinese Medicine is Unified TCM Language System. It consists of two parts: Basic Medical Word Base System and Medical Headings and Concepts Join Subsystem. The Medical Word Base has collected over 400,000 basic words in this domain. It analyses, collects and organizes the related words in all kinds of correlative heading table, classification table, databases, dictionaries and reference books, and becomes the core of the entire medical index system.

ACKNOWLEDGEMENT

We gratefully acknowledge helpful discussion with other members in the Grid Computing Lab of Zhejiang University. This work is supported in part by the Grid-Based TCM Dynamic Information Resource Management and Knowledge Service subprogram of the Foundational Technology and Research Program, China Department of Science and Technology, and in part by the China 863 Research Program on Intelligent Workflow Technologies supporting Creditable E-Commerce under Contract 2001AA414320, and in part by the China 863 Research Program on Core Workflow Technologies supporting Components-library-based Coordinated Software Development under Contract 2001AA113142.

REFERENCES

Ian Forster, Carl Kesselman, 1999. *The Grid: Blueprint for a New Computing Infrastructure*. Morgan Kaufmann. San Fransisco, 1st edition.

Stuart Russell, Peter Norvig, 2002. *Artificial Intelligence: A Modern Approach*. P.273-275. Prentice Hall. New Jersey, 2nd edition.

Michel Klein, March/April 2001. *XML, RDF, and Relatives*. IEEE Intelligent Systems, Vol. 16, No.2, pp. 26-28.

Jeff Heflin, James Hendler, March/April 2001. *A Portrait of the Semantic Web in Action*. IEEE Intelligent Systems, Vol. 16, No. 2, pp. 54-59.

Ying Ding, Dieter Fensel, Michel Klein, Borys Omelayenko, 2002. *The semantic web: yet another hip?* Data & Knowledge Engineering, Vol. 41, Issue 2-3, pp. 205-227.

Ian Foster, Carl Kesselman, Steven Tuecke, 2001. *The Anatomy of the Grid*. Intl J. Supercomputer Applications

Boris Motik, Vlado Glavinic, 2000. Enabling Agent Architecture through an RDF Query and Inference Engine. *in: IEEE Proceedings of the 10th Mediterranean Electrotechnical Conference*, MEleCon.

James G. Schmoize, Thomas A. Lipkis, 1983. Classification in the KL-ONE Knowledge Representation System. *in: Proceedings of Int. Joint Conference on Artificial Intelligence*, Karlsruhe, West Germany, pp. 330-332.

Jeen Broekstra, Michel Klein, Stefan Decker, Dieter Fensel, Frank van Harmelen, Ian Horrocks, May 2001. Enabling knowledge representation on the Web by extending RDF Schema. *in: Proceedings of the 10th International World Wide Web Conference (WWW10)*, Hong Kong.

Zhaohui Wu, Huajun Chen, Jiefeng Xu, December 2002. The Anatomy of the Knowledge Base Grid. *in: Proceedings of the International Workshop on Grid and Cooperative Computing (GCC 2002)*, Hainan, China.

Xuezhong Zhou, Zhaohui Wu, May 2002. *UTMLS: An Ontology-based Unified Medical Language System for Semantic Web*. Technical Report, Grid Computing Lab, Zhejiang University.

MEMBERSHIP PORTAL AND SERVICE PROVISIONING SYSTEM FOR AN INFRASTRUCTURE OF HUBS
Managed e-Hub

Jing Min Xu, Ying Nan Zuo, Shun Xiang Yang, Zhong Tian
IBM China Research Laboratory, 4/F, No.7, 5th Street, Shangdi, Beijing 100085, PRC
Email: xujingm@cn.ibm.com

Henry Chang, Liang-jie Zhang, Tian Chao
IBM Watson Research Center, Route 134, Yorktown Heights, NY 10598, US
Email: hychang@us.ibm.com

Keywords: Managed e-Hub, B2B Exchange, Infrastructure of Hubs, Service On-boarding, Service Subscription, Service Provisioning

Abstract: The goal of Managed e-Hub research prototype is to build a common infrastructure of hubs so that businesses can develop B2B exchanges meeting their business needs based on it. In this paper, an open and extensible framework for Managed e-Hub is presented and the hub fundamental services are discussed in detail as well. The service provisioning system of Managed e-Hub not only provides a way of integrating other services into the hub by means of service on-boarding and subscription, but also provisions these services with their required provisioning information.

1 INTRODUCTION

B2B exchanges are online marketplaces for businesses to buy and sell goods and services from other businesses. At their most effective, these marketplaces match buyers and sellers, reduce transaction costs, enhance sales and distribution, deliver value added services and streamline trading relationships (Gilda, 2001). The goal of Managed e-Hub research prototype is to build a common infrastructure of hubs so that businesses can develop B2B exchanges meeting their business needs based on it. Compared to building B2B exchanges from scratch, it significantly improves efficiency and reduces costs and time-to-market.

In order for the hub infrastructure to be able to support the myriad demands of customers while minimizing hub management efforts, Managed e-Hub is designed to have the following traits:

1) Extensible, multi-entity data model to facilitate true many-to-many processes.

2) Open architecture to make it easy to find and integrate any types of services (including Web Services) into the hub by service publishing, subscription and provisioning.

3) Rich built-in services such as business flow management, data format and business protocol translation to offer cost and time-to-market advantages.

4) Great capability in dynamic service composition to deliver business processes to end users according to their requirements.

5) Flexible framework to allow multiple virtual hubs sharing the same information infrastructure and interacting with each other.

Figure 1 shows the framework of Managed e-Hub (Liang-Jie, 2002) which includes multiple connected hubs sharing the same information infrastructure. Each hub is a six-level model that consists of core infrastructure services, system management, horizontal business services, vertical industry applications, service outsourcing manager and value added services.

O. Camp et al. (eds.), Enterprise Information Systems V, 323-330.
© 2004 *Kluwer Academic Publishers. Printed in the Netherlands.*

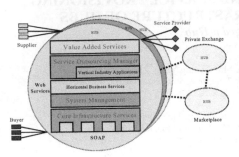

Figure 1: Managed e-Hub Framework

Managed e-Hub itself is made up of discrete services. The fundamental services provided by the hub include the directory service, the enrollment service, and the three other services that make up the service provisioning system: the on-boarding service, the subscription service, and the provisioning service. The service provisioning system aggregates services, such as system management, security, horizontal and vertical business services into the hub and provisions them for system or user access. The service outsourcing manager is built on top of the hub model to provide business process on demand service via dynamic service composition. Also it can be used by the internal applications to build a new value-added service using the existing services hosted by the hub or other community hubs (Liang-Jie, 2002).

Managed e-Hub has its user interface, the membership portal, which provides web based personalized workspaces for e-hub users to perform business operations. What a user can see and can do in the portal depends on the role(s) he plays. All e-Hub defined roles and the corresponding permissible operations are listed in the Table 1.

This paper introduces the underlying technologies of the e-hub fundamental services. As you will see, these technologies adhere to all kinds of industry standards to the maximum extent, which helps to make Managed e-Hub an open and extensible infrastructure of hubs.

Table 1: Roles and Permissible Operations in Managed e-Hub

Roles	Permissible Operations	Comments
e-hub administrator	• Approve top level organization registration requests • Approve service registration requests • Manage self-defined groups • Manage e-hub defined roles	
organization administrator	• Approve employee registration requests • Approve sub-organization registration requests • Manage self-defined groups • Manage organization defined roles	Each organization should have at least one organization administrator
Service provision manager	• Publish services • Approve service subscription requests from organizations • Manage self-defined groups • Manage service defined roles	One organization can have multiple service provision managers, each of them may be responsible for publishing different services respectively
Service subscription manager	• Subscribe to services on behalf of their organizations • Approve service subscription requests from employees • Manage self-defined groups	One organization can have multiple service subscription managers, each of them may be responsible for subscribing to different services respectively
organization employee	• Subscribe to services that have been subscribed by their organizations	

2 E-HUB FUNDAMENTAL SERVICES

2.1 Directory Service

The directory service is the cornerstone of Managed e-Hub as it enables businesses to quickly, easily and dynamically find and transact with one another. It stores information about hub members and their operational relationships in a single repository and provides access to the information for authorized services or applications. LDAP has become prevalent as a worldwide, open directory standard. Its flexible schema and referral capabilities make it suitable for even the most intricate directory integration needs in a heterogeneous environment. For this reason, we built the hub directory service on top of IBM SecureWay LDAP server.

The hub LDAP schema defines a comprehensive data model in XML format, which describes the structure of information stored in the hub directory. The relationships amongst hub members can be defined at different levels: business - user relationship (BUR), business - business relationship (BBR), user - user relationship (UUR), business - service relationship (BSR), user - service relationship (USR) and service - service relationship (SSR). These relationships are very important information for composing and executing dynamic business process integration (Liang-Jie, 2002).

- *Business - Business Relationship (BBR).* An organization can be either an independent organization or a sub-organization of one and only one existing organization. Furthermore, a set of organizations can be grouped as an organization group for a specific purpose, for example, to form a virtual enterprise.
- *Business - User Relationship (BUR).* A user must belong to one and only one organization. Inversely, each organization must have users to play roles of *business administrator, service provision manager* and *service subscription manager*, who are respectively responsible for administering the organization, publishing services to the hub and subscribing to services on behalf of the organization.
- *User - User Relationship (UUR).* A set of users can be grouped as a user group for a specific purpose, for example, to form a project team across an enterprise.
- *Business - Service Relationship (BSR).* An organization can publish services to the hub as a

service provider or subscribe to services published by other organizations as a service consumer.
- *User - Service Relationship (USR).* A user can only subscribe to services that have been subscribed by his belonging organization or its ancestors.
- *Service - Service Relationship (SSR).* A set of services can be grouped as a service group for a specific purpose, for example, to compose a business process.

What is worthy to note is that a sub-organization is recommended to be created for publishing or subscribing to services as a relatively independent business entity, whereas a user group is defined for other purposes. If it is possible, it is recommended to use user group rather than sub-organization to group a set of users.

UDDI, as an open, Internet based standard, has started to be adopted by businesses for publishing their services, finding and transacting business with partners (Stewart, 2001). If UDDI gains critical mass, it could become an important service hub in its own right, but only as a kind of horizontal intermediary between vertical service hubs and the service providers whose services are registered in the UDDI registry (UDDI, 2002).

The directory service of the hub is well integrated with UDDI by the bi-directional synchronization between the e-hub directory and public or private UDDI registries:

1. From UDDI to Managed e-Hub
   - Retrieve businesses and/or services information from a public UDDI registry and register them with the hub directory
2. From Managed e-Hub to UDDI:
   - Extract businesses and services information from the hub directory into UDDI format and publish them to a public UDDI registry
   - Directly update the private UDDI registry in the hub with businesses and services information.

By integrating with UDDI, Managed e-Hub also benefits a lot from the powerful functionality provided by UDDI. For instance, the BE4WS service in the hub allows hub applications to efficiently and effectively look up one or more UDDI registries by constructing an XML script based request (BE4WS, 2002).

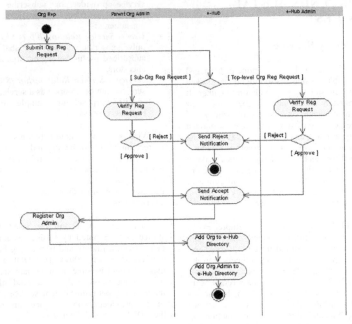

Figure 2: Standard Organization On-boarding Process

The directory service exposes two kinds of APIs to authorized applications: EJB (Enterprise Java Bean) and Web Services. EJB APIs are for services that are tightly coupled with the hub, for instance, the hub built-in services and the hub hosted services. In contrast, Web service APIs are for services that loosely coupled with the hub, for instance, services hosted by other third parties.

2.2 Enrollment Service

The enrollment service manages the on-boarding processes of organizations and users. These on-boarding processes are driven by workflows, so different flows can be used for different organizations to meet their specific requirements.

Figure 2 shows the standard on-boarding process for an organization. Two roles are involved in the process: a representative for the organization, a hub administrator or an administrator of the parent organization (for sub-organizations). The process includes the following steps:

a. The organization representative initiates a registration by completing an enrollment form. The specifics of the registration attributes will depend on the e-hub data model. The enrollment form is dynamically generated based on the XML schema represented data model, so no code change is required if the model changes.

b. If the organization requires to be enrolled as a sub-organization of an existing organization in the hub, the administrator of the parent organization will review and verify the request. Otherwise, the hub administrator will take on the job. The organization representative will be notified as soon as the request is processed.

c. If the request is approved, the organization representative will be asked to register an organization administrator with the hub. The organization representative completes the enrollment form for the organization administrator and submits it to the hub.

d. The hub directory gets updated and the organization is enabled to function as a business.

The standard user on-boarding process is similar to the above. But this time, the hub is no longer involved. The organization's own administrator is responsible for all the user registration request. In addition, a user can be assigned as a service provision manager to manage its service publishing or as a service subscription manager to manage its employees' subscription to services.

The hub also provides a bulk on-boarding process for quickly and easily getting an organization (including all its descendant organizations and users) onboard. The bulk on-boarding process lets the organization representative submit an XML file containing all information required to set up the organization. An authorization code is required to perform the bulk enrollment, which is issued by the hub administrator through other means such as e-mail, phone, etc.

The e-hub data model only defines the common information that is supposed to be shared by all services in the hub, so the organization or user profile will not contain information specific to a service. However, the hub does have the capability of collecting organization or user information specific to a service and delivering it with the common information to the service when the organization or user subscribes to the service.

The organization or user profile can be updated at any time after the enrollment. The change may need to be propagated to services that the organization or user has already subscribed to so that the profile can be kept synchronized.

2.3 Service Provisioning System

The service provisioning system in Managed e-Hub is responsible for:

- Enrolling services into the hub as its managed resources
- Managing service subscription
- Managing (setup, amend & revoke) user or system access and entitlement rights to services

These three tasks are accomplished by its three constituent services respectively: the service on-boarding service, the service subscription service and the service provisioning service.

2.3.1 Service On-boarding

The service on-boarding service manages two processes: the service registration process and the service enabling process. The service provision managers in an organization are responsible for

registering and enabling services with the hub on behalf of the organization. At service registration time, the service provision manager is asked to provide the basic information about the service to the hub. The hub administrator reviews the service registration request and decides whether or not to approve the request. The service information will be added to the hub directory if the hub administrator approves the request. However, a registered service is not available for subscription until it is enabled. The service provision manager needs to provide the following information to the hub for enabling a registered service:

- Service access information such as access URLs, technical specifications, etc.
- Service access control model, which defines what access controlled objects the service currently has, what the aggregation relationships between these objects are and what permissions and roles are defined by each of these objects. Based on the model, the service subscription service can allow the service subscription managers to grant permissions and roles to their employees for their access to each access controlled object in the service when they process their employee subscription requests.
- Service provisioning data model, which defines the information that the service expects to get from organizations and users for enabling their accesses to the service. The service subscription service is in charge of collecting the information from organizations or users based on the model when they subscribe to the service. Along with the information, the common information contained in the organization or user profile is also provisioned to services.

The enabled services are published for subscription. A service may be a business level service or a user level service. The business level services do not involve the human interaction, so it is not available for user subscription. The user level services are available for both organization subscription and user subscription. But a user can only subscribe to services that have been subscribed by his belonging organization or its ancestors, that is to say, the organization subscription must happen before any user subscription happens. This makes sense: an application instance may need to be created and all kinds of resources may need to get allocated specifically for the organization before its employees subscribe to the service.

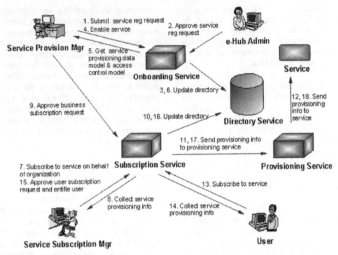

Figure 3: Service On-boarding and Subscription Processes

2.3.2 Service Subscription

The service subscription service manages the service subscription processes: the organization subscription processes and the user subscription processes. The service subscription manager in an organization is responsible for subscribing to services on behalf of the organization. The service provision manager in the service provider side reviews the organization subscription request and decides whether or not to approve the request. But the service provision manager is in charge of processing the user subscription requests to the user level services.

The service subscription service has the capability of dynamically generating web forms based on the service provisioning data model and the service access control model for collecting the provisioning information and access control information. This capability makes the hub provisioning system adaptive to the dynamic hub environment where the number of services published in the hub keeps growing and the diversity of the provisioning data models and access control models of these services make the situation more complicated.

A bulk subscription process is also available for the service subscription managers enabling a bunch of users to access to a service at a time. This process relieves the service subscription managers of

spending many laborious hours on manually approving a lot of user subscription requests. This is realized by submitting an XML file containing all provisioning information and access control information required to subscribe these users to a service.

Figure 3 shows a high-level schematic of the service on-boarding and subscription process stated in the above two sections.

2.3.3 Service Provisioning

Non-intrusive provisioning is a main design goal of the hub provisioning system. Services published in the hub are not required to be developed for the hub provisioning system in order to utilize the hub provisioning service. They may be the existing applications, Web services located somewhere on the Internet, or other services hosted by third parties. In order to do so, an adaptor is needed for each service to interact with the provisioning system. The following outlines the interaction process:

- The provisioning system constructs a provisioning request, communicates with the application adapter and passes the request on to it.
- The application adapter parses the request and calls the appropriate application programming interfaces for fulfilling the request.

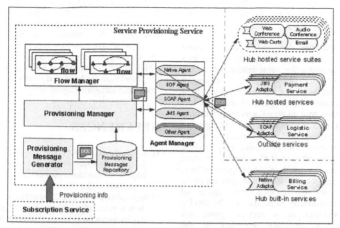

Figure 4: The Provisioning Service Architecture

- The application adapter notifies the provisioning system whether the provisioning operation succeeds or not.

The data format of the provisioning request and the transport protocol between the hub provisioning system and application adapters are two important issues. There are several standards focusing on these two aspects: ADPr (ADPr Specification), XRPM (XRPM Working Document) and SPML (Service Provisioning Markup Language). XRPM set out to define the set of standards required to facilitate inter-operation and functioning at the Provisioning-System-to-Provisioning-System level. In contrast, ADPr set out to define the set of standards required to facilitate inter-operation and functioning at the Provisioning-System-to-Managed-Resource level. The PSTC in OASIS has been formed to work through both areas of potential standardization with the goals of defining SPML as a single XML-based framework for the exchange of information at both levels. Unfortunately, SPML are still under discussion. So we are taking a hub proprietary approach while trying to use other standards to the maximum extent.

The SYNC_CUSTOMER BOD (Business Object Document) defined by Open Application Group (OAG) (Open Application Group) is chosen to be the provisioning data format because of its extensibility. The User Area segment in the OAG BOD provides the ability to extend the OAG XML DTD to convey the service specific provisioning information. The CONFIRM BOD is used by application adapters to send responses to the hub service provisioning system. The application adapters will be responsible for mapping the SYNC_CUSTOMER BOD into the data structures expected by the application interface and vice versa, mapping the data from the application interface into the CONFIRM BOD.

In order to meet the diverse requirements of diverse applications, multiple transport protocols are supported by the provisioning system: native Java, IIOP, SOAP and JMS. We classify the application adapters by the transport protocols they support, so there are 4 kinds of adapters: Native adapters, IIOP adapters, SOAP adapters and JMS adapters. To interact with each kind of adapters, a corresponding agent is implemented on the side of the service provisioning system. The agent manager component of the provisioning service is responsible for managing the life cycle of these agents: loading agents, unloading agents and choosing a right agent to serve a service provisioning request.

The native adapters are local Java classes that implement a hub specified interface, whereas the IIOP adapters are remote EJBs that implement a hub specified remote interface. These two kinds of adapters are extensively used to provision the hub built-in services and the hub hosted web applications. The SOAP adapters are implemented as Web services that have a hub specified WSDL, so they can be used to provision services located outside the e-hub operating environment. The JMS adapters are often used to provision legacy applications hosted by the hub. However, the above combinations are not prescriptive and some other

329

combinations are also acceptable. For example, the SOAP adapters can also be used to provision the hub built-in services.

A service provider may bundle two or more services together as a service suite. All services in a service suite can share the same infrastructure and leverage each other to bring the maximum productivity to its consumers. However, they might need to get provisioned in a specified sequence. For example, assuming that an e-mail service, a calendar service and a personal information management (PIM) service are bundled as a service suite, the provisioning sequence for the service suite may be required to be: PIM → e-mail → calendar. In order to resolve this kind of problem, the hub provisioning system allows service provision managers grouping two or more service together as a service group and specifying a provisioning workflow for the service group. All services in a service group get provisioned in a sequence specified in the provisioning workflow for the service group.

Figure 4 presents the architecture of the service provisioning service. The PMG (Provisioning Message Generator) component receives the service provisioning information and packages the information as a provisioning message containing one (if the provisioning target is only one service) or more (if the provisioning target is a service suite) SYNC_CUSTOMER BODs. For assured provisioning, the provisioning message is persisted in a provisioning message repository. The PM (Provisioning Manager) component picks up the provisioning message from the provisioning message repository and work in concert with the flow manager to get services in a service group provisioned following the specified provisioning workflow for the service group. For provisioning each service, the provisioning manager hands off the URL of the target adapter and the associated BOD to the agent manager, which in turn chooses a right agent to serve the provisioning request.

3 CONCLUSION

In this paper we have introduced the open and extensible framework of Managed e-Hub and its fundamental services: the directory service, the enrollment service, and the service provisioning system in particular, so that businesses can build (multiple) B2B exchanges based on it. The hub service provisioning system not only provides a way of integrating other services into the hub by means of service on-boarding and subscription, but also

provisions these service for system or user access. The ability to support multiple transport protocols for flexible provisioning and the capability of collecting the service specific provisioning information from service consumers make the hub provisioning system highly adaptive to the dynamic e-Hub environment. These fundamental services lay the foundation for Managed e-Hub to be an open and extensible infrastructure of hubs.

REFERENCES

Gilda Raczkowski (2001). The B2B Marketplaces: The Long Road to Success, special to dash30. From http://www.worldcom.com/us/resources/library/reports/ebiz/b2b.pdf

Liang-Jie Zhang et al (2002, October). A Manageable Web Services Hub Framework And Enabling Technologies for e-Sourcing, In IEEE International Conference on Systems, Management and Cybernetics

Liang-jie Zhang et al (2002, June). Web Services Relationships Binding for Dynamic e-Business Integration, In IC 2002, International Conference on Internet Computing

Stewart McKie, (2001, December 5). Hub Connection, Intelligent Enterprise Magazine, From http://www.intelligententerprise.com/011205/418infosc1_1.shtml

UDDI Version 2 Specifications (2002). From http://www.oasis-open.org/committees/uddi-spec/tcspecs.shtml#uddiv3

Business Explorer for Web Services (BE4WS) (2002) Form IBM alphaworks, http://www.alphaworks.ibm.com/tech/be4ws

ADPr Specification, From http://www.adpr-spec.com/profile/spec.htm

XRPM Working Document, (2001, August). From http://www.xrpm.org

Service Provisioning Markup Language, From OASIS Provisioning Services TC, http://www.oasis-open.org/committees/provision/

Open Application Group, http://www.openapplications.org

AUTHOR INDEX

331